WISCONSIN

WISCONSIN

A Guide to the Badger State

*Compiled by Workers of the Writers' Program
of the Work Projects Administration
in the State of Wisconsin*

ILLUSTRATED

AMERICAN GUIDE SERIES

*Sponsored by
The Wisconsin Library Association*

HASTINGS HOUSE · *Publishers* · NEW YORK

Republished 1974
SOMERSET PUBLISHERS—a Division of Scholarly Press, Inc.
22929 Industrial Drive East, St. Clair Shores, Michigan 48080

Library of Congress Cataloging in Publication Data

Writers' Program. Wisconsin
    Wisconsin, a guide to the Badger State.

    Original ed. issued in series: American guide series
    Bibliography: p.
    1. Wisconsin--Description and travel--Guide-books.
I. Title. II. Series: American guide series.
F586.W97   1973   917.75'04'4   72-8451
ISBN 0-403-02198-7

PRINTED IN THE U. S. A.

Foreword

The American regional guide is not so modern or bizarre an idea as some may suppose. More than one hundred and twenty years ago Timothy Dwight published in four stout volumes his "Travels in New England and New York." That was essentially a guide to the region covered by Yale's motor-minded president in the course of some twenty long vacation periods. He traversed the most important highways, riding in a two-wheeled gig drawn by a single horse, stopped at all villages, towns and many country houses, and gave his reader some account of what was most noteworthy at every point of observation.

The *Wisconsin Guide,* like all others published under the auspices of the Work Projects Administration, is a product of cooperative effort by numerous writers working to a definite plan under the supervision of a State director and the National Director. It is distinctly a guide, not a systematic history of the State, which would be a task for trained historians. But numerous essays of a historical nature supplement the guidebook features and, so far as can be discerned in a rapid survey, these were not only carefully planned and honestly worked out, under direction, but have been conscientiously checked by experts in the several fields represented. Accordingly, readers who are interested in a short account of Wisconsin Indian trade, in the early settlement, in the State's agriculture, fisheries, lumbering, manufacturing, transportation, political history, arts and numerous other topics can find in the book helpful short statements which can be read with confidence in their general accuracy.

These essays, it should be added, usually are presented in very readable style and even the tours, which are necessarily constructed of disjointed series of short items, have been edited with such care and skill as to make them interesting for their geographical information, though especially designed to aid the traveler or tourist.

JOSEPH SCHAFER
State Historical Society
Madison, Wisconsin

Preface

In one of the *Idler* papers, Dr. Samuel Johnson remarks on the lack of solid information in the many travel journals of his day. He writes,

"It may, I think, be justly observed, that few books disappoint their readers more than the narratives of travellers. . . .

"The greater part of travellers tell nothing, because their method of travelling supplies them with nothing to be told. He that enters a town at night, and surveys it in the morning, and then hastens away to another place, and guesses at the manners of the inhabitants by the entertainment which his inn afforded him, may please himself for a time with a hasty change of scenes . . . but let him be contented to please himself without endeavoring to disturb others. . . ."

The *Wisconsin State Guide* attempts to be such a book as, by its method at least, would not seriously have irritated the good doctor. The writers have travelled up and down Wisconsin, note-books in hand, taking mileages on the main highways, prowling about towns, scouring local libraries, and annoying good citizens by their questions; then checking and rechecking by letter, interview, and arduous hours in the State Historical Library the information they had secured. It is hoped that "he who enters a town at night, and surveys it in the morning" will know more about that town because he has read himself to sleep by this book; that as he leaves the town in the morning the roadside will reveal not merely a succession of acres vaguely changing shape and color, but a land that people have plowed and planted and lived by; that as he urges his car from one destination to another he will occasionally lighten the foot that presses down his accelerator, or steer into some brown side road to observe Wisconsin; and that he who stays at home through the long Wisconsin winters may take vicarious journeys.

This book, however, proposes to be more than a guide to places; for places, unless they present a spectacular break with the mild stretches of ordinary nature, are usually interesting chiefly for the people who inhabit them. This book hopes in some measure to guide the reader to Wisconsin's people, down through the years as well as across the miles, telling of the land the people found, how they cleared it, broke it, and built upon it the changing institutions that reveal their changeful thoughts and desires.

The design follows from the intention. The book is divided into three parts. The first of these is a series of essays, most of them historical in nature, intended to paint in large strokes the State's development and to furnish a background against which the detailed information that follows may become more intelligible. The second section describes the State's nine largest cities. Here the histories of the cities are briefly sketched and their points of interest described for the traveller who wishes to look about him. The third section is a series of selected tours covering the main highways. It is written with two intentions. The first is obvious—to guide the motorist through Wisconsin and furnish him, as he goes, with some knowledge of the land he passes through, some notion of where he might go next and how to get home from there. But this third section has another, less practical intention —to present the State once again, not in the large outlines of the first section, but, as it were, in mosaic; isolated bits—chips of description, of history or legend, of geographic or economic situation—are pieced together to make a variegated but single picture of Wisconsin. If, in the end, this book seems representative rather than exhaustive, that is because Wisconsin is too big for most of it to be pressed into a book of this size.

Working alone the Writers' Project could not have pieced together the puzzle of Wisconsin. To name the hundreds of people who have given us information by letter, by casual word of mouth, or by formal conversation would be impossible; nevertheless, our thanks are due the many people who have so generously answered our persistent questions. Our thanks are also due to the long line of Wisconsinians who have veined that gold-mine of information, the State Historical Library, where all who wish to know about Wisconsin must go digging. We are indebted to the late Dr. Joseph Schafer for reading much of this material in manuscript and most of it in galley proof and Dr. Louise Phelps Kellogg for criticizing, out of her great store of information, the articles on *History, The People Who Came, Indians, Green Bay, Kenosha, Racine,* and the *Chronology.* We wish to thank Charles E. Brown for answering the phone calls we have rained upon him and for reading all the galleys of the *Tours;* E. F. Bean and F. T. Thwaites for helping us over the humps of *Geology* and *Geography;* for advice on *Flora,* Professor N. C. Fassett; on *Fauna,* Professor G. W. Wagner; on *Conservation,* various members of the Conservation Commission, and especially Ernest Swift and H. W. MacKenzie, as well as Professor Aldo Leopold. We wish to thank Professor Ralph Linton for his invaluable aid on *Indians;* Professors Charles Bunn and Grayson Kirk, Dr. Joseph Schafer and Dr. Elizabeth Brandeis for their reading of *Political History;* Professors Selig Perlman and Harold Groves for their suggestions on *Labor;* Professor Edwin Witte and Samuel Toepfer, on *Industry, Commerce,* and *Transportation;* William Kirsch and Professor Groves (who made one of his own manuscripts available to us for consultation), on the *Cooperative Movement;* Mr. Kirsch and Professors Andrew Hopkins and George S. Wehrwein, on *Agriculture;* E. G. Doudna and other members of the State Board of Education, on *Education;* the Reverend J. N. Davidson and Father William Mahoney, on *Religion;* Fred Rhea, on *Recreation;* Professor G. M. Hyde, on *Newspapers;* Professor W. E. Leonard and A. O. Barton, on *Literature;* Professor L. Schemeckebier and Miss Charlotte Partridge, on *Painting and Sculpture;* Professor E. B. Gordon, William Arvold, and John Bach, on *Music;* Hamilton Beatty, on *Architecture;* Professor A. H. Sanford, on *La Crosse;* A. O. Barton on *Madison;* and Dr. A. R. Schultz for special work on *Sheboygan.*

But while all these consultants have read, either in manuscript or in galley proof, the material here connected with their names, the research and the writing of this book have been done by the members of the Writers' Project of Wisconsin, in large part under the direction of Marie G. Dieter, Editor of the Tours Section, and Harold E. Miner, Assistant State Supervisor. Many more errors might have occurred in the *Wisconsin Guide* had not these writers had easy access to the resources of the State Historical Library; acknowledgment and thanks must go to the librarians there who were unfailingly understanding, courteous, and helpful.

As the Guide went to press before the 1940 census figures were available, the 1930 figures are used throughout the text. There is, however, an alphabetical list of the 1940 figures in the Appendices.

There remains one more debt to be acknowledged. Nature herself, long-abused, deserves at least such piquant thanks as the poet-traveler Lord Byron once gave her:

"Nature, tortured twenty thousand ways,
Resigns herself with exemplary patience,
To guide-books, rhymes, tours, sketches, illustrations."

JOHN J. LYONS,
State Supervisor

Contents

Part I. General Background

Part II. Cities

Part III. Road Ahead

Part IV. Appendices

Illustrations

THE LAKES AND RIVERS
Between pages 64 *and* 65

Near Red Banks
Rainbow Falls on the Wolf River
Dells of the Eau Claire River
Dells of the Wisconsin River
Big Smoky Falls
Control Gates on Federal Dam
near La Crosse
The Fox River

Power Dam on Wisconsin River
Fishing Village
Lifting a Trap Net
The Gulls Come
Free Automobile Ferry Across the
Wisconsin River
A Village on the Mississippi Bluffs
A Northern Lake

Lake Michigan

HISTORY
Between pages 94 *and* 95

Marquette and Joliet Discover the
Upper Mississippi, 1673
The Landfall of Jean Nicolet,
1634
"The Spirit of the Northwest"
Log Cabin of a Pioneer
"The Grand Loggery"

Proclamation of Statehood
The First Capitol
Trading Post
The Indian Agency House
The Roi-Porlier-Tank Cottage
William Dempster Hoard,
"Father of Wisconsin Dairying"

THE FARMLANDS
Between pages 156 *and* 157

Architecture of the Dairylands
Stacking Pea Vines
Model Dairy Farm
Small Grain Elevator
Typical Cheese Factory
Coulee Country Farm

Winter Landscape
Contour Plowing
Tobacco
Cherry Blossoms
Apple Blossom Time
Harness Racing at a County Fair

Pulling Contest at a County Fair

INDUSTRY
Between pages 218 *and* 219

In the Cooper Shop of a Brewery
Forty-Ton Ladle
Old Brewery
Brewing Kettles
Lead and Zinc Mine
Automobile Frames

Paper Mill
Sawmill
Interlake Steamer Loading Ore
Green Bay Harbor
Lake Steamers Loading Grain
Milwaukee's Back Door

Factories at Racine

Maps

General Information

(State map shows highways and Transportation map shows routes of railroads, airlines, bus lines and water transportation)

Railroads: Chicago, Burlington & Quincy R.R. (Burlington); Chicago, Milwaukee, St. Paul & Pacific R.R. (Milwaukee); Chicago & North Western Ry. (Northwestern); Duluth, Missabe & Iron Range Ry. (Duluth); Duluth, South Shore & Atlantic Ry. (South Shore); Minneapolis, St. Paul & Sault Ste Marie Ry. (Soo); Chicago, North Shore & Milwaukee R.R. (North Shore); Green Bay & Western R.R. (Green Bay); Illinois Central R.R. (I.C.); Milwaukee Electric Ry. and Transport Co. (Milwaukee Electric); Northern Pacific Ry. (NP).

Highways: State traffic patrol but no border inspection. Traffic officers have authority to make arrests for traffic violations. Gasoline and water available everywhere. Gasoline: State tax 4¢, Federal 1½¢. (*For highway routes see State map.*)

Bus Lines: Interstate lines include Northland Greyhound Lines, Stewart Bus Lines, Southern Wisconsin Transportation Co., Peoria Rockford Bus Company (Central Trailways), Interstate Transit Lines, Wisconsin Power and Light Co. (Orange Line), Land O' Lakes Bus Co., Hiawatha Stage Lines, Green Bay Stages, Gray Transportation Co., and Cardinal Lines.

Air Lines: Northwest Airlines planes stop at Milwaukee, Madison, and Superior; Pennsylvania Central Airlines Planes stop at Milwaukee.

Waterways: Pere Marquette Railway Co., fast automobile ferry service; route, Milwaukee to Ludington, Mich., 2:00 a.m., 10:00 a.m. & 6:00 p.m. (CST) daily.

Motor Vehicle Laws: No specified speed limit on rural highways. Unlawful: speed endangering lives or property. Spotlights allowed if properly adjusted. Parking prohibited on traveled portion of highways, crest of hills, bridges and curves. Visiting cars retain license plates according to reciprocal requirements of visitor's State. No fee for trailers under 3,000 lbs. gross weight. No restrictions for cabin trailers. (*For local traffic information see General Information for larger cities.*)

Accommodations: Numerous tourist camps, small hotels, large resort hotels, restaurants, roadside picnic grounds. State parks for camping.

Recreational Areas: Northern half is largely forest. More than 7,000 lakes—largely in northern part; all lakes have fish. Deer in northern forest. Two national forests, 8 State forests, 12 State parks, 4 State monuments and historic sites, 5 State wayside parks; all open to tourists and all reached by improved highways.

Fish and Game Laws: Game fish include muskellunge, northern pike, large and small mouthed black bass, wall-eyed pike, german brown, rainbow, steel-head, brook and lake trout, white, silver and rock bass, blue gills, crappies, perch, bullheads, herring, catfish, smelt, sturgeon.

Open seasons: Muskellunge usually from May 25 to Jan. 15; large and small mouthed bass from June 25 or July 1 to Jan. 15, depending on the locality; trout from May 1 in counties bordering Lake Superior and May 15, elsewhere, continuing until Sept. 7. For all other kinds of fish except lake trout and sturgeon the season is usually from May 15 to Jan. 15 or Feb. 1, depending on the locality. The season for lake trout is from April 15 to Sept. 30. Sturgeon fishing in Lake Winnebago is usually from Feb. 1 to Mar. 1, and in certain other defined waters from Sept. 5 to Oct. 15. All non-resident fishing licenses expire April 30.

Licenses: No fee for resident hook and line fishing with one line. Resident rod and reel, or more than one line, $1, age limit 18 years old and over. Non-resident hook and line fishing either with or without reel, $3, age limit, 16 years old and over.

Limits: Vary in counties and from year to year. Usual limitation, muskellunge, 1 per day, minimum length, 30 in.; trout (all varieties except lake trout) 15, 7 in.; northern pike, 8, 18 in.; black bass, 6, 10 in.; wall-eyed pike, 7, 13 in.; lake trout, 5, 19 in.; silver bass and crappies, 25, 7 in.; blue gills, 25, 6 in.; bullheads, 25, no size limit; perch, 25, 6 in.; catfish, 15, 15 in.; sturgeon, 5 each season, no size limit. Conservation commission regulates fishing and furnishes explicit details of seasons and limits in each county with license.

Prohibited: No person shall take, catch, kill, or fish for fish of any variety with more than two lines, or two poles with one line attached to each pole and with one hook to each line, or more than one artificial bait to each line, except that fly fishermen may use two flies to one line, or with any fish line or lines and hooks left unattended in any of the inland waters of the State. The use of spears at night, snag lines, set lines, dip nets for taking game fish or minnows in trout streams is prohibited by law. Throughout the State are certain areas established as game refuges the boundaries of which are posted. Within such posted areas the possession of fire arms is prohibited unless they are unloaded and either knocked down or cased.

Open season for hunting: Deer, bear, red fox, raccoon, muskrat, mink, otter, beaver, skunk, gray squirrels, snowshoe, jack and cottontail rabbits, pheasant, Hungarian partridge, ducks, geese, snipe, and woodcock may be hunted during specified seasons in designated areas. Summary of seasons and areas given with license. Wolves, coyotes, wildcat, gray fox, opossum, badger, weasel, woodchuck, gophers and red squirrels are not protected and may be hunted at any time, but a license is required.

Licenses: Resident hunting, $1. Non-resident hunting, exclusive of deer, $25; including deer $50. Trapping licenses are available only to legal residents of the State at $1.

Limits: The Conservation Commission regulates the open seasons and bag and possession limits, releasing information prior to the opening of the season.

Prohibited: No person shall carry with him in any vehicle or automobile any gun or rifle, unless the same is unloaded and knocked down, or unloaded and enclosed within a carrying case. It is unlawful to enter upon the enclosed or cultivated lands, or woodlots connected therewith, for the purpose of hunting, fishing, trapping, netting, gathering fruit, nuts, straw, turf, vegetables, or herbs, without the consent of the owner or occupant thereof.

Calendar of Annual Events

JANUARY

Last week	at Milwaukee	Orchid Exhibit at Mitchell Park Conservatory
No fixed date	at Oconomowoc	Amateur National Skating Competition, U. S. and Canada
No fixed date	at Oconomowoc	Amateur U. S. and Canada Ski Meet
No fixed date	at Plymouth	Central Ski Association Meet
No fixed date	at Wausau	Winter Frolic
No fixed date	at Chippewa Falls	Ski Tournament
No fixed date	at Milwaukee	Auto Show
Sundays (extending through February)	at Lake Geneva	Ice Harness Races

FEBRUARY

First	at Portage	State Curling Bonspiel
Second	at Beloit	Founders' Day at Beloit College
First Friday	at Madison	Little International Livestock and Horse Show at University Stock Pavilion
First weekend	at Madison	Rural Dramatic Festival at University Theater
First week	at Madison	Wisconsin Farm and Home Week at State College of Agriculture
Third week	at Madison	State Dramatic Guild Festival at University Theater
No fixed date	at Superior	Curling Club Bonspiel
No fixed date	at Eagle River	Winter Carnival
No fixed date	at Stevens Point	Winter Sports Carnival

MARCH

First three weeks	at Madison	Annual National Intercollegiate Photographic Salon at Memorial Union
Last week	State-wide	Wisconsin Dairy Day
Twentieth (extending to April 5)	at Marinette	Smelt Carnival
No fixed date	at Superior	Tri-State Dairy Congress
No fixed date	at Bayfield	Paul Bunyan Dinner Outing

APRIL

No fixed date	at Madison	Madison Maennerchor Concert
No fixed date	at Madison	Woman's Club Chorus Concert
No fixed date	at Milwaukee	Milwaukee Art Institute Exhibition
No fixed date	at Madison	Haresfoot Production

MAY

Twenty-ninth	State-wide	Wisconsin Day (Statehood Anniversary)
Thirtieth	at Madison	Yacht Club Regatta on Lake Mendota
First Friday	State-wide	Arbor Day
First or second Sunday	at Prairie du Chien	Formal Opening and Tea at Villa Louis
Third weekend	at Madison	Parents' Weekend at University of Wisconsin
First week	State-wide	Conservation Week
First week	State-wide	Wisconsin Vocational Education Week
Second, third, fourth weeks	at Madison	Student Art Exhibition in Memorial Union
No fixed date (usually last week)	at Sturgeon Bay	Cherry Blossom Week
No fixed date	at Solon Springs	Northern States Amateur Field Trial Association Meet for Bird Dogs
No fixed date	at Oshkosh	White Bass Festival
No fixed date	at Gays Mills	Apple Blossom Week
No fixed date	at Beaver Dam	Tri-City Music Festival

MAY—continued

No fixed date	at Waukesha	Carroll College May Day Fete
No fixed date	at Madison	Wisconsin Schools Music Festival
No fixed date	at Madison	West Side Garden Club Flower Show

MAY OR JUNE

Corpus Christi Day	at Keshena	Corpus Christi Day Celebration by Indians on Menominee Indian Reservation

JUNE

Between tenth and eighteenth	at Madison	Wisconsin University Crew Races on Lake Mendota
Fifteenth-twenty-first	at Madison	State 4-H Week and Institute for Leaders at College of Agriculture
Third week	at Madison	University of Wisconsin Commencement
Sunday nearest eighteenth	at Madison	Robert Marion La Follette Memorial Services at Forest Hill Cemetery
No fixed date	at Chetek	National Outboard Boat Races
No fixed date	at Milwaukee	Desert Plant Exhibit at Mitchell Park Conservatory
No fixed date	at La Crosse	Tri-State Trapshooters' Association Annual Shoot
No fixed date	at Brule	Trout Season Celebration
No fixed date	at Madison	Madison Garden Club Flower Show

JULY

First (extending to tenth of September)	at Wisconsin Dells	Evening Indian Ceremonials (each night)
Fourth	at Eagle River	Water Carnival
Fourth	at Madison	Yacht Club Regatta
First week	at Bayfield	Strawberry Festival
Second weekend	at Madison	All-State Band Novelty Concert Sponsored by Music Clinic

Fourth weekend	at Madison	Final Festival All-State Band Concert Sponsored by Music Clinic
Fourth weekend	at Madison	Final Festival All-State Orchestra Concert Sponsored by Music Clinic
Last weeks	at Ashland Junction Spooner Sturgeon Bay Marshfield Hancock La Crosse Madison	Agricultural Field Days
No fixed date	at Milwaukee	Mid-Summer Festival at Juneau Park
No fixed date	in Door County	Cherry Harvest Time
Last week (or first week August)		Men's Amateur State Golf Tournament
Last week		Qualifying Round for Men in the National Golf Tournament

AUGUST

First Friday	at Ephraim	Regatta
First week	at Milwaukee	Three-day State Trapshooters' Annual Shoot
First week	at Chippewa Falls	Northern Wisconsin District Fair
First or second week		Women's Amateur State Golf Tournament
Last week	at Milwaukee	Wisconsin State Fair
Last week	at Superior	Tri-State Fair
No fixed date	at Amery	Water Carnival
No fixed date	at Sturgeon Bay	Aquatic Meet
No fixed date	at Pittsville	Indian Ceremonials
No fixed date	at Keshena	"Otcikona" Indian Pageant on Menominee Reservation

AUGUST OR SEPTEMBER

No fixed date	at Milwaukee	Home Show

Labor Day	at Madison	Yacht Club Final Regatta
Labor Day	Winneconne to Neenah	25-mile Rowboat Derby
Labor Day	at Red Granite	Three-day Celebration
Last week (or first week October)	at Madison	High School Livestock Judging Contest at College of Agriculture
No fixed date	at Cumberland	Two-day Rutabaga Festival and Fair
No fixed date	at Solon Springs	Northern States Amateur Field Trial Association Meet for Bird Dogs
No fixed date	at Wisconsin Rapids	Cranberry Festival
No fixed date	at Spooner Warrens Minong	Cranberry Harvest Time

SEPTEMBER, OCTOBER, OR NOVEMBER

| No fixed date | State-wide | Wisconsin Resources Week |

OCTOBER

Ninth	State-wide	Leif Ericson Day
Eleventh	State-wide	General Pulaski's Memorial Day
Third week	at Madison	Junior Livestock Show at Stock Pavilion
Last week (or first week November)	at Madison	University of Wisconsin Homecoming
No fixed date	at Rice Lake	State Potato Show
No fixed date	at Stevens Point	Potato Festival
No fixed date	at Evansville	Coon Dog Trials
No fixed date	at Milwaukee	Tropical Fish Exhibit at Mitchell Park Conservatory
No fixed date	at Milwaukee	Food and Radio Show at Auditorium
No fixed date		State Cornhusking Contest
No fixed date	at Ft. Atkinson	Plowing Contest Sponsored by Future Farmers
No fixed date	State-wide	Wisconsin Parent-Teachers' Week

NOVEMBER

Night before Thanksgiving	at Madison	Haresfoot Follies in Memorial Union
Last two weeks	at Madison	Wisconsin Salon of Art in Memorial Union
No fixed date (extending to March)	at Madison	Madison Art Association Lecture Series
No fixed date (extending to May) '	at Madison	Civic Music Association Concert Series in Masonic Temple
No fixed date	at Madison	Madison Maennerchor Concert

NOVEMBER OR DECEMBER

No fixed date	State-wide	Wisconsin Cheese Week

DECEMBER

First two weeks	at Madison	Wisconsin Salon of Art in Memorial Union
Twenty-fourth	at Milwaukee	Community Christmas Tree Celebration
Thirty-first	at La Crosse	Midnight Fireworks from Granddad's Bluff
No fixed date	at Madison	Woman's Club Chorus Concert
No fixed date	at Madison	State High School Forensic Association Dramatic Productions
Sunday before Christmas	at Madison	Public School Nativity Play in State Capitol
No fixed date	at Ashland	High School Nativity Play

PART I
General Background

Natural Setting

WISCONSIN'S area of 56,066 square miles, in the north central portion of the United States, is defined by a ragged boundary. Lake Michigan lies on the east, Lake Superior and the Menominee, Brule, and Montreal Rivers on the north, the St. Louis, St. Croix, and Mississippi Rivers on the west. Only the southern border and some relatively few miles at the State's northern limits follow a line unsuggested by natural water courses.

The topography today is essentially the same as it was immediately following the Ice Age. Broadly, it may be described as a composite of large areas of plains, smaller areas of stream-cut plateaus, and large areas of erosion-worn mountains. Elevations above sea level range between 581 feet where Wisconsin's eastern border edges Lake Michigan to a highest point of 1,940 feet at Rib Mountain near Wausau. The mean altitude for Wisconsin is 1,050 feet. Generally speaking, the elevation of the north is higher than that of the rest of the State.

Streams to the west of Wisconsin's major watershed, a broad land arch extending north and south through the middle of the State, empty by way of the Mississippi River into the Gulf of Mexico. Chief among these streams are the St. Croix, Chippewa, Black, and Wisconsin Rivers, the latter the State's largest interior waterway. Each joins the Mississippi at some point along Wisconsin's western border. The Rock River and some few small streams flow through Wisconsin into Illinois, where they join the Mississippi system. Streams to the east of the watershed empty into the Atlantic Ocean by way of Lake Superior or Lake Michigan. The St. Louis, Brule, Bad, Nemadji, and Montreal Rivers find their way to Lake Superior; the Menominee, Peshtigo, Oconto, Wolf, Sheboygan, and Milwaukee Rivers, together with numerous smaller waterways, are a part of the Lake Michigan system.

Wisconsin is bordered by more than five hundred miles of Lake Michigan and Lake Superior; the State possesses close to 4,000 mapped interior lakes. To the northeast, chiefly in Vilas, Oneida, and Iron Counties, are the hundreds of small waters of the highland lake district. In the northwest, especially in Sawyer, Barron, Polk, Burnett, and Washburn Counties is a second group of small, closely set lakes. Eastern and southeastern Wisconsin have a generous number of moderate-sized, scattered lakes. Lake St. Croix, an interruption of the St. Croix River, and Lake Pepin, a widening of the flow of the Mississippi, are

3

both long narrow bodies associated with hundreds of small flood plain lakes within the bottom lands that line these rivers. Of all Wisconsin lakes, Winnebago, in the Fox River Valley, is largest, covering 215 square miles.

CLIMATE AND SOILS

A mean annual rain and snow precipitation of 31 inches is one of the chief climatic factors that make the State a uniformly humid region with a constant water supply for all but the smallest of streams. The heaviest rains fall in the spring and summer months. As well as plentiful rain, there is plentiful sun; half of Wisconsin's days are shiny.

Wisconsin's position between 42° 30′ and 47° north latitude places it in the belt of prevailing westerly winds and within the temperate zone. Weather changes are numerous and rapid and there is a marked difference between summer and winter. Lakes Superior and Michigan have only a very limited influence in checking the temperature extremes of the very cold winters, like those of northern Sweden and central Russia, or of the hot summers, comparable to those of France, Germany, and southeastern England. Fifty degrees below zero to 111 degrees above are the recorded limits of Wisconsin temperatures. Within these extremes, temperatures vary according to the altitude of a given region, according to the northern or southern position of that region, and according to the proximity of lake bodies. Thus the growing seasons range between a shortest season of 75 days for a small part of Wisconsin that borders Michigan and a longest season of 175 days for the southwestern corner of the State.

Among Wisconsin's greatest natural assets are its soils, many of them immensely rich deposits of the glaciers. The latter, including tills or unsorted clays and sands, assorted gravels and sands, and red clays of glacial lake beds, cover the larger part of the State. Other Wisconsin soils are divided between residual—products of weathering of underlying rocks—and those transported by the wind. The residual and wind-blown soils include a sandy soil, the results of the weathering of sandstone, and a clay soil mixture composed of weathered limestone and a wind-brought silt called loess.

GEOGRAPHIC AREAS

Geographers divide the State into five major areas, three of which lie in the belted plain covering all of central and southern Wisconsin. This belted plain is so named because it includes a ring of ridges, each with a short steep descent on one side and a long gentle slope on the other, marking the junctures of weak sedimentary rocks with more resistant, overlapping formations. Such ridges are called cuestas.

First of the three areas within the belted plain is the Western Upland, which begins in southern Polk County and widens southward until, at the Wisconsin-Illinois border, it extends from the Mississippi River to beyond the middle of the State. With elevations above sea level ranging between 900 and 1,200 feet, it has the highest altitudes of the belted plain. Two cuestas—the Galena-Black River and the Lower Magnesian, of much greater length—are salient land features in this region of 13,250 square miles. The Baraboo Ranges intersect the Magnesian Cuesta at Sauk County. A section of the Galena-Black River Cuesta, extending from Fennimore to Mount Horeb, is widely known as the Military Ridge. The Green Bay-Prairie du Chien Military Road, built in 1835, followed the crest of the cuesta. Other well-known heights are Blue Mounds of 1,716 feet, highest point in southern Wisconsin, situated near Mount Horeb; and Platte Mounds and Sinsinawa Mound in the vicinity of Platteville.

Most of the Western Upland was never covered by the glaciers and therefore retained its early rugged landscape. But in the eastern part of the Baraboo Ranges the ice tore away huge blocks of the quartzite rock, deposited moraines, and created Devils Lake; in a region near the St. Croix and Chippewa rivers the glaciers deposited a thick drift. Nearly all of that portion of the Magnesian Cuesta which extends for 35 miles through Polk and Barron Counties is covered by glacial deposit. Drift left by some of the earliest ice sheets is spread throughout the Upland near Beloit and Monroe. The area north of the Baraboo Ranges affords good examples of glacial lake deposits.

Chief rivers of the Western Upland are the Chippewa, St. Croix, Trempealeau, Black, La Crosse, Wisconsin, and the Mississippi on the western border. The latter two have terraced their valleys and cut exceptionally deep gorges; the gorge of the Mississippi is cut to a point more than 500 feet below the level of the Upland Ridges. Interstate Park on the St. Croix River, Perrot, Merrick, and Wyalusing State Parks along the Mississippi, and Devils Lake and Tower Hill State Parks are regions of great natural beauty.

The province known as the Eastern Ridges and Lowlands covers 13,500 square miles in eastern and southern Wisconsin. Its western boundary reaches southwest from the Menominee River in Marinette County to the Wisconsin River in Sauk, thence southeast to the southern limit of the State in Rock County. The eastern boundary touches on Lake Michigan from the tip of Door County south to the Illinois line. Along this eastern boundary abandoned beaches, wave-cut cliffs, and terraces are found at varying distances inland. Door, Racine, and Kenosha Counties possess the best preserved of the ancient shorelines of the glacial predecessors of Lake Michigan.

The Eastern Ridges and Lowlands is a glaciated plain, flanked by northeast-southwest running cuestas of Lower Magnesian and Black River limestone on the west, and by a broader and higher parallel escarpment of Niagara limestone on the east. In contrast to the cuestas of the Western Upland the escarpments are generally of lower altitude and are simpler in outline. Between the two cuesta flankings a lowland, underlain by Galena-Black River limestone and St. Peter sandstone, provides the level topography and fertile soil which make this province the foremost agricultural portion of the State.

For a distance of some ninety miles in the upper part of this Green Bay-Lake Winnebago-Rock River Lowland the topography is that of a smooth plain, made so by evenly spread glacial lake deposits. From here south topography is progressively more irregular until in the southern lowland the area is marked by a glacially made landscape of modified hills, moraine and drumlin mounds, many small streams, and lakes. A great kettle moraine, an irregular mass resulting from glacial accumulation between two lobes of the ice sheets, and marked by deep hollows and knobs, is an important topographical feature of the area from Kewaunee County south to Walworth County.

The principal lakes of the Lowland are the Oconomowoc group and the Lake Geneva group in the south, a large group north of the Oconomowoc group, the Madison chain, and Lake Winnebago; the chief river systems are the Rock and the Fox of Illinois in the south and the Fox of Wisconsin in the north. A series of rapids in the northern Fox River provides the most valued water power in the State. Important manufacturing cities have developed at the sites of the rapids, and these, with Fond du Lac, Oshkosh, Madison, and the cities of the Lake Michigan shore, make the Eastern Ridges and Lowlands region the most highly populated and industrialized of the five geographic provinces. The lake regions, Terry Andrae, Peninsula, and Potawatomi State Parks, and the coastal islands and mainland of Door County are notable for their scenery.

Between the Western Uplands and the Eastern Ridges and Lowlands is the great crescent-shaped Central Plain. With the exception of a small area in the northwest portion which is floored by Keeweenawan lavas, all of the area is immediately underlain by Cambrian sandstone. Elevations vary from 685 feet above sea level (at Ellis Junction) in the eastern end of the plain to 1,242 feet at the western end.

Within the 13,000 square miles of the crescent are both driftless and glaciated areas. The unglaciated Camp Douglas country extending from Wisconsin Dells through Mauston and Camp Douglas to Tomah, and from Camp Douglas through Wyeville and Black River Falls to Merrillan and Humbird, a flat expanse of sandy, arid-looking landscape broken frequently by isolated buttes and mesas, is typical of Central Plain "driftless" country. Roche à Cris, standing 225 feet above the plain, and Friendship Mound, even higher, are well known among scores of castellated ridges and mounds.

Though the Camp Douglas country was never overridden by the glaciers, the water from the melting ice sheets covered the region with lake deposits—sand, gravel, and clay. Some of the Camp Douglas country is within a much larger area, which was once the basin for glacial Lake Wisconsin, and much of the Camp Douglas sand is sand of that lake bottom.

The glaciated landscape of the Central Plain is one of low, rounded hills and moraines, with occasional castellated hills, called nunataks, which were surrounded by the ice during the glacial period but never overridden by it.

Three-quarters of a million acres of swampland lie within the Central Plain. One great swamp covers an area of 300,000 acres between Wisconsin Rapids, Camp Douglas, and Black River Falls.

Lakes are few within the crescent. Some lie in the northwestern part of the section and a few others in the east within Waushara County. Green Lake in Green Lake County is deepest of all inland Wisconsin lakes; Lakes Shawano and Poygan, associated with the Wolf River, are among the largest lakes of the Central Plain. Major rivers are the Wisconsin, Wolf, Fox, Black, Chippewa, and St. Croix. The Wisconsin and the St. Croix rivers have both cut deep gorges, the beautiful Dells of the Wisconsin at Wisconsin Dells and the Dalles of the St. Croix at Interstate Park near St. Croix Falls. Rapids on the Chippewa River provide water power for the furniture factories and paper mills at Eau Claire.

With the exception of a relatively small area touching on Lake Superior, all of Wisconsin outside the belted plain is Northern or Lake Superior Highland. This plain, covering 15,000 square miles, shield-shaped and gently arched—with elevations ranging between 700 and 1,700 feet—is part of a great upland area which reaches beyond Wisconsin to Canada, Labrador, and Hudson Bay. Its moderate topography and underlying pre-Cambrian rock are evidence of the Wisconsin which was once all lofty mountains. Now only in the Northern Highland and a few other places are the early gneisses, quartzites, granites, schists, and lavas exposed.

Certain ridges and monadnocks are remnants of the early landscape. These more resistant metamorphic rocks stood above the ancient plain much as they do now. The eighty-mile long Penokee-Gogebic Range in the northern part of Ashland and Iron Counties is an outstanding example of a pre-Cambrian ridge. The quartzite Barron Hills of Barron County, the Flambeau Ridge of Chippewa, and quartzite Rib Mountain near Wausau are prominent. The latter, rising 1,940 feet above sea level, is the highest known outcrop in the State. The mountain summit has been designated a State Park.

Most of the Northern Highland was glaciated, but a small area near Wausau, Stevens Point, and Wisconsin Rapids escaped the ice. Some hundreds of square miles in Marathon, Wood, Clark, Taylor, Lincoln, and Langlade Counties are within an old drift area which was abandoned by the ice earlier than other parts of the highland. Here the lakes and swamps have practically all been drained and filled, the landscape shows great erosion, and the pre-Cambrian rock is almost everywhere very near the surface.

Areas of younger glaciation have abundant lakes and swamps and many moraines and drumlins; they are covered with a great thickness of drift. Lakes of the glaciated Northern Highland fall into two groups—those of northwestern Wisconsin, of which Lakes Court Oreilles, Upper St. Croix, Chetek, and Namekagon are probably best known, and those of the extreme northern part of the State in Vilas, Oneida, and adjacent counties. The latter, the Highland Lakes group, are numbered in the hundreds. Most of the lakes lie in holes, called kettles, that were left by the melting of ice blocks buried in the drift.

Principal rivers of the Northern Highland are the St. Croix, Chippewa, Menominee, Wolf, and Wisconsin. All of these rivers have rapids and waterfalls and are a source of water power. Extensive marshes, numerous boulders, and frequent areas of poor sandy soil that are found in the glaciated parts of the Northern Highland, combined with a short growing season, make much of this region better suited to forestry and recreation than to farming.

The Lake Superior Lowland, fifth and last of the geographic provinces, is a comparatively small region of 1,250 square miles—all within Douglas, Bayfield, and Ashland Counties in the northwest corner of the State. It is essentially a plain, with altitudes ranging between 600 and 1,000 feet above sea level.

Presumably this area was one part of a great pre-Cambrian peneplain which included the area now occupied by Lake Superior, the Northern Highland, and areas extending northwest into Minnesota and northeast into Canada. Unlike the hard bedrock of most of the peneplain, a relatively small part of the area was of weak sandstone and shale. In a period of uplift the rock weathered and was worn away to such an extent that the area became a lowland. Eventually the continental ice sheets covered the lowland, scoured its surface in some places, and left deposits in others. The water from the melting glaciers formed a mammoth lake whose waters spread and retreated, becoming finally the present Lake Superior.

The Lake Superior Lowland is covered by the deposits made when the lake extended farther inland; abandoned beaches and shorelines are frequently evident. The sand and clay soil, largely compounded of Lake Superior deposit, makes the region better adapted for grazing and for hay production than for grain and general agriculture. Glacial drift is thick in certain parts of the lowland and contains some native copper.

For a considerable distance inland from Lake Superior the post-glacial streams have cut deeply into the plain, and here the landscape is one of ravines and hills.

The most prominent relief feature of the Lowland is the escarpment which extends southwest to northeast from the Wisconsin-Minnesota line to the Apostle Islands and marks the boundary between Superior Lowland and Northern Highland. A companion escarpment edges a lowland of Minnesota. The two indicate the abutment of weak sandstone against the hard lavas and other older rocks of the Northern Highland. The Superior escarpment appears at Ashland as a low sloping wall and, south of the city of Superior, as the South or Douglas "Copper" Range.

As the St. Louis, Nemadji, Brule, Bad, and Montreal rivers descend over the Superior escarpment to the lake, they have developed cataracts which are among the steepest in the State. The Copper Falls of the Bad River and the falls at the juncture of Tylers Fork and the Bad River may be seen at Copper Falls State Park near Mellen. Little Falls and Manitou Falls on the Black River (tributary to the Nemadji) are in Pattison State Park south of Superior. Manitou Falls, one hundred and sixty feet, is the highest cataract in Wisconsin.

GEOLOGY

Successive geologic changes by which visible Wisconsin was shaped are revealed in exposed rock masses in many parts of the State. Oldest of these, the Archean fire-born stones of the north, found at Wausau, Rhinelander, and Chippewa Falls, may be remnants of the earth's primeval crust. They are part of the foundational body of the early North American Continent, which extended from Alaska to Labrador and thence south to the present latitudes of southern Missouri and Tennessee. This land was a barren expanse surrounded by seas that held only the simplest of single-celled life. Wind, rain, frost, sun, and all corrosive chemistries slowly planed the heights. Then, with a downward movement of the earth's crust, the continent sank into the sea where surface waste had already been deposited.

Into the waters covering what is now Wisconsin poured sediments from southern and eastern shores; they settled and eventually became thick deposits of hard crystalline sandstones and conglomerates. Finally the sunken land began slowly to rise again, and, as it presented its new face to the elements, portions of the great mass folded and fractured to form mountains. During the process molten rock welled up from deep within the earth and invaded the roots of the mountains. Pressure and heat metamorphosed sandstone into quartzite, shale into slate, limestone into marble. This period of flood and subsequent land elevation and the period of like action which immediately followed are known as the Lower and Upper Huronian stages in Wisconsin's geologic history. The purple-grey rocks seen in the present Baraboo Ranges are quartzite of these periods. Huronian slate and marble are both revealed near Mellen. Some of the rock formations are rich in iron; good examples are found at Hurley.

The alternation of deposition and erosion continued. Still a third sea terminated millions of years of levelling. Differing from the previous oceans whose beds lay quietly gathering their sedimentary stores, the third presented a restless floor. Alternate short terms of erosion and deposition occurred as the ocean's bottom frequently emerged from the deep, then sank again. Volcanic activity accompanied these processes, and great surface areas were covered with the hot spread of lavas. Upon cessation of volcanic action sandstone was deposited. A final movement upheaved the earth's crust again, and mountains were made. Thereafter northern Wisconsin was depressed in a mighty downward fold of the earth, the Lake Superior syncline. St. Croix Falls, Mellen, and Superior afford good outcroppings of the Keeweenawan masses of lava, sandstone, and conglomerate. In places the formation reaches a thickness of 55,000 feet.

With the end of the Keeweenawan period more than half of the earth's estimated billion years of record had passed; living things had developed slightly in complexity but, without backbone or shell, were still confined to water.

Then began a long age of land rest, with the bulk of Wisconsin protruding above waters whose northern boundary lay close to the present Illinois-Wisconsin line. The elements continued to wear away the land until the only heights that remained were a few rock masses in the central part of the State and the early Huronian mountains, including the Baraboo Ranges. The waters gradually crept over the land until northwest Wisconsin became an extensive peninsula companioned only by offshore islands of rock. With complete inundation came the deposition of sands, fine muds, and clays that form the Cambrian series of rocks, examples of which are present at Madison, La Crosse, Eau Claire, Camp Douglas, Trempealeau, and Lodi. Soft and porous, the Cambrian sandstones are the natural reservoirs that supply water to many Wisconsin cities.

While the ancient sea sometimes covered Wisconsin, sometimes claimed only parts, two more geologic periods passed. Animal and plant life had progressed materially. Shelled fauna were plentiful, corals built their limey colonies, and earliest fishes swam through the weeds. In southern and eastern parts of the State the stacked formations of Ordovician and Silurian times lie in ordered sequence save where complete erosion of a formation or insufficient deposition has caused a "lost interval"; in such places rocks of one series lie directly upon those of an older series, without trace of the missing term in the structural record.

First of the Ordovician deposits is the lower Magnesian limestone, a heavy rock quarried near Madison and La Crosse and used for road building and general construction. Frequently complete erosion of this particular limestone resulted in a "lost interval," indicated by the abutment of the second Ordovician formation immediately upon the Cambrian series.

St. Peter sandstone, a formation of the second Ordovician deposit, which appears, for example, at Viroqua, is a source of water supply for southern and eastern Wisconsin. Because of insufficient St. Peter deposition the next formation, Platteville limestone, rests in some places upon Lower Magnesian limestone.

Two limestone deposits, Platteville followed by Galena, were made in Ordovician time. Small quantities of lead and zinc are distributed throughout the Galena formation and are most concentrated in southwestern Grant, Iowa, and Lafayette Counties. A thickness of one hundred to five hundred feet of shale completes the Ordovician system in the State. Along the east side of Lake Winnebago near Fond du Lac, Richmond shale is dug out and used in the making of tile and brick.

Clinton iron ore is derived from deposits made in the Silurian period. Once mined at Iron Ridge in Dodge County, the low grade ore of the Clinton formation is not in sufficient demand to be profitably mined. Directly above the Clinton deposits is a series of limestone beds known as the Niagara formation. It is believed that these thick deposits are in part compounded of extensive coral reefs which were reduced to sedimentary muds by erosive water action. Appearing as a line of west-facing cliffs all the way from a point slightly north of Waukesha to the tip end of Door County, the formation is known as the Niagara escarpment and is a prominent physiographic feature of Wisconsin. Racine, Waukesha, Chilton, Sturgeon Bay, and Green Bay lie on or near it.

Devonian time was a signal period in the State's geologic evolution. Shallow seas deposited limestone and shale—the Milwaukee formation —in a small area along the Milwaukee shore of Lake Michigan. After Devonian time all the area that is now Wisconsin rose above sea level, and there, as far as can be ascertained, it remained. Millions of years passed; through erosion old mountains were again exposed; the Baraboo

Ranges took their place as surface features. Animals and plants became more detailed in bodily structure, more varied in kind.

Another radical altering of surface features began within the Pleistocene period, one million or more years ago, when great ice sheets advanced upon the continent; in their course they covered all but the southwestern quarter of Wisconsin. Moving cumbrously over ridges, deep valleys, and rounded hills, the glaciers ground away the hill tops and filled the valleys with the accumulation of their grinding and scouring. Sand, clay, gravel, and even huge boulders were all parts of the glacial load. In periods of warm temperature the forward parts of the ice sheets melted, but each time when the cold returned the glaciers again extended south. There were four major advances or forward movements of the ice.

When the continental glaciers melted away, probably only a few tens of thousands of years ago, they left a vastly changed Wisconsin, with only the "driftless" or unglaciated area of the southwest representative of previous surface features. Irregular humps and depressions were now characteristic configurations. The former are the kames, eskers, drumlins, and moraines—mounds of glacial accumulation which the ice sheets dropped in temporary periods of melting or in their final recession. The valleys, which were dammed by glacial deposit, and the depressions left where buried ice masses melted are the basins for most of the lakes in the State.

PLANT LIFE

Once great forests, rising 65 to 125 feet above the mold, covered most of what is now Wisconsin; only in the southern and western hilly sections were there tracts of open prairie. Lakes and streams were plentiful in the northern and eastern forest regions; the southwestern portion, which the glaciers had missed, presented a diverse landscape of green-topped crags, rich valleys, and flower-strewn prairies. Today, despite the work of lumbermen and farmers, much of the native flora remains; the only surviving stands of virgin timber are preserved in State, national, and county forests or in a few privately owned tracts.

In general the northern part of the State held a coniferous type of forest. On its best soils were pure stands of hardwood or mixed forests of conifers and hardwoods. Norway pine grew where the soil was sandy or gravelly, and the sandy barrens of the north were also favorable to the jack pine. Farther south were forests of deciduous trees. Bogs with sphagnum and heath undergrowth and tamarack and spruce stands lay in the low areas throughout the State.

After 1870 lumbering became an important industry and the forests of the north began to disappear. Here the white pine was most plentiful. Other evergreens—Norway pine, jack pine, white spruce, tamarack, balsam, fir, and white cedar—were interspersed with deciduous species such as the paper birch, aspen, red and burr oak, black and white ash, and the yellow birch. On richer soils throughout this area a shrub stage of red raspberry, blackberry, pin cherry, and sumac followed in the wake of fires and lumbering; aspen and white birch saplings sprang up in some sections. The sandy regions of the northern and central parts of the State now grow only jack pine, sweet fern, bracken fern, blueberries, and June berries.

The many shrubby plants replacing the ruined forests of the north are not without beauty. In the thinned woods and along old fencerows grow beaked hazel, chokecherry, northern gooseberry, wild black currant, and bush honeysuckle. In winter the shiny, leathery leaves of the pipsissewa and the delicate needles of the yew and juniper are green beneath the snow. When it is warmer, even before the snow has disappeared, the pink trailing arbutus blossoms over rocks and mulchy forest floors. The bogs, low meadows, and wet woods of the north support dwarf birch, wintergreen, bog rosemary, mountain fly honeysuckle, red-berried elder, cranberry, willow, and red osier dogwood.

Aside from the many kinds of mushrooms, grasses, sedges, and rushes, the northern coniferous area shelters various herbaceous plants. The commonest ferns are the brake, shield fern, and beech fern. One of the most interesting of the mosses is the club moss or ground pine, the spores of which are sometimes gathered and marketed as Lycopodium powder, a modern representative of a family that flourished in the coal-forming era. Early in the spring the hepatica puts forth a small, enamel-like blossom, varying from bluish-lavender to pink; then come the straw-colored Clintonia and the dwarf Solomon's seal, a mass of white flowerets. Ladyslippers, including the yellow and pink moccasin, grow widely, as do the related rein orchis and saprophytic coral root. In bogs and swamps are the pitcher plant, whose streaked purple leaves trap insects for nourishment, and the sundew, which also captures insects, but with the glue-tipped tentacles on its leaves. The fragrant pink twin-flower and the waxy, white, bell-shaped flowers of the shinleaf are found in late spring. In the fall evergreens and mixed broadleafs, turning yellow, orange, red, and purple, blend with goldenrod, purple asters, and scarlet swamp maple-gleam.

Near Bailey's Harbor lies a 400-acre tract of ridges and valleys with a wealth of plant varieties typical of northern Wisconsin. Here are found 30 of Wisconsin's 45 species of native orchids, the bird's-eye primrose and fringed gentian, rare elsewhere in the State, and all but two of the State's evergreens.

Common to all or most of the State are such trees as red oak, wild plum, quaking aspen, black willow, cottonwood, hornbeam, and hickory, and various bushes such as raspberry, gooseberry, and currant. Many herbaceous plants are likewise common, among them the white water lily, wild rose, and violet. The violet, of which Wisconsin has at least 20 species, was selected as the State flower by the vote of school children on Arbor Day of 1909. No particular species was chosen, but probably the children had in mind either the common early blue violet or the pale blue bird's-foot violet. Other common species are the yellow, the arrow-leaved, and the small fragrant white violet. The white water lily blooms in early summer in many Wisconsin lakes and rivers; and the American lotus, once in danger of extinction, has lately become abundant in lakes and in the sloughs of the Mississippi.

Originally the southern part of the State was covered with forests consisting mostly of hard maple, slippery elm, beech, white elm, burr oak, red oak, and ironwood. Less common were aspen, basswood, black cherry, green ash, hackberry, hickory, and butternut. Along the Mississippi and the lower Wisconsin Rivers a few trees characteristic of the Kentucky-Tennessee forest area reached their northern limit—the honey locust, chinquapin oak, and black maple; others, such as black oak, shell bark hickory, black walnut, and wild crabapple, also common in this forest area, extend farther up the State. Characteristic shrubs were the prickly and Missouri gooseberries, the thornapple, chokecherry, June berry, prickly ash, staghorn sumac, alternate-leaved dogwood, round-leaved dogwood, poison sumac, nannyberry, and honeysuckle; there were also a few climbers—the bittersweet, wild grapevine, Virginia creeper, and moonseed.

The southern part of Wisconsin is made up of three distinct regions: the southwestern uplands, the central sandy plain, and the southeastern marshes, woodlands and prairies.

At the northwest end of the deep-cut southwestern plateau, the valley bottoms and narrow ridges were originally covered with a deciduous forest. On the prairies of the broad upland levels Pasque flowers, growing by the millions, spangled the wheat grass, beard grass, and buffalo grass. Later each spring came a profusion of rich blue bird's-foot violets, and white and pink shooting stars blossomed in mid-May. Though most of the prairie vegetation has been destroyed by cultivation and grazing animals, the steeper southern slopes and railway right-of-ways are still full. Among the remaining prairie plants, besides a wide variety of grasses, are the grass-like herbs called blue-eyed and yellow star grass and the herbs curiously named for fruit trees—ground plum, ground cherry, and prairie apple. A few plants, mostly lower forms such as mosses, are peculiar to this region and the central sand country, both of which were not glaciated, while other plants such as leatherleaf and small cranberry grow everywhere else in the State but in these two regions.

Northeast of the region of broad highland prairies and narrow wooded valleys, in the central part of the State, is an extensive, oval-shaped terrain with mesa-like bluffs and characteristic vegetation. Originally this area, where bogs and marshes are now abundant, was covered by forests of white pine, jack pine, jack oak, and red pine. Now only some of the tamarack and spruce bogs of the undrained lowlands, and the meadows of sedges and rushes, retain their original vegetation; the remainder of the area consists of cutover land grown to jack pine and aspen. Bogs that have been drained and burned are largely covered with aspen and with thickets of blueberries, raspberries, and blackberries.

Conspicuous plants of the marshy areas are the sedges, bulrushes and cat-tails, the swamp milkweed with its rose-purple flowers, the blue iris, the arrowhead, and various willows. In the bogs and on the sandstone ledges are labrador tea and blueberry; huckleberry and bearberry thrive on the rocky banks and bluffs. In May the sandy open woods and fields are dotted with blue spiked lupine and orange hoary puccoon.

The southeastern part, by far the most fertile in the southern half of the State, was originally covered by deciduous trees, except for scattered bogs and marshes and for prairie openings throughout the south. Where the soil was boggy, tamarack was the most common tree. In the marshes and sloughs the usual reeds, sedges, rushes, and cat-tails mingle with a variety of moisture-loving plants—the arrowhead, water crowfoot, water persicaria, iris, water cress, swamp milkweed, water hemlock, water parsnip, tufted loosestrife, marsh marigold, and sticktight. The forest edges along the oak openings contained shrubs and small trees such as the dogwood, bladder nut, raspberry, bittersweet, hawthorn, and hazel.

In spring the woodlands throughout the south have large-flowered trilliums, fawn lilies, spring beauties, and a few large yellow ladyslippers. Though much of the undergrowth has died out, many of the more striking species of herbaceous plants remain.

In the rich soil of densely shaded slopes grow Virginia grapefern, interrupted fern, maidenhair fern. Among the first flowers to appear are the pink and lavender hepatica, the milk-white bloodroot, and the marsh marigold. Often the waxy-white golden-centered trillium and purple-striped Jack-in-the-pulpit grow here, and the showy ladyslipper, with purple hood arched over its white spur-like lip. Bellwort, Dutchman's breeches, violet and purplish-brown ginger blossom in early May. Phlox and Jacob's ladder form patches of pale lilac or blue, and the mitrewort extends its spike of flowerets. Spring beauties, which close when a cloud obscures the sun, make solid sheets of pink in the hardwood copses before the trees put forth leaves. In low-lying wooded lands and in ravines among the ostrich fern, shield fern, lady fern, and green dragon, the fawn lily expands large white flowers. The water leaf also grows here, and the jewelweed, with pendant orange and yellow flowers to attract the humming bird. More common in the upland woods are the yellow ladyslipper and the rattlesnake plantain—Wisconsin's only orchid with variegated leaves—the rein orchis, and the shinleaf. The red-flowered columbine grows in rocky places; bees, growing impatient, often cut into its nectar cup from below, leaving the task of pollination to the ruby-throated humming bird.

ANIMAL LIFE

Animal life in Wisconsin was once as varied as the topography. Fur-bearing animals attracted white men to the northwest territories, but, as the areas of human occupation widened, many of the larger animals retreated northward. Today many species originally found over the entire State live only in the northern part, and some species have altogether disappeared.

Within the evergreen forests of northern Wisconsin lived the wild-cat, the wolverine, the Canada lynx, the marten, and fishers, all now rare, weasels, otters, minks, muskrats, raccoons, and beavers. In the northern lakes region roamed herds of elk and northern Virginia deer; the latter is the only member of the deer family that remains. The only moose reported in recent years were a pair that strayed across the border from Minnesota, roamed about for a short time, and then returned to their haunts. The herd of some 30 elk in Vilas County is not native but is the progeny of two carloads imported in 1915 from Jackson Hole, Wyoming. Timber wolves and black bear are now comparatively rare, but brush wolves, or common coyotes, are numerous. The red fox, the porcupine, and the smaller mammals—the chipmunk, deer mouse, woodchuck, skunk, snowshoe hare, star-nosed mole, shrews, and squirrels—are still abundant. The flying squirrel, red-backed vole, bog lemming, marsh shrew, and several species of bat are common to all parts of the State.

At one time the elk, black bear, eastern cougar, timber wolf, and beaver lived not only in the northern forests but also in the deciduous forests farther south. These deciduous forests came within the Alleghanian faunal area, and in them a large number of animals reached the northern limit of their range. Typical small species in the south were the southern flying squirrel, fox squirrel, striped ground squirrel, gray squirrel, woodchuck, cottontail rabbit, long-tailed weasel, Wisconsin gray fox, prairie mole, opossum, small shrew, and prairie vole.

In the thickets edging the forest openings of the southeast the Franklin ground squirrel, skunk, jumping mouse, chipmunk, and short-tailed shrew are still to be found, and in the prairie openings themselves live some pocket gophers, prairie jumping mice, and badgers. Large herds of bison formerly grazed the more extensive prairie of the southwest, home of the prairie red fox, the coyote, the white-tailed jackrabbit, the ground squirrel, and pocket gopher. However, most of the large native mammals of the southern half of the State have been exterminated; such imported pests as the Norway rat and the house mouse thrive where once deer, bear, and porcupine lived in great numbers.

Whereas such species of reptiles and amphibia as the garter snake, the snapping turtle, painted turtle, and mud puppy are found throughout the State, the swamp tree frog, cricket frog, skink, milk snake, and racer live only in the southern area. Parts of the southeast are favorable to the pickerel frog, the bullfrog, the soft-shelled musk, spotted and map turtles, the green and the garter snake, the bull snake, and the rock rattler.

Wisconsin's fish fauna, with over 200 species, is rich and varied. Once the many lakes and rivers swarmed with fish. Now fish are less abundant, especially in the south, where conditions favorable to breeding have not been maintained. The northern lakes and streams still abound in game and near-game fish. Among them are brook trout, German brown trout, bluefin, largemouthed black bass, a common whitefish, smallmouthed black bass, black crappie, pickerel, and wall-eyed and other varieties of pike. The lake sturgeon is now comparatively rare. But king of all game fish and the fisherman's dream is the hard-fighting muskellunge, a species peculiar to the lakes of northern Wisconsin and Minnesota.

A few of the fishes common to the Mississippi River and its tributaries are the spoonbill, shovel-nosed sturgeon, the fish-destroying gar pike, river lamprey, common buffalo fish, carp, sucker, eel, the Mississippi catfish, and the hickory shad. Many other species, also plentiful farther northward and eastward, abound in this area—the channel catfish, common bullhead, common sucker, golden shad, yellow perch, yellow bass, sheepshead, and the smallmouthed and the largemouthed black bass.

Bowfin, mooneye, short-nosed pike, mud minnows, common pike, grass pickerel, white crappie, rock bass, burbot, pike, perch, red-spotted and blue sunfish are common in nearly all Wisconsin lakes. The smaller lakes and streams are rich in brook stickleback, nine-spined stickleback, mud cat, black bullhead, stone cat, tadpole cat, yellow cat, common red-horse, green sunfish, long-eared sunfish, Miller's thumb, and several species of darters (small fish belonging to the perch family).

The hog sucker is found occasionally in some rivers. New species that have been introduced into Wisconsin waters include the rainbow and brown trout and the German carp, now widely distributed. Smelt, first introduced from Green Lake, Maine, into Lake Michigan in 1906, now occur there in great numbers. In Lake Michigan also, and in the State's deeper lakes, the whitefish, Menominee whitefish, lake herring or cisco, bluefin, perch, and yellow bass are abundant.

Lying within the path of the mid-continental spring and fall migration, Wisconsin is visited by great flocks of birds. Of the hunted migratory waterfowl the Canada goose, flying in great V's, honking over cornfields, resting by the thousands on Lake Wisconsin, is perhaps the most spectacular and the most familiar. The fish-eating mergansers migrate in greatest numbers along the Lake Michigan shore and breed regularly in Door County. Mallard, blue-winged teal, black duck, and shoveler breed within the State, as does the beautiful wood duck. Canvasback, redhead, and pintail attract hunters yearly during the fall migration. Of the non-breeding migrants the lesser scaup, or little blue-bill, occurs in greatest number.

Wisconsin's first settlers found the region particularly rich in upland game birds. The sharp-tailed grouse was originally common in the southern half of the State. This species has since retreated to the northern half, and the "prairie chicken" of southern Wisconsin is now the pinnated grouse. Ruffed grouse still occurs in well-forested areas, and bobwhite is fairly common except in the extreme north and in counties bordering Lake Michigan. The Canada spruce grouse is found in the northernmost counties. The wild turkey has disappeared as a native Wisconsin bird, and the sandhill crane is reduced to a remnant. Woodcock and jacksnipe are still taken as game. The Eastern Chinese ring-necked pheasant and the Hungarian partridge have been introduced and are increasing in numbers. In 1939 the chukar partridge was introduced.

The common loon breeds on Wisconsin's northern lakes, and the red-throated loon is sometimes seen on Lake Michigan, especially in winter. The little pied-billed grebe is a frequent summer resident, and the handsome horned grebe a common migrant. Holboell's grebe is a rare breeder. There are nesting colonies of the double-crested cormorant, the great blue heron, and the black-crowned night heron. On inland waters the green heron is always a familiar sight. The American egret used to breed regularly in Wisconsin, but for a time it disappeared entirely as a breeding bird and for years was only a rare straggler from the south. More recently juvenile birds have occurred regularly in July and August, and at least three pair of egrets bred in the State in 1939.

Wisconsin marshes harbor coots, Florida gallinules, king, Virginia, and sora rails, American and least bitterns, and black terns. Herring gulls breed on the islands of Green Bay. Except for the spotted sandpiper and the killdeer, most shorebirds are known as migrants only, although the upland plover and the Wilson's phalarope breed in small numbers.

Raptors are well represented among Wisconsin's birds. The most abundant hawks are Cooper's, marsh, and red-tailed. The duck hawk breeds here and there on limestone cliffs. The bald eagle is much less rare than the golden. Sparrow hawks nest in small numbers, but the pigeon hawk is rare. Goshawks and snowy owls occur in the northern part of the State and are occasionally seen farther south. The barn owl, which has a relatively southern range, is not common here. There are long-eared and short-eared owls, barred owls (especially in the Wisconsin River bottoms), and great horned owls. The screech owl is very common, the saw-whet much less so.

Hairy, downy, and red-headed woodpeckers are common permanent residents, although many redheads leave in winter. Flickers are abundant in summer, and yellow-bellied sapsuckers are commonest during migrations in the southern counties. Well-timbered country provides the breeding habitat for pileated woodpeckers, and in the northern counties there are a few nesting pairs of American three-toed and Arctic three-toed woodpeckers. The red-bellied woodpecker is fairly common in the Wisconsin River bottomlands.

Other birds peculiar to the Wisconsin River country are the lark sparrow, the blue-gray gnatcatcher, the Kentucky warbler, and the yellow-breasted chat. Blue-winged and golden-winged warblers breed here, and the two hybrid forms, Lawrence's and Brewster's warblers, have been found. The beautiful prothonotary warbler nests in holes in bottomland timber, and sometimes nests in wren houses or tin cans. In the southern part of the State the yellow warbler, northern yellow-throat, and redstart are common breeders. More warblers, of course, nest in the northern counties. Both the northern and Louisiana water-thrushes are seen in migration, and ornithologists look for the western form, Grinnell's.

Many western birds, such as the yellow-headed blackbird, the western meadowlark, the western grebe, Brewer's blackbird, and Gambel's sparrow occur in greater or lesser numbers. Certain southern species, such as the cardinal and the tufted titmouse, are extending their range in the State.

In the fall the prairie horned lark is replaced by the northern horned lark, the migrant shrike by the northern shrike. The common seed-eaters in Wisconsin fields include the slate-colored junco and the tree sparrow. In severe weather the regular winter residents may be joined by such winter visitants as the Lapland longspur, the snow bunting, the pine and evening grosbeaks, and the Bohemian waxwing.

CONSERVATION

Men still remember when virgin forest covered five-sixths of Wisconsin. Today these woodlands are all but gone. In many areas soil has been exhausted or eroded, water levels have shifted, and wildlife and natural beauty have departed with the timber. The effects of exploitation are being more and more widely understood, and public opinion stands back of almost any program that promises to restore what has been lost or maintain what is left.

Closed seasons to protect some species of game, birds, and fish were established as long ago as 1851, and a fish inspector was appointed in 1866. At about the same time John Muir offered to purchase a tract of the rapidly vanishing prairie meadow in Columbia County and to give it to the State as a wildlife sanctuary, but his offer was rejected. In 1867 the legislature authorized a commission to study Wisconsin forest resources but little came of it, for the emphasis of the period was on exploitation. When Carl Schurz, then United States Secretary of the Interior, assailed timber thievery ten years later and proposed the establishment of controlled forestry, such as that practiced in Germany, an indignant Congress reduced the scanty funds already appropriated for an investigation of thefts of Government timber.

As Wisconsin tardily became conscious of its losses, a number of unrelated and inadequate agencies arose, were consolidated, and branched again, until the formation of the conservation commission in 1915 combined most activities under one administration. In 1933 a chair of game management was established at the University of Wisconsin, and independent studies in the biology, botany, and agriculture departments of the University are developing a science of conservation. These studies, together with those made at the commission's State game and fur farm, are revealing the complex interrelationship of all aspects of conservation work. In 1935 a number of voluntary groups of nature lovers joined themselves into the Wisconsin Wild Life Federation. Despite their great differences in organization and approach, these three agencies have the same end in view. The conservation commission, applying its slogan, "Conservation means wise use," seeks to modify the use of organic natural resources into sustained-yield harvesting; the Wild Life Federation seeks to educate people to an intelligent interest in nature; and the University experts explore the delicate system of balances by which one natural resource sustains another. Conservation activities are also integrated with the broader designs of the State Planning Board (see *Agriculture, Industry*).

An important part of conservation work is forestry, for forests, in addition to their value for industry and recreation, shelter wildlife and hold soil and water. During the years of exploitation the lumber industry steadily devoured itself, and by the 1930's Wisconsin's virgin timber, once thought illimitable, was virtually gone.

Great fires accompanied the reckless cutting. The history of almost every northern county records at least one great conflagration that overwhelmed settlements and ravaged forests. The annual destruction, according to the 1880 census, was about 400,000 acres. The Peshtigo fire of 1871 completely swept six counties and killed more than 1,000 people. Axe, fire, and plough drove wildlife northward. Buffalo, elk, wild turkeys, and other species fled or were annihilated. Migratory waterfowl, mercilessly harried by hunters, sought in vain for the wild marshes where they formerly roosted and fed. Plant life likewise retreated north; many native grasses and flowers are now virtually extinct in the State. Unshaded streams became so warm that game fish could not survive; silt, washed from denuded slopes, filled the stream beds, and even carp could not live where once large trout had flourished. The silt thus lost was irreplaceable topsoil which had been millions of years in the making.

The State now owns 187,000 acres of forest and 13,000 acres of fairly well wooded parks; the counties own 1,886,000, and the Federal Government, 1,300,000, including the two national forests, Chequamegon and Nicolet. The greater proportion of actual or potential forest land is held in private or semiprivate tenure in the north. Some lies in poor, half-cleared farms whose owners may at any time abandon them; some is held speculatively in the forlorn hope of sale; much is tax-delinquent. One of the principal obstacles to a comprehensive reforestation program are legal complications regarding land tenure.

The Forest Crop Law was enacted in 1927 to relieve forest lands from the pressure of general property taxation, which often impelled owners to snatch what profit they could and then abandon the deforested land. If an owner agrees to devote his land to sustained-yield forestry he is relieved from taxes until he harvests timber, paying in the meantime only a small flat acreage fee from which the counties are exempt. Taxes are taken on the value of the timber after it is actually cut; if the cutting is done destructively the taxes are doubled. Counties now own about five-sixths of the land entered under this plan, and their holdings are increasing as more tax-delinquent land is taken up and the State's new and unique rural zoning ordinances (*see Agriculture*) become effective.

These operate chiefly in northern Wisconsin where people have reluctantly become convinced that much of the region is worthless for private individual development. Attempts to settle it, they realize, result only in increased costs to local governments and the destruction of natural resources. Large and carefully designated areas, therefore, have been permanently and totally closed to further year-round residence and are deliberately destined to revert to wilderness. In time the region will receive direct communal benefits from forest products, recreational resources, and the less tangible assets of watershed, wildlife cover, and natural beauty.

To protect slowly regrowing forests from fire is of primary importance. There are ten forest protection districts, covering 13,600,000 acres in 30 counties. Fire fighting and fire prevention agencies are mobilized in these areas as efficiently as the conservation commission's resources will permit. The 122 steel lookout towers are placed so that almost every acre of protected forest region is within the view of two of them, and the system is linked by telephone.

In places where forest growth fails to reestablish itself naturally, young trees are distributed at the rate of twenty-five to thirty million a year from State nurseries. The trees are planted by the conservation commission, the Civilian Conservation Corps, 4-H and school groups, and farmers. Almost 2,978 miles of triple-row shelterbelt have already been planted in six counties of the sandy central plain as part of a program to check wind erosion. This device, now being extensively applied in the "dust bowl" and elsewhere, originated in Wisconsin where the University has been experimenting with it for a quarter of a century.

There is a growing recognition of the value of types of natural cover other than forests, such as the great peat marsh that once overlaid a large area in central Wisconsin. Here, intermingled with open bog-meadows, the earliest settlers found stands of tamarack which they burned to make place for wild hay. The entire region—bog-meadows, wild hay, and the grainfields surrounding the swamps—formed ideal wildlife cover. But as a result of a series of promotion schemes, ditches were cut to drain the marsh and the dry bogs were burnt off. Now there is danger that the underlying sand will be exposed and will blow over the surrounding land; and aspens, which replaced the earlier lush swamp growth, supply no shelter for wildlife.

To save what is left of the marsh means that the drainage ditches must be plugged. The Federal Government offers labor and funds to block out odd holdings; the State is prepared to operate the tract if restored. But restoration cannot begin until farmers are removed and county governments are satisfied regarding costs and potential revenue. Only then will the experts be able to approach the intricate problem of restoring wildlife under conditions in which it can survive.

Though hunters and trappers were reconciled to seeing wild game disappear with the forests, fishermen somehow expected their sport and business to continue unabated. Dozens of varieties of fish are scattered throughout the unmeasured spread of Wisconsin's inland and coastal waters. As cool, rapid forest streams were clogged into muddy pasture creeks, and as paper mills and factories dumped poisonous by-products into lakes and rivers, there came an outcry to save the fish. While other conservation efforts were largely at a standstill or proceeding slowly, primitive measures were adopted to protect and propagate game fish.

Such measures were not always well-considered. The most serious mistake was the introduction of carp into Wisconsin streams. Carp are good sewage scavengers and will live in warm or semi-stagnant waters where trout die; in some regions they are considered edible fish. Accordingly 136,409 carp were dumped into southern streams in 1881. As, little by little, conservationists learned to improve fish life conditions in streams and to propagate and distribute more desirable species, they found their efforts made useless by the presence of the fast-breeding and voracious carp. In 1900 commercial fishermen were licensed to remove rough fish from public waters under permit; but they found this so profitable that they often kept the captive carp in pens long enough to spawn before shipping them to markets. After several ineffectual attempts to regulate contract fishing, a more stringent inspection system was begun in 1935, and the conservation commission acquired equipment which enables its own men to remove tons of carp each year. The fish are taken to a cannery set up experimentally in 1936; the preserved meat is fed to adult game fish in State hatcheries and to animals at the State game and fur farm, or it is sold to mink farmers.

Since 1936 the distribution of fry from the State's 34 hatcheries and the numerous rearing ponds maintained by groups that cooperate with the conservation commission has been expanding at an unprecedented rate; during 1937 the conservation commission stocked creeks, lakes, and rivers with approximately 1,096,000,000 fish, and in 1938 with 1,124,000,000. Formerly these were sent to untrained volunteers to be dumped into neighborhood streams, but the mortality rate was so high that in 1935 the conservation commission inaugurated two methods of improving the system of distribution. It permits fry to attain some growth in rearing ponds before they are planted, and the planting is supervised by agents of the commission.

The environment in which fish grow and breed has been given careful study, and the regulation of disposal of sewage and industrial waste has greatly reduced stream pollution. Civilian Conservation Corps crews and other agencies have restored miles of streams by shading barren banks, building spawning beds, and placing log V-dams. Small fish, hatched in shallow ponds at flood time and stranded when rivers recede, are rescued in millions and replanted in inland streams. Refuges are established where fish habitually swarm to prevent their mass destruction. Laws regulating size, bag limit, seasons, and licenses are continually revised on the basis of a flow of information from wardens and volunteers. In this way protection is adjusted to the needs of localities and species.

In dealing with wildlife, problems of protection and propagation are as difficult as in the case of fish. The Federal Upper Mississippi River Wildlife and Fish Refuge, lying partly in Wisconsin along the river's bottom land, is of continental importance as a resting and breeding place for migratory waterfowl. The State has set aside 400,000 acres as deer refuge and has established fish and fowl refuges, while local governments, too, have game refuges. During closed season for deer the refuge area is more than doubled. Farmers and other private individuals cooperate by hatching the eggs of upland game birds and caring for the fledglings until they are old enough to be released into the woods. In winter they set up rough shelters and provide grain for birds and hay for deer. Equally important to some forms of wildlife is food and shelter on the farms themselves. It has been found that by the accident of ordinary use most southern farms have either food or cover, but only a fourth or less have both. With little change in farming practices, each farm could harbor wildlife.

Both the commission and the University carry on some study of animals and birds, and many volunteers assist with game censuses and reports on field conditions. At the State's game and fur farm at Poynette (see Tour 7) experts experiment with cross-breeding and study diseases, parasites, and the adaptability of exotic specimens to Wisconsin conditions.

Some attention is being given to the mysterious ebb and flow in wildlife population called the game cycle. At one time certain birds and animals flourish, and at another they are so infested with diseases and parasites that as many as 90 per cent of a species may die. The geographical extent of this phenomenon and the range of species it afflicts are, like its causes, unknown. Some attribute it to sunspots; others point out that it affects least those species which maintain a "saturation level" or are susceptible to other natural checks on population. Though too little known to be of much use to conservationists, the cycles are roughly considered in relation to limitation of seasons and other protective measures.

Erosion control is recognized as an essential phase of conservation work. Wind erosion is sometimes severe in the light soils of the flat central plain, and the ravages of water have been particularly noticeable in the hilly region of the southwestern driftless area, where a single heavy rain has been known to remove more than an inch of topsoil. Such loss of soil capital far exceeds the value of a season's crops.

At Coon Valley, near La Crosse, Federal and State agencies, working with 315 cooperating farmers in an extensive demonstration area (see Tour 20), have studied erosive action, the efficacy of various devices for checking it, and ways in which erosion control can be integrated with the rest of the conservation program. They have found by measurement how much soil of any given local type is carried off from slopes of various pitch covered with different kinds of growth. They have learned when terracing is sufficient protection and what kinds of crops must then be used; when pasture gives better protection than crops; how forest cover is sometimes useless as a check against erosion; how gullies may be stopped from forming and how they may be filled once they form; how to build check-dams and culverts; and many other facts by which farmers may save their soil. At the same time they demonstrated methods of integrating and reorganizing the use of farm land so that game, fish, songbirds, plant life, and scenery may be protected, while the interests of forestry, soil conservation, and flood control are advanced by practical but scientific farming. So successful was the experiment that since January 1940 the work has been carried on by State and local agencies.

Without the aid of such agencies as the Work Projects Administration and the Civilian Conservation Corps the conservation program would be many years behind its present position. In the State parks, which are intended to be kept permanently as wild and unspoiled as is consistent with public access, CCC crews have done no "cleaning up," but have instead built shelters, provided water and sanitary facilities, and made trails. In the woods they build observation towers, string emergency telephone lines, cut fire-breaks, make truck trails for fire fighting, eliminate fire hazards, fight fires, survey and tap shallow underground water supplies, and keep water tables; they campaign against all kinds of tree and plant diseases, insect pests, and rodents; they thin, plant, brush, and improve forest growths; they estimate timber, improve public campgrounds, plant fish, shelter wildlife, and shade streams; they dredge, plow, landscape, build dams, and clean up road and trail sides; they build check-dams, quarry limestone, and survey lands in the interest of erosion prevention.

Education is carried on to make the public aware of conservation problems. The law requires that conservation be taught in public elementary schools, though materials are lacking and formal work is yet in its early stages. In 1935-36 a series of pictures and descriptions of 56 native trees was published in the daily press to be clipped and used in schools; similar series on birds, flowers, animals, and fish are tentatively planned. Wide use is made of the press, radio, and public meetings. The conservation commission formerly devoted all its publicity efforts to teaching the people within the State to care for their resources. The establishment of a recreational publicity department in 1936, with special appropriation for advertising, marked the first change in this policy.

Indians

WISCONSIN was probably occupied by aboriginal peoples as early as fifteen thousand years ago. While the receding continental glacier still locked the northern part of the State, hide-clad men may have hunted the hairy mammoth and lived in spaces which the ice had cleared; some authorities believe that the probability of the presence of man in Wisconsin at the close of the glacial period is very high.

For ages after the ice was gone a succession of tribes pushed northward into Wisconsin to make temporary homes or to live out a history and be scattered. Men built and destroyed towns, traded and fought, hunted and fished, and broke the ground to farm, mine, and inter treasure or the dead. There is rich material proof of prehistoric man's existence. Village sites, mounds, and artifacts are found throughout the State; by these cultures of Wisconsin prehistoric stocks are interpreted. Odd implements belonging to tribes whose position in the order of occupancy has not yet been determined are occasionally discovered in Wisconsin, but the bulk of archeological evidence supposedly comes from a series of southern migrants, first of which began to move upon the State from two to four thousand years ago. Good authority, undecided concerning the racial stock of previous peoples, states that the invaders are to be definitely identified as Indians.

Whatever their race, they produced civilizations which, by comparison with the cultures that followed them, were high. Sites of the invaders' camps and villages, gardens, cornhills, and enclosures line the shores of nearly every lake and stream in Wisconsin. These are focal points for the collection of pottery fragments, arrow and spear points, knives, bone, and copper implements, and the skeletons of animals that were used for food. Gulf sea shells found with these artifacts and remains point the great distance to which tribal trade extended. Among the several thousand villages and campsites that have been discovered, Aztalan is unique and archeologically famous. Here on the quiet bank of the Crawfish River near Lake Mills was once a town whose towered wall was a skillfully devised shield for the cannibal dwellers within.

Knowledge of metal working was frequent among the peoples who had pushed northward along the Mississippi. Of Wisconsin's metals men prized the native copper most, but they knew and extracted various other minerals within their range. The State, in places, is pocked with diggings and quarries, sources for the copper, silver, meteoric iron, flint, pipestone, quartz, and quartzite from which many artifacts were fashioned. Wisconsin lead apparently was not used as a metal until historic time, but the prehistoric men from the south ground the small cubes of galena, made a lustrous mixture of the metal dust, and painted their bodies with it. The presence among tribal properties of foreign minerals such as hornstone, chalcedony, Minnesota pipestone, and dark bits of obsidian from the glass cliffs of Yellowstone are additional testimony to the scope of tribal trade.

These details relating to cultures of aboriginal peoples from the south are not to be considered as necessarily common to all groups in the series of migrations. Each culture had its own peculiar character, with qualities similar to, or at variance with, those of other cultures within the series.

Two major characteristics united the successive tribes—all knew how to raise corn and all heaped up the earth in ceremony and in burial of their important dead. The earthworks in Wisconsin made by the prehistoric southern migrants are of two structural types. Conical or round heaps, found singly or in groups, are common throughout the State. Butte des Morts (Hill of the Dead) near Neenah is one of the best known. Platform mounds, rarest of the mound types in Wisconsin, exist now only at Aztalan. These earthworks, flat-topped squares or pyramids, their sides sometimes terraced, were strikingly like constructions of the great Mexican and Central American civilizations that antedated mound civilizations of Wisconsin, and are held by some ethnologists as evidence for the theory that ancient peoples of Mexico and Central America and those of the State are culturally linked—that persistent memory and tradition, carried northward, expressed themselves again in Wisconsin.

Far more mounds were erected for burial than for ceremonial purposes. By virtue of a custom which called for deposition of objects with the dead, the mortuary mounds—some of them the accumulated pilings resulting from a number of community funerals widely spaced in time—are points for massed artifactual findings. Occasionally they yield rare pieces such as effigy pipes and the three clay portrait masks unearthed in 1936 at Rice Lake, the only pieces of their kind found in North America.

The culture of the mound-building peoples from the south probably reached a peak before 1000 A. D., but their descendants continued to make earth heaps and to live in a manner which, if inferior to the past, still retained salient features of the higher civilizations.

During the thousands of years of mound cultures Wisconsin was tenanted by other tribes than those from the south; tribes from a great Canadian Indian stock of peoples were already settled in the State when the first of the southern migrations to Wisconsin began. These, the Algonquians, lived mainly upon the fish, wild rice, and water fowl of Wisconsin's lakes; they made pottery and textiles but knew no agriculture. They, too, built mounds, at first small circular ones for burial. Later they constructed the linear mounds, limited largely to the southern half of Wisconsin, and the effigy, or emblematic, earthworks which occur so frequently in company with mounds of conical or linear structure. The effigy mounds are the most interesting of Wisconsin mounds. They are in the form of large-scale undetailed depictions of animals, birds, reptiles, and, rarely, man; some have the prodigious length of six hundred feet or more. A Man mound, preserved near Baraboo, is notable. Intaglio depictions (excavated rather than raised above ground level) are exceedingly rare variations of the emblematic earthworks. One such lies in Riverside Park at Fort Atkinson.

The Algonquian earthworks and those of the peoples from the south and east once totalled twelve thousand or more in Wisconsin. Lying within the great Atlantic-to-Mississippi, Florida-to-Wisconsin-and-Michigan area where mound building civilizations existed, Wisconsin is one of the States most richly studded with earth monuments. The southern half of the State is the most concentrated area of mound instance, Madison and environs alone still possessing two hundred and fifty earthworks.

There must have been a first time when peoples from the two great Indian stocks, widely separated in learning, language, and in manner of living, faced each other across Wisconsin terrain. Thereafter, by paths of peace or hostility, the Algonquians slowly absorbed the higher cultural patterns of the invaders. All the while both stocks were making an inevitable adjustment to their environment. When French explorers, first of the Europeans to pierce the western wilderness, met the Wisconsin natives they found the tribes living in ways which were not greatly dissimilar. Differences between tribal cultures were largely those of detail and emphasis.

The Indians then dwelt in forest areas and based their diversified economy in great part on existing plant and animal resources. They are classed among the Woodland tribes. All of the Wisconsin tribes were sedentary or semi-sedentary and established fixed villages of bark or rush lodge homes. They hunted and fished, and cultivated corn, beans, squash, and tobacco in planned gardens. From season to season they gathered the natural yield of edible roots, nuts, wild rice, and fruit. Social organization divided a tribe into kinship groupings or sibs, within each of which members traced their descent from an ancestor common to the sib. If the ancestor were female, anthropologists call the group a clan; if male, a gens. A child born into a family within a clan reckoned his blood relationship through his mother, and a child born into a family within a gens traced lineage through his father. In some tribes each clan or gens had its own chief, and frequently, among the more highly organized of the tribes, specific functions and jurisdiction. One provided all war chiefs for the tribe, another all civil guards or poli ᵕmen, and still another the tribal chief. The several sib chiefs and the single tribal chief were endowed with particular rights and council powers. Sib organizations within a tribe were either exclusively gens or exclusively clan.

Marriage between members within the same sib was expressly forbidden. The ties of acceptable union were loose and could be dissolved on grounds of infidelity, infertility, or unhappiness. Monogamy was most frequently practiced, but polygamy, more common among some tribes than among others, became a privilege extended to male members of wealth or social distinction.

A basic belief in the inherence of supernatural or magic powers in the objects of nature gave rise to numerous rites identified with significant events, such as birth, coming of age, death, war, the hunt, the harvest, and the advent of the seasons. By fasting, prayer, and propitiation, groups or single individuals, according to the dictates of ritualistic tradition, would attempt to gain some one of the supernatural powers and make it subservient to group or individual needs. Tribal members who were believed to have acquired power, and who in the process had experienced similar or related revelations, banded together in secret societies to celebrate certain religious rites known only to the band. Priests or medicine men were leading members of the societies. These spiritual advisors were intermediaries between individual tribesmen and supernatural powers. Disease, regarded as an unhappy mystery among the Indians, was brought to the medicine man for cure. The treatment often mixed primitive medical practices with magical healing.

All of the tribes showed skill in handicrafts. Clothes of fur and hides were sewed with bone needles and sinew threads, and ornamentation of garments and other articles often took the form of intricate geometric or floral patterned appliqués of dyed porcupine quills. Bags and mats were made of reeds and vegetable fibers, vessels and containers were improvised from tortoise shells, birch bark, or wood, and pottery was hand-molded from clay.

Not even the most primitive of wheeled vehicles had been devised. Neither was the horse and its carrier uses known. Land travel was by foot; birch bark and log canoes were the means of water transportation.

In 1634 the Frenchman Nicolet found a people living on Green Bay, their lodges spread in a number of villages between the bay shores and Lake Winnebago. These people, called Winnebago, were a pocket of Siouan stock which remained in Wisconsin during the course of the great Siouan migration from the southeast. According to Winnebago tradition they were once a great nation with a population far exceeding their number at the beginning of historic time; again according to tradition the Winnebago were said to have constructed mounds, a tradition whose claims recent excavations may verify. Pride, arrogance, and valor characterize the tribe's members—war was one of the most important elements in tribal life. The Iowa and Dakota tribes who lived in Wisconsin at the time of Nicolet's visit (though not discovered until later) are thought to have belonged originally to the Winnebago Nation. By ties of related heredity and mutually intelligible languages Winnebago, Iowa, and Dakota are all members of the Siouan stock.

In the Wisconsin of 1634 only one tribe of Algonquian stock was known certainly to have been resident. This was the Menominee who live today where they did over three hundred years ago—west of Green Bay.

Because of tribal wars and Indian hostility the route which Nicolet had pioneered was little used for French enterprise for twenty years thereafter. During the earliest of those years the Chippewa, or Ojibwa, an Algonquian people, came from a point to the northeast and settled along the shores of Lake Superior, but, in spite of this addition, the Indian population of the State was reduced by the attacks of disease and of warring Illinois tribesmen upon the Winnebago. For a time central Wisconsin woods were almost empty of human life. Then in disordered flight from Michigan came a number of Algonquian tribes seeking asylum. They had been driven from their homes by a confederation of tribes belonging to a third linguistic stock known as the Iroquoian, who, in the expansion of a warrior civilization and in the security of firearms procured from Dutch traders, had carried hostilities from New York and Pennsylvania thus far westward.

The Hurons and Neutrals of Canada and the Upper Lake country had already been defeated by the Iroquois when the latter made war against the Algonquians in Lower Michigan. By 1654 the Ottawa, Fox, Sauk, Mascouten, and Kickapoo tribes and the defeated Hurons had made a desperate entry into Wisconsin to hide behind the water barriers of Lake Michigan and Green Bay. The Potawatomi and Miami came to the State with these tribes or arrived here a few years later. For a decade or more central Wisconsin was a place for frightened refugees whom the thin ranks of native Winnebago were powerless to force out. Miami, Hurons, and Ottawa, still fearful of attack from the Iroquois, moved even further westward, to the Mississippi and beyond it. However, with a lessening of hostilities between Algonquians and Iroquois, they returned to Wisconsin, the Miami to found a permanent village as the tribes who remained in the State had done, the Hurons and Ottawa to reside only temporarily on their way back to their Michigan homes.

The influx of Algonquian peoples, who settled for the most part in the rich territory about Green Bay and the Fox River, created a western center of Indian population in the country that lay between the two greatest water systems of North America. Thus Wisconsin became a center for French explorers, missionaries, and traders who forged westward from Canada. Alliances made by the French with Huron and Algonquian in the early penetration of Canada were continued in the French-Indian relationships in Wisconsin. Friendliness of the Indians was essential to the success of Jolliet and Marquette in charting the Mississippi, to the efforts of the mission priests in carrying Christianity to the pagan tribes, and to the bartering between white man and red, which reached such proportions that it revolutionized Indian life.

Individuals within the tribes were converted to Christianity, but none of the Wisconsin tribes in the time of the missions was wholly Christianized. Ultimately the French zeal for spreading belief among the reluctant natives waned. After 1679 the number both of conversions and of missionary workers was small.

The white man's material culture was not rejected. Cloth, blankets, cheap jewelry, trinkets, metal tools and utensils, guns and liquor could be had from the French in exchange for the pelts of buffalo, beaver, and other fur-bearing fauna. To attain these treasures the Wisconsin Indians turned their efforts more and more toward hunting, and Indian economy became largely dependent upon trade.

The French regime held in this region for 129 years. The Indian territory which then constituted Wisconsin was formally annexed to France as part of her western colony, trading posts were established at places of Indian assemblage, and trade was extended to include the Siouan tribes dwelling along the Mississippi. The fortunes of the Indians rose or fell with the fur traffic as it was affected by French trade policy, and by conditions of peace or hostility between French and British or among the tribes.

Various hereditary enmities between Algonquian tribes and the Siouan tribes to the west were intermittently pursued. A sequel to the first Iroquois wars, which had reached a truce in 1670, began in 1682 when the Iroquois invaded Algonquian territory in search of furs to supply the English trade. This conflict continued until the end of the century. At its close another inter-tribal warfare began. The Fox and confederate tribes of Sauk, Mascouten, and Kickapoo arrayed themselves against the French and their Indian allies. In this outbreak the Fox, fiercest of Wisconsin tribes, gave vent to long resentment against French rule and to an inclination, shared by some of the tribes still in alliance with the French, to transfer their loyalties to the English and thus enjoy the more generous offers of British trade. In spite of several massacres and frequent defeat the Fox maintained their wars until 1740, when they were conclusively subdued by the French.

By the time of the second Iroquois war a great shift in Wisconsin Indian population had begun. Concentration of tribal settlement around Green Bay and the Fox River had so depleted the supply of natural foodstuffs that a famine occurred, and some of the tribes in the region began to scatter. The Mascouten moved to the Illinois River; the Miami also passed southward beyond present State boundaries; a part of the Kickapoo moved to a point on the Milwaukee River; and the Fox who still remained in the area left the Upper Wolf to locate themselves at Butte dès Morts. There was greater movement of Algonquian tribes as a preliminary to the Fox outbreak. At the invitation of the French a number of the tribes in the Green Bay region removed to Michigan, some of them returning to the site of earlier homes. These were the Fox and their allies who, at the beginning of the Fox wars, were driven back into Wisconsin. At the conclusion of the war the Fox and Sauk settled along the Wisconsin River, the Fox at Muscoda and Prairie du Chien, the Sauk at Sauk Prairie; the Potawatomi pushed southward along the entire Lake Michigan shore and inland to the Fox River country of Illinois; the Winnebago gradually spread out over the four lakes area of Madison, along the Fox, Rock, and Wisconsin Rivers, and beyond the State boundary to the south; and the Chippewa, freed from their fear of the Fox, settled at Lac du Flambeau and at Lac Court Oreilles.

The region passed from French to British rule in 1763, but not before a number of engagements had taken place in which Wisconsin native forces were employed. Indians of almost every tribe joined the ranks of the French in the colonial wars fought east of the State. When the British won, the Menominee, Winnebago, Sauk, Fox, and Sioux accepted most willingly the change in control. Under the British occupancy a general restlessness of the tribes was evident, but this subsided enough to allow the fur trade to reach its greatest height.

English forces had been in control for only fourteen years when the American Revolution began. In the early years of the conflict the British governed the Indian situation completely, and neither the Indians nor the fur traders were much affected; but in the following years of continued struggle the fighting services of the Wisconsin Indians were solicited by both sides, and trade suffered from the discord. At one time during the conflict Chippewa, Ottawa, Potawatomi, Sauk, Fox, Iowa, and Winnebago were strongly attached to the American forces; during the last years of the Revolution, Indian allegiance wavered between the Americans and the British. At the same time Spain was at war with England, and also sought the aid of Wisconsin Indians.

Spain held territories west of the Mississippi and in Upper Louisiana and had earlier established an extensive trade in Wisconsin. Many Wisconsin Indians preferred a Spanish alliance to a British or American.

Though nominally under American control after 1783 (when Great Britain had ceded the Northwest to the United States and had reached a peace with Spain) Wisconsin and the Indians continued largely under the influence of British traders who remained in the territory. The British fur traffic, maintained much as it had been before the war, was opposed only by a few American traders. Wisconsin Indians, resentful of American succession to the Northwest, were active in a long series of wars directed against American expansion. Every form of white settlement was resisted. At the same time there flared an intertribal war between old enemies, the Sioux and the Chippewa.

American authority was not firmly established in the region until 1816, after another war between America and England wherein Wisconsin Indians, more persistently pro-British than during the American Revolution, were used in large groups during the western operations of the British. After English monopoly of the fur trade and control of the Indians were finally broken, American settlement moved rapidly upon Wisconsin, and great sales of Indian land were corollary to the movement. In 1820 an estimated total population of ten thousand Chippewa, Menominee, Winnebago, Potawatomi, Sauk, and Fox Indians held ownership of Wisconsin properties that was recognized by the Government. Some land sales to the United States had already been made. Money from these, and from the bulk of sales thereafter, reduced the Indians' desire to hunt. The white man's goods could be obtained easily with cash; with a diminishing game supply, furs were increasingly hard to obtain.

As early as 1810 the Sauk and Fox particularly began to supplement hunting with the mining of lead in the southwestern part of the State. Prehistoric peoples had dug for the minerals here, but the historic Indians thought lead of little value until after firearms had been introduced. White settlers spread to the mining region as well as to fertile agricultural areas. Indian resentment mounted against the thousands of American miners who pushed their claims in the lead district, and there was a growing Indian dissatisfaction with the terms of a land transfer involving the mining region and adjoining territory.

Further discontent was felt by both Indians and white settlers as the result of a migration to Wisconsin of groups from four New York tribes. Eastern land speculators and missionaries directed a willing removal to Wisconsin of the Christianized Stockbridge, Brothertown, Oneida, and Munsee Indians. In 1821 the eastern tribes bought land in the Fox River Valley from the Menominee and Winnebago. The bargain was popular neither with the vendors nor with those of the New York Indians who arrived on the site, and in subsequent council the Menominee were persuaded to accept the New York tribesmen as joint owners with themselves of all Menominee lands. This arrangement brought more ill feeling as the eastern Indians, in the following ten years, took up residence near Green Bay, on the Lower Fox, and near Lake Winnebago.

The migration had been badly mismanaged. Elsewhere, grievances of Indians and white settlers ripened for conflict, and several Indian outbreaks aggravated a situation which was climaxed by the Black Hawk War.

In 1816 a Sauk band maintained a considerable village on the Rock River in Illinois. When, in that year, the Federal Government declared that the lower Rock was outside the prescribed boundary of lands owned or to be occupied by Indians, Black Sparrow Hawk, popular Sauk leader, held that the terms of certain land treaties had been violated, and he and his band remained on their grounds. By 1823 white settlers had begun to move in upon the Sauk and to harass them. In the spring of 1830 the Indians, returning from the winter hunt, found their village site preempted by whites, their cemetery plowed under. Indignant at the squatters' acts, Black Hawk and his people sought advice of the British at Malden in Canada. Urged to resist the white aggression, the Sauk band returned to their village, where Black Hawk threatened the squatters with force if they did not promptly leave. The Illinois militia was called out immediately, and Black Hawk fled west of the Mississippi to Iowa, agreeing to remain there unless permission to return were given him by the Government.

But famine in Iowa and promises of assistance from other tribes brought the Sauk leader, 500 warriors, and the women and children of the band back across the Mississippi in the spring of 1832; Black Hawk intended that the band should raise a crop at the Winnebago village at Prophetstown and then, if conditions were favorable, should go on the warpath in the fall. Alarm over the Sauk "invasion" spread among the whites; regular troops and volunteers were called out; and the Hawk with his band retreated up the Rock River. When it was evident that the promised assistance of other tribes was not to be had, the Indians made a brief stand at Stillman's Creek in Illinois and despatched a truce party to the enemy. But the party was slain and the enraged Hawk, ambushing the Illinois militia, fought to an unexpected victory. Encouraged by his success here, he engaged in a series of forays along the Illinois-Wisconsin border. Two hundred whites and almost as many Indians lost their lives in these skirmishes.

By July the forces in pursuit of Black Hawk numbered almost 4,000 men. The Sauk leader retreated before this army to a base near

Lake Koshkonong in Wisconsin, from which place, after gathering together women, children, and properties, he fled overland with his entire band toward the Wisconsin River. The battle of Wisconsin Heights took place near Sauk City on July 21; and the Battle of the Bad Axe began eleven days later while Black Hawk and his exhausted, famished people were attempting to cross the Mississippi. At both battles Black Hawk tried to surrender, but both attempts were disregarded. The Sauk leader escaped from Bad Axe, but was shortly captured. With the tragic defeat on the Mississippi the Black Hawk War and Indian resistance of white expansion in Wisconsin came to an end.

Thereafter the tribes pliantly ceded to the United States their remaining properties. By 1856 Indian title to Wisconsin lands covered only a few reservations. The Grand Council of 1825 at Prairie du Chien, in which United States Commissioners and Wisconsin Indians established the boundary lines of tribal lands, had been preliminary to a period of most concentrated Indian land transfer between 1825 and 1837. In those years, under a Government policy of removing Indians to points west of the Mississippi River, most Wisconsin tribes left the State. Portions of some of the tribes later returned.

The New York tribesmen, except for a number of Stockbridge who migrated to Kansas, were among the tribes remaining in Wisconsin. A controversy between one faction of resident Stockbridge, who favored individual holding of lands received from the Government, and another faction favoring tribal ownership involved the Stockbridge and the Government in a long legal and legislative tangle that was not concluded until 1912.

Close to twelve thousand Winnebago, Chippewa, Potawatomi, Menominee, Stockbridge, Oneida, Brothertown, and Munsee in Wisconsin today make up a State Indian population ranking ninth in America. For the most part they are concentrated in Indian reservations or in local districts. The Chippewa, by far the largest tribal group in the State, occupy four reservations: Red Cliff (*see Tour 14A*), Bad River (*see Tour 14*), Lac du Flambeau, and Lac Court Oreilles (*see Tour 15*). There is also a body of Chippewa at Danbury (*see Tour 13*). The Menominee are located at their reservation northwest of Green Bay (*see Tours 4 and 4A*). A number of Stockbridge live on lands adjoining the southern edge of the Menominee Reservation (created in 1937 and not yet declared a reserve), while others of the tribe are grouped with Brothertown and Munsee Indians along the eastern shore of Lake Winnebago (*see Tour 6*). One hundred and fifty to two hundred Oneida families are on properties at Duck Creek near Green Bay, which formerly constituted an Oneida reservation. Winnebago are widely scattered throughout the Black River Falls-

Tomah-Neillsville territory (*see Tour 19*), and there is a concentration of Potawatomi in Forest County, especially at Blackwell (*see Tour 16*).

The Wisconsin Indians' cultural adjustment to white civilization has not been generally successful. Hunting, fishing, logging, agriculture, the picking of seasonal crops, and manufacture of trinkets for tourist trade are the bases of their economy. The general level of Indian life is very low. In 1936 public aid in some form was administered to 6,690 Indians, 58 per cent of the Wisconsin representatives of a race which, little more than three hundred years ago, had had no contact with the civilization that was to rule them under three flags.

History

THE search for a northwest passage to China led to the discovery of Wisconsin. Champlain, the Governor of New France, having heard of a "People of the Sea" living to the West, sent an expedition to find out about them. In 1634 Jean Nicolet came to Green Bay and visited the Winnebago Indians who lived along its shores around the mouth of the Fox River (*see Tour 1*). Twenty years later two fur traders, Groseilliers and Radisson, entered this region by way of Green Bay and explored the country inland to the west and north to Lake Superior. These three opened Wisconsin to the Europeans, and for the next two hundred years desire for wealth in furs, which in turn necessitated political control, was the dominating factor in its development, whether under French, British, or American control.

Groseilliers and Radisson were followed in the 1660's by other fur traders accompanied by Jesuit missionaries, Father Ménard and Father Allouez. In 1671-72 Allouez established a center for missionary work at what is now De Pere on the Fox River, near Green Bay. The Jesuits, though motivated by religious zeal, served the practical purpose of cementing the friendship of the Indians and the French and of making the country known to the outside world through their reports, *Jesuit Relations*.

In 1671 representatives of fourteen Indian nations gathered at Sault Ste Marie to hear the Northwest claimed for Louis XIV of France. Two years later the Jesuit Marquette and the explorer Jolliet paddled up the Fox River, crossed the portage to the Wisconsin River, and on June 17, 1673 arrived at the Mississippi (*see Tours 13, 22, 23*). This journey was the signal for an influx of explorers, traders, and missionaries. Among the better known were La Salle, authorized by the French Government to build posts in the Mississippi Valley; Father Hennepin, a Franciscan friar who explored the western boundaries of Wisconsin; Duluth, who explored the western end of Lake Superior, the headwaters of the Mississippi, and the connecting waterways; and Perrot, who in 1685 became "Commandant of the West" and the next year built on Lake Pepin a fort to serve as a center for control of the fur trade and protection of the traders.

In the struggle between the French and the English for the Northwest and its fur trade the chief factor was the cheapness of the goods which the English sold to the Indians. This made the French monopoly difficult to maintain, for there was always the danger of the Indian allies of the French going over to the English and the Iroquois. The most important geographical factor of the French fur trade was the Fox-Wisconsin waterway. With scarcely a mile of portage between the two rivers, this waterway, joining Lake Michigan and the Mississippi, was the connecting link between French centers at Quebec, Montreal, and New Orleans and was therefore vital to French control of the region. The waterway was controlled by the Fox Indians who were hostile to the French because they paid less for furs than the English and because they traded with and supplied arms to the Sioux, the Fox enemy. The Fox tried to stop the French trade, first by charging a heavy toll, then by closing the waterway, and finally by negotiating with the French-hating Iroquois.

The French posts around the Great Lakes served as a bulwark against English penetration. But in 1696, in order to maintain prices by creating an artificial scarcity in furs, the king ordered these forts abandoned and all licenses revoked. The Fox then began to treat the French in a high-handed manner. A massacre of the Fox at Detroit precipitated a bitter war in which other tribes formerly friendly to the French rallied round the Fox. Though the Fox were completely subdued by 1740, nevertheless the war contributed to the downfall of New France by irretrievably undermining French sovereignty. With her center line of defense broken and many Indian allies alienated, France was not able to withstand the pressure of the French and Indian War with England (1754-63). Part of a world-wide war resulting from clashing economic interests of the two nations, this conflict resulted in the fall of New France and the transfer of the fur trade to the English.

With only a temporary lull during Pontiac's conspiracy (1763-64), the British fur trade continued profitable and uninterrupted until the War of 1812. In order to systematize the trade, the larger British traders combined to form the North West Fur Company and other companies; the French-Canadian employees of the company continued to make contacts with the Indians. Because of the value of the fur trade the British remained in possession of the Northwest until 1816, though the Americans came into nominal control at the close of the Revolution in 1783 and with the surrender of the forts to American garrisons in 1796.

In 1784 the Continental Congress passed a so-called "Northwest Ordinance" which provided a plan for settlement of western lands, north and south of the Ohio, and for division ultimately into 14 or 16 states; and in 1785 Congress adopted a scheme for the surveying and sale of these western lands ceded to the United States by Massachusetts,

Connecticut, New York, Virginia, and some other States. From then on the plan laid down in the ordinance was followed in the sale of all public lands. The American territorial system was established by the Northwest Ordinance of 1787. This applied only to the region north of the Ohio, and provided that, when the population justified, not less than three or more than five States might be formed from this territory. These States would enter the Union on a basis of equality with the older States—a solution of genius to the problem of colonial organization. Included in the ordinance was a compact between the older States and the territory which promised political and religious freedom, the encouragement of education, and no slavery.

Before 1800 there were not more than 200 whites in Wisconsin. The largest group, numbering about 56 families, was at Green Bay, occupied in 1764 by the fur trader, Augustin de Langlade, and his son Charles. The only other real settlement was the trading post established at Prairie du Chien in 1781 (*see Tour 13*). In 1795 Jacques Vieau, an employee of the British North West Company, established posts at Kewaunee, Sheboygan, Manitowoc, and Milwaukee. A few traders carried on their activities near what is now Kaukauna, but at the portage of the Fox and Wisconsin rivers there was only one settler, a Frenchman who made his living by transporting boats and cargoes.

Regardless of the change from French to English and from English to American sovereignty these settlements remained French in language and customs. The lives of the traders were relatively comfortable and pleasant. They intermarried with the Indians and had Indian slaves to do their work. Agriculture was on a small and primitive scale. The problem of government hardly existed. Disputes were settled in private until 1803, when Charles Reaume, commissioned by the Governor of Indiana Territory, became justice of the peace at Green Bay. The law of his court was French, like his accent, though he wore a British red coat and owed allegiance to the American Government.

At the close of the War of 1812 American occupation of the Northwest began. In 1816 Fort Crawford was built at Prairie du Chien and Fort Howard at Green Bay. The following year General Zachary Taylor took command of Fort Howard, which rapidly became the focal point of settlement from the East. Military rule continued until 1818, when Wisconsin became a part of Michigan Territory and was divided into two counties, Brown and Crawford, with centers at Green Bay and Prairie du Chien respectively. County officers were appointed, but boundary and land-title disputes continued to be settled by the participants themselves. Voluntary subscription rather than taxation paid for the necessary government services.

Until 1834 furs continued to be the basis of the Wisconsin economy. With England's hold on the fur trade broken by the War of 1812, the

American Fur Company came into control. Because the Indians still preferred British goods, which were cheaper and better, John Jacob Astor had a law passed restricting the fur trade to American citizens. His agents undersold their competitors, and he acquired huge tracts of land by taking mortgages in payment of goods for the fur trade. Thus he built up a monopoly from Lake Michigan to the Mississippi. But by the 1830's the fur trade in Wisconsin was diminishing, and Astor relied upon richer hunting grounds to the west.

Meanwhile, lead mining had begun to take the place of fur trading. The Indians mined lead in southwestern Wisconsin before the white man arrived. Then the French took it up. Lead mines in the Fever River district were known to the Americans as early as 1816 and here, in 1822, large scale mining began. In the following years it became so profitable that for a decade after 1825 there was a rush to the mining area from the States to the south.

The French, who had come to Wisconsin to trap and trade lived side by side with the Indians, but between the Indians and the Americans, who came to settle, there was a fight to the finish. The hostilities of 1827, directed chiefly against the southwestern miners, led to the re-establishment of the fort at Prairie du Chien and the building of Fort Winnebago at the Fox-Wisconsin portage. In 1831 and 1832 Chief Black Hawk led his Sauk braves in the last great war against the white usurpers (*see Indians*).

TERRITORIAL PERIOD

The defeat of Black Hawk in the summer of 1832 served to advertise Wisconsin to future settlers. In 1834 the government lands in the vicinity of Green Bay were surveyed, and land offices opened there and at Mineral Point; two years later a land office was opened at Milwaukee. The first Wisconsin newspaper, the Green Bay *Intelligencer,* was founded in 1833. Settlers poured in from New England and Canada, from Ohio and Pennsylvania, but especially from New York. And Southerners continued to come into the lead region.

So rapid was the increase in population that it was not long before land speculators and lead miners alike began to demand a separate Territorial government. James Duane Doty, a land speculator from Green Bay who had been made circuit judge of the entire region in 1823, and Albert G. Ellis, the publisher of the *Intelligencer,* were leaders in this movement. In April 1836 the "Territory of Wiskonsan" was organized to include what is now Wisconsin, Iowa, Minnesota, and part of the Dakotas. The Governor appointed by President Jackson was Henry Dodge, leading citizen of the lead-mining area. In October 1836 the territorial legislature met at Old Belmont (now

Leslie, Lafayette County), in the lead country, where nearly half the population was concentrated. The chief business of the first session was the choice of a site for the permanent capital. One of Doty's speculative ventures had been the lands around the Four Lakes, and here the legislators were persuaded to locate the new capital, which was named Madison. The townsite was surveyed and platted in 1837.

Economic activity in the territorial period was centered around lead and land. The production of lead increased steadily during the period until it reached its height in 1847. The interest in land was for speculative purposes, there being as yet only self-sufficing agriculture. Not until the late forties did wheat-growing become profitable, and then small flour and grist mills sprang up in the settled portions of the Territory; what little lumbering there was took place in the west along the tributaries of the Mississippi. But treaties with various tribes gave the Territory title to most of the Indian lands, and these were held for speculation with the hope of increasing their value through the construction of internal improvements. Banks were incorporated in 1836, at Dubuque, Mineral Point, and Milwaukee. Government land offices hummed. Fraud was rife. In the valuable lead region Government lands were sold privately before they were opened to public sale. Then came the panic of 1837, and unredeemed debts and bank failures left their mark on the State about to be born.

The movement for statehood developed out of the need for internal improvements and boundary adjustment. The question of Wisconsin boundaries has engendered long and bitter quarrels. In the first place, in order that Illinois might have an outlet on the Great Lakes the Illinois boundary was moved north to include Chicago. Then the northern peninsula of Wisconsin, a region rich in copper and iron, was turned over to Michigan in payment for territory taken from her by Ohio. No attention was paid to Doty's appeal in 1842 for the restoration of the old boundaries. In 1843 the Territorial government of Wisconsin offered to trade boundary adjustment for internal improvements which should include a railroad from Lake Michigan to the Mississippi, the Fox-Wisconsin River improvement, and harbors on Lake Michigan. This offer was not accepted, and the drive toward statehood was accelerated. Finally, in 1846, an enabling act was passed by Congress, and the first constitutional convention met in Madison. The constitution which was drawn up was rejected by the people and another, submitted by a second constitutional convention, was adopted in 1848. On May 29th of that year Wisconsin became the thirtieth State.

THE STATE

The years following admission to the Union witnessed a great influx of German and Scandinavian immigrants. The population of Wisconsin increased tenfold in the decade of the 40's and more than doubled during the 50's. Railroads opened the interior of the State to farmers; by 1854 the Milwaukee and Mississippi Company had extended its tracks to Madison and three years later to Prairie du Chien. There was a rapid increase in mileage during the next decade.

During the 50's the lead-mining industry declined and wheat took its place as the basis of the Wisconsin economy. In 1856 and through the 60's the wheat crop was seven times what it had been in 1849. Flour mills flourished in the Fox River Valley, and small grist mills were everywhere, Milwaukee, with a population of 18,000, being now an important port for the shipping of wheat.

The constitution demanded a free public school system and set up two school funds, one for a university and one for the common schools. It was not, however, until 1879 that schooling became compulsory and then for only twelve weeks a year for children between the ages of 7 and 12. The State University, founded in 1848, was unpopular at first. The legislature's appropriations were inadequate, and the sale of university lands, hastily, carelessly, and even at times fraudulently administered, was not as lucrative as it should have been. The monetary panic of 1857 and the Civil War decreased its funds even more. Not until after the Civil War did it become coeducational.

The Ordinance of 1787 prohibited slavery in the Northwest Territory, but a few slaves were brought into Wisconsin by Southern miners and Southern military officers. Anti-slavery sentiment crystallized in an abolition society formed in Racine in 1840, a second formed for the Territory in 1842, and in the publishing of a paper, the Waukesha *Freeman*. Wisconsin citizens helped runaway slaves through the "Underground Railway," and in 1854 the State supreme court declared the Fugitive Slave Act unconstitutional. In the same year a united front of anti-slavery Whigs, Free Soilers, and Democrats formed the Republican Party in protest against the extension of slavery. The Republicans were immediately successful, electing two Congressmen in 1854 and the Governor of Wisconsin and a United States Senator in 1855. In 1856 the State voted for Fremont and four years later for Lincoln.

Several months before the Civil War was declared the Wisconsin Legislature prepared for the conflict by passing acts that provided for the defense of the State and empowered the Governor, in case of war, to cooperate immediately with the National Government. Fort Sumter fell on April 14, and next day President Lincoln issued his call for 75,000 three-months volunteers. Within one week 36 Wisconsin companies had offered their services, and on April 22 the First Wisconsin Volunteer Infantry was organized. During the first year of the war 16 regiments were mustered in, and central camps were established in Milwaukee, Madison, Fond du Lac, and Racine.

Governor Randall was succeeded in 1862 by Louis P. Harvey. A few months later Governor Harvey led a relief expedition to aid the hundreds of Wisconsin soldiers left wounded on the battlefield of Shiloh, and, on his return journey, was drowned in the Tennessee River. Lieutenant Governor Edward Salomon, who succeeded him, faced the most depressing period of the war. The mounting costs, the great loss of lives, and the opposition of a minority group within the State were beginning to show their effects.

President Lincoln's call in August 1862 for 300,000 volunteers (the State's quota was 12,000) had to be met in Wisconsin by a draft. Serious anti-conscription riots resulted in the German settlements around Port Washington. Many of the Germans had come to America to escape military service and had settled where conditions for farming were so unfavorable that to leave the half-cleared land would have been to deprive their families of support. But more than that, these Germans, who had aligned themselves with the Democratic Party, were opposed to the Republican cause, associating it with the Whig Party, in which a Nativist group was "avowedly hostile to Catholic foreigners and unfriendly to others who were of non-English speaking races." When troops were sent in to enforce the draft and rioters were arrested and sent to Camp Randall, the feeling of bitterness among the Ozaukee County Germans was intensified.

In 1863 the Harvey Soldiers' Hospital, named in honor of Governor Harvey, was opened in Madison, and a year later James T. Lewis became the fourth wartime Governor. On April 13, 1865, recruiting ceased in Wisconsin, and during the summer and autumn of that year most of the State's troops were mustered out of service. Wisconsin sent 91,379 men to the Civil War; its death roll was 10,752, and its war expenses amounted to over eleven and a half million dollars.

After the Civil War industry began on a large scale. The rapid increase of railroad mileage, which by 1880 reached 2,960 miles, made possible the development of the lumber industry. Previously limited to a few miles on either side of a river, the lumber companies were now independent of natural highways. By 1880 lumbering had come into second place among the industries of the State, flouring and grist mill products being first. But the production of wheat was declining. The opening of superior wheat lands in the States across the Mississippi drew away many Wisconsin farmers; the land in southern Wisconsin was wearing out; and the northern cutover lands, sold to farmers by the lumber interests, were unsuitable for wheat growing. Furthermore, insect pests were becoming ruinous. In the face of such a situation William Dempster Hoard and others determined to turn the Wisconsin farmers from wheat growing to the raising of livestock (*see Tour 19*). For this purpose Hoard established the Wisconsin Dairymen's Association in 1872.

The State continued to grow. The unoccupied lands of the North were widely advertised by railroad agents. In 1860 the total population of Wisconsin was 775,881; in 1870, 1,054,670; in 1880, 1,315,497; in 1890, 1,693,330; and in 1900, 2,069,042. With the invention of Babcock's butter-fat tester in 1890 the agricultural revolution was complete. In 1880 dairying ranked sixteenth among the enterprises of the State; by 1900 it had jumped to fourth place. The lumbering industry continued to expand until between 1890-1910 it outranked all the other industries of the State; in 1900 Wisconsin was the first lumber-producing State in the country. By 1890 the railroads had laid down 5,640 miles of new track, an increase of 90 per cent since 1880; in the next decade another thousand miles were added.

By 1880 the seeds of the later industrial development in Wisconsin were beginning to be sown. Localities were offering special inducements to industry. Between 1880 and 1900 the number of factories doubled and the number of workers was multiplied two and a half times. With the decline in wheat growing and the increasing importance of the lumber industry, flour mills were superseded by paper and pulp mills. The change to livestock farming brought with it the meat-packing industry and the manufacture of shoes and leather goods. The metal industry grew out of Wisconsin's location between the iron of Minnesota and the coal of Illinois and Indiana; proximity to western wheat fields led to the manufacture of agricultural implements.

But these were disquieting years for labor. The rapid development of industry and the supplanting of men by machines led to several violent strikes. The office of commissioner of labor and industrial statistics was created in 1883, and in 1885 a factory inspector was appointed. The agitation for an 8-hour day was intense. Labor disturbances reached their height in 1893, the year in which the Wisconsin State Federation of Labor was formed, but the depression which followed the monetary panic of that year called a halt to the militancy of organized labor. The only attempt on the part of the government to soften the effects of the depression was the formation in 1896 of the bureau of immigration for protection against fraud in land sales.

Following the Civil War wealth and political power became more and more concentrated in the hands of a few men. Popular opposition to the growth of monopolies was crystallized in the Granger Movement of the 70's and again in the political struggles that took place at the end of the nineteenth and the beginning of the twentieth centuries. The career of Robert M. La Follette, Sr., was an expression of this latter anti-monopoly sentiment. Three times elected Governor of Wisconsin, he went in 1906 to the national Senate where he was active until his death in 1925. In 1924 he ran for President of the United States on an independent ticket.

Wisconsin's part in the World War was commensurate with that of other States. About 120,000 went into military service. There was opposition from the Socialists of Milwaukee and from La Follette, who suffered abuse and ostracism for the stand he took, but the conservative Republican faction, under the leadership of the chief executive, Emanuel Philipp, was zealous in the conduct of the war.

Since 1900 the history of Wisconsin has been marked by the growth of large-scale industry and the concentration of population increases in industrial areas, especially in the southeastern and lakeshore counties and in the Fox River Valley. Accompanying this concentration there has been a shift from rural to urban population. The 1930 census shows that approximately one-third of those employed worked in manufacturing enterprises, one-fourth in agriculture and forestry, and one-eighth in trade. Significant developments of the 1900's have been highway construction, conservation activities, rural land zoning, and the growth of cooperatives. These important subjects are treated in separate chapters.

The People Who Came

HALF the people of Wisconsin (50.2 per cent of the total 2,939,-006 according to the census of 1930) were either born in foreign countries or born in this country of foreign or mixed parentage. Of these, 41.2 per cent claimed Germany as their country of origin, 9.4 per cent were from Poland, 9.2 per cent from Norway, 4 per cent from Czechoslovakia, and 3.9 per cent from Sweden. With the ebb and flow of settlement other nationalities have at different periods been numerically predominant.

Nearly two hundred years of fur trading preceded the first real settlement in Wisconsin. In the middle of the seventeenth century came the French explorers, hunters, and missionaries. Their century of occupation left little in material development, but a lasting reminder of their early presence exists in the many colorful place names they gave to settlements, lakes, and rivers. Prairie du Chien and Eau Claire, Lac Vieux Desert and Butte des Morts, Flambeau and St. Croix all speak of the days when the land was part of New France.

The coming of the British after 1763 extended the fur trade but did not bring permanent settlement. The region was still a wilderness, known only to traders, explorers, missionaries, and soldiers. But by 1820, four years after America had finally taken control of the Northwest Territory, the population was sufficiently localized in the trading posts of Green Bay and Prairie du Chien to be enumerated at about 500 in each place.

The earliest wave of settlement into Wisconsin, between the years 1820-50, brought Southerners up the Mississippi River into the southwestern lead-mining area, now Grant, Iowa, and Lafayette counties. Some of the pioneers who, during the Great Migration which ended with the admission of Missouri in 1821, had moved west along the rivers from Virginia, Kentucky, and Tennessee, within the next decades came into Wisconsin from Illinois and Missouri. In 1830 nearly half the 3,245 people in Wisconsin were living in the lead region and the remainder in Green Bay and Prairie du Chien.

Negro slaves were brought from the South at this time. In 1822 a Kentuckian with a party of slaves encamped where Galena (Illinois) now stands and began lead-mining operations on the most extensive scale yet known in the lead country. Prior to the World War there were fewer than 3,000 Negroes in the State; afterwards the labor shortage brought many from the South. Of the 10,739 Negroes recorded in the 1930 census, 7,501 lived in Milwaukee.

The second wave of settlement, bringing Yankee farmers into the southeastern counties of Wisconsin, began after Black Hawk had been defeated in the summer of 1832. After the last great Indian war the United States acquired title to all the land in southern Wisconsin south of the Wisconsin and Fox Rivers and opened this area for settlement. In 1834 land offices were established at Mineral Point in Iowa County and at Green Bay in Brown County and, with the influx of settlers during 1835-36, at Milwaukee in 1836. The territorial census of 1836 showed a total of 11,683. In 1840 Wisconsin's population had increased to 30,945; in 1842, to 44,478; in 1846, to 155,277; and in 1848, to 210,546. Though the population of the lead-mining region was growing, the population of the eastern shore was growing faster. In 1840 Grant and Iowa Counties had 25 per cent of the total population; in 1847, 13 per cent.

Out of 197,912 native-born Americans living in Wisconsin in 1850, 191,143 had come from the States north of the Ohio and east of the Mississippi. The State which contributed the largest number was New York; in 1850 New Yorkers exceeded by 5,000 the number of persons born in Wisconsin. The second most important source was Ohio, followed by Vermont and Pennsylvania. The Easterners settled in the two southern tiers of counties east of the lead region and then spread northward to the Lake Winnebago region, into Columbia, Dodge, Fond du Lac, Marquette, and Winnebago Counties.

In 1850 more than a third of the total population of Wisconsin was foreign-born, the largest number having come from the British Isles. Cornish miners had begun to arrive in the southwestern lead region in 1830; by 1850 they numbered 7,000. But discovery of the California gold fields, besides diverting immigration, caused almost half of the Cornishmen to leave. When the lead mines were exhausted, those who remained began farming. People from Scotland, who also came in the 1830's, farmed in Racine and Rock Counties. Though never numerically important, subsequent Scottish settlements were established in central Wisconsin. Welsh settlers came chiefly during the decade 1840-50, some mining at Mineral Point and Dodgeville, others, who were noted as stock breeders, farming in eastern Columbia and Waukesha Counties.

The Irish immigrants in 1850 outnumbered the English and were three times as numerous as the Scotch and Welsh combined. Until 1880, when they were exceeded by the Norwegians, the Irish were second only to the Germans in number; they settled in scattered townships throughout the State, but especially in the central and southern portions as far north as St. Croix County and from Lake Michigan to the Mississippi.

In 1845 a group of Swiss, organized in Switzerland in the Canton of Glarus, settled in and around New Glarus, Green County, where, with later immigrants, they developed a famous center of Swiss cheese production (*see Tour 23B*). Other Swiss settlements are in Buffalo, Sauk, and Taylor Counties.

In 1850 there were fewer German-born than British-born inhabitants of Wisconsin. But between 1850 and 1860 there was such increase in immigration from Germany that since the latter year the Germans have been the predominant element of foreign stock in the State. This first great wave of German settlement, which reached its crest in 1854, followed the unsuccessful Revolution of 1848 and brought with it a large number of German intellectuals and liberals, including the notable Carl Schurz. A second great wave of immigration, from 1881 to 1884, brought the largest number of Germans who ever entered the State. Spreading first along the lakeshore from Milwaukee into Manitowoc County, the Germans fanned westward along the rich meadows of the Rock River in Jefferson and Dodge Counties. They early ranked among the State's best farmers, built tanneries and sawmills, and started the brewing industry in Milwaukee. Later immigrants journeyed still farther northward, settling counties which lie in the center of Wisconsin up to and including Marathon and Shawano.

Between 1840 and 1860 a large number of Norwegians also came into the State; the first, who arrived simultaneously with the Germans in 1839, settled on Jefferson Prairie in Rock County. The most important focal points of early settlement were Muskego in Racine County and Koshkonong in East Dane and West Jefferson Counties. From here the Norwegians spread to southern and southeastern Wisconsin in the 1840's and 1850's. During the 1850's and 1860's they moved into western and northwestern Wisconsin. By 1870 their areas of settlement were fairly well marked out: in the south, Dane and the circle of counties surrounding it; on the west, an area from Crawford County to Polk County concentrated in Vernon, La Crosse, and Trempealeau Counties; in the north-central section, Portage and Waupaca Counties; and in the northeast, Manitowoc County.

Subsequent immigration brought various nationalities, including other Scandinavian groups. The Danes, for the most part, went northwest into Polk, Barron, and Clark Counties, though they also settled from Juneau down through Rock County and in Racine County. The Danes also share Washington Island with the only group of Icelanders in America, who came there as fishermen in 1870. Swedish people also migrated to the northwestern part of the State; their chief southern center is in Waukesha County. The Finns, who came about the same time as the Scandinavians, settled in the north.

After 1863 Poles began to come to Wisconsin, settling in and around Marinette, Stevens Point, Berlin, Menasha, Manitowoc, Beaver Dam, La Crosse, and Independence. The largest Polish immigration came, however, between 1910 and 1920, when thousands settled in Wisconsin's industrial centers, especially Milwaukee. Since 1920 the Poles have been the second largest foreign national group in the State.

Dutch immigrants settled in Sheboygan County as early as 1848, later spreading from this center to La Crosse, Outagamie, Fond du Lac, Calumet, and Milwaukee and Brown Counties. Belgians, who began to enter Wisconsin in 1854-55, settled chiefly in Brown County and in southern Door and northern Kewaunee Counties. More numerous and more widely scattered than either of these groups are the Czechoslovakians, who are predominant in Kewaunee County and are found in small settlements in the west, from Grant County to Trempealeau, in a few central and northern counties, and in the south in the cities of Racine and Milwaukee.

At the beginning of the twentieth century laborers from southern Europe came to Wisconsin's growing industrial cities. Greeks, Lithuanians, Hungarians, and Yugoslavs, although proportionately small in number, constitute an important part of the industrial population. Half the Italians are concentrated in southeastern cities; the rest are scattered in other parts of the State.

Political History

IN 1828 there was a political revolution in America. Small farmers on the frontier and workers in the growing cities, revolting against the domination of government by the commercial and financial centers of the East, elected Andrew Jackson President. Backed by the masses of people but opposed by the manufacturers and financiers, Jackson fought to advance in practice the political concept that government should serve the people. The seat of Jacksonian frontier democracy was the land beyond the Appalachians, and the constitutions which embodied its ideals were those of the Mississippi Valley States formed during and shortly after the depression of 1837-45. Of these Wisconsin was one.

The constitutional convention which met in Madison in October 1846 was composed, as a contemporary expressed it, of "the Retrograding Democracy, the Progressive Democracy, and the Whigs." Progressive Democracy was in control. Democratic dislike of bankers was responsible for the most important issue before the convention. Although in the rest of the Mississippi Valley feeling against the vested interests, especially banking capital, was in general hostile, the situation in Wisconsin was complicated by the existence of two distinct sections. The eastern section on Lake Michigan, settled after 1834 by New Englanders and New Yorkers who were interested in land values and the development of the Territory, reflected the political ideals of the eastern seaboard. The southwestern lead-mining region, settled in the 1830's by Southerners, mirrored the Jacksonian ideals of the Mississippi Valley. Residents in the eastern section belonged either to the Whig Party, which in the Nation at large was the party of property, or to the right-wing "Hunker" faction of the Democratic Party; those in the southwestern section were Progressive Democrats, known to their opponents as "Tadpoles" or "Barnburners." The failure of all the banks that had been incorporated by the Territorial government and the "swindling operations" (as a contemporary called them) of the Wisconsin Marine and Fire Insurance Company of Milwaukee, which continued to do banking and to issue paper money after the revocation of its charter, led to the introduction of an anti-banking article. Drawn up by Edward G. Ryan, of Racine, it prohibited the incorporation of banks, the issuance of paper money, and the circulation of bank paper. The Whigs and Hunker Democrats, who wanted easily available capital, demanded a free banking system and called the Progressives defaulters. It was the anti-banking clause more than any other which split the Democratic Party.

A second acute question was whether or not the homestead should be exempted from seizure for debt. The Madison *Wisconsin Democrat* remarked, "After a poor man by dint of the closest economy and prudence has succeeded in securing to himself a forty acre lot of land, we want it engrafted upon our constitution that whatever reverses may come . . . we want that land, that homestead, secure from the grasping avarice of any creditor." Small farmers remembered the evictions and forced sales which followed the depression of 1837, but the Whigs and Hunker Democrats called this article a repudiation.

The third disputed article was the married women's property clause, which permitted married women to own property in their own names. Marshall M. Strong, a conservative from Racine, was so bitter in his opposition to this clause that he threatened to leave the convention and swore to defeat the constitution on account of it. "Woman is to be transferred," he said, "from her appropriate domestic sphere, taken away from her children and cast out rudely into the strife and turmoil of the world, there to have her finer sensibilities blunted, and ruling motives of her mind changed, and every trace of loveliness blotted out."

The difference between the eastern and the western temper was again apparent in the fight on the judiciary article. Easterners were used to appointive judges, while Westerners were accustomed to their being elected. The Lancaster *Herald* remarked, ". . . it may be said that it is an old federal axiom that the people are not to be trusted. If this axiom be true, we cannot too soon change our form of government. Those savants who assume to be invested with extraordinary wisdom, and to be themselves the peculiar guardians of conservatism ought to ask for letters patent of nobility. No, the people must govern, and no disguise about it. As power with us has but one source, let it be simple and direct in its application. We say—let our judges be elected directly by the people. We shall then have a simple, effectual power of correcting abuse, a power lodged where it ought to be, in the hands of those who suffer by abuses, and who, depend upon it, know when reform is needed as well as anyone can tell them."

There was general agreement in the convention upon the necessity for internal improvements; the question was whether these should be undertaken by the State or by private individuals. The Whigs favored the former method, the Democrats the latter. Private competition was considered to be the repository of human rights. The Jacksonians distrusted government, especially the legislative branch in which a political aristocracy had developed. It was argued by them that corruption and an increased incentive toward speculation would result from having the State construct internal improvements; the good of the people would not be considered. The States neighboring on Wisconsin had been bankrupted by the canal-building orgy, and the effects of the panic of 1837 were not easily forgotten. So restrictions on public debt were insisted upon. The articles on internal improvements and State debt, as finally adopted by the convention, read, "This state shall encourage internal improvements by individuals, associations, and corporations, but shall not carry on, or be a party in carrying on, any work of internal improvement" and "The credit of the state shall never be given, or loaned, in aid of any individual, association, or corporation."

The white citizenship clause caused no trouble, since the "Nativist" Whigs now realized the political folly of opposing this measure. It stipulated that one year's residence, the filing of intention papers, and an oath to support the constitution were the prerequisites for voting. Negro suffrage was not included in the constitution but was submitted to the people at the same time as a separate article.

Despite opposition on the floor of the convention, the Progressives, because of their majority, had been able to draw up the kind of constitution they wanted. But the struggle for ratification told a different story. With the Democratic Party definitely split, a Whig-Hunker coalition used all available means to set the people against the constitution. The New Yorkers of Milwaukee organized a society to clarify the difference between them and the people of southwestern Wisconsin. Ryan, fighting almost single-handed in the eastern section for the constitution, had this to say: "The opposition may talk about married women and exemption, but here along the Lake Shore at all events, the real opposition is to the restrictions against banks, internal improvements, and state debt."

Additional opposition came from the abolitionist Liberty Party which objected to the exclusion of Negro suffrage. When the vote was finally taken in April 1847 the constitution was defeated. Brown and Iowa Counties, where the old settlers were still dominant, and Washington County, with its large German population, were the only ones to ratify. Negro suffrage was also defeated; the largest vote in favor came from those Yankee counties in southcentral Wisconsin which were most strongly opposed to ratification.

Before the second constitutional convention the Democratic Party received a scare that emphasized the dangers of a factional conflict. Moses M. Strong, a "Tadpole," was running for Territorial delegate to Congress against John H. Tweedy, a Whig. The Democratic split threw the election to Tweedy. This determined the Democrats to work together in the second convention.

The constitution was completely rewritten, but the changes were more in wording than in substance. The legislature was to hold a referendum on the banking question and, if an affirmative vote were recorded, was to pass a general banking law which would have to be ratified by the people. Instead of the exemption clause, the Bill of Rights contained a section demanding the exemption of "a reasonable amount of property." The married women's property clause was omitted, but there was no prohibition of such legislation. The internal improvements, State debt, and elective judiciary clauses were retained.

With only the Liberty Party in opposition (because again Negro suffrage was submitted as a separate article) the constitution was ratified, and in May 1848 Wisconsin became the thirtieth State. A compromise between the two factions enabled the Democratic Party to elect Nelson Dewey Governor.

The constitution of 1848 is still in use. In it, without any great burden of detail, the fundamental law was laid down in terms broad enough to preclude the necessity of frequent amendment, and the amending process was made difficult. Until the turn of the century amendments dealt chiefly with the structure of government. Since 1900 there has been the problem of fitting a constitution drawn for a sparsely settled rural area to the needs of a thickly populated and increasingly industrialized State. In 1902 the State was empowered to pass a general banking law and in 1908 to levy an income tax. The constitutional prohibition of government participation in the making of internal improvements has necessitated amendments to allow highway construction (1908) and reforestation (1924). Several unsuccessful attempts have been made to amend the constitution to allow the State to generate and distribute electric power, on the ground that water power is a natural resource which belongs to the people and not to private interests. During the debate in the second constitutional convention, a delegate remarked that by the time the people were ready to vote for internal improvements by the State, the constitution they were making in 1847 would have outlived its usefulness and been superseded by another. Such has not been the case, and today, though the attitude toward the role of government has changed, the State is prohibited from undertaking internal improvements which are permissible in other states.

Frederic L. Paxson says that the constitution of Wisconsin marked "the high water mark of Democracy in the Northwest before the tide began to ebb." Already in the Nation at large the power of the Democratic Party was beginning to wane. Polk's veto of the river and harbor bill in 1847 antagonized many Democrats of the Northwest. Young capitalist enterprises needed the tariff, which the party was not willing to provide. Finally, the slavery issue was an obstacle which could not be overcome. As early as 1840 anti-slavery sentiment was becoming crystallized in Wisconsin Territory. As we have seen, the Liberty Party fought both constitutions because they provided for white male suffrage only. Negro suffrage was submitted to the voters of the State in 1849 and adopted. (A majority of those voting at the election did not vote on this particular question. It was therefore assumed that Negro suffrage had not been adopted and two subsequent referenda were held at which Negro suffrage was defeated. But in 1865 the State supreme court decided that the result of the first referendum was valid.) In 1854 the Fugitive Slave Act, which made it a Federal criminal offense to assist a runaway slave, was declared unconstitutional by the Wisconsin supreme court in the Booth case, and Judge Crawford, who dissented, was defeated for reelection in 1855. The doctrine of nullification was further upheld by the people in the election of Byron Paine (Booth's lawyer) to the supreme court in 1859.

The Republican Party was formed in Wisconsin (as in several other States) in 1854 by a united front of Whigs, Free Soilers, and anti-slavery Democrats, in protest against the extension of slavery as embodied in the Kansas-Nebraska Act. In its first year the new party elected two of Wisconsin's five Congressmen: Cadwallader C. Washburn and Charles Billinghurst. In 1855 a Republican Governor, Coles Bashford, was elected and a Republican, Charles Durkee, was sent to the Senate. Subsequently public offices were rapidly filled with Republicans. Since 1856 there have been only three Democratic Governors, each one borne into office on the wave of some crisis which temporarily discredited the Republicans. The Granger revolt against the railroads and the German revolt against the Graham Liquor Law elected William R. Taylor in 1873. The Bennett Law, making compulsory the teaching of English in the schools of the State, was bitterly opposed by the foreign-born population and brought about the defeat of all Republicans in the election of 1890, at which time George W. Peck became Governor. In 1932 Governor Albert G. Schmedeman came in on the Roosevelt landslide, at the lowest point of the great depression.

One of the earliest struggles in Wisconsin's political history centered about the railroad problem. This struggle began with the financing of the first railroads in the 1850's. The constitution prohibited State aid for internal improvements, but increased transport facilities were essential. Because railroads had to be built, local governments went into debt and farmers mortgaged their property to build them. When the panic of 1857 struck, the railroads failed. The farmers, facing ruin, turned to organization for protection. Leagues of farm mortgagors were formed throughout southern Wisconsin. In 1858 they obtained the passage of a law invalidating farm mortgages, based on the argument that the railroads had no power to accept in payment for stock anything but cash. But the State supreme court decided that the railroads could legally receive notes and mortgages and declared this law unconstitutional on the ground of impairment of contract. (Cor-

nell v. Hichens, 11 Wis. 353—Clark v. Farrington, 11 Wis. 306—
Blunt v. Walker, 11 Wis. 334.) The farmers declared in their organ,
The Home League, "The doctrines laid down in this opinion (Clark
v. Farrington) apply to all corporations. If they are the law, the
rights of the people must soon lie buried beneath the crushing weight
of irresponsible monopolies." This paper further insisted that the court
and the press were both against them, "the former deciding adversely
to the mortgagor and the latter justifying and extolling the unrighteous
judgment." In 1861 the mortgagors put through a law making foreclosure proceedings so difficult as to be ineffective. To give this act a
fair chance in the courts, the farmers attempted to elect their own
candidate, James H. Knowlton, to the supreme court. But they failed,
and the law was thrown out. In 1864 and 1867 legislative attempts to
obtain jury trials in farm mortgage cases were also blocked by the
judiciary. Though unsuccessful, these organized attempts of the
farmers to protect themselves paved the way for the Granger revolt
of the next decade.

The railroads soon became the greatest power in the State. They
seemed, in fact, to be above the State. In 1856, when Congress made
two land grants to Wisconsin, Byron Kilbourn, president of the La
Crosse and Milwaukee road, was accused of bribing the Governor, the
Lieutenant-Governor, and legislators to obtain the grant he wanted. The
facts of this scandal came out in a legislative investigation in 1858, but
Kilbourn charged that the Chicago, St. Paul, and Fond du Lac road
had used similar methods to obtain the other grant. (Report of
the Joint Select Committee to Investigate into Alleged Frauds and
Corruption in the Disposition of the Land Grant by the Legislature of
1856, May 13, 1858, Senate Journal, Appendix, 1858. Milo M.
Quaife, *Wisconsin, Its History and Its People,* v. I, pp. 533-38.) In
the immediate post-Civil War period, when the only thought was to
push back the frontier and provide opportunity for all, law after law
was passed making possible the exploitation of the natural resources of
the State. Congress would make grants of land to the State, and the
State would give these lands to the railroads in order to develop its
resources, thus making the roads a quasi-public enterprise. Then the
railroads would sell the grants cheaply to the lumber companies, which
were actually composed largely of many railroad men. In this way
politics and business went hand in hand, and the farmer was helpless.
Excessive freight costs, rate discriminations between localities and between individuals, and discrimination in storage rates were common
practices.

Sharpened by the panic of 1873, agrarian discontent crystallized
throughout the Northwest in the Granger Movement. In 1873 Wisconsin elected a Granger Governor, William R. Taylor, and a railroad

regulation law was passed at once. The Potter Law of 1874 provided for a railroad commission and the regulation of passenger and freight rates. Though a weak law, under which the commission was given too little power to be effective, it was the first real challenge to the railroads. It also marked the formal entrance of the railroads into politics, for the railroads saw that they had to control the State or it would control them. Alexander Mitchell, president of the Chicago, Milwaukee and St. Paul, and Albert Keep, of the Chicago and North Western, announced to the Governor their intention of disregarding the act; they were, however, enjoined from so doing by the Wisconsin supreme court. Chief Justice Ryan's decision established the principle that corporations are subordinate to the State:

> In our day the common law has encountered in England, as in this country, a new power, unknown to its founders, practically too strong for its ordinary private remedies. The growth of great corporations, centers of vast wealth and power, new and potent elements of social influence, overrunning the country with their works and their traffic throughout all England, has been marvellous during the last half century. It is very certain the country has gained largely by them in commerce and development. But such aggregations of capital and power, outside of public control, are dangerous to public and private right; and are practically above many restraints of the common law, and all ordinary remedies of the common law for private wrongs. Their influence is so large, their capacity of resistance so formidable, their powers of oppression so various, that few private persons could litigate with them, still fewer private persons would litigate with them, for the little rights or the little wrongs which go so far to make up the measure of average prosperity of life. It would have been a mockery of justice to have left corporations counting their capital by millions—their lines of railroads by hundreds, and even, sometimes, by thousands of miles—their servants by multitudes—their customers by the active members of society—subject only to the common law liabilities and remedies which were adequate protection against turnpike and bridge and ferry companies . . . with capital and influence often less than those of a prosperous village shopkeeper. The common law remedies, sufficient against these, were, in a great degree, impotent against the great railway companies. . . . Every person suffering, or about to suffer, their oppression by a disregard of corporate duty, may have his injunction. When their oppression becomes public, it is the duty of the attorney general to apply for the writ on behalf of the public.

The railroads, having failed in the courts, determined to force their will. Money and free passes were distributed lavishly. All construction on railroad lines was stopped and train service was in many instances discontinued. The press flayed Taylor, holding him up to the ridicule and hatred of the people. The voters defeated him after one term and the Potter Law was repealed in 1876. From 1876 to 1905 there was practically no regulation of railroad rates.

During the turbulent 1870's the State government began to enter other fields of social control. In its first decade of statehood, Wisconsin had assumed the responsibility for the care of the blind, the deaf and the dumb, the insane and the criminal. In the succeeding decades of the nineteenth century the State began to assume increasing responsibilities in regard to public health, conservation, education, agriculture, and industry. The State board of health and vital statistics, established in 1876, was followed by appointment of a State veterinarian, and boards of pharmaceutical, dental, and medical examiners. The bureau of labor statistics was entrusted with factory inspection and the enforcement of State safety regulations. The commission to receive fish spawn, appointed in 1874, developed into a body which operated State fish hatcheries and controlled the activities of numerous State fish, game, and forest wardens. In 1878 an insurance commission was set up by a law which regulated the conditions upon which foreign corporations could do business in Wisconsin. Held constitutional in an opinion written by Chief Justice Ryan, this law laid the basis for more stringent insurance laws in the State.

In 1873 Chief Justice Ryan made a speech at the graduation exercises of the University of Wisconsin Law School, in which he said:

> There is looming up a new and dark power. I cannot dwell upon the signs and shocking omens of its advent. The accumulation of individual wealth seems to be greater than it ever has been since the downfall of the Roman Empire. The enterprises of the country are aggregating vast corporate combinations of unexampled capital, boldly marching, not for economic conquests only, but for political power. For the first time really in our politics money is taking the field as an organized power. . . . Already, here at home, one great corporation has trifled with the sovereign power, and insulted the State. There is grave fear that it, and its great rival, have confederated to make partition of the State and share it as spoils. . . . The question will arise, and arise in your day, though perhaps not fully in mine, "Which shall rule—wealth or man;' which shall lead—money or intellect; who shall fill public stations—educated and patriotic free men, or the feudal serfs of corporate capital?"

One young man who heard this speech never forgot it. Robert M. La Follette, born in Primrose, Dane County, in 1855, was graduated from the University of Wisconsin in 1879. The following year he was admitted to the bar and was elected district attorney of Dane County, in spite of opposition from the Republican machine, by appealing directly to the voters over the head of "Boss" Keyes. Using similar direct tactics he was elected to Congress in 1884 and was re-elected until 1890, when almost all the Democratic candidates were swept into office.

Since 1874, interlocking railroad and lumber interests had controlled the State. The Republican leader of Wisconsin for fifteen years was Philetus Sawyer, a rugged millionaire lumberman. Soon after he went to Congress to look out for lumber's welfare, he sent to the Senate John C. Spooner, counsel for the Chicago and North Western Railway, to stand by the railroads. While in the Senate Spooner acted as chief counsel for the railroads on trial before the United States Supreme Court. A third important figure was Henry C. Payne, Secretary of the Republican State Central Committee and intimate friend of Dave Rose, Chairman of the Democratic Committee. Both were interested in Milwaukee street railways and utility franchises. The Governor's office was occupied by a succession of Civil War veterans who, La Follette said, "outwardly dwelt upon the glories of the past and inspired the people with the fervor of patriotic loyalty [while] these corporation interests were bribing, bossing, and thieving within." A panic, beginning in 1893, intensified the popular hostility toward the group in power. It was this opposition to monopoly control of State and Nation which, like the popular revolt that expressed itself in Jackson in 1828, now expressed itself in Wisconsin in the person of La Follette. His concern was the restoration of competitive conditions and his creed was "The cure for the ills of democracy is more democracy." If government failed in its primary duty of carrying out the will of the people, then the laws and techniques of government needed to be changed. Production should still be for profit, but government should be for the "use of the people."

In 1891 war broke out in earnest between La Follette and the Republican organization. During his congressional service La Follette had kept the peace. The immediate cause of his change in tactics was a break with Sawyer. It had been the custom for some twenty years for the State treasurers to loan out official funds to favored banks, keeping the interest. When the Democrats came into office in 1891 they brought suit against the treasurers. Sawyer, as one of the chief bondsmen, would have lost hundreds of thousands of dollars. La Follette accused Sawyer of attempting to bribe him to talk to his brother-in-law, Judge Siebecker, who was to try the cases. Having antagonized the most powerful man in the State, there was nothing for La Follette to do but take the offensive, thus splitting the party between the Stalwarts and the Progressives. He put up Nils P. Haugen as his candidate for Governor in 1894. He himself ran in 1896 and 1898. None of these campaigns was successful, but La Follette was finally elected in 1900, the first native of Wisconsin to be so honored.

Albert R. Hall, a leader in the fight to break the regular organization, had in 1899 succeeded in putting through an anti-pass law. The La Follette platform of 1900 called for direct primaries and railroad regulation, but a Stalwart legislature prevented the enactment of this program. The session of 1901, however, has one important accomplishment to its credit—provision for a legislative reference library. This was set up by Dr. Charles McCarthy to provide a research service for legislators and to give them the benefit of the expert training of lawyers and scholars in the drafting of legislation.

One of the chief instruments of the Republican organization was the party convention. To put the nomination of officers in the hands of the rank and file of the party, the legislature of 1903 passed a direct primary law. At the same session a bill was passed which provided for the taxation of railroads according to the value of their property so that the roads would bear a fair share of the taxes of the State. Up to this time the railroads had been taxed at a lower rate than other property in the State because of the licensing system of taxation based on earnings per mile, which had been in use since 1854. (Report of the Wisconsin Tax Commission, 1898, p. 134. A. R. Hall, *Railroad Taxation in Wisconsin,* 1899. Briefs of the Chicago, Milwaukee & St. Paul and Chicago & North Western Railway Companies submitted to the Wisconsin Legislature, 1903.)

By 1904, when he was elected Governor for the third time, La Follette had won Wisconsin. The La Follette wing had at last wrested control of the Republican Party from the Stalwarts. He had fought against tremendous odds. The money of a powerful machine and almost the entire press of the State had been against him. His support had come from the voters, from the farmers to whom he had talked for hours on end, bringing figures to substantiate their knowledge that the railroads were bleeding them. The Norwegians were the first to rally to his cause. Two Norwegian papers, one in Chicago and one in Minneapolis, supported him. The Germans were convinced less readily, but when they were their support was strong and valuable. The Milwaukee *Sentinel* supported him until it was bought in 1901 by Charles Pfister, for many years one of the leaders of the Republican organization. Then Isaac Stephenson, a rich lumberman who had deserted to La Follette, backed the Milwaukee *Free Press* as a Progressive organ.

With the legislature at last on the administration side, La Follette's program was secure. But it could not have succeeded without a civil service law, because the whole Progressive program depended upon confidence in the administrators. John R. Commons, professor of political economy at the University of Wisconsin who drafted the civil service law, pointed out that, in his opinion, "administration [was] more important than legislation. Legislation furnished the authorization. Administration was legislation in action." The Civil Service Act was passed in 1905 at La Follette's request. The most important piece of legislation of the 1905 session was the railroad regulation bill, a necessary supplement to the ad valorem tax bill of the previous session. Without supervision it would be possible for the railroads to shift the burden of higher taxes to the consumer. The bill provided for an appointive railroad commission of non-political experts which would have power to regulate rates, not according to a set schedule, but to meet the reasonable requirements of each company as determined after a hearing. If a railroad took a commission order to court and there presented new evidence, the commission was given a chance to review this additional evidence and rescind or amend its order. The bill also .prohibited rate discrimination and rebates.

Passed despite violent opposition from the carriers, the act was soon tested in the State courts and declared constitutional. In upholding the principle of rate-fixing by commission, Chief Justice Winslow argued that since railroad business had become so complex that a legislative body could not regulate it, there would be no regulation at all if the legislature had to do it. "Such contention would make the mere implications of the constitution greater than the constitution itself, and would lose sight of the main and paramount purpose of the creation of the State and the adoption of the constitution. . . . This is called by counsel the doctrine of expediency but . . . we think it is the doctrine of common sense that forbids implications from an instrument which tend to render nugatory or to destroy that instrument." (Minneapolis, St. Paul & Sault Ste. Marie Railway Company v. Railroad Commission of Wisconsin, 136 Wis. 146.)

La Follette went to the United States Senate in 1906. Progressive victories, however, continued uninterruptedly under his successors, Governor James O. Davidson and Governor Francis E. McGovern. In 1907 the railroad commission was given control of all public utilities. The legislature of 1909 made provision for the office of revisor of statutes, whose duty it is to make a continuous revision of the statutes, selecting between contradictory statements and striking out all dead letters, and to publish after each regular session a new edition of the *Wisconsin Statutes*. In that same year, in response to popular demand, interim committees were appointed to make preliminary studies of necessary social legislation, workmen's compensation, income taxation, and part-time schools. In addition, these committees studied the question of the best type of administration and decided upon the three-man commission as being more satisfactory than a single administrator for handling cases of vital importance both to the public and the private interest.

Meanwhile, the Socialist movement had been developing in Milwaukee and extending into the industrial centers of the lower lake region. The Social-Democratic Party was organized in June, 1897 by Victor L. Berger and Eugene V. Debs, the Wisconsin branch being the largest and most influential group in the national organization. In 1898 the Socialists put up their first candidates for city election and received 2,500 votes. By 1904 they had succeeded in sending four assemblymen and one senator to the State legislature, all of whom had been elected in Milwaukee. The first Socialist representatives from outside of Milwaukee were not elected until 1918.

In Milwaukee, in 1906, after a grand jury had exposed several cases of corruption, six Socialist aldermen were elected to the common council. In 1910 a surprising victory swept many Socialists into office, including the mayor and 21 out of 35 aldermen. They captured not only the city, but nearly all county offices, while the largest group of Socialists ever elected to the State legislature, 12 assemblymen and two senators, were sent to Madison. During the fall election of the same year Victor L. Berger was elected the first Socialist in the United States Congress.

In the 1911 session of the legislature the Socialists from Milwaukee County worked with the Progressives for the passage of liberal legislation. This session was remarkable for the boldness of its attack and the broad scope of its achievement. The findings of the interim committees appointed by the 1909 legislature were enacted into law. To administer the workmen's compensation law, an industrial commission was set up. From the decisions of this three-man board appeal could be made to the Dane County circuit court, but, in the absence of fraud, the commission's findings of fact were to be conclusive in order to avoid litigation. In subsequent years the industrial commission has been given the task of administering all the factory and labor laws of the State, the constitutionality of which was basically established in the first test case of the Workmen's Compensation Act. Chief Justice Winslow's opinion reflects the broad social vision of many decisions of the Wisconsin supreme court:

> It is a matter of common knowledge that this law forms the legislative response to an emphatic, if not a preemptory, public demand. . . .
> When an eighteenth century constitution forms the charter of liberty of a twentieth century government must its general provisions be construed and interpreted by an eighteenth century mind surrounded by eighteenth century conditions and ideals? Clearly not. This were to command the race to halt in its progress, to stretch the state upon a veritable bed of Procrustes. . . .
> . . . the changed social, economic and governmental conditions and ideals of the time, as well as the problems which the changes have produced, must also logically enter into the consideration, and become influential factors in the settlement of problems of construction and interpretation.

A second important piece of legislation in 1911 was the income tax law, made possible by a constitutional amendment of 1908. Surviving the election of 1912 and a test in the courts, this law brought in $4,000,000 in its first year and has since provided an important source of taxation. It has been possible to drop entirely the State property tax. The successful operation of the Wisconsin act paved the way for the establishment of an income tax by other States.

At the same session a board of vocational education was set up by a law which also provided that cities over 5,000 must have vocational schools. A corrupt practices act was passed to limit and publicize campaign expenditures. Provision was made for a State life insurance system and a teachers' retirement fund. The incorporation of cooperatives was legalized. Other laws covered apprenticeship training and maximum hours of labor for women. The 1913 session contributed to the program of social legislation a mother's pension act and a minimum wage law for women and children.

The La Follette philosophy of government and the methods used to put it into practice have come to be known as the "Wisconsin Idea." According to Dr. Charles McCarthy, the originator of the phrase, this idea is impossible to define; its very essence is a willingness to experiment in meeting the changing needs of the economic order. Its motivating concept is government by the people and for the people within the framework of constitutional procedures. Commissions of non-political experts are appointed to safeguard the interests of the people. Scientific investigation precedes the drawing up of all important legislation so that in meeting the needs of the people it will not be unfair to business. Laws are drafted with great care, and the experience of other States— wherever any such can be found—is used to avoid weaknesses which might bring invalidation by the courts. Public hearings are held to give everyone a chance to speak.

The long reign of the Progressives was terminated by the election of Emanuel L. Philipp in 1914, on the issues of lowering taxes and increasing government efficiency. Governor Philipp stated that "the victory is a complete repudiation of the much heralded Wisconsin Idea," which was characterized by administration supporters as "reform run wild, humanitarianism without common sense, education to the verge of bankruptcy and an insolent interference with the liberties of the people." Governor Philipp stated that, "in the past ten years this state has made a national reputation for so-called progressive legislation. Business men declare that we have been fighting business." During the six years of Governor Philipp's regime the only "progressive" legislation repealed was the provision for a second choice in the primaries. Though State boards and commissions were consolidated, their functions were expanded rather than curtailed. This expansion of the regulatory and service functions of the State has continued to the present, on the whole unaffected by the alternations of Progressive and Stalwart control of the State government.

Worthy of emphasis is the change in the structure of government which took place gradually as appointive administrative commissions were set up. Established to meet the needs of an increasingly complex economic system, these commissions have grown in importance until their orders are now as voluminous as the statutes. Their activties are both legislative and judicial, but safeguards are provided in public hearings and the right of review by the courts.

Although administrative departments have regulatory, licensing, and enforcing functions, their most important activities are the supply of services to the citizen-consumer. More than 90 per cent of the expenditures of the State government go into service activities. Highway construction and upkeep account for more than a third of the total expenditure. Education ranks second in financial importance. The department of agriculture offers information to the farmers of the State, aids them in the control of disease, and assists cooperative enterprises. The industrial commission, in addition to its regulatory duties, operates a State employment service providing a network of public employment offices throughout the industrial areas of the State. Among other service bodies are the conservation commission and the department of health.

The administrative boards were at first decentralized and to a certain extent co-equal with the legislative, executive, and judicial branches of government; the constitution, in fact, set up the administrative as a fourth branch. The constitutional provision was not complete, however, since it mentioned only the elective administrative officers and not the administrative boards. Continuing appropriations made these boards partly independent of the legislature, and, because most of them were three-man commissions, one Governor in a single term had an opportunity of appointing only a minority of the members. In recent years, however, the trend has been toward centralization in the hands of the Governor. As the people have come to hold the executive more and more responsible, that branch of government has become increasingly important. Governor Walter J. Kohler (Republican, 1929-31) did much to strengthen its position. He established a budget bureau and bureaus of purchasing, personnel, engineering, and printing whose directors should be appointed by the Governor and responsible to him. In addition he set up an emergency board, with the Governor as chairman, to handle unforeseen contingencies. In 1930 executive control of finances was further increased when the Governor was given power to veto separate items of appropriation bills. A State planning board was set up in 1935 to take over the duties of the former director of regional planning; its activities cover the whole field of the physical and economic development of the State.

During the last few years a complete realignment of political forces has developed. From the days of "Old Bob" La Follette's struggle with the Republican machine, the Progressives gathered around him had operated as a wing of the Republican Party. The struggle between the Progressives and the Stalwarts centered in the primary elections. But after the Republican defeat of 1932 the Progressives ended the anomalous situation in which men and women opposed to the Republican practices and program yet voted in the Republican column. Feeling that the party had ceased to represent their views, and that votes would be lost rather than won by continuing under the old label, the leaders of the Progressive wing called for the formation of a new party. At a convention held in Fond du Lac in 1934 the Progressive Party was officially born. In 1934 Philip F. La Follette was elected Governor and Robert M. La Follette, Jr., Senator on the new Progressive ticket.

The formation of this new party was motivated partly by a desire to forestall insurgency among left-wing Progressive groups. These groups had been seeking the formation of a new party which would contain the words "Farmer-Labor" in its name. In 1935 nine Socialist, farmer, and labor organizations, not entirely satisfied by the creation of the Progressive Party, formed the Farmer-Labor-Progressive Federation. The Socialists withdrew from the State ballot, choosing to use the Federation as their political vehicle. The conception of the Federation was of a disciplined bloc of members who would support a single candidate in the Progressive column of the open primaries. Though nominating no candidates for Governor in 1936 or 1938, the FLPF elected some lesser officers and a number of assemblymen and senators.

Meanwhile some leaders of the Republican and Democratic Parties have been trying to effect a consolidation of the conservative forces. A working coalition of Republicans and conservative Democrats developed in the legislature after the elections of 1932 and prevented the Progressives from controlling more than one house until the session of 1937. In the primaries of 1938 a coalition slate of the old parties ran identical candidates for most State offices in the Republican and Democratic primaries. Coalition candidates won some nominations on both tickets and, forced by law to choose, ran as Republicans or withdrew in favor of Republicans. When the Democratic State committee met to fill the vacancies in its ticket, it selected a list of conservative candidates who made an unsuccessful fight against the victorious Republicans in the 1938 election.

In the spring of 1938 Governor La Follette announced at a mass meeting in Madison the launching of a new national third party, the National Progressives of America, believing that the Roosevelt leadership could not eventually create a liberal Democratic Party. Philip F. La Follette has announced that he will continue to try to organize this third party, though the Wisconsin Progressive Party was overwhelmingly defeated in the autumn of 1938 when the Republicans elected Julius P. Heil Governor and Alexander Wiley U. S. Senator. A legislature was elected containing Republican-Democratic majorities in both houses. The 1940 elections illustrate the present instability of party lines in Wisconsin: Julius P. Heil was reelected Governor on the

The Lakes and Rivers

NEAR RED BANKS ON THE GREEN BAY SHORE
WHERE NICOLET LANDED IN 1634

RAINBOW FALLS ON THE WOLF RIVER, MENOMINEE
INDIAN RESERVATION

DELLS OF THE EAU CLAIRE RIVER, MARATHON COUNTY

DELLS OF THE WISCONSIN RIVER

BIG SMOKY FALLS ON THE WOLF RIVER,
MENOMINEE RESERVATION

Above

**CONTROL GATES ON FEDERAL DAM,
MISSISSIPPI RIVER NEAR LA CROSSE**

Above Left

**POWER DAM ON THE WISCONSIN RIVER
AT PRAIRIE DU SAC**

Below Left

THE FOX RIVER AT DE PERE

FISHING VILLAGE, GILLS ROCK, AT THE TIP OF
THE DOOR PENINSULA

LIFTING A TRAP NET, GREEN BAY

THE GULLS COME WHEN THE
FISH ARE CLEANED

FREE AUTOMOBILE FERRY ACROSS THE WISCONSIN
RIVER, FROM STATE 113 AT MERRIMAC

A VILLAGE ON THE MISSISSIPPI BLUFFS, LYNXVILLE

A NORTHERN LAKE—ONEIDA COLONY

LAKE MICHIGAN AT CAVE POINT—DOOR COUNTY

Republican ticket; Robert M. La Follette was reelected United States Senator on the Progressive ticket; Franklin D. Roosevelt, a Democrat, received a majority of the votes for President; and a dominantly Republican legislature was chosen.

CHRONOLOGICAL LIST OF GOVERNORS

TERRITORY OF WISCONSIN

Henry Dodge 1836–1841	Nathaniel P. Tallmadge .. 1844–1845
James Duane Doty 1841–1844	Henry Dodge 1845–1848

STATE OF WISCONSIN

Nelson Dewey 1848–1852	William D. Hoard 1889–1891
Leonard J. Farwell 1852–1854	George W. Peck 1891–1895
William A. Barstow 1854–1856	William H. Upham 1895–1897
Arthur McArthur 1856–1856	Edward Scofield 1897–1901
Coles Bashford 1856–1858	Robert M. La Follette 1901–1906
Alex W. Randall 1858–1862	James O. Davidson 1906–1911
Louis P. Harvey 1862–1862	Francis E. McGovern 1911–1915
Edward Salomon 1862–1864	Emanuel L. Philipp 1915–1921
James T. Lewis 1864–1866	John J. Blaine 1921–1927
Lucius Fairchild 1866–1872	Fred R. Zimmerman 1927–1929
C. C. Washburn 1872–1874	Walter J. Kohler 1929–1931
William R. Taylor 1874–1876	Philip F. La Follette 1931–1933
Harrison Ludington 1876–1878	Albert G. Schmedeman ... 1933–1935
William E. Smith 1878–1882	Philip F. La Follette 1935–1939
Jeremiah M. Rusk 1882–1889	Julius P. Heil 1939–

Industry and Transportation

WISCONSIN'S geographical setting has many elements favorable to the development of heavy industry. About half the coal in the country lies near the Great Lakes, and 85 per cent of the Nation's iron ore is in the immediate vicinity of Lake Superior. Only one other region in the world, the Ruhr-Lorraine-Luxembourg district in western Europe, approaches the Great Lakes area for known concentration of these two vital minerals in close proximity. The lakes provide cheap water transportation, and in addition Wisconsin streams have a potential hydroelectric generating capacity of about a million horsepower.

Thus, even though Wisconsin has little mineral ore of its own and does no smelting of iron, 37 per cent of the value of its manufactures comes from industries which depend upon readily available iron. Their expansion has kept pace uniformly with the development of the Nation at large, for since 1910 in every year save one Wisconsin has ranked tenth among the States in the value of its manufactures. But this mature industrial development was reached only after a long process of adjustment in which more immediately available resources were exhausted.

For a long time after its penetration Wisconsin remained a forest wilderness, inhospitable to settlers, and valuable to its possessors only for the fur trade. Fur seekers opened the Fox-Wisconsin waterway linking the Great Lakes and the Mississippi, built trading posts around which later communities clustered, and gradually sent word out to more settled districts of the richness of the region. During its later phases, when John Jacob Astor began his successful warfare against the Hudson's Bay Company, the fur trade took on some of the characteristics of big business; but Astor himself had abandoned the region before Wisconsin became even so much as a Territory.

Gradually nuclear communities arose at the mouths of rivers both on Lake Michigan and on the Mississippi, and small areas of settlement spread out from the shelter of the two forest forts at Green Bay and Prairie du Chien. In the southwest, where lead lay virtually on the surface of the ground, miners began filtering into the Galena hinterland about 1824 and by 1830 had founded a dozen or more rough and busy communities (*see Tours 12 and 24*). Before 1840 the mining country was producing almost half the Nation's output of lead and its population had risen to about 25,000; but until the arrival of the railroad in 1852 the region was commercially dependent upon the Illinois river port of Galena. From Galena radiated crude, crowded forest roads which provided practically the only communication between these settlements and the outside world.

After the defeat of Black Hawk in 1832 had quieted fear of attack by Indians there came a swift inrush of settlers, who spread rapidly throughout the southern portion of Wisconsin and up both eastern and western borders. Steamboats ascended the Mississippi to serve the boom, and on them came speculators, traders, and farmers, who settled in ever-increasing numbers among the hills and along the rivers of the western boundary. Wildcat banks empowered to issue their own currency rose and collapsed; land speculators sold lots in cities which did not exist, sometimes building the cities afterward. The tiny lake ports became crossroads of commerce. Settlers piled over the sand bar at Racine in little boats and thronged into the rich territory behind the harbors of Milwaukee and Kenosha; they descended the Fox-Wisconsin waterway in canoes, bateaux, and barges, rode up the Mississippi on paddle-wheel steamers, or drove overland in prairie schooners whose drivers handled teams of 8 to 12 oxen with whips 27 feet long. Fifty to sixty steamboats and an unrecorded number of sailing craft plied Lake Michigan before 1848. The military road of 1835, originally nothing but a blazed track through the forest, became the main highway of the region, and along its route heavy wagons bogged in the marshes, overturned in the unbridged streams, or broke to pieces on the roots and stumps of the forest.

Lumbering began early in the 1830's along the Chippewa, Black, and St. Croix Rivers. Rude sawmills powered by water wheels rose in the woods on their banks, and settlements grew around the sawmills. Every spring the streams were carpeted with rushing logs, and every summer rafts of sawed lumber drifted down the Mississippi. A great log harbor serving the entire northwestern quadrant of the State rose among the semi-stagnant sloughs at the mouth of the Chippewa (*see Tour 13*). Except for lead mining and lumbering, however, manufactures throughout the Territorial period were largely a matter of home handicraft; farms were almost self-sufficing, butter was marketed locally at insignificant prices, wheat was ground at local gristmills, and clothing was often homemade, even to shoes. Imported articles were brought in mainly by peddlers with packs or wagons.

As population slowly increased during the next decade, means of communication were somewhat improved. Inland waterways were utilized more fully than at any other period; the Wisconsin, the St. Croix, the Fox, and the Chippewa became great freight routes. Barge and steamboat canals were widely proposed, and a number of people lost money trying to promote them. Though the highways were by no means comparable to even the poorest of modern roads, they spread into a network serving an ever-increasing traffic; stagecoach routes established in the previous decade became busier and more regular, and ox-drawn prairie schooners were replaced by more comfortable vehicles.

Since even the best of the early highways were too often blocked by mud or snow, plank roads came into use for a brief period—the first hard-surfaced country roads in the State. Four-by-four oak stringers were laid upon leveled grades, and across them planks eight feet long and two or three inches thick were spiked, making a road that looked something like a wooden sidewalk. At one time several hundred miles of such all-weather plank roads radiated from the principal eastern cities, built as private business ventures and paid for by tolls charged every five or six miles; but when the railroad competition became too strong they were abandoned. Only one plank road made money; the failure of the others involved both communities and farmers, many of whom had gone into debt to help finance their construction. Caught up in the ensuing railroad boom, the people pledged their resources to replace the planks with steel rails.

Meanwhile the Wisconsin wheat crop had become second largest in the Nation. From 4,000,000 bushels in 1849, the yield multiplied itself seven times within the next seven years, then remained fairly constant at 28,000,000 bushels through 1860. Little water-powered gristmills arose beside streams, and flour mills were built on the banks of the Fox River between Green Bay and Lake Winnebago. Wheat flour in 1860 made up 40 per cent of the total volume of the State's manufactures; its total value was nearly 12 times that of any commodity except lumber.

During the Civil War mine operators in the southwest, who previously had thrown away zinc ore in their anxiety to get the lead with which it was mingled, now found it profitable to install the more costly zinc-refining processes. The mining industry revived, but the new boom was different from the old. Small, independently-owned diggings were replaced by corporately-owned mines, and the corporations merged into constantly larger and more powerful units. Later in the century, however, the industry gradually declined, largely because of the discovery of better deposits elsewhere.

After some 20 years of hesitation railroad lines began to reach back into the country. In 1836, only a year after its formal organization, the village of Milwaukee had sought rail connections between its harbor and the Mississippi. Aided by Congressional appropriation, surveying began in 1837. By 1851 the tracks had reached Waukesha, 16 miles

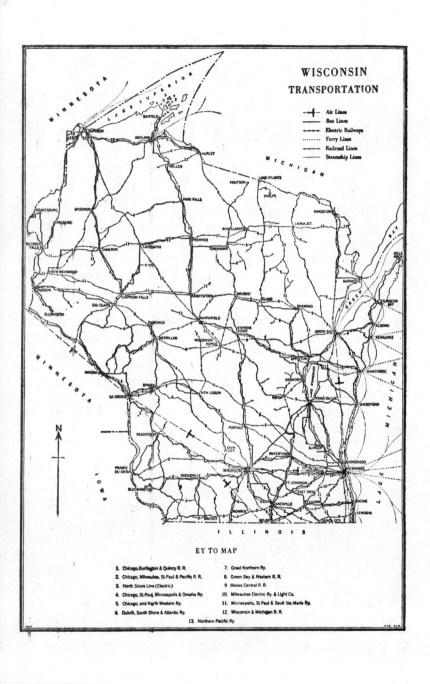

WISCONSIN
TRANSPORTATION

	Air Lines
	Bus Lines
	Electric Railways
	Ferry Lines
	Railroad Lines
	Steamship Lines

EY TO MAP

1. Chicago, Burlington & Quincy R. R.
2. Chicago, Milwaukee, St. Paul & Pacific R. R.
3. North Shore Line (Electric)
4. Chicago, St. Paul, Minneapolis & Omaha Ry.
5. Chicago, and North Western Ry.
6. Duluth, South Shore & Atlantic Ry.

7. Great Northern Ry.
8. Green Bay & Western R. R.
9. Illinois Central R. R.
10. Milwaukee Electric Ry. & Light Co.
11. Minneapolis, St. Paul & Sault Ste. Marie Ry.
12. Wisconsin & Michigan R. R.

13. Northern Pacific Ry.

away, and in 1854 they had spanned the 80-odd miles to Madison. Then suddenly, within six years, 905 miles of track were laid, and in the decade 1860-70, 620 additional miles were built. Milwaukee became linked with Lake Winnebago and the Mississippi settlements by several interconnected routes. Wherever tracks went down changes occurred in the life of the region. Land values tripled and quadrupled along the rights-of-way, river steamboat lines were abandoned, settlements sprang up, vanished, or were relocated, and economic self-sufficiency broke down.

Between 1860 and 1870 the value of manufactures increased from $27,000,000 to $77,000,000. The frontier period in southern Wisconsin was ended, and a new type of exploitation had begun.

In 1870 five-sixths of the State was still covered with virgin forest. The early lumbering industry along the western ·boundary, unable to operate far from the riverbanks, had done little more ·han nibble at the edges of the great northern wilderness. Formidable rapids in the upper reaches of the streams, and a barren sandy plain sprawling across the center of the State, had been effective barriers to any extensive infiltration of industry.

Gradually, however, the wealth of timber ready for reaping in the north woods began to attract exploitive enterprise. Sawmill machinery was dragged up the Wisconsin and its tumbling tributaries with great difficulty, sometimes on rafts and canoes, sometimes on human backs. Little sawmills were built, bought, sold, and merged into bigger mills, until finally the volume of their output drew rails across the sand hills and into the forests. Once the railways had arrived, lumbermen fell upon the pine with avidity.

Year by year the forest's edge was crowded farther north. Lumberjacks swarmed through the woods, and logs leaped down the rapids, sometimes piling into eight-mile jams containing 70,000,000 feet of timber. Fortunes were extracted from the forest; lumber operators won quick wealth and founded cities, then faded into legend as the timber neared extinction. Lumbering was the State's second industry in 1880 and its first in 1890, and it remained first until after 1910.

It was confidently expected that, as the forests were removed, settlers would take over the denuded land and turn it to agriculture. Promoters began speculating in land. The State gave millions of acres to railroads, and the rails followed the receding timber without waiting for more stable enterprise. Between 1870 and 1880, 1,435 miles of new track were laid; in the next decade 2,624 more miles went down; and by 1900 there were 6,530 miles of railroad in Wisconsin, only 600 miles less than the mileage today. Thus within three decades the State was covered with a network of railways which, while spoliation of the forests and speculation in land continued, made enormous profits, even though for miles they tapped only a stripped and barren wilderness.

Wherever railroad building seemed imminent, communities bonded themselves to the limit to bid against each other with subsidies. In the period between 1870 and 1875 alone, $7,000,000 worth of municipal bonds were issued to finance railroad construction. Localities ignored by railroads had to spend even more than those which were favored, for they had to build their own narrow-gauge connecting lines in order to have access to the outside world. Individuals, like communities, were caught up in the boom; many farmers and businessmen mortgaged everything they owned in order to buy railroad stock.

The railroads, in the meantime, fought one another bitterly. Sometimes they built parallel tracks through the same region, ignoring equally profitable regions nearby, intent only on annihilating their competitors. Since their warfare was financed largely by levies upon public treasuries and stockholders, these investors were the real losers. As one road after another failed or was absorbed, individuals and local governments alike faced ruin. Laws designed to invalidate their debts were declared unconstitutional, but the roads themselves later took up notes of some of the distressed farmers in order to qualify for Federal land grants. The small narrow-gauge connecting lines all eventually became involved in financial difficulties and were taken up by the large companies at the price of the mortgage debts.

Simultaneously another force was slowly becoming important in the State's economic life. The last of the great wheat crops was the 26,000,000-bushel harvest of 1872. In that same year, culminating a hard-fought campaign led by William Dempster Hoard, the Wisconsin Dairymen's Association was formed. From then on cash crops dropped to a relatively unimportant position, agriculture shifted more and more toward a livestock system, and gradually crossroads cheese factories sprang up. The ultimate industrial repercussions of this movement were not felt immediately, but eventually the increased prosperity and stability of agriculture had far-reaching indirect effects upon industry, commerce, and the development of transportation.

As wheat raising declined after 1870, so the milling industry declined after 1880. The flour mills along the Fox River were abandoned, and in their place rose paper and pulp mills, whose output soon began to rank high among the State's manufactures. The State's position on Great Lakes waterways between the Minnesota iron mines and the Illinois and Indiana coal fields began to attract metal-working industries; its proximity to the new wheatfields of Minnesota and the Dakotas gave rise to the manufacture of agricultural implements. The new livestock farming brought in meat-packing plants; shoes and leather goods were made in increasing quantities; by 1892 the brewing of beer had already reached an annual production of 2,000,000 barrels. Between 1870 and 1880 the number of factories within the State doubled and the number of workers tripled; by 1900 manufactured products were valued at $360,000,000, and already manufactures made up almost 70 per cent of the value of the State's total production.

Thus by the turn of the century most of the significant transitions had already taken place, and the State's industry was ready to develop along new and more modern lines.

As industries based on the manufacture of iron and other metals rose along the Great Lakes, freight traffic on those waters increased. Wisconsin harbors became great ports, handling south- or east-bound ore and north-bound coal simultaneously. The interstate Duluth-Superior harbor grew to one of the most important in the world for volume of commerce; Milwaukee, Ashland, and eleven other Wisconsin harbors rose to high rank in Great Lakes traffic. The first car ferry crossed between Kewaunee and Frankfort, Michigan, in 1892; soon powerful ice-breaking boats traveled the year round out of Milwaukee, Manitowoc, Kewaunee, and Marinette, and ferrying on Lake Michigan became more extensive than anywhere else in the world. The peak of water-freight volume was reached in 1920 but began to drop after 1925, presumably because package freight was diverted to other agencies.

Railroads, in the meantime, stopped expanding trackage about 1900, though car loadings increased to a peak in 1927. With the decline of lumbering and the failure of agricultural development in the north, the roads found themselves maintaining service into regions too poor and thinly settled to yield profit. Though the public service commission has been reluctant to permit roads to abandon service to such regions, trackage since 1920 actually has declined by 555 miles. The railroads have long since sold most of their grants of land and spent the proceeds, but they still are among the largest private landholders in the State. Their financial and corporate structure has been much manipulated, and in 1937 many important roads were bankrupt.

Truck traffic increased as the rails declined. Tonnage at point of origin of freight handled by trucks in 1932 was 44 per cent of that transported by rail and included a much larger proportion of the higher revenue-producing types. Though most truck traffic is relatively short-haul in comparison with railroad service, the greatest gains in Wisconsin trucking recently have been made in hauls of 100 and 150 miles or more. Bus lines, in some of which the railroads have a minority interest, also have made considerable inroads into the railroad passenger business. To meet such competition the rails have had to reduce rates drastically below post-war levels, so that the growth of highway carriers has meant a loss to railroads greater than the tonnage and passenger figures alone might indicate.

Modern highway building began on an extensive scale with the close of the World War, though the program had been planned and legalized since 1909. Previous to then the narrow, poorly surfaced roads had been made for wagon traffic only. By 1940, 9,980 miles of State highway, 15,351 miles of county highway, and an estimated 66,423 miles of town and city roads and streets were open to automobile traffic most of the year. The entire State system is dustless, and about 4,513 miles of it is paved with concrete. Wisconsin was the first State to use the number system for marking highways, devised here in 1918.

Some revival of Mississippi River traffic seems imminent. The War Department is building 27 dams across that river, 10 of which are in Wisconsin (*see Tour 13*), to maintain a 9-foot channel between Alton, Illinois, and Minneapolis.

Though there was a spurt of activity during the World War and a lesser one in 1935-37, lead and zinc mining have virtually ceased. Partial exhaustion of the mines, and, more important, the competition of newly exploited deposits in other States, have reduced them to a marginal level where they can operate only during sustained periods of high prices. In other parts of the State, however, miscellaneous mining and quarrying have become a $20,000,000 industry.

Dairying has become vastly important to the State within the present century. The invention of the Babcock milk test in 1890 was the foundation of modern dairy enterprise, and, immediately after its release, creameries and condenseries began to spring up throughout the State. After the close of the World War the production of butter, cheese, fluid milk, and condensery products rose rapidly; the manufacture of dairy products became a leading industry, and Wisconsin has ever since ranked first in the Nation in this field. Dairying is a local industry of small producing units requiring a widespread network of transportation services: 88 per cent of the cheese is produced in plants with an annual output of 2,500,000 pounds or less, and 74 per cent of the butter in creameries with per-unit capacities of less than 400,000 pounds.

After 1910 the lumbering industry slumped badly, fell to seventh place among the State's industries in 1920, and to fourteenth in 1930. In its place has risen a diversified group of wood-products industries. Paper and pulp, pails and tubs, veneering and furniture, sashes, doors, and floors, excelsior, matches, shingles, lath, casks, and caskets, all feed upon domestic crops of wood growth too small to be sawed as lumber, or upon raw materials shipped in from near-by States and Canada.

Though Wisconsin itself mines very little iron, and smelts none at all, a group of metals-manufacturing industries has risen which in the aggregate constitutes the most important industrial activity in the State. Iron manufactures stand first, but in the processing of non-ferrous metals, such as aluminum and brass, the State also maintains high ranking. Thus during the present century another widely diversified list of products has taken its place in the statistics of important Wisconsin industries: sheet metalwork, foundry products, farm machinery, electrical machinery, engines and pumps, plumbing supplies, tools and hardware, automobiles and tractors, refrigerators, precision instruments, and many other products.

The only automatic motorcar frame factory in the world, with a theoretical capacity large enough to supply all the frames needed by the industry, is among the plants in the State. The Panama Canal was dug by 77 steam shovels built in Wisconsin and 30 from another State, and the three largest Diesel engines ever manufactured in this country were made in Milwaukee for use on the Canal. Wisconsin has built the world's largest mine hoist; it furnished outboard motors, batteries, electric flashlights, radio equipment, and all the ship *Bowdoin's* marine engines for MacMillan's polar expedition. Turbines, hoists, ore crushers, hydroelectric units, furnaces, concrete mixers, castings, and engines go from Wisconsin to such projects as Boulder Dam; in the Milwaukee area alone 600,000 tons of steel are annually fabricated into such specialized giant machinery.

Serving these industries, and constituting a considerable industrial group in themselves, are the various public utilities. The water power which first drove flour mills and later turned the wheels of sawmills and paper mills is now used to generate electricity. The State has, in fact, been important in the history of electric utilities; the first hydroelectric plant in America was built in Appleton in 1882, and the first trackless trolley ran in 1903 at Merrill, which also was the scene of other early electrical experiments.

But though the maximum potential water power of the State is great, the flow of its streams is so variable as to make much of it financially worthless, since plants built to use the maximum head must be supplemented by steam generators in time of low water, an unnecessary duplication of equipment. Many small communities nevertheless owe their electric power to the fact that hydroelectric development has been possible near by.

On January 1, 1940, there were 120 public utility hydroelectric plants in the State with a generating capacity of 394,792 horsepower, and 57 industrial power plants that can generate 117,765 horsepower. Undeveloped potential water power in the State was estimated by the United States Geological Survey in 1928 at 480,000 horsepower during 50 per cent of the time, but only 285,000 horsepower is available as much as 90 per cent of the time. It is sometimes more economical to produce electricity by steam, and the largest power plants are not on rivers but near coal docks in Lake Michigan harbor cities. Of the 152 electric utilities of all types in the State, 66 are privately owned and

86 are municipally owned, but the municipal plants serve only 11 per cent of the consumers and generate only 8 per cent of the current.

The 1937 status of other utilities may be briefly summarized: there are 747 telephone companies, of which one, the Wisconsin Telephone Company, branch of the American Telephone & Telegraph Company, collects 81 per cent of the total revenue; nine other Class A and B companies earn 10 per cent; 185 small companies get 8 per cent; and 552 tiny farm, cooperative, and other exchanges together get only 1 per cent. Twenty-eight gas companies, whose growth has been rather slow, serve all cities over 7,000 and 26 cities between 3,000 and 7,000 in population. Water is supplied by 288 water companies, of which the 268 municipally owned concerns collect 93 per cent of the total revenue. There are 11 heating and hot water utilities, 8 of them privately and 3 municipally owned, located in cities ranging in size from Waterloo (population 1,272) to Milwaukee. Electric railway systems, both urban and interurban, have suffered considerably in recent years from the competition of buses; only seven cities now have them, including Kenosha with its trackless trolley. Their revenues have increased considerably since 1934 but are still far below pre-depression levels.

Post-war highway development has made recreation one of the State's major commercial resources, particularly in the north.

These main lines of enterprise by no means include all the State's industry. Altogether, Wisconsin is individually represented in about 100 of the 308 industries listed for report by the 1935 U. S. Census of Manufactures; that is, one-third of all types of American manufactures are represented in this State in sufficient magnitude to take them out of the "all others" class. In 79 of these 308 industries Wisconsin ranks twelfth or better among the States.

Within the State, the following manufactured products (in order of importance) were most valuable in 1935: iron, foundry, and machine-shop products; paper; motor vehicle bodies and parts; meat products; agricultural implements; cheese, condensed and evaporated milk, and butter; malt liquors; boots and shoes; electrical machinery; knit goods; tanned goods; canned goods; and bread. In addition Wisconsin produces nationally known makes of bedsprings, automobiles, flashlights, scales, malted milk, floor waxes, plows, batteries, fountain pens, paper tissue, hosiery, mineral water, and bathtubs. Eighty-nine of the State's 126 lines of industry in 1930 ranked in the million-to-hundred-million-dollar group, and four others were in the more-than-a-hundred-million-dollar classification.

This industrialization is concentrated in certain districts. In 1935 the total value of all manufactures was $1,334,913,670, of which 61 per cent was produced in the three southeastern lakeshore counties and Rock County. Non-ferrous metallic industries are largely by Lake

Michigan north of Milwaukee; paper and pulp production are heaviest along the lower Fox and upper Wisconsin Rivers. But because dairy manufactures, woodworking plants, canneries, breweries, and tourist commerce are widely dispersed, almost all sections derive some revenue from non-agricultural sources.

A few summaries will further reveal the extent to which Wisconsin, rural in appearance and tradition, is also an industrial State. The value of its industrial products is approximately five times that of its agricultural produce; even the value added to material by manufacturing processes is estimated at two and a half times the value of farm products. Though approximately equal numbers of workers are engaged in each form of enterprise, industry pays its workers about half again as much as agriculture. The average wage in 1935 was $1,043 for each of the 200,893 workers then industrially employed.

Most of Wisconsin now is in the Western Trunk Line freight zone, to which it serves as eastern gateway; for this reason it suffers a disadvantage of from 5 to 15 per cent in freight rates to New York in comparison with points in Illinois similarly distant, and pays a rate of $1.60 per hundred pounds to Liverpool compared with 94¢ for New Orleans. The State derives little advantage as a gateway to the West, for manufacturers find it cheaper to ship to the Pacific Coast via New York and Panama, or, if rail is to be used, to freight through favored Chicago. This is perhaps the greatest single handicap to further industrial development in Wisconsin.

The scope for expansion of Wisconsin's industry can only be conjectured. The State's regional planning board, selecting only six among many other possible commodities for study, has discovered that the State produces only 13 per cent of the flaxseed it uses, only 16 per cent of the building paper and roofing, 16 per cent of the cement, 28 per cent of the pipe and tile, 44 per cent of the pulpwood, and 45 per cent of the brick; and that all of these products can be produced in quantity within the State. The St. Lawrence Waterway proposal also promises great potential benefits to the industry and commerce of the State.

Labor

BEFORE 1890 Wisconsin was an agricultural State. Industry was centered in a few eastern cities, particularly Milwaukee; only 2 to 4 per cent of the population was industrially employed; and wage-conscious labor was a relatively small element. But near the turn of the century came an expansion of industrialization. Increasing numbers of farmer boys were drawn into urban districts; 7 to 10 per cent of the population became wage earners, and the labor movement took on new significance to the State as a whole.

At the same time a spirit of liberalism was growing, expressed politically in the rise of the La Follette Progressive organization within the Republican Party and in a number of projects for governmental reform, which are referred to collectively as the "Wisconsin Idea." The fact that a powerful group opposed the new liberalism added zeal to the incessant crusades by which its aims were advanced.

Labor obtained considerable influence among those who were shaping the liberal tradition and consequently was able to avail itself of political action more fully here than in many States. To some extent legislative successes removed the necessity for economic action, and until recently Wisconsin ranked low in the proportion of workers organized in unions; but in the upsurge of the past few years a favorable political climate has contributed to the gains in organization made by labor, and Wisconsin is now one of the most completely unionized States.

Though labor has contributed to and benefited from Wisconsin liberalism, the benefits have not descended like manna. In order to attain its ends, labor has had to exercise unwearying vigilance and effort, for the Wisconsin liberal movement is largely agrarian and middle class rather than urban and wage-conscious. Nevertheless, labor here has been emancipated from the traditional Gompers strategy of waiting to see which of the two major parties might be inclined to trade a few concessions for a body of votes, of "rewarding your friends and punishing your enemies." The development of Socialism and Progressivism has to a considerable extent allowed Wisconsin labor to be openly and methodically partisan and to reap the fruits of partisan victories.

The close of the Civil War brought a Nation-wide unrest among industrial workmen, stimulated by rising commodity prices and the mechanization of certain trades. During this period Wisconsin labor first became conscious of itself, and through the seventies and eighties organizations sprang up with increasing vigor. The Knights of St. Crispin, an organization of shoemakers, was formed in Milwaukee in 1867 to combat technological change; it grew to be the largest union in America, weakened itself with many strikes, and collapsed during the depression of 1873. Until 1880 most organizations were more or less ephemeral, but in subsequent decades Wisconsin workmen learned to build unions that could survive, and a number of organizations which date from the eighties are flourishing today.

In 1881 some of the independent Milwaukee organizations grouped themselves into the Milwaukee Federated Trades Association, dominated by the Knights of Labor and the cigarmakers. After the disastrous 8-hour day demonstrations of 1886, however, the Knights slipped out of the picture. When unions of printers, cigarmakers, and iron molders organized the Milwaukee Federated Trades Council in 1887, they affiliated with the new American Federation of Labor.

The formation of the Wisconsin State Federation of Labor in 1893 welded sporadic groups into a State-wide labor movement; seven years after its formation, the federation represented 86 local unions and 10 city central bodies; and by 1915 it had 219 locals and 15 city centrals. Its growth thereafter was continuous but slow until 1932-37, when another furious burst of organizing activity more than doubled the 1915 totals.

Outside the federation, also, union activity has prospered. The independent railroad transportation brotherhoods have some 20,000 members in the State and are as firmly entrenched here as elsewhere. Other railroad unions with a State membership of about 25,000 are affiliated with the American but not with the State Federation. These groups in the main have been unobtrusively content to let the federation act for them politically, and federation prestige has suffered little from their non-affiliation.

In the meantime, labor had been trying its strength in conflict. The period 1880 to 1900 was, in Wisconsin as in the Nation, one of the most turbulent in labor history. The first outbreak of any consequence occurred in Eau Claire in 1881, when eight companies of the National Guard were summoned during a strike of sawmill operatives. Next year the cigarmakers, fighting vainly against the extinction of their craft by machines, conducted what the State commissioner of labor called the most important and disastrous strike Wisconsin had ever had. At the same time a strike of Milwaukee telegraphers and printers won national attention.

This also was the period of 8-hour day agitation, which culminated in plans for an international strike on May 2, 1886. Though the strike was generally a fiasco, the intensity of the outbreak in Milwaukee was surpassed only by the Chicago Haymarket riots. For the first two days 3,000 workmen milled about the streets; on May 2 and 3 they redoubled their demonstrations; and by May 4 more than 7,000 were participating. The appearance of National Guardsmen provoked open rioting, which finally was quelled on May 5 after five lives had been lost.

The period of strikes continued into the 1890's, reached its height in the boom year 1893, then subsided during the ensuing depression. One of the most serious outbreaks in the State's history occurred in 1898, when workers in Oshkosh wood-working plants turned out in demonstrations which reached the proportions of riots. But by 1900 militancy had begun to give way to conciliation, in an effort to obtain public support and overcome employer resistance.

The Milwaukee Socialists were mainly responsible for putting Wisconsin labor into politics. A Socialist party basing its beliefs largely on Marxist theories was active in that city as early as 1870, and when Victor Berger emerged as its leader about 1894, he introduced the distinctive modifications which have become known as "Milwaukee Socialism." At this same time, and mainly in this same city, trade unionism was taking shape; it was quite natural that about 1899 the Milwaukee trade unions and the Socialist Party, with overlapping memberships, should become closely allied, the unions representing the economic, and the party the political aspect of the same mildly radical movement. In 1910 the Socialists first won control of the city and began that long career of remarkably good government which has brought Milwaukee international attention. Previously, however, they had sent to the State legislature two men who led labor's battles for many years thereafter: Frederick Brockhausen, elected in 1905, and Frank J. Weber, founder of the Wisconsin State Federation of Labor, first elected in 1907.

Berger, Weber, and Brockhausen gave to Wisconsin labor an individuality in theory and tactics which it still retains. Samuel Gompers, labor's national chief, had committed the American Federation to a nonpartisan policy of rewarding its friends and punishing its enemies among the politicians. But Berger, Weber, and Brockhausen, ardent and disciplined unionists though they were, disagreed strongly with this attitude; Weber called it "a policy of deceiving organized workers by asking them to search for labor's friends among the ranks of the enemy—the Democratic or Republican parties."

The Socialist Party alone, however, never has been able to dominate the State legislature, and most of its successes have been won through none too stable alliances with La Follette Progressives. The similarity in immediate aims between these two anti-monopoly parties sometimes has obscured their great differences. The Wisconsin Socialists concentrate upon three types of reform: (1) labor legislation; (2) the improvement of civic government in Milwaukee; and (3) the achievement of ultimate Socialist objectives such as "production for use rather than profit." The Progressives, on the other hand, are a heterogeneous party, including not only non-Socialist trade unionists, but many small business men and farmers, whose attitudes often conflict with those of labor. Two elements have been influential in linking these groups: the intellectuals, friendly to labor and to reform movements but by no means committed to Socialism, have been important in the development of Progressive ideology; and the politicians, particularly the Progressive Party leaders, acquainted with the prejudices of all groups, have been able to interpret each to the other in the interests of a liberal program. The importance of such leadership can hardly be over-emphasized; for, due to their diverse constituencies and theories, when Socialists and Progressives work together they are not so much like two well-matched and friendly horses trotting placidly in harness, as like a whole troupe of temperamental and quarrelsome ponies kept briefly in line by skillful political ringmastership.

The great year in Wisconsin labor legislation was 1911, when seven labor laws of major importance were enacted. Previous to this year the Progressives under the senior La Follette had been engrossed with civil service, primary, and utility reforms, while the Socialists had introduced bills designed mainly to facilitate agitation. But now, marshaled by Progressive Governor Francis E. McGovern of Milwaukee, and inspired by a wave of liberal sentiment that was sweeping the Nation, all liberal groups co-ordinated their efforts on behalf of a comprehensive and politically practical farmer-labor program, and Socialists and Progressives achieved a unity unique in the State's history. Progressives were dominant, though without full control, in 1921-27 under John J. Blaine, and in 1930-31 and 1934-38 under Philip F. La Follette, but in none of those years was labor as successful as in 1911. It is apparent, therefore, that the heterogeneous Progressive organization is by no means solely responsible for labor's legislative successes.

The State Federation of Labor has always had its own legislative program, which it has advanced by lobbying and pressure politics as well as by ballot. Early local committees, which scrutinized the records of individual legislators, were replaced in 1920 by local farmer-labor leagues, the first of several attempts to reconcile the often conflicting viewpoints of rural and urban workers. In 1925 such local action became much less important as the federation concentrated on another plan first inaugurated in 1919—that of calling special joint legislative conferences at Madison shortly before each session of the legislature. Local representatives from all districts attend and study the labor program, especially the more intricate proposals such as unemployment compensation. The federation also maintains a continuous lobby which has been headed by J. J. Handley since 1912.

As labor has developed these methods of applying legislative pressure, its opponents have devised others to counteract them. Historically, the principal opposition to labor has come from the Wisconsin Manufacturers' Association and the Employers' Council. The influential association, founded in 1910, grew out of the Milwaukee Merchants' and Manufacturers' Association, which had been founded in 1894. Although it is inclined to prefer the status quo and often opposes labor before legislative and administrative bodies, in seeking to foster the best interests of its members it often takes the attitude that compromise with labor is more expedient than open conflict. The Employers' Council, dissolved late in 1937, was, however, more militant, its chief purpose having been to oppose labor organizations. Because it refused to recognize or confer with trade unions, it generally did not have much success in influencing either legislative or administrative action; but in the courts it won several victories.

Farm interests also have often opposed labor legislation, for farmers in their capacity of occasional small employers have feared the imposition of restrictions which labor designed mainly for industry. Employers have taken advantage of this feeling by appealing to the individualism of farmers, which contrasts with the collective attitude of organized labor. To meet such opposition, labor has resorted to a number of more or less successful expedients: it has ceaselessly attempted to obtain some sort of alliance with farm groups through farmer-labor political organizations; it has backed laws favoring farm co-operatives; its leaders have forged working agreements whereby farmer and labor forces trade support for one another's measures; and it has developed a technique of drafting laws which benefit industrial workers without applying to agricultural pursuits. Through this latter principle, particularly, it has sometimes won the tolerance if not the active support of farmers. But farmers are far from a homogeneous group politically, and it is significant that both Progressive Party strength and the success of labor legislation have been greatest when the rural-radical ferment among farmers was most active: during 1905-15, when the Society of Equity was rising; in the middle 1920's, under the influence of the Nonpartisan League; and in the 1930's, as the Farmers' Union expanded after the milk strikes.

Socialist trade-union tacticians have been able to achieve many legislative successes, although backed by only a relatively small voting strength and opposed by powerful forces. One reason why the Socialist Party retained its dominance in the State federation for so many years was the ability of its leadership.

The all-important connecting link between labor and government in

Wisconsin has been the industrial commission, the quasi-judicial body which administers labor laws. Prior to its establishment in 1911 this function had been apportioned among a number of separate agencies; but because of the quantity of labor legislation enacted in that year, some reorganization of administrative machinery became almost imperative.

The conception of this commission has been called "nothing less than a work of genius." It was devised by Prof. John R. Commons of the University of Wisconsin and Dr. Charles McCarthy as an agency to apply the general policies approved by the legislature. Its handling of safety regulations will illustrate its general procedure.

The safety law of 1911, instead of prescribing a long and inflexible list of prohibited practices and conditions, merely stipulates that employers and owners of public buildings shall provide places which are safe to employees and frequenters. It is the duty of the commission to put this statute into effect, and its requirements have full force of law. The commission accordingly has adopted some 1,300 separate regulations, all drafted by advisory committees made up of representatives of employers and employees, assisted when necessary by the commission's own engineers.

Thus the commission's procedure provides flexibility and accuracy and permits a maximum of co-operation between employer, employee, and legislating body. At the same time reformers are spared incessant vigilance and strife to secure the enforcement of laws. Through innumerable conferences the commission has become remarkably skillful in promoting harmony and a spirit of compromise between otherwise varying interests. Many bitter old quarrels and deadlocked issues, which otherwise would have had to be fought through doubtful and lengthy legislative battles, have been settled through its intervention. The industrial commission is not primarily, however, a mediating body, but rather one for the formation of regulations; its decisions make up most of the actual substance of labor legislation.

Only once was the commission's authority seriously questioned. Deciding that the provisions of the 1911 law restricting the hours of employment for women were too inflexible to be applied to the pea-canning industry, the commission set up new regulations and proceeded to prosecute refractory canneries. One cannery defended itself on the ground that, in being permitted to exercise legislative as well as administrative powers at once, the commission had been delegated an unconstitutional amount of authority. The State supreme court ruled against the commission, despite its contention that it was merely exercising lawful police powers. Thereupon the commission informed all canners that they must go back under the inflexible restrictions of the 1911 law. Then not only the commission and the canners themselves, but also laundries, shoe manufacturers, and the State Federation of Labor joined in petitioning the supreme court for a rehearing and in submitting briefs on behalf of the commission. The court, persuaded of the wisdom of their claims, overlooked its previous legal reasoning and reversed itself.

The mass and varied history of Wisconsin's labor legislation permit only a summary of its salient features here:

The State's workmen's compensation law was the first to take effect, though not the first to be enacted, in the Nation. It now provides a maximum death benefit of $6,000, and a scale of lesser amounts for non-fatal injuries. Before its enactment workmen had to sue and prove negligence by the employer in order to get damages for injuries, but the compensation principle declares that employers must pay for injuries incident to employment. Employers, finding that 50 to 90 per cent of their liability expenditures went for litigation and insurance costs, eventually joined labor in backing the law, and it was passed in 1911. Employer acceptance was optional until 1931, but non-complying employers faced suit by injured employees with most of their legal defenses removed. In 1931 the law was made obligatory for all employers to whom previous stipulations had applied. The principal opponents of compensation were farmers, who were pacified by an amendment excluding employers of four persons or less. Insurance companies, trying to prevent extension of compensation into other States, successfully delayed the law for a year and a half by charging exorbitant rates, but were brought into line by the competition of newly-arisen mutuals. Subsequently the law was made more and more liberal until by 1938 only two States had slightly more generous provisions.

Ineffectual attempts to regulate child labor date back as far as 1867. The present code, enacted in 1911, was drafted largely by Professor Commons, who combined and modified previous laws and added new features. The reform movement was notable because of the vigorous participation of a number of disinterested groups affiliated for the purpose into a child labor committee. Cherry growers blocked further legislation regulating child labor in agricultural pursuits until 1925, when they were persuaded by the Industrial Commission to abandon their opposition. Then the enactment of the present law, restricting child labor in the production of sugar beets, cherries, cranberries, and certain canned products, made Wisconsin one of six States which have even this much regulation of child labor in agricultural industries. Despite opposition by the conservative farm press, Wisconsin in 1926 became one of the first four States to ratify the national child labor amendment. The State thus has kept well abreast of the field, but has not pioneered. Its principal innovation is the provision of triple compensation for children injured while illegally employed.

The Wisconsin apprenticeship law, unique in the Nation, and its vocational education law, first of the kind subsequently popularized by the Federal Smith-Hughes Act of 1917, were both enacted in 1911.

A law regulating the hours of employment for women workers was enacted in 1911 and has since been modified. It applies to women employed in beauty parlors, factories and laundries, hotels, mercantile or mechanical establishments, confectionery stores, telegraph offices, express and transportation establishments (other than street cars), restaurants, and telephone exchanges. Usually these laws require a 9-hour day and 50-hour week, though in some occupations much longer hours are permitted. Wisconsin's rules regarding night work rank among the best, but probably about 12 States have better regulations for daytime hours.

A law enacted in 1913 empowered the Industrial Commission to fix minimum wages for women employees. The commission failed to act during the World War years, but in 1919 set forth a system of wage rules. After the United States Supreme Court in 1923 ruled unconstitutional a similar law passed for the District of Columbia, the Wisconsin Supreme Court refused to enforce the Wisconsin law. The 1925 legislature therefore substituted an "oppressive wage" law, forbidding the payment of wages insufficient to compensate for the services rendered. When the United States Supreme Court recently reversed itself in another minimum wage case, the State legislature promptly repealed the "oppressive wage" law and re-enacted the 1913 law. To help modernize the wage scales, an advisory committee was appointed to make recommendations to the Industrial Commission regarding proposed scales.

Heretofore trade unions have been lukewarm on the issue of protecting women workers by legislation, preferring to organize them into unions. Some farmers have opposed liberalization because farm girls are already too strongly inclined to leave home, and a few women's groups have opposed reform on the ground that special favors to women offend their conception of equality between the sexes. The minimum wage scales at present enforced, though below generally prevailing rates, have eliminated extremely low pay in some chain stores, telephone exchanges, and other industries.

A law declaring "yellow dog" contracts contrary to public policy and null and void was passed in 1929, the first of its kind in the Nation. Laws prohibiting this type of contract had been passed by several States, but in 1908 the United States Supreme Court declared these acts unconstitutional. A "yellow dog" contract is one in which a workman, upon entering into employment, agrees not to join a labor union. Labor has fought such contracts for years. An 1899 law was declared unconstitutional by the State Supreme Court in 1902, and the present law, based on a model drafted by the American Federation of Labor, was passed only because it is so phrased as also to protect producer co-operatives against private corporations.

A law requiring 48 hours' notice to the adverse party before an injunction or restraining order can be issued in a labor dispute was enacted in 1923 to remedy one of labor's historic grievances against court procedure. Wisconsin's legislation taking civil contempt in connection with labor disputes out of equity, declaring contempt actions independent of previous court acts, and requiring unanimous jury decisions for conviction, also favors labor more than that of any other State. After being vetoed by Governor Kohler in 1929, it was reenacted in 1931 and signed by Governor La Follette.

A law requiring licensing and bonding of detective agencies which work in industrial disputes, and of all their detectives, was passed in 1925 and subsequently was strengthened in order to end industrial spying. No important national agency doing such work now maintains offices in Wisconsin.

A fraudulent advertising law, providing that strike-bound employers advertising for help must mention the strike, was enacted in 1911 and was subsequently improved.

Wisconsin pioneered in unemployment compensation. At first even the American Federation of Labor opposed the principle, fearing that it would weaken unions by removing one of the benefits they had previously offered to members, or that it would compel union men, on penalty of forfeiting benefits, to accept work in non-union shops. Politically-minded Wisconsin labor, however, fought for it for ten years. With the onset of the depression, unions no longer could afford to care for all their unemployed, farmers and taxpayers found relief costs intolerable, and an unemployment compensation law, devised by John R. Commons, Harold M. Groves, Paul Rauschenbush, and Elizabeth Brandeis, was enacted in January 1932, with the approval of almost everyone but the employers. Until the passage of the Federal Social Security Act, it was the only law of its kind in the Nation. The Wisconsin law provides for contributions by employers only. Not only did legislation tend to favor the theory of passing these costs on to consumers and society in general through the employers, but its proponents believed that it would help reduce preventable unemployment in the same way that compensation has reduced accidents—by giving employers themselves an incentive to work toward the desired end. The Wisconsin plan strengthens this incentive by providing individual unemployment reserves for each employer rather than a general fund. A study published by the special Citizens' Committee on Public Welfare in 1937 indicates that the plan is working; employment has tended to stabilize—and so has unemployment.

A 1931 law empowers the industrial commission to collect back wages due to workmen who might find litigation costs prohibitive.

A labor relations act designed to protect unions and their members, to outlaw company-dominated unions, and to force employers to bargain collectively with their employees, was modeled, with modifications, after the National Labor Relations Act and went into effect in 1937. The enforcement of this difficult and controversial legislation was entrusted to a labor relations board, whose procedures, decisions, and court cases began forming another mesh of rights and responsibilities between organized labor and the State government. The enactment of this law coincided in time with a sudden outburst of strikes, stimulated partly, perhaps, by the legally protected right to organize, but deriving also from the upswing of business in 1937 and the activity and rivalry of the American Federation of Labor and the new Committee for Industrial Organization. In 1938 the board drew elaborate praise from both sides for its part in the peaceful settlement of serious controversies in the Allis-Chalmers plant, Wisconsin's largest. Nevertheless, the hostility of some employees and inter-labor strife involved both the law and the board in controversy, and they were abolished by a dominantly Republican legislature in 1939.

A mass of miscellaneous legislation, often modified or strengthened after its first enactment, includes regulation of hours and wages for workmen on public works (1909); provision for one day's rest in seven (1919); establishment of public employment offices (1901); licensing and supervision of private employment agencies by the industrial commission (1913); and license laws for various trades. Until recently license laws were generally opposed by organized labor on the ground that they impose standards rather than allow the craftsmen themselves to devise and enforce their own as the situation might require. Usually they have been enacted only when self-regulation has broken down.

Attempts to stop the practice of letting prison labor out on contract to private firms have thus far (1939) been unsuccessful. A 1934 law was permitted by Democratic Governor Albert G. Schmedeman to die by pocket veto.

The effect of all these laws may be altered by legislation too recent for its consequences yet (1939) to be evaluated. In 1939 a coalition of Republicans and conservative Democrats, controlling the legislature, passed two far-reaching laws affecting employer-employee relations and the conductance of labor disputes. One forbade picketing any place where a labor dispute was not in progress and provided that only a majority of the employees in any plant unit could wage a recognized labor dispute, thus outlawing such traditional labor tactics as secondary picketing and "public opinion" picketing. The other, called an "employment peace" act, was sponsored by a group of farmer co-operatives banded into a Council of Agriculture.

The employment peace act recognized the right of employees to collective bargaining under certain carefully circumscribed restrictions and set up lists of unfair labor practices for both employers and employees. Employers are forbidden to coerce or discriminate against employees either to induce or prevent their joining labor organizations; are forbidden to spy upon employees or keep blacklists, or to start, finance, or dominate employee organizations. Employees are forbidden to coerce or intimidate other individuals. Mass picketing and such practices as blocking entrances to a plant or obstructing roads or streets are forbidden, as is any picketing whatsoever unless a majority of the employees in a plant unit have voted to strike. Sit-down strikes and secondary boycotts, strictly defined, are outlawed, and employees may not hinder anyone from obtaining materials or services in any way. An employer is permitted to enter into collective bargaining only with a majority of the employees of any unit, and can sign a closed shop agreement only after it is approved, through secret ballot, by 75 per cent of the employees. A check-off is permitted only upon written order of each employee. Workers must give ten days' notice before waging a strike affecting raw agricultural products or those in the initial stage of processing—a provision designed mainly to protect such enterprises as canneries, condenseries, and cheese factories. One provision states that no employee guilty of an unfair labor practise may have his name upon any ballot, legally represent fellow-employees, or exercise any rights under the act; this clause severely restricts union officers and negotiators. Miscellaneous provisions provide that either employers or employees may ask for plant elections on various issues, even though previous elections on the same subject already have been held; that all representatives of employees must submit annual financial statements to each member in the form of a balance sheet and operating statement; and that a one-year limitation shall apply.

Meanwhile, as labor pursued its legislative interests, organization of new unions had slackened, though the slow growth of the State federation continued, and its political successes constantly enhanced its prestige. During the 1920's a policy of entrenchment replaced that of expansion, and education became an important union activity. First the federation attempted to sponsor local discussion groups which met periodically to discuss labor problems and economic events. These groups gradually disappeared, but in their place rose the Wisconsin Summer School for Workers in Industry, conducted under the auspices of the University of Wisconsin. Open originally only to women, this school met with such immediate response that its curriculum was broadened, men were admitted, and soon it was endorsed by the federation as part of its educational program.

When the Wisconsin Emergency Relief Administration was set up, the federation obtained its support in hiring unemployed teachers to conduct workers' education classes. In 1937 the legislature, for the first time in any State, included in the university budget provisions for a new department of workers' education to be conducted on a full-year basis throughout the State as an extension service offered by the University; this was abolished, however, by the 1939 legislature. The federation also has made comprehensive surveys of the State public school system, has sought improvements in the education of youth for industry, has submitted an educational program to the State board of education, and has endeavored to obtain labor representation on local school boards. Occasionally there has been local discrimination against the Wisconsin Federation of Teachers. Labor, therefore, has a twofold interest in obtaining influence with school authorities: it seeks to guard against anti-union instruction and to protect its own members.

With the onset of the depression the federation did not immediately rise to the organizational opportunities presented under section 7a of the National Industrial Recovery Act; but, after the Wisconsin Workers' Committee, an organization of the unemployed, set about unionizing some of the State's largest plants, organization work by the federation was intensified. Organizers found thousands of workers newly susceptible to the union idea, and between 1933 and 1937, 332 new locals joined the federation, more than doubling the previous total. This wave of expansion brought with it a new series of strikes.

Led by the Workers' Committee, employees of the J. I. Case Company in Racine formed an independent union in 1934 and prevented strike breakers from taking their places by reporting for work each morning and sitting idly at their machines all day. Thus two years before sit-down strikes became generally known in America, these workers applied their own form of the strategy. In the same year a strike against the Milwaukee Electric Railway & Light Company elicited one of the most remarkable demonstrations of public sympathy ever known in the State. Originally only about 75 of some 1,000 workmen walked out, but the Workers' Committee sent 5,000 men to assist in picketing. Then virtually the entire public turned against the company, and by the fourth day of the strike some 75,000 people gathered about the great Lakeside Power Plant and the company's car barn. A man was somehow electrocuted, and feeling became very bitter; but because the police aided in preventing non-strikers from trying to enter the plant, there was little physical violence on the part of strike sympathizers. This is in keeping with the peaceful history of labor disputes in Milwaukee, due, according to former Mayor Hoan, to the fact that strikers have been guaranteed "the full enforcement of their legal rights."

Noteworthy also was the bitter strike for union recognition, in which two strikers were killed, begun in 1934 against the plumbing equipment plant of former Governor Kohler, at Kohler, near Sheboygan. Though Kohler's political record was attacked by labor, his factory and its village had constituted a highly publicized example of paternalism, and the State was stunned to learn of the outbreak. The strike has not yet (1940) been formally ended.

The strike of the newly formed American Newspaper Guild against the *Wisconsin News,* Hearst-owned Milwaukee daily, in 1936, was nationally recognized as a test of the guild's efficacy as a fighting union. While the compromise settlement fell short of the guild's demands, it is generally interpreted as a significant victory for editorial workers over a powerful newspaper chain.

During the winter of 1935-36 the Committee for Industrial Organization brought into Wisconsin its program for gathering hitherto unorganized workers into vertical-type unions. In the organizing activity that accompanied the upswing of business in 1936, the CIO has been at least as busy as the AFL. Authentic membership figures are not available, and, in the case of the still unstabilized new organizations, would not long be valid in any event; but by 1938 the two groups claimed almost identical numbers of new unions "listed," or accredited as bona fide for collective bargaining purposes, by the State Labor Relations Board. Wisconsin was the third State to have a State central CIO body chartered by the national committee, and the first to hold a State convention of CIO unions; the 1937 national convention of the United Automobile Workers of America, an important CIO affiliate, was held in Milwaukee.

In the organizational competition between the CIO and the federation, both sides have been spurred into intensive efforts, so that thousands of laborers who until recently were never approached by any union now find themselves solicited by two. The Labor Relations Board from its inception was faced with the delicate and trying task of maintaining the freedom of the workers to decide the issue as they chose without employer interference, while at the same time protecting employers who manifested no preference from being drawn in spite of themselves into a jurisdictional dispute between rival labor organizations. The operations of the board were ended when the 1939 employment peace act took effect.

The conflict in Wisconsin is, for historical reasons, unusually keen. The tradition of militancy among laborers that permitted the CIO to organize here has made federation leaders particularly bitter against it, for in their eyes the CIO is an upstart revolt offering nothing that the federation has not been doing efficiently for a quarter of a century. Even the vertical structure distinctive of the CIO has been endorsed and fought for by Wisconsin federation men within the American federation for some time. The CIO, on the other hand, points to the organizational apathy of the federation between 1915 and 1934 and claims credit for injecting new inspiration and virility into the labor movement. Thus the rivalry here is unusually confused and its course is not typical. In one large plant the AFL found itself insisting that office and factory workers should vote in an election as a vertical plant unit, while the CIO demanded that the vote should be split among different functional classes of workers—a direct reversal of the theoretical viewpoint of each group.

In the meantime tension has also developed in the political field, centering around the Farmer-Labor-Progressive Federation, which was founded in 1935 at the instigation of the Wisconsin State Federation of Labor, led by its president, Henry Ohl, Jr.

Because of the success of its lobbying and the growing importance of negotiation before such bodies as the Industrial Commission, labor had tended to become less partisan in its political activities. Nevertheless, prior to 1935 labor had been becoming uncomfortably suspicious that the two political groups upon which it still placed its main reliance— the Progressives and the Socialists—had become more concerned with maintaining party supremacy than with promoting liberal causes. It particularly desired to reform the Progressive organization, which then was still a faction within the Republican Party. Labor leaders sought accordingly to combine all the diverse liberal groups in the State into a united third party, whose name would include the term Farmer-Labor. Shortly before these plans could be brought to fruition, however, the Progressives seceded from the Republican Party.

With so formidable a third party already in the field and bidding for liberal support, Farmer-Labor leaders had to relinquish some of their plans. Instead of seeking a place on the ballot, they united nine farm, labor, and partisan bodies into a political alliance called the Farmer-Labor-Progressive Federation, which pledged itself to a program generally progressive but included the old Socialist slogan "production for use." This program it seeks to advance by concentrating its potentially great pressure upon party leaders and legislators, for it plans to endorse candidates at each election. To avoid carrying the jurisdictional conflict between CIO and AFL into the political field, affiliation with the FLPF was placed upon an individual rather than an organizational basis; thus it is indirectly possible for both factions to cooperate, when they choose, in election and pressure activities. In 1940 the FLPF changed its name to the Progressive Party Federation.

Agriculture

THOUGH financial figures indicate that Wisconsin is more an industrial than an agricultural State, agriculture can properly be called its basic activity. While means of communication and manufacture were still primitive, and long before recreation had become a business, agriculture supported the settlement and development of the State. Even now, outside of Milwaukee and the eastern industrial regions, almost all commercial, manufacturing, and professional life is closely related to rural prosperity.

A century or so ago there were no farms at all. Sixty years ago six-sevenths of the State was still blanketed with virgin forest. Thirty years ago a thousand sawmills were cutting two and a half billion feet of lumber annually from a region still heavily timbered. But now about 200,000 farms occupy three-fifths of all the land in the State, and agriculture has progressed from a one-crop type based on wheat to a diversified crop and livestock system crowned by the richest dairy development in the world. For the time being, at least, major trends are stabilized.

The Wisconsin landscape, incessantly varied in pattern but almost universally unvarying in essentials, is a visible summary of the State's rural economy. Woodlots crown the ridges, pastures cover the slopes, and fields of hay or grain lie in the valleys, illustrating at a glance the prevailing farm formula: crops support livestock, and livestock supports the farmer. This formula holds good for all regions, for there is not a single county in which dairying and its supporting feed crops are not predominant, from the hilly, stream-cut western border country to the intensively developed southern and eastern areas; from the flat, sandy plain in the center of the State, where agriculture is otherwise restricted to a few specialized crops, to the newly opened dairy belt in the north. Even in the cut-over country, with its short growing seasons and pioneer methods, it serves in rudimentary form as the basis for subsistence farming.

Since competition has arisen in the dairy industry leaders have been striving with every resource of science and education to increase the diversification in the direction of a more balanced agriculture. The depression, repeal of prohibition, and recent droughts have helped to introduce changes which may in time cause a considerable alteration in the general farm picture. None of these influences has yet brought drastic change, but together they give some indication of the direction of contemporary trends.

Farming in Wisconsin began as a sideline. After the voyageurs had brought their spring cargoes of furs to traders at Prairie du Chien and Green Bay, they spent the summer raising a little maize to take with them when they went back into the forest the next fall. Lead miners in the southwest, forbidden until 1847 to cultivate more than 1½ acres of each 220-yard-square claim, ignored the ruling entirely and began supplementing their earnings with farm produce almost as soon as permanent settlement began. In 1834 the Federal Government threw its lands open to sale at $2.50 an acre and opened land offices at Mineral Point and Green Bay.

From the pioneer stage of self-sufficing homesteads emerged an agricultural economy based upon wheat. Wheat was the chief cereal in American diet; it could be grown almost immediately on new soil, and the processes it required were simple and traditional; farmers reaped it with scythes and cradles and winnowed it with flails. In 1849, one year after Wisconsin achieved statehood, the crop was 4,000,000 bushels; seven years later it was 28,000,000 bushels. It maintained that level through 1860, fluctuated somewhat during the unsettled Civil War period, and resumed its former volume after the cessation of hostilities. The wave of railroad building just before the war opened thousands of acres which distance had formerly withheld from markets; the demobilization of armies sent hundreds of footloose men into frontier regions to build farms and found families. As lumbermen began their onslaught upon northern forests, the wheatfields crept northward along the edge of the receding timberline; and as old land was exhausted in the south, new land was opened in the north. Wheat was by far the State's major product, and Wisconsin was one of the leading wheat States all during this period; even in 1872 it still ranked high, with a 26,000,000-bushel harvest.

But symptoms of a permanent decline had become manifest. Chinchbugs had ravaged Wisconsin fields in periodic invasions of increasing frequency; soil exhaustion was ruining the productivity of southern fields; expansion northward was checked by short growing seasons and poor soils. To the west, in Minnesota and the Dakotas, settlers were breaking ground better suited to wheat raising than Wisconsin's had ever been. As long as the State clung to wheat as its major crop, its agriculture would tend ever more toward a marginal level.

William Dempster Hoard, editor of a weekly newspaper in Fort Atkinson, had been arguing that Wisconsin could no longer depend upon grains, and that the future prosperity of the State lay in dairying. First he devoted a column to his campaign, then a page, and then a separate section of the paper; eventually *Hoard's Dairyman* became an independent weekly of Nation-wide circulation and influence. Speaking, writing, touring the State from one end to the other, Hoard hammered his gospel into the consciousness of the people. His policies were by no means immediately popular; the farmer of the early 1870's was inclined to resent being "tied to a cow." But farm leaders saw the value of Hoard's program, and his doctrines began to take root among the Germans and Scandinavians who were used to handling livestock in their native countries. When Hoard and Chester Hazen founded the Wisconsin Dairymen's Association in 1872 the agricultural revolution was fairly on its way; in the same year the State dairy and food commission was formed.

Wheat production dropped almost immediately to a comparatively minor position, and cheese making gradually rose to replace it. Hazen had opened the State's first cheese factory at Ladoga in 1864; and, though his example was not generally followed for more than a decade, by 1880 small plants had already begun to dot the crossroads. But the expansion of processing industries for a time was retarded by the backwardness of dairy farming. Few of the first cattle were purebred; the sciences of feeding and breeding were rudimentary. There was no standard of quality. Modern concepts of dairy sanitation were unknown, and so were most of the facts concerning the health of cattle and the transmission of bovine tuberculosis from cows to human beings through milk.

Experts at the University's agricultural experiment station began a many-sided attack upon these problems. Outstanding among their successes was Prof. Stephen Moulton Babcock's butterfat tester, invented in 1890. It provided for the first time a simple, convenient means for determining the richness of milk. The culling of herds, the development of dairy breeds, the selection of stock, and the marketing of fluid milk were at once put on a practical basis. With de Laval's separator, Babcock's butterfat tester was the foundation of modern dairying; after its release creameries rose beside the crossroad cheese factories, and commercial butter making began.

H. L. Russell, hearing of Koch's work with tuberculosis in Germany, visited him and brought back information that led to the first tuberculin tests in America. Wisconsin ever since has been a leader in the fight against bovine tuberculosis. A relentless campaign went on for 35 years, first under the Livestock Sanitary Board, later, after a departmental consolidation, under the department of agriculture. Despite much bitter opposition, and sometimes in the face of shotgun fire, agents tested and condemned herd after herd. In 1915 the State began paying indemnities to owners of infected cattle, and two years later the Federal Government began contributing. By 1934 Wisconsin became "modified accredited"—in no county were more than 0.5 per cent of the cattle tubercular. Its herds now constitute by far the largest and most valuable body of tuberculosis-free cattle in the world.

In the meantime W. A. Henry contributed a series of researches which established the importance of balanced rations in livestock feeding, and F. H. King developed the round silo, now an integral part of dairy farming. The campaign against Bang's disease, or contagious abortion, the worst modern plague of dairy cattle, began 20 years ago and has been carried further than in any other State. The agricultural experiment station and the university's college of agriculture were developed into agencies with broad scope and many direct contacts with farm life and problems; the department of agriculture and markets grew out of many smaller independent agencies into an organization dealing with every phase of agricultural economics.

Not until after the World War did the dairy industry reach its present magnitude. Statistics on the value of the State's output of butter, cheese, and condensed and evaporated milk reveal the trend:

Year	Rank in State	Value of Products
1880	16	$ 1,501,087
1890	7	6,960,711
1900	4	20,120,147
1909	3	53,843,000
1919	1	221,447,000
1929	2	203,339,004
1935	..	156,816,069
1937	..	175,539,638

At the time that dairying was becoming the foremost enterprise within the State, Wisconsin rapidly assumed national preeminence in the production of fluid milk, cheese, and condensed milk, though it remains only third in butter production.

Changes in other lines of farming also occurred. Corn and oats were raised widely as secondary cash crops between 1850 and 1880; the production of hay in that period increased sevenfold. Canning peas, introduced in 1870, quickly found favor as a cash crop and have remained important. After 1880, as dairying displaced grain farming, the production of both corn and oats shrank with that of wheat, though oats remained the leading grain for some time. Hay and peas maintained their place through the transition period and for a time were the outstanding crops. In 1910 potatoes emerged as the State's largest cash crop, a position they so far maintain, though competition from other States is causing them slowly to be displaced by other products. Barley, a leading grain during the same period, was virtually eliminated when prohibition destroyed the malting industry. The tobacco crop rose during the 1920's to 45,000,000 pounds; alfalfa, long kept out by

History

MARQUETTE AND JOLIET DISCOVER THE UPPER MISSISSIPPI, JUNE 17, 1673

THE LANDFALL OF JEAN NICOLET, 1634. NICOLET WAS THE FIRST WHITE MAN KNOWN TO HAVE VISITED WISCONSIN

Statue by Sidney Bedore at Green Bay

"THE SPIRIT OF THE NORTH-
WEST"—MISSIONARY, EXPLORER,
AND INDIAN

LOG CABIN OF A PIONEER, DUDLEY

"THE GRAND LOGGERY," GOVERNOR DOTY'S HOME
AT NEENAH-MENASHA, BUILT IN 1845

Proclamation.

By James Duane Doty

Governor of the Territory of Wiskonsan –

Whereas the compact between the United States and Virginia and the Ordinance of Congress of 1787 secure the right to form a permanent constitution and State Government to each of the states whose boundaries were established by the said Ordinance, "whenever any of the said states shall have sixty thousand free inhabitants therein":

And whereas it is the opinion of many citizens that there are now more than sixty thousand inhabitants in that part of the fifth of the said states which is at present under the Territorial government of Wiskonsan; and that, to obtain the Constitutional liberty enjoyed by the citizens of the United States; to secure an economical administration of government by the Executive and Legislative departments; to establish a more efficient Judiciary system; to prevent an increase the Public debt of Taxation, and to discipline Legislation the time has arrived when the preliminary steps ought to be adopted to restore to the people of this state the right of self government to the extent that it is enjoyed in either of the states of the Union:

And whereas the Legislative Assembly has failed to provide by law the time and place for the said inhabitants to vote upon the question whether the preliminary steps ought to be taken to form a permanent government for the said Fifth State, or not:

Now therefore, in order that the public voice may not be stifled by its failure but that it may be fully expressed to the Congress of the United States and the Legislature of the Territory be thereby instructed, I do recommend to the said inhabitants to deposit with the Judges of the Election in their county, on the day of the General Election, (viz: the fourth Monday of

PROCLAMATION OF STATEHOOD, WRITTEN BY
TERRITORIAL GOVERNOR DOTY IN 1843

...tember next a ballot with the two Words "Yes" or "Nay" therein as they
may be in favour of or against the formation of a ———— permanent
...ment for the State of Wiskonsan.

And I do respectfully urge that the said judges of the election
...cincts do receive the said ballots and canvass and certify
...same to the clerks, in the same manner as they are required
...law to return the votes given for Members of the Assembly; and
...the said clerks do make return thereof to the Secretary of
...Territory of Wiskonsan.

In Testimony whereof I have hereunto subscribed
my name and caused the Great Seal of the Territory
to be affixed.

Done at Madison this twenty third day of
August A. D. one thousand eight hundred and
forty three.

J. D. Doty

THE FIRST CAPITOL, AT OLD BELMONT. THE FIRST
TERRITORIAL LEGISLATURE MET HERE IN 1863

AMERICAN FUR TRADING COMPANY POST (1835),
PRAIRIE DU CHIEN

THE INDIAN AGENCY HOUSE (1832), PORTAGE

THE ROI-PORLIER-TANK COTTAGE, GREEN BAY.
BUILT IN 1776 BY A FRENCH TRADER, THIS IS THE
OLDEST BUILDING STANDING IN WISCONSIN

BUST OF WILLIAM DEMPSTER HOARD—
"FATHER OF WISCONSIN DAIRYING"—
AGRICULTURAL CAMPUS, UNIVERSITY
OF WISCONSIN, MADISON

the acidity of most Wisconsin soils, began about 1925 to be grown on ground fertilized with commercial lime; and silage corn expanded northward as University experts adapted new strains to shorter growing seasons. After the repeal of prohibition in 1932 barley production rapidly revived; but tobacco, potatoes, and other cash crops declined sharply during the depression, and shortage of dairy feed during drought years threatened to change the balance of livestock.

During the 1920's, while farm income in most places remained well below the prices of things that farmers buy, the milk index followed the general price line fairly closely. Consequently, Wisconsin farmers were less affected than most by the prolonged agricultural depression of the 1920's. But even dairy markets slumped at the impact of the depression of the 1930's, and in Wisconsin droughts aggravated the distress. The State's reputation for purebred, high-yielding, tuberculosis-free cattle had made its stock desirable for breeding, so a market for live animals was opened briefly just as the unregulated milk market sagged and Wisconsin farmers found it necessary to liquidate their herds; but this advantage was soon lost.

During the Nation-wide readjustment of agriculture to the depression, the State's primacy in dairying has been threatened. Other regions compete in the production of its chief commodity, cheese; the State is not in a position to control the price of butter, which is the determinant of the whole dairy market. Even within the State dairying has not been growing as fast as a number of other branches of agriculture. With a 4 per cent annual increase in livestock, the number of cattle is actually decreasing, while horses, sheep, poultry, and minor cash crops are becoming more important. Agricultural leaders, aware that the once comfortable position of the dairy industry may have been permanently impaired, are intensifying their efforts to help farmers find new products with which to stabilize their shaken finances. The department of agriculture and markets looked with favor upon a tendency to consolidate processing plants into larger flexible units (*see Cooperative Movement*). The experiment station has broadened the scope of its investigations to include studies of marketing and general economic conditions; the rural zoning movement, for example, inaugurated to help local governmental economy and developed mainly by conservationists, was first devised by agricultural economists. Thus the State seeks to adjust its agriculture to current changes.

Status in 1938: Wisconsin's two million head of dairy cattle constitute the most valuable collection in the Nation. Numerically they lead the second State by more than 400,000 head. In production they furnish more fluid milk, more condensed and evaporated milk, and more cheese than those of any other State. In 1935 Wisconsin produced 93 per cent of the brick and muenster cheese, 70 per cent of the Swiss cheese, 75 per cent of the Limburger cheese, 55 per cent of the American, and 42 per cent of the Italian type cheese of the United States, as well as 160,000,000 pounds of creamery butter. There are 70 milk cows in Wisconsin for every 100 human beings, and before recent droughts depleted herds, the State exported about 80,000 head of breeding stock a year to many parts of the world. Almost half the State's farm income is derived directly from milk.

The production of milk for sale in fluid form occurs mainly near the cities, where it brings better prices than milk marketed in any other way. The perishability of the product requires short, quick hauling, while its relatively low bulk value prohibits much freight handling; cities, furthermore, have set up stringent sanitary regulations and require periodic inspection of each farm. Regions a little too distant for fluid milk marketing turn profitably to condenseries, which are concentrated mainly along Lake Michigan and the Fox River Valley, though they are also spreading throughout newer northern districts. Most cheese production is even farther from market centers: American cheese is produced mainly in the northern dairy belt, a strip of counties running east and west across the State somewhat north of the middle; other forms of cheese are made widely throughout a triangle comprising the southeastern third of the State. Butter, which has the highest value of all in proportion to its bulk, is produced chiefly in the extreme western counties.

Some special areas are noteworthy. Green and Lafayette Counties on the southern border produce between them nearly half the Nation's Swiss and Limburger cheese. Dodge County, a trifle north and west of Milwaukee, alone produces 59 per cent of the brick and Muenster cheese of the United States. Calumet County, farther north and east, yields more milk per square mile than any other county in the Nation— 59,031 gallons. Of the top hundred milk-producing counties of the Nation, Wisconsin has 37.

About four-fifths of the dairy cattle are grades or pure-bred. More than half are Holsteins; but though few counties list Guernseys as their principal breed, that strain is increasingly favored in the newer dairy districts in the north.

Apart from their value as producers of milk and cream, the State's cattle as livestock account for about half its total animal capital. There are 3,230,000 head of cattle, of which only two-thirds are dairy animals. Bulls and beef breeds alone make up more than an eighth of the total livestock value; calves, herd culls, and breeding stock add another considerable fraction. In 1934 the total value of Wisconsin cattle was estimated at $73,836,000, a value greater than that of all other livestock combined, but still only one-third of what it had been five years previously for a smaller number of animals.

Other forms of livestock are usually added as a supplementary line after dairy herds are established, so in general they are most abundant in districts where agriculture is oldest and best developed. The half-million horses, raised mostly in the west and north central districts, make up a third of the total livestock capital. About a million and a half hogs are raised in the southwestern areas where corn ripens; their value has ranged from $6,500,000 to $41,500,000. Poultry yields about a tenth of the total farm income, though the 1934 valuation of $7,000,000 is only 45 per cent of the value in 1930, when there were considerably fewer birds. Sheep, wool, honey, and beeswax together bring in less than one per cent of the gross farm income.

Fur ranching is a natural outgrowth of the days when trapping was a major industry. The 300 or more silver fox farms have about 50,000 aristocratic animals classified as domestic livestock and valued at $20,-000,000, which yield two-fifths of the Nation's fox pelts. The sale of foxes for breeding stock, formerly a large part of the business, has declined considerably as the industry nears saturation. Other fur-bearing animals—mink, raccoon, muskrat, skunk, otter, and beaver—remain under the jurisdiction of the conservation commission as protected wildlife but may be farmed under permit; the commission issues about 1,000 such permits annually.

Essential to the support of this livestock are the State's crops. Because so few of them are marketed directly, these crops bring in little more than a fifth of its cash farm income. But only one out of every five cultivated acres is devoted to raising cash crops; feed crops form the major part of the production and are essential to the prosperity of the State.

Pasture occupies 8,500,000 acres—25 per cent of all land, 40 per cent of the farm land—of which almost 7,000,000 are permanently withheld from cultivation because of rough topography or poor soils. The rest is land temporarily withdrawn from cropping for replenishment of fertility. Corn is the most valuable crop and is a close second in acreage to tame hay. In the extreme south it is husked and fed to hogs; in other regions it is used principally for silage. Tame hay occupies more acreage than any other crop and is second in value. Two-thirds of the total hay crop is timothy and clover, a sixth is wild hay, and another sixth is alfalfa, though the acreage of alfalfa is increasing. Five out of every six farms raise some oats, which account for more than a third of the total crop value; practically the entire harvest is fed to cattle. The production of barley has increased greatly since beer was legalized, and in 1935 this grain accounted for almost a fifth of the value of all crops; at the same time it is becoming more popular as a feed. Rye at one time was grown almost everywhere, but now it is concentrated definitely within the sandy plain in the middle of the

State. Other grains are unimportant. Spring wheat is used mainly for chicken feed; buckwheat is grown locally as a cash crop; soybeans promise to increase under the stimulus of new industrial demands.

Potatoes are the State's most valuable cash crop; the Wisconsin harvest ranks high in the Nation. They are raised almost everywhere, but most of the commercial crop comes from Langlade County in the north and from the central sand country, slightly north of and overlapping the rye region. From a peak $38,000,000 crop in 1922, they declined until by 1935 their $9,000,000 yield was less than a tenth of the total crop value. Half the canning peas in the United States are grown in Wisconsin, but most farmers raise them as a sideline under contract with canneries, for peas are a sensitive crop requiring ideal conditions of warmth and moisture and prompt harvesting. Since the pea-pack lasts only about six weeks, many canneries are equipped to handle other less highly seasonal crops, including snap beans, cucumbers, cabbage, beets, and corn; thus the production of truck vegetables has become important in some districts. Between 1920 and 1930 the State raised about 45,000,000 pounds of tobacco annually, but since 1932-33 the acreage has fallen from 28,000 to 8,500, and the 11,000,000-pound harvest in 1934 was worth only $840,000. Little tobacco is grown above the southern third of the State; most of it comes from two small areas, one near Viroqua on the western border, the other southeast of Madison.

In most areas small fruit provides an auxiliary farm income. The Door County Peninsula on Lake Michigan is one of the most important cherry-growing districts in the United States. Its cherries are marketed fresh, canned, or packed in sugar and refrigerated so that they retain much of their original quality all winter. Apples are grown in Door County, in the southwestern Kickapoo Valley, and along the Lake Superior shore. Marshy districts of the southwestern driftless area, the north woods, and the northwest are turned to profit in the production of cranberries; Wisconsin's 60,000-barrel harvest is second largest in the Nation. Maple trees yield 80,000 gallons of syrup and 20,000 pounds of sugar a year. Sugar beets are rapidly increasing in importance. Other minor products include onions, strawberries, melons, grapes, flax, hemp, popcorn, ginseng, and sphagnum moss for florists; Wisconsin leads the Nation in production of the last two.

Public Agencies: The development of the State's agricultural system has been closely associated with the University of Wisconsin's agricultural experiment station, set up to mobilize the research facilities of the University on behalf of agriculture and to serve farmers somewhat as industries are served by their laboratories. Its staff largely coincides with that of the University's college of agriculture, the main distinction between them being one of function: the station gathers facts and the college disseminates them. Eight substations located in various soil type areas help bring investigations closer to field conditions.

An agricultural department was established at the University of Wisconsin under the Federal Morrill Land Grant Act of 1862, but for the next fifteen or twenty years it was little more than an adjunct to the chemistry and botany departments. In 1883 a tentative sort of experiment station was established under Prof. W. A. Henry; but its effective history dates from 1887, when Congress passed the Hatch Act giving Federal aid to such institutions.

Some of the most notable work of the station's history was done by Henry, Babcock, Russell, and King soon after it was established. Rivaling their classic researches are recent discoveries and inventions in the field of vitamins. In 1927 Dr. Harry Steenbock announced the invention of his irradiation process, in which ultra-violet light is used to build the antirachitic Vitamin D in foods. To protect this process from improper exploitation its patents have been turned over to the Wisconsin Alumni Research Foundation, which releases it under franchise to manufacturers who use it legitimately and without exaggerated claims. Set up originally to handle the Steenbock patents, this foundation now also controls a dozen other discoveries made by Wisconsin scientists, and its income is used to finance further research. In 1937 Professor Conrad Elvehjem announced his discovery of the cure for pellagra.

Two significant current investigations concern methods of managing pasture to furnish economical six-month grazing, and methods of making an alfalfa silage almost equal to summer pasturage in enabling cows to yield milk rich in Vitamin A and growth-promoting elements. The station also devises tests and cures for plant and animal diseases; analyzes fodder, soils, and milk; identifies weeds, grasses, and fungi; and tests seeds and crops for their adaptability to Wisconsin growing conditions. Two new strains of corn adapted to Wisconsin's short growing season, Silver King and Golden Glow, were developed by R. A. Moore at the station. B. D. Leith perfected the heavy-yielding Wisconsin Ped. 38 barley. L. R. Jones went into a region where the yellows, worst foe of cabbage plants, was raging, selected a tough old head that had defied the disease, and from it brought forth a new yellows-resistant variety. Coddling moths and apple maggots were ruining the orchards of the Kickapoo Valley; within two years the station had perfected a means of bringing these pests under control. The station pioneered in experimenting with shelter belts and is a leader in the study of erosion control. Such processes as wiring farm buildings, grinding grain at home, and loading barns and silos have been notably improved by engineering studies at the station. The station is also devoting an increasing share of its attention to the social and economic status of Wisconsin farmers, investigating such matters as cooperative and marketing problems and the social welfare and future of rural youth.

Through the facilities of the extension division and its 69 county agents, through the regular use of the two radio stations operated by the department of agriculture and markets, and through publication of annual reports and numerous other bulletins, the station endeavors to keep the public fully informed of its studies as soon as they are finished. Extension work began in 1885 with the enactment of a law providing for farmers' institutes, the first organizations in the world to teach scientific agriculture to active farmers. In 1911 the legislature appropriated $10,000 for sending extension workers out among farmers, and thus the county agent system was founded. Since 1914 it has been aided by Federal support. In addition to instructing farmers in procedural problems, the extension service energetically sponsors such rural social activities as public discussion groups, rural beautification, food and clothing improvement, "buymanship," book and magazine lending groups, homemaking, family relations, improved housing, dramatics, music, recreation, dancing, education, and sports.

Four-H (Head, Hand, Heart, and Health) organizations began 20 years ago, and, supported by State and county governments, now enroll 31,000 members in 1,800 clubs whose purpose is to train children to become better farmers and homemakers. With their projects for home and community beautification, their bands, orchestras, and drama groups, ball teams, games, and picnics, 4-H clubs have become a vital part of rural life. Their more practical activities, such as handicraft, home making, gardening, and breeding and judging livestock, are of considerable educational and economic value. So efficiently are these clubs organized that in Lincoln County they superseded a languishing county fair association and successfully conducted the county fair. Another organization, the Future Farmers of America, has a membership consisting solely of high school pupils with rural backgrounds; its purpose is to train its members to represent rural interests in public life.

More important than any other single agency in consciously determining the directions and policies of Wisconsin agriculture is the department of agriculture and markets. By 1915 a number of agencies were combined into a department of agriculture. A separate department of markets was formed in 1919, and in 1929 these two departments were merged with the old dairy and food commission into the department of agriculture and markets. Under the reorganization of 1938 and 1939 the three commissioners who directed this department were replaced by a single director who has charge of all administrative matters, and a seven-man policy-making board. At the same time the department again became known as the department of agriculture.

Now the department protects farmers against fraudulent products and impure seeds through its division of feed, fertilizer, and weed control; inspects nursery stock and enforces plant quarantines through the division of insect and plant disease control; seeks to improve horse breeding in its stallion and dog license division; and, through the division of agricultural statistics, compiles records of agricultural enterprise. It also protects the public by standardizing and inspecting farm produce; by regulating the size and fill of spice and liquid containers, the sale of oleomargarine, the use of imitation colors and flavors and deceptive packaging; by licensing peddlers, milk dealers, and itinerant merchants; by inspecting fish, fruit, and vegetable markets and eggs, meat, beer, and dried fruits; and by maintaining bacteriological laboratories. Its two radio stations, WHA in Madison and WLBL in Stevens Point, still are used by the department for the dissemination of market and other information to farmers.

The division of markets slowly is remaking the machinery by which farm products are released and sold. Since 1919 it has manifested a friendly interest in the promotion of cooperatives, since 1921 it has given them direct aid, and in 1929 it set about actually promoting them (*see the Cooperative Movement*). Finding farmers victimized by monopolistic control of fluid milk distribution, in 1932 it set prices to be paid to the producers, soon afterwards fixed consumer prices, and saw its regulations upheld in the courts. It also manages the State fair and aids in marketing Wisconsin farm and dairy products.

The land economic inventory preceded and still serves as field survey agency for the State planning agencies. Since 1927 it has been attempting to study and describe every rod of rural land in the State. It notes topography, soil type, stoniness, and forest cover; takes inventory of timber, vegetation, farms, clearings, buildings, lakes, and streams; and lists and studies existing industries and resources and the economic potentialities of the future. Based on such knowledge, there has arisen a philosophy of conscious research and directed development by which Wisconsin seeks a solution to some of its major problems.

Two Rural Regions: Most of Wisconsin's agricultural activity lies south of a line from Hudson on the west to Green Bay on the east, about two-thirds of the way up the State. North of that line the land is largely half-wild cutover, and rural life sometimes approaches pioneer conditions. It is of regions like this that the National Resources Board said, "Evidently a very large proportion of the farmers . . . produce little, if any, more farm products and sell little, if any, more than the typical European peasant." This fact is of double significance: it means that most of the production cited for the State as a whole actually is accomplished within the southern two-thirds of the State; and it means also that here there are two radically different types of rural life and economy, one abundant, the other meager.

For many years the north impatiently awaited the time when it would develop into a region as rich as the south. Ever since the lumbermen removed the forests, northern citizens have been aggressive colonizers. The concept of sub-marginal land had no place in their minds; their institutions, their businesses, their hopes and plans, all were based on the theory that eventually all the land would be put into farms. The collapse of this theory has taken away from many districts the foundations of their institutions and has brought down upon them a swarm of problems.

Though most of the good land in the north was soon taken up, the settlers continued to come. Indomitable and tenacious pioneers went into the poorer regions, struggled, and failed. City people, attracted by the cheap price of the land, came out seeking new opportunity during the depression; an astonishing number chose their tracts purely by "want ad" and generally got the worst that the agent had to offer. Too often they thought of farming as a way of living, not as a combination of a business and a hard job. When they arrived, they found, instead of the pastoral life they had envisioned, merely interminable, unclocked labor, logging, brushing, stumping, stoning, draining, fencing, and breaking ground. The region demands a toll of at least one failure for each piece of land successfully brought to cultivation; of the relatively poor land left, much could be sold and resold, and ruin settler after settler, without ever becoming more productive than a sand dune.

In six northern Wisconsin counties the average gross farm income in 1936 was less than $600—the lowest, in Vilas County, was $417. Three more counties averaged between $600 and $700. In a solid block of sixteen northern counties, not one reported an average annual income as high as $1,000. Though farmers under such circumstances cannot adequately support local government, they require schools and roads, even though they may be so scattered and isolated that only a few families can use each unit. In 1929 taxes rose as high as 9 per cent of the valuation of property. Though the State's highly developed system of State aids defrayed 25 to 40 per cent of northern county expenses, property tax rates still were 50 to 75 per cent higher in proportion to value than in richer southern counties. As taxes rose, delinquencies increased, sending tax rates still higher and delinquencies still deeper. As far back as 1927, in 17 northern Wisconsin counties, more than two and a half million acres were put up for tax sale; by the middle of the depression delinquencies had mounted to proportions that virtually defied computation.

During the 1920's agricultural economists became increasingly impressed by the futility of the land-agent-settler-sheriff-land-agent cycle. Convinced that the State had arrived at "the age of social and economic planning," the land economic inventory had been gathering the detailed information upon which land-use planning programs could be based; now it began laying groundwork for rural zoning and resettlement programs. By 1927 the delinquency situation had become so acute that the legislature appointed an interim committee to study causes and seek remedies. As early as 1923 the State had empowered counties to zone into residential and industrial districts; in 1928 the law was amended to permit zoning for forestry, recreational, and agricultural purposes. Immediately the University's college of agriculture and the conservation commission, at the request of county boards, began intensive surveys regarding current land uses, which, though completed for only six counties, demonstrated that problems in all cut-over regions were resolvable into a few factors applicable to the entire area.

Meanwhile Oneida County had been grappling with the old problems in the old way. According to the 1930 census eight of the townships in that county had fewer than 25 farms, four fewer than 12; yet these townships like all others had to maintain schools, roads, and local governments. The county appointed a colonization committee to sell land to which the county held tax deeds. This committee, however, also was instructed to study the general problem of the disposition of sub-marginal lands. The committee, finding that prospective settlers constantly sought to buy cheap lands in areas which it knew should not be settled, sought the aid of the college of agriculture in evolving a zoning plan. After a half year of conferences between the personnel of the college of agriculture, the conservation department, the Attorney General's office, and the county agent and local officials, the Oneida County zoning ordinance, first of its kind in the world, took effect in July 1933. A procedural method had been worked out, and as other northern counties hurried to join the zoning movement they had simply to follow the Oneida form. Twenty-four zoned counties now form a solid block across the northern third of the State. Other States have followed Wisconsin in enacting rural zoning laws, but Wisconsin still leads in their effective application to land utilization and settlement control.

At first the counties zoned themselves into only two districts, one for forestry and the other unrestricted. Later ordinances included three districts in which recreational functions were differentiated from those of forestry; in recreation districts year-round residence is permitted. Following zoning, the next step envisioned is the relocation of the non-conforming users—people who were on the land before the zoning ordinances were passed and who, under the law, are permitted to stay and demand the same governmental services as before.

The present inhabitants of restricted areas cannot be removed without compensation, even though further settling is forbidden. Until they are driven out by loneliness, failure, death, or the knowledge that the area never will be developed, public services must go on. But local authorities envision great eventual savings. Towns, like the sparsely settled ones in Oneida County, can be merged; school districts can be eliminated or consolidated; counties may even find it profitable to alter their boundaries to reduce the costs of government. The transformation of town roads into fire lanes, the administration of fire protection and other measures of conservation, and the elimination of public services may be facilitated by adjustments in State-aid plans which at present tend to encourage the continuance of unnecessary services. Meanwhile, conservation authorities are planning ways to use restricted areas for restoring vanished natural resources (*see Natural Setting*).

Despite the poverty of the north, census figures reveal the State as a whole to be better supplied than most with the conveniences that indicate a high standard of living. Except for two counties in the central sandy plain, all districts south of the cut-over belt have average farm incomes higher than $1,000, and four counties average higher than $2,000; the highest is Kenosha County, with $2,322 (1934). And not only do southern farms yield greater incomes, but their operation apparently leaves more of the cash income for family spending.

In the State as a whole, more than nine-tenths of the farms have automobiles; during the depression the proportion of car-owning farmers increased by 3 per cent. Three-fifths of them have telephones and one-fourth have electric lights; the Rural Electrification program may cause this proportion to increase rapidly. These figures are at least 50 per cent higher than those for the Nation as a whole.

In addition to their automobiles, a full third of the farmers have trucks, more than a quarter of them have tractors, and three-fifths use gas or electric engines or motors. More than half of the farms of the State are on hard-surfaced or graveled roads. Approximately half the farm homes have washing machines, an eighth have their own milking machines, and about a third have furnaces. Seventeen per cent have running water in their kitchens, thirty-six per cent have it in their barns; and on a tenth of the farms there are water-heating systems. Wisconsin has more silos than any other State. About half of all farms are free of mortgages. Farm population increased from 920,037 in 1920 to 930,515 in 1935.

In reading such statements the divergence between north and south must constantly be borne in mind. Statistically, rural Wisconsin ranks high among the States in ownership and consumption of the goods and services that make for fuller living. As the northern regions are much poorer than the averages for the State as a whole, so the southern regions are correspondingly richer. But wherever its soil permits, the north apparently is entering into a newer, sounder, and more orderly phase of development.

Cooperative Movement

TWO general types of cooperative are now at work in Wisconsin, one concerned with marketing, the other with purchasing. The first type, handling much of the produce from Wisconsin farms, aims at influencing markets in order to keep distribution steady and prices stable. In certain types of cooperatives supply is controlled through membership and contract agreement, so that each farmer-member may escape the wavering prices of market gluts or market shortages. Present day cooperative marketing strives more and more toward centralization, merging the market operations of local cooperative associations into State-wide systems for particular commodities. Consumers' cooperatives, on the other hand, operate stores or other enterprises to supply their members' needs: farm machinery, oil, medicine, housing facilities, or whatever they may be. Savings made as a result of purchasing cooperatively are handled as the group decides.

Both cooperative marketing and purchasing are fundamentally unlike a corporation. In a corporation the ownership of stock gives the owner control of the enterprise, while in a cooperative association control of the enterprise is in the hands of all the members, who have equal rights regardless of economic status. To attain this democratic ideal the Wisconsin law governing the organization of cooperative associations provides, among other things, that each member shall have one and only one vote; that the rate of dividend upon stock shall be limited to 8 per cent; and that the net proceeds shall be distributed on the basis of patronage. This part of the law is modeled after principles that were drafted by a group of flannel weavers of Rochdale, England, in 1884, and are therefore known as the Rochdale principles.

Farmers and farmer sympathizers in Wisconsin have been behind the cooperative movement since its start. They have backed it with campaigns, money, and legislation, setting in motion a federated machinery of terminal markets, collective bargaining agencies, and cooperative retail and wholesale units. Poverty-stricken single enterprises have been able, with such help, to spread their influence and trade beyond the radius of farms, then beyond cities, and sometimes even beyond the State. In 1855 there was but one cooperative farmer store open in Wisconsin, and that failed in less than a year. Today there are as many cooperative memberships as there are farms, and each farm averages more than $300 a year in volume of cooperative business. Wisconsin has one-tenth of all cooperative groups in the Nation, about one-tenth of all the cooperative business, averaging $133,820,000 a year, and one-seventeenth of all the membership. Its number of cooperative marketing and buying organizations is well over 2,000, the second largest of any State. These organizations, with handicaps to overcome such as chain-store underbidding, meager capital, and scattered small production areas, have grown steadily, thus far totaling 185,800 members among farmers alone. They adjust production, standardize quality, offer financial assistance, and undertake large programs of education and recreation.

National farmer groups were first to experiment with cooperation in the State. The largest of these, the "Patrons of Husbandry," better known as the Grange, signed up many members here during the post-Civil War depression, when markets were almost completely disrupted. Beginning in 1874, the Grange intended to "discountenance the credit system" and introduce the Rochdale Plan into its farmer stores. In spite of a strong beginning the Grange suffered Nation-wide slumps in power and membership only a few years later; its business volume in Wisconsin, $164,445 in 1877, had dropped 50 per cent by 1878. From a peak of 17,000 in 1875, its membership fell off sharply. Small savings, poor quality in goods, order delays, and the requirement of cash with orders caused the failure. The stringent cash clause especially tended to drive farmers over to credit stores where they could get time extensions or could barter butter and eggs for merchandise. However, the Grange did constitute the first powerful move towards collective farmer strength, its small stores laying the groundwork for future cooperative action.

While the Grange had been at work, cooperative thought had reached trade and industry in the State; in the early eighties a cooperative newspaper lasted seventeen days and then stopped printing for lack of capital. Other ventures were a cooperative wagon works at Fond du Lac in 1880 and a cooperative cigar factory at Milwaukee in 1882, both short-lived. Cheese and butter factories made further attempts during the nineties, but actually no durable cooperatives were set up until the opening years of this century. In 1903 the Society of Equity, general in its purpose like the Grange, began vigorously organizing in Wisconsin as a political, educational, and propagandist society aiming at "better business methods on the farm." At the same time another group called "The Right Relationship League" was circulating its agents among Wisconsin farmers, persuading them that "cooperation is sound," and getting their support for a few small cooperative stores.

The years between 1905 and 1915 were filled with intense cooperative campaigns by labor, Equity, and Right Relationship groups. In

1911 farm and labor interests, working together as never before or since (*see Labor*), forced the passage of a law providing for the incorporation of cooperatives.

Though local cooperation developed in Wisconsin at an early period, and though the Wisconsin Cranberry Exchange had been in existence since 1906, the real beginnings of large-scale cooperative marketing occurred between 1915 and 1920. More than any other organization it was the Equity which helped crystallize cooperative aims in that period. It was able to influence farm legislation considerably, being represented by fifteen or twenty legislators. It also helped to found the Wisconsin Cheese Producers' Federation, now known as the Wisconsin Cheese Producers' Cooperative. But after 1920 the Equity national treasury collapsed under a series of heavy losses, and thereafter the organization operated only in Wisconsin. With its roll call of 29,000 dwindling rapidly, Equity's next step was to merge with the Farmers' Union (organized in Wisconsin in 1930) under the name of The Wisconsin Division of the Farmers' Educational and Cooperative Equity Union of America. Known in Wisconsin simply as the Equity Union, the group claims a membership of 15,000 persons, including secondary educational clubs and a junior union. At the present time the union operates in the State about thirty bulk oil plants, several stores, and about thirty shipping associations. It further maintains lobbies at Madison and Washington, active politically on behalf of liberal farm reforms.

State assistance to cooperatives has long since passed the stage of mere encouragement, regardless of whether or not the cooperatives compete with other businesses. The reason for this is that the State recognizes that neither the farmer nor the State, if one works independent of the other, is able permanently to secure better markets for farm produce. It is believed that the only way by which farm markets or marketing methods can be improved is through group action among the farmers themselves. The State justifies its attitude, therefore, on the ground that it is aiding markets by aiding cooperatives. In fact, State law requires that the department of agriculture "promote and assist in the organization of cooperatives." Encouragement has been given to the Pure Milk Products Cooperative, a collective bargaining agency with a membership of about 3,000 among farmers who sell their milk to condenseries. The agency cooperates with farmers by installing checking and testing machinery in each of its plants, which insures correct weights and tests. Not to be confused with the condensery group is the Pure Milk Association of farmers in the five southeastern counties, which supplies fluid milk to the Chicago market. Also important in the southern part of the State is the Farm Bureau Federation, which conducts educational sessions and supports lobbies for more favorable cooperative laws. The bureau campaigns for better schools, elimination of dairy substitutes, and facilities for farm cooperative marketing.

There are approximately 2,882 dairy plants in Wisconsin, including 1,900 cheese factories, about 600 creameries, and 75 condenseries. These are scattered throughout the State. To market the products of all these plants presents a complicated problem. Thus far two types of solution have been charted for this problem. The first type is represented by the Wisconsin Cooperative Creamery Federation, consisting of a number (fluctuating around eighty) of local creameries, blocked off into districts. Their main services are the consolidation of butter shipments in order to save on freight costs and the employment of field men whose duty it is to work on the improvement of butter quality. The second type of solution lies in the centralized power of large concerns like the Land O'Lakes Creameries, Inc., operating from Minneapolis. Its membership of more than five hundred creameries is spread extensively through Minnesota, Wisconsin, and Iowa, about forty creameries being contracted in Wisconsin. At the present time its agents concentrate most effectively on the distribution and sale of butter and cheese. Land O' Lakes is also marketing the cheese produced in the sixty cheese factories that are members of the Wisconsin Cheese Producers' Federation Cooperative. In Shawano County, a few years ago, there were approximately ninety-five competitive cheese factories, each expensive to operate because of the small volume handled. In order to bring about more economical manufacturing and marketing of their dairy products, dairymen of the county have organized the Consolidated Badger Cooperative. Membership is limited to actual producers of milk. Likewise, Langlade County farmers established the Antigo Milk Products Cooperative, operating since 1931, to take the place of numerous small cheese factories, both cooperative and private. Their combination plant is at Antigo. Both of these large cooperatives market their products through Land O' Lakes Creameries.

Cooperation is widespread among the two-hundred-odd shipping associations in Wisconsin, whose function is to assemble and ship livestock. Instead of selling their hogs, cattle, and sheep individually to local buyers, members of these associations bring their stock to local yards and ship it collectively to terminal markets for sale. To understand the significance of cooperative selling on terminal markets it should be remembered that local cooperative shipping associations are limited to local action, and what is needed for the greatest advantage and savings is cooperation through the terminal markets themselves. Contact with the markets can be maintained by locally controlled cooperative sales agencies and organizations. The only cooperative terminal organization in Wisconsin is the Equity Cooperative Livestock Association at the Milwaukee Stock Yards, which returned $31,357 in dividends to its members during 1936, from a total of 6,392 carloads of livestock. In spite of low charges the association was able to make substantial savings, as shown by the dividends paid. Many farmers living in the northwestern part of the State ship their livestock through a cooperative terminal association in St. Paul, the Farmers' Union Central Exchange and the Central Cooperative Association.

To bring about an orderly marketing of the Wisconsin wool clip, the wool growers of the State organized the Wisconsin Cooperative Wool Growers' Association which markets a considerable per cent of the wool produced in the State. This State-wide cooperative collects, grades, and stores wool for its members, feeding the national wool market in Boston at regular intervals. In a period of six years their orderly method has netted association members three to four cents more per pound than was paid by independent dealers. Central offices keep in close touch with the Agricultural Experiment Station, profiting by the latter's discoveries concerning production, control, and the treatment of sheep diseases and insect pests. During selling season the association sends out weekly letters to sheep locals, with information on the price of wool in the eastern market as well as the bulk of wool that the organization sells between times.

Since the State began sponsoring cooperatives their rise has been rapid. The department of agriculture has been active in organizing and assisting the Wisconsin State Potato Exchange, the Pea Growers' Association, the Farmers' Union branch of the poultry and egg markets, various beekeepers, the Northern Wisconsin Tobacco Pool, and numerous beet growers' cooperatives. Partly because of department help, the National Silver Fox Fur Breeders' Cooperative at Wausau now controls about 70 per cent of the national production of silver fox pelts. All these groups have shown in their operation that, while they have been successful in a reduction of handling costs, their products still have been at the mercy of fluctuating prices in the large terminal markets. The remedy possibly will be consolidation—locals into regional organizations, and federations into national organizations.

While Wisconsin ranks third in the Nation in the value of products handled by producer cooperatives, in purchasing association transactions it ranks seventh. This is probably because the producer type is comprised of more central industries such as cheese making and dairying, while buyers' cooperatives consist of diversified and comparatively small-scale activities such as rural electrification, petroleum sales, and banking and insurance transactions. No complete census of these many scattered cooperatives has ever been taken, nor is information concerning their various failures available. It is known, however, that the volume of farm purchasing association transactions for 1936 totaled over $15,800,000 in Wisconsin alone.

Expansion from initially small capital is demonstrated by the histories of now flourishing concerns, such as the Central Cooperative Wholesale Society of Superior. Its controlling unit, with a net worth of $200,000, handling an annual volume of business in excess of $3,000,-000, set out in 1917 with a hat collection of $15.50 to serve as a working fund. In 1939, in addition to its large central exchange and warehouse, the society conducted a training school, sponsored a health association, and provided an education and auditing department for the benefit of its one-hundred-odd member stores.

Superior, mostly because of the Central Cooperative Wholesale, is internationally known as a cooperative stronghold. "At Superior," says H. G. May, British cooperative leader, "we reach the principal center of consumers' cooperation in the United States." For besides the great Cooperative Wholesale the city shelters a thriving retail group known as the People's Cooperative Society, which carries on extensive advertising and house-to-house campaigns for the furtherance of the movement. Here, also, at least a dozen credit unions, a cooperative health association, a workers' mutual savings bank, a cooperative club, a youth league, and a women's guild actively contribute towards education and efficiency in the movement. Other localities having conspicuous cooperative retail organizations are Prentice, Madison, Racine, and Milwaukee. The first has the Prentice Cooperative Supply Company, the Price County Cooperative Oil Association (supplying both the local cooperative and the Brantwood Cooperative Supply Company), a credit union, and an educational group called the Prentice Cooperative League. In Madison the movement is represented by a cooperative dairy, a petroleum cooperative, and a cleaning and tailoring cooperative. Racine, where the cooperatives are supported mainly by the labor movement, has a large meeting hall, four service stations, a coal yard, auto repair shop, grocery store, bulk oil plant, electric equipment shop, and credit union. Milwaukee, which only recently began to organize cooperative retail buying, has a modern and successful People's Cooperative Association, a store begun in 1936 by Negroes.

One of the earliest of the fifty to seventy-five cooperative general stores in the State was the Patron's Mercantile Company of Black Earth, which, organized in 1886, now does an annual sales business of over $200,000. Two other pioneers are the Medford Cooperative (1911), and the Brule Cooperative Association (1920). The latter carried on its first business transactions in a horse barn, but now it takes care of more than 90 per cent of the retail work in its area. The first attempt to organize this type of cooperative was a little store started in 1855 at Sussex, Wisconsin, which lasted only a year.

In Wisconsin, as in the rest of the United States, the membership of oil and petroleum cooperatives is rapidly growing. As yet mainly rural in character, oil cooperatives in the State date back to 1921, when four stations were begun simultaneously at Manawa, Casca, New London, and Van Dyne. Petroleum cooperatives have since sprung up like mushrooms; figures from 1930 to 1936 show a growth from 37 to 163, an increase of over 450 per cent. At least 75 of these 163 local retail cooperatives are branches of the Midland Wholesale Cooperative in Minneapolis, founded in 1926, the oldest cooperative wholesale petroleum exchange in America. Likewise a Minnesota concern, The Farmers' Union Central Exchange has about thirty-two bulk oil branches in Wisconsin, credited by union statisticians with having saved Wisconsin farmers more than $75,000 during 1936 alone.

Credit unions have increased and thrived only since laws aiding their organization have been in effect. Although a credit union law was passed in 1910 in Wisconsin, it contained so many defects that incorporation under it was almost impossible. When it was altered in 1923, there was immediate response; two unions, the Milwaukee Federal Employees Union and the Milwaukee Municipal Credit Union, were at once established. The number of credit unions grew to 52 in 1931, 333 in 1935, and, in 1936, to 445 chartered institutions. Requiring interest only on unpaid balances, they accomplish for their 80,382 members considerable reductions in credit costs. Centers in the State are Milwaukee, La Crosse, Green Bay, Kenosha, Appleton, Beloit, Madison, and West Allis, Milwaukee heading the list with about ninety unions. Because Wisconsin had the greatest number of such unions per capita in the Nation, in 1935 the National Association moved its headquarters to Madison.

Largest among the 240 insurance cooperatives in the State is the Cooperative Insurance Mutual, which was begun in 1936 at Appleton and within a year had more than 1,000 policies in force. This cooperative, through the incorporation of fifty small associations, is able to supply automobile insurance on a strictly non-profit basis. Another large insurance cooperative, the Mutual Cooperative Insurance Association in Superior, backed by the Central Cooperative Wholesale, concentrates on property fire insurance, although it intends also to grant individual policies on urban property. In this way it secures steady patronage at a small amount of risk.

The Wisconsin Rural Electrification Coordination was established by the legislature to aid farmers in gaining a portion of the Federal fund allocated for rural electrification purposes: this helped the State to obtain an apportionment of $3,613,600 for REA purposes. Its advisory committee, selected by State, farm, and cooperative groups, guides and explains the policies of the State REA. There are now 26 electricity and two power cooperative projects in Wisconsin, and four more projects are being organized. In its short life cooperative electrification has already accomplished, at least in rural areas, a 15 to 20 per cent reduction in the cost of line construction as well as a substantial cut in retail rates.

Though there are only six telephone companies listed under the cooperative law (all but one without a switchboard), well over 400 companies actually operate under some cooperative plan. They comprise, however, only a small part of the State's total telephone business. The single cooperative telephone exchange of any magnitude is the Wood County Telephone Cooperative; this has about 3,500 members and serves a large portion of the central Wisconsin River area.

Cooperative buying has begun in locker plants, furnishing mass refrigeration that enables rural consumers to preserve meats and vegetables in large quantities. Of some sixty locker plants in the State, most of them placed in cheese factories in and around Green Bay, many are cooperative. A start was made in cooperative medicine a short time ago when farm and labor groups around Superior organized the Cooperative Health Association. Members take a $5 share of stock and pay a fixed fee which has been temporarily set at $2.90 per month. For this sum members are entitled to all normal medical care by the association's doctors and to hospitalization in certain hospitals.

Hundreds of groups and individuals carry on the educational work of the cooperative movement in both producer and consumer centers. The Central Cooperative Wholesale, the Northern States Cooperative League, the Northern States Women's Cooperative Guild, the Midland Cooperative Wholesale, the Wisconsin Cooperative League, the Farmers' Educational and Cooperative Equity Union of Wisconsin, and the Extension Division of the University of Wisconsin are important groups. Most helpful in the matter of education has been the 1935 Wisconsin statute, the first of its kind in America, which requires that the essentials of cooperation be taught in every State high school and vocational school as part of the regular curriculum. Another law, passed earlier, provides for State supervision of bonded warehouses. Through the department of agriculture, the State maintains a staff of employees, agriculturists, economists, attorneys, accountants, and organizers, all of whom aid in the organization and operation of cooperative enterprises and give expert assistance in drafting technical contract provisions, especially those involving prices of farm produce. The law also provides means for issuing State certificates of inspection, thus guaranteeing reliable standards of quality and measure. The statute of 1937 protects electrical distribution cooperatives from encroachments by private utilities.

Cooperative methods of business have won favor among Wisconsin people. Benefits to both producers and consumers are apparent, as is the growing importance of cooperative enterprise in the economic life of the State.

Recreation

OVER the whole northern half of Wisconsin lies a forest wilderness, smelling of pine pitch and brush fires, where rivers thunder across trap-rock ledges or flow quietly on clean sand beds. The land is pitted with swamps, hidden ponds, and uncounted lakes, and wildlife abounds in both the uplands and the lowlands. A third of the northern boundary juts out into Lake Superior, in the disconnected series of the Apostle Islands. Southeastern Wisconsin, in contrast, is now a farmland, cleared and plow-broken, between mazes of lakes and a labyrinth of drumlin chains. Here corn and bluegrass wave and the countryside is patched with mild wooded ridges, groves, reedy creeks.

Bordering the entire eastern length of the State are the cold green waters of Lake Michigan, split to the north by the slim thumb of the Door County Peninsula. In the southwest sprawls the coulee country, steep and irregular, veined by streams, rivulets, and rivers—tributaries of the Mississippi. Apple orchards smother the ridges with pink and white blossoms, and the highways rise and circle high above slopes of sugar bush and abandoned ginseng beds. The Mississippi moves slowly here, in a broad 250-mile path that divides Wisconsin from Minnesota and Iowa.

Recently Wisconsin has come to realize the possibilities of this natural scene as an important source of income. Already recreation brings in a revenue of about 250 million dollars annually and ranks high as a State industry. Its program is of two types, that undertaken by local, Federal, and State agencies, and that undertaken by individual promoters, real estate men, and chambers of commerce. The first type is recent in origin. Before 1936 individual steps towards a paying program of recreation were timid, balked on every hand by limited cash. Money was not available for extensive advertising, and such bulletins and pamphlets as were published by independent proprietors reached only scattered groups within the State. But since 1936, when the conservation commission established a recreational publicity department, the situation has changed rapidly. Concentrating on adding to the State income, and incidentally to private income, the publicity department began a scientific advertising campaign. Neighboring States, particularly in the corn belt, have become more aware of a countryside only a day's drive away that contrasts sharply with their own prairie-land. Recreation publicity directs its appeal to people in Chicago and other centers of population throughout the Midwest.

Conservation and recreation are linked together, and "Wise Use," the conservation commission's slogan, has come to mean the most profitable treatment, from a long range view, of park areas, forests, and submarginal lands. Unproductive regions are used most profitably and pleasantly as recreation centers while they slowly revert to their natural wild state.

The State's many waters are probably its greatest recreational asset. It has 8,500 counted lakes, 10,000 miles of trout streams, 500 miles of Great Lakes shoreline, several large rivers, and innumerable springs. All Wisconsin waits for the opening of the fishing and swimming seasons. When ice melts from the rivers and streams that empty into Green Bay, Lake Superior, and the Mississippi, anglers trek into the open country and the wilderness, to the Brule River, the Wisconsin, the Peshtigo, the Wolf, the Namekagon, the Evergreen, the Flambeau, the Pine, the Black Jack, the Thunder. Fifty-one of the 71 counties of Wisconsin have trout in their streams. Black bass, wall-eyed and northern pike, crappies, blue gills, perch, silver and white bass, and sunfish and other pan fish are caught in nearly all the lake regions within the State. Muskie are not so generally distributed, their main haunts being the headwaters of the St. Croix, Chippewa, Flambeau, and Wisconsin Rivers. The Mississippi contains all these and also bullheads, catfish, sturgeon, and rough fish such as sheephead, buffalo, carp, red horse, and suckers.

Lakes for swimming, boating, and all water sports are sprinkled in great clusters over the north central, the northwest, and the southeastern portions, some of them mossy pools deep in the forest, others reaching the size of Lake Winnebago, Lake Geneva, and the lakes that surround Madison. Lake Superior's shore, broken into high, red, intricate cliffs, is more suitable for sightseeing and boating than for swimming. But the Lake Michigan shore is made up mostly of sand dunes, sloping down flatly to the water; its natural beach is marked off for swimming holes at intervals all the way from Kenosha to the tip of the Door Peninsula. In the Great Lakes harbors—Ashland, Superior, Green Bay, Sister Bay, Ephraim, Sheboygan, Milwaukee, Racine, and Kenosha—trim sailing craft course far out on the horizon, while fast outboards and bug-like racing boats churn the water nearer shore. The inland lakes, too, have regattas, yacht cruises, and all types of water frolic.

Gathering places for thousands of summer vacationists are the State Parks, the roadside parks, and the forests that are scattered throughout Wisconsin. Peninsula State Park, on three limestone bluffs in the heart of the Door County cherryland, faces north across Green Bay. Dense groves of white cedar grow from the moist ledges of these bluffs, close to clusters of juniper and yew trees. In Door County also is Potawatomi State Park, its wooded bluff and headland looking over the bay. A hundred miles south on the Lake Michigan shore, just below Sheboygan, is Terry Andrae State Park, a long, glistening sand beach with a backdrop of white pine woods. The four State Parks—Wyalusing, Perrot, Merrick, and Interstate, on the western side of Wisconsin—border the Mississippi. Wyalusing is high up in the bluffs above the confluence of the Wisconsin River and the Mississippi; a long welter of sloughs, woods, bayous, islands, and prairie reach to the distant skyline. Perrot is famous for Trempealeau Mountain, which rises out of a maze of Mississippi backwaters near the site of an early French wintering post and fort. Merrick, on a flat but pleasantly-wooded site on the upper river, is used principally by campers, golfers, and fishermen. Oldest of all the State Parks is Interstate, partly in Wisconsin and partly in Minnesota, looking down from timbered banks to the boiling waters of the St. Croix River. Here towering columns of rock and pot holes, made by some prehistoric waterfall, lie within a wild, natural valley.

In the Baraboo Range is Devils Lake Park; cottages, camping and boating facilities, and a beach center around Devils Lake, a quiet, clear body of water. Rib Mountain State Park, near Wausau and above the Wisconsin Valley, is probably the highest point of land in the State; its rocky escarpments of quartzite look out for many miles across the Wisconsin, Rib, and Eau Claire river valleys. Two other State Parks are Copper Falls and Pattison. Copper Falls is hidden in a northern forest just outside Mellen; here the raging red waters of the Bad River and Tyler's Fork meet in a series of wild cascades, falls, and gorges. At Pattison, some dozen miles south of the city of Superior, Big Manitou Falls, the highest waterfall in the State, is carved by the Black River tumbling northward over a rocky range on its way to Lake Superior.

Smaller areas have been set aside as State Parks because of their historic interest. First Capitol Park, two acres of flat ground near Belmont, contains the building where the first legislative session in Wisconsin was held in 1836. Cushing Memorial spreads over a green slope on the banks of the Bark River as it flows through Delafield; a granite shaft commemorates the "Three Wisconsin Cushings," soldiers of the Civil War period. Tower Hill, close to Spring Green, is a single precipitous bluff hanging over the Wisconsin River. Here lead shot was made during the last century in the now extinct village of Helena. The State has also established little parks along main-travelled roads as temporary stopping places for weary drivers. Rocky Arbor, a few miles north of Wisconsin Dells, has cool woods and curious rock formations, and Ojibwa Park, fronting the Chippewa River in Sawyer County, is equally pleasant. In New Glarus Woods at New Glarus are 40 acres of natural oak forest.

People seeking seclusion during the summer often park their trailers or pitch their tents in the Northern State Forest in the central part of Vilas County. Here the State owns 100,000 acres of dense forest, in which the Eagle Chain of Lakes and many nameless streams are interspersed with hills and bare levels of sandy land. More difficult to reach by highways is the Flambeau River Forest, 3,000 acres of virgin hardwood timber on the upper reaches of the river. American Legion State Forest, in Oneida County, is similar in character to Northern State Forest. The Wisconsin River, draining from the thickest network of lakes in the north, provides bathing, fishing, and beautiful campsites. Brule River State Forest is a series of State-owned wooded tracts on the Brule River, famous for trout. The two National forests, Chequamegon and Nicolet, blanketing thousands of acres in northern counties, are wild enough in spots for the most adventurous of sportsmen; and the many county forests are open to sightseers or to hunters and fishers.

Golf courses, baseball diamonds, shooting galleries, bowling alleys, and tennis courts are found in profusion throughout the whole State, especially in the large resort areas such as Lake Geneva, the Door County Peninsula, Hayward, Eagle River, Tomahawk, Green Lake, Wisconsin Dells, Oconomowoc and the Milwaukee region, and Bayfield and the Apostle Islands. Gradually, however, such sports are being supplemented by diversified, all-inclusive programs, some of them purely experimental, others permanent. In all the State Parks CCC boys and WPA workers are finding out what sports and activities are most popular. Nature tours, for instance, are being tried; a guide points out little known types of flowers, trees, and animals, or explains the geology of queer formations. At Devils Lake, evening campfire sings, and at Tower Hill, outdoor plays put on by children are proving successful A chain of youth hostels is springing up throughout the southeast and the coulee country. Experimental activities include the cooperative camps of out-of-state businessmen, who build their own cabins but run their camp life cooperatively. There are over a hundred privately run summer camps for adults or children.

With autumn comes a new group of sportsmen. Hunters find Wisconsin well stocked with wild game. Grouse, pheasant, prairie chicken, partridge, quail, woodcock, jack rabbits, squirrels, cottontails, and foxes hide in the tall dry grass of the southern prairies. With the first frost, teal and mallards wing over gray Wisconsin lakes on their way south. Various farms, refuges, and shelters help keep game abundant.

Recreation in Wisconsin has thus far been charted principally against a summer and fall scene, leaving the advantages of a typical northern winter to the local people who take their vacations when the snow falls. They fish through lake ice in the quiet wilderness or hunt rabbits by moonlight over crusted snow. The tracks of bear, deer, wolves, or bobcats cross over snowy clearings down to the brink of frozen rivers. Most cottages are boarded up, and drifts cover doors and windows.

But winter sports are becoming fashionable throughout the country and Wisconsin is wisely following the general trend. Furnaces and huge comfortable fireplaces are being built into lodges and cottages for winter living. Ski-tows are installed on the long northern hills, and some northern lakes are equipped for hockey games, ice boating, skating, and skate-sailing as well as for summer swimming. The popularity of winter fun in the north was demonstrated by the junior ski-jumping tournament held at Eau Claire in 1937, when 400 young people participated in the largest junior ski-meet ever held in the world. Rib Mountain, with its long smooth slopes, Eagle River, where resort properties keep open all year, and Oconomowoc, with several snow-sheltered lakes, are rapidly becoming centers for skiing and ice carnivals. Elsewhere, particularly in the coulee region, the terrain is more suitable for tobogganing, snowshoeing, jumping, cutter riding and sleigh riding, skijoring, dogsled mushing, and hunting. Rhinelander, a northern town, appropriates funds for a full-time sports director and for publicity. Snow trains now leave Chicago and Milwaukee every week end from Dec. 23 to Feb. 17 for Ashland, Devils Lake, Eagle River, La Crosse, Phelps, Rhinelander, and Lac du Flambeau. Winter sports in all these places are energetically conducted, chiefly by men of Scandinavian stock, who serve as professional teachers, guides, and athletes.

Though recreation advertising campaigns mainly reach out-of-state tourists, Wisconsin people are helped to discover their own State. The northern lakes offer ideal retreats for two weeks of fly and plug fishing, for wolf, bird, and deer hunts. The northern Indian reservations, such as the Menominee, the La Pointe, the Lac Court Oreilles, and the Lac du Flambeau draw visitors from the southern part of the State. New trout streams are still discovered each year and not even the conservation commission has counted all the lakes.

Education

BEFORE Wisconsin was organized as a Territory in 1836, there was no provision for public education in the region. The officers at the military posts had schools for their children, and the well-to-do mining families in the southwest, following the southern custom, maintained small private schools through subscription and fees. With the establishment of the Territory there was some agitation for free schools. Michael Frank of Southport (now Kenosha) tried in 1840 to get a bill through the legislature authorizing taxation of property for this purpose, but was defeated. A law of 1841 provided for a discretionary county or town school tax but set property qualifications for voting in district meetings and required a three-fourths vote for a tax for teachers' wages. Since counties and towns were not eager to levy the permissive tax, a charge was made for each child in school; the poorest were therefore excluded. Dissatisfaction with this system strengthened the movement for free schools. In 1845 popular pressure, organized under the "Friends of the Free School," forced the passage of Frank's bill, and in 1846 a free school was opened in Southport.

With the coming of statehood Wisconsin acquired on paper a complete system of public education, but not until thirty years later was anything really accomplished. The constitution of 1848 provided for free schooling for all children between the ages of four and twenty; an attempt in the convention to limit free schools to white children was defeated. Legislative action in 1849 set up the district system of common schools almost exactly as it is today, the entire burden being placed on local school districts; not until 1885 was there a State tax for schools. In 1867 a law required consolidation of school districts in nearly all cities and villages, thus becoming the basis of the city school system. In 1901, as a result of the public's desire for something other than the one-room school in rural and small village areas, the first State graded school law was passed. In 1939 there were 712 State graded schools, many of which are consolidated schools in fact though not in name. The closed school law further raised the level of educational opportunity in rural areas by providing for the closing of many one-room schools and the transportation of children to the neighboring district; a total of 525 schools have been closed to date. The 1928 Equalization Law makes it possible for every rural district to maintain, through State and county aid, a school of required standards. Wisconsin's rural supervisory program is unique in that the State pays the salary and expenses of at least one supervising teacher in every county.

The Federal Government appropriated for the support of the common schools of the State more than 1,500,000 acres of land, but much of the potential income from these lands was never realized. Eagerness to attract settlers led to the selling of these lands too cheaply. In 1852, when the market price was $10 to $20 an acre, the legislature set the minimum price of school lands at $1.25. Appraisals were often as low as 5¢ or 10¢ an acre, and as much as 30 years credit was allowed. Sales were often made below the assessed valuation. These were the days when the development and settlement of the frontier was being pushed, when speculation was rife, and before there was a modern system of bookkeeping. In addition, as a legislative investigation in 1856 revealed, there were doubtless irregularities and abuses by the land commissioners. Today the income from the school funds is less than 2 per cent of the cost of public education.

Exactly 30 years after the establishment of free public schools the first compulsory school attendance law was passed (1879). Children from 7 to 15 were required to attend school for 12 weeks out of the year, but since any excuse was valid, this law was ineffective. The superintendent of schools reported that 34 per cent of the school population was not enrolled. Only in 1903 was a school attendance law passed which did not exempt poverty-stricken children. But this law was not enforced. In 1907 the first effective compulsory school law was enacted; however, the total attendance required differed for children in Milwaukee, in second and third class cities, and in towns and villages. The present law demands regular attendance up to 16 and part-time up to 18, but the same variation between localities is in effect. It is also difficult to enforce this law beyond the age of 16.

Elementary schools were the first to be set up, but the constitution provided for a complete system of public education from the kindergarten to college. The first kindergarten in the United States was opened by Mrs. Carl Schurz in Watertown in 1855; regular kindergartens in the schools, however, did not come until after 1872, when a beginning was made in Milwaukee.

Secondary education was early in the hands of private academies and seminaries, and only gradually did public high schools supplant these. In 1849 Michael Frank obtained a free high school for Kenosha; other cities followed, but not until 1875 was there effective general high school legislation. This legislation permitted school districts to join to form a high school district with taxing power. Today only 20 per cent of the State's total area falls into these high school districts, the localities outside being required to pay the tuition of any student who may wish to attend high school elsewhere. But transportation is not required by law (except in the case of union free high school districts) and is provided in only 15 or 20 per cent of the cases. It is estimated that about 60 to 62 per cent of the children in rural areas who are graduated from the eighth grade attend high school.

The private preparatory schools fought the establishment of free high schools and, when they saw that it was a losing fight, turned to teacher training in order to receive State funds. In 1857 an act was passed appropriating money to academies with normal departments, but in 1867 this aid was withdrawn, and by 1879 there were only 25 private schools left. Today several well-known private colleges survive (*see Tour 18*).

Teacher training in private academies was not satisfactory. In 1862 the nine academies which were receiving State money had a total of 106 students in the normal course. To remedy this situation a normal school act was passed in 1865, and the first school opened at Platteville the next year. Since then numerous facilities for the training of teachers have been developed. The State now offers 28 county normal schools and 9 teachers' colleges, in addition to the university and private colleges.

The Wisconsin Institute of Technology, established at Plattville in 1907 and called successively the Wisconsin State Mining Trade School and the Wisconsin Mining School, received its present name in 1939. It offers three- and four-year engineering courses in practical mining and in highway construction. The Stout Institute at Menominee, which was taken over by the State in 1911, is the only institution in the United States devoted exclusively to training teachers in the special fields of home economics and industrial education. Special acts of the legislature have empowered it to grant Bachelor and Master of Science degrees.

A branch of education in which Wisconsin pioneered and still holds a position of leadership is vocational training. In 1909 the legislature appointed a committee to study the need for industrial education. In 1911 the first vocational education law in the country was passed, drawn up after extensive research in Europe by Dr. Charles McCarthy, chief of the legislative reference library. Provision was made for general and civic courses as well as for pure vocational training. The first school was opened at Racine in 1911, and in the next year twenty others were established. Today every city of 5,000 in the State has a vocational school, that in Milwaukee being the largest in the world housed in one building. It offers a complete high school course, in addition to the usual part-time schooling for adults, apprentices, and youths under 18 who have not finished high school.

The University of Wisconsin at Madison was incorporated in 1848 as an integral part of the public education system of the State. It was opened in 1849 but for a quarter of a century received no appropriation from the State and was entirely dependent for support upon the sale of lands. As in the case of the common school lands, these funds were dissipated through mismanagement. The era of wild speculation, ending with the panic of 1857, had a disastrous effect upon the University, and the Civil War almost destroyed it. Struggling against such odds, the institution was barely able to maintain itself as a small liberal arts college.

The first extension of its field of activity came in 1866, when agricultural, mechanical, and military training courses were added to comply with the terms of the Morrill Land Grant Act. At this time 100 women were formally admitted. In 1872 the legislature began to appropriate money, and a new era dawned. During the presidency of John Bascom (1874-1887) the central college grew strong and began to make a reputation for itself beyond its own bounds. In 1883 an agricultural experiment station was founded, the most important contribution of which was the Babcock butter fat test completed in 1890. A winter short course for farmers was established in 1885. Reorganized in 1932 to emphasize not only vocational efficiency but also social and cultural values, it is today one of the outstanding services of the University to the State.

During the 1890's the institution was transformed from a college into a University, with expansion in technical research and graduate study. The culmination of this program was the establishment of the graduate school of political science and history, with Richard T. Ely at the head. It was chiefly from the work of this department that the University of Wisconsin obtained its reputation for liberalism, in spite of the fact noted by Professor John R. Commons (in *Myself,* published in 1934) that 90 per cent of the faculty is conservative. In 1894, following labor trouble growing out of the depression, Dr. Ely was investigated for alleged subversive activities. He was exonerated by the board of regents in these words, which became the slogan of the University: "Whatever may be the limitations which trammel inquiry elsewhere we believe that the great state University of Wisconsin should ever encourage that continual and fearless sifting and winnowing by which alone the truth can be found."

The University was at its height during the administration of President Charles R. Van Hise (1903-1918) who, from the original conception of President Bascom, developed the application of the "Wisconsin Idea" to education. During Van Hise's presidency the University became known nationally for its services to the State, for the idea that a university has an obligation to the public which it pays by extension work and by the participation of its experts in government activities. These services to the State have taken the form of experimentation in dairying and farming methods, rural education through local farm institutes, medical and public health services, and expert assistance in drafting social and labor legislation.

With the outbreak of the World War "the service of the university to the state was interrupted by its service to the nation." An overwhelming majority of the faculty plunged into war work, and 400 members, in February 1918, signed a "round robin" to "protest against those utterances and actions of Senator Robert M. La Follette which have given aid to Germany and her allies in the present war."

Since the World War, the University has undertaken various experiments in educational method. Also it has been the center of political controversy, the significance of which it is not yet possible to evaluate. Continuing in Wisconsin's liberal tradition, the legislature, in 1923, made military drill a non-curricular subject, thus establishing the University as the first land-grant college under the Morrill Act of 1862 to offer such drill as optional.

Of the many experiments that have been tried in the University during the last 20 years the most noteworthy is the Experimental College, which continued from the time of its establishment in September 1928 until 1933. The college, under the leadership of Dr. Alexander Meiklejohn, aimed to develop a broad social outlook in a day when training tended to become more and more specialized. Students in the Experimental College lived in dormitories apart from the rest of the student body. Classes were abolished and the tutorial system was established instead. The method of the two-year curriculum was to give the students a comprehensive view of two diverse periods of civilization, through which they might discover interrelationships that would help them to understand their own age. The first year was given to the study of Greek civilization, the second year to that of the nineteenth century. In lieu of examinations, the students made studies of regional cultures.

Outstanding among the occasional struggles between academic and non-academic groups was the Senate investigation in 1935 of alleged "communistic" activities at the University. Charges of encouraging such activities were leveled against Dr. Glenn Frank, then president of the University, and at the time of his death (1940) chairman of the policy committee of the Republican Party. The Senate, without the concurrence of the Assembly, empowered a committee to investigate these charges. After numerous public hearings the committee recommended that "individuals or societies offering or expounding un-American doctrines be expelled from the university or other State educational institutions, or refused their facilities." No legislative or other action was taken on the report.

Wisconsin has many excellent private colleges and universities: Marquette University (1938 enrollment, 3,388), Milwaukee-Downer College (284), and Mount Mary College (385) in Milwaukee; Beloit College at Beloit (598); Carroll College at Waukesha (565); Lawrence College at Appleton (753); Milton College at Milton (151); Mission House College and Seminary at Plymouth (169); Northland College at Ashland; Northwestern College at Watertown (120); Ripon College at Ripon (353); St. Francis College at Burlington; St. Norbert College at West De Pere. There are also several important theological seminaries and private academies.

In 1931 a legislative interim committee, appointed to make a survey of the public school system, published a report entitled *A Plan for Reorganizing Wisconsin's System of Education*. Under this plan the entire system would be centralized in a single State board of education, to be appointed by the Governor, thus making possible a unified program and eliminating competition for funds among the various units. The committee further recommended that a county system of schools be established to consolidate rural school districts and to equalize educational opportunity. In connection with teacher training it was proposed that responsibility be centralized by eliminating over-lapping agencies, and that standards of training be raised by instituting a modern system of teacher certification.

Religion

THE coming of religious denominations to Wisconsin follows closely the pattern of immigration to the State. Catholicism came with the French missionaries and, nearly two centuries later, with the Germans, the Irish, the Italians, the Poles, and the Bohemians. English Protestantism entered with the Yankees from the East; and Lutheranism with Germans, Norwegians, and Danes, who grouped themselves into congregations using their mother tongues.

When defeated Hurons fled to Wisconsin from northern Canada, Jesuit missionaries followed them. The first, Father René Ménard, visited the Huron village on the Chippewa and Black Rivers in 1660. When the Hurons crossed to the Wisconsin River, he followed, but disappeared at a portage and was never heard of again. In October 1665, Father Claude Allouez, named by Bishop Laval as vicar-general "for all the countries to the North and West," reached the Ottawa and Huron villages at Chequamegon Bay and built the first house of worship in Wisconsin, the Mission of the Holy Ghost, about three miles north of where Ashland now stands. "We have erected there a small chapel of bark, where my sole occupation is to receive the Algonquin and Huron Christians, instruct them, baptize and catechize their children."

In 1669 Father Jacques Marquette came from Sault Ste. Marie and took over the Holy Ghost Mission. Father Allouez immediately sought new soil and founded in the same year the Mission of St. Francis Xavier among the Mascouten Indians at what is now De Pere. By 1670-71 Jesuit priests were conducting twenty missions among as many tribes, though the work of Allouez was the most far-reaching. In 1670 he founded the Mission of St. Mark among the Outagamies, on the Wolf River near the present site of either Iola or New London; among the Mascoutens he founded the Mission of St. James near Portage; and, among the Green Bay Indians, the Mission of St. Michael at the mouth of the Menominee River.

The *Jesuit Relations* records graphically the work of the missionaries, such as that of young Father Louis André, who came in 1671 to work among the Indians of Green Bay:

". . . [He] makes a strong impression on the minds of the savages by songs, composed in the Indian tongue, but sung to French airs, which he accompanies with a flute. These songs, many of them expressly directed against their superstitions, he teaches to the children, and with a band of these little savage musicians, he goes about the village to declare war on the jugglers, and those who have several wives."

The work of the Jesuit priests in Wisconsin continued until the first of the Fox Wars in 1720, after which all missionary efforts ceased for many years. Half a century later religious gatherings were being held in homes in the white settlements at Green Bay and Prairie du Chien, and an occasional itinerant priest said mass and administered the sacraments of marriage and baptism. With the establishment of American forts at these places the French Catholics began to request the regular services of a priest, and in 1817 the Trappist monk, Father Prior Marie Joseph Dunand, came to Prairie du Chien from Missouri. He established missionary services, blessed the grounds for a cemetery, and urged the building of a church. Father Dunand, however, remained at Prairie du Chien only thirty days, and it was ten years before another priest, Father Francis Vincent Badin, came this way to serve Prairie du Chien during parts of 1827, 1828, and 1829. At Green Bay in 1823 Father Gabriel Richard began construction of a mission church that was completed two years later by Father Francis Vincent Baraga, the first resident pastor. With the arrival of Father Samuel Mazzuchelli in 1830, survival of the Catholic religion in Wisconsin was doubly assured, for Father Mazzuchelli was also an architect and designed churches throughout the region. At Green Bay in 1830-32 he built the Church of St. John the Baptist, the earlier church having been destroyed by fire. In 1839-40 he planned and directed the building of the present stone Church of St. Gabriel at Prairie du Chien. The history of the Catholic religion in Wisconsin for the next thirty years is closely connected with the work of Father Mazzuchelli.

In the summer of 1835 Father Frederick Baraga built an Indian mission at La Pointe, on Madaline Island. Father Theodore Van den Broek served the Indians of the Green Bay territory from 1834 until his death in 1851. In 1848 he effected the emigration to Little Chute of a Holland Catholic group which fifty years later numbered 1,400 souls. In 1839 Father Patrick O'Kelly built the first Catholic church in Milwaukee; this was the Church of St. Peter's, which stands now on the grounds of St. Francis Seminary. During the period from June to December, 1842, Father Martin Kundig organized nineteen congregations throughout the State. In 1843 the Diocese of Milwaukee, which had hitherto been included in the Diocese of Detroit, was established with Father John Martin Henni as the first bishop. In the next four years the number of priests in the new diocese increased from four to thirty. By 1866 it was necessary to set up two new dioceses, Green Bay and La Crosse; in 1875 the Diocese of Milwaukee became an archdiocese, with Bishop Henni as Wisconsin's first archbishop.

Among the early activities of the Catholics was the founding of schools and colleges. Sinsinawa, under Father Mazzuchelli, became the seat of St. Clara's Academy and of the Congregation of the Most Holy Rosary, a teaching order which spread into many States. Of more than State-wide influence are also the St. Francis Seminary near Milwaukee, established in 1855, Marquette University in Milwaukee, which developed from Marquette Academy founded by Jesuits in 1857, and the Capuchin Monastery and College at Mount Calvary in Fond du Lac County. The mother house of the School Sisters of Notre Dame is located in Milwaukee; over 4,000 accredited teachers have been sent from the mother home to all parts of the country.

English Protestant ministers came into Wisconsin as missionaries to the Indians who moved from New York in 1822. In 1820 an Episcopal lay-reader, Eleazer Williams, came with a preliminary party of Oneidas who settled at Duck Creek, near Green Bay. This settlement, under the auspices of the Domestic and Foreign Missionary Society of Philadelphia, became the center of Protestant Episcopal mission work, and here in the late 1820's Christ Church was built. From 1829 to 1834 Christ Church and an Indian mission school, later known as Hobart University, had an able leader in the Reverend Richard Fish Cadle. In 1835, with the appointment of the Reverend Jackson Kemper as missionary bishop of the Northwest Territory, the Episcopal Church began a rapid development. In 1841 Kemper brought four young clergymen from the East to conduct missionary work and to institute religious training. Settling temporarily at Prairieville (now Waukesha), they moved to Upper Nashotah Lake where they founded the renowned seminary, Nashotah.

The Presbyterians and Congregationalists joined in missionary work under the auspices of the American Board of Commissioners for Foreign Missions and the American Home Missionary Society. In 1827 the Reverend Jesse Miner, a Presbyterian minister, was sent as missionary pastor to the Stockbridges at Statesburg (now South Kaukauna), who since their departure from New York in 1818 had had an able religious leader in the Indian layman, John Metoxen. In 1827 or 1828 Miner built the log church described by the Reverend Calvin Colton in his *Tour of the American Lakes*. After Miner's death in 1829, the Reverend Cutting Marsh, who had studied medicine as well as theology, came to work among the Stockbridges; he remained with them until 1848, when the Indians were removed.

Beginning about 1829, the Reverend Aratus Kent, a Presbyterian minister of Galena (Illinois), worked in the Prairie du Chien district as representative of the joint body. The Reverend Sherman Hall and other pastors worked among the native Wisconsin Indians at La Pointe on Madaline Island, beginning their activities in 1830; in 1833 they organized the first Congregational Church body in Wisconsin. Later the mission was removed to the mainland. In 1836 Marsh and Moses Ordway organized a Presbyterian (now Congregational) Church in Green Bay; in 1857 they organized the first Church in Milwaukee. Through a long period Presbyterians and Congregationalists, led by the Reverend Stephen Peet, continued to work together under the assumption that one strong church in a community was more desirable than two weak ones. A prospective parish was given the right to choose the denomination by which it wished to be designated, and until 1884 the two denominations were still to some extent meeting in joint conferences.

In 1832 Methodist missionary work began under the Reverend John Clark among the Stockbridge Indians in Kaukauna, but the Methodists had earlier turned their attention to the white settlers of the southern lead mining country. In 1828 the Reverend John Dew was appointed by the Illinois Methodist conference to work in Grant and Lafayette Counties, with headquarters in Galena. When southeastern Wisconsin began to be settled the Methodists established churches there. The outstanding figure in the early history of Methodism in Wisconsin was the Reverend Alfred Brunson who, in 1835, came as missionary to the Northwest Territory and as sub-Indian agent to the tribes on the Upper Mississippi. He rode the circuit, organizing parishes in an area that extended from the Mississippi near Galena (Illinois) east about 75 miles and north as far as Lake Superior; later he was named presiding elder for the Territory. In 1847 the jurisdiction of the Illinois Conference over the Wisconsin area was transferred to the newly-formed Wisconsin Conference. An interesting phenomenon was the growth of Methodist Churches among European nationalities traditionally of other faiths. In 1851 at Cambridge the first Norwegian Methodist Church in the world was formed; later, German and Italian Methodist Churches were founded.

The Baptists, under the American Baptist Home Missionary Society, began their work among the Brothertown Indians who had settled about 1828 east of Lake Winnebago. The leading spirit of the Baptist mission was elder Thomas Dick, who, with his wife Deborah, came in 1834 and remained as lay pastor until his death in 1841. The Reverend Richard Griffin came to Wisconsin as emissary of the society, visited the mission, made plans for missionary work in the Green Bay community and in other parts of Wisconsin, and himself organized nearly all Wisconsin's early Baptist Churches. By 1839 there were churches at Sheboygan, Waukesha, and Delavan, with mission churches in other towns. The Free Will Baptist Church was founded at New Berlin in 1840 by Rufus Cheney, a settler from New Hampshire, who held revival meetings and performed baptisms in nearby creeks and springs. In 1856 the first Danish Baptist Church in the United States was organized at Raymond, in Racine County, by Lars Jorgenson Hauge; a second Danish Baptist Church was founded at Racine in 1864.

The English Protestant denominations were organized in Wisconsin under the direction of outside agencies, but German and Norwegian immigration groups themselves brought the Lutheran doctrine to the State and proceeded to build with their own labor and tools a church for each community that they settled and to make provisions for a pastor as soon as immediate practical matters were taken care of. For them, as well as for the Catholic groups who came from Germany, the village church was an essential part of community life. The first Lutherans to come to Wisconsin, in 1839, were German religious refugees under the leadership of an army captain, Heinrich von Rohr. Some of this group settled near Milwaukee, at a place which they named Freistadt to honor their new freedom; others settled in Milwaukee. In the fall of 1841 these German Lutherans organized St. Paul's Lutheran congregation and called an ordained pastor. Like others who came after them in the forties and fifties, these immigrants were orthodox Lutherans who felt that they could not conform when King Frederick Wilhelm III of Prussia declared in 1817 a union of the Lutheran and the Reformed Churches.

An important function of the Lutheran Church, as well as of the Catholic Church in the early days, was the establishment of parochial schools. Among the immigrants from Germany these schools were conducted in the German language by native teachers called especially for that purpose. When the Bennett compulsory education law of 1889 specified instruction in the English language, a storm of protest was aroused and Lutherans and Catholics united to defend what they considered their civil and religious liberties. Although the law was repealed, it had had its effect, for efforts were made to introduce more and more English and otherwise to bring the parochial schools into conformity with the public school system.

The oldest Norwegian Lutheran Church in America to have a continuous existence was founded in 1843 at Muskego. During the forties, as Norwegian settlement spread, other churches were built at Koshkonong, Skaponung, and Bergen. With the coming of the Danes, so-called Scandinavian Churches, composed jointly of Danes and Norwegians, were organized. The first of these, founded at Racine in 1841, later became pure Danish and is today the oldest Danish Lutheran Church in America.

Although before 1858 people of the Hebrew faith were meeting together in the cities where they settled, the first synagogue and Jewish center in Wisconsin was built in that year, the Shaare Shamayim edifice, erected at Madison by immigrants from Bavaria (*see Madison*). The first Jews in Wisconsin were French and English who came from Canada. They were followed by immigrants from Holland and Switzerland, then by larger groups from Germany, Austria, and Bohemia, and by still larger groups from Poland and Russia (including Lithuania, Latvia, and the Baltic provinces), Hungary and Rumania. Some of the cities where Jews first met for reading and devotions were Green Bay, Marinette, La Crosse, Wausau, Madison, and New Glarus. Both the orthodox and the reformed congregations are represented in Wisconsin. In recent years a turning to the orthodox religion is observable in Wisconsin, and on days of real significance many of the smaller, remote orthodox temples are filled to overflowing. The orthodox synagogues maintain Talmud Torahs, where the children, after public school hours, learn Hebrew and study the ancient books of their people.

The first Protestant Dutch colonies in the State, at Cedar Grove and Oostburg, near Sheboygan, were planted by the Reverend Peter Zonne, who in 1848 founded a Presbyterian Church among the Hollanders in Sheboygan County. Not long afterward another Presbyterian Church and several churches which affiliated with the Dutch Reformed Church of America (now the Reformed Church in America) sprang up in the vicinity.

Welsh settlers in Racine and Waukesha Counties organized a Welsh Calvinistic Society, after which they erected their first church near Waukesha in 1845. A. M. Iverson, leader of a band of Scandinavian immigrants in Milwaukee, organized his followers into a Moravian Church in October 1849 (*see Tour 1*). This group moved to Green Bay the next year. In Green Bay Iverson and another leader, Nils Otto Tank, had differences, and in 1853 the little band of the followers of Iverson moved to Door County where they founded the village of Ephraim.

Under the auspices of the Western Unitarian conference, the Unitarian Church carried on missionary activities in the West between 1865 and 1880. The first Unitarian Church in Wisconsin was founded at Kenosha in 1865 by Zalmon G. Simmons and others. A Wisconsin conference, which was at the same time a local organization for missionary work, was established at Sheboygan in the following year.

Other denominations, although numerically small, play an active part in the religious life of the State. In 1840 the Universalist Church was organized at Racine, and in 1864 the Seventh Day Baptists founded at Milton a church and a college. A Christian Science edifice, erected in 1886 at Oconto, is still in use. Its first pastor, the Reverend Lanson P. Norcross, later became pastor of the Mother Church in Boston.

New sects and congregations have arisen since these pioneer churches were established, but none has enrolled large memberships. Today there are approximately 5,000 church edifices, with about one-half of the population participating in religious activities. Wisconsin ranks twenty-second among the States in the number of churches and eleventh in church membership. The Roman Catholic Church, embracing Irish, South German, Polish, Bohemian, and Italian elements, now includes somewhat less than one-half (44 per cent) of the church membership in the State, and the Lutheran Church, embracing North German and Scandinavian elements, includes one-third—thus reflecting the unusually heavy immigration of European peoples. The English Protestant denominations, drawn largely from descendants of New England pioneers, make up only a very small percentage; together with members of more than 50 other denominations, they comprise the remaining one-fourth. Milwaukee is largely Roman Catholic, with slightly over one-fifth of the population adhering to the Lutheran faith. Church membership during the past two decades has grown at approximately the same rate as the population.

Newspapers and Radio

WISCONSIN'S journalism was born of schemes of land promotion, personal rivalries, and partisan politics. A century of growth was needed to develop the comparatively detached and sophisticated journalism of the 33 dailies and 320 country weeklies that today express and mold public opinion in Wisconsin. Political loyalties provided the State's papers with their most fervid causes, the cue for journalists always coming from Milwaukee or Madison, where the struggle between parties was sharpest and the alertness of the public added intensity to the strife. Control of a prominent newspaper was an advantage every Territorial politician could understand, affording him the opportunity of spreading propaganda in his own and his party's behalf.

Land, which created the first wealth in the new Territory, gave inspiration to frontier journalism. Enticing the immigrant with golden promises, the Green Bay *Intelligencer,* a weekly, was founded by John V. Suydam and Albert G. Ellis in December 1833, the first newspaper in Wisconsin. The four pages of blurred type soon stopped praising the glories of the new land and plunged into partisan politics, siding with the Democrats and ardently championing James Duane Doty in his contest with Morgan L. Martin, in 1834, for an appointment as Michigan's Territorial Delegate to Congress. Out of this controversy grew Wisconsin's second newspaper, the *Wisconsin Free Press,* founded by Martin at Green Bay in 1834 to compete politically with the *Intelligencer.*

The discord of political life in Green Bay was not sufficient to focus the limelight on its papers for very long. With the establishment of the Milwaukee *Advertiser,* 1836, and the *Wisconsin Enquirer* in Madison, 1838, the center of Wisconsin's newspaper activity shifted to the two metropolitan areas, where it has since remained.

The Milwaukee *Advertiser,* like its Green Bay predecessor, originally concerned itself with land development and called attention to the new town growing at the mouth of the Milwaukee River. Soon, however, the *Advertiser's* interest in such projects as the Rock River Canal became linked with politics, and the paper became the mouthpiece of Byron Kilbourn, promoter of Milwaukee's West Side, who was engaged in a political feud with Solomon Juneau, promoter of Milwaukee's East Side. This feud resulted in another paper, the fourth in Wisconsin, known as the Milwaukee *Sentinel*, which was started by Juneau in 1837. In 1884 it came into the possession of John S. Fillmore and David M. Keeler, who attempted to publish both daily and weekly editions. At the end of the year the weekly *Sentinel* went out of existence; the daily still exists.

The early Milwaukee newspaper battle between the *Advertiser* and the weekly *Sentinel* epitomizes the rivalries which inspired the pioneer Wisconsin press. Juneau held considerable land on the east side of town, which he divided and offered for sale; Kilbourn had purchased land on the west side of the river and encouraged settlement there. The stakes were high, and so were the motives which the papers imputed to themselves. The *Sentinel* helped Juneau promote his east town plot, linking his real estate future with the destiny of the Whig Party, and opposed the candidacy of Henry Dodge, Democratic nominee for Congress. In 1841 Dodge's friends managed to obtain a lien on the presses of the *Sentinel,* and, taking advantage of a brief absence of the editor, seized the plant with the backing of a court writ. Whig politicians, finding their paper in opposition hands, sent Elisha Starr to Chicago to purchase the plant of a dying weekly. From this second-hand press emerged the Milwaukee *Journal*. After election day the *Sentinel* was returned to its former owners, and the *Journal,* having served its purpose, died on February 16, 1842.

Two years after the founding of the Milwaukee *Advertiser* Madison entered the newspaper arena with the establishment of the *Wisconsin Enquirer*, by J. A. Noonan. The bad luck which attended the efforts of editors to establish newspapers in this city earned for Madison the name of "the graveyard for newspapers." A minor catastrophe was connected with the launching of the *Enquirer* in 1838. Noonan, the editor, ordered a press and printing equipment in Buffalo, N. Y., to be shipped by way of the Great Lakes. The bill of lading arrived, but weeks passed and nothing was heard of the equipment. News finally arrived that the press had been tossed overboard during a storm on Lake Erie to prevent the sinking of the ship on which it was being carried. Despite these difficulties, the *Enquirer* was finally launched, the first issue appearing on November 8, 1838.

The *Wisconsin Express,* forerunner of the present *Wisconsin State Journal,* appeared on December 9, 1839, as Madison's second newspaper, with William W. Wyman as editor. A Whig organ, it supported General Harrison for President in the "log cabin" campaign. The precarious existence of these two early Madison newspapers resulted in frequent changes of ownership. The *Enquirer,* during its five years' existence, had six owners in a variety of partnership combinations. During the first 12 years of Madison's newspaper history, from

1838 to 1850, seven newspapers were founded, of which only four, the *Wisconsin Argus,* the *Wisconsin Democrat,* the *Wisconsin Express,* and the *Wisconsin Statesman* survived the year 1850. In 1852 David Atwood, one of the State's most able editors, changed the name of the foundering *Express* to the *Wisconsin State Journal,* a paper which is still flourishing. Later, in 1868, the Madison *Democrat* was established by A. E. Gordon, and these two held the field exclusively, defeating all attempts to start a third paper until 1917, when the *Capital Times* was founded.

Between 1833 and 1850 newspapers appeared at thirty different points throughout the State. A few continued permanently, but many lived a year and died, having completed their mission of aiding in the selling of land or obtaining a trunk highway for the community. Fickle in their allegiance, these early papers were crude but virile, and often violent in their practices. The experiences of the Platteville *Northern Badger,* founded in 1840 in the lead-mining region, were far from unique; this publication had the distinction, during its brief three years of life, of being first a non-partisan, then a Democratic, and lastly a Whig paper.

Not all the papers, however, were provincially bickering over land schemes. A typical example was the Belmont *Gazette,* founded in 1836 when the first legislature met. This little weekly published elaborate and accurate reports of the debates of the Territorial legislature. When the legislature moved to Burlington, now in Iowa, the *Gazette* packed up and went with it. In Burlington it changed its name to the *Wisconsin Territorial Gazette and Burlington Advertiser,* and it remained in that city when the Wisconsin capital was shifted to Madison.

The abolition movement was sweeping the North, and William Lloyd Garrison's creed found champions in Wisconsin, which had always been free territory. In 1843 C. C. Sholes established the Milwaukee *Democrat,* which quickly changed its name to the *American Freeman* and actively opposed Negro slavery. In 1844 this paper was moved to Waukesha, a station on the Underground Railway and a center of anti-slavery sentiment. Sherman M. Booth brought it back to Milwaukee, changed its name to the *Wisconsin Freeman* and then to the *Free Democrat,* and made it a journal of great influence in the abolition movement and the formation of the Republican party.

The political leaders of the early days gave little attention to the growing foreign language press in Wisconsin. But a group of German political refugees, literate, well-educated, artistic, and liberal in their political views, were organizing their fellow-countrymen into a force of some political importance and fostering a broad and distinctive cultural development through publishing and writing for German-language newspapers. The German press antedates Wisconsin's entry into the

Union by four years. In 1844 the *Wiskonsin Banner* was first published as a weekly in Milwaukee by Moritz Schoeffler, and six years later it became a daily. Its life was prolonged when it merged in 1880 with the thriving *Freie Presse,* a morning daily. Meanwhile, Carl Schurz's Watertown *Anzeiger* was ardently supporting the radicals of the day who were making their first bid for power with the Republican Party. The leading German daily of America, however, was not founded until the appearance of the *Milwaukee-Herold* in 1861. This paper was known as the *Germania-Herold* during the critical years of 1913 to 1918, but resumed its old name until its cessation in 1932.

With each wave of immigrants new publications in the languages of the foreigners came into being: first in German, and then in Norwegian, Polish, Yiddish, and Finnish, until from the presses of Wisconsin rolled a polyglot stream of folk information, telegraph news, criticism, and literary translations. Wisconsin, the cradle of the Norwegian press in America, witnessed the birth of the *Nordlyset* in Racine County in 1847. With over two-thirds of the Norwegian immigrants concentrated in Wisconsin, it is not surprising that before long seven publications were issued in the Norwegian language, giving information about everything from household arts to Indian lore. In Racine, also, the first Bohemian-American newspaper, the *Slovan Amerikansky,* was established in 1860, coming to prominence in 1861 as the Racine *Slavie* under the editorship of Karel Jonas. Today 24 foreign language papers are being published in the State, of which 12 are German, 4 Polish, 2 Finnish, 2 Yiddish, 1 Norwegian, 1 Slovene, 1 Bohemian, and 1 Hungarian. The only foreign language dailies in Wisconsin today are *Die Deutsche Zeitung* and the two Polish papers, the *Kuryer Polski* and the *Nowiny Polskie,* all three of which are published in Milwaukee, and the Finnish daily, the *Tyomies,* published in Superior.

The technique of newspaper editing advanced little in Wisconsin between the days of the *Intelligencer's* birth and the Civil War. Wisconsin editors followed the staid, uninteresting make-up of their eastern predecessors, using worn type and presenting smudgy papers to their public. However, at the beginning of the Civil War, A. N. Kellogg, editor of the Baraboo *Republic,* invented patent inside sheets and thus took the first steps which have earned for Wisconsin the name of the birthplace of the newspaper syndicate. A shortage of typesetters, created by the drafting of men for the Union Army, forced Kellogg to order pages of printed material from the *Wisconsin State Journal* in Madison. Kellogg printed local news on the backs of these ready-printed pages and discovered he had turned out a newsier paper with less cost than before. About the same time A. J. Aikens of the Milwaukee *Evening Wisconsin,* who also is sometimes acclaimed as the inventor of the newspaper auxiliary, began publishing a similar service for weeklies for which he solicited syndicated advertising. Both Kellogg and Aikens became prosperous by organizing syndicates which supplied hundreds of weekly newspapers with ready-printed news and advertising material.

In the years following the Civil War newspapers took root, traditions grew, "founded in" appeared on the mastheads, and the liberal voice of Horace Greeley echoed from the editorial rooms of the New York *Tribune* across the prairies. The purely political outpourings of the early weeklies were largely replaced by articles of general information, short stories and serials appeared, and the telegraph was supplemented by the cable, bringing to Milwaukee news of the Paris Exposition of 1867, the Franco-Prussian War, and the German Empire's expansion. Newspaper type dress brightened with the introduction of new and larger type and the use of larger headlines, a direct result of the craving for news fostered by the Civil War. The *Sentinel,* under General Rufus King, became the outstanding political organ in the State and a leader in the educatio..al progress of the city, setting the pace for the smaller papers throughout Wisconsin.

As the century drew to a close the Republican party, dominated by Charles L. Pfister, Philetus Sawyer, and a group of railway men, acquired control of the State with the support of most of the larger newspapers. As Robert M. La Follette began to challenge the party leadership in the nineties, the Milwaukee *Sentinel* began a vigorous attack upon the Pfister-Sawyer group. Though the fight was protracted and exciting, eventually, on February 19, 1901, an announcement appeared that Pfister had bought the *Sentinel* for an immense sum. The new editor of the *Sentinel* offered to support La Follette if he would change his attitude toward the railways and relinquish his demand for a primary election law. When La Follette refused, the paper threatened, "If that's your attitude, the *Sentinel* will begin skinning you tomorrow." Nevertheless, La Follette's influence grew, his followers relying upon the sawdust trail and a few country weeklies to spread their doctrines. For twenty years his faction flourished and won elections without the support of a single important daily newspaper save the Milwaukee *Free Press.* La Follette men always included a denunciation of the press in their speeches, urged an attitude of skepticism towards newspapers, and made "kept press" a political byword.

Meanwhile the German Socialists of Milwaukee, led by Victor L. Berger, founded the Milwaukee *Vorwaerts* in 1893. This was the second German Socialist newspaper to come to Milwaukee; the first was a *Vorwaerts* established in 1878 and published for only one year. In 1901 the *Social Democratic Herald,* a weekly, was brought to Milwaukee from Chicago by the Socialists, and it continued until 1913. The Milwaukee *Leader,* founded as a daily in 1911, plunged into the fight for trade unionism and Socialist reforms. The *Leader* attained national newspaper notice, October 3 to 5, 1917, when it was denied the use of the Government mails because it allegedly had opened its columns to matter designed to harass the Government in its conduct of the World War. Its editor, Congressman Berger, former editor of the *Vorwaerts,* was indicted by a Federal grand jury on a charge of espionage. Loss of its mail rights was a severe blow to the *Leader,* for, of its total circulation of 40,600, fully 25,000 subscribers lived outside the city of Milwaukee. For many years the *Leader* was the official organ of the Wisconsin Socialist Party, but in 1938 it was forced to reorganize. Division in the labor movement and the depression had contributed to a gradual loss of circulation.

In the tense atmosphere of the World War, the *Capital Times* was launched in Madison, taking a strong stand against American participation in the World War. William T. Evjue, its editor, was immediately accused of being pro-German, and attempts were made to wreck the *Times* with charges of espionage. Evjue, however, was finally absolved by Federal investigators. In 1921 the *Wisconsin State Journal* bought the Madison *Democrat,* leaving the *Journal* and the *Times* as the only two newspapers in the city. Today, the *Times,* a liberal paper, has the largest circulation of any newspaper in Wisconsin outside of Milwaukee.

Chiefly because the Milwaukee *Leader* and the *Capital Times* did such efficient service for the labor movement in Wisconsin, an independent labor press never gained a firm foothold in the State. *The Progressive,* a weekly founded December 7, 1929, by Robert M. La Follette, Jr. and William T. Evjue, serves as a pro-labor organ of the Progressive Party. However, the industrial communities along the lake shore and in the Fox River Valley are becoming conscious of the need for local labor organs, and in Racine, Kenosha, Oshkosh, and Waukesha papers devoted to the labor movement have been published. The Sheboygan *Times,* a labor weekly, struggled along for four years but finally succumbed in April 1938.

Milwaukee is still the newspaper center of Wisconsin. The present Milwaukee *Journal,* launched on November 16, 1882, by the late Lute Nieman, has become one of the most modern and wealthy newspaper properties in the country, with a circulation far exceeding that of any other paper in the State. In 1919 the *Journal* gained national recognition when it was awarded the Pulitzer prize for its campaign for Americanism as the "most distinguished and meritorious public service rendered by an American newspaper during the year." Until January 1939 the Hearst-owned Milwaukee *News,* formerly the *Wisconsin News,* and the *Journal* divided the afternoon field in Milwaukee; the *Sentinel,* merged by Hearst with the *News,* but retaining its own name, holds undisputed control over the morning editions. In January 1939 the *News* abandoned publication. At the same time the Milwaukee *Leader* reorganized, expanded its size, and changed its name to the *Evening Post*. It is now owned and run cooperatively by its employees as a liberal paper.

In January 1940 there were 48 daily papers in Wisconsin. Milwaukee had seven, including three foreign language papers; Madison had three, including the University student paper; Racine two and Superior two. The other 34 dailies were dispersed throughout the State, in cities ranging in size from Stoughton and Berlin, both under 5,000, to Kenosha.

It is the unspectacular, unsung weekly newspaper, however, which provides the great mass of readers in Wisconsin with their news. Weekly newspapers, 360 in number, represent an investment of $3,000,000 and employ 1,700 workers. They are linked by the Wisconsin Press Association, originally founded in 1853, when 39 editors organized to exchange news. The association was the first of its kind in the country and provided the model for numerous groups in other States. In Wisconsin the association acts as a clearing house for trade news and maintains a clipping bureau for its 200 members.

The weeklies have a flavor all their own. As contrasted with their partisan predecessors, the *Intelligencer* and the *Free Press,* they are non-combatants, generally maintaining a fair measure of impartiality and aloofness. This has often been cited as their weak point, since their editorials scrupulously avoid controversial questions. Many of them run pictures, and nearly all serve as outlets to the feature syndicates for short stories and occasional serials. Their contents are dictated by local needs—civic improvements, public parks, and the local schools being their man concern. The major portion of each issue is devoted to personal affairs, commonly known as "personals," to marriages, deaths, births, and church events.

Supplementing the weeklies are the farm journals, the most prominent of which is *Hoard's Dairyman,* founded in 1870 by William Dempster Hoard at Fort Atkinson. Dealing with agricultural problems and farm economics, this journal has done staunch service in promoting Wisconsin's dairy products. Also important is the *Wisconsin Agriculturist and Farmer,* founded in 1849 in Racine as the *Wisconsin Farmer,* and merged in 1929 with the *Wisconsin Agriculturist,* which had been established in Racine in 1877. Consumer and producer cooperatives are now supporting publications of large circulation, such as the *Co-operative Builder,* which combine news of the agricultural or commercial world with educational material on the benefits of united selling and buying organizations. Although the farmer's budget limits the amount of reading matter coming to his home, most Wisconsin farmers subscribe to their local weekly newspaper and to at least one of the farm journals.

RADIO

Wisconsin's radio history goes back to 1909, when wireless experiments were conducted in the laboratories of the department of physics of the University of Wisconsin. "Point-to-point" communication led to the development of broadcast service in 1915 over station 9XM, later WHA. During the World War, when the Navy Department ordered most stations closed as a precautionary measure, 9XM continued experimenting until, in 1919, the first clear and scheduled telephonic broadcast was heard from the University by the Great Lakes Naval Training Station. In 1920 the first daily scheduled weather reports were begun; then followed market and produce reports for farmers and bulletins on road conditions.

In 1922 9XM was licensed as WHA, and in the same year the Department of Agriculture established a new station at Waupaca, licensed as WPAH. In 1924 this station, with its call letters changed to WLBL, was moved to Stevens Point, where it was used primarily in the service of rural people, stressing market reports and agricultural and home economics. WHA is concerned with keeping the highly trained personnel and technical services of all State agencies in direct and frequent contact with the people. Its programs are generally educational in purpose. It has 40,000 regularly enrolled listeners in addition to the thousands who form the usual radio audience.

Commercial broadcasting began in 1925 with the licensing of WIBA at Madison. Sixteen commercial stations now (1939) serve the State, many of them hooking up with national broadcasts. All Wisconsin's stations, however, are limited to 5,000 watts or less, none having a fully cleared channel. Milwaukee has several stations of State-wide importance: WTMJ, the Milwaukee *Journal* station; WISN, the *Wisconsin News* station; and WHAD, at Marquette University, over which regular programs were broadcast as early as 1922.

Literature

THE bulk of Wisconsin's literature has been written by men well known in public life, who have set down comprehensive accounts of their own ideas and experiences. The memoirs, reminiscences, and formal autobiographies of these men—politicians, artists, economists, scholars, farmers—together make up a solid and uniform body of writing that extends from the wilderness days of 1700 down to the present. There were the diaries of the first missionaries and travelers; there was the life story of a defeated Sauk chieftain, of a Liberal and reformer during Lincoln's administration, of a frontier farmer and of frontier humorists, of a Spiritualist preacher of the 1890's, of a fighting states-man during World War years, of a modern revolutionary architect; a lumberman, a chief justice of the State supreme court, a poet-professor, a labor economist, a pioneer sociologist; each presents a fairly complete picture of the man and his field of activity. These books are the root and substance of Wisconsin's literature; even more than the writings of many professional authors they convey the day-to-day flavor, the social excitement, the ferment and activity that characterize Wisconsin life.

The French Jesuit priests, trained observers and recorders, often the first white men in regions of the Northwest, wrote detailed accounts of their own adventures and hardships and of the lives and customs of the Indians. These accounts were sent in instalments to France over a long period, from 1611 to 1768, and came to be known as *The Jesuit Relations.* Outstanding among the contributing priests was Father Jacques Marquette, who crossed what is now Wisconsin with Louis Jolliet. *The Jesuit Relations* were translated and edited (1896-1901) in seventy-three volumes by Reuben Gold Thwaites. About thirty volumes deal specifically with Wisconsin.

Another priest, the Franciscan friar Louis Hennepin, is remem-bered for his vivid writing in *A New Discovery of a Vast Country in America* (accessible in a 1903 version edited by Reuben Gold Thwaites). Father Hennepin tells of a voyage that he made to Green Bay in 1679 on the ill-fated *Griffon* in company with Robert Cavelier, Sieur de la Salle.

An important book touching on Wisconsin during the British regime is Jonathan Carver's *Travels through the Interior Parts of North*

America in the Years 1766, 1767, 1768, first published in London in 1778. This book, in its day a best seller in Europe, has been a storm-center of controversy among historians. It records the explorations of an energetic young American soldier who had fought with the English against the French and who subsequently had sought help from Major Robert Rogers, commandant at Michilimackinac, in the organization of an expedition through Green Bay up the Fox River to the upper reaches of the Mississippi. Carver traveled thousands of miles among twelve nations of Indians, and jotted down such observations as the following:

> Among these people [the Indians] I eat of a very uncommon kind of bread. The Indians, in general, use but little of this nutritious food; whilst their corn is in the milk, as they term it, that is, just before it begins to ripen, they slice off the kernels from the cob to which they grow, and knead them into a paste. This they are enabled to do without the addition of any liquid, by the milk that flows from them; and when it is effected, they parcel it out into cakes, and enclosing them in leaves of the basswood tree, place them in hot embers, where they are soon baked. And better flavored bread I never eat in any country.

A famous passage in Carver's journal describing the memorial harangue of a Naudowessian chief over the dead body of an Indian warrior was converted into German poetry by Friedrich von Schiller and attracted the favorable attention of Goethe.

After Carver's work no writing of importance appeared until 1834, the date of Chief Black Hawk's *Autobiography* (interpreted by Antoine Le Claire). In his story Black Hawk, still bitter from the defeat of the Sauks two years before, tells simply and unaffectedly of his early life and native countryside, of his tribe's courtship and marriage customs, the War of 1812, the death of his children, the Battle of Wisconsin Heights, and the historic massacre at Bad Axe.

Mrs. Juliette Kinzie, wife of an Indian agent at Fort Winnebago, gives another view of Indian Wisconsin in *Wau-Bun* (1856) (Ojibway, dawn). Written during the dawn of social life in the Northwest, the book includes accounts of the Winnebago uprising in 1827 and of the Black Hawk War of 1832, and several well-written portraits of the half-civilized French-speaking savages.

> The chief was a large, raw-boned, ugly Indian, with a countenance bloated by intemperance, and with a sinister unpleasant expression. He had a gay-coloured handkerchief upon his head, and was otherwise attired in his best. . . . Among the various groups of his people, there was none attracted my attention as forcibly as a young man of handsome face, and a figure that was striking even where all were fine and symmetrical. He too had a gay handkerchief on his head, a shirt of the brightest lemon-coloured calico, and abundance of silver ornaments, and, what gave his dress a most fanciful appearance, one legging of blue and the other of bright scarlet. I was not ignorant that this particular feature in his toilet indicated a heart suffering from the tender passion. The flute, which he carried in his hand,

added confirmation to the fact, while the joyous, animated expression of his countenance showed with equal plainness that he was not a despairing lover.

James Gates Percival, born at Kensington, Connecticut, lived in Wisconsin during his last years. Percival was graduated in medicine from Yale and was interested in history, linguistics, and natural sciences, but it was his melancholy romantic poetry that attracted greatest attention. The publication of his *Poems* in 1821, and of subsequent volumes, made him the most famous poet in America until the appearance of Bryant's work. However, Percival gradually lost interest in poetry. In 1835 he accepted the position of State Geologist of Connecticut; sixteen years later he was employed by the American Mining Company to survey the lead region of Illinois and Wisconsin. Until his death at Hazel Green, Wisconsin, Percival was mostly absorbed in geological studies and for a short time was State Geologist of Wisconsin.

With the exception of the *Voyage of Père Marquette* (1860), a long poem in stiff eighteenth-century couplets, by Elizabeth Farnsworth Mears of Oshkosh, no writing of significance was published until the time of the Civil War. The *Battle of Gettysburg,* by Colonel Frank A. Haskell of Madison, who was killed in 1864, is one of the worthiest of its genre and has been included in the Harvard Classics. Another true memoir in story form was John Azor Kellogg's *Capture and Escape* (1908). Kellogg, from Mauston, was in the thick of more than a score of battles; he tells of his capture during the Fight in the Wilderness, his imprisonment at Lynchburg, Danville, Macon, and Charleston, and his escape by jumping from a moving train. Equally exciting are *Civil War Letters* (1936) written by Colonel Hans Christian Heg to his family back in the Norwegian settlement at Muskego, and *Star Corps* (1865), an account by the Reverend George S. Bradley, of Racine, telling of Sherman's famous march to the sea. The *Artilleryman's Dairy* (1914) of Jenkin Lloyd Jones, Welsh settler of Spring Green, the uncle of Frank Lloyd Wright, describes many great battles, including those of Vicksburg and Chattanooga.

During the late sixties and seventies, when "local color" became fashionable all over the country, a number of humorists appeared in Wisconsin. By using dialect, bad spelling, and other devices they stripped off the traditional elegance of book-characters, bringing them down to homely levels. Comic roughnecks, bumpkins, and small-town philosophers were set against their native backgrounds. Typical of these writers were Marcus (Brick) Pomeroy, author of *Nonsense and Sense* (both 1868), and Lute A. Taylor, whose *Chip Basket* (1874) displays a range of cracker-box subjects from tooth-pulling to radicalism. Wisconsin's two best known humorists were George W. Peck, onetime Governor of the State, and Edgar Wilson Nye of St. Croix

County.   Peck wrote the *Peck's Bad Boy* series (1882-1900), tales of a mischievous young man and his rascally father.   Nye, the most versatile, was nationally famous for his lyceum speeches with James Whitcomb Riley (made between 1885 and 1900) and for a long line of semi-autobiographical books, rich in the local color of town, city, and frontier, ending with *Bill Nye, His Own Life Story* (1926), compiled by his son.

In contrast with the humorists Hamlin Garland portrayed humble types seriously, attempting not only to present them with accuracy but to interpret their social situation.   As a boy on a western coulee farm he had known all the rigors of frontier life.   Garland, the "first dirt farmer in literature," a friend of William Dean Howells, Henry George, and Theodore Roosevelt, was born in West Salem and spent his childhood as a farm boy.   He began his career with the writing of *Main-Traveled Roads* (1891), *Prairie Folk* (1893), and *Rose of Dutcher's Coolly* (1895), bitter tales of farmers exploited by land-sharks and mortgage-holders.   Summer and winter his men toil in dirt and mud; the women grow ugly and sad from overwork.   "The song of emigration," he wrote, "had been in effect the hymn of fugitives." But later, perhaps because his own living had become more secure, Garland came to believe that "the poor are almost obsolete."   During this phase of his career he wrote romances of the far West, *Her Mountain Lover* (1901), *The Grey Horse Troop* (1902), *The Light of the Star* (1904), idealizing the mountaineer, the plainsman, and the Indian.   However, in his old age Garland renewed his theme of the "pilgrimage from hope to hopelessness" in the autobiographical *Middle Border* books.   Though colored and softened by reminiscence, they contain much of the writer's earlier power and an added breadth of interpretation.   *A Son of the Middle Border* (1917), the first of this series, traces out the Wisconsin part of Garland's life, his boyhood shortly after the Civil War.   Its sequels, *A Daughter of the Middle Border* (1921) and *Trailmakers of the Middle Border* (1926), are autobiographical tales of the Garlands and the McClintocks, of their restless migration from one frontier to another.   *A Son of the Middle Border* has become a classic in Wisconsin public schools.

Hamlin Garland easily overshadows the work of others who were writing before 1900.   Warren Chase's *Forty Years on the Spiritual Rostrum* (1888), first among the autobiographies of Wisconsin political reformers, is notable for its account of Fourier Socialism and the brief life of a communal colony established near Ripon (*see Tour 5A*). Ella Wheeler Wilcox, like Chase a Spiritualist, began writing in 1880, at the age of nine, with a novel called *Minnie Tighthand*.   Her auto-biography, *The Worlds and I* (1918), centers around the posthumous messages of her husband, who before death had promised that "should he precede me to the realm beyond, he would importune God until he was allowed to communicate with me." Mrs. Wilcox characterized herself as a "poet of passion," and the characterization was apt.

> Sometimes I feel so passionate a yearning
> For spiritual perfection here below,
> This vigorous frame with healthful burning,
> Seems my determined foe.

She was also a spirited opponent of the liquor traffic; one of her hundreds of poems, called "Two Glasses," a dialogue between a wine glass and a water glass, was once a favorite recitation at school and temperance meetings. Ella Giles Ruddy, a friend of Mrs. Wilcox, was the author of *Bachelor Ben* (1875), Wisconsin's first novel. Quite as prolific as Mrs. Wilcox was General Charles King of Milwaukee, writer of more than sixty books on the army and army life, whose autobiography, *Memories of a Busy Life* (1922), tells of his activities from West Point to the Philippines.

In 1908 and 1913, two of Wisconsin's greatest men, Carl Schurz and Robert M. La Follette, published their autobiographies. Schurz, already the author of a life of Henry Clay and a penetrating sketch of Lincoln, describes in his *Reminiscences* the first forty years of his varied career. He tells of his activities as a republican during the unsuccessful German revolution of 1848, and of the forced flight that brought him finally to Watertown, Wisconsin; of his entrance into the political controversies that centered about anti-slavery, monopoly, and the spoils system; of his work as Secretary of the Interior under Hayes and as diplomat in Spain under Lincoln, as brigadier-general during the Civil War, and as United States Senator from Missouri. Wide travel and acquaintance sharpened his knowledge of character and of the English language, enabling him to write lively portraits of Douglas, Ward, Seward, Davis, and of four Presidents: Jackson, Lincoln, Grant, and Hayes. The three stout volumes of *Reminiscences* are beautifully written, subtle, and informative; they are one of the high watermarks of Wisconsin's literature.

Senator La Follette's *Autobiography*, like Carl Schurz's *Reminiscences*, is incomplete. It begins with an account of his determination to become district attorney of Dane County, Wisconsin, in 1881, and it ends with the text of an address delivered before the Periodical Publishers' Association in Philadelphia in 1912. This address was keyed to his favorite theme—"the encroachment of the powerful few upon the rights of the many." La Follette expressly disclaims a literary intent in writing this book. But the story of his youthful ambitions; of his six-year struggle with Wisconsin bosses; of the problems that he had to meet as Governor; of his election to the United States Senate;

and of his growing distrust of Theodore Roosevelt are models of direct narrative, inspired by enthusiastic devotion to the democratic ideal.

Chronicles of other Wisconsin personalities deserve mention. Roujet Deslisle Marshall, in his *Autobiography* (1923-31), tells of his life in a pioneer environment and his rise to the State supreme court. *The Voice and Pen of Victor L. Berger* (1929) is a valuable record by a Milwaukee Socialist editor and United States Congressman. Another former Milwaukeean, Ernest L. Meyer, like La Follette and Berger an opponent of America's entrance into the World War, recounts in *Hey, Yellowbacks!* (1930) the humiliations he underwent at Camp Taylor and Camp Sherman, where he was imprisoned as a conscientious objector along with Mennonites, Pentecostals, and members of other religious sects.

Economists, philosophers, historians, and other scholars of the University of Wisconsin have written books with literary interest. Rasmus B. Anderson, in addition to translating and editing notable Scandinavian works, has written a *Life Story* (1915), which, with a wealth of anecdote, covers nearly the whole period of Norwegian settlement in Wisconsin. Contemporary with Anderson was Grant Showerman, a Classics professor, author of *Eternal Rome* (1925) and two semi-humorous autobiographies, *A Country Chronicle* (1916) and *A Country Child* (1917). In *Myself* (1934), John R. Commons describes his long study of the evolution of American industrial society. Edward A. Ross' travels and the development of his social thought are the subject of his autobiography, *Seventy Years of It* (1936). *What Does America Mean?* (1935), by the liberal educator, Alexander Meiklejohn, is an attack on pragmatism and the mechanization of living; it is a plan for a cooperative society, based on traditional American values. Historians such as Louise Phelps Kellogg and Joseph Schafer, who have concentrated on studies of Wisconsin, and Frederick Jackson Turner and Frederic L. Paxson, famous for their interpretations of the frontier and the section, have furnished a detailed background for an understanding of the State. Together with the autobiographies, they fairly represent Wisconsin's character.

Workers in various fields outside the University have contributed to the literature of the State. The naturalist John Muir, in *The Story of My Boyhood and Youth* (1913), tells of his childhood in Scotland and on a crude farm in Columbia County, and of his years at the University. An *Autobiography* (1932) by Frank Lloyd Wright is a beautifully designed book that tells of a hardworking childhood, rebel years at the University and in Chicago, his first experiments in building, and his attainment of artistic maturity, tracing the growth of his conception of architecture. Clinch Calkins has written two social studies. *Some Folks Won't Work* (1930), dealing with the demoralization of

America's unemployed, and *Spy Overhead* (1937), "the story of the American industrial worker caught in a trap of commercialized espionage and violence."

Of the novelists following Hamlin Garland, Zona Gale of Portage was most widely known. Her characters are always humble, undistinguished people set in an ordinary country town. The early books, *Friendship Village* (1908), *Mothers to Men* (1911), *When I Was a Little Girl* (1913), and others written before 1920 are pervaded by a gentle irony. Miss Gale, as Carl Van Doren has said, "varied the same device; that of showing how childlike children are . . . how motherly are mothers . . . how lovely are lovers of whatever age, sex, color, or condition." But in *Miss Lulu Bett,* written as a novel in 1920 and as a play that won the Pulitzer Prize in 1921, the vision has sharpened; the town is revealed as dull, its people bigoted and petty. *Faint Perfume* (1923) is notable as an experiment in the inner monologue. *Borgia* (1928), one of Miss Gale's most forceful attempts to "reveal the infinitely familiar as the infinitely strange," is the story of a girl obsessed with a sense of her own evil because of the disasters which overtake those who associate with her. Her publication, *Light Woman* (1937), describing a superficial city woman who succumbs to small-town conventionality, mingles the realism of *Miss Lulu Bett* with the sentimentality of *Friendship Village*. *Magna* was published posthumously in 1939. A biography of Zona Gale, *Still Small Voice,* by August Derleth, appeared late in 1940.

The books of Edna Ferber and Glenway Wescott describe many Wisconsin places and characters. *Dawn O'Hara* (1911) derives from Miss Ferber's early life, part of which was spent as a reporter in Appleton and Milwaukee. *Come and Get It* (1936), among the latest of her many novels, is a robust, brawling story of the lumbering and mill-working industries of northern Wisconsin, a sort of case-history of many of those self-made lumber barons whose feverish aggression hurried the State's industrial life.

A single theme runs through Glenway Wescott's novels—the isolation of a sensitive young man in a provincial society and his attempt at orientation. Though set in typical Wisconsin small towns and farming regions, his books deal with problems of expatriation common to many American writers of the 1920's. In *The Apple of the Eye* (1924) the principal character is a Wisconsin farm boy, uncertain whether to accept the strict moral code of his parents or the lax principles of his friends. Since writing this book Wescott has lived in the eastern States and in France, returning only intermittently to Wisconsin. His second novel, *The Grandmothers* (1926), which won the Harper Award for 1927-1928, was written in Europe. It is formed of the thoughts of the expatriate Alwyn Tower, who tries to come to an understanding of himself through recalling the lives of his ancestors in early Wisconsin. In their example, their working out of pioneer problems, he finds reason for being "proud and content to be an American." But a short time after returning to the State Wescott wrote *Goodbye, Wisconsin* (1928), in which he declares himself unable to accept his home world. "How much sweeter to come and go than to stay; that by way of judgment on Wisconsin." *Babe's Bed* (1930) concerns the homecoming of a young man and his reflections on the future of midwestern generations.

Recently several of the State's novelists have gained recognition. The work of Margery Latimer is important chiefly for the intensity of the sensations it records. The most significant of her books, *This Is My Body* (1930), written a few years before her death, describes the life of a high-strung girl in college and later in Greenwich Village, following her hysterical search for "reality" among dilettantes and Philistines. Miss Latimer's subjective and highly personal prose style has been compared with that of Katherine Mansfield. Samuel Rogers, Associate Professor of French at the University, author of six novels, has been praised by critics for the quality of his style and for his delineation of character. *Dusk at the Grove,* which was awarded the 1934 Atlantic Monthly Prize, concerns the life of a New England family between the years 1909 and 1931, revealing in an interwoven story the experiences of a small parish minister, his wife, and children. August Derleth of Sauk City has published some twenty books, all but eight of which belong to his Sac Prairie Saga, the most ambitious attempt of any Wisconsin author to record and interpret from its beginnings to the present the life of a Wisconsin community. Among the prose volumes of the Saga are *Place of Hawks* (1935), *Still Is the Summer Night* (1937), *Any Day Now* (1939), *Restless Is the River* (1939), *Atmosphere of Houses* (1939), *Bright Journey* (1940), and *Country Growth* (1940). Three volumes of poetry, a part of the Saga, have been published. When completed, Derleth's monumental work will include 50 volumes. Sterling North writes of farm life in the southern part of the State; in *Night Outlasts the Whippoorwill* (1936) the setting is a small Wisconsin town during the year and a half after America entered the World War. Edward Heth, of Milwaukee, has described the history and beauty of a German-American city in his two novels, *Some We Loved* (1935) and *Told With a Drum* (1937). In the latter, a small boy of German descent tells of the plight of his family during the World War, their ostracism by neighbors, and the conflict between the German grandfather and his Americanized daughter. A third novel by Heth, *Light Over Ruby Street,* appeared in 1940. The single novel by Mark Schorer, *A House Too Old* (1935), covers a century in the life of a small Wisconsin town, and against the background of its growth, traces the slow degeneration of an aristocratic family (*see Tour 22*). Helen C. White has written two novels on medieval times, *A Watch in the Night* (1933) and *Not Built with Hands* (1935). *To the End of the World* was published in 1939. Honore Willsie Morrow is known chiefly for her series of novels on Lincoln, *Forever Free* (1927), *With Malice Toward None* (1928), and *Last Full Measure* (1930). Though born in Madison, Thornton Wilder, author of *The Bridge of San Luis Rey* (1927) and of *Our Town,* Pulitzer Prize Play for 1938, has had little connection with the State. Nevertheless, he has recently said that *Our Town* was based largely on memories of Madison.

In the meagre history of Wisconsin poetry it is William Ellery Leonard whose reputation seems most assured. Through years of changing poetic fashions he has remained an isolated figure in American letters. Although Professor Leonard's literary preferences are largely for the epic and the classical, his work is marked by intense personal experience. It is significant that the early *Sonnets and Poems* (1906) opens with a poem called "Anti-Rococo," for Leonard has always sought directness and simplicity of statement. His concern with plain but dramatic diction and with ethical themes is expressed in a sonnet published in 1934:

> Plain words be mine, afoot, ahorse, afloat,
> That say big things; like that high wooden sign
> On Yukon's north bank, near the Porcupine,
> Where one reads "ARCTIC CIRCLE" from the boat;
> Or Schwitzer's Alpine letters pointing south,
> "ITALIA," chiselled on the boundary-stone;
> Or at the fork, for Trailers facing drouth,
> Plains, thunder, Rockies: "ROAD TO OREGON."
> Be *my* words smokeless where they flash or hit,
> Aimed not at stabbed deer nor at carrion-bird,
> But at the Lords—to force, even where they sit,
> Surrender from the bleeding Gods—each word
> Edged and compact as steel, steady and bright
> As glint of sunshine on a rifle-sight.

Vaunt of Man (1912) is memorable for its strong judgment of friends and enemies. After the World War Leonard's ethical preoccupation is shown still more intensified in the angry poems, "The Lynching Bee," "The Mountain of Skulls," "Saecla Ferarum," "Tom Mooney," "The Heretics," and "The Old Agitator." *Two Lives* (1925), a narrative sonnet sequence about his disastrous first marriage, is Leonard's most sustained poem. Besides these original poems and some scholarly articles, Leonard has published important translations of *Empedocles* (1908), *De Rerum Natura* (1918), *Beowulf* (1923), and *Gilgamesh* (1934). Leonard's well-known autobiography, *The Locomotive God* (1927), containing an analysis of his neuroses and their source in childhood, furnishes a key to the emotional intensity of his poetry.

Wisconsin has produced a few other poets of standing. Horace Gregory, born in Milwaukee and now living in New York City, is widely known for both his verse and his literary criticism. *Chelsea Rooming House* (1930) marks the beginning of his attempt to combine what he calls "the idiom of contemporary life" with early classical influences. His two subsequent volumes of poetry, *No Retreat* (1930) and *Chorus for Survival* (1935), reveal a greater command of lyric form and a persistent interest in social themes. Kenneth Fearing's satires on the bourgeoisie in urban America are more bitterly insurgent. He pieces together shots and cross sections in a sort of news-reel technique, "as American as the Loop, the tabloids and the subway." Clinch Calkins, whose poems are tense and often ironic, and Marya Zaturenska, whose *Cold Morning Sky* won the 1938 Pulitzer Prize, are two women poets who have lived in Wisconsin. Others who have gained some reputation as poets are Glenway Wescott, Grant Hyde Code, Raymond Larsson, Edward Weismiller, winner of the 1937 Yale Young Poets' Prize, and Herbert Bruncken, all of whom have lived or still live in Wisconsin. Those who have had only a slight association with the State include Carl Sandburg, who for a time was secretary to Daniel Hoan, the Socialist Mayor of Milwaukee; Adelaide Crapsey, who was educated at Kemper Hall, Kenosha; and Lew Sarrett, who lives part of the time in Laona.

An exhaustive list of poets who have lived in Wisconsin or whose lives have touched it briefly has been compiled in *Poetry out of Wisconsin* (1937), an anthology edited by August Derleth and Raymond Larsson. While the poetry, as a whole, is not of a high order, it represents interestingly the struggle for esthetic expression in a State that only a century ago was a wilderness and whose most forceful literature has come from its pioneers, its scholars, and its men of action.

Painting and Sculpture

BEFORE the arrival of Europeans in the State, Indians were making brightly-colored geometric designs by sewing porcupine quills, small feathers, or crude beads on buffalo hide or buckskin. Because curves were difficult to produce with the straight porcupine quills, diamond, triangle, vertebrae, and forked patterns were very frequent. Curves were more common in beadwork, and large beads were strung together to make breast ornaments and necklaces. The Winnebagoes added conventionalized floral motifs to their geometric patterns. They also wove storage bags of fibre, nettle, and buffalo hair. There was little pictorial design, though tepee hides were sometimes decorated with paintings and drawings of angular symbolic figures of men, animals, birds, and implements of war. The combinations of primary colors—produced from bark, plants, and soil—in both sewed work and painting were often excellent. When the missionaries and traders of the seventeenth century brought finer beads, steel needles, cotton thread, and woven fabrics, Indian work became more varied. The women learned the arts of appliqué work, embroidery, and knitting, which the white settlers had brought with them from Europe. Richer floral patterns and more subtle colors were used, and pictorial designs, such as horses, pipes, guns, arrows, and men, made their appearance upon beaded vests and ceremonial aprons. Indians who were converts to Christianity began to introduce the cross and pictures of churches into their designs.

A single ostensorium of sterling silver, now in the Green Bay Museum, has been preserved from the period of French settlement. It was long after the traders and missionaries had come that American artists began to appear. The inhabitants generally had little interest in art, but at the beginning of the nineteenth century eastern painters were being sent into the Territory, commissioned by the War Department to depict the dress, ceremonies, and domestic habits of the Indians and to record the topography of the area between Green Bay and Prairie du Chien. Free-lance artists were making solitary canoe trips up and down the Fox-Wisconsin River route, painting Indians in much the same spirit as Audubon painted birds.

The first painter known to have traveled in Wisconsin was Samuel Seymour (1797-1872), staff artist to Major S. M. Long. In 1823,

when Long was ordered to explore the headwaters of the Mississippi
and Minnesota Rivers, Seymour accompanied the expedition, crossing
by land from Chicago to Prairie du Chien, thence by boat to Lake
Superior. Lithograph copies of the paintings made on this trip, principally broad sketches of local river bluffs, plains, and Indian encampments, were published in Keating's *Narrative* (Philadelphia, 1824).
Seymour's primary concern was accuracy, and his Indians may be
identified by the faithfully depicted tribal ornaments.

Another Government painter was James Otto Lewis (1799-1858),
whose career and work resembled Seymour's. Having previously
traveled into the Northwest Territory as a copperplate engraver,
draughtsman, and portrait painter, Lewis was commissioned by the
Government in 1823 to make portraits of Wisconsin Indians. The
first pictures he sent back East, a series of twenty Indian heads and
one general view of a fort, tribes, and soldiers were "painted on the
spot," as he said, at the Great Treaty of Prairie du Chien, where
nine tribes were gathered. Ten years later Lewis published his
Aboriginal Port-Folio (Philadelphia, 1835), which contained seventy-
two colored lithograph plates dealing with Indians.

Considerably more lively than Lewis' Indian paintings are those of
Seth Eastman (1808-75), who came to Wisconsin in 1829 to do
military duty at Fort Crawford, Prairie du Chien. Winnebago,
Menominee, and Fox Indians frequently visited the Fort, and Eastman
drew them at their games and ceremonies; his many paintings and
sketches pictured a wide range of Indian customs. In 1853 he published
an *Aboriginal Portfolio* (Philadelphia), which contained sketches of
*Squaws Playing Ball, Dressing a Buffalo Skin, Spearing Fish from a
Canoe,* and other close-ups of typical Indian activities. A contemporary
of Eastman, Peter Rindisbacher, the State's first resident artist, left only
one painting (1829, now owned by the Wisconsin Historical Society),
a sharply-detailed miniature of *Isaac Winnescheek,* a Winnebago chief
of La Crosse Village.

The most inventive and enterprising of the early painters was
George Catlin (1796-1872), who set out to visit every tribe of Indians
in North America, "for the purpose of procuring portraits of distinguished Indians of both sexes in each tribe, painted in native costume,
accompanied with pictures of villages, domestic habits, games, mysteries,
religious ceremonies, etc., with anecdotes, traditions, and histories re-
specting the natives." In 1835, with a single canoe companion, he stopped
at Prairie du Chien to paint Wabasha's Indian band; by 1836 he had
reached Green Bay, after working his way along the Fox and Wisconsin
Rivers. After ten years of traveling (1830-40) over the entire Midwest, sometimes penetrating to spots where no white man had ever been,
he exhibited 310 portraits, 93 landscapes, 25 sporting scenes, 77 scenes

of customs and amusements, and 4 religious pieces, many of which had been painted in Wisconsin. It was Catlin who more clearly than any other artist expressed the aim of the painters of Indians when he wrote:

> I have flown to the rescue, not of their lives or their race (for they are "doomed" and must perish), but to the rescue of their looks and their modes, at which the acquisitive world may hurl their poison and every besom of destruction, and trample them down and crush them to death; yet, phoenix-like they may rise from the "stain on the painter's pallette," and yet live again upon canvas and stand forth for centuries to come. . . .

While in Wisconsin Catlin also painted, among others, portraits of James Madison, De Witt Clinton, Eleazer Williams (ca. 1835, Wisconsin Historical Museum) (see *Tour 2*), and an oil, *Spearing Fish by Moonlight*. It was probably during his stay in Wisconsin that he did his famous "22 Self-portraits," now hanging in the Neville Museum at Green Bay, which depict *Rage, Joy, Lunacy, Sadness, Contempt,* and other psychological states. Drawn in charcoal and white pencil on butcher's wrapping paper, these portraits display unusual deftness and clarity; they are the most imaginative work accomplished on the Wisconsin frontier.

Another artist to work in Wisconsin was Paul Kane, author of *The Wanderings of an Artist Among the Indians of North America,* published in 1859. In 1845 Kane toured from Toronto to Green Bay, then down the Fox River, painting the "Manomanee" Indian camp near Lake Winnebago. Like Catlin he made a drawing of *Spearing Fish by Torchlight in the Fox River.*

Characteristic of early settlement in Wisconsin was the portrait art of "itinerant limners" who traveled through the countryside with stocks of pictures complete except for the face. These early painters often ground their pigments from berries and soil and made their brushes from straw and horsehairs.

Wisconsin, with its great variety of national groups, has produced many examples of folk art. Sometimes these embody traditions brought from Europe during the nineteenth century; Scandinavians, Finns, and Swiss are among those who carried on their folk arts to some extent after settling in the State. The styles are rarely as strong or clear as in the old country, in part because of the more simple manner of living; and often the only attempt at art was the cutting of designs on working implements. A few inlaid chests and simply ornamented baskets have been preserved. Carving on wood and horn has not been uncommon among sailors, lumberjacks, and workers in other industries. Architectural ornaments, such as crestings, finials, rosettes, and grills, were made by craftsmen in the State. Women did much textile work, making shawls, quilts, samplers, and laces after patterns originated by themselves or brought in from the eastern States. There was also a curious fashion for memorial wreaths; these were made of human hair, wax, feathers, yarn, seeds, or skeltonized leaves. The finest collection of the State's folk art is in the Wisconsin Historical Museum.

The advance of the frontier was helping to inspire American artists and public with an interest in landscape. During the 1840's a number of panoramas painted by artists outside the State were exhibited in Milwaukee. These huge canvases were unrolled on wooden spools, often to the accompaniment of music and the explanations of a commentator. At first religious subjects were treated, but these soon gave way to river scenes and to views of foreign lands such as Ireland and Italy. The earliest panoramist known to have worked in Wisconsin was Henry Lewis (1819-1904), who during the years 1847-49 painted a view of the Mississippi River from St. Anthony Falls to New Orleans. The canvas, more than half a mile in length, was enlivened with historical scenes along the way, with no regard for their time sequence; among those set in Wisconsin are scenes of Cassville in 1829, Prairie du Chien in 1830, showing old Fort Crawford, and the Battle of Bad Axe, 1832. Later, in Germany, Lewis issued *Das Illustrirte Mississippithal*, describing his journey along the river and containing a number of lithographs of sketches reworked from the panorama.

Meanwhile, townsites were being laid out, and the population was becoming more settled. A growing interest in the history of the State can be seen in the activities of the Wisconsin Historical Society. Under the leadership of Lyman C. Draper, first secretary of the society, the institution formed a large art collection. In 1855 the first published proceedings announced that "the design of the Historical Society is . . . to preserve all mementoes of the past that yet remain to us. . . ." The specific plan was to secure as many portraits as possible of State governors, Congressmen, judges of the supreme court, Indian chiefs, early pioneers and settlers, and many views, backgrounds, and pictures of historic houses.

Among the first painters to be commissioned by the Historical Society was the English-born Samuel Brookes (1816-92), among whose paintings are portraits of *Solomon Juneau* (founder of Milwaukee), *Chief Oshkosh, Souligny* (Pierre le Duc), and a view of the *Wisconsin Heights Battlegrounds*. His portraits, filled in with backgrounds in the English manner, often show a lack of technical ability, especially in the hands and clothing; but he was able to catch some of the stern character of the early settlers who sat for him. About 1855 Brookes also worked with an artist named Thomas H. Stevenson, of Madison and Milwaukee, painting battleground scenes for the Society and a series of ten river scenes for the Fox-Wisconsin River Improvement Society. Seeing better opportunities in the West, he moved to California, where he attracted attention as a painter of fish and birds.

During the middle years of the century many artists had difficulty in earning a living. Bernard Isaac Durward (1817-1902), who came from Scotland to Wisconsin with his wife and two children, was forced to exchange portraits for food. After several difficult years he was commissioned to paint *Solomon Juneau,* and this soon brought him other orders. It was in portraiture that he was best; paintings such as *Bishop Henni* and *Joshua Hathaway* (both now in the Wisconsin Historical Museum) mark an advance over earlier Wisconsin portraits. In 1852 the family moved to a glen near Baraboo, where Durward painted nature, still life, and religious subjects. He made his inks from native berries and his drawing pens from feather quills. For some years he shared his Milwaukee studio with George J. Robertson (died 1870), also a Scotsman, who had come to Wisconsin after ten years of study in London. Together they attempted to form a Wisconsin Academy of Fine Arts, but got no further than drawing up incorporation papers. Robertson remained in Milwaukee as a portrait painter for several years and then went to Rockford, Illinois, to teach painting and drawing in a young ladies' school.

Wisconsin was introduced to a kind of neo-classicism by the Englishman, Mark R. Harrison (1819-94), who came to the State in 1849 and finally settled in Fond du Lac, where he remained until his death. Harrison gained a considerable reputation with his large, colorful canvases portraying religious and historical scenes—*The Deluge, The Angel Delivering Peter from Prison, Peter Listening to the Cock Crowing,* and *Cleopatra's Triumph,* picturing the queen's return with Mark Antony to Alexandria. A number of his portraits now in the Wisconsin Historical Museum are marked by a soft, rather hazy quality. Harrison's comparative isolation from his surroundings can be seen in the romantic handling of his Indian paintings, *Minnehaha, The Defeat of Black Hawk,* and *The Sioux Chiefs under Sitting Bull.*

New photography studios were springing up throughout the State, and many artists who had come upon hard times were offering to do either painting or photography. The Art Gallery of the State Historical Museum had changed its title to Paintings and Photographs, and the museum was beginning frankly to discourage even the presentation of oil portraits as gifts, since photographs took up far less space.

Among the artists who divided their time between painting and other activities were Frederick Stanton Perkins (1832-99) and Conrad Heyd (1837-1912). Perkins, who was born in New York, came to Burlington in 1836, and returned to his native State for a period of study with a painter of the Hudson River School. Perkins painted a number of portraits of prominent Wisconsin men, but his most important work was in archeology. He devoted much of his time and money to collecting copper and stone antiquities, and made watercolor reproductions

of many of his nearly 50,000 carefully recorded Wisconsin relics. Like
Catlin's, his approach stressed accuracy and completeness of detail.
Heyd was well known as a painter of portraits and landscapes. Many
leading Milwaukeeans patronized him, and he became known outside
the State as the "foremost artist" of Wisconsin. Heyd spent part of
his time coloring photographs.

Eastman Johnson (1824-1906), important in American art as a
genre painter, worked for a period in Wisconsin as a portraitist. His
Sarah Fairchild Conover, now owned by the Wisconsin Historical
Society, was painted at Superior in 1856. It is more finished in color,
texture, and chacterization than any early portrait executed in the State.

Many artists sought to stimulate public interest by occasional exhibits, art-books, and prints. Art unions and schools were formed. A
new impetus was supplied by the German immigrants, political refugees
and others, who arrived in Milwaukee. The city, with its displays of
scenes of the 1848 German revolution, was said by artists to be "as
German as Düsseldorf." A good share of the Milwaukee Germans
had an excellent cultural background; they sponsored art as a matter
of course and set no narrow limits on subject matter.

Heinrich Vianden (1814-94), one of the best of the artists with Old
World training to come to Milwaukee, exerted, through his teaching,
a great influence on Wisconsin art. Vianden attempted to instil in his
pupils a reverence for nature and that concern for local detail that
marked the Düsseldorf style; owing to him, trees were for twenty
years the favorite subject. One of Vianden's best-known works, now in
the Milwaukee *Journal* Gallery, was *The Old Oak* (1890).

A few Wisconsin artists had already studied the Düsseldorf,
Munich, and Paris styles, and a number of native-born men went to
Europe for training. Among these were Charles Durward (1844-75),
Bernard's son, who studied in England and later built a studio at his
father's glen, where he painted Madonnas and other religious subjects
in the Italian manner; Julius Segall (1858-1925), who spent several
years in Europe making copies of pictures of Venetian galleries and
cathedrals; Edwin C. Eldridge, first curator of the Layton Art Gallery
in Milwaukee, who painted and taught in the manner of the French
Academy.

During this period, Milwaukee sponsored two art projects, a sculptured *Soldier's Monument* and a set of murals for the local chamber of
commerce. Both were contracted by John S. Conway (1853-1926),
who came to Wisconsin from Ohio in 1871 and remained to paint portraits until 1881. His Chamber of Commerce mural, *Agriculture and
the Industries Bringing Their Tribute to Milwaukee,* shows the extent
to which European academic methods were being copied. Figures nude

or in classical robes are set, without much regard for composition, beside such objects as a stock-ticker and a coal truck.

Contemporary with Conway was James Reeve Stuart (1834-1915), who lived in Madison from 1872 until his death. During that time he painted many prominent persons in the city; there are portraits by him in more than a hundred Madison homes, as well as 35 portraits in the State Historical Museum. Stuart was patronized mainly because of the photographic quality of his painting; in fact, he sometimes copied from photographs, as he did in his full-length portrait of *Ole Bull* (Wisconsin Historical Museum).

The predominance of portrait and classical subjects was cut short in 1885, when twenty German-trained artists came to Milwaukee and revived the painting of panoramas in a program sponsored by William Wehner, a Milwaukee German. A special building, round and spacious, was acquired to accommodate the huge canvases on which they worked. Battles of the Civil War were popular subjects, and each of the twenty artists specialized in painting human figures, animals, or landscapes. These panoramas, costing about $25,000 and requiring from six months to a year and a half to complete, were exhibited in large circular halls in the principal cities of the Middle West. Because of them Milwaukee's reputation as an art center increased.

When panorama painting was discontinued in Wisconsin, a number of artists turned to teaching as a means of livelihood. F. W. Heine (1845-1921), who had done much of the finest work on the panoramas, was among the most popular of these teachers. Later he turned to water colors, often of marine scenes. Heine accompanied George Peter, also a former panoramist, to Jerusalem, where they made drawings for a religious panorama to be shown at the St. Louis Exposition of 1905. Before 1914 he painted a panorama for Wehner in San Francisco, *The Battle of Manila*. His water colors continued to sell until the eve of America's entry into the World War, when support of most German artists ceased. Heine's studio was burned to the ground by a mob. In his last years he painted church murals.

Wisconsin's contribution to sculpture has been meagre. Among the leading sculptors of the State two have been women. Vinnie Ream (1847-1915), born in Madison, soon left the State for Missouri, then went to Washington, where her life-size model for a statue of Lincoln won her a ten thousand dollar commission from the Federal Government. Traveling in Europe, she made the acquaintance of such personages as George Brandes, Gustave Doré, and the Queen of Rumania. Besides the Lincoln statue, her work includes the *Farragut Monument* in Washington, D. C., *Miriam, The West, Sappho,* and *The Spirit of Carnival,* the last of which is in the Wisconsin Historical Museum. Helen Farnsworth Mears (1878-1917) began her short career at the

age of fourteen with a figure, *Repentance,* which attracted the attention of Saint-Gaudens. At the age of eighteen she made her *Genius of
Wisconsin,* now in the State Capitol, which represented Wisconsin
at the Columbian Exposition. Later she studied art in New York and
Europe and then returned to America, where she completed a number
of statues before her death.

After the Civil War Wisconsin's industrial development was rapid.
With the increasing prosperity, galleries and collections of European
art were begun, and communication with the Continent became more
common. Many artists born in the 1850's and 1860's got the greater
part of their training in Europe.

Outside the earlier art movements of Milwaukee and of the State
was Theodore Robinson (1852-96), born in Evansville, the first American to be represented in the Louvre and the Luxembourg. His early
study in Chicago was financed by portrait drawings. It was during a
second period in Paris, when he came in contact with Monet, that he
reached his full power. With Maurice Prendergast, Twatchman, and
a few others, he was among the first American impressionists; but while
Monet had considerable influence on him, he succeeded in maintaining
his individuality. After his return to America he painted figures and
Delaware and Hudson River scenery. Robinson died without obtaining much recognition; today his paintings may be seen in the Metropolitan Museum of Art, New York City, in Philadelphia and Kansas
City galleries, and in the private family collection in Evansville.

Robert Koehler (1850-ca. 1923), born in Hamburg, Germany, and
brought to Milwaukee at the age of four, was a pupil of Vianden. In
1873 he went to Munich, where, except for a period in New York, he
studied and maintained an art school until 1892. In America Koehler
allied himself with the New York Art Students' League, and his work
is distinguished by a concern with social problems, represented in such
paintings as *The Strike* and *The Socialist.* Richard Lorenz (1858-
1915), born in Voigstaedt, Germany, was among those who came to
Milwaukee to join the panorama group. Trained at Weimar, Lorenz
became interested in painting characteristic American scenes. Much
of his time was spent in the West, and, after the death of Frederic
Remington, Lorenz became the leader of western genre painting. Carl
Marr (1858-1934), early associated with the Royal Academy at Munich
as student, teacher, and director, was more German than American,
though some of his early years were spent in Milwaukee. He is represented in Wisconsin by his large historical canvas, *The Flagellants,* in
the Milwaukee Auditorium; *Christmas Eve,* at the Milwaukee Art
Institute; and *Silent Devotion,* at the Layton Art Gallery. George
Raab, born in Sheboygan in 1866, was a student at Weimar and Paris;
his painting is influenced by the work of Whistler and Puvis de Chav-

The Farm Lands

ARCHITECTURE OF THE DAIRYLANDS

STACKING PEA VINES

PASTURE SCENE

MODEL DAIRY FARM AT FORT ATKINSON. THIS IS MAINTAINED BY "HOARD'S DAIRYMAN" MAGAZINE FOR EXPERIMENTAL WORK

SMALL GRAIN ELEVATOR AT ARLINGTON

TYPICAL CHEESE FACTORY

COULEE COUNTRY FARM IN SPRING

WINTER LANDSCAPE—MURAL BY GEORGE ADAMS
DEITRICH IN THE LAKE GENEVA POST OFFICE

CONTOUR PLOWING

TOBACCO

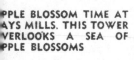

CHERRY BLOSSOMS
DOOR COUNTY

PPLE BLOSSOM TIME AT
AYS MILLS. THIS TOWER
VERLOOKS A SEA OF
PPLE BLOSSOMS

HARNESS RACING AT A COUNTY FAIR

PULLING CONTEST AT A COUNTY FAIR

annes. Louis Mayer (1869-   ), who studied in Milwaukee under Otto von Ernst and Richard Lorenz, and later in Weimar, Munich, and Paris, was one of the early art leaders in Milwaukee. Since 1912, when he went to New York, he has made busts of Emerson, Whitman, Lincoln, Debs, Robert La Follette, Sr., Victor Berger, and Daniel Hoan. Karl Knaths (1891-   ) was born in Wisconsin and his early work reflected the rural atmosphere of his native place.

Georgia O'Keeffe, outstanding modernist painter, was born in Sun Prairie in 1887, but left the State early in her career. Her reputation is founded upon a series of brilliant close-ups of flowers and arrangements of exotic objects and scenes, among which the seashore, the desert, and New York skyscrapers are favorite themes. Her work contains a marked element of abstraction and never treats the human figure; yet the shapes and colors of her compositions succeed in expressing strong emotion.

Recent painting in Wisconsin is varied in scope and method, and throughout the State artists, too many to enumerate or describe individually, are doing vigorous work. Milwaukee remains the art center. Among the Milwaukee painters are Emily Groom (1876-), who paints brightly colored flower-studies and landscapes; Robert von Neumann (1888-), well known for his studies of grouped figures, usually of fishermen working or resting together in boats; Gerritt Sinclair (1890-), most prolific of the Milwaukee artists, who tends to use subdued tones in his carefully-designed scenes of houses, lawns, and country life; Myron Nutting (1890-), many of whose paintings contain figures set against a background of sky and cloud. Other outstanding Milwaukee men are Peter Rotier, Howard Thomas, George Dieterich, Dudley Crafts Watson, Gerhardt Bakker, Forrest Flower, Charles Thwaites, Lester Bentley, and Paul Clemens. In Madison the best-known painter is John Steuart Curry (1897-), Resident Artist in the University of Wisconsin College of Agriculture. Curry, who is among the leaders of American regional art, is now engaged mainly in painting rural Wisconsin scenes. In 1939 the Nation-wide competitions for murals in each State resulted in Wisconsin artists receiving five of the 72 commissions awarded. These five artists, all of them between 25 and 35 years of age, are executing murals in Wisconsin, Illinois, Minnesota, and Northern Michigan.

A number of younger artists are at the present time employed on the Wisconsin Art Project in Milwaukee. A group of these are making exact reproductions in water colors of various handicraft objects, domestic designs, and other examples of folk art preserved from the early days of the State. The reproductions will be included in an Index of American Design, which is reminiscent of the early collections of Frederick Stanton Perkins. Other members of the project are painting oils, water colors, and murals for public buildings. A number of sculptors are also employed, doing bas-reliefs and sculptures of figures and animals. Some are at work on statuary for the Park Lawn housing area. Through the project a group of young artists is creating murals, easel paintings, and sculpture allocated to Wisconsin public institutions.

Societies throughout the State have been encouraging artists with exhibitions and awards. The most influential of these are the Wisconsin Society of Painters and Sculptors, Milwaukee, and the Madison Art Association, both of which hold annual shows. There are smaller clubs in various other cities such as Oshkosh and Fond du Lac. The art collection of Beloit College is among the most important in the State. The teaching centers are Milwaukee and Madison. The Art Education Department of the University of Wisconsin, under the direction of William H. Varnum, is assisted unofficially by John Steuart Curry. Milwaukee, with its Art Institute, Layton Art Gallery, and Milwaukee State Teachers College, has developed a strong teaching tradition, and has trained many of Wisconsin's leading contemporary artists.

Music

W HEN Europeans came to Wisconsin in the seventeenth century they found Indians of Algonquian and Siouan stock. Music was deeply rooted in the lives of these people. It was, apparently, neither an isolated art nor a medium of entertainment but an essential part of work, play, war, and religious ritual. The music of the different tribes within these two great families varied and, partly for this reason, the entire subject of Indian music is highly technical. There is an authoritative body of literature in this field, with notable contributions by Frances Densmore, George Herzog, and other specialists. Without harmony, in the European sense of the word, the music of the Indians frequently imitated natural sounds, such as thunder, winds, animal, and bird cries. There were songs for corn planting and harvesting, songs of celebration, lullabies, and dance music for the sick. Songs were looked upon as earthly possessions, and at the approach of death an Indian often bequeathed as a definite legacy his own medicine song, acquired in the first dream of his youth.

The first European music that the Indians heard was the *Vexilla Regis* chant of the French Jesuits. In a short time the songs of the voyageurs were also heard, and when the nineteenth century opened French boatmen were still singing their old songs on the rivers of Wisconsin. Juliette Kinzie, who brought one of the first pianos into the territory, writes that a crew of voyageurs sang as they rowed her down through the wild rice mazes of the Fox River, in 1830. Later, when social life and music began to center in the military posts of the wilderness, at Green Bay, Portage, and Prairie du Chien, the *chansons* of the French were heard less and less frequently. While soldiers held weekly evenings of song at the frontier forts, people far from the main settlements were gathering at surprise parties, birthday parties, and weddings, dancing to *Devils Dream, Money Musk,* and *The Wind that Shakes the Barley,* accompanied by a single violin or, sometimes, by a bass viol or dulcimer. Old newspapers mention military bands that played for Independence Day celebrations and torchlight processions.

The Germans, first coming to Wisconsin in 1839, brought a fine musical tradition. All over the State, and particularly in Milwaukee, the newcomers started *Männergesangvereine, Männerquartette,* and *Männerchöre.* Intelligent leadership was given these societies by the

German immigrants of 1848-49, who settled in large numbers in the villages and cities of the southeastern lakeshore counties. Having been educated in schools that taught music as a basic subject, these newcomers were able to read melodies from the musical staff as easily as they read words from the printed page. Wherever they made their homes musical societies sprang up.

One of these refugees was Hans Balatka, an energetic, gifted man, who soon became director of Milwaukee's important *Musikverein* (1850) and later founded the Northwest *Sängerbund,* which still is active. Germans founded societies in Sheboygan, Portage, Watertown, Madison, La Crosse, and other cities. When families could afford it their children invariably learned singing, violin, or piano from a German master.

The entire middle century was filled with folk song, for the German, Welsh, Scandinavian, and Irish settlers kept alive the music of their homelands. Welsh farmers continued the traditional *Eisteddfod,* a yearly contest-festival in which most of the participants sing by ear original songs and the technically difficult works of the masters—Bach, Haydn, Handel, and Beethoven—which they have known since childhood. *Eisteddfodau* have long been held in such places as Oshkosh, Wales, and Columbia County; other festivals of song and poetry are part of Welsh life at Sparta, Waukesha, Wales, and other communities in the State. Different in character are the *cymanfaoedd canu,* gatherings for the singing of hymns, instituted originally as a secular custom in Wales. *Hen Alaw, Rhyd-y-Groes,* and *Pebyll yr Arglwydd* are hymns which have been sung in Wisconsin Welsh centers for nearly a century.

The Swiss, clustered together on the farms of Green County, continued to sing melodies learned from their parents, songs quick and light-hearted, full of joyous yodels. Today Swiss orchestras from New Glarus, made up of instruments played in the native land, such as zither, shepherd's pipe, concertina, and violin, have gained a fairly wide reputation through radio and concert performances. The Belgians, who settled in Door County in 1884, have clung to their custom of the *Kermiss,* their old religious harvest festival. Three days of the week during the six weeks of this celebration old and young people in bright Belgian dress dance and play games and gather into choirs to sing Belgian songs and Catholic hymns. Choirs sometimes sing hymns to the Virgin at roadside shrines on the Door Peninsula.

Wisconsin was a haven for Scandinavian as well as German dissenters. By 1850 nearly half the Scandinavians in America were in Wisconsin. Settling first in the southern and eastern counties of the State, by 1870 they had spread throughout the north; *Vor Gud han er sa a fast en borg* soon took its place in worship with *Eine feste Burg ist unser Gott.* In Swedish and Norwegian communities, even today, folk song is deep-rooted in the lives of the people. The most common native instruments of the Swedes are the flute and zither guitar; of the Norwegians, the *langeleik,* the *salmodikon,* and the *Hardangerfelen,* an eight-stringed violin. Probably the man who did more than any other to develop Scandinavian musical expression in Wisconsin was Ole Bull, the great violinist. During his periods of residence in Madison, between 1870 and 1880, he gave several benefit concerts to aid the establishment of a Scandinavian department in the University. His popularizing of Norwegian folk tunes and his concerts, held in public halls, his own music pavilion, or out-of-doors, helped Wisconsin people to overcome their musical isolation. When Bull first visited Madison in 1856 he brought with him a small Italian girl of thirteen, Adelina Patti, who joined him in a recital. In 1879 he invited the *Normanna Sangerkor* (1869) of La Crosse, reputed to be the oldest Norwegian singing society in America, to share the program of a concert which was held the same year before an enormous audience in Madison.

Before the Civil War, many churches were without organs or any instruments for accompaniment; nevertheless, hymn-singing was kept vigorous through singing schools, which conducted a sort of popular music education. Excited attention was given the concerts of famous musicians, though these were still rare in Wisconsin. Frontier people followed with interest Jenny Lind's chain of eastern successes. Local newspaper editors disputed, on the front page, the possibility of her appearing in Wisconsin, and many women wore faddish "Jenny Lind" hats. Ole Bull attracted crowds from more than a hundred miles beyond Madison. Performers began to find that certain cities of Wisconsin paid as well as Cincinnati or Chicago.

Though the Civil War left remote places untouched, it seriously drained rural settlements and larger villages and cities of their musicians. In Milwaukee, Manitowoc, Wausau, Sheboygan, Watertown, La Crosse, and Madison musical societies found their memberships shrinking rapidly as one after another of the singers and orchestra men joined the Union Army. German singing societies often united to form a volunteer regiment. Yet when the war was over there were many new bands and folk-song combinations that had been formed during the high pitch of martial excitement. Many of the national groups had sung and marched together, and it was not uncommon to find Yankee and Bohemian fife-and-drum corps, German and Irish, or Irish and Swedish musical units suddenly familiar with each others' marches, dances, and songs. German melodies were being used for Yankee hymns, and Yankee tunes for German drinking songs. Everyone was singing the sentimental words and airs of Joseph P. Webster (1819-75) both during and after the war. His *Lorena,* though written with the North in mind, was highly popular with the Confederate troops (it recurs all through *Gone with the Wind*). *She Shines in Honor Like a Star,* the *Irish Volunteer, Brave Men, Behold Your Fallen Chief,* and others were sung nationally during this time. Webster, a resident of Elkhorn from 1856 until his death, is remembered best for his music to the hymn *In the Sweet Bye and Bye.*

During the 1870's Milwaukee's reputation as the *Deutsch Athen* of America was growing fast, in part because of its musical activity. The *Männerchor* of the *Musikverein,* after taking part in the huge La Crosse *Sängerfest* of 1871, made a highly successful tour to St. Paul and Minneapolis. In the same decade several other choruses were formed that are still singing today; among them are the *Männerchor Hermannssöhne* formed in 1870, the *Baden Männerchor* in 1872, the *Sozialistischer Männerchor* in 1876, the *Milwaukee Liederkranz* in 1878, and the *Schweitzer Männerchor* in 1879. A short-lived Philharmonic Society, founded about this time, served as a forerunner to the Arion Musical Club (1876), out of which grew, in 1877, the Cecilian Choir, a women's chorus. National attention was given Milwaukee and Wisconsin when Milwaukee, in 1886, was host to the great North American *Sängerbund.*

Meanwhile, in the north woods, gangs of lumberjacks were creating their own songs, freely adapting ballads of the Maine and Canadian woods to their experience on Wisconsin streams and in the logging camps. Out of the forests came various crude instruments, among them an imitation of the salmodikon, an instrument with one string and a fretted neck that was used in the old Christian church of Norway to give pitch for the singing of hymns. Attempting to copy it, Norwegian lumberjacks used a crackerbox for the tone chamber and a broomhandle for the neck. They played the single guitar string with a violin bow borrowed or bought from any wandering fiddler who happened to come through camp. The Irish shantyboys, trying to fashion bull-fiddles, mounted the tone chambers of their instruments on pitchforks. Bohemians, Swedes, Norwegians, and Irish played hand-made cigar-box fiddles, harps, "squeezebox" accordians, and odd kinds of birchbark instruments. Now and then a Norwegian was fortunate enough to own a Hardanger fiddle. At night in the bunkhouse, accompanied by one or more of their instruments, the lumberjacks sang *River in the Pines, The Fatal Oak, My Name is Yon Yonson,* and other folk songs. As they floated the rafts down the rivers, one of their favorites was *Jack Haggerty's Flat River Girl.*

> I'm a heart-broken raftsman, from Greenville I came,
> My virtue's departed, alas! I declaim.
> The strong darts of Cupid have caused me much grief,
> Till my heart burst asunder I will ne'er find relief.

I am by occupation a raftsman where the Flat River rolls,
My name is engraved on its rocks, sands and shoals.
In shops, bars and households I'm very well known,
They call me Jack Haggerty, the pride of the town.

At the turn of the century musical activity, centering in Milwaukee, expanded with the social and industrial growth of the State. Operas were held daily in Milwaukee's Schlitz Park, and many new musical societies were formed. Eighteen ninety-five saw the birth of the *Gesangverein Bavaria,* the Milwaukee A Capella Chorus, and the *Sozialistische Liedertafel* (recently dissolved). In 1896 Dr. Daniel Protheroe, famous Welsh musician, founded the Lyric Glee Club, which has since become the nationally-known Lyric Male Chorus. Later Dr. Protheroe became director of the Arion Club, and it was during this period that year after year he traveled to Wales to conduct the annual national *Eisteddfod* there. A composer as well as a director, he published nearly a thousand songs during his lifetime. Before the World War the *Männerchor Edelweiss* (1902), the *Damenchor Saxonia* (1902), the *Bäcker Liederkranz* (1908), the *Nordseite Damenchor Freiheit* (1909), and the *Kärnthner Gesangverein* (1912) were begun in Milwaukee. Until 1914 these societies drew much of their support from local businessmen, but when the World War came this support ceased. Many societies were forced to merge with one another or dissolve altogether. Only two conspicuous German societies have risen since then: the *Damenchor* (1925) and the *Schweitzer Damenchor* (1927).

Following Joseph P. Webster, no prolific composer of popular music appeared in Wisconsin for some years. The words to *Silver Threads Among the Gold,* by Eben E. Rexford of Shiocton, and the song, *The Little Brown Church in the Vale,* by W. S. Pitts of Rock County, are noteworthy among the few written between Webster's time and the 1890's, when Charles K. Harris of Milwaukee made his fortune with *After the Ball.* Other tunes by Harris included *Break the News to Mother* and *Hello, Central, Give me Heaven.* Probably the most beloved songs were those written by Carrie Jacobs Bond, a native of Janesville, composer of *Just a-Wearyin' For You, I Love You Truly,* and *A Perfect Day.*

As the twentieth century advanced, interest in civic and public school music grew throughout the State. The *Wisconsin Journal of Education,* which since 1855 had been carrying on a continuous campaign for the teaching of music in the schools, partially achieved its end in 1906 when several cities introduced incomplete music courses in their curriculum. Teachers, trained at the university, were hired for the "experiment" only one day a week and were not accorded regular standing as teachers. Yet within a few years regular singing hours had been established in most of the schools in Wisconsin, and, side by side with them, hundreds of bands and glee clubs. Though music in the schools was optional, nearly every school board soon agreed that some form of music was essential to child training. The vogue of school music has continued to spread rapidly.

School music got a firm start in August 1920 at Reedsburg, wher William Arvold, local music director and now president emeritus of the Wisconsin School Music Association, arranged for the first Wisconsin tournament of high school bands. Three towns responded to Reedsburg's invitation; by December the Wisconsin Boy's Band Association was formed by fifteen bands. Their two-day tournament at Elkhorn in June 1921 was filmed by Pathe News as an innovation; there were bands from New Holstein, Marshfield, Richland Center, Beloit, Delavan, Kilbourn, Lake Geneva, Mauston, Reedsburg, and Elkhorn; two of the world's best cornetists, Herbert Clark and Frank Simon, were present. At this time the name of the association was changed to the Wisconsin Juvenile Band Association, and girls were encouraged to participate in coming tournaments. By 1933 band music had been supplemented in the schools by solo, ensemble, orchestral, and vocal work, largely as a result of the efforts of the Wisconsin School Music Association. The number of tournament contestants in this organization has grown so large that it surpasses even the enrollment of the national tournaments, and today State contests in Wisconsin are forced to limit themselves to solos and ensembles.

Outstanding young musicians from the high schools often attend the Wisconsin Music Clinic, arranged by the University School of Music in co-operation with the School Music Association. The clinic is a summer session of training for both teachers and students, offering private as well as ensemble lessons during most of July. Musicians of national standing are hired to direct an all-State Band, orchestra and chorus, made up of students, which gives a concert at the end of the session. In 1940, 500 high school players and 40 directors came to Madison for their eleventh annual meeting and study session on the University campus. A Music Clinic Opera, recently introduced, has thus far produced Penn's *Lass of Limerick Town* (1937) and Balfe's *Bohemian Girl* (1938).

Some high school players, if they wish to become teachers or supervisors of music in public schools, go on to the various State teachers colleges, the Wisconsin Conservatory, the Milwaukee Institute, the independent colleges, or the school of music of the State university. The extension division of the college of agriculture and the department of rural sociology are both working in the rural areas of the State, helping to promote music education. Young farmers, who attend the short courses offered in the midwinter at the university, may join a glee club or orchestra; all the short course students are offered two hours a week of community singing. Sight reading, rhythmic exercises, vocal drill, and discussions on topics from folk-song to symphonies are a part of the curriculum. The department of rural sociology offers help through its State music specialist in planning county musical events and in training volunteer music leaders. One- and two-day training schools are held in those counties wishing help from the specialist; leaders who attend such schools usually are interested in furthering music in rural schools and churches, and in farm organizations.

This interest often leads to the formation of county music and folk festivals, drawing their attendance from a forty-mile radius of farms and small towns. For the past few years selected groups from these county events have attended the State Rural Music Festival, held annually at the State Fair Park. Questionnaires sent out from the department of rural sociology show that the second, third, and fourth generation descendants of immigrants like best to sing their ancestral songs—such as the German *Come Let Us be Joyful,* the Slovakian *Morning Comes Early,* and the Irish *Galway Pipers.*

Farmers and people from small towns participate in community music through the broadcasts of the two State-owned stations, WHA in Madison and WLBL in Stevens Point. Professor E. B. Gordon's pioneer course, *Journeys in Musicland,* was first heard on the air in 1931. Now, in its tenth year, 2,000 teachers and 35,000 children are registered for the course, and it has recently taken highest award in its field at the Ohio Institute of Radio Broadcasting. In *Music Enjoyment for Younger Children,* another radio course, boys and girls hear simple classics like *The Bee, In a Clock Store, March of the Dwarfs,* and *Traumerei.* Other State-station broadcasts for both education and entertainment in music are offered by the *College of the Air, Music of the Masters,* organ recitals, and the regular university *Music Appreciation* course, broadcast directly from the classrooms of the school of music.

Today Madison and Milwaukee are the music centers of Wisconsin. The first has the Madison Civic Symphony and the Madison Civic Orchestra, the Madison Civic Chorus, one mixed chorus, one women's chorus, and four male choruses. In Milwaukee the Lyric Male Chorus, the A Capella Club, the Arion Club, the Symphonic Male Chorus, and the Musical Society are outstanding. The Chicago Symphony Orchestra gives a series of ten concerts each year, and there is a summer festival in which the music clinic of the University takes part. Two days of the festival are given over to folk dances, singing, and band music. Many of the old German singing societies still perform, some of them with a solid membership of Swabians, Saxonians, Swiss, or Bavarians. Polish, Jewish, and Greek singing societies are active.

The Greeks, members of the Orthodox Church, sing their old hymns and chants to the accompaniment of clarinet, violin, mandolin, and *bouzouki* (lute). Folk-music is kept vigorous in a Croatian women's chorus, a Greek folk-song group, three Jewish singing societies, various German societies, and an Italian opera chorus, which sings both in Italian and English. In the annual Harvest Festival of Many Lands in Milwaukee, twenty-two nationalities are represented, wearing traditional costumes, playing traditional games, and singing folk-songs.

Helping to spread a knowledge of music in Wisconsin are the Wisconsin Music Project and the Adult Education and Recreation Department of the Work Projects Administration. The music project, furnishing employment for professional musicians, has organized concert orchestras, small ensembles, and choral groups that give public concerts for audiences who formerly lacked the opportunity to hear good music. The most popular of Milwaukee orchestras, aside from the Young People's Symphony, is the WPA-sponsored Wisconsin Symphony. Until recently this organization was directed by Hugo Bach, son of the beloved Christopher Bach, who years before had led the Little Symphony of the *Turnverein*. Dr. Sigfrid Prager, conductor of Madison's Civic Orchestra and Chorus, is the present director. The adult education program is attempting to train leaders who can awaken latent interest in music. In Milwaukee County more than twenty groups have begun to study music under WPA direction; they include instrumental classes, orchestras, bands, glee clubs, harmony clubs, a Mexican and an Italian chorus. Work such as this is particularly valuable in preserving the folk-music of the Finns and Italians in northern counties not reached by any other agency.

At present more than twenty-five vocational and adult education schools in Wisconsin sponsor musical programs; those found in Beloit, Milwaukee, Shorewood, Sheboygan, and Madison are probably the most carefully organized and best equipped. Some have all-inclusive programs for bands, orchestras, A Capella choirs, choruses, Hawaiian bands, children's choruses, opera, drum corps, courses in harmony and music appreciation. Band shells dot nearly every city and town, and every community has its church choirs, local musicians, singing groups, and school bands. Ashland has a particularly fine reputation for all-round musical activity.

During the past forty years Wisconsin, at one time or another, has been the home of several composers, among them Alexander MacFayden (1879-1936) of Milwaukee, author of a long list of piano pieces and songs. His *Inter Nos, Cradle Song,* and many others have been included in the concert repertoire of Joseph Hofmann, Schumann-Heink, and Florence MacBeth. Carl Eppert has been active since 1919 in the Wisconsin Conservatory of Music, the Milwaukee Institute of Music, and the Wisconsin College of Music. Performances of his *Symphony of the City, The Road to Mecca,* and *Symphonic Tonette* have been given by several of the great symphony orchestras of both America and Europe. Hugo Kaun, Eppert's teacher, internationally known in the field of musical composition, lived in Milwaukee during his youth. Cecil Burleigh (1885), professor of violin and composition at the State university, is best-known for two violin concertos and numerous *Indian Sketches.*

Edgar Stillman Kelly (1857-1937), who was born and grew to manhood in Sparta, wrote *The Headless Horseman* and *The Royal Gaelic March* for piano, *Ben Hur, The Pit and the Pendulum,* the *New England Symphony,* and *Pilgrims Progress* for symphony orchestra, and the songs *Phases of Love, Eldorado, Israfel,* and *My Captain.* Other composers are Gilbert Ross, head of the school of music at Smith College; William T. Purdy, who wrote *On Wisconsin;* Jacob Reuter, author of numerous violin pieces; and Theodore Steinmetz, composer of the *32nd Division March.*

Perhaps the most important musical development of the last few years has occurred since the reorganization of the University School of Music under its new director, Professor Carl Bricken. Integral to the three-fold aim of the School—to provide teacher training, a major in applied music, and a major in composition and theory—is Professor Bricken's unfolding plan for "education through performance." To accomplish this plan there has been a serious and increasingly successful attempt to raise the level of performance of the University orchestra and chorus. In the spring of 1940 the *Pro Arte* String Quartet, a European ensemble of great distinction, played the entire cycle of Beethoven quartets in a music festival that ended with the performance of the Beethoven fourth concerto for piano and orchestra, with Profesor Gunnar Johansen as soloist, and the Beethoven ninth symphony, with Professor Bricken as conductor. In the autumn of 1940 the *Pro Arte* quartet was added to the faculty of the School of Music; the members of the quartet not only teach in the School but perform with the University orchestra in concerts of great merit.

The Theater

THE German theater in Milwaukee, during its long life, was the most illustrious foreign-language organization in America—with the possible exception of the pre-war German troupes in New York. Notable both for the catholicity of its repertory and the high standards of its acting and production, it dominated Wisconsin theatrical history for almost 85 years. The record of this organization is, in effect, a record of the theater in the State until the second decade of the twentieth century.

The beginnings were meager. In February 1850 the printers and typesetters of the *Banner und Volksfreund* produced a play in Market Hall and continued for a few months with occasional performances. Between February and December of the same year a *Liebhaberverein* made several sporadic offerings of German drama and then collapsed. There was an interlude when the German theater lived a hole-in-the-wall existence, playing in beer gardens and one-flight-up halls. Several theatrical enterprises rose and succumbed until 1868, when Heinrich Kurz built the first theater for German drama in the Midwest.

Through the enthusiasm and energy of the Kurz family, this group gradually emerged from amateur and semi-amateur status, freed itself from the conditions of the music hall, and attained a vitality that presently flowered in the remarkable company of the Stadt Theater. In repertory there was a shift from vaudevilles, farces, and the plays of Kotzebue and Charlotte Birch-Pfeiffer to the mature drama of Hebbel, Kleist, Ibsen, Goethe, Grillparzer, Schiller, and Shakespeare.

Heinrich Kurz's first theater was a 900-seat structure in the heart of the German district of Milwaukee's Second Ward, on Third Street between Wells and Cedar. Almost at the same time semi-professional groups took possession of the North and South Side *Turn* Halls for dramatic performances. In March 1868 the German-speaking Bohemian actress, Fanny Janauschek, appeared in Milwaukee with her own troupe as the first European actress of eminence to cross the ocean since Rachel's American visit of 1855. Pictures and contemporary accounts portray her as a woman of beauty and superb power, an actress in the grand style of those who "shake the heavens and uproot the earth." As Medea, Mary Stuart, and Adrienne Lecouvreur, somber and magnificent, she brought her brief season to a triumphant conclusion. Her visits became seasonal and soon opened the way for a train of illustrious actors from the great stages of Germany and Austria.

Both in repertory and personnel the Stadt Theater progressed steadily and smoothly, until by 1879 its position in the community was assured. In that year, owing to a rupture in the organization, part of the company opened a rival theater in the Grand Opera House, only to fail promptly and disband. For the next five years the German theater lacked its former quality. The management found it necessary to bring forward the frothier part of its repertory. This recession, however, did not affect the flow of glittering talent from Central Europe: Seebach, Barnay, Mitterwurzer, Haverland, Raabe, Ernst von Possart, and others appeared briefly as guest actors, supported by a company that yearly moved nearer its former standard. By the season of 1884-85 the balance between the troupe and play-list was restored.

The Stadt Theater hesitated so long over the production, daring at the time, of Ibsen's *Ghosts* that another Milwaukee group deprived it of the honor of a first American performance. Except for Madame Modjeska's Louisville presentation of *A Doll's House* in 1883, the production of *Ghosts* by the Thalia *Verein* of the North Side Theater in 1886 was the first noteworthy performance of Ibsen in America. A tremendous uproar ensued, but the outraged public came to see the play in such numbers that the Society transferred its production to a downtown playhouse. The Stadt Theater staged *The Pillars of Society* in 1889, and thereafter Ibsen dramas remained a staple on its list. By 1894, when a New York audience strenuously rejected an English version of *Ghosts,* it had been a repertory piece in Milwaukee for three years. Similarly, the works of Shaw, Wilde, and Strindberg were familiar to Milwaukee audiences in German translations at a time when they were still exotic fare even in New York.

In 1890 Captain Frederick Pabst bought the Grand Opera House and reconditioned it in order to provide the German theater with a more commodious home. At this time the organization began adapting itself to the rising school of naturalism in acting. This was necessary, for it was apparent that the older technique—suitable for the rhetorical type of drama then in vogue—could not portray the realities and psychological subtleties of the "new drama" born in Norway.

Joseph Kainz, who came to the Milwaukee theater in 1891-92 at the height of his fame, was peculiarly equipped to help the group with this problem. Much has been written about Kainz. When he joined the Stadt theater his life as a power in Bavaria at the court of Ludwig II was only a few years behind him. One of the Bavarian king's line of favorites, which also included Richard Wagner, he was expelled from his paradise after a quarrel and went back to the serious business of becoming a great actor. In Meiningen and later in Berlin Kainz began to develop a style of acting that adjusted the artificialities of the stage to the necessities of the new type of drama. By the time he reached Milwaukee he had achieved remarkable power in interpreting both realistic plays and those of the earlier, more romantic school.

In January 1895 the Stadt Theater burned and the organization faced a dubious future. But Captain Pabst, whose generosity rushed to meet the occasion, again contributed largely to building the most sumptuous auditorium and well-equipped stage in the region. The good days continued. The repertory, made up of the dramas of Ibsen, Bjornson, Hauptmann, Maeterlinck, Rostand, Gorki, and Tolstoi, and the regular classic and lighter fare, kept pace with the Continental stage for the next quarter century. The company, recruited almost entirely in Central Europe, was worthy of the virtuosi whom it supported.

As far back as 1870 the theater had made a five-year experiment with operetta—had, in fact, introduced the genre on this continent with a production of Offenbach's *Orpheus in Hades*. In 1912 the directors, at great expense, added a musical wing to the troupe, which for a while successfully performed the latest products from the *Theater an der Wein*, along with standard light opera pieces.

But this development was short-lived. Within a few years the powerful anti-Germanism of World War years destroyed what neither fire, feud, nor civil war had touched more than lightly. The company that had been so carefully picked and trained was disbanded; the theater planned as a "temple of dramatic art" stood vacant and dark. When the war was over a few enthusiasts who remained from the older generation set about to restore the company, and for a time performances were resumed. But the population of Milwaukee was no longer predominantly German, and the spirit of the times had changed. After a futile struggle, the German theater was finally abandoned in 1935.

But meanwhile another kind of dramatic activity had arisen in the State. The little theater movement in America had its significant beginnings at Madison in December 1910, when Professor Thomas H. Dickinson established the Wisconsin Dramatic Society. Its inception preceded other harbingers of a movement which was to affect the entire country. The first American tour of the Irish Players from Dublin's Abbey Theater came some months later, and it was not until the following year that the short lived Lake Forest (Illinois) Theater opened its doors, and Maurice Browne launched his little theater in Chicago.

Dickinson's association at first consisted of a group of amateurs and a few semi professionals, who presented plays unlikely to be seen in the commercial theater to an audience of participating subscribers. In the words of its manifesto, the general aims were "to raise the standard of dramatic appreciation in the community; to encourage the support of the best plays; to encourage the reading of good plays in English and in translations from other languages; to encourage the translation, composition, and publication of good plays; to conduct companies for the production of high-class plays at low prices." It further proposed to eliminate theatrical claptrap in acting, writing, and production; to emphasize the dominant idea of the whole play by harmonizing all elements, in opposition to the distortions of the "star system"; to abolish such traditional pests as the curtain-call, the entr'act orchestral number, and between-curtain arrivals and departures. The repertory theater was seen as a goal. The scenic side of production was necessarily limited by slight financial resources, and emphasis was placed upon acting and direction.

Soon after its beginning in Madison the Society extended its activities to Milwaukee, where a branch worked separately under the direction of Mrs. Laura Sherry, an actress of professional experience from the company of Richard Mansfield. For four years the two sections continued to gather and train talent and to produce plays. Performances were exchanged and engagements filled throughout the State. Play-reading in groups, translation, and lectures were added to the regular activities. Two volumes of *Wisconsin Plays* and eight issues of a quarterly magazine, *The Play Book,* were published, containing (among other contributions) the early work of two writers who later acquired national reputations, Zona Gale and William Ellery Leonard.

Professor Dickinson left the University in 1916, and the Madison organization dissolved. But Mrs. Sherry's group in Milwaukee continued to flourish under the name of the Wisconsin Players. At the invitation of Maurice Browne, they appeared twice at the Fine Arts Theater in Chicago in 1914 with such success that they were asked to return for a longer engagement. They again played in Chicago throughout April 1916, winning the esteem of the reviewers with a repertory of plays by Wisconsin writers and a number of European works translated by the members. The next year they acted for two weeks at the Neighborhood Playhouse in New York and evoked an interest that indicated their national standing. Though the organization has not maintained the position it held at the height of the little theater movement in 1916 and 1917, it still functions at 355 Van Buren Street in Milwaukee and shares the non-commercial field with the Milwaukee Little Theater. Mrs. Sherry, who is writing the history of the Wisconsin Players, was State Director of the Federal Theater Project of the Works Progress Administration.

In 1923 the Reverend Mathias Helfen started a Catholic dramatic movement in Mapleton which eventually became international in scope. His purpose was to combat the spread of communism among young Catholics by interesting them in the drama. The organization is still active in Mapleton and has extended into 9,700 parishes in the United States, and to India and Australia.

The Experimental College of the University of Wisconsin, established in 1927 under Dr. Alexander Meiklejohn, devoted the freshman year to an integrated study of Athenian civilization. Under Professor Walter Agard and a student director, Victor Wolfson (later to become prominent as an actor and playwright), the College gave semi-yearly performances of Greek plays, translated by its members or in the standard versions.

Though representations of Greek classic drama had from time to time been attempted at the University in its open-air theater and elsewhere, the Experimental College undertook a different method of production. The conventions of the Greek theater—the masked chorus, the all-male cast, the formal movements of the chorus in its semi circle preceding the scene, and the seating of audiences in an amphitheater above the actors—were observed. Suggestive lighting and movement were used to heighten the action, after the fashion of Max Reinhardt in his revivals of classic plays. These performances were continued with some success until the Experimental College was abolished in 1932.

The University's contribution to the Wisconsin theater has not been confined to the Greek play productions. Well coordinated courses in acting, production, and design, as well as the more usual history of the drama, are given under the department of speech. For some twenty years this department has also sponsored a dramatic organization which has developed several well-known actors of stage and screen.

In 1938 construction was started on what is considered the finest theater-plant in the State, under the supervision of Lee Simonson, well known scenic designer and a member of the New York Theater Guild. This structure is a part of the University's student social-center, the Memorial Union, and serves a variety of functions, as theater, music hall, lecture room, and auditorium for the public recitals of the University's renowned dance division. There is an adjustable proscenium; two sets of curtains, hidden in the walls, to reduce the size of the audience-room, which has a full seating-capacity of 1300; and modern equipment for lighting, scene-shifting, and radio-broadcasting. The building also contains a small experimental theater, rehearsal rooms, dressing-rooms, storage facilities for scenery, and a spacious lobby which is used for art exhibitions.

The German theater of Milwaukee, the little theater initiated by Dickinson, and the work of the University of Wisconsin have influenced the development of the more usual theater activities, particularly in the non-commercial field. A summer theater is now being established at Oconomowoc along the lines of those on the north Atlantic seaboard.

The larger cities now have their amateur dramatic groups, and the 4-H clubs and similar agencies sponsor plays and contests. The home talent tournament of the extension division of the College of Agriculture has been particularly effective in stimulating interest in this form of rural and community recreation.

Architecture

LIKE THAT of other midwestern States the architecture of Wisconsin is to a great extent a record of fashions that were brought from the East. But it is often the less pretentious houses, devoid of obvious stylistic earmarks, and unaffected by the trends of other regions, that have greatest value as architecture.

The finest early buildings of the State were erected in the Green Bay and the southwestern regions, where French traders and American soldiers were stationed. The Porlier-Tank Cottage at Green Bay, oldest house in the State, was built by the fur-trader François Roi. The walls of the original building were wattled, made of branches and twigs woven over rough timber uprights and plastered with mud. This framework was covered with rough clapboards, cut with a whipsaw. In 1850, when the cottage passed into the hands of Otto Tank, it was finished with neat clapboarding; at that time wings were placed at both ends. Shortly after 1800 a number of houses were erected in the vicinity, some by an architect named Jackson, but few of them exist today. The Fort Howard Hospital Building (1816), a graceful structure in the Georgian Colonial style, was constructed by a company of American soldiers; the millwork had probably been executed at one of the Lake ports.

In the southwest is the Brisbois house, built in 1815 by one of the first white settlers of Prairie du Chien. This simple two-and-one-half story building, with gable roof and a wooden porch at the front, is the oldest stone house in the State. Fort Crawford (1816), one of three forts built by Americans early in the century, was a bare, low, rectangular structure with a surrounding open porch. The Florentine Dominican, Samuel Mazzuchelli, is important in southwestern Wisconsin history both as a missionary and as an architect. In 1831 he built his first Wisconsin church at Green Bay. Later, when stationed in the lead region, Mazzuchelli built stone, brick, and frame churches at Prairie du Chien, Burlington, Shullsburg, and Sinsinawa; in addition he made plans for the Saint Clara College of Sinsinawa.

The character of most early Wisconsin houses was largely determined by the materials that could be obtained near by. While an architect might have balked at the severe limitations, the settler-builders were concerned mainly with adequate shelter. As a result their dwellings were simple and integral with the landscape. Among the poorer inhabitants during the first part of the nineteenth century log cabins were most common. Set in pine and hardwood forests, they afforded a tolerable protection against the elements. They had roofs of shakes, rough shingles slabbed with a broad-ax; the chimneys, which sometimes occupied all of one side of the house, were made of field stones and clay; the thick walls were chinked with moss, chips, and clay or mortar. Since glass was a rare commodity in the backwoods, windows were covered with shutters, oiled skins, or paper. The inside walls were left rough, and the floors were laid with puncheons, logs split in two with the rounded side down. If the settler brought no furniture with him, he built a few stools and benches of wood and laid boards over two of the provision barrels for a table. Later, as his needs and resources increased, he added lean-to's, wings, another story, or perhaps an entire cabin to the original structure, and it was not uncommon for him to cover the outside of the building with boards.

Until late in the nineteenth century schoolhouses were almost always constructed of logs, especially those in the interior of the State, and many communities could not afford frame or brick churches. With the advent of towns, roads, and stage coaches some pioneers established inns to accommodate the ever increasing number of travelers. Until around 1840, when lumber from mills became more available, most of these were log buildings a story and a half high. A number of log houses remain from those days, though the forests of which they seemed a part are gone and even the contours of the surrounding land have been changed. Among these are the Christian Turck house (1830) near Kirchayn, Washington County, the Deleglise house near Antigo, the Jorgenson house, Vermont township, the Annen, Lappley, and Schopp houses of Springfield township, in western Dane County.

The Cornish miners, who came in the 1830's to the lead and zinc region of the southwest, were the first Wisconsin settlers to use stone houses extensively. Living where sandstone and limestone were accessible, they were able to build homes after the simple pattern of those in their native country. Their houses, usually two stories high, are rectangular, with sloping roofs, and a fireplace in each main room. On the principal façade the stone is laid in 15-inch courses, with side and rear of random ashlar. The walls, approximately 20 inches thick, provide deep reveals at the doors and windows. Floors are of pine boards varying in width, laid over log or sapling joists that have been evened on one side. Like the log cabins, these small squat dwellings were designed mainly to serve as shelters. Their simplicity precluded the confusion and faults of later periods, and they fit well into the surrounding countryside.

The poorest inhabitants of the cleared prairie lands first lived in sod huts, but most of the Yankees who came to Wisconsin had enough money for more adequate dwellings. The first cabins of the plains were of dressed logs neatly pointed up with mortar; they had floors of sawed boards, and glass in the windows. But the settlers were dissatisfied with these homes and soon replaced them with buildings of wood brought from the new lumber mills. Most of these were two stories high, with separate rooms, two fireplaces, and heavy well-constructed doors, staircases, and cellars; many had porches on two sides of the house. Though the original structures lacked the grace of many New England homes, often their lines became less harsh with the addition of wings and lean-to's. When new frame houses were built they followed the L-shape of the enlarged older houses.

The early builders in the Fox and Rock River valleys, the Madison, and the Lake Michigan coastal regions used native stone with considerable originality. In valleys and on hillsides they set up houses that fitted with the white, yellow, and gray outcroppings of Cambrian and Niagara formations. The William T. Bonniwell house, between Thiensville and Cedarburg, built in the late 1830's, is made of stone plastered over and carefully scored. The mantel, staircase, and other woodwork were fashioned by hand. This remarkable backwoods house, now dilapidated, apparently followed the Italian Renaissance style. Three miles southwest of Big Bend, Waukesha County, is the 1848 Jessie Smith Cobblestone Inn, a popular tavern during stagecoach days. The thick walls are of small varicolored field stones; the interior is especially interesting for its array of cabinets, cupboards, and fireplaces.

Builders soon began to make use of the brick clay beds found in many parts of the State. In 1840 the first brick house was finished at De Pere. Farm and village buildings in north and central Wisconsin were constructed of local red brick. Along the east coast cream-colored brick was popular, especially in Milwaukee, which came to be known as the Cream City. For some decades cream brick was a common material for churches, homes, office buildings, breweries, and factories. Most of these buildings are now gloomy and black with soot. The most notable old brick structure in Racine is the 1851 Presbyterian Church. Designed by the architect Lucas Bradley, it shows refinement and excellence of proportion and bears a marked resemblance to work of Christopher Wren. In the southwestern part of the State are numerous houses constructed of red brick that was brought up from St. Louis by riverboat.

About the middle of the century Wisconsin took up the Greek Revival movement that had started earlier in the eastern States. Many ambitious houses were built with temple façades. The majority of the builders had received their training in the East and undoubtedly had access to such handbooks as those of Asher Benjamin and Minard

Lafever. A typical Greek Revival building is Luther Hall, Burlington, with its four front columns and walls of variegated stones over which several coats of plaster have been applied. The 1859 Iowa County Court House at Dodgeville, rectangular and built of limestone, is among the finest structures of this period. The axes of the corner columns in the front of this building have been tilted subtly to give a greater feeling of solidity. The Court House is an example of the taste of the Southerners who settled in the lead region.

During the decade 1850-60 yellow sandstone houses began to appear in the central southern section, and these soon became distinctive of Wisconsin architecture. The Cornish miners had used native limestone, but with less originality than did the builders of these new homes. The stone was quarried crudely from near-by ledges, and the settlers seemed to know that its endurance depended upon laying it in the same position it had had in the ground; many of the houses are still in good condition. Harmony with the landscape was achieved by the use of L-shaped structures with three roof levels. The walls were extremely thick, the windows tall and narrow, with deep reveals; the rooms were high-ceilinged and spacious, with large stone fireplaces, concealed stairways, pine paneling, and hardwood floors.

Sandstone houses were also numerous in the cities, especially in Madison and Milwaukee. In Madison a fine yellow sandstone was common. Often the buildings were elaborately decorated, but some of the best were rather simple, relying on the quality of the stone to produce a pleasing effect. Among these are North and South Halls on the University campus, the Dudley house (present German Club), and the City Hall. Age and weather have had no ill effect on their outer walls. During the latter half of the century brownstone was the fashion for the elaborate and stately mansions of the well-to-do. It was this Cambrian sandstone, quarried in the Lake Superior region, which was extensively exported to Boston, New York, and other eastern cities, giving its name to the houses of an era. Typical of the public buildings of the time was the old brownstone Milwaukee Court House (1870), designed by L. A. Schmidtner in heavy Italian Renaissance style.

During the period of building activity that began around 1880 many public and business buildings were erected in a variety of European styles. Houses were decked out with meaningless pinnacles and lush ornamentation. The results of this heydey of eclecticism can best be seen in Milwaukee, especially along Prospect Avenue, where dozens of ponderous imitations were built. As in other States, the Columbian Exposition of 1893 had a strong influence in Wisconsin. Most of the banks, libraries, and post office buildings of the period were patterned after the ornate neo-classic buildings of the Exposition, with their columns, pediments, elaborately molded classical cornices, and domes. The Milwaukee City Hall (1895), designed by Koch and Esser, is in modified Flemish Renaissance style. Set at a convergence of streets, the building is in the form of a triangle, with a high stone bell tower rising at the front. The lower stories are constructed of granite and limestone, the upper of pressed brick and terra cotta. The present State Capitol at Madison (1907), the most expensive building in Wisconsin, was designed by J. B. Post and Sons, New York City. It is in mixed French and Italian Renaissance style, with four wings containing offices, and a heavy dome rising above the center. That the influence of the Exposition has been kept alive well into the century may be seen in the Milwaukee County Court House (1931), a massive structure designed by Albert Randolph Ross on which the influence of classical architecture weighs heavily.

The movement to break away from the eclectic styles of the so-called Carnegie era in order to create a more indigenous architecture centered around Frank Lloyd Wright, the internationally famous architect born at Richland Center and now living near Spring Green. Wright's teacher, Louis Sullivan of Chicago, the first strong critic of the period of classical imitation, designed three Wisconsin buildings— Das Deutsche Haus, Milwaukee (1890), the Bradley House (now Sigma Phi House), Madison (1909), and the Merchant's Union Bank, Columbus (1919). Around the turn of the century Wright designed several buildings at Lake Delavan, Hillside, and Madison. But the greater number of his patrons were in Illinois, especially at Oak Park, where he erected the best examples of his early "prairie architecture," with their horizontal lines and extending roofs, believed by Wright to be appropriate for the Midwestern landscape.

In 1906, at a time when buildings were laden with ornament, Wright erected the largest of his early structures, the straight-lined, efficient Larkin Administration Building in Buffalo, New York, the first office building in the United States to use magnesite as a building material. The Imperial Hotel of Tokio (1920) is one of Wright's finest achievements in architecture and engineering. It is a low building with predominant horizontal lines and planes handled with skill and variety. So that it would be earthquake proof, the hotel was set on long piles and sunk into its 60-foot bed of mud.

Taliesin (1925-6), Wright's present home near Spring Green, is a low spacious house closely following the contours of a hill. It is built of brown stucco and of limestone that was quarried near by. As Wright has written, it is "an example of the use of native materials and the play of space relations, the long stretches of low ceilings extending outside over and beyond the windows, related in direction to some feature in the landscape." Some distance away on the 200-acre tract stand the workshop and playhouse, where students of the Taliesin Fellowship do much of their work (*see Tour 20*).

Recently constructed at Racine, the S. C. Johnson Administration Building is among Wright's most ambitious works. It is a low red-brick structure, complex but unified. The plain rear wall is broken at one end by a car entrance; on the roof a narrow bridge leads to an open squash court. In the center of the building two "nostrils" are designed to draw in air for ventilating; lighting is secured by means of glass tubes stretched around the sides of the building. A circular pattern is carried out, from ground floor to roof, in the 20-foot concrete units supported by dendriform columns. These columns, narrowing to 9 inches at the base, though able to hold upwards of 60 tons give the interior an appearance of grace and lightness.

Most of Wright's clients have been able to pay .the cost of the architect's ingenuity, but the Herbert Jacobs home, outside of Madison, finished in November 1937, is an experiment under stricter cost limitations. Flat and L-shaped, it is constructed of red brick, natural-finished wood, and fibre board. The principal façade is plain, except for a narrow band of windows near the roof, with an entrance and car shelter at one end; in the rear the glass doors of the living room and the bedrooms open into a garden. Excessive heat, light, and rain are intercepted by a low, extending roof. The living room is amiable and well-lighted; plain waxed-wood bookshelves extend along one wall, and there is a brick fireplace simple and pleasing in design. The Jacobs house is one of the first houses in the modern world to use integral heating, the pipes being laid in a bed of gravel under the concrete floor.

Wright's work is essentially simple but is never merely the result of leaving off ornament. His buildings are all designed for specific localities and planned as an integral part of the landscape.

Examples of sound and original modern architecture are not numerous among the private residences built during the last few decades, most of these homes being variations of Colonial or other styles. But there are a few younger men in Wisconsin who have based their work on contemporary architectural theories. Hamilton Beatty, Allan Strang, and William Kaeser have built a number of houses in or near Madison. George Frederick Keck, now practising in Chicago, has designed houses at Watertown and Madison. His glass and steel "House of Tomorrow," designed for the Century of Progress Exposition, was partly inspired by the Octagon House of Watertown. Most of the work of these men is severe in design and bears more resemblance to contemporary European architecture than to that of Wright.

Recently attempts have been made to simplify the architectural styles of public buildings. The Chicago firm of Holabird and Root has designed a number of buildings in the State, the best of which, perhaps, is the well-designed and efficient A. O. Smith Research Building in Milwaukee, wherein glass is freely used for lighting and for wall material. The Federal Forest Products Laboratory, occupying a broad open area in Madison, is convenient and highly modern, though slightly mechanical in conception. Tiers of windows stretch along the lower stories; the higher central part, deeply set in from the lower walls, contains windows arranged vertically and trimmed with aluminum-covered wood. The Racine County Court House, designed by Hola-bird and Root, represents another departure in civic architecture. The simple front façade is varied by stone carving; the predominantly vertical lines of the structure produce a pleasing effect. Another excellent modern building is the Sheboygan County Court House, designed by W. C. Weeks.

There have been two recent experiments in low-cost housing in Wisconsin. Parklawn, Milwaukee, consisting of 518 living units, is a purely urban housing development of the United States Housing Administration. Greendale, near Milwaukee, is one of the three Green-belt towns of the Resettlement Administration. It consists of 572 dwelling units—in detached, semi-detached, and group houses—occupying a site of 3,410 acres. These two settlements are important as experiments in town planning, though perhaps not equally significant architecturally. The houses are constructed of cinder-concrete blocks and other durable materials, but scarcely differ in style from those of an ordinary residential district.

Wisconsin, being a highly agricultural State, has had to meet the problem of rural as well as of urban building. The houses on farms have not differed greatly from those in the towns; they are constructed of wood, brick, or stone after the same general patterns, though the addition of wings and lean-to's has been more common in the country. On the whole, farm dwellings are older in style, but the number of modern rural homes is increasing. Often these are Tudor or Colonial adaptations stylistically indistinguishable from those of the city.

The structure of the agricultural buildings has been dictated almost entirely by functional considerations. The earliest silos, used first in Europe and the eastern States, were simply a type of trench. Soon after 1882, the year of the report on silos by the United States Bureau of Agriculture, the first cylindrical silo was demonstrated in Wisconsin.

With the increasing importance of dairying as an industry in the State, it became necessary to plan buildings that would accommodate 15 to 100 animals. Problems of feeding, ventilation, and temperature had to be dealt with in the most economical fashion. The high, long barn and the tall silo became familiar in the countryside. In 1889 F. H. King, of the University of Wisconsin engineering department, designed the Wisconsin Round Barn, a type which is to be seen in almost every part of the State. It is a distinctly practical barn except for the fact that it cannot be expanded.

To allow for future expansion, the typical Wisconsin dairy barn is rectangular, two stories in height, with gambrel or straight-pitched roof. The first story, often constructed of stone when it can be obtained easily, houses the livestock and gives access to the silage. The second story is used for keeping grain and hay. It was the storage problem that determined the adoption of the basement barn, whose first story, set into a bank on the north side, gives a more even temperature, protects the stock from north winds, and facilitates the storage of hay since it is possible to drive into the second story from the ground level. A row of windows along the top of the first story in the south wall accents the long horizontal lines of the roof and of the junction between the first and second stories, particularly when these are of different materials. The method of enlarging a barn depends upon the contours of the land. It may simply be made longer; or a wing may be added to the south at the west end, which then acts as a windbreak against northwest winds. Appreciation of the value of light and sun in the dairy barn has resulted in a growing emphasis upon window space, and Wisconsin architectural engineers are now considering the practicability of glass bricks for walls.

PART II
Cities

Green Bay

Railroad Stations: Oakland Ave. Station, 6th and Oakland Aves. for Chicago, Milwaukee, St. Paul and Pacific R.R.; NE. corner Dousman and N. Pearl Sts. for Chicago and Northwestern Ry.; foot of W. Mason St. for Kewaunee, Green Bay, and Western R.R. and Green Bay and Western R.R.
Bus Station: 229 Main St. for Green Bay Stages, Grey Transportation Co., Cherry Transportation Co., Oneida and Seymour Bus Lines, Orange Line, and Shawano and Wausau Bus Line.
Airport: Brown County Airport, 1.5 *m.* S.W., at Ridge and 9th Sts.; no scheduled service.
City Busses: Fare 10¢. Three tokens for 25¢.
Taxis: Fare 10¢ to 25¢ within city limits.
Traffic Regulations: Regulation traffic lights in business district. Forty-five-minute parking limit from 9 a.m. to 7 p.m. in downtown section; two-hour limit in rest of business section; no overnight parking in any part of city; no U turns in downtown section.

Accommodations: Thirteen hotels; municipal tourist camp on US 41 between De Pere and Green Bay; tourist rooms in and near city.

Information Service: Association of Commerce, 206 W. Main St.

Radio Stations: WHBY (1200 kc.); WTAQ (1330 kc.).
Concert Hall and Motion Picture Houses: Columbus Club Auditorium, 115 S. Jefferson St.; four motion picture houses.
Swimming: Non-commercial pool, YMCA; Municipal Beach on Bay.
Golf: Municipal course 3 *m.* S. on State 57, 18 holes, greens fee, 40¢ for 9, 65¢ for 18 holes; municipal course in suburb of Shorewood, 18 holes, 50¢ for 9 holes, 25¢ for second nine.
Tennis: Municipal courts at East High School, 1415 E. Walnut St.
Professional Football: Green Bay Packers' Stadium, Walnut and Baird Sts., Sept.-Jan.
Fishing: Black bass, perch, herring, smelt, lake trout in the Bay.

Annual Events: Brown County Fair, last days of August.

GREEN BAY (590 alt., 37,415 pop.), the oldest settlement in the State, lies at the southern extremity of Green Bay, spread out along the east and west banks of the Fox River. Entered from either the south or the north, the city seems intensely industrial. A capacious harbor, open from April until December, allows the largest lake steamers to dock and empty their cargoes of coal, lumber, and steel. Long miles of railroad tracks and warehouses line the riverbanks; heavy smoke from paper mills rises above them; and during the day the bridges, connecting the east and west sections of the city are often raised high in the air in order to allow the bulky freighters to ply the river. The bayshore is sandy and vacant. Wild rice grows in the stagnant water along the beach, and terns, sandpipers, and migratory waterfowl find food and cover in the long swamp grass.

On the east bank of the river, near the mouth, is the main business district, where small, weatherbeaten wooden houses are crammed between tall office buildings, fashionable dress shops, and restaurants. South of this section, strung out in tended gardens, a few leading down to the river, and shadowed by long avenues of trees, are the spacious Victorian homes of the businessmen. Docks and mills line the west bank, and behind them, in rows of cottages and low houses, the factory workers live.

Descendants of the French, British, and Yankees, who first occupied the site, compose the majority of Green Bay's population. The workers in the mills and factories are for the most part native-born, children of the German, Belgian, Dutch, and Irish laborers who came to the city between 1870 and 1890. Only 2,742 of the total population are foreign-born; of these Germans, Belgians, and Polish are most numerous.

French *voyageurs* and *coureurs de bois,* roaming independently through the woods and streams of the Northwest, trading with the Indians, discovering new waterways without bothering to record them, probably knew of the site of Green Bay before 1634. But in that year Jean Nicolet, commissioned by Champlain, the Governor of New France, arrived at the *Baye de Puans,* and claimed the region in the name of the King of France, thus making it a recognized part of New France. In his account of the voyage Nicolet recorded that at a feast given here in his honor 120 beavers were the main course. For two hundred years fur, principally beaver, was accepted currency.

For a period of 30 years after Nicolet's exploration, very little attention was given to La Baye. Only after 1669, when Father Claude Allouez, Jesuit missionary, founded a mission, did La Baye and the Fox River become important. Allouez went up the Fox as far as Berlin, in Green Lake County; Marquette and Joliet, in 1673, penetrated the entire length of the Fox, crossed the portage, and found the way to the Mississippi. Thus a continuous natural waterway was charted between the St. Lawrence and the Gulf of Mexico, and La Baye, at the end of the Michilimackinac-Great Lakes waterway and at the entrance to the Fox-Wisconsin, became the natural trading center and rendezvous for everyone interested in the abundant furs of the Wisconsin region.

Indian villages were settled in and around La Baye; traders built log cabins along both banks of the river; missionaries, French soldiers, and *coureurs de bois* had temporary shacks along the river as far south as the present De Pere. The entire region became so significant in the French occupation of the Northwest that in 1684 Nicolas Perrot, one of the most brilliant men in Northwest history, was appointed commandant of the region of La Baye.

A crude frontier fort and trading post, built in the same year, served as his headquarters. As official representative of the French

Government, Perrot made alliances and trade treaties, settled inter-tribal disputes, and listened to the grievances of Indians and traders. His tact and knowledge of Indian ways and languages so won the trust and confidence of the Indians that in May, 1689, he was able to hold a great ceremony at Fort St. Antoine on the shore of the upper Mississippi River, formally declaring all the lands drained by the upper Mississippi the possession of the French Empire. From then until 1700 La Baye and the entire Fox-Wisconsin waterway was the most productive fur trade region in all of New France.

But by the end of the century French fur trade had diminished; Perrot was recalled to Canada, most of the trade licenses were revoked, and by 1703 the Fox Indian wars had begun. In 1716 the diplomatic policy of Perrot was abandoned for a military policy, and Sieur de Louvigny, sponsored by important fur companies in Canada, led an expedition of 500 against the warring Fox. To control the waterway and keep it open to trade Fort La Baye was built on the west bank of the river. In 1728 a second Indian war flared up and a second military expedition was sent to La Baye. When the French retreated they destroyed the fort. In 1733 the French officer, Coulon de Villiers, was killed by Black Bird, a Sauk chief, and a fort was again established. By 1740 the Fox had been intimidated and the fur trade flourished again.

The presence of the fort gave a new stability and permanence to the trading settlement. Instead of coming to the Bay in the spring, bartering with the Indians, and returning to Canada in the fall, traders began to build permanent establishments and homes, to cultivate the land for winter supplies, and to make marriage contracts with the Indians. As early as 1718 these settlers are mentioned, but the first settler of importance was Augustin de Langlade who about 1745 came from Mackinac and built a trading post on the east bank of the Fox River. Langlade's knowledge of the Indian languages, his gentility, honesty, and generosity soon won for him the complete support of the Indians and almost complete monopoly of their trade.

Around the Langlade family a genuine society grew, a patriarchy made up of Augustin, his son Charles, his sons-in-law, nieces, grand-daughters, and nephews. The Langlades, Grignons, and Porliers, all related to one another, controlled the trade and commerce of La Baye and the Fox River during the French and British regimes. They owned huge tracts of land that extended as far as Kaukauna, married into the Menominee tribe, and had a consistent policy of friendliness toward the Indians. The political and social affairs of the community were conducted by the families with justice and grace. And thus they managed to produce a self-contained community all but formally independent of the political and economic control of a distant French King.

Trade and commerce at La Baye continued in comparative peace and prosperity until the French and Indian War (1755-60), when the soldiers at the fort, Langlade, and some of the Indians went to the Ohio and Canada to help fight against the British. At the end of that period the British had gained control of the Northwest Territory, and in 1761 old Fort La Baye was occupied by British soldiers under the command of Lieutenant James Gorrell. Gorrell rebuilt the fort and named it Fort Edward Augustus. Although the French citizens continued to call the site La Baye, the British traders called it Green Bay, because the water and the shore assumed green tints very early in the spring. The old French title was gradually dropped and Green Bay became its permanent name.

In terms of trade and occupation the signing over of the Northwest Territory to the British had little effect on the French citizens of Green Bay. The British needed French help and cooperation, and the French tolerated the British because they needed British good-will. During the French occupation fur trade licenses had been few and issued only to select groups, but the British, trying to get as much wealth from the Northwest as possible, issued licenses freely, both to Britons and to the French. Even the Pontiac uprising of 1763 had slight effect on the settlement at Green Bay, beyond resulting in the abandonment of Fort Edward Augustus. The fur trade reached its height during the British regime; the first self-sustaining farms in the State were established (these were the French-Canadian "ribbon farms" that were as narrow as a city lot but extended from the river banks as far back into the wilderness as the owner wanted to cultivate); and a crude gristmill was set up. Between 1763 and 1780 Green Bay was a rich community, carrying on a lucrative business in trade, friendly with the Indians, producing its own foodstuff, building graceful cottages, and having dances and festivities.

In 1783 the Northwest Territory was officially declared the property of the United States, but French and British traders continued to trade and live there. Independent American traders who tried to share in the fur traffic met with difficulties on all sides. The French and British, once enemies, were now united against a new, common enemy. And although the United States government had nominal control of Wisconsin, the Americans were not to share fully in the fur trade until after the second war with England in 1812. In this war the citizens of Green Bay took commissions in the British forces and were greatly impoverished by the demands for food and supplies.

At the end of the war John Jacob Astor's American Fur Company, organized in 1808, gained control of the major portion of the trade. But the early French-Canadian settlers continued to occupy their homes, trade with the Indians, and be assigned deeds to large tracts of land by the Americans. Grignon, Lawe, and Porlier were such influential citizens that in 1815 Astor found it good business policy to form a trade association with them and make them agents for the American Fur Company. In 1816, partly because of Astor's demands for protection, military forts were built at the two ends of the Fox-Wisconsin waterway, Fort Howard at Green Bay, and Fort Crawford at Prairie du Chien. For another 20 years fur trade at Green Bay continued to flourish.

The completion of the Erie Canal in 1825 and the defeat of Black Hawk in 1832 combined to give impetus to the settlement of the West. Farmers from New England, hearing of the cheap, fertile lands in the West, began using the easy water transportation of the canal, the Great Lakes, the Bay, and the Fox-Wisconsin waterway. Green Bay again became an important port. As more and more of the Fox River and Bay region was settled, Green Bay developed as a trading center for this new population. The first crude gristmill was replaced by a flour mill, general stores were established, hotels and inns for the new arrivals were built along the riverbanks, domestic animals were bought and sold, passenger boats arrived daily, a permanent, reliable mail route was established, the Green Bay *Intelligencer*, the first newspaper in Wisconsin, began its weekly publication in December, 1833, by advertising the lands of the Green Bay region, and a land office was opened in 1834.

In 1829 Daniel Whitney, who had purchased land on the north end of the east bank, platted the first section of present Green Bay, naming it Navarino. In 1835 Astor platted his town on the south end of the east bank and built the Astor Hotel, flamboyantly advertised as "the largest hotel west of N. Y.," to attract settlers and speculators attending land sales. The land platted had originally belonged to Grignon, Porlier, and Lawe, but they had lost it to Astor through indebtedness. Whitney sold his claims at a moderate price, and the north section grew rapidly. But the growth of the south end of the city was retarded by the high prices Astor's company put on the claims. Though speculators did buy the claims, permanent settlers did not, and the "town of Astor" held back the settlement of Green Bay until 1857, when the hotel burned to the ground and the Astor Company relinquished its claims.

During the 1850's Germans, Belgians, Hollanders, and Scandinavian farmers settled in the region around Green Bay. The city soon became a farm market center. In this period, when Green Bay was developing as a wholesale and retail food center, pine lumber was in great demand. Consequently, while fur trading was almost entirely over, lumbering was fast taking its place. In 1854, the year Green Bay was incorporated, this description of the city was written: "The many mills in this vicinity make it a rendezvous for owners of mills and the large number of men engaged by them for the pineries. Men, oxen, horses, and provisions are here supplied. . . . There will be sawed by these mills, water and steam, the present year, 80,000,000 feet of pine lumber [which will employ] 1,500 men, 300 yoke of cattle and 100 span of horses."

As long as timber remained within hauling distance of Green Bay, sawed lumber was the main manufactured product. Wholesale and retail trade was next in importance; between 1873 and 1880 there was a fairly active iron furnace industry; in 1880 shipping and railroad transportation employed some 200 men. Except for the slump following the financial panic of 1873, Green Bay has experienced no serious setback in its growth. In 1880 the population jumped from 4,666 to

7,464; in 1890 it had reached 8,069; and by 1900 the population reached 18,684, owing to the importation of cheap labor by the lumber and railroad industries. Employment agents at New York met incoming Germans, Belgians, and Scandinavians and offered them two weeks' room and board and free transportation to the mills and factories in Wisconsin. Many of them settled in Green Bay.

By 1910 there were 102 manufacturing establishments producing paper and paper products, iron and steel, foods, and building materials. These industries still constitute the principal occupation of the wage earners of Green Bay. According to the 1930 census, four paper mills, manufacturing principally tissue paper, employ approximately 1,400 men and women; iron and steel plants employ 1,000 workers; the railroads employ 1,500 workers; and food plants employ 600 workers. One hundred and fifty million pounds of cheese, 75,000 tons of paper, and 30,000 tons of pulp are produced annually. These industries are supplemented by a large wholesale and retail trade engaging some 3,000 men and women.

POINTS OF INTEREST

1. The MORGAN L. MARTIN HOUSE (*private*), 1008 S. Monroe St., a white, one-and-a-half-story frame house set far back from the road, is the former home of Morgan L. Martin, prominent early citizen of Green Bay. Surrounded by a landscaped lawn and old elms, this American post-Colonial home with its colonnaded porches on street and river side, and its dormer windows, is one of the most charming houses on the Fox River. Born in New York and trained as a lawyer, Martin came to Green Bay in 1827. He was a member of the legislative council of the Michigan Territory in 1834, and president of the convention that drew up the Constitution of Wisconsin. He fostered the Fox-Wisconsin River improvement. When the project for the improvement of the waterway was finally decided upon, land along the river sold rapidly. Martin's home, built between 1837 and 1839, and known at the time as "Hazelwood," is on one section of the large tract that he purchased.

GREEN BAY. Points of Interest

1. Morgan L. Martin House
2. Site of Astor Place
3. Site of the First Bank of Wisconsin
4. Kellogg Public Library
5. Courthouse Square
6. Moravian Church
7. Site of The Sauk Indian Village
8. Green Bay Packers' Stadium
9. Northern Paper Mills
10. Fort Howard Hospital and Surgeon's Quarters
11. Site of Fort Howard Stockade and Parade Grounds
12. Roi-Porlier-Tank Cottage

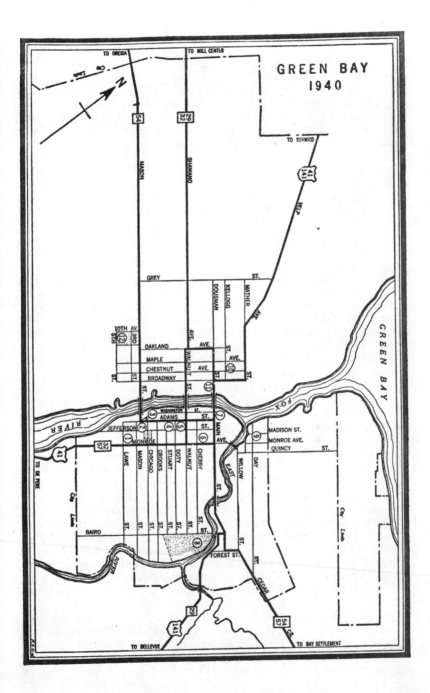

2. The SITE OF ASTOR PLACE, intersection of E. Mason, S. Washington, and Adams Sts., designated by a white wooden sign, is the location of the business section of the Town of Astor, platted in 1835. Here, before the American Fur Company bought the land, stood the first Catholic Church in Green Bay, the earliest in Wisconsin. In 1823 Father Gabriel Richard, Vicar Apostolic of the Northwest, began the construction of the church, and two years later Father Stephen Badin, first resident pastor and missionary, finished it. Slightly northeast of this area was the first Catholic Cemetery, used from 1735 to 1835.

3. The SITE OF THE FIRST BANK OF WISCONSIN, indicated by a bronze plaque on a building at the NW. corner, Chicago and S. Washington Sts., was part of the town of Astor. The business offices of the American Fur Company and the Astor trading house were in the bank.

4. The KELLOGG PUBLIC LIBRARY (*open 9-9 weekdays*), 120 S. Jefferson St., a two-story, gray stone building of neo-classic design with Ionic pedimented porticos, is noteworthy for its wealth of source material concerning the earliest days at La Baye and the frontier developments of the first city of Wisconsin. Attached to the south side of the library is the NEVILLE MUSEUM (*open 9-12, 2-5 daily*), one of the most outstanding local history museums in the country, containing such valuable pieces as Charles de Langlade's uniforms and journals, pictures of Indian chiefs and warriors, the china, glass, and furniture taken from the old homes of Green Bay, particularly from the Tank Cottage, the 22 self-portraits by George Catlin, coins, stamps, newspapers, Indian weapons and pottery, and a large natural history collection. Most important of the items is Nicolas Perrot's silver ostensorium, the oldest relic of the French regime in Wisconsin. Perrot presented the piece to Father Nouvel, of the St. Francis Xavier mission at De Pere, in 1686.

5. COURTHOUSE SQUARE, Walnut St. between Jefferson and Adams Sts., extending to Doty St., contains within its landscaped block the BROWN COUNTY COURTHOUSE, a three-story gray stone building with a red brick base, the POST OFFICE, constructed of the same materials and in the same neo-classic style, and the JAIL. At the SE. corner of the square, facing Walnut and Jefferson Sts., is the *Spirit of the North-West*, a seven-foot statue of gray granite, sculptured by Sidney Bedore, student of Lorado Taft, and resident of Suamico, a small village a few miles north of Green Bay. The three figures represent Nicolas Perrot, Father Claude Allouez, and a member of the Outagami tribe; they honor the three types of men who developed the great Northwest. The statue was purchased by Green Bay in 1931.

6. The MORAVIAN CHURCH, Cherry St. between Monroe and Madison Sts., a single-story, white frame church, reflects the simple austerity of the Moravian religion, first introduced here by Nils Otto Tank in 1850. Many of the Moravians, displeased with Tank's methods, removed to Ephraim in 1853. But those who remained, although

they discontinued the common ownership of land taught by Tank, continued to practice their religion.

7. The SITE OF THE SAUK INDIAN VILLAGE, Main and N. Washington Sts., is designated by a bronze plaque on the corner of the Beaumont Hotel. It was on this site that the French officer, Coulon de Villiers, and a number of other French soldiers were killed, in 1733.

8. The GREEN BAY PACKERS' STADIUM, Walnut and Baird Sts., is the playing field for the Green Bay Packers, one of the best known professional football teams in America, and a member of the oldest pro-football league in the country. The squad of 23 men, made up of football stars chosen from colleges all over the United States, is sponsored by a non-profit corporation. Every Sunday, from September to January, that the Green Bay Packers are playing a home game, this stadium, holding 22,500 spectators, is filled. In 1929, 1930, 1931, 1936, and 1939 the team won the world's championship in professional football, playing against such opponents as the New York Giants, the Brooklyn Dodgers, and the Chicago Bears.

9. The NORTHERN PAPER MILLS (*not open to public*), Day and N. Madison Sts., is one of the largest tissue mills in the country. Covering an area of some 100 acres along the shore of the Fox River and its small tributary, the East River, the mill is constructed of brick, steel, and concrete and includes a steam power and electric energy generating plant. The company has a steam freighter which every six days from April to November makes a trip to Lake Superior, bringing back 60,000 cords of spruce, balsam, poplar, and hemlock. The peeled logs are stacked in long, high piles in the yards, then power-cut into small chips and placed in high-pressure steam and chemical cookers where they are converted into pulp. The pulp, reduced to the proper consistency, is run out over sheets of wire screen, which drain off the excess moisture from the pulp and give it tensility; from there it goes through a long battery of steam-heated dryer rolls. The paper comes out of the machines in large, wide rolls called parent or jumbo rolls, and is then sent into the converting department where it is cut, embossed, and folded into paper napkins, toilet tissue, and paper towels. The quality of the product depends upon the amount of pure cellulose in the wood and the chemicals and other treatment to which it is subjected. Spruce produces the highest grade of paper. The Northern Paper Mills employs about 600 workers, has five paper machines, uses nearly 130,000 cords of lumber annually, and produces approximately 125 tons of paper a day. It is a self-contained mill, manufacturing its own pulp and paper and converting it into the finished and packaged merchandise.

10. The FORT HOWARD HOSPITAL AND SURGEONS' QUARTERS (*open 10-5 daily; adm. 25¢*), N. Chestnut and Kellogg Sts., is a white frame structure designed in the post-Colonial style. Erected in 1816 by a company of American soldiers to house the surgeons, patients, and some officers of the fort, it is now the only remaining building of the dozen odd that once stood on the west bank of the

river. Constructed of logs and later clapboarded, the building appears very much the way it did when occupied by the American soldiers. The hospital was placed outside the picketed enclosure of the fort, and was for a time the only hospital for the entire community. Its wide soft-wood board floors and large stone fireplaces, spacious rooms, dormer windows, and delicate floral wallpaper are characteristic of the nineteenth century period. The redecorated interior contains many of the original pieces of furniture that the young officers brought to the fort from their homes in the East. Beds, desks, rugs, and curtains of the same period have been added.

11. The SITE OF FORT HOWARD STOCKADE AND PARADE GROUND, foot of Dousman St. Bridge, near Chicago and North Western Ry. Depot, is marked by a white flagpole. This was the site of the first crude fort, built in 1684. In 1717 the fort was rebuilt and called St. Francis. It was evacuated in 1760 and then occupied by the British forces from 1761-63. It was occupied again on the arrival of the American troops in August 1816. By the spring of 1817 Fort Howard was completed. The soldiers cut the logs, erected the buildings, planted vegetable gardens and fields of grain, and built the high stockade. The buildings were painted white; at the four corners of the log stockade there were tall blockhouses, each containing a small cannon.

12. The ROI-PORLIER-TANK COTTAGE (*open 10-5 daily; adm, 25¢*), 10th Ave. and 5th St., is the oldest house standing in Wisconsin. The graceful lines of the structure, the absence of superficial decorations, the simple, functional details of the doors, windows, and chimneys are characteristic of the type of architecture used by early fur traders in the Northwest. Today the exterior of the house, consisting of a main central portion and added wings, is a more finished structure than it was in 1780; the interior retains a nice balance in the divisions of rooms and the slim French windows. The central section is built according to a wattled type structure used frequently in early French-Canadian homes. Roughly sawed uprights were planted in the ground, boughs, withes, and twigs were woven between the supports, and the whole was plastered with clay or mud.

The middle section of Tank Cottage, built in 1776 by Francis Roi, an early French trader, was originally on the west bank of the Fox River, close to the edge of the water. In 1805 Judge Porlier bought the property and made it his residence. During the War of 1812 English officers gathered here for conferences. At this time the house was a small cabin, two rooms and an entrance and stairway downstairs, a rough fireplace at one end of the living room, and two bedrooms, store-room, and small bathroom upstairs. The windows were protected by heavy wooden shutters. In 1850 Nils Otto Tank, a Norwegian and the leader of the Wisconsin Moravians (*see Tour 1B*), bought the property, covered the rough interior and exterior of the house with clapboarding, plastered the inside walls, painted the wide softwood floors black, and added a wing on either side. The one to the right was 14 feet wide and ran the length of the entire side of the house. This was the meeting place and prayer room of the Moravians. The left wing was the dining room and kitchen. From Holland, the home of Tank's wife, came many beautiful furnishings, china, pottery, linen, glass, and copper, spelter, and pewter utensils.

After the death of Mrs. Tank, the house was sold to the Rice Box Company, which later deeded it to the South Side Improvement Association and the Green Bay Historical Society. They moved it to its present site and furnished it with many of the original articles belonging to the Tanks.

POINTS OF INTEREST IN ENVIRONS

Stone Lighthouse (1848), on Tail Point in the Bay, 3 *m.;* Red Banks, 7 *m.* (*see Tour 1*); Fort Howard Cemetery, 2 *m.;* State Reformatory, 3 *m.;* Duck Creek, 4 *m.* (*see Tour 2*).

Kenosha

Railroad Stations: 5410 13th Ave. for Chicago & North Western Ry.; 2703 63rd St. for Chicago, North Shore & Milwaukee R.R.; 800 55th St. for The Milwaukee Electric Ry. & Transport Co., interurban.
Bus Stations: 617 57th St. for Greyhound Lines; 800 55th St. for Chicago & North Western Stages and Wisconsin Motor Bus Lines.
Airport: Kenosha Municipal Airport, 0.6 *m.* S. of city limits on 22nd Ave., taxi fare 50¢; no scheduled service.
Trackless Trolleys: Fare 7¢.
Taxis: Fare 25¢ single, 5¢ each additional passenger within city limits.
Traffic Regulations: No left turn off 6th Ave. in downtown area; no U turns in downtown area.

Accommodations: Three hotels; tourist homes.

Information Service: Chamber of Commerce, U. S. Nat'l. Bank Bldg., 625 57th St.

Motion Picture Houses: Six.
Athletics and Recreation: Lakefront Stadium, 58th St. and lakefront for track meets, football, city celebrations, etc.; Washington Bowl, Washington Park, 22nd Ave. and Washington Blvd. for bicycle races; Lincoln Park, 68th St. and 18th Ave., for tennis, boating, softball, football, picnicking.
Swimming: Alford, Pennoyer, Simmons' Island, and Southport Parks, Lincoln Park.
Tennis: Municipal courts at Washington, Pennoyer and Simmons' Island Parks.
Golf: Municipal course at Washington Park, 22nd Ave. and Washington Blvd., 9 holes, greens fee 15¢; Petrifying Springs Park Golf Course, 4 *m.* W. on State 43 then County H, 18 holes, greens fee 25¢ for 9 and 50¢ for 18 holes.

Annual Events: Annual horse show, June; Flower show, June and Sept.; Amateur Bicycle Races, during summer; Road Race Thanksgiving Day.

KENOSHA (612 alt., 50,262 pop.), a highly industrialized city in southeastern Wisconsin, lies along the shore of Lake Michigan north and south of the point where Pike's Creek enters the lake. Compact and trim, its streets running in an orderly fashion, Kenosha spreads out across the flat level of the land, broken only by the narrow, slow creek widening into a small harbor at its center. One factory stands on the harbor's edge, a long, dark building shadowing the yacht club basin, where slim sailboats and fishing dories anchor side by side. The long lakefront is a series of pleasant green parks that overlook wide waters and the passing bulk of freighters and steamers. On misty days the sound of a foghorn cuts through the air, and the smoke from tall factory smokestacks hangs low over the city.

The costly homes in deep gardens along 3rd Avenue near the lakefront reflect the prosperity of Kenosha. North of the creek and back from the lake parks are the substantial and neat homes of the Italian workers employed in the large factories. In their own business sections there are small wooden flower stalls, restaurants, and cafes. The main business district consists of a few blocks along 6th Avenue in the mid-town area and branches west and north beyond the bridge. West of it, covering five blocks, stands the formally landscaped Civic Center. Beyond are the long, even blocks of tree-lined residential streets.

Kenosha, an industrial town manufacturing such products as machinery, autos, beds, and hosiery, has a population derived largely from the immigrant factory workers who came here in the 1900's. More than 64 per cent of the people are foreign-born or of foreign-born or mixed parentage. Of these, Germans, Italians, and Poles are the most numerous.

Kenosha began modestly and grew without spectacular changes. In December, 1834, the Western Emigration Company was organized at Hannibal, Oswego County, New York, for the purpose of settling a colony on land in the newly opened West. Shares sold for $10, and representatives were sent to purchase sites on the western shore of Lake Michigan, then considered the most desirable section of Wisconsin. The buyers found the price for land too high at Milwaukee, failed to negotiate at Racine, and made no purchase. The agents having returned East, the company then appointed John Bullen, Jr., as its sole agent. In June, 1835, Bullen arrived at the mouth of the Pike River. Wider and deeper than it is now, the river had two outlets a mile apart. The southern outlet was called Pike Creek, and Bullen, seeing the possibility of creating a lake port at the latter site, claimed land there.

Eight New York families came to Pike Creek in the summer of 1835, settling either as farmers in the fertile country beyond the lake plain or as the first members of a new village lying along the small harbor. The financial failure of the Western Emigration Company in the first winter left no organization to settle land claims between the rival squatters, and many disputes occurred. One reputed claim jumper awoke one morning to find that the vengeful villagers had fenced him into a single acre during the night. Another settler found a field of young corn growing where no corn had been visible the day before; he was able to prove that the corn had been transplanted during the night by a rival claimant. Events such as these resulted in the formation of a Pike River Claimants' Union in February 1836, with a board of arbitration that assumed local jurisdiction. Soon this union merged into the larger Milwaukee Claimants' Union.

By the fall of 1836 the best prairie groves of the surrounding country were occupied by New England farmers. Wheat was then the most marketable crop, and the prairies and meadows were quickly plowed and planted to it. Timber in this area was scattered and difficult to transport; consequently, the new farmers had to buy sawed lumber for their homes and farm buildings. The villages of Racine and Pike Creek competed for this commerce—wheat to be exported by the lake steamers to the East, lumber to be imported into the new West. But the first cargo-bearing boat that arrived at the Pike River, in July, 1835, was unable to dock. The water was so rough and the channel so uncertain that the lumber had to be thrown overboard, floated to shore, and there picked up by the anxious villagers. During the next few years passengers from steamboats had to be brought to shore in small scows or lighters; whole cargoes were occasionally ruined i. storms; valuable commerce in wheat and lumber was lost because Pike Creek had no suitable harbor. Aroused by the urgent need for a harbor, in 1837 the 150 citizens of Pike Creek raised money to send a representative to Washington to ask for Federal appropriations for dredging the creek. Although he failed, Pike Creek hopefully changed its name to Southport and continued to man the lighters every time a steamer made its appearance.

The village grew very slowly; in 1840 its population was only 337. In 1842, B. F. Cahoon, at his own expense and despite the ridicule of rival towns, completed a wharf that reached some distance out into the lake, at which boats and steamers could dock. This and subsequent piers allowed Southport to share in the exportation of wheat and lead and the importation of lumber. That year marked the upturn in Southport's growth; by 1843 the population had increased to 1,132, and in the same year 165 buildings were erected.

The early settlers, largely Americans of the third and fourth generation, had practical training in the Eastern tradition of free schools, community cooperation, and political action. Besides launching Wisconsin's first literary magazine, the *Garland of the West and the Wisconsin Monthly Magazine,* they agitated for free public schools. When C. L. Sholes, the man who later invented the typewriter, brought a printing press from Green Bay in 1840 and became the editor of the Southport *Telegraph,* Colonel Michael Frank used the paper to campaign for free schools. A bill introduced in the Territorial legislature in 1844 failed, but next year a law was passed giving Southport the authority to tax itself for the establishment of a free school within its corporate limits, provided that the Territorial legislature's enabling act was approved by a majority of Southport voters. After a number of stormy meetings the voters accepted the authority to tax; however, no adequate levy was made until 1849. In that year the first free public school in Wisconsin was established at Southport.

Another social experiment was the chartering of the Wisconsin Phalanx under the leadership of Warren Chase. At one of the weekly meetings of the Franklin Lyceum, an editorial in the New York *Herald Tribune* urging the formation of a colony patterned after Fourier's socialism was the point of debate. The young intellectuals took enthusiastically to the idea and in May, 1844, formed the Wisconsin Phalanx, sold stock at $25 a share, and organized a party to claim land in the northwestern section of Fond du Lac County. On May 20, 1844, nineteen men and one boy left Southport and settled in what is now the first ward of Ripon, naming their settlement Ceresco (*see Tour 5A*).

The year 1844 marked the beginning of a number of Federal appropriations for harbor improvements: $12,500 in 1844; $15,000 in 1845; $10,000 in 1852. With each successive appropriation the volume of export and import business increased. The wheat export increased from 71,000 bushels in 1842 to 1,003,992 bushels in 1855. Lumber was still the chief import, averaging approximately 3,000,000 feet a year in the 1850's. But still the growth of Southport was slow. For although Irish, English, and German immigrants had increased the population to 3,455 in 1850, and the harbor was bringing valuable trade, compared with cities such as Madison, Milwaukee, Racine, and Oshkosh, Southport was backward. The completion of the Lake Shore R. R. through the city in 1855 had the immediate result of suddenly increasing harbor traffic; it was only later that the railroad stripped the harbor of its usefulness. But for all the improvements and the general civic concern for lake commerce, Southport's harbor was small and dangerous compared with the Milwaukee and Racine harbors; consequently, relatively small amounts of merchandise came to its port.

In 1850 Southport changed its name to Kenosha (Ind., pike or pickerel), was incorporated as a city and made the seat of the newly created Kenosha County. During the few years following 1850 political and religious refugees from Germany came to Wisconsin, and some settled in Kenosha. Their influence, combined with that of the Easterners who had first settled here, kept the city alive with lyceums, lecture courses, and partisan discussions of the controversies of the day. Many families subscribed to four or five newspapers and pamphlets, liberal social measures were freely advocated, and the anti-slavery doctrine was almost universally accepted. Prominent citizens, workers, and seamen were united in forming a Kenosha station of the Underground Railroad.

By 1884 the Federal Government had appropriated $215,307 for the improvement of the harbor, and lake commerce was still the most important activity of the city. The type of merchandise exported and imported had changed slightly; wheat by 1860 had fallen off considerably; lumber imports increased; cheese, butter, beef, and eggs were exported, coal and stone imported. But by 1885, for all the continued improvements, the harbor activity had so diminished that receipts by boat were only 4 per cent of those by rail, and shipment only 1 per cent. Extensive manufacturing, later to become the means for the life and growth of the city, was limited to two factories, the Allen Tannery and the Bain Wagon Works, both established before 1870, although in 1870 there were 40 or 50 shops and small factories operating in the city. But the decade between 1890 and 1900 marked the beginning of large-scale manufacturing and the sudden rise of Kenosha as an important city in Wisconsin.

The removal of the Chicago Brass Company to Kenosha in 1886, the expansion of the present Simmons Company from a small cheese box factory to the Northwestern Wire Mattress Company, and the founding of the Chicago and Rockford Hosiery Company in 1893 established Kenosha as a manufacturing center. By 1900 the population had risen from 6,532 to 11,606 with over 3,000 persons engaged in industry. In the same year the Thomas B. Jeffrey Company, makers of Rambler bicycles, was added to the growing list of factories. By 1910 the population almost doubled, reaching 21,371, and a third of the people worked in the plants. In large part the increase was due to the immigration of Italians and Poles, and smaller numbers of Lithuanians, Russians, Czechs, and Bohemians, who had been establishing themselves in Kenosha between 1895 and 1910. The city rose from sixth to third place in the State as a manufacturing city.

In 1915 Charles W. Nash bought the Thomas B. Jeffrey Company, and by 1920, when the population had reached 40,472, Simmons and Nash were each employing between 4,000 and 5,000 men. Among the cities in the State having 10,000 or more inhabitants in 1928, Kenosha ranked third in total value of products, third in pay roll, and fourteenth in the number of manufacturing establishments.

Before 1928 Kenosha had had a peaceful labor history, and wages averaged approximately $32 per week, but in February of that year a bitter strike began at the Allen A (silk hosiery) plant, which lasted 18 months. Labor lost the strike, and Kenosha remained an open-shop town. In the fall of 1933 the Wisconsin Workers' Committee was organized (*see Labor*). The next labor disputes occurred in 1933 and 1934 when Nash and Simmons workers struck. The strikers succeeded in gaining recognition of their union at Simmons and at Nash established one of the first auto-workers' locals. Union membership increased from 3,700 in the early 1930's, to a total of 9,000 in 1938 in the American Federation of Labor and the Committee for Industrial Organization together. Both organizations continue to act together in the Trades and Labor Council. Unionism is strong enough in Kenosha to support a weekly labor paper, Kenosha *Labor*.

In 1925 Kenosha won the State-wide "better cities contest," placing first in seven out of the ten points considered by the judges. The city-manager form of government, in which an elected council determines policies and an appointed manager executes them, has lowered the government cost and increased efficiency.

POINTS OF INTEREST

1. SIMMONS' ISLAND PARK reaches from the harbor north to 45th St. and from Lake Michigan west to the lagoons of Pike Creek. From the bridge that crosses the lagoons into the park there is a view of the harbor, with fishing boats and yachts, red sentinel lights, a shining white Coast Guard Station, and to the southwest the long buildings of the Simmons plant. The park itself is landscaped, sloping down to the wide, sandy beach of Lake Michigan. The MUNICIPAL BATH-HOUSE (*open 1-9:30 daily; adm. adults, 10¢, children free*), has a pavilion overlooking the lake. Life guards are on duty during the

open hours of the Bathhouse. On the wooded bluffs back from the lake are picnic tables, slides, swings, tennis courts, and basketball fields.

2. The SIMMONS COMPANY (*open by permission at office*), 55th St. and 5th Ave., is housed in a six-story, dust-darkened cream brick building overlooking the harbor and the lake. The main building and many wings occupy five square blocks. Founded in 1870 by Zalmon G. Simmons, the plant has grown until today it employs approximately 2,500 men at capacity production, manufacturing mattresses, springs, steel beds, steel furniture, and allied products.

3. LAKE FRONT PARK, 58th St. and Lake front, designed for use as a public recreation area, contains two football fields, softball diamonds, and a track field. The FIELD HOUSE, a one-story fireproof building of modern design, dedicated in July, 1936, was planned by Chris Borggren. The small STADIUM, of modern design, is used for high school meets, football games, and city celebrations. In 1937 Joe Louis trained here for his fight with Jim Braddock.

4. KEMPER HALL, 6501 3rd Ave., is an Episcopalian private academy for girls. The center building, constructed of cream brick and designed as a residence in the manner of the mid-nineteenth century townhouses of the East, was built in 1861 by Charles Durkee, who was one of the founders of Southport in 1835; served terms in the territorial legislature; Congressman 1849-1853; Senator 1855-1861; and in 1865 was appointed Governor of Utah Territory, serving in that capacity until his death in 1870. In 1865 it was sold on generous terms to the trustees of an association for the establishment of a school for young ladies. Founded by Bishop Armitage, in memory of Bishop Kemper, first Episcopalian Bishop of the Northwest Territory, the school graduated its first class in 1874. Since that time a gymnasium, chapel, and dormitory have been added. The average annual enrollment is 120 girls. The academy offers them high school and college preparatory courses.

5. The FIRST SOLDIERS' MONUMENT IN THE STATE is in Green Ridge Cemetery, Sheridan Road and 66th St., set about 100 yards back of the gate house in a plot surrounded by an iron railing. The simple stone shaft marks the grave of Captain Augustus Quarles, who commanded the only company from the Wisconsin Territory in the Mexican War, and was killed at the battle of Cherubusco. The monument, dedicated in 1848, was erected by the Legislature of the Wisconsin Territory, by the citizens of Southport, and by the relatives of Quarles.

6. LIBRARY PARK, 7th Ave. between 59th Pl. and 61st St., extending to 8th Ave., contains the GILBERT M. SIMMONS LIBRARY (*open 8:30-9 weekdays; 2-5, 7-9 Sun.*). Z. G. Simmons donated the funds for the construction of the library, and in May, 1900, the building was dedicated to his son. D. H. Burnham designed the building to conform to the architecture of the 1893 World's Fair. In neo-classic style, it is a low, one-story building with Corinthian columns and a dome, constructed of Bedford limestone. The LINCOLN MONUMENT,

NE. corner of the park, a bronze statue of Lincoln seated in a chair, was the gift of Orla Miner Calkins to the city in 1909, and is a replica of the monument, sculptured by Charles H. Niehaus, at Muskegon, Mich. The SOLDIERS' AND SAILORS' MONUMENT in the north section of the park, a granite Corinthian column with the figure of a winged victory on top, is dedicated to the Civil War veterans.

7. A BOYS AND GIRLS LIBRARY (*open 2-6 Mon.-Fri.; 9-12, 2-6 Sat.*), 5810 8th Ave., is housed in a grey stone Gothic Revival building, originally constructed in 1907 as a Unitarian church. In April, 1929, the church was dedicated for use as the only separate boys' and girls' library in the the State. Still retaining much of the mellow beauty of a church interior, the library has small children's tables and chairs, diminutive exhibits, and low book cases. This is one of the five branches of the Gilbert M. Simmons Library.

8. The CIVIC CENTER, Sheridan Road to 10th Ave. between 56th and 57th Sts., is a small green park covering one block, faced on four sides by public buildings. The KENOSHA HISTORICAL AND ART MUSEUM (*open May-Oct., 9-5:30 weekdays; Oct.-May, 9-9 weekdays, 1:30-5 Sun.*), west side of the square, a one-story ivy-covered building, constructed of Indiana limestone, with Ionic columns, contains one gallery for painting, sculpture, and photographic exhibits, another hall for science and history collections, including a permanent exhibition of sculpture by Lorado Taft, and an auditorium with a seating capacity of 250. Formerly the old post office, in 1934 the building was moved intact several blocks to its present location. It was opened for use as a museum Jan. 2, 1937. The KENOSHA COUNTY COURTHOUSE, north side of the square, contains the offices of Kenosha County and the KENOSHA COUNTY HISTORICAL MUSEUM (*open 8-5 weekdays*) in the Courthouse basement. A large, three-story limestone building, it is of Italian Renaissance design, with tall monolithic columns as the principal decoration. The firm of Lindle, Lesser and Schutte designed the building, and in 1925 the courthouse was opened for use. The central entrance lobby is decorated in Botticino marble and hand-wrought iron work. The murals on the dome and walls, depicting *Civil Law, Knowledge, Power, Mercy,* and *Force,* are the work of

---

KENOSHA. Points of Interest

1. Simmons' Island Park
2. Simmons Company
3. Lake Front Park
4. Kemper Hall
5. First Soldiers' Monument in State
6. Library Park
7. Boys and Girls Library
8. Civic Center
9. Site of First Free Public School in Wisconsin
10. R. H. Deming House
11. American Brass Company
12. Lincoln Park
13. Nash-Kelvinator Plant

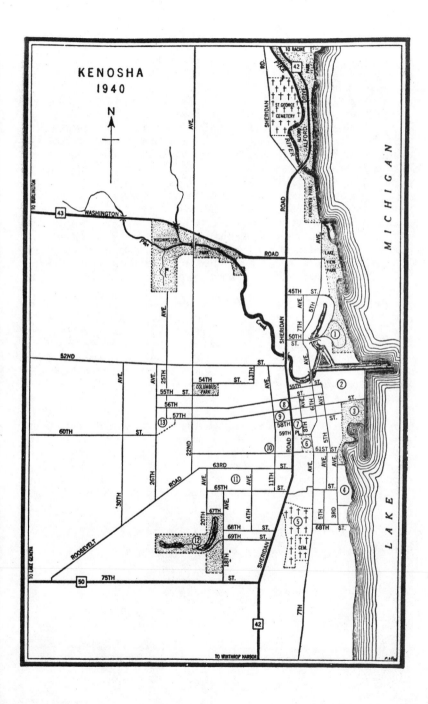

A. E. Foringer. The POST OFFICE, on the east side of the square, is a neo-classic structure of Indiana limestone, with Corinthian columns. It was planned under the supervision of James A. Wetmore and completed in 1932. The HIGH SCHOOL, in the same classic style, occupies the south side of the square.

9. A glacial boulder, NE. corner 58th St. and 11th Ave., marks the SITE OF THE FIRST FREE PUBLIC SCHOOL IN WISCONSIN.

10. REVEREND R. H. DEMING HOUSE (*private*), 1118 61st St., a two-story yellow frame house, formerly stood on the NE. corner 59th Pl. and 7th Ave. and was a station on the Underground Railroad during the 1850's.

11. The AMERICAN BRASS CO. (*open by special permission*), 1420 63rd St., formerly the Chicago Brass Company, and now a subsidiary of the Anaconda Copper Mining Company, occupies twelve blocks in the heart of the south side of Kenosha. A yellow-brick wall surrounds the two buildings, so that from outside only the gable roofs and tall smoke stacks can be seen. This plant, employing 2,000 men at capacity, manufactures brass, copper, nickel silver, and other copper bearing alloys, in the form of sheets, tubes, rods, wire, and extruded shapes.

12. LINCOLN PARK, 68th St. and 18th Ave., is traversed by LINCOLN DRIVE. The LINCOLN PARK BOTANICAL GARDENS are in the center of the park. Sometimes called the Sunken Gardens, they are reached by descending steps. On one side they are bordered by a low hill, on the other by a lagoon used for boating in summer and ice-skating in winter. Flowers are so arranged and placed that the garden is continuously in bloom throughout the warm months. In the western section of the park are the ROCK GARDENS.

13. The NASH-KELVINATOR PLANT (*tours 10-2 Mon.-Fri.; guides*), 57th St. and 25th Ave., the largest factory in the city, is the main plant of Nash Motors. Its low cream and red brick buildings are connected by a series of covered arcades and are spread out over an area of eight square blocks. The factory, containing a foundry and a drop forge plant, manufactures some parts for all the Nash factories. The Ambassador Model and all its parts are made in this plant.

POINTS OF INTEREST IN ENVIRONS

Petrifying Springs Park, 7.5 *m.*, on State 43, then County H.

La Crosse

Railroad Stations: 200 Pearl St., for Chicago, Burlington & Quincy R.R.; Andrew and Caledonia Sts., for Chicago, Milwaukee, St. Paul & Pacific R.R.; 301 Vine St., for Chicago & North Western Ry.
Bus Stations: 301 S. 4th St., for Northland Greyhound Lines; 601 N. 3rd St., for Mississippi Valley Public Service Co.
City Busses: Fare, 10¢.
Airport: La Crosse County Airport, 5 *m.* NW. on French Island; no scheduled service.
Taxis: Fare, 25¢ single, 5¢ each additional passenger within city limits.
Traffic Regulations: Regulation traffic lights in business district. Two-hour parking limit from 7:00 a.m. to 7:00 p.m. in business districts; no daytime limit in other sections; all-night parking prohibited in entire city.

Accommodations: Five hotels; tourist camp; tourist rooms and lodges in and near city.

Information Service: Chamber of Commerce, Stoddard Hotel, 4th and State Sts.; American Automobile Association, 3rd and State Sts.

Radio Station: WKHB (1380 kc.).
Theaters and Motion Picture Houses: State Teachers College Auditorium, seating 1,000, used by students and local organizations for concerts and conventions, and by traveling theatrical companies; Vocational School Auditorium, seating 1,294; Logan High School Auditorium, seating 1,006; 7 motion picture houses.
Swimming: Municipally owned swimming pool, within Fair Grounds, near Myrick Park.
Tennis: Fifteen tennis courts: three in Copeland Park, city-owned; two in Myrick Park, city-owned; six at State Teachers College (State-owned, but can be used by city people when students are not using them); two at playground, 14th St. and South Ave.; two at playground, 7th and Farnum Sts.
Golf: Colonial Golf Club, 0.8 *m.* S. of city limits on State 35, 9 holes, greens fee 25¢; La Crosse Golf Club, W. end of Gillett St. in North La Crosse, 9 holes, greens fee 25¢.
Riding: La Crosse Riding Academy, State Road, route 1.
Fishing: Pike, black bass, trout, crappie, pickerel, bullhead, sunfish, and other kinds of fish in rivers and creeks.

Annual Events: Western Wisconsin Music Festival, May; Pig Club Contest, June; Interstate Fair, August; City-county farm picnic, August; Western Wisconsin Teachers Convention, October; New Year's eve celebration, fire-works display on top of Grandad Bluff at midnight.

LA CROSSE (649 alt., 39,614 pop.), lies in the Coulee Region where the confluence of three rivers, the La Crosse, the Black, and the Mississippi, forms a natural port. From the summit of Grandad Bluff, highest of the massive crags that overlook the city and form its eastern boundary, La Crosse is seen 570 feet below, on a narrow oblong terrace, limited on the west side by the irregular shoreline of the Mississippi. On a clear day sections of three States are visible: western Wisconsin, Minnesota across the river, and Iowa 25 miles southwest. For miles above and below the city rise the palisades that line both shores of the Mississippi, which lazily winds its way southward between marshy islands.

From a warehouse and compact business section near the shore of the Mississippi, La Crosse expands inland toward the bluffs. On the outskirts, to the north and south, close to the city's tributary rivers and railroads, are scattered factories, mills, and some of the workers' homes. Red brick colors the older district—the warehouses, breweries, taverns, hotels, and some of the public buildings. Here streets are narrow and brick-paved. Homes are simple except for some pretentious red-brick mansions built in the seventies and eighties by wealthy lumbermen. In the newer residential section extending toward the bluffs, homes are set in wide shady lawns; streets are wider and better paved; maples, elms, and oaks arch many boulevards.

Though two-thirds of the people are foreign-born or have foreign-born or mixed parentage, few of the Old World customs are retained. Various racial groups maintain special religious congregations, such as the Irish, German, and Bohemian Roman Catholics, the German and Norwegian Lutherans, and the Syrian Greek Orthodox.

La Crosse started as a trading post in Indian territory. Trail and river led to the prairie, a favorite gathering place for Indians. Here the French occasionally stopped to trade with the encamped Winnebago, calling the site Prairie la Crosse for a game they saw Indians playing that reminded them of the French game *la crosse*. Indian trade likewise attracted the first permanent white settlers. On November 9, 1841, 18-year-old Nathan Myrick, a New Yorker, ascended the Mississippi in a government keelboat from Prairie du Chien, where he had purchased articles for trade and barter. He built a temporary shelter on Barron's Island (now Pettibone Park), but the next winter he hired H. J. B. Miller, who later became his partner, to move supplies and timber across the ice to the treeless prairie, and raised the first log hut and trading post on the present site of La Crosse. In the spring of 1844 they floated logs from the Black River pineries to La Crosse, sorted and rafted them, and sent them down river to St. Louis. The same year, Mormons settled in the fertile valley now named Mormon Coulee. Though the land was well adapted to farming, they found themselves at odds with other settlers and left the following year. When John M. Levy, a young English merchant from Prairie du Chien, disembarked with his wife from the small steamboat *Berlin* in 1846, "like Noah from the ark," followed by animals—"a horse, cow, dog, two cats, a whole family of hogs and a zip coon"—there were only a few rough claim shanties huddled on the water front, housing nine men and four women. Two years later, when the Government removed the Winnebago to Minnesota and with them the main source of the settlers' income, the settlement's white population was only 30.

These early traders exchanged blankets, trinkets, firearms, and some money for pelts which they shipped to Mississippi markets. Supplies came from Galena, Illinois, and the whistle of the approaching steamboat signalled the entire population, white and red, to hurry to the river front, bearing pails, pots, and pans in which to carry home food and other provisions.

The first and largest group of settlers in the early fifties came chiefly from New York, Ohio, and Vermont. Among them were shrewd and aggressive men who quickly recognized the commercial possibilities of the site, bought up land, erected saw and grist mills, and promoted the coming of the earliest railroads. Through their efforts Prairie la Crosse was made the county seat in 1851. The next year the first sawmill was built, the nucleus for the industry that developed the settlement for the next 40 years. The same year A. D. La Due, a printer, brought his hand press from Prairie du Chien and edited the first newspaper, *Spirit of the Times,* a Democratic weekly. This paper, advertising the advantages of Prairie la Crosse, was sent to friends and relatives in the East and abroad, and greatly stimulated settlement. In 1852 the first churches were organized, the Baptist and Congregational, though Episcopalians were credited with conducting the first complete religious service, an early morning communion service on Grandad Bluff. (Methodist records indicate that a Methodist circuit rider commenced a service here in the late forties only to be interrupted by the warning whistle of his arriving steamboat.)

During the fifties many German and Norwegian immigrants, among them skilled artisans and professional men forced by the revolutions of 1848 to leave their homelands, were attracted by the extensive La Crosse and Black River pineries. Germans, the first and largest group to arrive, in 1855 organized their *Turnverein,* which provided facilities for physical exercises and maintained a liberal forum through which were discussed the political and economic problems of the Fatherland and the newer issues of America. The following year the La Crosse *Maennerchor,* a German singing society, later known as the La Crosse *Liederkranz,* was organized. This organization also served as a social center for the Germans of the community.

In 1856 La Crosse, which had grown from a struggling frontier settlement with scarcely 100 inhabitants at the beginning of the decade to a bustling river port of 3,000, received its charter as a city, dropping "Prairie" from its name. But only the next year La Crosse experienced its first depression. Many of the pioneers had lost their farms and savings when the La Crosse and Milwaukee Railroad Company went into bankruptcy during the panic of 1857. At this time businessmen started an odd custom. Wearing high silk plug hats and Prince Albert suits, they warmly greeted newcomers who disembarked from steamboats; they sauntered around hotels and the water front, hoping by their conversation and opulent appearance to induce strangers to settle here.

In 1858, only three years before the Civil War, the La Crosse and Milwaukee Railroad was completed. The war closed traffic on the Mississippi River below the Ohio, diverting it into east-west directions. Thus La Crosse, which had direct communication with the East, became the natural outlet for a large section of western Wisconsin and the Northwest seeking new markets.

During the war Mark M. "Brick" Pomeroy, editor of the La Crosse *Democrat,* became a strong partisan of the Southern cause. City and county were largely northern in sympathy, and shortly after Lincoln's assassination an enraged mob, blaming Pomeroy for instigating Lincoln's murder, gathered with the intention of marching to the editor's home and hanging him to the nearest lamp-post. But there was a brewery on the way. The mob stopped to quench its thirst and forgot to go on. One of the editor's of Pomeroy's *Democrat* was Wisconsin's humorist, George W. Peck, author of *Peck's Bad Boy.* His own newspaper, *Peck's Sun,* was published at La Crosse before it was removed to Milwaukee. Later Peck was Milwaukee's mayor and Governor of the State.

One of the most significant developments during the war occurred in the realm of industrial relations. An editorial of 1860 told of the awakening self-consciousness of labor:

. . . the working men of La Crosse have done more than all the petty aristocracy that has ever existed here and will continue to do so. This will be more fully shown when the *unwritten* history of La Crosse shall be written out.

As migration increased, La Crosse became the most important center between Dubuque and St. Paul for men and supplies traveling toward new frontiers. Steamboat companies opened offices here to care for the enlarged traffic. The Northwestern Union Packet Company had gained control of the steamboat packet business of the upper Mississippi and in 1866 had its office and a large shipyard at La Crosse. Commodore W. F. Davidson and his associates became dominant figures in the steamboat industry and in the economic life of the city. One of the earliest strikes on the Mississippi occurred when Commodore Davidson refused to raise the pay of his deckhands. He went to Cincinnati where he hired 400 newly liberated Negroes as strike breakers. Wages were reduced, and white deck-hands were no longer hired. Trade unionization, however, continued in other industries.

The first railroad bridge, erected in 1876, enabled trains to cross the Mississippi. New railroads came, and at the end of the seventies, with five railroads radiating from it, La Crosse became the most important distribution point between St. Louis and St. Paul. With new markets available manufacturing increased, and in 1877 La Crosse was the second most important manufacturing city in the State. Lumber and sawmill products, flour, cigars, foundry and machine shop products, agricultural machinery, furniture, sashes, doors, blinds, beer and malt products were the leading manufactures. There were more than 20 wholesale houses for the distribution of drugs, furniture, dry goods, and fruit. The rapid increase in trade and manufacturing was reflected in the population, which during the seventies grew from 7,785 to 14,505.

The period from 1880 to 1905 saw the lumber industry swell and subside. In the eighties, while railroads were rapidly creating new markets for lumber and sawmill products, La Crosse grew into one of the large lumber centers of America. The industry reached its crest in 1892, but within seven years the forests were depleted. The decline was startling: there were 1,795 mill hands employed in 1899; 480 in 1900; 445 in 1903; and 34 in 1905.

La Crosse survived the shock of losing its foremost industry because other industries had developed with it. Four large breweries, which in 1884 manufactured more beer than those of any other city in the State, extensive plow works, furniture factories, agricultural implement factories, foundries, woolen mills, tanneries, a large pork packing plant, railroads, all these, still expanding, helped absorb the unemployed.

During this period numerous social, political, and cultural organizations developed in La Crosse. A "19th Century Club" discussed the problems of the day, such as "Pauperism and Its Remedy"; a Law and Order Society existed to enforce Blue Sunday legislation. La Crosse was a musical center in those days, and steamboats and railroads often brought large crowds from the surrounding territory to attend music festivals here. German *Saengerfeste* and concerts of the *Normanna Sangerkor,* the oldest Norwegian singing society in the United States, organized in 1869, attracted many visitors.

Today the leading products of La Crosse manufactories are rubber boots and shoes, gauges, agricultural implements, heating and air-conditioning equipment, and beer. Photographic film development is an important industry. La Crosse, the largest city between Madison, Dubuque, and St. Paul, is a natural trading and shipping center for a rich and extensive agricultural area.

The Federal Government is creating a nine-foot channel in the Mississippi, with new locks and dams north and south of the city. Its completion in 1940 will assure a deep channel from Alton, Illinois, to beyond the Falls of St. Anthony. La Crosse is again looking to the river as a possible source of income.

POINTS OF INTEREST

1. The LA CROSSE PUBLIC LIBRARY (*open 9-9 Mon.-Sat., 2-6 Sun.*), NE. corner 8th and Main Sts., is housed in the oldest library building in Wisconsin, a brick structure completed in 1888, the gift of Governor C. C. Washburn, who endowed the library with $50,000. In 1909 the building was doubled in size and the brick was faced with stucco.

2. The ALLIS CHALMERS FARM IMPLEMENT PLANT (*tours by arrangement with office, 10-4 Mon.-Fri.*), 501 N. 3rd St., manufactures plows and other farm implements. This plant, consisting of four separate buildings, was originally locally owned. The first building was erected in 1890; the plant was taken over by Allis Chalmers in 1929.

3. RIVERSIDE PARK, foot of State St., an area of drives and landscaped gardens, borders the Mississippi River. Here the U. S. Bureau of Fisheries maintains a FEDERAL FISH HATCHERY for the propagation and distribution of rainbow, brook, and German brown trout to co-operators' propagating ponds throughout Wisconsin, Minnesota, and Iowa. In a near-by low area is a pond for rearing small-mouthed black bass for general distribution throughout this region. A FISH EXHIBIT (*open 8-5 daily*), displays fish native to the region.

4. In PETTIBONE PARK, on an island at W. end of Mt. Vernon St. bridge, grow nearly all the better known types of trees indigenous to the upper Mississippi. The park contains a band shell and picnic tables. Originally the land lay in Minnesota, but it was traded in 1917 to Wisconsin for a tract near Winona.

5. In ST. ROSE CONVENT, 912 Market St., maintained by the Franciscan Sisters, is ST. ROSE CHAPEL, noted for the exquisite beauty of its interior and as one of the few chapels of Perpetual Adoration in the country. In 1872 the cornerstone for the first chapel was laid. In 1886 this chapel was enlarged, and a new addition, begun in 1902, was consecrated in 1906 as "Maria Angelorum." The architectural style is that of a Romanesque basilica of the seventh to the twelfth century, the outside ornamented with red brick, carved stone, and terra cotta work. Mr. Eugene Liebert of Milwaukee was the architect of the new chapel, Mr. A. Liebig of La Crosse was the decorator, and Mr. Egid Hackner of La Crosse was the altar builder. The altars, designed by Mr. Hackner, are of Italian marble, decorated with cast bronze, onyx, and inlaid mosaic of glass and mother of pearl; and the Carrara marble statues on them are from Italy. The walls and arched ceilings have decorations of intricate patterns and delicate tones, and in the sanctuary and over various altars are several fine oil paintings, the work of Mr. Thadeus von Zukotynski. The statuary and some

---

LA CROSSE.   Points of Interest

1. La Crosse Public Library
2. Allis Chalmers Farm Implement Plant
3. Riverside Park
4. Pettibone Park
5. St. Rose Convent
6. State Teachers College
7. Myrick Park
8. Grandad Bluff
9. La Crosse Rubber Mills

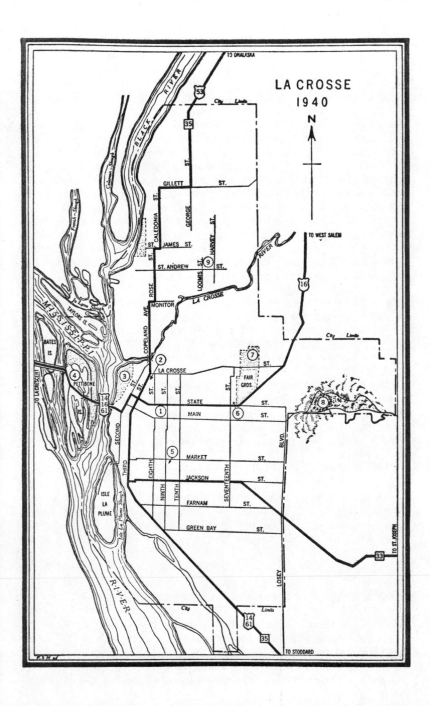

of the mosaics were executed in Italy from Mr. Hackner's designs. Windows of the chapel of Perpetual Adoration are exceptionally fine, the figures representing the Nine Choirs of Angels. One of the figures represents "Mary of Angels." The Zittler firm, one of the greatest in Europe, designed the windows in the chapel which were furnished by the Bavarian Art Company of Munich.

6. The STATE TEACHERS COLLEGE, State St. between 17th and 18th Sts., a co-educational college with a four-year course leading to a Bachelor of Science degree, is one of ten similar institutions in Wisconsin. An act of the legislature in 1905, together with a State appropriation of $10,000 to which the city of La Crosse added $15,000, made possible the purchase of the present site, eight acres on State Street. An additional State appropriation in 1907 resulted in the construction of the main building, which was completed two years later when the first session was held. Nearest State Street is Main Hall, for recitation and classroom work, a red-brick vine-clad structure set among blue spruce and other trees. Behind this is the Physical Education Building with separate swimming pools for men and women. The construction of two new buildings began late in 1938. A MUSEUM (*open 9-5 Mon.-Fri.*) on the second and third floors of the main building contains relics of American wars, displays of household utensils and lumbering implements, and mineralogical and biological collections.

7. MYRICK PARK, La Crosse St. E. of 17th St., was named for Nathan Myrick, who built the first hut and trading post on the mainland in 1842. On a hill, elevated about thirty-five feet, stands a large shelter house and band shell. The park contains a ZOO (*always open*) and on an artificial island, enclosed by a woven wire fence, are a number of monkeys. Other out-of-door enclosures contain birds, ducks, and raccoons. The only known INDIAN BURIAL MOUND in La Crosse, a "turtle" effigy, near the main drive of the park, is marked by a boulder and a plaque.

8. GRANDAD BLUFF, E. end of Main St., is the highest vantage point overlooking the city (1,150 feet above sea level and 570 feet above the terrace). From the summit, reached by an automobile road that winds its way around the bluff, there is a good view of the country for miles around. On the top is a PARK and shelter house, with running water and picnic benches, and near the crest is a large parking space for automobiles.

9. The LA CROSSE RUBBER MILLS (*open 9-12 Mon.-Thurs.; guides*), St. Andrew, Loomis and Harvey Sts., is one of the largest industries in the city, employing 1,900 men when operating at full capacity. It was organized in 1897 to manufacture rubber clothing. In 1906, however, it changed to the manufacture of tennis shoes and other rubber footwear, and now maintains an office in New York City for its export trade. To this large, many-windowed plant crude rubber is brought from plantations of Ceylon and the upper regions of the Amazon. The plant includes a chemical and physical testing laboratory

and a miniature rubber manufacturing plant where new compounds and methods are tested before they are employed in the factory.

POINTS OF INTEREST IN ENVIRONS

Oehler's Cave 6.5 *m.*, Mormon Coulee 5 *m.* (*see Tour 20*). Hamlin Garland's Home 10.8 *m.;* Pictured Rock Cave 7.1 *m.* (*see Tour 21*).

Madison

Railroad Stations: 644 W. Washington Ave. for Chicago, Milwaukee, St. Paul and Pacific R.R.; 201 S. Blair St. for Chicago & North Western Ry.; 602 W. Washington Ave. for Illinois Central R.R.

Bus Station: Union Bus Terminal, 122 W. Washington Ave. for Northland Greyhound, Wisconsin Motor Bus, and Orange Lines; Southern Wisconsin, Central Wisconsin, and East Shore Transportation Companies.

Airports: Madison Airport, N. end of North Street, taxi fare 25¢; Royal Airport, 3.8 *m.* on US 12 and US 18, taxi fare $1; Municipal Airport, 7 *m.* on US 51, taxi fare $1.50; planes twice daily each way, between Chicago and Minneapolis.

Taxis: Cruising cabs, and cabs on call, fare 10¢ and 15¢; zone system, fare 15¢ and 25¢; meter cabs, some 15¢ first m., 5¢ each additional 1/3 m., others 25¢ first 2 m., 10¢ each additional 2/3 m.; 5¢ each additional passenger.

City Busses: Fare 5¢.

Traffic Regulations: No left turn on or off upper State St.; one way traffic bears right around Capitol Square.

Accommodations: 14 hotels; tourist rooms; municipal campsite at Olin Park, Lakeside St. and city limits; trailer parks opposite Fairgrounds 2.4 *m.* S. on US 12 and US 18 and 5.9 *m.* on US 12, US 14, and State 13.

Information Service: Madison and Wisconsin Foundation, 122 W. Washington Ave.; Madison Business Association, Park Hotel, 22 S. Carroll St. with information booths open from Decoration Day to Labor Day at Wisconsin Ave. and Capitol Square; Wisconsin Division, AAA, 724 University Ave.

Radio Stations: WIBA (1280 kc.); WHA (940 kc.).

Motion Picture Houses: Seven.

Athletics and Recreation: Camp Randall Stadium, Camp Randall, Breese Terrace opposite Hoyt St.; Breese Stevens Field, E. Washington Ave. and N. Patterson St.

Swimming: Lake Mendota: Tenney Park, Sherman Ave. and the Yahara River, and the Willows, Willow Drive and the University of Wisconsin Intramural Fields. Lake Monona: Brittingham Park, South Broom St., and Lake Front Park, Lakeland Ave. between Hudson and Welch Aves. Lake Wingra: Vilas Park, NE. shore. South Shore in South Madison; piers without lifeguard service at many streets ending at a lake.

Tennis: Municipal courts at Brittingham Park, off 800 block of W. Washington Ave.; Tenney Park, E. Johnson St. to Lake Mendota, between Marston Ave. and the Yahara River; Vilas Park, NE. shore of Lake Wingra; East Side High School, Fourth St. and E. Washington Ave.; West High School, Regent St. between Highland Ave. and Ash St.

Golf: Burr Oaks, US 13 and US 14, beyond city limits, 9 holes, 25¢ for 9 holes, 20 rounds $4.00; Glenway (Municipal) W. city limits, Glenway and Speedway, 9 holes, 25¢ for 9 holes, 22 rounds for $4.50; Monona, US 51 and Lake Edge Park, 18 holes, 25¢ for 9, 50¢ for 18 holes, 20 rounds for $4.50; Westmoreland, Mineral Point Rd. just outside city limits, 9 holes, 25¢ for 9 holes, 20 rounds for $4. Private courses, cards may be secured from the Madison and Wisconsin Foundation, 122 W. Washington Ave.; Black Hawk Country Club, 18 holes, greens fee $1; Maple Bluff Golf Club, 18 holes, greens fee $1; Nakoma Country Club, 18 holes, greens fee $1 weekdays, $1.50 Sundays.

Fishing: In adjacent lakes.

Riding: Blackhawk Riding Club, Shorewood Hills; Fashion Stables, 2024 University Ave.

Boating: Lake Mendota: 624 E. Gorham St., canoes, rowboats, sailboats, iceboats and large launches; 412 N. Franklin St., canoes, rowboats and sailboats; University Boathouse, University Gymnasium, Langdon St., canoes, rowboats, sailboats, motorboats, launches. Lake Wingra: Conklin Park Boat Livery, off Monroe St., rowboats; Vilas Park Boat Livery, canoes and rowboats. Lake Monona: Brittingham Park Boat House, S. Bedford St., rowboats.

Winter Sports: Iceboating, sail-skating, skiing, on lakes and in vicinity.

Annual Events: Farm and Home Week at State College of Agriculture, Feb.; Little International Livestock and Horse Show at University Stock Pavilion, 1st Fri. in Feb.; University of Wisconsin Hoofers' Ski Meet, middle weekend in Feb.; Annual Meeting of the Friends of our Native Landscape, 2nd Thurs. in Feb.; Annual Horse Sale of Thoroughbred Draft Horses at the University Stock Pavilion, last Thurs. in Feb.; State Dramatic Guild Productions by State Authors and Players, 1st week in Mar.; Parents' Weekend Horse Show at the University Stock Pavilion, next to last Sat. in May; City Yacht Club Regatta on Lake Mendota, May 30; Washington or California State Crew Race with University of Wisconsin Crew on Lake Mendota, between 1st and 10th of June; Class B and C Yacht Club Regattas on Lake Mendota, Sats. and Suns. in June, July, and Aug.; Yacht Club Regattas, July 4; Dane County Fair, end of Aug.; Yacht Club Final Regatta, Labor Day.

MADISON (859 alt., 57,899 pop.), capital of Wisconsin and home of the State University, lies in the center of the dairylands of southern Wisconsin, filling a narrow isthmus between Lakes Monona and Mendota. The city widens fan-wise at either end and follows the miles of wooded bluffs and flats along the shore lines of these two lakes and little Lake Wingra to the southwest. Five lakes can be seen from the dome of the State capitol—the three that girdle the city, and Kegonsa and Waubesa to the southeast, linked by the same Yahara River that cuts through east Madison between Monona and Mendota.

On the isthmus heights the white granite capitol rises from landscaped grounds, surrounded by office buildings, theaters, shops, restaurants and hotels. Surmounted by the gilt figure of *Forward* facing the rising sun, circled by public roofwalks that overlook the city, the capitol dome, towering 285 feet from the ground, is visible for miles on any approach to Madison.

Here, where the isthmus is little more than a half-mile wide, no building is more than seven blocks from the waters of Monona or Mendota, edged with parks, piers, boathouses and beaches. Broad tree-lined blocks, filled with modern apartments, old mansions long ago converted into rooming houses, offices, clinics, clubhouses and public buildings, push inward from the lake shore to the capitol. Thus hemmed in, Madison's main business district fills the eight blocks fronting on the Square, extends into State Street between the capitol and university, and spills into the side streets.

The seven crowded commercial blocks of State Street link the Square to the University of Wisconsin in the western part of Madison. Partly wild, partly landscaped, the irregular beauty of the 200-acre campus runs nearly a mile along the ridge crests and slopes of Mendota's southern shore. The lake is as much a part of university life as the land. Students hike, ride, and drive along the willow-fringed shore road; they swim at the university piers and at "The Willows," a public bathing beach at the western end of the campus. In summer Mendota's blue expanse is alive with white sails, bright canoes, and motorboats; in winter skaters dot the frozen waters, iceboats whistle along, tobogganers swoop down from the campus slide, and from the towering ski-jump students take off for two-point or embonpoint landings on the ice.

Tree-grown residential districts make up West Madison and its suburbs, Shorewood Hills and Nakoma. Little Wingra's shores are almost entirely public property. Along the northeast is Vilas Park; along the southwestern shore is the University of Wisconsin Arboretum. The small isthmus between Lake Wingra and Lake Monona divides the West Side from the South Side. Landlocked by Olin Park and a fringe of better homes along Monona Bay, the modest cottages of South Madison stretch beyond the city limits, bordering the Dane County Fairgrounds.

East of the capitol, the lake homes of the oldest residential section of the city give way to smaller, newer homes and flats, and along the wide blocks bordering East Washington Avenue a few factories appear. Madison's 110 plants, most of them glass-walled, vine-covered structures, spread over a tree-filled area. The plants are scattered where the isthmus widens eastward, more concentrated near the eastern city limits where smokestacks and tanks overlook widely spaced railroad lines. Although Madison's other activities far overshadow its industry, the city ranks fourth in Wisconsin industrially, and a surprising variety of merchandise is manufactured. Tin cans, flashlights and batteries, air conditioning and radio equipment, hospital furniture, road machinery, automatic garage doors, metal garages and buildings, oil burners, water softeners, milking machines, bricks, chemicals, castings, culverts, bottle caps, cement stave silos, drugs, rennet extract, candy, ice cream, soft drinks, and meat are among the products manufactured here.

Lakeside parks, playgrounds, and the simple homes of workers and tradespeople flank the industrial section and the extensive East Side business area. The shore homes and estates in the wooded stretches of Lakewood and Maple Bluff along northeast Mendota are as expensively lovely as those of the exclusive communities in the West Side.

Though representatives of more than 20 different stocks are included in Madison's population, the foreign-born constitute less than 9.5 per cent; natives of foreign parentage constitute 29.5 per cent; nearly two-thirds of the people are descendants of native Americans. The largest national groups are German and Norwegian, still retaining cultural and religious societies. Irish, English, and Italians comprise the next largest divisions. Italians and Negroes constitute the only distinct and homogeneous groups.

Though town and gown tend to form two distinct societies, with separate sets of interests, at times they overlap. The Madison Literary Society allows a few from both groups to attend its solemnities; and the exclusive Town and Gown Club mingles the men of both sets. Members of the faculty, devoted to the "Wisconsin Idea," serve sometimes as public officials, sometimes as trade unionists, sometimes as advisers in the capitol. There is a floating population of students, famous visitors and legislators. When the legislature is in session the lawmakers claim the capitol—fighting for or against bills on the senate and assembly floors, conducting public hearings in the committee rooms, caucusing in private rooms. Lobbyists hover outside the chamber doors and at the bars where the solons occasionally drift during the day and frequently during the night.

"Beautiful but uninhabitable," pioneers considered Taychopera, the Four Lakes region where Madison stands today, and they left the land to the Winnebago Indians. Shrewd and opportunistic, Federal District Judge James Duane Doty saw something more tangible than beauty when he rode through the region in 1829. After losing his judgeship in 1832, Doty busied himself with exploring the Wisconsin wilderness and with land speculations. By 1836 he owned, among other tracts, 1,200 acres on the Four Lakes isthmus which he had bought in partnership with Stevens T. Mason, Governor of Michigan Territory. When the legislators of the newly formed Territory of Wisconsin met at Belmont that same year to draft a Territorial constitution and to consider the location of a capital, Doty was prepared for them. Poring over a map of "Madison," already named by Doty and planned according to his conception of the future city, the members of the legislature succumbed to his persuasion; they voted the virgin wilds of the Four Lakes isthmus, uninhabited by a single white family, as the site of the capital and of the University of Wisconsin. When the Territory was divided into counties by the lawmakers, Madison, still only on paper, became the seat of Dane County.

The first white family, Eben and Rosaline Peck and their son Victor, arrived in the spring of 1837 to open the Madison House, a crude log inn consisting of three large cabins joined together. The Peck house became the community center, serving in its first year as a boarding house for the occasional visitors and for some of the workmen who arrived in June to begin construction of the capitol. For a short time after the post office was established, mail was distributed from one corner of the Peck Inn. Before the year was out Simeon

Mills had opened a general store, and the first religious services had been conducted in a tavern barroom.

In 1838 Miss Louisa Brayton opened the first school, in Isaac Palmer's cabin; the Madison House, now under the management of Robert Ream, became a stopover for the stage coach running between Madison and Mineral Point; and on November 8 the *Wisconsin Enquirer* made its debut, published weekly by Josiah Noonan. Meanwhile, under the supervision of Augustus A. Bird, a crew of workmen quarried stone on Maple Bluff, hauled it across Lake Mendota in wooden scows, erected a steam sawmill to process wood for the capitol, and worked furiously to finish the building before the legislature convened. But the legislators who arrived in Madison in November, 1838, found the statehouse far from complete; the council members met in a small upstairs room of the new American Hotel, across the street, and the house members met in the basement dining room. When the legislators finally assembled in the capitol, ice-coated walls and floors, frozen ink, and the squeals of hogs quartered in the basement made their meetings miserable affairs. A legislative committee could not find accommodations for more than fifty persons in the village of less than a dozen houses, and the lawmakers were forced to sleep on floors, crowded together in cold rooms. Before the session adjourned on December 22 a savage resolution to move the capitol to Milwaukee passed one house and might have passed the other if the legislators could have been assured of better accommodations there. This was the first of many attempts to move the capitol elsewhere; not until 1848 was the statehouse finally completed.

A Protestant Episcopal parish, first religious organization in the village, was formed in 1839; in this year the Dane County jail was built, and W. W. Wyman launched the community's second newspaper, the Madison *Express*. Stagecoaches now left in five directions—for Chicago, Milwaukee, Galena, Green Bay, and Prairie du Chien.

The village was dormant for the next five years. Cows, pigs, and chickens monopolized the capitol lawns by day, and there at night citizens hunted wolves, bears, and deer. There were still no streets, and the markers that staked out the village were hidden in hazel brush. The population was 146 in 1840, when Clarissa Pierce opened a Select School for Young Ladies in a toolhouse left on the capitol lawn; there were about 35 buildings, including two stores, three public houses, three groceries, and a steam mill. In 1842, when the first issue of the *Wisconsin Democrat* was printed, there were only 172 residents.

In 1846 Madison was incorporated as a village with a population of 626, and Thomas W. Sutherland became president. The hotel lobbies were choked with legislators, lobbyists, and visiting politicians, and the press rebuked them for their horseplay, profanity, and hard drinking. More roads began to radiate from Madison, but there were still no streets. Development lagged until the arrival of Leonard J. Farwell, wealthy Milwaukeean. Farwell bought land in Madison in 1847; two years later he moved to the village and began large-scale

Industry

IN THE COOPER SHOP OF A BREWERY

FORTY-TON LADLE POURING LARGE CASTING

OLD BREWERY AT POTOSI

BREWING KETTLES IN A MILWAUKEE BREWERY

LEAD AND ZINC MINE NEAR SHULLSBURG

AUTOMOBILE FRAMES

PAPER MILL AT RHINELANDER

SAWMILL AT PARK FALLS

INTERLAKE STEAMER LOADING ORE AT
SUPERIOR. THIS IS THE LARGEST ORE
DOCK IN THE WORLD

GREEN BAY HARBOR

LAKE STEAMERS LOADING GRAIN, SUPERIOR. IN THE BACKGROUND IS GREAT NORTHERN ELEVATOR "S," THE LARGEST SINGLE BIN UNIT IN THE WORLD

MILWAUKEE'S BACK DOOR

FACTORIES AT RACINE

improvements. He replaced the circuitous Catfish (now Yahara) River channel with a canal between Lakes Mendota and Monona, dammed the Mendota end, and built a large grist and flour mill. He opened streets, drained the east side marshland, built side- and cross-walks, and planted thousands of shade trees. When Wisconsin became a State in 1848, the University of Wisconsin was established here, and the next year the first classes met in the Madison Female Academy, furnished rent-free by the village. In January, 1849, the first telegraphic report was received; the same year the Wisconsin State Historical Society was founded.

In 1850 the isthmus thickets were still so dense that the village was called an "inhabited forest," despite a population of 1,672. During the next five years business expanded tremendously. Commercial blocks were erected, three banks sprang up, the Yahara River was bridged, numerous machine shops, foundries and mills operated at full capacity, and a courthouse was built. However, the University of Wisconsin did not share this boom, despite the impressive inauguration of Chancellor John Lathrop in January, 1850. The curriculum was merely college preparatory; there was only one teacher. The first graduating class of 1854 consisted of two men. Non-denominational, the university was attacked in press and pulpit, and parents were warned to keep their sons away from the "godless associations of this atheistic institution."

Madisonians celebrated the arrival of the first railroad train in 1854; the streets were lighted by gas in 1855. Legislative sessions and conventions crowded the hotels; the capitol, courthouse, and churches were used for concerts, traveling shows, and lectures by such national figures as Bayard Taylor, James Russell Lowell, and Horace Greeley. The quickening literary interests of the citizens centered around the Madison Institute, which sponsored a lyceum and by 1855 possessed a library of 13,000 volumes. That year the population of 6,863 supported three daily and five weekly newspapers and one agricultural monthly. Madison became a city in 1856, and Jairus Fairchild was elected first mayor. The same year the first commercial educational institution in Wisconsin, now Madison College, was founded.

By 1857 the flimsy capitol could no longer house all the expanding State activities, and another legislative move to change the capital site to Milwaukee was barely frustrated. Alarmed by this threat to destroy the very basis of the city's growth, Madisonians voted to donate $50,000 in city bonds for reconstructing the building, and, on February 28, 1857, the legislature passed an act "to enlarge and improve" the capitol. But the plans and contract that were finally authorized provided for a second statehouse on the old site, and a fury of controversy arose when the public discovered that instead of "repairs" on the old capitol an entirely new capitol was under construction.

During these first months, as the erection of public schools, the city hall, and other buildings was begun, there was great clamor for the importation of skilled workmen from the East. But the financial panic that crippled the Nation in the second half of 1857 caught many of

Madison's businessmen, slackening building projects and trade. Stone-cutters waged one of the first labor strikes this year, protesting that the price of room and board consumed their weekly wages and left nothing for other necessities.

In 1861 the influence of the Civil War buoyed up Madison commerce. Transformed into Camp Randall, the State Fairgrounds became a training camp for many Wisconsin soldiers, and a Madison company was the first in the State to volunteer. Business stirred and employment increased as the city supplied food, fuel, and other necessities to the men concentrated in the barracks, 7,000 to 8,000 at a time. But the University received almost a death blow. Many of the students joined the army; the 1864 commencement was cancelled because only one civilian senior remained; professors struggled along on half pay. There was insufficient income to repay State loans for the construction of buildings, and the 1862 legislature ordered payments made from the University treasury, seriously depleting its capital funds.

Peace brought progress to the city. The bustling factories produced $433,856 worth of farm tools, tinware, cabinet ware, flour, beer, coal gas, clothing and shoes, and there were 9,191 citizens in 1865. The campus welcomed back its soldier-students, and university development really began. In 1866 the legislature passed a bill completely reorganizing the university; in 1867, recognizing that spending the capital fund for building construction was unjust, it voted to restore the money in annual installments of $7,303.76; in 1868 an agricultural department and college of law were established; and in 1870 the legislature made its first direct appropriation, $50,000, to erect a separate building for women students. By now recreation on Madison lakes was increasing each year; as early as 1867 the first steamboat on Lake Mendota, the *City of Madison,* was making excursion trips. In 1869 the first trains of the third railroad line to enter the city thundered in. In 1871 a combined Federal post office and courthouse, numerous factories, shops and residences were erected. The building program of 1873 cost $300,000 and included the new high school. When the Madison Free Library, first in Wisconsin, opened its doors in 1875, the city directory listed 450 factories and business houses, including 26 hotels and five banks.

Through the seventies and eighties the parade of municipal progress continued. Building increased steadily, cultural activities multiplied, university enrollment leaped after the 1872 legislature authorized free tuition for State high school graduates who could pass the entrance examinations. Telephones were installed in 1878, electric lights appeared in the early eighties, the city waterworks opened in 1882, free mail delivery and the appearance of mule-drawn streetcars were highlights of 1883 and 1884. The population was more than 12,000 by 1885; it was 13,426 by 1890, the year the Fuller Opera House opened. In 1892 gas was a common illumination for residences and public buildings, electric streetcars replaced the mule cars, telephones increased.

The Federated Trades Council emerged in 1893 to combine the strength of the many labor unions that had arisen.

The constant praise of visitors swelled civic pride in Madison's physical beauty, and meetings inspired by John M. Olin and E. T. Owen resulted in the organization of the Madison Park and Pleasure Drive Association in 1894. Citizens donated tracts of lake shore and forest bluff to the association, contributions averaging $20,000 a year began to accumulate for the improvement of scenic drives, parks and playgrounds, and in 1898 the city council inaugurated annual appropriations to the park association.

In the first 16 years of the 1900's the population grew from 19,164 to more than 32,000 and university enrollment increased from 2,619 to more than 7,500. In 1916 the city had 35 churches and there were 35 labor unions. The third Madison capitol, built to replace the statehouse partially destroyed by fire in 1904, was constructed between 1906-17, and by 1916 the park association had expended more than $300,000 that the public might enjoy 269 acres of parks and playgrounds, with a shoreline of almost eight miles.

In the war feeling of 1917, patriotic fervor reached such a height that Senator Robert Marion La Follette was burned in effigy by university students for his anti-war speeches and denounced for his pacifist attitudes in a "round-robin" letter signed by 399 members of the faculty. This year the entire medical school enlisted, faculty members became emergency food agents, and the university "released" 488 students for farm work because of the wartime clamor for increased crop production.

During the 1920's and 1930's Madison was comparatively unstirred by the booms and depressions that affected more industrial cities, because of the large proportion of families employed by governmental agencies and supported by tax funds. As late as 1930 only 27 per cent of gainfully employed Madisonians were engaged in manufacturing. Factory expansion has been in the number and variety of products and the extent of markets rather than in the number of plants and employees. Dwelling units increased from 7,751 in 1921 to 12,307 in 1930; the population rose from 39,984 to 57,899 during the same period. In a single century the isthmus wilderness from which Madison sprang has become a concentrate of Wisconsin activity—capital, college town, medical center, the lively scene of exhibitions, concerts, plays and lectures, and headquarters for numerous Federal, State, county, and municipal agencies.

POINTS OF INTEREST

(*Downtown and East Madison*)

1. The STATE CAPITOL (*open 8:30-12, 1:30-5; tours 8, 9, 10, 10:45, 1, 2, 3, and 3:45 weekdays; 1, 2, and 2:45 p.m. Sat. and Sun.; 9, 10, and 10:45 a.m. Sun.*) is situated in Capitol Park, the square of land bounded by Main, Carroll, Mifflin, and Pinckney Streets. The

plan of the building is in the form of a Greek cross; a massive dome rises from the intersection of four similar wings, which contain offices and legislative and judicial chambers. The structure, designed by

---

MADISON. Points of Interest

1. State Capitol
2. Site of the American House
3. City Hall
4. Grace Episcopal Church
5. Old Baptist Church
6. Park Hotel
7. David Atwood Home
8. Capitol Annex
9. Site of the Peck House
10. Lamp Home
11. Turner Hall
12. Wisconsin Foundry and Machine Plant
13. Fauerbach Brewery
14. Gisholt Machine Plant
15. Oscar Mayer Packing Plant
16. Tibbets and Gordon Brewery
17. Tenney Park
18. Site of the Old Walker Castle
19. Executive Mansion
20. Pierce House
21. College Women's Club
22. Central High School
23. Madison Free Library
24. Vilas Home
25. Braley Home
26. Dudley House
27. University Club
28. Men's Gymnasium and Armory
29. Memorial Union
30. Library
31. Administration Building
32. Science Hall
33. Radio Hall
34. Education and Engineering Building
35. North Hall
36. Bascom Hall
37. Carillon Bell Tower
38. South Hall
39. Law Building
40. Music Hall
41. Chadbourne Hall
42. Lathrop Hall
43. Biology Building
44. Chemistry Building
45. Wisconsin General Hospital
46. Wisconsin High School
47. Studio of the Artist in Residence
48. University Extension and Home Economics Building
49. Agricultural Hall
50. University Farms
51. Observatory Hill
52. Van Hise and Kronshage Dormitories
53. University Field House
54. University Stadium
55. First Congregational Church
56. Airplane House
57. Sigma Phi Fraternity House
58. Home of University Presidents
59. U. S. Forest Products Laboratory
60. Forest Hill Cemetery
61. Arboretum
62. Old Spring Hotel
63. Plow Inn
64. Edgewood Academy
65. Vilas Park
66. Olin Park
67. Giles Home
68. B. O. Webster Home
69. Dane County Courthouse
70. St. Raphael's Church
71. Former Synagogue

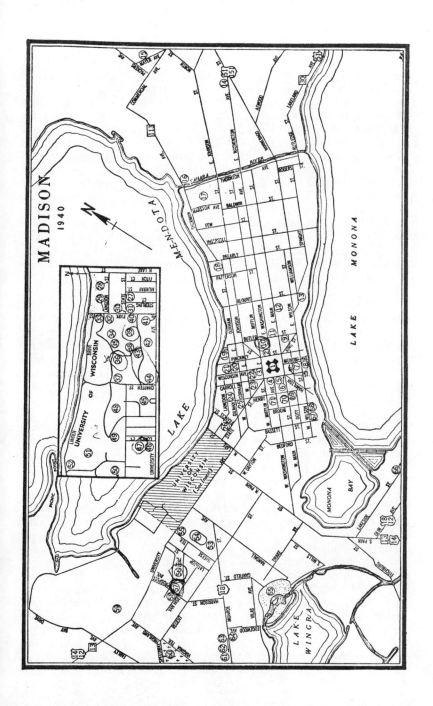

George B. Post and Sons in the Italian Renaissance style, was built at a cost of more than $7,200,000. The exterior of the building, the balustrade surrounding the formal terrace, and the copings along the walks are made of white Bethel Vermont granite.

Each of the four wings, which extend toward the cardinal points of the compass, terminates in a portico. The classical pediments are supported on tall Corinthian columns; in the tympana of the pediments are works of allegorical sculpture by Karl Bitter, A. A. Weinman, and Attilio Piccirilli. Four other entrances are provided by large circular pavilions, which are set in the angles formed by the wings; grand staircases lead to the second floor, and under these are passages for cars. Set along the colonnaded drum of the dome and overlooking the pavilions are four symbolic statuary groups by Karl Bitter. Above the row of Corinthian columns and high windows is a podium roof. The ribbed dome, which begins above a row of rectangular windows and a row of console brackets, is the one granite dome in the United States; it is second in height only to the dome of the National Capitol. Surmounting the lantern is a gilded bronze statue by Daniel Chester French symbolizing the motto of the State, *Forward*.

The interior is finished in a great variety of domestic and foreign marble and granite. From the octagonal rotunda, with its balustraded central well, there is an excellent view of the grand staircases leading to the four wings, and of *The Resources of Wisconsin,* the painting in the crown of the dome by Edwin Howland Blashfield. In the pendentives between the four arches of the rotunda are the glass mosaics by Kenyon Cox representing *Legislature, Government, Justice,* and *Liberty.* Murals by Albert Herter, C. Y. Turner, Blashfield, and Cox are in the Supreme Court Room, the Hearing Room, the Assembly Chamber, and the Senate Chamber, respectively. The most highly ornamented room in the capitol is the Governor's Reception Room, designed in Italian Renaissance style by Elmer T. Garnsey and Hugo Ballin, with ceiling and mural paintings by the latter.

In the Assembly Chamber is the first electric voting machine used by a legislative body, installed in 1917. This machine, an invention of B. L. Bobroff, Milwaukee consulting engineer, records a roll call in 11 seconds and develops a photographic record of all votes in 24 seconds. The G. A. R. Hall in the capitol contains numerous objects of historical interest. On the second floor, north wing, is the Legislative Reference Library, established in 1901.

The present capitol is the third built in Madison. The second Territorial capitol was begun in 1837 on the same site. The first statehouse, much more commodious than the preceding buildings, was erected during the period 1857-69 and additions were made in 1882-84. The decision to build a new structure was made by the legislature of 1903, which appointed a commission "to provide proper accommodation for the state law library and the supreme judicial department of the state. . . ." In 1904 fire destroyed most of the interior of the building, accentuating the need for a new and larger capitol. Construction of the present building was begun in 1906 and was completed in 1917.

2. The SITE OF THE AMERICAN HOUSE, 1 N. Pinckney St., an early small frame hotel, is occupied by the American Exchange Bank. Because construction of the capitol building, begun in 1837, had not been completed, the Territorial legislature of 1838 held its meetings here until the new statehouse was ready.

3. The CITY HALL, 2 W. Mifflin St., completed in 1858, designed by Donnell and Kutzbock, is a simple three-story building of modified Florentine Renaissance design, constructed of Madison sandstone. Rusticated stonework frames the arched doorways and windows of the first story. Above the high third-story windows is a heavy bracketed main cornice. Three bays of the side facade are brought forward in the form of a rusticated central pavilion. Almost from the date it was built the old hall has been too small for the city's governing forces, but repeated efforts to build a larger center have failed. In early days the top floor of the building was used as an opera house; Laura Keene, noted American actress, averted a fire panic here in 1866.

4. The GRACE EPISCOPAL CHURCH, 110 W. Washington Ave., was built in 1858 of rough-hewn sandstone in a simple Gothic style. The church congregation, the oldest in Madison, was organized in 1839.

5. The OLD BAPTIST CHURCH, 16 S. Carroll St., a square, flat-roofed building constructed of rust brick, was erected in 1854, and is now headquarters of the Wisconsin Telephone Company. Highly popular in its first years, the church was frequently used for concerts and lectures. Ole Bull and Adelina Patti, then a child of 13, appeared in a joint recital here in 1856. Lectures were held here by Bayard Taylor, Wendell Phillips, James Russell Lowell, and Horace Greeley. Lyman C. Draper, first secretary of the State Historical Society, for a while housed the library of the Historical Society in the church basement.

6. The PARK HOTEL, 22 S. Carroll St., was built in 1871 with the contributions of Madison citizens (who received only a dinner for their efforts) to accommodate legislators in the uncertain days when the removal of the capitol to Milwaukee, which had better hotel facilities, was feared. Milwaukeeans, conducting a tremendous lobby to get the capitol moved to their city, served the legislators with "Romeo and Juliet Cigars, old rye, piperheidseick," and much Milwaukee beer. Madison businessmen grew alarmed. Meeting to make plans for adequate hotel facilities, they agreed that the side of the square subscribing the most money should be favored with the location of the hotel. After a hot contest, subscriptions were combined and the present site was chosen. The Milwaukee lobbyists were silenced.

7. The DAVID ATWOOD HOME (*private*), 206-10 Monona Ave., a long brick Greek Revival building, was erected in 1851 by David Atwood, founder of the *Wisconsin State Journal,* and his partner, Royal Buck. It was constructed as a double residence, with a massive three-story central section, flanking wings and twin corner

porches. The wings and bracketed cornice are probably of later date. During Atwood's occupancy the house was a meeting place for public men of every calling—Governors, Congressmen, educators, jurists, and politicians.

8. The CAPITOL ANNEX, 1 W. Wilson St., is an 11-story white granite building, designed by R. C. Kirchhoff. Window casements, evenly spaced, form unbroken vertical lines from ground to roof. A bronze tablet on the front marks this as the site of the Jarius Fairchild estate, the home of Wisconsin's first State treasurer (1848-52). After the Fairchild house was razed in the late 1920's, plans for the Annex were made. The six-story wing to the southeast was built in 1932; in 1939 the 11-story center section was erected; and eventually another wing will be constructed to the southwest. The Annex houses various State departments and the Wisconsin Free Travelling Library, organized in 1896.

9. SITE OF THE PECK HOUSE, 122-124 S. Butler St., is now a parking lot. The Peck House was the first permanent home in Madison. It consisted of three log buildings joined together, one a tavern, another sleeping quarters, and the other a living room for the Pecks. When the family arrived in Madison in 1837, the structure had not yet been completed. A pen-like outdoor room was built under an oak tree, and it was here that the Pecks lived until the log house was ready for occupancy.

10. The LAMP HOME (*private*), 22 N. Butler St., was built for Mr. and Mrs. Robert Lamp in 1895, from a design by Frank Lloyd Wright. In the center of a block, now completely surrounded by houses, this small yellowish brick building stands on a slight hill. It is one of the earliest of Mr. Wright's houses, resembling, with its use of diamond leaded windows and striking mass, the early Oak Park homes he designed.

11. SITE OF TURNER HALL, 21 S. Butler St., which was destroyed by fire in November 1940. Built in 1863 to replace a former hall destroyed by fire, Turner Hall served as an Armory for the Governor's Guards in the late 1870's, and between 1884 and 1890 it was used for theatrical entertainments.

12. The WISCONSIN FOUNDRY AND MACHINE PLANT (*open to visitors by permission at office*), 623 E. Main St., was incorporated in 1910. It is housed in five one-story frame buildings. Here in rooms jammed with machines, other machines are designed, patterns made, moulds cast, and armatures wound. Approximately 75 skilled mechanics and draftsmen are employed.

13. The FAUERBACH BREWERY (*open by special permission*), 651 Williamson St., is a massive Victorian brick structure with Gothic and Richardsonian Romanesque features, such as the pointed arch windows of colored and frosted glass, the two marble columns at the entrance, and the brick tower at the corner of the building. Fauerbach's stands on the site of Madison's first brewery, built by Fred Sprecher in 1848. All the interior furnishings, the round oak tables, the huge

barrels, the elaborate staircase, and the long heavy bar are characteristically Victorian.

14. The GISHOLT MACHINE PLANT (*open 8-12 and 1-5 Mon.-Fri.; tours by arrangement at office*), 1245 E. Washington Ave., is the largest manufacturing concern in Madison. Founded in 1885 by John A. Johnson and incorporated in 1888, the company now employs approximately 1,000 workers, specializing in the manufacture of tools such as turret lathes, balancing machines, and tool grinders. The factory consists of a number of huge steel and brick buildings with skylights and modern factory windows. Great electric cranes run through the plant, carrying massive castings for the assemblage of large machinery.

15. The OSCAR MAYER PACKING PLANT (*open 7-4 Mon.-Fri.; 7-12 Sat.; guides*), 910 Mayer Ave., manufactures sausages, lard, ice, and other products. Its large red-brick buildings contain facilities for the butchering of livestock, the processing and storing of meats, and the receiving and shipping of poultry products. Approximately 1,000 men and women are employed.

16. The TIBBETS AND GORDON BREWERY, 1603 Sherman Ave., better known as the "Malt House," was built in 1849, and is now used as a tavern. It is a rambling old brick building, a series of rooms, sheds and shafts loosely joined together, on the banks of the Yahara River. Most of these sections were added in 1852 by the owner of the plant, in a period when business was so flourishing that the brewery had its own railway spur. Underneath the ground floor is a labyrinth of damp tunnels, leading to vats where beer was once aged and stored.

17. TENNEY PARK, E. Johnson St. between Marston Ave. and Yahara River, extending to Lake Mendota, was created in 1899 from useless marsh and swampland. About 16 acres were converted into lagoons, lawns and islands through the plans of O. C. Simons, landscape gardener and architect of Chicago. Of $41,480 contributed by 1912, $16,289 was given by D. K. Tenney, for whom the park is named. New plots were added, and today the park consists of 44 landscaped acres and a long lake frontage. The Yahara River runs through the park, and there are facilities for swimming, tennis, picnicking, skating and other outdoor activities.

18. The SITE OF THE OLD WALKER CASTLE, 930 E. Gorham St., is occupied by a private home. On this spot, in the early 1860's, Benjamin Walker, a wealthy Englishman, built a towered Norman structure as a home for himself and his family. It was made to look as regal as possible, for Walker had promised his wife a "real castle," complete with underground passages, towers, stables and a coat of arms. But in 1866 Mrs. Walker became dissatisfied, and the family returned to England. The castle became the property of Edward Thompson and his wife, but they also disliked the place, finding it damp, drafty, and hard to heat. Timothy Brown, the next owner of the building, left it vacant for years. The romantic subterranean pas-

sages were used for fraternity initiations. In 1887, when Fred M. Brown offered to restore and modernize the castle for his bride, she refused, for she considered it too far away from town. In 1893 the castle was torn down and its stones, large native sandstone blocks, were used in the construction of the house at 137 E. Gorham Street. All that remains of the original castle and its outbuildings is a stone fence, a porte-cochère, and the stables, now used as a garage.

19. The EXECUTIVE MANSION (*private*), 130 E. Gilman St., is the home of Wisconsin's governors. Built in 1854, the comfortable, square house is constructed of brown sandstone blocks, with evenly spaced windows, heavy bracketed cornice, and a flat-pitched roof. Running along the front and west side is a long, curved veranda supported by small white Doric columns. The grounds slope gradually down to Lake Mendota, visible through a screen of old trees. Senator J. G. Thorp, millionaire lumberman of Eau Claire, who purchased the estate in 1867, made it the social center of Madison. Thorp's son, J. G. Thorp, Jr., married Anna Longfellow, daughter of the well-known American poet; it was she who induced her father to write the lyric *The Four Lakes of Madison.* Sarah, daughter of Thorp, married Ole Bull (*see Music*), who terraced the lawn in Norwegian style and made other improvements. In 1882 Governor Jeremiah M. Rusk purchased the house and lived here during his term of governorship. In 1885 the State legislature bought the home from Rusk for use as the executive mansion.

20. The PIERCE HOUSE (*private*), 424 N. Pinckney St., built in 1858, and designed by Donnell and Kutzbock, was to be "the finest home that money could buy." It was constructed for A. A. McDonnell, who chose this site in the butternut woods, which then lay on the outskirts of Madison, on the tip of the long hill that slants down to Lake Mendota. McDonnell hired Italian stone carvers who had worked on the second Madison State Capitol to execute the elaborate architectural detail of his home. Constructed of light buff sandstone, brought from quarries at Prairie du Chien, the exterior walls are embellished with tall, arched mullioned windows of Italian Renaissance design, porches with elaborate iron grillwork, octagonal bays, and a heavy corbeled and gabled cornice. Inside, the doors and banisters of the steep winding staircase are made of solid hand-carved mahogany. "The finest house in Madison" still retains something of its old reputation, for though the plaster of the outer walls has weathered and the ironwork has rusted, the interior, with its white marble fireplaces, its wall niches, its excellent floors, carries something of the elegance it had 80 years ago. The George M. Pierce family occupied the house from 1906 till 1937.

21. The COLLEGE WOMEN'S CLUB, 12 E. Gilman St., headquarters of the American Association of University Women, stands some distance back from the street in broad, shaded grounds. Built about the middle of the century for J. T. Clark and enlarged in the 1880's for U. S. Senator William F. Vilas, the house, which seems

aged and rambling, has tall narrow windows with elaborate corniced and bracketed headings. Its red-brick walls are accented at the corners by gray sandstone quoins, and crowned with a wide bracketed cornice typical of the architecture of the late nineteenth century.

22. The CENTRAL HIGH SCHOOL, 200 Wisconsin Ave., a simple collegiate-Gothic, red-brick building, occupies the site of the old Madison Select Female School where the first university classes were conducted. The building, designed by Cass Gilbert of New York City, was completed in 1908. The Madison Public Vocational School, established in 1912, offering courses in arts, crafts, and business, has occupied one wing of the building since 1921.

23. The MADISON FREE LIBRARY (*open 9-9 weekdays all year*), 206 N. Carroll St., built of red brick with granite trim, is designed in the Tudor-Gothic style of old English university buildings. Its construction was made possible by Carnegie funds. Together with its 17 school branches and 5 public branches, it contains more than 127,000 books and a large number of newspapers and periodicals. From 1906 until 1938 the building served as quarters for the Wisconsin Library School, which in the fall of 1938 moved to 811 State St.

24. The VILAS HOME (*private*), 521 N. Henry St., was built of native sandstone in 1851 by Levi B. Vilas, fourth mayor of Madison. Three stories high, the square house is simply constructed, with slim columns, semicircular arched windows, and lofty rooms, today let out as apartments. Levi B. Vilas was the father of Colonel William F. Vilas, U. S. Senator, Postmaster General, and Secretary of the Interior.

25. The BRALEY HOME (*private*), 422 N. Henry St., is a hip-roofed brick structure. During the 1880's it was the home of Judge Arthur B. Braley, Shakespearean scholar and father of Berton Braley, local versifier. In his book, *Pegasus Pulls a Hack,* Berton Braley writes: "Ella Wheeler Wilcox, then Ella Wheeler, was in the house when I was born. . . . It was in our house that Ella wrote 'Laugh and the World Laughs With You,' probably the most famous and widely quoted of her verses."

26. The DUDLEY HOUSE, 508 N. Frances St., was begun about 1855 and completed shortly after the Civil War. The walls of the building are formed of ample buff sandstone blocks, set under wide eaves. Its large windows, set low near the floor, have a simplicity characteristic of pre-Civil War architecture. After the death of William Dudley and his son Charles, the house was used as a school for boys, later as a clubhouse and rooming house. Since 1924 it has been known as the "Deutsches Haus," a dormitory for women students and instructors of German at the university.

27. The UNIVERSITY CLUB, 803 State St., a red brick Tudor-Gothic building, with clustered chimneys, stepped gables, octagonal bays and stone trim, was constructed in 1908 and remodeled in 1924. The club has almost 400 members, all men with college degrees, 95 of whom live in this building. The only teacher's dormitory on the campus, the club is a favorite gathering place for the university faculty.

UNIVERSITY OF WISCONSIN
(Buildings open during school hours unless otherwise indicated.)

In 1849, while Madison was little more than a cluster of rough houses built on a ridge between two lakes, the hill at the western end of the village was unofficially selected as the site for the University of Wisconsin. At that time the slope facing the town was a tangle of blackberry bushes, and deer still ran wild in its woods. This piece of ground was purchased in 1850, two years after the incorporation of the university. Later a double row of elms was planted from the top of the hill to the bottom. North Hall, the first building, served for classrooms, mess hall and living quarters for students and faculty. In 1855 South Hall was erected opposite North Hall for use as a dormitory. Since then almost a hundred buildings have been added to accommodate a growing enrollment and an enlarged curriculum; and the campus grounds have been extended so that they now embrace not only the eastern slope of the hill and its foot, but also a mile-long strip on the western slope. Nearly every building erected since 1900 has been designed in a modified Italian Renaissance style by architects George B. Ferry and Alfred C. Clas, J. T. W. Jennings, and, more recently, Arthur Peabody.

Each year, from seven thousand to ten thousand students register at the university in one of the eight colleges or schools—Letters and Science, Agriculture, Law, Medicine, Education, Nursing, Engineering, or Graduate School. Best known for the wide range of its College of Letters and Science, and for the varied services offered to the State by its College of Agriculture, the university draws its enrollment from all States in the Union and from nearly every Nation. Courses range from Gaelic Literature, Labor History, Library Science and Medieval Latin Poetry, to Agronomy, Steam Engineering, Fur Farming, and Relativity Theory. But the limits of the university are not confined to the Madison campus; in a sense they are conterminous with those of the State (*see Education*).

Three adjoining sections comprise the present university grounds: the Lower Campus, the Upper Campus, and the Agricultural Campus. Theses are supplemented by outlying centers for specialized instruction, among them the University Extension, the Washburn Observatory, and the group of Medical buildings. Various other units, such as the University High School, football stadium, farms, and fieldhouse, are scattered in the western end of the campus.

The LOWER CAMPUS, at the foot of Bascom Hill, spreads eastward from the end of N. Park Street, penetrating the old residential section of the city.

28. The MEN'S GYMNASIUM and ARMORY (1894), Conover and Porter, architects, is the easternmost college building on Langdon Street. Designed in the manner of a Norman fortress, its red-brick towers and huge open floors are shared by the Military Department and the Physical Education Department, both of which use

the large play field just across Langdon Street. The gym has been the scene of many inter-party political rallies.

29. MEMORIAL UNION (*open to visitors only on the first Sunday of each month; the building at other times is for the use of students, members of the faculty, and their guests*), Langdon and Park Sts., the principal campus social center, was designed by Arthur Peabody (1928), who modelled it after the Renaissance palaces of Venice. The central unit and east wing provide lounges, recreation rooms, student offices, and a library, refectory, and rathskeller; the modernistic west wing (1939) contains a theater (*see Theater*), club and game rooms, studios, an arts-craft workshop, two radio broadcasting studios, and a small laboratory theater, known as the Play Circle. Michael M. Hare was the project designer; Lee Simonson was the theater consultant.

30. The LIBRARY (*open 8-4 weekdays in summer, 8 a.m.-10 p.m. weekdays during university sessions*), State and Park Sts., constructed of white stone, was built in 1900 to house the library of the State Historical Society. Founded in 1849 to collect and preserve the story of pioneer life, development, and settlement in Wisconsin, the society in 1854 appointed Dr. Lyman Draper secretary. It was under his administration that some of the most important manuscripts, documents, newspapers, journals, daguerreotypes, pamphlets and printed circulars were obtained. Dr. Draper's largest single contribution was his own collection of priceless manuscripts, gleaned primarily from the Ohio Valley, which he bequeathed to the society in 1891 and which were later bound into a set of 470 folio volumes and designated the *Draper Manuscripts.* The library now (1940) owns a collection of 305,739 volumes of books and bound newspapers and 333,144 pamphlets. The 44,136 volumes of bound newspapers form the second largest collection of newspapers in the United States. They cover all sections of the country and date from earliest Colonial times to the present. The Document Division has 87,844 books and 98,475 pamphlets.

Sharing the building with the Historical Society is the LIBRARY OF THE UNIVERSITY OF WISCONSIN, which owns approximately 443,000 volumes and 80,000 pamphlets. The Library of the Wisconsin Academy of Sciences, Arts, and Letters, also in the building, consists of about 6,000 volumes of reports and transactions of learned societies.

The STATE HISTORICAL SOCIETY MUSEUM (*open 8-4 weekdays in summer, 8-5 weekdays in winter*), occupies the fourth floor of the library. It contains portraits of notable pioneers, an Indian collection, a reconstructed pioneer home, a replica of an early drug store, old medical instruments, the clock John Muir made while a student at the university, Daniel Webster's carriage, and many other historical objects.

31. The ADMINISTRATION BUILDING, across State St. from the library, is a weatherworn limestone house. Once a private residence, it was remodeled in 1906 as offices for university business administrators.

The UPPER CAMPUS spreads over the four sides and top of Bascom Hill, rising in a long green slope westward from N. Park Street. The oldest halls are set along the two cement paths that lead from the Lower Campus up the hill to Lincoln Terrace and Bascom Hall at the top. A rough boundary to this campus is formed by Lake Mendota on the north, N. Park Street on the east, University Avenue on the south, and N. Charter Street on the west.

32. SCIENCE HALL, Langdon and Park Sts., a Richardsonian Romanesque building, was designed by A. C. Koch & Co., in 1888. Within its high red brick walls are classrooms, an anatomy laboratory, and a GEOLOGY MUSEUM (*open 8-5 weekdays*), on the second floor of the south wing, containing prehistoric skeletons, a cross-section of a lead-zinc deposit, many types of minerals, and other exhibits of geological interest.

33. RADIO HALL (*open 8-5 weekdays*), rear of Science Hall, is the headquarters and studios for WHA, claimed to be the oldest radio station in the United States (*see Newspapers and Radio*).

34. The EDUCATION AND ENGINEERING BUILDING, the first building on the north side of the hill, was designed by J. T. W. Jennings in 1901. Pink mortar laid between gray bricks gives its walls a purplish cast. Until 1939 this structure housed the main office and library of the College of Engineering; in that year much of the engineering equipment was moved to other quarters and part of the building was taken over by the School of Education.

35. NORTH HALL, the oldest building on the campus, was built in 1851 from a design by John F. Rague. Constructed of native sandstone in simple rectangular style, the one-time dormitory, where John Muir lived as a student, is used principally for mathematics classes. On the top floor is the U. S. Weather Bureau.

36. BASCOM HALL (1857), crowning the hill, overlooks the LINCOLN MEMORIAL TERRACE, and the large bronze STATUE OF LINCOLN, copied from a statue designed by Adolph A. Weinman and presented in 1909. Originally in the modified Roman Doric style, but since remodeled, Bascom Hall was designed by W. Tinsley. As the center of the University it contains many of the general administrative offices and the classrooms and offices of most of the Liberal Arts departments.

37. CARILLON BELL TOWER, a few yards northwest of Bascom Hall, was designed in 1934 by Arthur Peabody.

38. SOUTH HALL, downhill from Lincoln Terrace, was designed by Rague in 1855 as a twin to North Hall. Having outgrown the years it served as a faculty dormitory, South Hall now houses the Journalism Department, the Political Science Department, and the offices of the dean of men and the dean of Letters and Science.

39. The LAW BUILDING, directly opposite the Engineering Building, is headquarters for one of the university's two professional schools, with an independent library for which a new wing was recently constructed. It was built in 1893, designed by Charles S. Frost in a

modified Romanesque style; it is constructed of Lake Superior brown sandstone.

40. MUSIC HALL, fronting N. Park St., is a pseudo-Gothic building constructed in 1879, and is the headquarters of the School of Music, a branch of the College of Letters and Science.

41. CHADBOURNE HALL (1871) and BARNARD HALL (1912), N. Park St. and University Ave., are the two women's dormitories. When it was first built Chadbourne Hall took the place of South Hall as a college for women.

42. LATHROP HALL (1909), University Ave. between Brooks and Mills Sts., a massive structure of modified Renaissance design, with great arched windows and smooth walls, contains the women's gymnasium and the offices and classrooms of the women's Physical Education Department.

43. BIOLOGY BUILDING (1910), up the hill from Lathrop Hall, contains botany and zoology laboratories, a large herbarium, and, in its lobby, a NATURAL HISTORY MUSEUM (*open*), with specimens and models of land, sea, and bird life.

44. The CHEMISTRY BUILDING, University Ave. and N. Charter St., has an Italian Renaissance façade; the interior is squarely divided off into classrooms and laboratories. The School of Pharmacy, sharing these rooms with the Chemistry Department, has a permanent PHARMACEUTICAL EXHIBIT (*open*).

45. The WISCONSIN GENERAL HOSPITAL, 1300 University Ave., designed by Arthur Peabody in 1924 to conform with the Renaissance style of the rest of the buildings on the campus, serves as the combined State hospital and practice rooms of students in the School of Medicine. The Student Infirmary (1918, 1931), the Bradley Memorial Hospital (1919), the Orthopedic Hospital for Children (1931), and the Nurse's Dormitory (1925) are all branches of the main hospital and stand in the same block.

The AGRICULTURAL CAMPUS begins on the hill above Linden Drive and spreads broadly westward between Lake Mendota and University Avenue.

46. WISCONSIN HIGH SCHOOL (1913), University Ave. and Lorch Court, a yellow-brick structure with a red tile roof, serves as the university training school for prospective teachers. Wisconsin High experiments in the newest methods of education.

47. The STUDIO OF THE ARTIST IN RESIDENCE resembles a small country school except for the skylights on its northern side. It was built in 1937 for John Steuart Curry (*see Art*), the first artist in residence appointed by the university.

48. The UNIVERSITY EXTENSION AND HOME ECONOMICS BUILDING, overlooking the Medical building, contains the offices of the Extension Division, one of the largest in the United States, and the Department of Home Economics.

49. AGRICULTURAL HALL (1902), with its Greek pillars and quoins, looks south across the HENRY QUADRANGLE. This hall stands

in the same relation to its campus as Bascom Hall does to the Upper Campus; in it is the Agricultural Library containing 35,000 volumes.

50. The UNIVERSITY FARMS, containing various laboratories, horse barns, poultry buildings, beef cattle sheds, swine barns, and dairy barns, are spread out over 841 acres, some of which is reclaimed land.

The ANIMAL HUSBANDRY AND STOCK PAVILION (1908), west from Agricultural Hall, is used for stock exhibitions and occasionally for concerts. In April 1938 the National Progressives of America held their first political rally here. The HIRAM SMITH HALL (1892), of half-timber construction, is the chief dairy building of the University. Experiments in the production and purification of milk are conducted in this building.

51. OBSERVATORY HILL, the highest point on the campus, and well known since Irving Berlin's popular song of a few years ago, "On Observatory Hill," overlooks Lake Mendota and Picnic Point. CHAMBERLIN ROCK, a huge granite boulder brought by the Continental Glacier from ancient Pre-Cambrian bedrock in Canada and deposited on this section of the Wisconsin drift, was named as a memorial to Thomas Chrowder Chamberlin, State geologist (1873-77) and president of the university (1887-92). WASHBURN OSBERVATORY (*open 7:30-9:30 p.m. 1st and 3rd Wed. only*), a weathered yellow sandstone building, has offices, classrooms and a large telescope of the department of astronomy. A STUDENT'S OBSERVATORY, next to the larger observatory, is housed in a small gray frame building.

52. The VAN HISE AND KRONSHAGE DORMITORIES for men, at the foot of Observatory Hill, extend westward along the lakeshore.

CAMP RANDALL, a 42-acre lot extending from University Ave. to Monroe St., between Breese Terrace and Randall Ave., was donated in 1861 by the Wisconsin State Agricultural Society to the State legislature as a drill ground for Union soldiers, and named Camp Randall in honor of the war Governor, Alexander W. Randall. The camp became the center of Wisconsin military activities, and 70,000 men were quartered and trained here. After the war, the property became the State Fairgrounds, but in 1893 it was acquired by the university as an athletic field. In 1911 a section of the land was set aside as the Camp Randall Memorial Park, and a MEMORIAL ARCH, 36 feet high and 36 feet wide, completed in 1912, was dedicated to the Civil War soldiers. During the World War, the camp was again used as a drill ground for the soldiers, many of them university students.

53. UNIVERSITY FIELD HOUSE, NE. corner Breese Terrace and Regent St., was built in 1930 and is used for indoor sport contests, occasional university convocations, and the annual commencement exercises.

54. UNIVERSITY STADIUM, directly back of the Field House, Breese Terrace opposite Hoyt St., with seating capacity of 45,000, was built in 1918 and has since had five additions.

(West and South Madison)

55. The FIRST CONGREGATIONAL CHURCH, SW. corner University Ave. and Breese Terrace, a red brick building with white columns and a blue-tipped white tower, was designed in the Georgian Colonial style by W. Roger Greeley, Boston architect. Dedicated in 1930, it is a representative example of Georgian influence upon Colonial style in America. Its congregation is the largest of its denomination in Wisconsin.

56. The AIRPLANE HOUSE, 120 Ely Place, spreads over one of the highest points in Madison. Designed for Professor E. A. Gilmore by Frank Lloyd Wright in 1906, this low-slung brown stucco residence is typical of Wright's "Illinois Prairie" style. Its almost level roof projects out over long lines of windows, set in two wings that flank a center section. A long rudder-like garden wall and a pointed sleeping porch have helped give the house its name.

57. The SIGMA PHI FRATERNITY HOUSE, 106 Prospect Ave., was designed by George Elmslie and Louis Sullivan in 1910. The cantilever construction, used often by Sullivan's pupil, Frank Lloyd Wright, is employed in front and rear second-story porches; supporting the porches and extending beyond them are two great stained wooden beams, heavily carved. Other notable features of the exterior include two circular bays and a series of leaded windows, set back a little distance from the outer walls and ornamented with white glass inserts of geometric design. The low-pitched roof terminates in deep overhanging eaves. The walls are faced with dull red brick and brown shingles, cut off into long horizontal lines by white concrete trim. Professor H. C. Bradley, for whom the home was designed, sold his property to the fraternity in 1916.

58. The HOME OF UNIVERSITY PRESIDENTS, 130 Prospect Ave., is a three-story red brick house, with four attic gabled windows over a low pillared porch. The building was planned for John M. Olin in 1910. When Olin died in 1924 he willed it to the university as a home for its presidents. It has since served as a residence for Glenn Frank and Clarence A. Dykstra, presidents of the university.

59. The U. S. FOREST PRODUCTS LABORATORY (*conducted tours 2:30 p.m. Mon.-Fri.; 9:30 a.m. Sat.*), at the end of a concrete drive leading north from University Ave. between Allen St. and Highland Ave., is a five-story, limestone, U-shaped building, with two wings flanking a central court. Vertical wooden fins separating the many windows and the receding lines of the "step back" construction of the lower two stories add height and grace to the building. Constructed of white dressed limestone, it was designed in the modern industrial style by Holabird and Root of Chicago, and completed in 1932.

The laboratory was established in Madison in 1910, when it was housed in the University of Wisconsin's present Mining and Metallurgy building. For several years it was the only institution in the world conducting general research on wood and its utilization. Construction funds for the present building, valued at $1,500,000 with its equipment and later additions, were provided by Congressional act in 1930. The laboratory is operated by the Forest Service of the United States Department of Agriculture in cooperation with the University of Wisconsin for the study of wood, either in its raw state or in the converted forms of paper, plastics, cellulose, lignin, etc. Experimental equipment includes a sawmill, a Fourdrinier paper-making machine, dry kilns, gluing machinery and presses, humidity rooms, hydrolysis apparatus for chemical conversion of wood, and devices for testing paints, wood preservatives and fire retardants. More than 600,000 mechanical tests have been made to determine strength characteristics of 160 native woods, and experiments in boxing and crating are estimated to have saved $37,000,000 in claims against railroads for damages to goods in transit between 1920 and 1930. About 3,000 samples of wood are sent annually to the laboratory for identification, and important questions of commercial use or decisions in lawsuits often hinge on its findings; valuable evidence concerning the ladder used in the Lindbergh kidnapping case was supplied by a laboratory research worker. Broadly speaking, the research activities of the laboratory are directed toward the more efficient and diversified utilization of forest materials, thus contributing to the economic use of the 600,000,000 acres of forest land in the United States.

60. The FOREST HILL CEMETERY, Mineral Point Rd. and Regent St., was established by the city in 1857. On the right of Forest Hill Mausoleum, near the main entrance, is CONFEDERATE'S REST, containing the graves of 140 Confederate soldiers. At other spots are the tombstones of Louis P. Harvey, Lucius Fairchild, William R. Taylor, and Robert M. La Follette, former Wisconsin Governors. Adjoining the cemetery on the north, at the intersection of Regent St. and Speedway Rd., are the Catholic cemeteries of HOLY CROSS and CALVARY.

61. The ARBORETUM (*open parking spaces and shelter houses*), Manitou Way and Seminole Highway, consists of 900 acres of experimental and recreational land along the west and south shores of Lake Wingra. Owned by the University of Wisconsin, and maintained by the university and the Wisconsin Conservation Commission, the area is primarily a testing ground for the study and improvement of the State's natural resources in soil, flora, and fauna.

62. The OLD SPRING HOTEL (*private*), 3706 Nakoma Rd., a white trimmed, red brick house, was built in 1854, near a large spring. In those days a main mail route passed by the tavern, and many travelers came to its doors. The place was noted for its cookies and coffee. Robert M. La Follette, when a lad, used to stop for breakfast on the way from Primrose farm to Madison. Then it was known as Grandma Gorham's. Professor James Dickson, present owner, has added a two-story Georgian Colonial porch and made other alterations on the rear of the house. A bronze tablet identifies the old building.

63. PLOW INN, 3402 Monroe St., now a private residence, was a prosperous tavern and overnight stopping place in stagecoach days. Built in 1836 of native limestone, and designed in the post-Colonial style, the building has since suffered additions and alterations. A covering of stucco completely hides the original walls.

64. EDGEWOOD ACADEMY, 2209 Monroe St., consists of academy buildings, a chapel, and a home for the Dominican Sisters. The academy buildings, designed in 1927 by Albert Kelsey of Philadelphia, are constructed of cream-colored brick, with panels of embossed tan terra cotta tile. The friezes and entrance motifs are of Renaissance design. The academy began in 1881 as a school for girls when Cadwallader Washburn, former Governor of Wisconsin, deeded his 40-acre estate to the Dominican Sisters. In 1926 the school became coeducational. Its curriculum covers grades from kindergarten through junior college. Protestant children may attend. Several Indian mounds are on the grounds of the school.

65. VILAS PARK, S. end of Garfield St. on shore of Lake Wingra, covers 62.6 acres of land, various sections of which were donated by Colonel and Mrs. William F. Vilas as a memorial to their son, Henry. The park was created by dredging, filling, and tree planting on an area of sodden marsh. Three islands, a lagoon, and the main grounds have replaced a large strip of submarginal lakeshore. Besides tennis courts, ball grounds, fireplaces and picnic tables, the park contains a well-equipped Zoo (*open 7-5 daily*), housed in three main buildings and a number of smaller buildings, dens, and pond islands. There are monkeys, lions, tigers, bears, bison, elk, camels, deer, many varieties of birds, and, best known of all, Annie, the elephant.

66. OLIN PARK, at the southern city limits, left from Highway US 12, has 30 acres of grounds, with picnic tables, fireplaces, a pavilion, a swimming pier and a boat pier. The park was once the site of the old Lakeside Water Cure, built in the 1850's, and later of the Monona Lake Assembly, where thousands came each year to hear lectures and political speeches. It was purchased by the city in 1912 and in 1924 was named for John M. Olin, first president and leading spirit of the Madison Park and Pleasure Drive Association.

67. The GILES HOME (*private*), 451 W. Wilson St., was built in the middle of the last century by A. A. Bird, building commissioner for the first Capitol in Madison. The cream-colored brick cottage, designed in the Victorian manner with elaborate jig-saw ornament, was for many years the home of Ella Giles (*see Literature*), writer and close friend of Ella Wheeler Wilcox.

68. The B. O. WEBSTER HOME (*private*), 314 S. Broom St., is a two-story yellow frame house, built on an embankment close to Lake Monona. In the 1880's and 1890's it was the residence of Robert M. La Follette, and during those years it housed many distinguished guests, among them Theodore Roosevelt.

69. The DANE COUNTY COURTHOUSE, 207 W. Main St., is a massive red brick building, erected in 1885 on the site of an earlier

courthouse built in 1850. Brownstone, limestone, and brick, each of a different color, have gone into the construction of this building. Its round arched windows, corbeled cornices and heavy towers are characteristic of Richardson's Romanesque Revival style.

70. ST. RAPHAEL'S CHURCH, 200 W. Main St , was built in 1854 as Madison's second Catholic Church. Father Etschmann, resident priest at the time, toured Wisconsin and eastern States soliciting donations; he collected $1,200 and about 20,000 feet of lumber. The old church is long and high, and of simple design. The Georgian type steeple is reminiscent of Christopher Wren's work.

71. The FORMER SYNAGOGUE, 214 W. Washington Ave., was built in 1863 by the congregation Schaare Shomain and was one of the first synagogues in Wisconsin. Constructed of brick and sandstone blocks, the one-story building of Victorian Gothic design has successively served as a synagogue, a Unitarian society hall, a Woman's Christian Temperance Union headquarters, a chapel for three religious denominations, and now (1940) a funeral home.

POINTS OF INTEREST IN ENVIRONS

Lake View Sanatorium and Mendota State Hospital, 5.8 m. (see Tour 19B); Trailer Park, 5.9 m, (see Tour 20); dam and locks at outlet of Lake Waubesa, 9.1 m., Lake Kegonsa, 15.5 m. (see Tour 7).

Milwaukee

Railroad Stations: 321 W. Everett St. (Downtown) and 3315 W. Cameron Ave. (Northwest Side) for Chicago, Milwaukee, St. Paul & Pacific R. R.; 915 E. Wisconsin Ave. (Downtown) for Chicago and North Western Ry.; 231 W. Michigan St. for Milwaukee Electric Ry. and Transit Co. (interurban electric) and Minneapolis, St. Paul and Sault Ste. Marie Ry.; 537 W. Michigan St. for Chicago, North Shore and Milwaukee R. R. (electric).

Bus Stations: National Trailways System Depot, 631 N. 6th St., for Central Trailways; Public Service Bldg., 231 W. Michigan St., for Wisconsin Motor Bus Lines, Northland Greyhound Lines, Northwestern Stages, and Midland Coaches.

Airports: Milwaukee County Airport, E. Layton Ave. (County Y) between S. Griffin and S. Brust Aves., 9½ *m.* SW. of North Western Depot, for Northwest Airlines and Pennsylvania Central Airlines; taxi 95¢, time 30 min.; Milwaukee Seadrome, E. end of E. Wisconsin Ave., no scheduled service; Curtiss-Wright Airport, US 41 and W. Silver Spring Drive, 12 *m.* NW. of North Western Depot; no scheduled service.

Taxis: Zone system; 25¢ for first zone and 15¢ for each succeeding zone; one to five passengers; 15¢ for each extra stop.

Streetcars and Local Busses: Streetcars: fare 10¢, 6 tickets for 50¢; suburban fare, add 3¢ for each zone or 20 zone tickets for 50¢; weekly passes $1 to $1.75, according to zone. Busses: fare 10¢, weekly pass $1.25, no transfers. Chicago, North Shore and Milwaukee Local, fare 5¢.

Steamship and Car Ferry Lines: Operate daily and Sunday throughout year, weather permitting. 350 N. Plankinton Ave. for Wisconsin and Michigan Steamship Co.; sailings at 11:30 p.m. to Muskegon, Mich.; 1940 S. Kinnickinnic Ave. for Pere Marquette Ry. Co.; sailings at 2 a.m. and 10 a.m. from E. Maple St. docks and at 7:30 p.m. from E. Bay St. dock to Ludington, Mich.; foot of E. Bay St. for Grand Trunk Western Ry. Co.; sailings at 8 a.m., 2 p.m., 7 p.m., and about midnight to Muskegon, Mich. All lines except Grand Trunk carry automobiles. Dock at 324 N. Plankinton Ave. for Chicago Milwaukee Line; excursions during summer only between Milwaukee and Chicago. Boat arrives at Milwaukee 2 p.m., leaves at 5 p.m.

Traffic Regulations: Overnight parking on streets prohibited; U turns only at intersections without signs, lights, or traffic officers.

Accommodations: Eighty-three hotels; tourist camp in Grant Park on State 42, 9.8 *m.* south of North Western Depot.

Street Numbering: Base line for north and south numbering, E. Menomonee St. on East Side, and W. Canal and W. Stevenson Sts. on West Side. East and west base line N. and S. 1st St., Milwaukee River, and S. Chase Ave.

Information Service: Milwaukee Motor Club, 312 E. Mason St.; Milwaukee Association of Commerce, 611 N. Broadway.

Radio Stations: WTMJ (620 kc.); WISN (1120 kc.); WEMP (1310 kc.).

Theaters and Motion Picture Houses: Pabst Theater, 144 E. Wells St., plays, concerts, light operas, ballets and German films; Davidson Theater, 621 N. Third St., plays and outstanding films; 80 motion picture houses.

Baseball: Borchert Field, N. 8th and W. Chambers Sts., home of Milwaukee "Brewers" of American Association.

Football: Marquette Stadium, N. 35th St. and W. Clybourn Ave., State Teachers College Stadium, 3200 N. Maryland Ave., for college football; State Fair Park, S. 81st St. and W. Greenfield Ave. (West Allis), for professional football.

Swimming: Bradford, McKinley, and South Shore Beaches on Lake Michigan; Estabrook, Kletzsch, and Lincoln Park Beaches on Milwaukee River; outdoor swimming pools at Jackson, Greenfield, Sheridan, McGovern and Lapham Parks; indoor pools at 709 W. Highland Ave., N. 16th and W. North Ave., N. Jackson and E. Huron Sts., S. 4th and W. Mitchell Sts., E. Center and N. Richards Sts., W. Greenfield Ave. and S. Union St., S. 10th St. and W. Hayes Ave.

Tennis: Tennis courts in most parks and many of the larger playgrounds.

Golf: Public courses at Lake Park, E. Center St. and N. Prospect Ave.; Lincoln Park, on State 57, 6.8 m. N. of North Western Depot; Brown Deer Park, on State 57, 12 m. NW. of North Western Depot; James Currie Park on US 16, 9.2 m. NW. of North Western Depot; Greenfield Park on State 59, 9.5 m. SW. of North Western Depot; Charles B. Whitnall Park on US 45, 11 m. SW. of North Western Depot; Grant Park on State 42, 9.8 m. S. of North Western Depot; all courses 18 holes, greens fee 25¢ for 9, 35¢ for 18 holes; except Lake Park, two 9-hole pitch and putt courses, fee 15¢ for each course.

Boating: Artificial lakes and lagoons at Brown Deer, Humboldt, Mitchell, Silver Spring, Kletzsch, Washington, and Kosciuszko Parks.

Winter Sports: Skating rinks with warming cabins offering refreshments, checking service and rest rooms at most parks and many of the larger playgrounds; skiing and tobogganing at Gordon, Lake, South Shore, and Washington Parks.

Annual Events: Orchid Exhibit, begins first Sun. in Feb.; Easter Lily Exhibit, begins Palm Sunday; Central Intercollegiate Field Championship, first Fri. in June; Wisconsin Iris Show, June; Music Under the Stars, June, July, Aug.; Midsummer Festival, July; Italian Festival Days, honoring Saints Madonna del Lume, San Rocco, San Guiseppe, and Madonna Addolorata, during July, Aug., and Sept.; State Fair, last week in Aug.; State Dahlia Show, Sept.; Chicago Symphony Opera Season, begins Oct.; "Mum" exhibit through Nov.; Poinsettia Exhibit, begins Dec. 20; Municipal Christmas Tree Celebration, Dec. 24.

MILWAUKEE (581.23 alt., 578,249 pop.), the largest city in Wisconsin, covers an irregularly glove-shaped area of 44.1 square miles along the crescent curve of a bay in Lake Michigan's western shore. Toward the east Milwaukee looks upon a marine landscape animated by freighters, car ferries, excursion steamers, and the white flecks of yacht and sailboat. Westward, highways lead past wooded farmlands to dozens of inland lakes where affluent Milwaukeeans maintain year-round residences and the mildly prosperous have summer cottages. The life of the city itself verges toward the Lake Michigan shore with its three large parks, beaches, yacht clubs, Coast Guard Station, municipal water filtration plant, and long Government pier, haunt of lay fishermen. Three rivers emptying into the lake—the Milwaukee from the north, the Menominee from the west, the Kinnickinnic from the south —roughly quadrisect the metropolitan district; with their canals, they account for a score of bridges.

North along the high bluffs overlooking the lake are the town houses of the wealthy, some new and impressive, some old and baronial, many built years ago as the homes of pioneer brewers, tanners, and lumbermen. Wisconsin Avenue, the main thoroughfare, runs westward from the lake, through the heart of the city. Business in outlying areas concentrates in frequent neighborly clusters of shops and offices. The Menominee Valley is the chief industrial district, home of the city's second-ranking industry, meat packing; and shops of the metal trades, their output exceeding all other Milwaukee products, spread from the valley south over the city.

Milwaukee ranks twelfth in population among the cities of the United States and ninth in the value of manufactured goods. For health, safety, and solvency, it resolutely holds a place in the highest brackets among the 13 largest cities in the country. Milwaukeeans have ceased to be surprised at perennial announcements that their city leads in health, fire and crime prevention, or low death and accident tolls. In 1937, because Milwaukee had won the top health award with such frequency and regularity, the city was barred temporarily from competition so that other cities might have a chance at the prize. During the same year Milwaukee placed first in the national safety contest, winning the award for the fourth time. Simultaneously the city won additional honors by presenting the lowest homicide rate and the lowest motor death rate among all United States cities of more than 250,000 population; the general death rate and the record for fire prevention in that year gave Milwaukee second place among cities of its population class. Taxpayers found cheer in still another 1937 record when Milwaukee, for the second time, had the lowest per capita debt among the 13 largest cities. An alert police department and swift, incisive criminal court procedure gave Milwaukee its reputation for swift "24-hour justice." Of Milwaukee's way with transgressors, the Wickersham Committee reported to the United States Congress: "Milwaukee is often cited as a city free from crime or where a criminal is speedily detected, arrested, promptly tried, and sent on his way to serve his time. No other city has such a record."

Newcomers and visitors sense a reason for the record in the suburban, rather than metropolitan face that the city presents: the low buildings of the downtown area where only a few rise higher than 300 feet, the acres of field and forest in one of the country's outstanding park systems, the free sweep of Lincoln Memorial Drive along the lake, the neat cottages in the German and Polish neighborhoods, the pastoral look of lawns and gardens in even the less prosperous districts, and a nocturnal quiet that often produces the waggish comment, "You could fire a cannon down Wisconsin Avenue at midnight and never hit a soul!"

Night clubs and restaurants are relatively few because Milwaukeeans prefer the home dinner party, an evening of bridge, *schafskopf,* skat, or, more recently, bingo. Although the city has more than 2,000 taverns, only a few have inherited the look of the *Bierstuben* where whole families gathered when *Gemuetlichkeit* reigned and Milwaukee was the *Deutsch Athen* of America. Music and drama have little of the importance they had for the Milwaukee of 50 years ago; the legitimate theater is far from flourishing and musical events occur with only moderate frequency. Milwaukee, a city of homes and workers, boasts of a liberal school system, the largest municipally owned and operated museum in the United States, unusual social centers with activities suited to all members of the family, recreational facilities for each season of the year, and abundant safeguards for the well-being of its citizens.

The 1930 census figures show that 18.9 per cent of Milwaukee's population is foreign-born. Germans form the largest group of foreign stock, though the percentage of German foreign-born has shrunk considerably in recent years. In 1880, thirty-five per cent of Milwaukee's population was made up of foreign-born Germans, and Germans comprised 68 per cent of the total foreign-born; in 1930, eight per cent of the total population was composed of foreign-born Germans, and Germans comprised 37 per cent of the total foreign-born. Of the entire population, foreign-born Germans and Germans of the first generation (including Austrians) comprise 29.7 per cent. Assimilation of the German elements has accompanied the decline of German immigration to the city. Milwaukee no longer seems a city transplanted from the Rhine to the banks of the Milwaukee River; the German theater (*see The Theater*) has disappeared with the beer gardens; "Milwaukee German" is heard less and less frequently.

The Polish population has steadily increased; foreign-born Poles and their children were 11 per cent of the total population in 1930. Most of them live on Milwaukee's South Side, their life centered about their parish churches. They publish two newspapers, the *Kuryer Polski* and the *Nowiny Polski.* The Polish Alliance, a center for Polish activity, has far-reaching influence on the life of the city.

The Italians, concentrated largely in the third ward, give a special color to the city's life. In summer they hold frequent fiestas when strings of lights illuminate the streets, Madonnas ride in processions, and redolent sausages roast at sidewalk stands.

Negroes, brought to Milwaukee to fill a labor shortage, have settled here since the World War. In 1930 there were 7,501 Negroes in the city. Most of them live in the sixth ward, where they operate shops, cabarets, and a grocery cooperative.

As recently as the early nineteenth century, Milwaukee was still *Mahn-a-waukee Seepe,* "gathering place by the river," for various Indian tribes, among them the Potawatomi, Menominee, Winnebago, Chippewa, Sauk, and, earlier, the Mascoutin and Fox. Most numerous were the Potawatomi, who with the Menominee, their brothers in the great Algonquian language division, had come under French suzerainty in the seventeenth century.

The twilight of the Indian's day in *Mahn-a-waukee Seepe* began in the late eighteenth century when such traders as Joseph Le Croix, Jacques Vieau, Antoine LeClair, and Joseph Framboise, though friendly to the natives, opened the territory to the white man. The Indian went deeper into the forest, emerging to trade his pelts and furs for guns, ammunition, knives, tobacco, and calico. By the end of the century tribal chieftains had begun to fear that they must follow the example set by Virginia in 1784 in ceding claims on the Northwest Territory to the national government. In 1831 the Menominee relinquished claim to the land lying east and north of the Milwaukee River. Two years later, in a treaty made at Chicago, the United Nation of Chippewa, Ottawa, and Potawatomi gave the United States the large section south and west of the river.

In 1835, when the first lands in the Milwaukee region were surveyed and bid off at the Green Bay land office, three men formally came into possession of Milwaukee. Solomon Juneau, a French trader who had come to *Mahn-a-waukee Seepe* in 1818, obtained land between the Milwaukee River and Lake Michigan, calling it Juneautown. Byron Kilbourn, a New Englander, bought the tract west of the river, naming it Kilbourntown, and George H. Walker, a Virginian, purchased a section to the south. Though Juneau remained primarily an Indian trader, amassing great wealth for himself, he built the community's first courthouse and acted as interpreter and peacemaker between the Indians and the white settlers. He sold a portion of his land to his partners, Morgan L. Martin and Michael Dousman; Juneau and Martin planned the future city, investing $100,000 on improvements within a few years and recording the new village under the name of Milwaukee. Walker spent the first ten years on his land as a trader, fighting off squatters who tried to jump his claim. Kilbourn's dream of a great city prompted him to establish Milwaukee's first newspaper, the *Advertiser,* in 1836. His boat, the *Badger,* went down the Milwaukee River through a maze of grass and wild rice to greet lake vessels calling at Milwaukee on their Chicago route, and to carry all newcomers to Kilbourntown.

The year 1836, when Milwaukee County was established, brought an interval of phenomenal growth and prosperity to the new village. Eastern speculators and tradesmen came in on every boat. A score of Irish and Yankee settlers arrived; Germans, who later figured so powerfully in the cultural and political development of Milwaukee, began coming in that year. The boom times of 1836, when houses went up over night and every man had a pocketful of money, were poor preparation for the panic of 1837, which stunned the city, deflating its real estate values and freezing its currency.   In spite of the financial confusion, Milwaukee took time in 1838 to observe the departure of the Potawatomi, remnants of the once mighty tribe, who were moved by wagon caravan to a new home in Kansas.

Within the next two years the Indian's council ground became the white man's battle ground in the acrimonious rivalry between Juneautown and Kilbourntown.   Consolidation of the two villages in 1839 as the east and west wards of Milwaukee proved only a temporary armistice in what came to be known as the Bridge War.   The quarrel, centering around the payment for Milwaukee River bridges ordered by the 1840 legislature, raged for five years, reaching its climax when the East Siders awoke one morning to find the west end of the Spring Street (W. Wisconsin Avenue) bridge impassable and the west end of the Chestnut Street (W. Juneau Avenue) bridge being torn away by angry West Siders.   Equally angry, east ward citizens produced a cannon and trained it on Byron Kilbourn's house.   They were restrained from firing only by the news that Kilbourn's daughter lay dead in the house.   A few days later they assembled again and set about demolishing the Spring Street bridge.   The controversy ended in 1845 when the legislature provided that the cost of all bridges be shared equally by the two wards.   During the same year George Walker succeeded in a long struggle to acquire clear title to his land, and Walker's Point was consolidated with the other wards.

As smoke from the Bridge War cleared, Milwaukee found itself a city of 10,000 people, more than half of them Germans and the majority Catholic.   John Martin Henni was appointed bishop of the new Milwaukee diocese, the first German Catholic bishop in the United States.   *Das Wiskonsin Banner,* first of many Milwaukee German papers, was established in 1844.   Stagecoaches were making three trips a week to Chicago and Galena, Illinois.   In 1846 the city charter was ratified, and Solomon Juneau became the first mayor of the newly incorporated municipality.

Two years later the city's most significant immigrants had begun to arrive—the "forty-eighters"—men of high intellect, many of them wealthy and cultured, refugees from the unsuccessful rebellion against German monarchies in 1848.   Arriving with high dreams of building a free German republic, they plunged immediately into the professional, cultural, and political life of the city.   They founded theaters, music societies, *Turnvereine,* and Freethinker groups.   They published radical newspapers and pamphlets on every debatable subject from the existence of God to the tyranny of monarchy.   Among them were Peter Englemann, influential in the evolution of Milwaukee's school system; Fritz Anneke, a leader in the German revolution; his wife, Mathilde, noted feminist and dramatist; the painter, Henry Vianden; the German poets, William Dilg, Konrad Krez, and Edmund Maerklein; and Carl Schurz, who arrived later and became a major general in the Civil War and United States Secretary of the Interior.

Despite the decimating effects of cholera and other epidemics, Milwaukee's population leaped from 21,000 in 1850 to 46,000 in 1851. The State's first railroad, from Milwaukee to Waukesha, was opened in 1851 with passengers frequently sharing the duties of the crew. Gas lights appeared on the city streets in 1852. During the same year the exodus of the Indians neared completion when the Menominee were granted a reservation in northern Wisconsin.

Abolitionist sentiment flared to open fury in 1854 when Joshua Glover, an escaped slave, was arrested in Racine and placed in the Milwaukee jail. An enraged citizenry freed Glover and arranged for his transportation to Canada. The subsequent arrest of Sherman Booth, abolitionist editor of the *American Freeman,* for violation of the Fugitive Slave Act in the Glover incident marked the beginning of a legal battle which continued for seven years and ended only when Booth, his health and his fortune long since sacrificed in the fight, was released from jail by order of President Buchanan.

Meanwhile Milwaukee was moving steadily ahead. Shipbuilding had seen a marked increase, and in 1856 the schooner *Dean Richmond* carried Milwaukee's first transoceanic shipment of wheat direct to Liverpool. *Mohega, die Blume des Waldes,* a German opera written from Indian legends by a Prussian-born Milwaukeean, von Sobolewski, was received with wild enthusiasm in 1859. Abraham Lincoln spoke at the Milwaukee State Fair in September, 1859. In the next year 295 persons, most of them Milwaukeeans, drowned when the excursion steamer *Lady Elgin* collided with the lumber schooner *Augusta* and sank near Winnetka, Illinois. For weeks the city witnessed funeral processions. Numerous ballads were composed lamenting the event, and the mourning was muted only when Milwaukee stirred to the greater excitement of war-time and the increased prosperity produced by the Civil War. Closing of the Mississippi-Gulf route shunted shipping to the Great Lakes and created demands for manufactured goods, which meant the substitution of machine power for man power. Backyard shops became factories, and business sky-rocketed. This industrial change gave rise to Milwaukee's first major labor union, the Knights of St. Crispin, formed among boot and shoe workers by Newell Daniels in 1867. Labor continued to organize in direct proportion to the growth and concentration of industry. The value of goods manufactured in Milwaukee had tripled by 1869 and, despite the industrial depression of 1873, lake commerce and the extension of railroads made Milwaukee in 1875 the primary wheat market of the world.

Two tragedies darkened the 1880 decade. On a January night in 1883 fire destroyed the Newhall House, a leading hotel. Sixty-four persons are known to have perished, though loss of the hotel register made a correct estimate impossible. In 1886 five persons were killed and four wounded when State troops fired on a labor demonstration at the North Chicago Rolling Mills in Bay View. Death dealt out by the guns of the militia was a shattering blow to union morale and to the Knights of Labor, active in Milwaukee since 1880. It was two years before any great number of unions rallied to join the new American Federation of Labor.

Though "Lost on the Lady Elgin" and "Burning of the Newhall House" still were popular as ballads, the disasters they commemorated were eclipsed on the night of October 28, 1892, when fire laid waste 16 blocks of residential and business districts in the Third Ward between the Milwaukee River and Lake Michigan. Damage totalling $4,500,000 included the Chicago and North Western Railway's freight houses and 215 loaded cars. Suddenly homeless and destitute, the Irish who had settled in the Third Ward found refuge in the charity of their fellow citizens, who contributed $137,436 in a subscription campaign to aid the victims. Despite the fire and the panic of 1893, this was the golden age in the German theater and music societies, in the cafes and beer gardens, among them the famous Schlitz Palm Garden. *Gemuetlichkeit* prevailed. Even in the street railway strike of 1896 the public hilariously participated, cheering the strikers and jeering the police who aided the strike breakers. The decade also marked the amalgamation of Socialists and trade unionists as a political force (*see Labor*). Victor L. Berger, who later exerted so profound an influence on Milwaukee's political life, arrived in 1882. A few years of teaching in the public schools and editing the German daily *Vorwaerts* convinced him that the utopian Socialism of the "forty-eighters" was esoteric and stagnant, clearly unsuited to the needs of a new land. Under Berger's leadership, Socialists and the unions co-operated in the municipal campaign of 1894. Four years later Berger's platform became the foundation for a united Social Democratic party. At the turn of the century, when Milwaukee had 3,342 factories producing goods valued at $123,786,449, labor with Socialist support again was on the upswing. Victories for the combination mounted steadily until 1910 when the Socialists won overwhelmingly in the city and county elections. Emil Seidel was the first Socialist mayor. In the same year Berger was elected to Congress, the first Socialist in the House of Representatives. Graft investigations involving the two major political parties combined with the work of the "bundle brigade"—nearly 1,000 men and women who distributed Socialist campaign literature printed in 12 different languages—to effect the sweeping victory. During two years of undisputed Socialist control labor experienced a happy reversal of the old order. When the street railway workers again went on strike they received the aid of city and county authorities. Strikers, not strike breakers, were deputized. City officials frequently served as mediators in labor disputes with the result that disturbances were fewer, less violent, and of shorter duration.

This period of domestic peace and progress continued until distant rumblings of a World War began to reverberate in Milwaukee and finally stirred the city to a frenzied pitch of anti-German feeling. The statue of *Germania* was removed from the Brumder Building, which long had been a center of German commerce. Signs saying "English Spoken Here" were removed from shop windows. German streets and German foods underwent a new christening. In 1919 Victor Berger and four others who had opposed America's entrance into the war were convicted of conspiracy to violate the Espionage Act and sentenced to 20 years in Leavenworth. Bail, pending appeal to the U. S. Supreme Court, was set at a half-million dollars, which the Socialist party raised overnight. Berger's newspaper, the Milwaukee *Leader,* founded in 1911, was deprived of its third-class mailing privileges. Socialists peddled the paper in the streets. Though Berger was re-elected to Congress in 1919 and 1920, his seat was denied him. It was not until he was once more elected in 1922, a year after the Supreme Court had freed him, that he was allowed to serve his term.

Much that made Milwaukee so strongly German in flavor never revived after the war. In 1919 prohibition destroyed an industry that had brought the city an annual income of $22,500,000. Yet in the decade before 1929 Milwaukee increased the value of its manufactures from $576,161,000 to $912,261,503. In the early years of the depression, the Milwaukee County Board set up work relief projects for road building and park improvement, a program which served as a stop-gap until the Federal Government established the Civil Works Administration.

Though Milwaukee has earned a reputation for Socialist government and kept a Socialist mayor in office from 1916 until 1940, its common council has been largely nonpartisan. The police chief and the fire chief are Socialist appointees of the municipal fire and police commission, but most of the city's appointive offices are held by men and women of varying party faiths. Many observers believe that this system of political checks and balances is responsible for a city where solvency is the ideal, where an efficient fire department makes possible the lowest fire insurance rates of any American city but Detroit, where a constantly progressing health department has increased a newborn baby's chance for survival four-fold in 30 years, where a man's danger of being murdered, robbed, or struck by an automobile has been reduced close to a minimum. Whatever the concomitant factors, Milwaukee's record has kept it among the five highest ranking cities of its size during the last decade.

Through municipal planning and the cooperation of the Federal Government, nearly four miles of concrete breakwater to protect 1,200 acres of water, piers, lighthouses, and other aids to navigation, have been provided in Milwaukee Harbor. Although four trunk-line railroads make connections here, shippers depend upon water transportation for between one-third and one-half of the city's freight. The chief commodity is coal, placing Milwaukee as the second-ranking port on the Great Lakes. Passenger traffic averages between 150,000 and 200,000 persons a year.

Industrially, Milwaukee is known across the face of the earth. The metal trades and meat packing are closely followed in productiveness by tanning (more topside calf is tanned in Milwaukee than in any other city in the world), and the manufacture of liquor, malt, knit goods, boots and shoes. Out of the city's vast machine shops come products that range from turbines weighing 1,200,000 pounds to parts so minute as to be assembled only with the aid of magnifying glasses. Milwaukee steam shovels dug the Panama Canal; Milwaukee turbines harnessed Niagara Falls; Milwaukee tractors are in the fields of most of the world's agricultural regions; herring-bone gears made in Milwaukee operate mines in Africa and Mexico, sugar mills in South America, and rolling mills in Japan, India, and Australia.

It was beer, however, as the advertising slogan said, that made Milwaukee famous. Repeal restored a major industry and brought with it the return of a few old German cafes and beer gardens where zither music is heard on Saturday night and *Sauerbraten-mit-Knoedeln* accompanies the beer.

POINTS OF INTEREST

(Downtown)

1. MARQUETTE UNIVERSITY, W. Wisconsin Ave. between N. 11th and N. 16th Sts., is a nonsectarian, co-educational institution operated by the Jesuit order. The compact campus embraces ten buildings, some of them the former homes of the city's wealthy families. The university is composed of Colleges of Liberal Arts, Business Administration, Engineering, Journalism, and Nursing; Schools of Speech, Dentistry, Medicine, and Law; a Graduate School, night school, and summer school. For the first semester of 1938-1939 the enrollment was 4,865.

The university had its beginning in 1857 when two scholarly Jesuit priests established St. Aloysius Academy, with an enrollment of 50 pupils. This school was succeeded seven years later by St. Gall's Academy. In 1880 expansion forced removal to a site at N. 10th and W. State Streets purchased through a gift of $16,000 made in 1848 by Chevalier J. G. De Boeye of Antwerp, Belgium. The cornerstone of Marquette College, named for one of the first missionaries in the Northwest Territory, was laid in August 1880. The nucleus for the present campus was provided in 1906 when Robert A. Johnston, Milwaukee industrialist, presented JOHNSTON HALL, 1131 W. Wisconsin Ave., to the college.

Connected with its important medical and dental schools are the MARQUETTE-KIRCHER ANATOMICAL EXHIBIT, the PATHOLOGICAL EXHIBIT, and the BRIGHT'S DISEASE EXHIBIT (*open when the university is open*), in the Medical School Building, 561 N. Fifteenth Street. The exhibits are mainly for the use of medical students and contain medical and anatomical displays.

In 1917 the Marquette School of Journalism became an independent unit of the University. The course of study was increased to four years, requiring, in addition to journalism courses, all cultural studies necessary for a bachelor's degree. The 1933 session of the Wisconsin Legislature provided for the admission of all graduates of the Law School to the bar, upon presentation of diplomas to the State Supreme Court.

Within the Marquette campus stands spired GESU CHURCH, 1145 W. Wisconsin Ave., one of Milwaukee's finest examples of ecclesiastical Gothic architecture, the work of H. C. Koch of Milwaukee.

The Marquette GYMNASIUM occupies the length of a city block on W. Clybourn Street, between N. Fifteenth and N. Sixteenth Streets, and has a seating capacity of 2,000. The University STADIUM, with a seating capacity of 20,000, is at N. 37th and W. Clybourn Streets.

2. The WISCONSIN CLUB (*private*), 900 W. Wisconsin Ave., was once the home of Alexander Mitchell, one of the wealthiest of Milwaukee's industrial pioneers, connected with early railroad and banking industries. The rambling three-story yellow brick house, with a heavy mansard roof and prominent tower, stands behind a large landscaped lawn, dotted with flower beds, a miniature Dutch windmill and a pagoda. The originally square mansion, designed by E. Townsend Mix, Milwaukee architect, was altered in later years by the addition of a west wing and a tower. Founded in 1891 as the Deutscher Club, the Wisconsin Club took its present name during the World War.

3. COURT OF HONOR, a boulevard plot on W. Wisconsin Ave. between N. 8th and N. 11th Sts., includes the Washington Monument, the work of R. H. Parker, erected in 1885; a memorial to Civil War Soldiers, designed by John S. Conway of Milwaukee and dedicated in 1898; a carnival shaft, designed in 1900 by A. C. Clas, Milwaukee; and the Hiker memorial to Spanish-American War veterans, the most recent addition to the court, designed by A. Koenig, Evanston, Illinois, and dedicated in 1932. The Court of Honor is the setting for Milwaukee's annual Community Christmas Tree Celebration.

4. The MILWAUKEE PUBLIC LIBRARY AND MUSEUM BUILDING, W. Wisconsin Ave. between N. 8th and N. 9th Sts., covers more than half of a square city block. This four-story stone structure of Renaissance design, with characteristic details of both French and Italian styles, is the work of Ferry and Clas, Milwaukee architects. The symmetrical facade is designed with a rusticated first story and Corinthian colonnades and elaborate Palladian windows at the second story. The interior has a rotunda, open from the first floor to the dome, finished in Italian marble. The rotunda floor is one of the finest examples of mosaic inlay in the city.

In front of the Museum, contrasting sharply with the architectural design of the building, stands a large TOTEM POLE bought by the institution in 1921 from the Haida Indians on the Queen Charlotte Islands, British Columbia.

The LIBRARY (*open 8:30-9 weekdays; 1:30-5 Sun.*), founded in 1847 by a group of private citizens, changed residences many times before the present building was erected in 1898. Most of the library's books are on open shelves readily available to the reader. A system whereby readers charge the books they take from the library, subject to verification by the librarian at the door, makes for rapid handling and reduces losses. Eighteen branches throughout the city circulate 20,000 books daily and extend library facilities to more than 700,000 people. Traveling collections go to suburban schools and institutions, and an extension division brings library privileges to prison inmates and hospital patients. To adapt the facilities to individual and group needs, a reader's advisory bureau outlines specialized reading and research programs. A collection of children's books, some printed as early as 1700, is one of the most outstanding divisions of the library. Notable also is an immense volume containing the signatures of 2,300 nationally known persons, compiled by Lydia Ely, art patron, who hoped to pay for the Civil War monument in the Court of Honor with contributions accompanying the autographs. When her plan failed to bring the necessary revenue, Captain Frederick Pabst agreed to pay the balance in exchange for the book. Presented to the library years later, the autograph book is estimated now to be worth far more than the original cost of the monument.

MILWAUKEE. Points of Interest

1. Marquette University
2. Wisconsin Club
3. Court of Honor
4. Milwaukee Public Library and Museum Building
5. Milwaukee County Courthouse
6. Public Safety Building
7. St. Benedict the Moor Mission
8. Pabst Brewery
9. Milwaukee Vocational School
10. Milwaukee Auditorium
11. West Side Turn Hall
12. Milwaukee Journal Building
13. Pabst Theater
14. City Hall
15. Blatz Brewery
16. Cathedral Square
17. St. John's Cathedral
18. Milwaukee Art Institute
19. Layton Art Gallery
20. Madonna de Pompeii Church
21. Kosciuszko Park
22. St. Josaphat's Basilica
23. South Shore Yacht Club
24. Jones Island
25. Milwaukee Sewage Disposal Plant
26. Mitchell Park
27. Veterans' Administration
28. Juneau Park
29. Milwaukee Yacht Club
30. Lake Park
31. Water Purification Plant
32. Milwaukee State Teachers College
33. Milwaukee-Downer Seminary
34. Milwaukee-Downer College
35. Milwaukee University School
36. Estabrook Park
37. Lincoln Park
38. Linus N. Dewey House
39. Schlitz Brewery
40. Plankinton Packing Plant
41. Red Star Yeast and Products Plant
42. Miller Brewery
43. Washington Park
44. Research and Engineering Building of the A. O. Smith Corporation
45. Garden Homes Subdivision
46. Parklawn
47. Mount Mary College

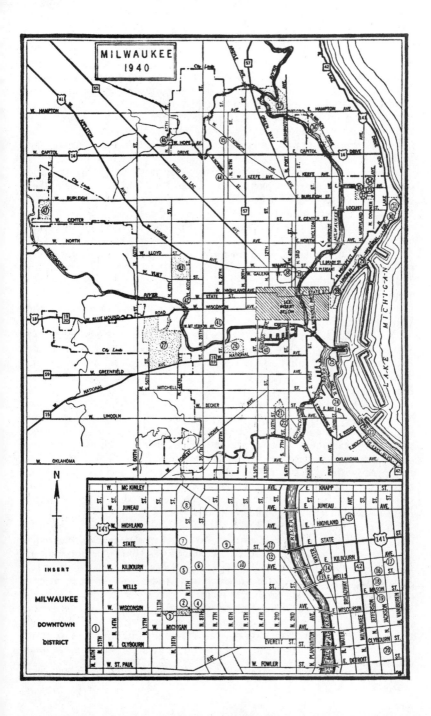

Instructive exhibits, environmental groups, and mural paintings in the several branches of the natural sciences, anthropology, and history occupy the MUSEUM (*open 9-9 Nov. 1 to May 1; 9-5:30 May 1 to Nov. 1; 1:30-5 Sun. and holidays*). The exhibits, ranging from archeological and zoological specimens to typewriters and ceramics, include 562,000 specimens. Many of them have been improved since 1932 through the use of $700,000 from the Federal Works Program. The museum conducts a program of free popular illustrated lectures and field excursions.

The museum is noteworthy for the extensive series of groups and dioramas in all of its departments. The Rudolph J. Nunnemacher collection of arms, the George A. West collection of aboriginal pipes, the Carl P. Dietz collection of typewriters, the B. F. Goss collection of birds' eggs, and the William J. Uihlein collection of philately are outstanding.

The museum maintains an extensive reference library, primarily for the use of its staff, but available to special students. There is, in addition, an extensive loan service of teaching aids to schools and other educational organizations of the city.

It is the largest municipally owned and operated museum in the United States.

5. The MILWAUKEE COUNTY COURTHOUSE (*open 8-5 weekdays*), 901 N. 9th St., stands on a low rise at the west edge of the Milwaukee River valley. The courthouse extends over a city block, dominating the area designated by the City Planning Commission as Milwaukee's Civic Center.

Designed by Albert Randolph Ross and completed in 1931 at a cost of $7,322,928, the courthouse attains distinction by the solid mass of its neo-classic architecture. Great arched windows and pedimented entrances break the severity of the lower half of the building; towering Corinthian colonnades support the simple top stories. The composition is topped with a classic attic story. The interior decorations are of travertine, Italian marble, and rich walnut paneling. Twenty-five murals by F. Scott Bradford, allegorical figures depicting historical incidents and civic virtues, adorn the courtrooms.

6. The PUBLIC SAFETY BUILDING (*open continuously*), 822 W. Kilbourn Ave., just east of the courthouse, was the first structure in the proposed Civic Center. Designed by Albert Randolph Ross, New York, and Alfred C. Clas, Milwaukee, it was completed in 1929. It is modern in design with an elaborate parapet and set-back at the sixth floor. Above its southern main entrance are bas-relief groups symbolizing *Safety, Justice,* and *Equity.* An ornamental frieze emphasizes the long lines of the facade. The interior is of marble and travertine. Its cost, $3,750,000, was shared by the city and county, who use it jointly for police and sheriff's departments, jails, and criminal courts.

7. ST. BENEDICT THE MOOR MISSION, 1004 N. 10th St., a Roman Catholic mission for Negroes, was established at its present

site in 1911. Work among the Negroes began in 1886 when a mission was started in connection with St. Gall's Church. Negroes were not numerous, and the mission served a small group. The activities of the mission increased with growth of Milwaukee's Negro population, and in 1911 the nucleus of the present group of buildings was dedicated. Today the mission school, dormitories, rectory, hospital, and other buildings occupy two city blocks. The Romanesque chapel, of variegated brick and limestone trim, faces W. State Street. Above the entrance, which is reached by a Y-shaped flight of steps, is a statue of St. Benedict.

The patron saint, a descendant of African slaves imported into Sicily, lived in sixteenth century Sicily and is generally regarded as the father of Catholic evangelism among Negroes. The Capuchin Order is in general charge of the mission, but Dominican Sisters teach in the school and Franciscan Sisters conduct the hospital.

8. The PABST BREWERY (*tours 9, 10, 11 a.m.; 1, 2, 3, 4 p.m., Mon.-Fri.; guides*), 917 W. Juneau Ave., is one of the largest breweries in the Nation. Spreading over five blocks, the older buildings embody many of the characteristics of medieval German architecture with their battlements and small windows; the newer buildings, much plainer, are more strictly utilitarian. Founded by Jacob Best as the Empire Brewery in 1842, the firm absorbed several smaller companies and was renamed in 1889 for Captain Frederick Pabst, an owner since 1864.

9. The MILWAUKEE VOCATIONAL SCHOOL, 1015 N. 6th St., has attained international recognition as the world's largest vocational school under one roof. Since 1926, when the present six-story brick building was erected at a cost of $4,000,000, its staff of 300 teachers has instructed an annual average of 35,000 students, ranging from young people who have not completed their secondary schooling to adults doing post graduate work. More than 50 courses in the day and evening schools fall roughly into ten classifications: apprentice, adult high school, adult preparatory, adult special, full and part time continuation schools, rehabilitation, nursing, technical, and vocational junior college.

10. The MILWAUKEE AUDITORIUM, 500 W. Kilbourn Ave., a quasi-public corporation of which the city is the majority stockholder, is the scene of large public gatherings. The building, filling an entire block on the site of the old Milwaukee Exposition building, is constructed of red brick. Though erected in 1909, the Auditorium is included in the Civic Center Plan. It has been host to three Presidents and numerous Presidential candidates on the Republican, Democratic, Socialist, and Communist tickets.

Within the Auditorium is the painting *Flagellants* by Carl von Marr, a Milwaukee artist who exhibited the canvas at the Columbian Exposition in 1893. Later it was purchased by Mrs. Emil Schandein, who presented it to the city in 1898.

11. WEST SIDE TURN HALL (*private*), 1034 N. 4th St., was once the cultural home of those German émigrés whose political philosophy helped lay the foundation for Socialism in Milwaukee and other

liberal movements in Wisconsin. Though the literal translation of *Turnverein* is "gymnastic club," discussion was as important as calisthenics to the Milwaukee Turners who organized in 1853. The building, of modified German Romanesque design, was erected in 1882. Gymnastic classes and exhibitions, musical programs, lectures, discussions and debates are still carried on in the hall.

12. The MILWAUKEE JOURNAL BUILDING (*tours upon request*), 333 W. State St., is the home of one of the city's large daily newspapers and its broadcasting station, WTMJ. Designed by F. D. Chase, Chicago, the five-story building of Kasota limestone is modern in design. Above the third-story windows are lunettes reproducing the emblems of twenty celebrated printers of eight nations. At the top of the building is an ornamental frieze depicting the history of printing. A portrait by Carl von Marr of the late Lucius W. Nieman, founder of the Milwaukee *Journal,* hangs in the lobby.

In 1936, the will of Mrs. Agnes Wahl Nieman provided that approximately $1,000,000 be given to Harvard University "to promote and elevate the standards of Journalism in the United States and educate persons especially qualified for journalism."

13. The PABST THEATER, 144 E. Wells St., once the home of the German repertory theater (*see The Theater*), remains as an example of ponderous German Renaissance architecture; with its grilled iron sidewalk canopy, it has an Old World appearance. Built in 1895 by Otto Straack for Captain Frederick Pabst, the theater was one of the first buildings in the northwest to provide unobstructed vision of the stage by eliminating interior columns and supports. The Pabst now houses concerts, occasional road shows, travel lectures, and German photoplays.

14. The CITY HALL (*open 8-5 weekdays*), 200 E. Wells St., for years has dominated the downtown skyline with its 350-foot clock tower and domed cupola. An eight-story building designed by Koch and Esser in the manner of a Flemish Renaissance town hall, it stands on an odd triangular shaped plot determined by converging streets. Built in 1894-5 on 25,000 piles driven into reclaimed marshland, it replaced a brick and wood city market. Around a center well, which extends the height of the building, are offices and assembly rooms.

15. The BLATZ BREWERY (*tours 10, 11, 1, 3 daily June through Sept.; guides*), 1120 N. Broadway, shows an exuberant nineteenth century German influence in its many huge buildings of weathered brick and rough stone. Founded by Johann Braun in 1844, it was taken over after his death in 1851 by his brewmaster Valentine Blatz.

The production of beer begins with barley being germinated or sprouted in huge bins in an air-conditioned malt house. The newly formed malt is ground with other cereals into a hot-water mash, and the malt enzymes form a liquid wort which is piped to copper cooking kettles. Hops are added, and the wort is cooked. Then the hopped wort is sent to cooling tanks in a "cellar," usually several floors of artificially refrigerated rooms. To the cooled wort a yeast culture is added, producing the final stage of fermentation; but the beer must still be aged. After aging for about three months it is piped to the chilled barrel-room, where warmly clad men operate batteries of pumps that fill several barrels in less than a minute. Normal temperatures prevail in the bottling and canning departments, noisy rotating machines fill thousands of containers daily. After pasteurization the canned and bottled beer is ready for shipment.

16. CATHEDRAL SQUARE, E. Wells and N. Jackson Sts., is a landscaped plat that lies in front of St. John's Cathedral. In 1836 Solomon Juneau donated this land as the site of Milwaukee's first courthouse. The last courthouse to stand here, erected in 1870, was closed in 1932 and demolished late in 1939. The "old courthouse," long an architectural landmark of Milwaukee, was a brownstone building with a two-story pedimented portico, arched windows, and a sixteenth-century style Italian dome, designed by Baron von Kowalski, the son of a royal architect of Russia.

17. ST. JOHN'S CATHEDRAL, 802 N. Jackson St., erected in 1847-53, is the Metropolitan Church of the Archdiocese of Milwaukee. Almost completely destroyed by fire in 1935, the church is being rebuilt at a cost approximating half a million dollars. The Italian Renaissance tower, rising in three stages with crowning dome and lantern, has long been a favorite subject for artists. It was spared by the fire. In 1880, the upper part of the original tower was torn down, and was replaced in 1892 by the two top sections of the present tower, designed by Ferry and Clas, Milwaukee architects. The cathedral will be 54 feet longer than the original edifice, and will accommodate about 1,350 persons.

18. The MILWAUKEE ART INSTITUTE (*open 9-5 daily, except Tues. afternoon, free*), 772 N. Jefferson St., now receiving an annual grant of $20,000 from the city, is the outgrowth of the Milwaukee Art Association, incorporated in 1888 by a group of Milwaukee painters. The present building, in Spanish Renaissance style, was remodeled from a lumber office in 1910 by Harry Bogner, Milwaukee. The permanent collection, valued at more than $150,000, is on exhibition during July and August. Noteworthy are the Buckner collection of oils, nearly all by American artists, and the Nunnemacher-Schuchardt collection of etchings and woodprints. Circulating exhibits are displayed from September to July. The Wisconsin Painters' and Sculptors' annual exhibit is held in April, and the Wisconsin Society of Applied Arts' and Milwaukee Printmakers' exhibit jointly during the autumn. Free art training for children is provided by the institute.

19. The LAYTON ART GALLERY (*open 9-5 weekdays; 2-5 Sun.; adm. 25¢ Tues. and Fri.*), 758 N. Jefferson St., for which Frederick Layton, English-born Milwaukee packer, provided the building and a $100,000 endowment fund, was opened in 1888. The gallery, in Hellenistic style, was designed by G. A. Audsley, an English architect, and E. Townsend Mix, a Milwaukeean. The permanent collection, with paintings by nineteenth century English, German, and American artists, has been enlarged steadily.

Exhibitions in the two galleries of contemporary art are changed monthly, one gallery being devoted exclusively to current showings of Wisconsin artists. Other activities include lectures, free Sunday afternoon concerts, and gallery tours.

The Layton School of Art, established in 1920, is affiliated with the Layton Art Gallery and offers four-year professional courses in sculpture, painting and illustration, advertising, industrial, and costume design, interior decoration, and teacher training. Evening classes are conducted for adults, and free Saturday morning art classes for children.

20. MADONNA DE POMPEII CHURCH, 419 N. Jackson St., a modified Italian Romanesque structure of "Cream City" brick, now badly discolored, is Milwaukee's largest Italian Roman Catholic Church. It is the center of frequent summer "fiestas" in the Italian ward. Originating with the church, the "fiestas" give "Little Italy" a chance to dress up the dingy neighborhood with brilliant lights and gay colors, and set off fireworks. National dishes are eaten at temporary stalls, and the statues of saints, with money gifts for the church pinned to their robes, are paraded through the roped-off streets.

(South Side)

21. KOSCIUSZKO PARK, W. Becher St., between S. 7th and S. 10th Sts., and extending to W. Lincoln Ave., is named for Thaddeus Kosciuszko, Polish general who contributed his services and his wealth to the colonists during the American Revolution. His statue by Gaetano Trentanove, erected in 1905, stands at the W. Becher Street entrance. A sweeping hill in the northeast section of the park provides a setting for outdoor pageants. An enclosed pavilion serves as a summer school where instruction is given in the Polish language and Polish arts. In the park are playgrounds, illuminated tennis courts, a lily pond, and a lagoon.

22. ST. JOSAPHAT'S BASILICA, SW. corner W. Lincoln Ave. and S. 6th St., one of the four Roman Catholic basilicas in the United States, is the center of worship for one of Milwaukee's largest Polish congregations. Designed by E. Brielmaier and Sons, Milwaukee, it was built in 1898 from materials salvaged from the old Chicago Post Office and Customhouse. The basilica, a favorite subject for painters and etchers, is a massive stone structure of Italian Renaissance design in the form of a Latin cross with a copper dome 204 feet high. Six granite columns at the entrance stand below a statue of St. Josaphat. Inside are many murals, some of them copies of originals in Polish galleries. Dedicated in 1901, the church came under the direction of the Franciscan Fathers in 1910 and was designated a basilica by papal decree in 1929.

23. SOUTH SHORE YACHT CLUB, E. end of E. Nock St., an unpretentious white frame building, was erected almost entirely by the cooperative labor of members in 1936. The club, organized in 1912, had its first quarters aboard the hulk, Lily E, which was burned

in 1914. More than 100 boats are now included in the club fleet, among them sailing craft that have won many racing honors. In 1938 South Shore made a clean sweep of the annual Chicago-Mackinac race by taking first, second, and third places. Two membership classifications for juniors are maintained by the club.

24. JONES ISLAND, N. end Lenox St., though now the site of the city's sewage disposal plant, retains some of the color of the days when it was a mighty fishing colony. Still standing on the island are seamen's shacks, and large revolving racks for drying nets. From the dock across the Kinnickinnic River slip, jaunty little tugs steam forth at dawn carrying their crews to the fishing grounds 20 or 30 miles out in Lake Michigan. Early in the present century, Jones Island was the rendezvous of Milwaukee's epicures who came to its taverns and eating houses for sea-food dinners. The fishermen, chiefly Poles and Germans, seined almost 6,000,000 pounds of fish annually during the island's heyday (1890-1915). Today the catch averages less than a quarter of a million pounds each year, and the number of flimsy homes has dwindled into one small group along a narrow dirt street. A few houses display signs, "Fresh and Smoked Fish for Sale." One tavern, operated by a retired boat captain, remains.

Though many early settlers left the island when the sewage disposal plant was built, those who remain cling to their rent-free squatters' rights, resisting the city's claim to the property since it was purchased for a proposed extension of Lincoln Memorial Drive.

25. MILWAUKEE SEWAGE DISPOSAL PLANT (*tours, 9, 10, 11, 1:30, 2:30, 3:30, Mon.-Fri.; guides*), at the northern tip of Jones Island, is internationally known for its highly developed commercial treatment of sewage. The plant, occupying 50 acres, utilizes the activated sludge principle. Incoming sewage is settled, treated with compressed air to supply oxygen, and inoculated with aerobic bacteria. Sewage so treated is allowed to settle, and the solids are dried. The dried solids are sold as fertilizer containing a high content of nitrogen. From an average of 125,000,000 gallons of sewage processed daily, 130 tons of artificial fertilizer, known as Milorganite, are extracted. This by-product returns $500,000 to the Metropolitan Sewage District annually.

Construction of the plant in 1925 followed years of experiment and represented an investment of $10,000,000; extensions have raised its value to about $15,000,000. The system has greatly reduced the pollution of local streams and the lake.

26. MITCHELL PARK, with its conservatory and botanical gardens, covering 63 acres on a bluff at the south end of the 27th St. viaduct, overlooks the Menominee Valley. It was here that Jacques Vieau, Milwaukee's first permanent fur trader, established an Indian trading post in 1795. A reproduction of his cabin, erected by the Old Settlers' Club, stands on a high bluff at the northeast corner of the park. A shaded boulevard winds past tennis courts, playgrounds, picnic

spots, and an artificial lagoon. The park also contains two baseball diamonds, one of which is equipped with a concrete stadium seating 1,000 persons.

The CONSERVATORY AND BOTANICAL GARDENS (*open 8-10 in summer; otherwise 8-5*), are the setting for seasonal flower shows. The orchid show in January, the Easter displays, and the chrysanthemum show in autumn are the most important of the exhibits. An outdoor sunken garden is illuminated at night. A grotto fed by a miniature waterfall is stocked with tropical fish.

27. The VETERANS' ADMINISTRATION, a landscaped 390-acre tract on W. National Ave. between S. 44th and S. 56th Sts., is known familiarly as the National Soldiers' Home. Its many buildings are in groups along winding roads and on broad meadows. A Federally operated medical and rest center for America's disabled soldiers, sailors and marines, it is the third largest institution of its kind in the Nation, serving a transient population of more than 3,000 veterans.

Each patient admitted to the Home—and there have been more than 65,000—is accustomed to military discipline. The institution is administered by a manager with assistants, all of whom are officers of the United States Army. There are, also, a chief attorney, and a Protestant and a Catholic chaplain. Thirty-six medical officers and 125 trained aides are attached to a hospital staff, which includes nurses, dietitians, pharmacists, laboratory technicians and occupational and physiotherapy experts. The remainder of the employed population of more than 1,000 is composed of laborers, gardeners, maids, and approximately 350 ward attendants.

Of primary importance are the institution's hospitals and infirmaries, which have been assembled gradually at a cost of several million dollars. There are wards and private rooms, sun porches and sleeping porches, reading and recreation rooms, and a thoroughly-equipped workshop. Ward Memorial Hall, a large theater, is equipped for sound motion pictures. In addition there is a three-story recreation building with a dance hall on the top floor, and a library building containing 23,000 volumes.

The national cemetery in the northwestern section is a 25-acre plot. High above the cemetery, overlooking the burial ground, stands a 70-foot monument surmounted by the statue of a soldier at "parade rest."

The Home was established to meet a need created by the Civil War. In April 1864 Milwaukeeans organized the Wisconsin Soldiers' Home association. Through solicitation and voluntary contributions funds were obtained to erect a building near what is now the corner of W. Wisconsin and N. Plankinton Avenues. When the United States Government decided to establish one of its three national soldiers' homes in Milwaukee, the local home made a $125,000 contribution. The institution was opened May 1, 1867, on a site purchased from Major John L. Mitchell.

(Northeast Section)

28. JUNEAU PARK, its terraces extending more than a mile north along Lake Michigan from E. Wisconsin Ave., was named for Solomon Juneau, who once owned a portion of the park. The main entrance is at the E. end of E. Mason Street. In the park are statues of Juneau, Leif Ericsson, and Lincoln. The Lincoln statue, by Gaetano Cecere of New York, commands the entrance to Lincoln Memorial Drive. The Ericsson statue was donated in 1887 by Mrs. J. T. Gilbert, who had it unveiled at night to avoid the publicity and formalities of a dedication.

On the landscaped lower level of "made land" are Lincoln Memorial Drive, planned eventually to extend along the lake front from the north to the south city limits, a lagoon where waterfowl find year-round refuge, paved and lighted tennis courts, and the United States Coast Guard Station.

From the upper level Juneau Park offers a magnificent view of Milwaukee's harbor, spreading north and south from the confluence of three rivers, the Milwaukee, the Menominee, and the Kinnickinnic. To the south of the harbor entrance is the Kinnickinnic basin, winter dock of the lake fleets.

29. The MILWAUKEE YACHT CLUB, 1700 N. Lincoln Memorial Drive, a white frame building with a green roof, was built originally on piles in Lake Michigan. The club fleet of 47 boats participates in most of the Great Lakes sailing events, including the annual regatta of the Lake Michigan Yachting Association each July 4. The club's crowded trophy room attests the nautical prowess of the members.

30. LAKE PARK, entrance at the N. terminus of Lincoln Memorial Drive, is the largest of the shoreline parks (which include about one-half of the lake frontage within the city limits). It is identified by the NORTH POINT LIGHTHOUSE, rising 154 feet above the shore, with a 300,000 candle-power beacon. A pitch and putt golf course, tennis courts, a bowling green, a field house, and tree-shaded tables are facilities offered park visitors. Lake Park is best loved by Milwaukeeans for its natural ravines, the largest of which, almost 50 feet wide, winds downward from the park plateau to the lake level. A spring-fed rivulet tumbles down the ravine, rustic bridges cross and recross the stream, and stairways lead to hidden nooks.

31. The WATER PURIFICATION PLANT (*open 2-5 daily; guides*), east of Lincoln Memorial Drive at the N. end of Lake Park, is a modernized Gothic stone structure, with massive, towered central section and flanking wings. It was designed in the City Engineer's office, with Alvord, Burdick, and Howson, Chicago, serving as architectural consultants. The plant covers approximately 24 acres of "made land" enclosed by a revetment wall 664 feet east of the original shoreline. Completed in 1939, the plant, employing the "rapid sand" filtration process, has a maximum capacity of 275,000,000 gallons daily.

To the total cost of $5,100,000, the Federal Government contributed $1,250,000 in a PWA grant.

The plant assures a water supply of uniformly good quality throughout the year, free from turbidity and unpleasant tastes and odors.

32. The MILWAUKEE STATE TEACHERS COLLEGE, 3203 N. Downer Ave., occupies a campus of approximately 32 acres. The plant of the college, on the east campus of 16 acres, consists of a three-story red-brick building of American Renaissance design, a combined gymnasium and field house, and a heating plant. A new library is in course of construction (1939).

The west campus contains a modern football field, track, concrete tennis courts, hockey and baseball fields. A small concrete stadium is being built (1939).

The school awards a bachelor of science in education degree. Noted for its fearless support of democracy in ideology and administration, the college also has acquired repute for high scholastic standards, for its division of exceptional children, which trains teachers for the deaf and mentally handicapped, and for its campus training school and art and music schools.

The college was established on its present campus in 1909 when increased enrollment forced it to abandon an earlier building where the school was founded in 1885 as the fifth State "Normal School."

33. MILWAUKEE-DOWNER SEMINARY, 2513 E. Hartford Ave., was a subordinate division of Milwaukee-Downer College until it became a separate school in 1910, when the college and the seminary outgrew one set of buildings. Housed in a group of three red-brick buildings, Tudor Gothic in design, it offers instruction from kindergarten to preparation for college. The school has received recognition for its teaching of French, fine arts, music, and dramatics.

34. MILWAUKEE-DOWNER COLLEGE, 2512 E. Hartford Ave., is a private school for women. Its eleven red-brick buildings in Tudor Gothic design stand on a wooded campus of 50 acres. In 1895 the school was founded through coalition of Milwaukee College, chartered under the auspices of the Congregational Church in 1851, and Downer College, chartered in 1855 at Fox Lake, Wisconsin. Milwaukee College, which had been started in 1848 as the Milwaukee Female Seminary, was reorganized in 1851 through the efforts of Catherine Beecher, sister of Harriet Beecher Stowe, author of *Uncle Tom's Cabin,* and of Henry Ward Beecher, abolitionist author and preacher. Although primarily a liberal arts college, Milwaukee-Downer has pioneered in art, home economics, and occupational therapy.

35. MILWAUKEE UNIVERSITY SCHOOL, 2033 E. Hartford Ave., drawing its enrollment from Milwaukee and suburbs, is a private school for boys and girls from pre-kindergarten age through high school. The present building, designed by G. J. de Gelleke, Milwaukee, in a modified Tudor style, was erected in 1926 to succeed an earlier school on N. Broadway near E. State Street, founded as the German-English Academy in 1851 by Peter Engelmann, German politi-

cal refugee. Because of World War sentiment the school changed its name.

36. ESTABROOK PARK, extending NW. from E. Capitol Drive for 1.4 miles along the east bank of the Milwaukee River, is a 115-acre tract touching three communities—Shorewood, Whitefish Bay, and the Town of Milwaukee. Extensive improvements since 1933 have made it an attractive outing spot. Stone steps lead to the river's edge and railed rustic bridges extend across natural ravines. A flood control dam extends across the river at the northwest end of the park.

Attracting many visitors is the BENJAMIN CHURCH HOUSE, moved to the south end of the park in 1938 from N. 4th Street, where it stood for almost a century. It was built by Benjamin Church, one of the city's earliest and wealthiest contractors. Designed in the Greek Revival style, it has four columns at the front, classic cornices, and well proportioned door and window openings. Its construction exemplifies the enduring sturdiness of pioneer building.

37. LINCOLN PARK, Port Washington and E. Hampton Aves., and extending west to N. Green Bay Ave., embraces 259 acres along the Milwaukee River and includes a public golf course, a bathing beach, tennis courts, picnic areas, shelters, and an illuminated archery court.

38. The LINUS N. DEWEY HOUSE (*private*), 1631 N. 4th St., is an octagonal two-story brick house with an octagonal cupola. Built in 1855 by Linus N. Dewey, a painter, it stands as a reminder of an architectural vogue for octagonal houses of the 1850's. The porch is of later date.

39. The SCHLITZ BREWERY (*tours every half hour 9-11:30, 1-4, Mon.-Fri., 9-11 Sat.; guides*), 235 W. Galena St., is the home of "The Beer That Made Milwaukee Famous." The variety of architectural styles in the many buildings graphically reveals the development of the brewery since 1870, when it was removed from its original site on W. Juneau Avenue. Older brick buildings, smudged with age, are burdened with steeples, towers and turrets. Newer buildings and grain elevators constructed along simple utilitarian lines with brick, tile, and reinforced concrete, are in sharp contrast to the earlier structures.

At the corner of W. Walnut and N. 2nd Sts., the stables, (adorned with sculptured heads of horses), recall the era when powerful teams of dappled Percherons, their harness glistening with brass, pulled rumbling beer wagons over the cobblestone pavements. Today a fleet of motorized trucks and trailers moves in and about the buildings.

The Brown Bottle (destination of the tours) is a refreshment bar that retains much of the old glamour of a brewing industry dominated by German traditions.

The brewery was founded in 1849 by August Krug. After Krug's death in 1856, Joseph Schlitz, his bookkeeper, married Krug's widow. In 1874 Schlitz organized the Jos. Schlitz Brewing Company with himself as president. Krug's nephews, five of the Uihlein brothers, became affiliated with the brewery and today are the owners, although the name remains unchanged as provided in Schlitz' will.

(Northwest Section)

40. The PLANKINTON PACKING PLANT (*tours 9 a.m., 1 p.m., Mon.-Fri.; guides*), 230 S. Muskego Ave., largest of the local packing companies, has facilities for processing 5,000 animals daily.

A one-room butcher shop was established by John Plankinton shortly after his arrival from Pennsylvania in September 1844. From this shop grew the packing company bearing Plankinton's name. The shop cost $110; the site was rented for $60 a year. Plankinton increased his business to $12,000 during the first year. Several reorganizations of the company followed, and the plant is owned today by Swift and Company. Plankinton was instrumental in the organization of the adjacent Milwaukee stockyards, which have a daily capacity of 15,000 hogs, 2,500 cattle, 2,500 sheep and 10,000 calves.

41. The RED STAR YEAST AND PRODUCTS PLANT (*open by arrangement with general office, 221 E. Buffalo St.*), 325 N. 27th St., is the third largest yeast producing plant in the United States. Located in the barley center of the world, it supplements its large volume of yeast manufacture with vinegar and alcohol, by-products of the yeast-making process. Until 1938 the company financed two research fellowships at the University of Wisconsin where a complete miniature yeast-making plant was maintained.

Founded in 1882 by August Grau, August Bergenthal, and Leopold Wirth as the Meadow Springs Distilling Co., the plant continued operation under that name until 1887, when it became known as the National Distilling Co. When prohibition was declared it took its present name.

42. The MILLER BREWERY (*tours on request 9-11:30, 1-4:30, Mon.-Fri.; 9-11:30 Sat.*), 4002 W. State St., was founded in 1846 by Charles Best. In 1856 Fred Miller became the owner.

43. WASHINGTON PARK, 150 acres of forest land bounded by N. 40th, N. 47th, W. Vliet and W. Lloyd Sts., is the second largest park in the city, its natural beauty heightened by an artificial lake and lagoon. It has a $100,000 band shell.

The park's chief attraction is the MILWAUKEE ZOOLOGICAL GARDENS (*open 9:30-5 daily*) where 85 species of animals and 210 species of birds live in houses and yards covering an area of 45 acres. This is the only zoo in America or Europe where polar bears, born in captivity, are successfully raised. The zoo is popular in the summer when monkeys take up their residence on Monkey Island, a rocky eminence surrounded by a moat.

44. The RESEARCH AND ENGINEERING BUILDING of the A. O. Smith Corporation, 3533 N. 27th St., popularly known as "the glass house," is a notable example of modern industrial architecture. Completed in 1931, it was designed by Holabird & Root, Chicago, in

cooperation with the corporation's architects. The outer walls are lined with a series of vertical V-shaped bays of aluminum and glass. The base and corners of the building are of black Benedict stone.

The function of the building created unusual architectural problems, requiring special treatments. An experimental model of a typical office was built to study the problem of heating and cooling the building, created by the large expanse of window area. All windows are sealed, and mechanical ventilation and air-conditioning are used. It was found that the V-shape of the window placement admits 30 per cent more light than conventional windows. Movable partitions permit changing of floor plans as occasion demands.

45. GARDEN HOMES SUBDIVISION, W. Atkinson Ave. and N. 26th St., represents the first cooperative housing venture between citizens and a local government in the United States. The group of 105 single family houses, 10 duplexes, and a single apartment house, built in 1921-23 on 29 acres of suburban land, was constructed at a total cost of $549,339, with a unit cost that the Milwaukee Housing Commission estimated to be $1,000 to $1,500 below the usual costs for similar homes. The project was financed by sale of five per cent preferred stock to the city, county, and general public and common stock to the members buying homes. Retirement of the preferred stock, planned for 25 years, was accomplished in about half that time. The houses are of uniform stucco construction, the narrow curved streets prevent rapid automobile traffic, and there are play spaces and a park.

46. PARKLAWN, a 42-acre tract with the main entrance at W. Hope Ave. and N. Sherman Blvd., is a low-cost Government housing project. Two thousand men, women and children live here at moderate rental fees. Built by the Public Works Administration, Parklawn was one of the first projects to employ Federal housing funds for other than slum-clearance programs.

A group of architects combined as the Allied Architects of Milwaukee to design nine blocks of brick and tile houses with uniform blue doors and red roofs. The buildings were completed in 1937 at a cost of $2,238,500. The 518 housing units occupy only 20 per cent of the tract; the rest is used for a park, playgrounds, baseball diamonds, and tennis, basketball, and horseshoe courts. A $50,000 community building houses a social center, staffed by the city's municipal recreation department, and home nursing and child welfare clinics supervised by the city health department. Occupancy is restricted to families within a limited income range.

47. MOUNT MARY COLLEGE, 2900 N. Menomonee River Dr., is an accredited Roman Catholic college for girls, conducted by the School Sisters of Notre Dame. A campus of 74 acres surrounds the two principal halls, Notre Dame (administration) and Caroline (residence). The buildings, constructed of Lannon stone in variegated colors with trimmings of buff Bedford limestone, are connected by a

cloister. The Gothic influence is apparent in the archways of the walk and in the halls, designed by Herbst and Kuenzli, Milwaukee architects.

Mount Mary, built in 1929, is a successor to St. Mary's established by the Notre Dame Sisters at Prairie du Chien, Wisconsin, in 1872. Besides cultural studies, Mount Mary offers special training in art, business, administration, dramatics, home economics, journalism, library science, medical technology, music, nursing, science, social service and teaching.

POINTS OF INTEREST IN ENVIRONS

Fox Point, 10.8 *m.* (*see Tour 3*); Sheridan Park, 7.8 *m.*, Grand Park, 9.7 *m.* (*see Tour 3A*); James Currie Park, 12 *m.*, Whitnall Park, 13.9 *m.*, Greendale, 15.5 *m.* (*see Tour 5*).

Oshkosh

Railroad Stations: 245 Broad St. (North Side), and foot of 10th St. (South Side) for Chicago & North Western Ry.; 84 Bond St. for Minneapolis, St. Paul & Sault Ste Marie Ry.; 21 Market St. for Chicago, Milwaukee, St. Paul & Pacific R.R.

Bus Stations: Union Bus Terminal, 60 Main St., for Northland Greyhound, Gray Diamond, Orange, and Yellow Motor Lines; Hotel Athearn 15 High St., for Sioux Limited.

Airport: Oshkosh Airport, 2.5 *m.* SW. at 20th Street Rd. and city limits; no scheduled service.

Taxis: Fare 25¢ single, 5¢ each additional passenger within city limits.
City Busses: Fare 10¢.

Steamship Piers: Municipal dock, Riverside Park, S. end of N. Main St.

Traffic Regulations: No left turn off or on Main St.

Accommodations: 9 hotels; tourist homes; lake cottages; municipal trailer camp in Menominee Park; tourist camps in environs.

Information Service: Chamber of Commerce and Winnebagoland, Inc., 124 Main St. during winter; during summer, information booth at foot of Main St. near bridge.

Motion Picture Houses: Five.

Athletics and Recreation: Menominee Park, between Hazel St. and Lake Winnebago; professional basketball, Merrill Gymnasium.

Swimming: Menominee Park, Hazel St. between Merritt St. and New York Ave.; West Side and South Side Beaches.

Tennis: Menominee Park, Hazel St. between Merritt St. and New York Ave.; South Park, S. Park Ave. between Georgia and Ohio Sts.; Oshkosh Tennis Club, between Merritt and Washington Sts., near Bowen St.

Golf: Municipal course, Lake Butte des Morts, NW. city limits, 18 holes, greens fee 25¢ for 9, 40¢ for 18 holes, 75¢ for all day; Maxcy's, NW. of city on State 21 and county oo, 9 holes, greens fee 25¢ for 9 holes, 40¢ for all day.

Fishing: Lake Winnebago; 32 varieties including sturgeon, black bass, white bass, perch, pike, pickerel, muskies, pan fish in general.

Hunting: Lake Winnebago and Lake Butte des Morts vicinity, in season.

Riding: Murdock St. near County Fairgrounds, N. city limits.

Annual Events: White Bass Festival, May (dependent upon weather); National Rowboat Derby, 25-mile course, Labor Day; County Fair, County Fairgrounds, early Sept.

OSHKOSH (761 alt., 40,108 pop.) lies on a marshy plain where the Upper Fox River flows into Lake Winnebago. Woodworking plants sprawl along the edge of the Fox, their yards stopping abruptly at the river, which sucks slowly at piles reinforcing the banks. The Fox makes hardly an eddy as it flows into the shallow lake. Far across the lake the blue edge of the Niagara escarpment lies low against the sky.

Oshkosh is a confusion of winding and irregular streets. Four bridges, which swing open for tugs and freighters, connect dissimilar sections of the city. The South Side is a Main Street town of shops, warehouses, and frame houses; the North Side preserves remnants of older and more elegant architectural styles. Here turreted public buildings, red brick with limestone trim, and office buildings of limestone or red brick stand as testimony to the energy of a young city that quickly rebuilt itself after the fire of 1875 had destroyed most of its business section. In the residential district, along Algoma Boulevard, which parallels the Fox River, are the austere wooden mansions built in the eighties and nineties. With glass-enclosed towers, large plate glass windows, and bracketed eaves, these houses stand empty and "for sale," their owners, many of them made rich by lumber, having left the city.

The citizens, businessmen, shopkeepers, and industrial workers, represent a typical fusion of many different stocks. Among the early peoples that migrated to Oshkosh vestiges of old world customs soon disappeared   Only the German-Russians and Poles, immigrants of a comparatively late date, have closely-knit national groups. The forefathers of the German-Russians had entered Russia in search of religious liberty during the reign of Catherine the Great. By the third quarter of the last century they were again subjected to religious and political persecution, and many of them migrated to America, some coming to Oshkosh. They are German-Lutherans, who through the years they lived in Russia, never lost their German customs or tongue.

In 1670 Father Jean Claude Allouez stepped ashore from his canoe at a point in what is now Menominee Park, to read mass to the Indians. Though many explorers passed the site during the next century and a half, it was not until 1818 that white men settled in the vicinity. In that year Augustin Grignon and Jacques Porlier established a trading post a mile below the present village of Butte des Morts as a midpoint stop on the Fox-Winnebago waterway between Forts Howard and Winnebago. In 1833, when the mail route between the Forts was shifted southeastward so that the trail crossed the Fox at a point below the foot of Lake Butte des Mortes—near the present W. Algoma Street Bridge—George Johnson erected a trading post, consisting of two log cabins. On the site of this post grew the village of Algoma (Ind., sandy place, or snowshoe).

In the next three years this combined trading-post, tavern, and ferry passed into the possession of James Knaggs, a half-breed, who named the post for himself and sold it to Webster Stanley. In 1836 Governor Dodge, returning from Cedar Island where a treaty had been concluded with the Indians, crossed the Fox River at Knaggs' Ferry; Webster Stanley and his partner, Chester Gallup, learning that the Treaty of the Cedars had terminated Indian possession of the territory north of the River, immediately laid claim to the angle of land between the north bank of the Fox and Lake Winnebago, the site of the future city of Oshkosh. A year later (1837) this small community on the shore of Lake Winnebago, now composed of the Gallups, Stanleys, Wrights, and Evanses, was known as Athens.

During the next decade Algoma and Athens were rivals in the developing lumber industry, and it was a question which of the two would absorb the other. In 1839 Conrad Coon built the first sawmill near Knaggs' Ferry in Algoma; in the same year the government offered to establish a post office in Athens. At the election in 1840 to determine the official name of the post office, fur traders from the Butte des Morts vicinity, foreseeing practical advantages in flattering the Indians, stampeded the rest of the population with arguments and drink into renaming Athens in honor of the Menominee chief, Oshkosh (Ind., claw or brave). A new stimulus to the development of both Algoma and Oshkosh came in 1844, when the *Manchester,* first of a long line of freight and passenger boats plying the Fox-Winnebago waterway, began carrying merchandise between Fox River ports. Three years later, two steam sawmills were built—one in Oshkosh, one in Algoma—and the lumber industry began to assume real importance. The rivalry between the two villages continued. In 1848 Algoma acquired the first gristmill, but by 1850 Oshkosh contained a sash factory, tannery, brewery, wagon and carriage shop, and foundry. Oshkosh had been the county seat for six years when, in 1853, it was incorporated as a city with a population of 2,500. Continuing to grow, the city in 1856 absorbed the village of Algoma as the Fifth Ward. In the autumn of 1859 the first railroad came to Oshkosh and soon took the major burden of freight away from the schooners which plied between Lake Winnebago ports. For several decades, however, water transportation continued, and boat building remained an important industry.

At the beginning of the 1860's, with a population of 6,086, Oshkosh straggled over the plain, a city of wooden houses, wooden walks, and wooden factories, manufacturing wood products. In 1867, after the revival of activity following the Civil War, its people, most of them Yankee, German, English, Irish, and Welsh, numbered more than 12,000. Steamers in the summer and stages in the winter provided transportation north and west of Oshkosh; the railroad connected with the south and east. In 1869, 20 sawmills and 12 shingle mills produced 84,000,000 feet of pine lumber and 141,000,000 shingles; six sash and door factories were forerunners of what is today Oshkosh's most famous industry. By 1870 some of its residents had established what is one of the oldest yacht clubs in the West. Although manufactured products were turned out in such volume that there was a shortage of railroad cars to export them, the Chicago & North Western Railway resisted all attempts to bring a competing line into the city. Though in 1871 the lumbermen themselves financed a short railroad, later leased to the Milwaukee & St. Paul Road, Oshkosh had already lost the opportunity to become an important terminus.

In 1875 the worst of several fires which had swept through Oshkosh burned an area a mile long and a quarter-mile wide, comprising nearly the entire business district. The slabs and sawdust waste from the plants along the river, as well as the wooden houses, stores, and factories, were easily set aflame. Oshkosh had been rebuilt with wood after the fires of 1859, 1866, and 1874, but damage was so great in the fire of 1875 that the business district was reconstructed with stone and brick. The growth of industry was only briefly interrupted by the catastrophe. Logging went on unabated, although the timber line was receding and dams were needed on the Wolf River to conserve the water for spring drives. Millowners began operations only after the logs had been delivered to the millponds, and toward the end of the 1870's milling and manufacturing from rough timber were becoming much more lucrative than felling and transporting logs. Lumbermen made fortunes, and Oshkosh, already the leading sash and door producing center in the world, became known as the "Sawdust City."

In these days the lumberjacks came roaring into town on pay day, stopping first at Otto Naus's saloon at the foot of Main Street. Naus had three inches of sawdust on the floor to prevent their cleated boots from ripping it to pieces. The lumberjacks would work up the Main Street saloons, hire buckboards, and then invite their ladies to a keg of whisky and some swimming in the river. The townsmen, having sold them supplies at high prices, would grumble tolerantly at the noise and fighting. These brawls moved north with the receding timber line, and Oshkosh began to experience the more serious struggles of labor. In 1898 a city-wide woodworkers' strike was called to abolish female and child labor and to obtain better hours, higher pay, and the right to organize. The women came with their men to the factory yards and, on occasion, fought beside them with eggs, bags of pepper, and potatoes which had been cached in tightly clutched aprons. The riots culminated in the killing of James Morris, sixteen-year-old striker. The strike was broken when the National Guard arrived from Milwaukee; the leaders, charged with conspiracy, were acquitted after Clarence Darrow led an eloquent defense.

By the turn of the century the city had made many civic improvements; it had gas and telephone service, a teachers' college, hospitals, an opera house, an electric light system, three railroads, a city hall, and an electric car line. The lumber business boomed in these years; the maximum for spring drives was reached in the early nineties when 150,000,000 feet of lumber were driven into Bay Boom in Lake Poygan for distribution to mills at Oshkosh and sawmill villages on the Fox. The long drives added a transportation charge which placed cities like Neenah and Fond du Lac at a disadvantage and enabled Oshkosh to continue rough lumber manufacture long after the best and most accessible of the Wolf River timber was gone.

In the first decade of the twentieth century 32 passenger and 48 freight trains arrived and departed each day from the city. The building of boats and the construction of marine motors increased. Three mills sawed almost as much lumber as 23 had produced a quarter-century before. But with the depletion of near-by forests, the sawing of rough lumber declined, and Oshkosh turned to the manufacture of finished wood products. After the last spring drive in 1911, Oshkosh had to import lumber to supply its woodworking plants, and lumberjacks disappeared from its streets as lumber came to town to the accompaniment of train whistles and the rumble of flatcars.

Immigration between 1890 and 1910 brought new national groups, the German-Russians and Poles, who came to America in answer to the advertisements of lumber companies, glad to escape the military service and religious persecution of their homelands. In contrast to the earlier German immigrants, who were in large part prepared to enter business, farming, or the skilled trades, these later immigrants came mainly as contract labor. Providing Oshkosh with an industrial population dependent upon the woodworking industry and superfluous without it, they strengthened the hold of lumber manufacturers upon the city.

Although still the major industry, the wood products trade has been supplemented by the manufacture of goods as various as "Oshkosh B'Gosh" overalls, four-wheel drive trucks, grass-twine, marine motors, coffins, lighting equipment, matches, machinery axles, and tents. Within the last decade the metal industry has grown rapidly in Oshkosh. The number of employees in this field probably equals that of any other industry in the city. The Fox-Winnebago waterway, responsible for the origin and early development of Oshkosh, still contributes to its activity, attracting tourists with fishing, boating, and swimming.

POINTS OF INTEREST

1. The WINNEBAGO COUNTY COURTHOUSE, NW. corner Algoma Blvd. and Jackson Drive, a five-story building of white Indiana limestone with terrace flagging and steps of Minnesota granite, was designed with formality and simplicity in a modern style by Granger and Bollenbacher, architects, and opened for use on June 16, 1938. The bas-relief decorations of the entrance portal, sculptured by Alphonso Ianelli, represent the functions of Winnebago County government. Other sculptural decorations on the exterior of the buildings, cut into the second floor window sills, depict historical and legendary figures identified with Winnebagoland.

2. The STATE TEACHERS COLLEGE, Algoma Blvd. between College and Forest Aves., extending to Elmwood Ave., is a small group of buildings dominated by the Collegiate Gothic MAIN HALL, finished in 1918, a large rectangular structure of red brick and limestone trim fronting on Algoma Blvd. The ROSE C. SWART TRAINING SCHOOL, completed in 1928 and harmonizing in style with the Main Hall, is to

its right. The PRESIDENT'S RESIDENCE, on the college grounds, was formerly the Oviatt house. A grey building of Romanesque design, it is constructed of rock-faced limestone. The college was founded in 1871 and now grants the Bachelor of Education and Bachelor of Science degrees, having continually enlarged its curriculum since its inception. A coeducational institution, it registers approximately 800 students per semester.

3. The OSHKOSH PUBLIC MUSEUM (*open 9-12, 2-5 week-days; 2-5 Sun.*), SW. corner Algoma Blvd. and W. Algoma St., is a three-story red brick structure designed in the English Gothic style with gabled roof and limestone ornamentation. Set in a big lawn among native trees and shrubbery, it is approached by a foot walk and a semicircular driveway which runs beneath a heavy marquee. The building was designed by William Waters and erected in 1908 as a home for Edgar P. Sawyer, wealthy lumberman, who in 1924 presented it to the city. Now a city museum, the first floor contains a fine art collection, objects used in pioneer days, and monthly art exhibits. Historical relics of the region are exhibited on the second floor; exhibits of the natural history and archeology of the region are shown on the third floor.

4. The JOHN HICKS HOME (*private*), SE. corner Algoma Blvd. and Congress St., is a white frame house built during the latter part of the nineteenth century and remodeled since. Colonel Hicks, who received his title as a member of the staff of Governor Rusk, was U. S. Minister to Peru under President Harrison, and Envoy Extraordinary and Minister Plenipotentiary under President Theodore Roosevelt. He was born in Auburn, New York, in 1847, but his family soon moved to Wisconsin. After the Civil War he worked as a reporter on the Oshkosh *Daily Northwestern,* becoming in turn editor, part publisher, and full publisher. The many public monuments he gave to the city bear witness to his varied interests.

5. The NATHANIEL PAINE HOUSE (*private*), NE. corner Algoma Blvd. and Congress St., is an imposing low rambling Tudor Gothic structure of brownish stone with multiple car garage, large organ, art gallery, and great transplanted trees. Approximately $800,000 was spent on its construction, yet it has never been occupied.

OSHKOSH. Points of Interest

1. Winnebago County Courthouse
2. State Teachers College
3. Oshkosh Public Museum
4. John Hicks House
5. Nathaniel Paine House
6. Paine Lumber Plant
7. Lighthouse
8. Clyde B. Terrell Aquatic Nurseries
9. Carl Schurz Monument
10. Menominee Park
11. Camp Bragg Memorial Park
12. Mears House

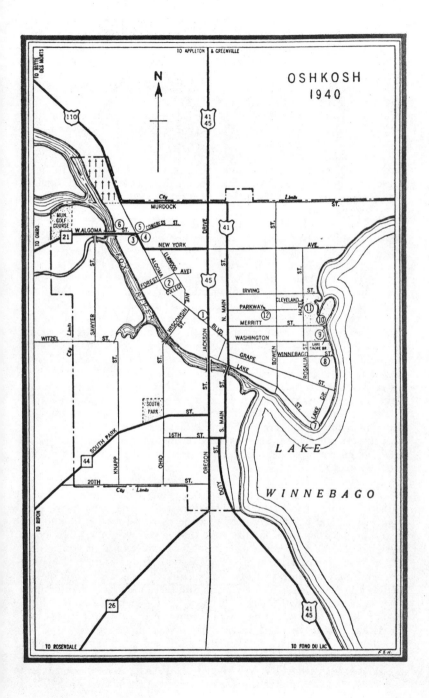

6. The PAINE LUMBER PLANT (*not open to visitors*), W. Algoma St. and the Fox River, is a remnant of what was once the largest sash and door factory in the world, employing thousands of men. Closed during the last depression, a small section was reopened in late 1937, employing a small fraction of its former employees. The factory today is a long row of rusting tin-roofed sheds, large brick buildings with ventilators bulging into the sky, and piles of broken masonry scattered over the ground.

7. A LIGHTHOUSE (*not open to visitors*), Lake Drive and Lake St., squats on a point of land at the mouth of the Fox. The lighthouse still guides lake traffic into the river, though it is so small—hardly more than twice the height of a man—that it is often referred to as "ornamental."

8. The CLYDE B. TERRELL AQUATIC NURSERIES (*8:30-12, 1:30-5 weekdays, tours arranged at office*), 240 Winnebago St., grew from a hobby of John K. Terrell, who in his travels down the Mississippi and in other localities made a study of the proper food and shelter for wildlife. The requests of friends for special foods which he began to grow on an aquatic preserve near Lake Butte des Morts soon led to the establishment of a business. Today there are three tracts on Lake Butte des Morts, one on the Fox River, and another farther west. The main purpose of the nurseries has been to supply aquatic vegetation, wild game, and food-bearing trees, shrubs and vines for wildlife, but it also furnishes specimens of hydra, frogs, tadpoles, newts, and mud puppies for schools and laboratories.

9. The CARL SCHURZ MONUMENT, Washington Blvd. and Lake Shore Drive, was presented to the city in 1914 by Colonel John Hicks; its sculptor was Karl Bitter. Inscribed to "Our greatest German American," the figure of this great German liberal, one of Wisconsin's most famous immigrants, stands in an informal pose, its back to Lake Winnebago. The pedestal is surrounded by a circular cement walk with smaller walks leading toward the monument.

10. MENOMINEE PARK, Hazel St. between Merritt St. and New York Ave., and extending to Lake Winnebago, is a wooded area with swimming and boating facilities and tennis and horseshoe courts. The STATUE OF CHIEF OSHKOSH in the northeast section, honors the man who gave his name to the city, and marks his grave. His bones were buried here after removal from a grave at Keshena in 1927. The city observed the occasion with a large parade headed by a band playing a funeral march. Born in 1795, Chief Oshkosh, who earned his reputation as a brave warrior under Tomah and Tecumseh, was the grandson of Cha-kau-cho-ka-ma (Ind., Old King). He never lifted his hand against the white men, fighting with them in their wars. The ALLOUEZ MARKER, also in the park, across the road from the grave of Chief Oshkosh, is a memorial to the first mass said in the vicinity when Father Jean Claude Allouez stopped here in April, 1670.

11. CAMP BRAGG MEMORIAL PARK, NE. corner Hazel and Cleveland Sts., marks the site of a military camp used in the Civil

War. Four 12-pound brass cannon, mounted on concrete bases, and a tablet indicate the place where the 21st and 32nd Wisconsin Regiments were organized and drilled before leaving for the front. The park was named for General E. S. Bragg of the Iron Brigade, at the request of Fond du Lac veterans.

12. The MEARS HOME (*private*), 71 Parkway, a simple frame structure with arched window frames, a small vine-covered porch, and shrubbery partly hiding the stucco foundation, was the home of an unusually artistic family. Mary Elizabeth (Farnsworth) Mears, writing under the pen name of "Nellie Wildwood," is said to have published the first book of serious verse in the State, the *Voyage of Père Marquette* (1860). Her daughter, Mary Mears, published *Bird in the Box* and *Breath of Runners* early in this century. Another daughter, Helen Farnsworth Mears, was a sculptress at the age of nine, exhibiting a head of Apollo at the county fair. When only sixteen, she executed a figure, *Repentance,* which so struck Augustus Saint-Gaudens that he offered her a place in his studio should she come to New York. A statue, the *Genius of Wisconsin,* now standing in the capitol at Madison, sculptured when she was eighteen, represented Wisconsin at the Chicago World's Fair of 1893.

Racine

Railroad Stations: State and Randolph Sts. for Chicago & North Western Ry.; 709-15 S. Wisconsin St. for Chicago, Milwaukee, St. Paul & Pacific R.R.; West Blvd. between Washington Ave. and 13th St. for Chicago, North Shore, & Milwaukee R.R.; 1510 Goold St. for Milwaukee Electric Ry. & Transport Co. interurban.

Bus Stations: 709-15 S. Wisconsin St. for Wisconsin Motor Bus, Midland Coach and Interstate Transit Lines; 1342 Washington Ave. for Greyhound Lines, Union Pacific Stages, and Chicago & North Western Stages.

Airports: Racine Airport, 12 *m.* W. on State 20; taxi fare, $3; Godske Airport, N. Durand Ave. beyond city limits; taxi fare, $2; no scheduled service at either field.

Taxis: Fare 25¢ anywhere in city, one to four passengers.

Busses: Fare 7¢.

Traffic Regulations: Turns in either direction at all intersections except where prohibited by traffic officers or lights; all-night parking on streets prohibited.

Accommodations: Eight hotels; tourist rooms; tourist park in Washington Park, Washington Ave., 12th St., and Valley Dr.; trailer camps on outskirts.

Information Service: Association of Commerce, Hotel Racine, 6th and Main Sts.

Radio Station: WRJN (1370 kc.).

Motion Picture Houses: Nine.

Athletics: Horlick Athletic Field, Forest and St. Patrick Sts., Washington Park Recreational Center.

Swimming: Municipal Beach, foot of Kewaunee St.; Island Park Pool, at Root River; Washington Park Recreational Center Pool.

Golf: Shoop Park, 4 *m.* N. of city limits on Lake Michigan at Wind Point Lighthouse, 9 holes, greens fee 20¢; Washington Park, Washington Ave., 12th St. and Valley Drive, 9 holes, greens fee 20¢; Herbert Fish Johnson Memorial Park, 3 *m.* NW. on State 38, 18 holes, greens fees, 20¢ for 9 holes, 35¢ for 18.

Tennis: Municipal courts at Douglas, South Shore, Cedar Bend, and Lake View Parks.

RACINE (629 alt., 67,542 pop.), the second largest and most highly industrialized city of the State, is on Lake Michigan at the mouth of the winding Root River, which bisects the community. Factories are scattered along the riverbank west from the lake front and north and south along the route of the Chicago & North Western Railway tracks through the center of the city.

The most attractive view of Racine is from the lake. Gulls dip about the basin within the break-water, and the city rises in a low, broad mound with smokestacks and water towers etched against the sky and steeples breaking through the foliage. At night buoys flash on the lake, revolving beams of lighthouses sweep the harbor, the lights of Kenosha wink along the coast 12 miles south, and Racine stands out in tiers of vari-colored illumination.

The retail center of Racine is an area of old three- and four-story buildings huddled closely along the streets about Monument Square. The factories are scattered, and the homes of wage earners lie in all sections. These homes are neat and comfortable, for Racine's average wage rate is one of the highest in the State.

The proportion of foreign-born decreased from 28 per cent to 21 per cent during the decade 1920-30, but even in 1930 only 37 per cent of the population was of native-born parentage. There are special religious congregations of at least 14 racial or national groups, with the peoples of northern and central Europe slightly leading. Though people of Danish and German extraction still predominate, immigration since 1900 has consisted almost entirely of central and eastern Europeans. At the height of immigration to Racine several foreign-language newspapers flourished, only to pass gradually from existence. The Welsh preserve their ancient tongue through the *Cymdeithas y Meibon Tabernacl* (Men's Guild) of their Presbyterian Church, and the Bohemians, Danes, and Poles retain strong national societies.

Because the Root River was choked with snags and roots the Indians called it *Kipikawi,* or *Chippecotton,* meaning root; the French called it Racine, meaning the same. Louis Jolliet (1673), Fr. Jacques Marquette (1674), St. Cosme, the first to specifically identify the stream (1698), and Henri de Tonty, all investigated its snag-choked channel, which they found unsuitable for canoe travel. Later a trader named Jacques Vieau, known to the Indians as Jambeau, settled near by at Skunk Grove to traffic with the Potawatomi. In 1833 the United States disposed of Indian claims by treaty and the following year Captain Gilbert Knapp, a former officer on a U. S. revenue cutter, took claims on both sides of the river mouth and induced settlers to occupy the land. The settlement was originally called Port Gilbert in his honor. In 1836 the imports were worth $52,853, the exports only $225.

Despite the panic of 1837, when lots on Main Street sold for as low as $2, the population by 1840 had reached 300. In that year the first bridge across the river was built, inspiring the citizens to jerk out 120 oak stumps from the middle of Main Street. The village was incorporated under the name of Racine in 1841.

The early community's principal handicap was lack of an adequate harbor. Cross-currents drifted perversely about the river mouth, so blocking the channel with sand that dockage had to be provided with piers into the lake. Farther out a semicircular sand bar extended from dangerous Racine Reef around to the north beach, and people and goods usually had to be landed in lighters from ships anchored out in the lake. As the community grew this inconvenience became a serious obstacle to commerce. When Congress, in 1842-43, voted down a proposal to improve Lake Michigan ports, meetings of indignation and defiance were held all over the county. The village raised several thousand dollars by subscription and tax, levied two days labor or its equivalent in cash from every citizen, and set out to construct its own harbor works. A little pier went up, and dredgers cut a groove through the sand-choked channel. In July, 1844, escorted by a band and hailed by a special edition of the *Advocate,* the steamboat *Chesapeake* officially opened the port. In 1848 the city government was chartered.

Before 1850 there were no roads worthy of the name, no rails, no important manufactures; the community lived on trade, and the harbor was its only source of supply. By 1851 imports had increased to $979,558 and exports to $579,704. The Crimean War of 1853-55 sent the price of wheat to $2.10 a bushel at Racine, and wheat growing, thus stimulated, remained important for a quarter of a century. Farmers drove in from 100 miles around and sometimes waited 15 hours for their chance to unload; after the railroad came, 100 cars of wheat sometimes arrived in a single night. Eight wheat warehouses and one large elevator were built.

Meanwhile the seeds of industrialization were slowly germinating. The Racine & Mississippi Railroad joined Racine with Beloit and Milwaukee in 1855 and began to absorb an increased proportion of freight, though not until two decades later did it become a serious rival to the busy harbor. In 1857-58 small factories were making wagons, agricultural implements, books, boats, cigars, soap, and a dozen other articles. Within the next decade the agricultural implement industry grew in importance, the city was one of the Nation's chief producers of fanning mills, and there were 11 tanneries. Whereas the Federal Government between 1844 and 1864 had granted only $22,500 to Racine harbor, between 1864 and 1873 it gave $134,875. The 6½-foot channel was dug to 8 feet, then to 10 feet.

At the same time came an influx of foreign-born. Bohemian political refugees began arriving in such numbers in the 1850's that the city was called the "Czech Bethlehem." Later English, Irish, Germans, Danes, and other Scandinavians filtered in. All these nationalities were represented by active well-educated men who founded charities, societies, churches, and foreign-language newspapers. The first Bohemian-American paper in America, the *Slovan Amerikansky,* was founded here in 1860. Karel Jonas (1840-96), a Bohemian leader, through his Racine *Slavie,* led his people almost to a man into the Republican Party, led them out again into the Democratic Party near the close of Grant's administration, became Consul to Prague in 1886-89 and Lieutenant-Governor of the State in 1890-92, and between times wrote books on political and social topics, the first Bohemian-English dictionary, and a textbook on the Bohemian language. Between 1870 and

1876 three Danish newspapers were added to the city's foreign-language press. The Bohemian society *Narodni Jednota,* founded in 1876, rose to considerable local prominence.

In 1880, with a population of about 16,000, the city still had no sewage system; householders dumped their ashes in the open roadway, and the streets were cleaned only twice a year. Industries relied less and less on the market provided by farms of the surrounding territory. Between 1890 and 1900 Racine experienced a boom; 8,000 people, many of them Slavs, came or were brought to work in the mills; the industrial output rose to unprecedented figures, and the city attained national importance in the production of farm machinery and wagons. Other types of industry were attracted to the city, among them the manufacture of malted milk, waxes, polishes, paints and varnishes, rubber goods, knit goods, trunks, and iron. As lake boats increased in size the channel was deepened to 17 feet; however, despite constant dredging, the sand flowed in as swiftly as ever. Then in 1893 the Federal Government began the 20-year job of building a mile-long breakwater, which was finished about the time large-scale lake traffic ceased.

Racine gained its present industrial importance near the turn of the century. For a time the harbor, symbol of the old era, remained fairly busy, but although the Federal Government had invested more than a million dollars in harbor improvements before 1916, by the World War period large cargo ships had virtually ceased to arrive. In the 1920's two freight lines picked up package freight daily, but even they abandoned the port by 1930.

The hinterland no longer shapes the city's industry. The agricultural implement industry is proportionately the same size, but it now serves a national market. The one remaining tannery does a business larger than the total handled by its 11 predecessors. Castings, forgings, machined metals, jacks, trunks, autos, auto parts, electrical equipment, rubber goods, printing, floor waxes, and related products form the bulk of the manufactures.

Many shops were unionized during the World War, though their organizations succumbed to an open-shop drive in the early twenties. After passage of the National Industrial Recovery Act, in 1933, the Workers' Committee, an early depression organization of relief workers, inaugurated another wave of unionization, which continued with increasing vigor through 1937. Racine labor was then approximately 85 per cent organized, with most of the workers affiliated with the Committee for Industrial Organization. During this period there were a number of strikes, notably at the Case and Nash plants, involving recognition and collective bargaining agreements, with labor generally winning its point.

POINTS OF INTEREST

1. MEMORIAL HALL, E. end 7th St., is a large Corinthian colonnaded building in the neoclassic style, designed by Howard Shaw

and erected in 1924. The building houses all local patriotic organizations and is the nucleus of the proposed South Side lakeshore development. In the auditorium conventions, dances, boxing matches, and other events are held. Its balustraded walk affords a view over the lake.

2. The PUBLIC LIBRARY (*open 9-9 weekdays*), 7th and Main Sts., is a large two-story building of Italian Renaissance design with brick and tan stone alternating in rather bizarre horizontal rows, designed by John Lawrence Mauran of St. Louis. It houses a well-organized institution which, with its six branches, circulates more than 700,000 volumes annually. On the second floor is the HOY BIRD COLLECTION, containing specimens collected within 10 miles of Racine and mounted by Dr. P. R. Hoy between 1847 and 1891. Dr. Hoy wrote several works on Wisconsin antiquities, was internationally known as an amateur ornithologist, and was one of the founders of the Wisconsin Academy of Arts and Letters.

3. The COURTHOUSE, 7th and Wisconsin Sts., is a 10-story white stone structure designed in modern functional style by Holabird and Root, who also did the interior decoration and furnishings. Reliefs at the entrance were designed by Carl Milles, Swedish sculptor. The building was erected in 1931 at a cost of two million dollars. On the first floor is the HISTORICAL ROOM (*open 8-12 and 1-5 weekdays, 8-12 Sat.*), containing photographs and cases of museum exhibits. An outstanding item is the first light bulb made by Thomas Edison.

4. The FIRST PRESBYTERIAN CHURCH, SW. corner College Ave. and 7th St., is a Greek Revival structure, designed by Lucas Bradley. Built in 1851 of cream-colored bricks with massive columns at the entrance and a wooden spire, the edifice is notable for its fine proportions and extreme simplicity.

5. The TAYLOR HOUSE (*private*), 1135 Main St., is a Greek revival building erected in 1853, outstanding for its excellent propor-

---

RACINE.   Points of Interest

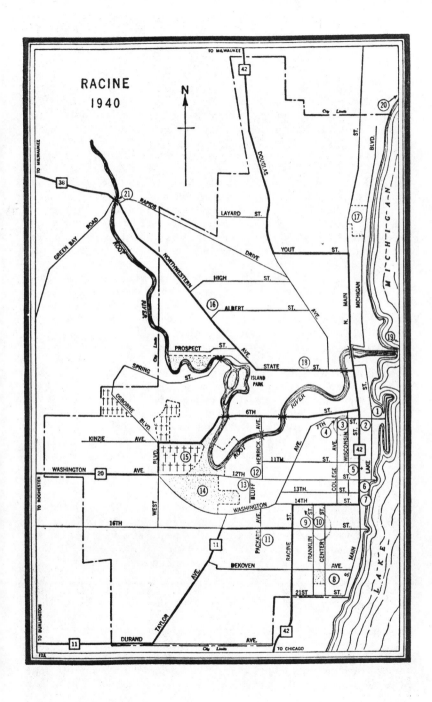

tions.   The two-story central section, with the main entrance flanked
by Doric columns, has one-and-a-half-story wings.   The white color is
set off by green shutters and three bright red chimneys, one on each
section.   The fireplaces have marble mantels and original hob grates.

6. The KNIGHT HOUSE (*private*), 1235 Main St., is a Cots-
wald type structure with leaded windows, steep gables, and ornate eaves
surrounded by Lombardy poplars.   It was built in 1842 by a bachelor
tailor who, taking the brick in payment of a debt, built it himself but
forgot to include a pantry or any closets, which he had to add later.

7. The HUNT HOUSE (*private*), 1274 Main St., is another
Greek Revival structure built about 1848 "without the guiding hand
of an architect."   One-story wings flank the one-and-a-half-story central
section, finished with vertical matched boards in front, siding at the
sides and rear.   The beautiful metal grille in the tympanum of the
west pediment, like all the wood trim, was shipped in from Buffalo.
The columns are Ionic; the entire building is notable for its fine proportions and careful detail.

8. The SPORER HOUSE (*private*), 1319 Main St., was designed
by Frank Lloyd Wright in 1906 and restored at the suggestion of
some of Wright's assistants in 1938.   Standing atop a bluff overlooking
Lake Michigan, it is designed in two horizontal planes almost like a
steamship; creosoted wood trim emphasizes the horizontal lines of the
stucco walls.   At the time of its construction it aroused considerable
architectural comment.

9. The DeKOVEN FOUNDATION FOR CHURCH WORK
(*private; driveways through grounds open*), S. Main St., and DeKoven
Ave., occupies the ivy-covered Collegiate Gothic brick buildings of old
Racine College.   Children are sent here each summer for recreational
activities on the spacious, shady grounds and quadrangles.   During the
rest of the year the buildings are used for church conferences and
retreats.   In 1853 the Episcopal Church founded Racine College as a
preparatory school for prospective priests.   In 1859 a four-year college course in arts and sciences was added, and by 1870 the institution
had become a nationally-known high church school.   In 1889, because
of insufficient endowment, the college courses were dropped and the
school continued as DeKoven Academy, operated under military discipline.   Closed from 1918 to 1923, it reopened as a military academy
but closed again in 1933.   In 1936 the Sisters of St. Mary's, an Episcopal order, formed the present institution, popularly known as St.
Mary's Home for Children.

10. The S. C. JOHNSON & SON OFFICE BUILDING, 16th
St. between Howe and Franklin Sts., was designed by Frank Lloyd
Wright.   The building process was an almost continual experiment.
A streamlined, wing-shaped penthouse spans a built-in driveway.   Two
tubular glass bands, emanating light both night and day, encircle the
windowless one-and-a-half-story main structure; the roof is almost
entirely of glass.   Structural support is provided by tee-columns, nine
inches in diameter at the base and 17 inches across the top.   The hollow

In the Cities

MILWAUKEE COUNTY COURTHOUSE

STATE STREET, MADISON

STREET SCENE, LA CROSSE

WELLS STREET BRIDGE AND CITY HALL, MILWAUKEE

STATUE OF CAPTAIN FREDERICK PABST,
PABST BREWERY, MILWAUKEE

THE WISCONSIN
(FORMERLY THE
GERMANIA) CLUB,
MILWAUKEE

ST. JOSAPHAT'S
BASILICA, MILWAU-
KEE. HERE IS THE
CENTER OF POLISH
WORSHIP IN
MILWAUKEE

FLOAT IN CHEESE DAY PARADE, MONROE

CAROUSEL AT STREET CARNIVAL IN THE ITALIAN
DISTRICT, MILWAUKEE

IN THE NEGRO
DISTRICT,
MILWAUKEE

EAST CLAYBOURNE
STREET,
MILWAUKEE

Courtesy of the United
States Housing Authority

MILWAUKEE HARBOR

RACINE

cores of these columns serve as wiring conduits. Ventilation is provided by two cylindrical built-in shafts that Wright calls the "nostrils" of the building. Within, the structure is one vast room, with a mezzanine floor for superior ranking employes, and a penthouse for executives. There is provision for a carport, storage space, and recreation.

11. The JOHNSON PLANT (*tours 10-11:30 and 2-3 Mon.-Fri.*), 1012 16th St., manufactures nationally known waxes, household and automobile polishes, paints, varnishes, enamels, lacquers, and other finishing materials. The company is noted for its liberal labor policies, which include a five-and-one-half day week, profit sharing, vacations for all employees, company unemployment and life insurance, non-occupational disability benefits, retirement pensions, and broad shop training and rotation of work to alleviate seasonal unemployment.

12. The NASH MOTORS PLANT (*open 10-4, Mon.-Fri.; arrangements for tours must be made at office, Packard Ave., S. of 17th St.; guides*) is an assembly plant where La Fayette cars are made. Chassis, motors, wheels, and body are built into finished road-worthy machines. Nash history in Racine is connected with the great Mitchell wagon plant. Like many other wagon works, the Mitchell people turned to the manufacture of automobiles and their plant was taken over by the Nash Motors Company in 1925. The plant at capacity employs approximately 1,000 persons. In 1938, when Nash sought to remove this plant to Kenosha, Racine labor picketed and successfully struggled to keep it for Racine.

13. CO-OP CORNERS, 12th St. and Herrick Ave., is completely occupied by the Racine cooperatives, formed during a movement that began locally in the mid-depression era. The first co-op meeting was held in 1934 and was attended by only two persons; by 1937 cooperatives included a bulk oil plant, four automobile service stations, a repair garage, grocery store, coal and oil business, and an electrical appliance store.

14. The HERRICK HOUSE (*private*), 1635 12th St., is a frame building of English design. The west section was built in 1846 by Captain Thomas J. Cram, West Pointer and U. S. topographical engineer, who surveyed Racine harbor in 1839 and surveyed and mapped the Wisconsin-Michigan boundary. For a time the house was occupied by Eliphalet Cram, his brother. The eastern section was built in 1883, the central section later. The house is 96 feet long, has 12 steep dormer windows with finials above, six steep gables, four bays, and four chimneys, two of them hooded. Behind it are two narrow sheds, miniatures of the house.

15. WASHINGTON PARK, Washington Ave., 12th St., and Valley Drive, has a 9-hole golf course, an outdoor amphitheater, skating rink, tourist park, tennis courts, flower nursery, and bird retreat.

16. MOUND CEMETERY, West Blvd. between 12th St. and Kinzie Ave., derives its name from 10 oval Indian burial mounds at the eastern end. In addition to a SPANISH-AMERICAN WAR MONUMENT, dedicated in 1909 and now diffidently claimed to be the first erected in

the United States, there is a marker designating the GRAVE OF ELISHA RAYMOND, prominent early pioneer.

17. The HORLICK MALTED MILK PLANT (*not open to public*), 2109 Northwestern Ave., is a series of massive cream-colored brick buildings of Tudor Gothic architecture with square castellated towers, its design based on that of Medieval castles. William Horlick and his brother James began making food products in Racine in 1877. The company developed a number of new products, among them malted milk, which Mr. Horlick invented in 1887. The family is prominent in Racine, and has given its name to schools, parks, and hospitals.

18. ZOO PARK, Michigan Blvd. between Goold and Augusta Sts. extending to N. Main St., is a sunny, open tract atop the bluff on the north side of the city. Its grassy lawns overlook a wide expanse of Lake Michigan. The Zoo (*open*) consists of a row of cages along the northern extremity of the park. The collection, begun in 1923, contains about 200 animals and a like number of birds. Recreational facilities include a sailboat lagoon and, in the winter, a skating pond.

19. The J. I. CASE CO. PLANT (*open by arrangement at office, 700 State St., 9-3 Mon.-Fri.*), covers an area of 120 acres and employs several thousand persons. The firm was founded by Jerome I. Case, who built his first threshing machine in 1844. In early days the plant was concerned only with the manufacture of agricultural implements. Later it took over the Pierce Motor Company, which had made Pierce-Racine automobiles here since 1899, and manufactured autos until 1926 under its own name. The Case plant perfected the first modern steel thresher in 1904 and marketed America's first practical gasoline tractor in 1911. Since then its products have attained international reputation.

POINTS OF INTEREST IN ENVIRONS

20. REEF LIGHTHOUSE (*open to visitors*) 2 1/8 *m.* offshore, looks like a Swiss chalet deposited in the lake. Atop a heavy concrete base is a steep-gabled house with a balconied tower. Here live four men who normally see their families eight days of each month. In winter they may be marooned for weeks on end since the ice freezes thick around their tower, sealing doors and windows, and completely burying their elevated boathouse and derrick. They welcome company, but it is up to the visitor to arrange his own transportation with some fisherman or boat-owner.

21. WIND POINT LIGHTHOUSE is in Shoop Park, 4 *m.* N. on Lake Michigan.

22. HORLICK MILL, 1.5 *m.* NW. on Northwestern Ave., was built by William See in 1836. The original dam, now unused, still stands. The mill has been rebuilt and enlarged; the machinery in the basement is still used.

Sheboygan

Railroad Stations: Pennsylvania Ave. and S. 12th St. for Chicago and North Western Ry.; 411 N. 8th St., for Milwaukee Northern Electric Line.

Bus Station: 411 N. 8th St., for Orange Line and Green Bay Stages.

City Busses: Fare 5¢.

Taxis: Fare 10¢ per person to most sections of city; other rates according to distance.

Traffic Regulations: Half-hour parking limit from 8 a.m. to 6 p.m. except Sundays and holidays on 8th St. downtown section; two-hour limit in rest of business section. L-turns prohibited where warnings posted; no U-turns in downtown section.

Accommodations: Ten hotels; municipal tourist camp; tourist rooms and lodges in and near city.

Information Service: Sheboygan Association of Commerce, 605 N. 8th St.

Radio Station: WHBL (1300 kc.).

Concert Hall and Motion Picture Houses: Central High Auditorium, 901 Jefferson Ave.; North Side High Auditorium, 1210 North Ave.; six motion picture houses.

Swimming: Non-commercial pool, Central High School; North Side Municipal Beach, N. 3rd St. at Ontario Ave.; South Side Municipal Beach, S. 7th St. at Kentucky Ave. Beaches at numerous near-by inland lakes.

Tennis: Municipal courts, Deland Park, N. 3rd St. at Erie Ave.; Vollrath Park, N. 3rd St. at Bluff Ave.; South Side Junior High, 1019 Union Ave.; Cooper Ave. playground, N. 20th St. at Cooper Ave.

Golf: Pioneer Public Golf Course, Upper Falls Road at Evans Ave., 18 holes, greens fee 50¢; Riverdale Public Golf Course, 1½ miles south of city limits on County Trunk KK (extension of S. 12th St.), 18 holes, greens fee 50¢.

Baseball: Baseball Park, 18th St. at Superior Ave., Tri-State League.

Fishing: Game fish in near-by lakes and streams; perch in Lake Michigan.

Annual Events: Sheboygan Skating Derby, January; Easter Sunrise Service at Vollrath Bowl, interdenominational; Conservation exhibit, May; Memorial Services for Kohler Workers, July 27; Luther Day, July; Park and Recreation Day, August; German Day, August.

SHEBOYGAN (589 alt., 39,251 pop.), is built along the shore of Lake Michigan around the mouth of the Sheboygan River. Coal docks, factory buildings, and warehouses are grouped in the river flats, while the higher outlying districts, marked into checkerboard blocks, are residential and shop areas. Except for a few streets near the lake shore, where the larger, more pretentious houses stand, the architecture is staid and undistinguished, its only charm being a certain natural simplicity. Native limestone has been used very little in any type of construction; a few old houses of yellow brick are to be found. The neatness and orderliness of the streets and houses is part of the German atmosphere which pervades the city. With as much regard for frugality as for beauty, the citizens cultivate every plot of earth, giving the city a trim, gardened face. In the moist, lake-tempered climate green parkways and front lawns flourish.

The citizens are home-loving and home-owning people; in 1930 eighty per cent of all houses were owned by their occupants. Of the racial groups which are represented in Sheboygan, German-Americans predominate; German-Russians who came to America from the Volga region before the World War, Dutch, Austrians, Jugo-Slavs, and Lithuanians are next most numerous. Representatives of all parts of the Homeland have settled in the city—Low-Germans from Hanover, Pomerania, and Mecklenburg, High-Germans from Hesse-Darmstadt, Rhenish Prussia, Saxony, and Lippe-Detmold, to name the most important. Dialectal differences between these groups, which settled in compact colonies in different sections of the city and county, are clearly recognizable even today. The English spoken in the country is richly flavored with phrases and mannerisms borrowed from the German dialects.

It is believed that the Chippewa named the river Shawb-wa-way-gun, (Ind., wind or rumbling underground) because of the rushing sound of the falls three miles upstream. The earliest settlement in the region occurred in 1835, when a sawmill, built at the center of what is now the city of Sheboygan Falls, began to saw pine and oak timber. In 1836 prospectors took land and built twenty frame buildings, including a hotel, on the site. But permanent settlement was not made at the mouth in that year, for in the depression of 1837 the little boom in real estate crashed and the buildings were torn down and moved to other towns, only one family remaining behind. By the next year the settlement had been all but reabsorbed into the wilderness. In 1838, however, Sheboygan County, sparsely settled by Yankee traders and farmers, was organized by the territorial legislature, and roads were built to Madison via Horicon; in 1843 a road was built to Fond du Lac. In the same year the community struck roots with the building of a store, stocked with necessities of frontier settlers that included snuff, crackers, pins, salt, codfish, striped peppermint candy, and whisky. By 1844 "The Mouth," as the town was called, had a post office, a dock, a warehouse, and a pier at the lake front; the harbor was brightened by a lighthouse. The town was a convenient disembarking point for settlers entering the Northwest Territory from the Great Lakes and was the winter home of many lake sailors.

When in 1846 it was granted a village charter, Sheboygan began its first period of expansion. The pier having been improved in 1845, Captain Powell began building a fleet of lake-going vessels with their home port at the village. Steamships from Chicago and Buffalo visited the port daily, during the years 1845-1848 bringing more than 16,000 immigrants. Each load brought permanent settlers for the county, so many that between 1846 and 1850 the population of the county increased from 1,600 to 8,300. Of these newcomers the majority were Germans who had left their homes because of economic difficulties or religious oppression, Sheboygan having been recommended to them by promoters' pamphlets which were being widely distributed in Germany. Many Lutherans had been driven from Germany for resisting the attempt of the Prussian Government to unite the two branches of Protestantism—the Lutheran and the Calvinist churches. Others had split from the church at home over questions of church government. The other important group of immigrants were the Dutch, members of the Free Separate Reformed Church, who left Holland in search of religious freedom. In 1849 they began publishing the *Niewsbode* as their official organ in America. This paper (later absorbed by the German weekly *Zeitung*) is claimed to be the first newspaper in the Dutch language published in the United States. Other church missions formed before 1850 were the Catholic, Congregational, Episcopal, German Methodist, and Methodist. By 1850 the community had a hotel, blacksmith shop, machine shop, foundry, brewery, three weekly papers, and several retail shops.

In the 1840's and early 1850's, the Germans tackled the job of clearing the land and practiced the vocation they had learned in Germany—farming. The Yankees, as a rule, were entirely willing to turn their uncleared holdings into cash at highly profitable prices, moving to the towns and entering business, leaving the harder work to the sturdy peasant folk. The clearing proceeded rapidly, and the first crops were phenomenal. The settlers raised oats, potatoes, and wheat, and found a good market for their grain. In 1849 the first of many grain elevators was built, and Sheboygan exported nearly 30,000 bushels of wheat that year, in addition to lumber, whitefish, barreled pork, and wool.

By 1850 the era of frontier trading was ended. The distinguishing feature of the city's next thirty years of economic development was the founding of industries and the development of dairying. Despite the lull caused by hard times in the 1850's, the village was steadily growing, having in 1852 a population of 2,000. Charters were granted for the building of plank roads to penetrate the interior. Corduroy roads were also built. The Sheboygan-Fond du Lac plank road was finished in 1852; a road extending to Manitowoc County was finished in 1859. In 1852 Congress appropriated funds for the improvement of the harbor, and in the next year, with a population of 3,500, the village received a city charter and held its first election. In this year J. J. Vollrath began making implements and engines in his foundry, a barrel factory and a tannery were opened, and a shipyard began to construct vessels for lake traffic. In 1856, the year of the founding of the German Bank, the town was doing an export business of $700,000 annually.

By 1860 there were twenty flour mills in the county. Wheat raising, however, was soon to reach its peak and gradually to be supplanted by other crops. When the soil showed signs of exhaustion from repeated grain sowings, farmers turned to the raising of peas and, especially, to dairying. Hiram Smith began the manufacturing of cheese in the county in 1859, and the first cheese factory was built in 1864.

In the 1850's several new parishes were formed—German Baptist, German Reformed, and Lutheran. The intensity with which these congregations, kept apart by differences of dialect and customs, practised their chosen forms of worship at first prevented much inter-mingling of the nationalities. The first to bring about wider participation in the community life were those who sought in America political rather than religious freedom—men of the "generation of 1848." Sheboygan had a small leavening of these men of education and enlighten-ment who were interested in perpetuating German cultural traditions in their new home and for whom the Turner Society served as a meeting ground. Organized in 1854, the Turners provided physical culture from the beginning, setting up their wooden exercising horses in the public square even before they owned a building. More important, however, were their political and cultural activities, their active support of the Republican Party, their sponsoring of discussions, lectures, musical and dramatic entertainments. In 1860 the Concordia Society was established and, with several other singing societies, it cultivated choral music, competing in annual *Sängerfeste* held in the district. In 1861, 2,200 men from the county enlisted in the Union Army.

After the 1860's transportation loomed less important in the econ-omy of the city than it had in earlier decades. Not until 1872 was there rail connection with Milwaukee. Manufacturing, however, was continually expanding. Several large furniture and woodworking fac-tories were opened, producing millions of chairs annually, and also wagons, ships, brooms, and wooden shoes. Wisconsin cheese com-manded higher prices than the Eastern products and dairying was profit-able; in 1875 there were forty-five cheese factories in the county, pro-ducing two million pounds annually. Sheboygan's main exports were chairs, cheese, wheat, clover seed, peas, limestone and lime, gloves, and pianos. In this era of prosperity the characteristic brick buildings, many of which are still standing, were erected on the main streets. In 1880 there were five weekly newspapers, and 900 pupils were en-rolled in the schools. The city had new bridges and gas mains, a new county asylum and a county courthouse.

Two developments characterize the history of the period 1880-1900. One is the phenomenal growth in population; the other is the develop-ment of large-scale industry. While in 1875 the city had had a popula-tion of less than 7,000, in 1890 it had 16,300 inhabitants, and the county had 34,260. The highwater mark of immigration was reached shortly after 1880, when in a few years 15,000 North German laborers and peasants came to the town. Woodworking continued to dominate the scene; a toy factory and several huge furniture factories were opened. The Kohler foundry, which in 1883 began the manufacture of enameled plumbing fixtures, in 1899 moved to Riverside, a site west of the city, later named Kohler. New improvements of these decades were street railways, a water system, a sewer system, and cedar block paving on the main streets. The town had a public library, hospital, and five school buildings.

While in previous decades the citizens of Yankee descent had dominated the business life of the town, after 1880 German influence asserted itself. German drama was occasionally performed in the 1890's at the *Turn-Halle* and Opera House and at the inland resorts where famous German artists and actors from the East spent their vacations. Of the six papers published in the city in 1895, three were German. There was a *Militär-Kapelle,* a symphony orchestra, a Social-Democratic Club, and several mutual aid societies and lodges with purely German membership. In line with liberal tradition, by 1900 many labor unions had been formed. It was only in the twentieth century that other national groups erected churches of their own, the Lithuanians in 1903, and the Slavonic Catholics, immigrants of the 1890's from Carniola and Styria, in 1910.

In the twentieth century dairying became the county's leading agricultural activity and its most important source of income. The county in 1938 was the largest cheese-shipping center in the Nation. Industry, on the other hand, has undergone serious changes since the peak of the woodworking activity. As long as Wisconsin afforded lumber, the "Chair City" hummed with furniture factories, but since 1918 at least forty of these businesses stopped operations, displacing thousands of workers. A similar trend is observable in the shipping business, for although as late as 1911 more than 500 steamers visited the port annually, by 1938 the port had no regular steamship service except for coal shipping. The manufacture of enamelware and plumbing fixtures grew in importance over furniture manufacturing, in 1938 supplying jobs for some 5,000 persons. Other manufactured goods in 1938 were tannery products, shoes, clothing, toys, bread wrapping machinery, beer and malt.

In its most prosperous days Sheboygan was known as the city of "cheese, chairs, children, and churches," and though the citizens still used the phrase in 1938, it had lost part of its meaning. Sheboygan, in 1930 the seventh largest city in the State, did little more than keep up on the level of industrial activity reached a decade ago. Few enterprises arose to replace those that left; the city was off the main routes of transportation in the region. Despite this, Sheboygan is a town of stable, thrifty population, with good municipal credit and many expensive civic improvements.

POINTS OF INTEREST

1. SHEBOYGAN COUNTY COURTHOUSE, NE. corner N. 6th St. and Center Ave., was designed in the modern style by W. C. Weeks, and built in 1933. The building is a striking example of setback architecture, its massive walls broken by the lines of heavy buttresses.

2. NORTH POINT, E. end of Lake St., a narrow promontory overlooking Lake Michigan, affords a view for many miles up the north shore and southward to the harbor. In the distance on the riverbank are the coal docks, with loading machinery hung above black pyramids of coal. LAKE SHORE DRIVE parallels the shore from the point southward.

3. VOLLRATH PARK, N. 3rd St. between Vollrath Boulevard and Park Ave. and extending to Lake Michigan, contains the VOLLRATH BOWL, a deep, natural ravine which has been turned to use for outdoor gatherings, concerts, and theatricals. The CITY ZOO (open at all times) is in the NE. section of the park.

4. EVERGREEN PARK (picnicking and playground facilities), 1 mile north of the city limits on Calumet Drive, owned by the city, preserves a stand of 85 acres of the timber of the region, mostly pine and cedar. In the SW. corner the city maintains its KIDDIES' CAMP (open daily 3-5 p.m. except Sunday during July and August), where during July and August undernourished children are cared for. Across the highway is the abandoned water-filled LIMESTONE QUARRY, formerly the Sheboygan Lime Works, which was opened in the 1860's.

5. VOLLRATH PLANT (open by special permission at office), N. 18th St. at Michigan Ave., is the home of the first manufacturers of gray enamelware in America. The process of enameling was introduced in 1874 by J. J. Vollrath, who brought the so-called "wet process" of enameling from Germany.

6. LAKE VIEW PARK, S. 6th St. between Wilson Ave. and city limits and extending to Lake Michigan, formerly called Shooting Park, is a natural picnic spot on a bluff overlooking Lake Michigan. To the south along the beach are sand dunes and pine forests, the site of former Indian pow-wow grounds and summer encampments.

KOHLER VILLAGE, 4 miles west of Sheboygan on the north bank of the river, is a charmingly planned and carefully gardened community of 450 cottages, surrounding many acres of factory yard of the Kohler Company. This town, which accommodates about one-sixth

---

SHEBOYGAN.   Points of Interest

1. Sheboygan County Courthouse
2. North Point
3. Vollrath Park
4. Evergreen Park
5. Vollrath Plant
6. Lake View Park

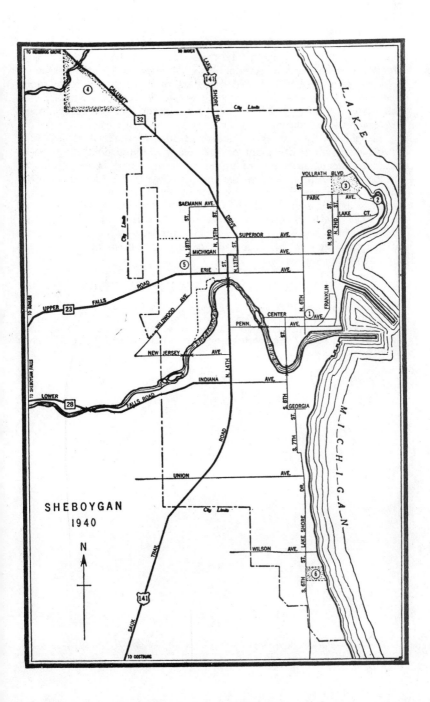

of the workers in the plant, has won national recognition as a community of outstanding beauty and architectural harmony, achieved by rigorous control and zoning. To the southeast, above the river, is built the WAELDERHAUS, a reproduction of a large Austrian forest-house with broad eaves, dark-stained walls set on white stone foundations, and typical landscaping. Below the town to the west lies RIVER BEND, the estate of Walter J. Kohler, who was chairman of the Company and Governor of Wisconsin.

KOHLER CO. PLANT (*tours at 10 a.m. and 2 p.m. weekdays, June-Sept.*), High St., plant of the company founded in 1873, is devoted to the manufacture of plumbing fixtures and home appliances, the best known of which are the smooth white-enameled bathroom fixtures. These are cast and moulded at the foundry and then given coatings of dry enamel, which is applied to the forms while they are at red heat and thus fused on the metal. There is also a pottery, where vitreous china bowls are moulded and finished; a foundry for brass fittings, an electrical plant for the making of home-light systems; and a plant for heating systems.

POINTS OF INTEREST IN ENVIRONS

Terry Andrae State Park, 8 *m.* (*see Tour 3*); Taylor Park and City Water Reservoir, site of pioneer residence and largest overhead tank in the world, 2 *m.* on State 23; Mission House College, 14 *m.* on County M; Elkhart Lake and Crystal Lake, 17 *m.;* Sheboygan Marsh, park, game refuge, 19 *m.* on County J.

Superior

Railroad Stations: Union Depot, Oakes Ave. opposite Broadway St., and 2111 Central Ave. (South Superior) for Great Northern Ry. and Northern Pacific Ry.; 25th Ave. E. and 5th St. for Northern Pacific Ry.; 1615 Winter St. for Duluth, South Shore & Atlantic Ry.; 1615 Winter St. for Minneapolis, St. Paul and Sault Ste Marie Ry.; 818 Ogden Ave., and 2039 E. 9th St. (East End) for Chicago, St. Paul, Minneapolis and Omaha Ry.

Bus Station: Hotel Superior, SE. corner Belknap St. and Tower Ave., for Northland Greyhound and Wisconsin Northern Bus Lines.

Inter-City Bus: Duluth-Superior interstate bus; local stops with transfer privileges in either city. Fare 10¢ within city limits, 6 tokens for 45¢.

Airport: Hammond Ave. and 46th St.; no scheduled service.

Taxis: Fare 15¢ first ½ m., 5¢ each additional 1/3 m.

Traffic Regulations: Visitors' cards obtainable from Police Dept., NE. corner Hammond Ave. and Broadway St.; parking restricted in busy section of Tower Ave. only.

Street Order and Numbering: In West Superior and South Superior, avenues run N. and S., numbered from Bay S.; streets run E. and W., numbered from Harbor W. to River. In E. Superior avenues run perpendicular to Harbor, numbered from N. to S.; streets run parallel to Harbor, numbered from Harbor inland. Hill Ave. is the dividing line between E. and W. Superior; streets and avenues marked E. refer to those in East Superior.

Accommodations: 18 hotels; tourist rooms and cottages; Nemadji municipal campsite on Nemadji River between East End and Allouez; tourist cabin camp on Tower Ave. (State 35) at 42nd St.

Information Service: Association of Commerce, Androy Hotel, 1213 Tower Ave.; Junior Chamber of Commerce, Indian Head Booth, Belknap St. and Tower Ave.

Radio Stations: WEBC (1290 kc.); WDSM (1200 kc.).

Motion Picture Houses: Six.

Swimming: Osaugee Beach on Lake Superior; Billings Park on St. Louis River.

Tennis: Municipal courts at Central Park, Y.M.C.A., Nelson Dewey School ground, Wade Athletic Center.

Golf: Municipal course, 58th St. and Bardon Ave., 18 holes, greens fee 50¢; Gitchie-Nadji Public Golf Links, 21st St. and St. Louis River, 9 holes, greens fee 35¢.

Riding: Tower Ave. and 33rd St.

Fishing: Plentiful in vicinity.

Hunting: Throughout the region in season.

Excursion Trips: Boats leave Daisy Mill Dock, foot of 22nd Ave. for Park Point Recreational Center every hour from 8 a.m. to 9 p.m. during summer months.

Annual Events: Annual Bonspiel, first week end in Feb., with the northwestern curling championship as the main event; Annual Ice Follies, middle of Feb.; Annual Skating Races (Municipal), Feb.; Northwest Amateur Golf Championship, end of July; Tri-State Fair, late August.

SUPERIOR (629 alt., 36,113 pop.), on the southern shore of Lake Superior's western tip, is an outlet for the iron ranges in Minnesota and the agricultural lands of the Northwest. The city extends across a flat plain pinched by the confluence of the lake on the northeast and by the St. Louis River on the northwest. Across the lake and river, on a range of hills, lies Duluth, Minnesota. Two long thin tongues of land, thrown up by lake waves buffeting the silt-laden waters of the river, extend toward each other from the Wisconsin and Minnesota shores. They provide a natural harbor for the twin ports, Duluth and Superior, the western extremity of a waterway that reaches to the Atlantic Ocean. Though Duluth-Superior harbor is icebound between four and five months a year, fully ten thousand vessels arrive and depart during the navigation season between spring and fall. Along the harbor front stand skeleton coal cranes, high grain elevators, long slender ore docks, and scrap iron docks that bear great hills of rusty metal. Grain purrs from the chutes of the elevators, piling into the holds of freighters tied alongside; ore thunders from the docks into the hatches of long boats. In the many-tracked railroad yards, whose spurs reach to the water's edge, stand row after row of freight cars, ready to carry goods from the hinterland to the harbor, from the harbor to the hinterland.

The 42 square miles of Superior form a triangular plat sparsely covered with buildings. Everywhere wide streets trail off into dirt roads, for the city is separated into three sections that fringe a prairie not yet crowded outside the city limits. In West Superior, the northern tip of the triangle, modern stores, restaurants, and office buildings rise neatly from wide streets, and a mixture of frame houses and fortresslike brick apartment buildings line the residential back streets. In East Superior, connected by Belknap and a few parallel streets with West Superior, fine old mansions, their turreted frames still strong, front Superior Bay. Small houses fill the spaces between them. South Superior, a workers' residential district, is huddled about the center of the city's southern limits, a clump of frame dwellings in the middle of a plain.

Scandinavians, Finns, Canadians, Germans, and Poles are the largest groups among the foreign-born population in Superior; the Finns and Scandinavians have been the most important foreign groups in shaping the present character of the city. These peoples have established at

Superior such a strong cooperative movement that the city has been called the "consumer cooperative center of the United States" (*see The Cooperative Movement*). The People's Cooperative Society, founded in 1915, a member of the Central Cooperative Wholesale, has 1,000 shareholders. Before the depression it was largely a Finnish and Scandinavian workers' society, but in recent years people of other nationalities have been entering the cooperative in increasing numbers. Within the last five or six years, teachers, doctors, and other professional men and salaried workers have taken shares in the Society. The People's Cooperative Society maintains three groceries and a garage and service station for all consumers and a credit union limited to members only. It is affiliated with other retail cooperatives in the vicinity into a regional society which obtains bulk commodities, such as lumber, cement, and coal, for its members. *Työmies*, a Finnish language daily published in Superior, formerly handled official cooperative news. Though it still serves to maintain a kind of national unity among the Finns, the official cooperative news is handled by a nationally circulated weekly, *The Cooperative Builder*.

Chippewas from the Lake Superior region journeyed eastward to Quebec in 1634, and French fur traders soon repaid the visit. Pierre Esprit, Sieur Radisson, and Médard Chouart, Sieur de Groseilliers paddled up the St. Louis River in the fall of 1661 and camped on the site of the present city in the summer of 1662. Five years later Father Jean Claude Allouez came to the head of Lake Superior from his headquarters and mission at Chequamegon Bay. Daniel Greysolon, Sieur du Lhut, known to have been in the region in 1679, is thought to have established a trading post near the Superior site. Indian hostilities during the next century retarded trade in the Northwest, and little is known of what occurred in the Superior region during that time. The fur traders, however, reestablished themselves, for in 1787 the North West Fur Company found a Hudson's Bay post here and drove it out. In 1816 John Jacob Astor's American Fur Company replaced the North West Fur Company but abandoned the post within a few years. The white men who followed were itinerant prospectors in search of copper ore, which always proved too scattered for profit.

In 1852 George R. Stuntz, U. S. Surveyor, platted the township lines and State boundary in the region. A year after his survey, when news reached St. Paul that ground had been broken for the "Soo" Canal, three young men, R. R. Nelson, Judge D. A. J. Baker, and Colonel D. A. Robertson, held a secret meeting and dispatched representatives to claim land at the western extremity of Lake Superior. They soon followed the men they had sent and claimed land bordering the Nemadji River and Wisconsin Point in order to control the future harbor. Rivals from St. Paul, headed by Henry M. Rice, quickly followed, but, finding the land along the Nemadji occupied, they settled to the west. The later group was connected with Washington, politically and financially. Men of such national importance as William Wilson Corcoran, Washington banker, Stephen A. Douglas, U. S. Senator from

Illinois, and John C. Breckenridge, U. S. Senator from Kentucky and later Vice President of the United States, were financially interested in the projected city. The first actual settlers were transplanted Yankees; soon, however, Kentuckians came north to the new settlement. Within a year an unusual number of visitors for a wilderness town came to the settlement. The English lord and the rich Southern planter were given no more than a squatter's comfort—they all slept on the floor of the half-finished hotel.

For two years Superior communicated with outside points by Indian trail or river and lake routes. Then, in January, 1854, a road from Superior to the St. Croix River was started, Judge Baker furnishing the supplies and others volunteering the labor for the undertaking. On January 2, fourteen men started out, leaving behind them a track 20 feet wide; they arrived at the St. Croix, 57 miles away, on February 18. Thus Superior was connected with lumbermen's trails, with the land office at Hudson, and with St. Paul to the south. But this stumped road was good only as a winter substitute for the water route. A railway was needed. When the Minnesota legislature made a land grant for railroad construction from the Nemadji River to St. Paul, Superior boomed, and though Congress repealed the Minnesota land grant, the fever for land continued. Another railroad, the St. Croix and Lake Superior, was immediately projected, but all that materialized was a pleasant state of anticipation lasting a number of years.

Speculators with ambitions larger than the lands they possessed rivalled one another in the race for titles. Three groups struggled for dominance: the Nelson party, which had settled the East End; Hollinshead, Rice, Becker, and their followers, who claimed the West End; and an Ontonagon group from Michigan who squatted near the St. Louis River. The Nelson and Rice parties consolidated into a land company called "Proprietors of Superior," and advanced large sums of money for building a hotel and pier and for grading the streets. By August, 1857, the holdings of the "Proprietors" were valued at more than $4,000,000 while sales and transfers averaged $200,000 a week. During this era of squatting and swapping, the young city concerned itself mainly with sheltering hopeful owners and prospective buyers. It is doubtful whether there were more than 150 acres in all of Douglas County under actual cultivation; improvement was neglected in the excitement of possibilities.

After the panic of 1857 had spread to Superior in early September, all who could go left immediately. From nearly 3,000 the population fell to less than 1,000; after the prolonged Indian scare of 1862, during which stockades were built to protect the settlement, the population was reduced to approximately 500, where it remained for nearly 20 years. The harbor, which had been first surveyed in 1823-25 by Lieut. Henry Wolsey Bayfield of the British Navy, was resurveyed in 1860-61 by Capt. George Gordon Meade, later in command of the Union forces at the battle of Gettysburg. Sporadic proposals for railroads no longer excited the people; railroad owners saw little commercial prospect in the then sparsely populated Northwest, and though a railroad reached Lake Superior in 1870, its terminal was among the rocks of Duluth rather than upon the plain of Superior. A proposal for a spur collapsed with the panic of 1873, and it was not until December, 1881, that the first railroad, the Northern Pacific, reached the city.

In 1883 iron ore was discovered in the Gogebic Range, and a year later the first shipment of ore was sent from the Vermillion Range in Minnesota. Superior boomed again, this time with something more than hope as collateral. New York and St. Paul financiers organized a corporation headed by General John Henry Hammond which sponsored the platting of West Superior in 1885. Lots were given away in order to draw settlers, and settlers were brought in to preempt lots. Less than two years after receiving a village charter in 1887 Superior became a city that included "Old" Superior at the East End, West Superior, and the land formerly settled by the Ontonagon group.

It was during the period of the second boom that foreigners filtered into the city as lumbermen or as workers connected with the mines, the ore docks, and the railroad. Finns followed the Scandinavians as timber workers in the region and, though some remained as farmers in the cutover area, the majority, together with Poles, furnished workers for the growing industries. Within five years of the platting of West Superior, grain elevators, merchandise docks, warehouses, coal docks, coking ovens, schools, churches, electric street railways, and graded streets covered the burnt over plain. Shipping had increased from 21 arrivals and departures in 1883 to 900 in 1889, and, with interruptions, has been rising ever since.

Between 1890 and 1900 the population of Superior increased so rapidly that by the turn of the century Superior was the second largest city in the State. MacDougall whalebacks, designed to withstand the sharp, choppy waves of the Great Lakes, were launched by the dozen from Superior shipyards. Home industry and distribution facilities increased; by 1910 millions of dollars for improvements and construction were being spent each year; millions of tons of ore, millions of bushels of grain, were being stored at or shipped from Superior. The founders, who had hoped to build a city that would rival Chicago, were now followed by those who envisioned Superior as "the Pittsburgh of the West," hoping to manufacture their own steel from native ore. However, the development of the Duluth harbor offered a more direct access from the Mesaba Range to the water and so tended to make Duluth the major ore-shipping center. This diverted the potential ore supply from Superior. Though the West Superior Iron and Steel Company operated intermittently between 1889 and 1910, when a United States Steel plant opened in 1915 it was at Duluth; Superior furnished the railroad facilities.

World War demands increased general industrial activity. The Government call for ships in 1917 resulted in a tremendous increase in shipbuilding, but at the end of the war there was an inevitable slackening. Superior participated in the general commercial prosperity of the late 1920's. Labor relations in the last twenty-five years have been comparatively peaceful, and the Railroad brotherhoods, the American Federation of Labor and the Committee for Industrial Organization unions, with an aggregate membership of 6,000, have worked together without friction.

Although the receiving and shipping of freight have been, and still are, the dominant activities of the city, other industries include the manufacture of briquets of coal, colored and flavored toothpicks, seminola (macaroni flour), doorcatches, windmills, and pumps, the canning of vegetables, and a dairy association which ships butter, cream, and evaporated milk.

POINTS OF INTEREST

BILLINGS PARK DRIVE, bordering the St. Louis River between 21st St. and Central Ave., five miles of quiet scenery within the city limits of Superior, in part follows the winding shore of the river. Little inlets reach into the land, and low wooded islands lie offshore. Duluth rises on hills across the waters. Band concerts are given in the park in summer.

1. THE GREAT NORTHERN ELEVATOR, St. Louis Bay W. of Banks Ave., the largest working house grain elevator in the world, has a total storage capacity of 12,000,000 bushels of grain, and an effective operating capacity of 10,000,000 bushels. Working house grain elevator is a technical term used to distinguish this type from the ordinary storage grain elevator. All grain elevators have some working house facilities, i.e., they sort the grain into kinds and grades. The Great Northern, since it handles shipments from many different concerns, not only sorts the grain but keeps various lots belonging to different shippers distinct from one another. The great, blank brick and steel walls of Elevator "S", the working house, rise 243 feet above the ground, and the structure has a working storage capacity of 2,500,-000 bushels. Grain is unloaded here, or at Elevator "X", a wooden structure which is equipped to dry grain containing too much moisture or to wash it if smutty. Ordinarily the grain is sorted and graded in the working house and then conveyed to one of three annexes, groups of cylindrical, reinforced concrete storage bins with an average height of 133 feet, where it is stored. When ships are ready for loading the grain is returned to the working houses, where bucket conveyors feed it into chutes through which it drops into the holds of freighters. The Great Northern Elevator has handled as much as 45,000,000 bushels of grain in one year.

2. The CENTRAL COOPERATIVE WHOLESALE (*open, 9-12; 1-5, Mon.-Fri., 9-12, Sat.*), 1901 Winter St., is a five-story loft building with basement housing the office and warehouse of the CCW and the Cooperative Publishing Association which publishes the *Cooperative Builder* and the *Työvaen Osuustoimintalehti* (Finnish Cooperative Weekly). The Wholesale services more than 100 retail

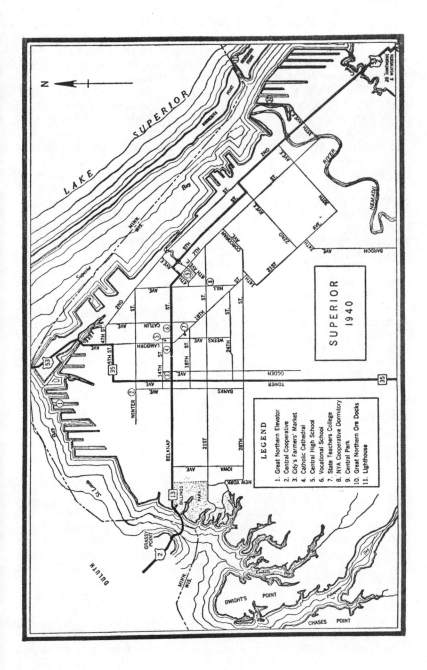

SUPERIOR
1940

LAKE SUPERIOR

LEGEND

1. Great Northern Elevator
2. Central Cooperative
3. City's Farmers' Market
4. Catholic Cathedral
5. Central High School
6. Vocational School
7. State Teachers College
8. NYA Cooperative Dormitory
9. Central Park
10. Great Northern Ore Docks
11. Lighthouse

cooperatives in Minnesota, Wisconsin, and Michigan, and handles an annual volume of business worth $3,000,000. Trucks owned by the retail cooperatives scattered within hauling distance of the CCW load from platforms at the side of the building, and the many cars parked in front give evidence of the lively activity within.

3. The CITY FARMERS' MARKET, SE. corner Ogden Ave. and 14th St., is a long, gray shed marked off into stalls. The city rents these compartments to farmers who sell their produce directly to city folk. Because of this direct exchange, the farmer gets more money for his wares, and the market furnishes fresh vegetables to the city without a middleman.

4. The CATHEDRAL OF CHRIST THE KING (Roman Catholic), 1115 Belknap St., which opened on Christmas morning of 1927, was designed by Louis Preuss, and is a replica of the Church of Santa Maria Maggiore, standing outside the walls of Rome. It is a basilica type church, with a Romanesque tower, walls of soft-colored Indiana limestone, and long banks of steps leading to the slender columned portico.

5. CENTRAL HIGH SCHOOL, 1015 Belknap St., is a three-story brown-stone and red-brick building with double Ionic columns guarding its entrance. It was the summer capitol in 1928 when President Coolidge, vacationing at Cedar Island Lodge on the Brule River, conducted official business from an office here. A large BUST OF JAMES J. HILL, on a granite base, stands in front of the school. It is a replica of the bust sculptured by H. H. Frolich in 1909 that stands on the campus of the University of Washington at Seattle. This cast was erected here in 1926 in honor of the "Empire Builder," by Great Northern Railway associates and the citizens of Superior.

6. The VOCATIONAL SCHOOL, 805 Belknap St., is a three-story red-brick building with limestone trim. It was erected by WPA labor and first opened in the fall of 1938, and offers a complete list of vocational courses, together with an apprenticeship program common to other vocational schools in the State. An agricultural vocational course is conducted in connection with the NYA cooperative dormitory.

7. The SUPERIOR STATE TEACHERS COLLEGE, 18th St. and Grand Ave., is a fully accredited institution conferring the degrees of Bachelor of Education and Bachelor of Science. The MAIN HALL, fronting on Grand Avenue, is a three-story brick building with white sandstone trim and square windows; McCASKILL TRAINING SCHOOL is on its immediate right. Facing Main Hall across Grand Avenue is CROWNHART HALL, the women's dormitory, where Colorado spruce frames the entrance walk; porch balustrades are topped with garden boxes. To the right of Crownhart Hall is the GYMNASIUM. The small dome of the KIWANIS OBSERVATORY (*open for all special astronomical events*), housing a six-and-a-half inch telescope, stands on the roof of the heating plant to the left of Crownhart Hall. GATES FIELD, seating 3,000 spectators and provided with floodlights for night football, is to the left of the heating plant.

8. The NYA COOPERATIVE DORMITORY, Hill Ave. and N. 21st St., one of the first National Youth Administration training centers of its kind in the United States, is a one-and-a-half story, gray, shingled building with a small porch in front. It houses students from small farms and villages in surrounding counties who work in and about the demonstration farm and conservation project half the time, devoting the remainder to school. It is intended that this dormitory shall be self-sustaining in time. Some students attend the State Teachers College, and others are enrolled in either the Vocational School or other educational institutions in the city.

9. CENTRAL PARK, E. 7th St. and 4th Ave., covering six blocks, was once rough and matted ground, but is now a landscaped area. This site was the scene of a dramatic clash—more ludicrous than serious—between the rival parties settling Superior during the first boom. The Ontonagon and Hollinshead groups, rivals for unsurveyed land, raced feverishly towards each other from opposite ends of Superior. It was over the slough running through Central Park that Brunson, leading man for the Ontonagon group, and Thomson, heading a contingent of the Hollinshead party, came face to face with each other armed and ready to fight. But their followers, unarmed, refused to fight.

10. THE GREAT NORTHERN ORE DOCKS, foot of 35th Ave. E., is the largest group of ore docks in one location in the world. Duluthians call them "The Necklace," for, when lighted at night, so they seem from their city's hills. Strings of ore cars averaging 30 cars to a train, and containing 60 to 80 long tons of ore per car, are shunted from the railroad yards over the docks, where they dump their loads into large storage pockets. There are 1,352 pockets. As the ore runs into the hatches of the ships from the pockets, dropped through long chutes, water ballast, which keeps the ships navigable when empty of ore, is pumped out. The total storage capacity is 441,800 tons, and 16 vessels can be loaded simultaneously without interference. The largest annual shipment of ore occurred in 1937, when 20,271,959 tons passed through these docks. The average for the last 15 years has been approximately 11,650,000 tons annually.

11. The LIGHTHOUSE (*open 8-4 daily, during navigation season, at own risk*), on Wisconsin Point, foot of 35th Ave. E., is a squat, conical tower poised on the end of the breakwater reaching into Lake Superior from Wisconsin Point. During storms the high seas ride over the breakwater and the keepers are isolated in the lighthouse. From the tower one can see the complete expanse of Superior, Duluth, and the long narrow finger of Minnesota Point with Superior-Duluth harbor beyond.

POINTS OF INTEREST IN ENVIRONS

Bird Sanctuary, 38.7 *m.* (*see Tour 10*); Big Manitou Falls and Little Manitou Falls in Pattison State Park, 13 *m.* (*see Tour 13*); Amnicon Falls in James Bardon Park, 14.9 *m.*, Village of Brule, 31.1 *m.*, Northern Wisconsin Cooperative Park, 35.7 *m.* (*see Tour 14*); The "Dutch" Windmill, 12.7 *m.* (*see Tour 14A*).

PART III
Road Ahead

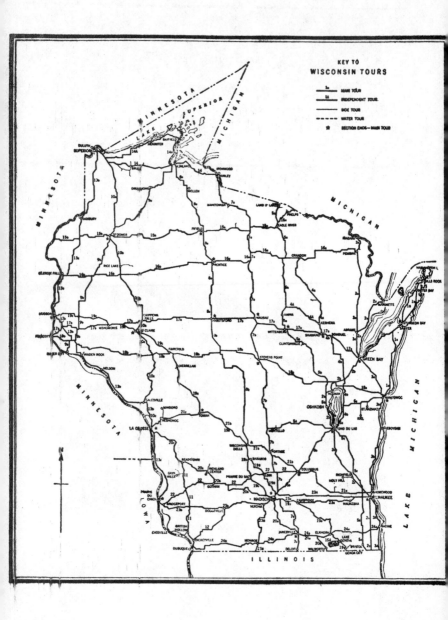

Tour 1

Green Bay—Sturgeon Bay—Sister Bay; **73.1** *m.* State 57.

Bus lines parallel route throughout.
Concrete roadbed.
Accommodations numerous; rates higher during summer months.

Wisconsin is acutely conscious of Door Peninsula, the most conspicuous feature of its shore line—the spout, as it were, of the Wisconsin teakettle. Protruding into Lake Michigan, its rocky and sometimes precipitous shore line suggests New England rather than the Middle West. At times the road overlooks water and cliffs; at other times it crosses an irregular, varied, and beautiful interior; and altogether it touches upon two State parks, a series of fishing villages, and Belgian and Moravian communities whose people have transplanted traditions and beliefs from the Old World. Here is one of the great cherry-growing districts of the world. At blossomtime the hillsides are like perfumed drifts of flowering trees.

The peninsula is a prolongation of the ridge of the Niagara Escarpment, which here rises out of Lake Michigan as in other places it rises above the inland plain. Waves have carved long expanses of the rocky shores into a high relief of caves, arches, and ripple-worn ledges. On some of the higher cliffs these caves are many feet above the present level of the lake, revealing the action of an older, far larger sea that rolled here after the glaciers melted. At the tip of the peninsula, separating it from the outlying rocky islands, is a dangerous channel known as the Porte des Morts (Death's Door), from which both Door County and Peninsula take their name.

Section a.   GREEN BAY to STURGEON BAY; 42.6 m., State 57

GREEN BAY, 0 *m.* (590 alt., 37,415 pop.) (*see Green Bay*).
State 57 follows Main St. eastward from its junction with Monroe St. to Cedar St., 0.8 *m.* Here is the junction with State 29 (*see Tour 17*), US 141 (*see Tour 3*), and US 41 (*see Tour 2*). Left on Cedar St. to Willow St.; R. on Willow St. to the outskirts of the city.
At 4 *m.* is the junction with County A, Nicolet Rd.

Left on County A, which follows the lakeshore roughly parallel with State 57. At 7.7 *m.* is RED BANKS, a privately owned park (*open to public, picnic tables*). It was presumably in this vicinity that Jean Nicolet, emissary of Governor Champlain of New France, landed in 1634, clad in elaborate robes and firing pistols with both hands, while naked savages came out of the forest and bowed before him. Nicolet was seeking a route to China and had come equipped to meet the mandarins in what he considered their own costume. This was the first time any white man touched soil now governed by Wisconsin. A MONUMENT here commemorates the event.

What happened between the time when Nicolet landed and the time of permanent white settlement is uncertain and garbled. Nicolet himself left no writings, but Father Vimont, a friend, recorded some of the things Nicolet described. It seems that the Winnebago had established here an encampment of some 5,000 warriors living behind fortifications. Plagues and warfare are believed finally to have destroyed the city. The first white settlers noticed traces of earthworks, since obliterated by erosion.

In 1831, when a Government appointee came to Milwaukee to negotiate the purchase of Wisconsin lands from the Indians, he met a group of Menominee who claimed possession of the entire shore, and forthwith bought it from them. The Potawatomi of the Door Peninsula were surprised when Federal agents came to evict them, for they had owned and inhabited the territory for centuries and had not sold it to anyone. The Government was not interested in intertribal details, however; it had bought land from "the Indians" and it expected "the Indians" to give it over. The rights of the Potawatomi never received more than perfunctory consideration.

At 8.9 m. is the junction with State 57 (see below).

Although this is one of the oldest settled regions in Wisconsin, wild brush covers the land and surrounds the farms as in the cutover farther north. State 57 turns inland from the Green Bay shore and climbs to the crest of the Niagara Cuesta, where, partly concealed by a screen of trees, the immense concave slope of the escarpment sweeps backward to the farms of the bayshore lowland. At 5.5 m. all of Green Bay is visible below, its houses and harbor works a smoke-blurred cross hatching on the floor of the plain.

BAY SETTLEMENT, 7.7 m. (201 pop.), is a small village with deep-windowed stone houses, a few veneered with brick or stucco, many whitewashed. It is one of the oldest settlements in the State, dating from French and Indian days. North of here the road still overlooks the downward sweep of the escarpment face, and at 8.6 m. POINT SABLE, once the boundary between Potawatomi and Menominee territory, extends like a long finger into the bay.

At 9.4 m. is the junction with County K.

Right on County K to the ROBINSONVILLE CHAPEL, 6.2 m., a popular Belgian shrine established in the 1860's by Sister Adele Brice who is buried in an adjoining cemetery. Sister Adele had a childhood unremarkable save for her reputed modesty and religiousness. The Virgin appeared to her twice without speaking, but on October 9, 1858, while she was returning from mass, the Virgin appeared a third time and spoke to her in French, requesting her to devote her life to the service of the Virgin and the Catholic faith and to build a chapel on the spot. Miss Brice followed her instructions. "From farm to farm, from one log cabin to another she went through rain, snow, and heat. She gathered the children in one place and gave them instructions; then she went forth for another meeting. God blessed her work and soon, through the help of some generous souls, she found the means of building a little school and chapel." Sometime in the 1860's the first chapel was built and later it was surrounded by a church, schoolhouse, and convent. The present chapel was built in 1880 and the present convent in 1885.

Sister Adele died on July 5, 1896. Her companions continued the work until October 1902, when the two remaining sisters joined the Sisters of St. Francis, of Bay Settlement, who took over the school. In 1933 the school was remodeled and converted into a Home for Crippled Children.

The countryside becomes wilder and poorer. Leafy low brush grows in clumps at the roadside and wild hay chokes the ditches. Sandy cart tracks occasionally wander into the interior; small birds and animals dart among the rocks and stumps; old foundations pit the brush-grown clearings; and a few antique rail fences are tottering into heaps of rotting poles. At 12.5 *m.* is the junction with Nicolet Rd. (*see above*). Here is one of a series of lookout points, a wide, graveled area enclosed with wooden railings and equipped with benches, from which the out-flung escarpment face and bay appear as in an aerial survey. At 12.7 *m.* and at 13 *m.* are similar lookouts, and at 13.5 *m.* is a larger park-like ground (*picnic tables*). At 17.5 *m.* State 57 drops down a dip in the ridge to a shallow bay enclosed by a reedy sand bar.

DYCKESVILLE, 17.7 *m.,* grew up around a trading post established about 1860 by Louis Van Dyke, retired sailor. He prospered well, and when he left, two of his neighbors helped him load $100,000 in gold into his wagon; but when he started a bank in Green Bay, his partner absconded with all the cash.

Farms are fairly numerous near the village, but north of Dyckesville State 57 traverses the brush once more. The outline of the escarpment is lost, and the lake is rarely visible. Gray, weather-beaten log buildings or structures of native limestone, still in use though more than half a century old, stand in neatly fenced fields. At 27.3 *m.* is a ramshackle roadside resort that once served as stagecoach tavern and post office for the town of Brussels.

BRUSSELS, 27.9 *m.* (275 pop.), was settled by Belgians in 1854-55. Though at first the settlers lived in log huts and supported themselves by hauling cordwood across the ice to Green Bay, in time many of them acquired great farms, not all in one piece but in tracts so widely scattered that after an estate had been split up among one or two generations of heirs a landowner found it an all day job to visit his fields. They bought beer by the barrel and ate five meals a day; after two breakfasts of apples fried in pork fat, one at 6 and another at 8, they had dinner at 12, dessert and coffee at 4, and a heavy supper at 7. Their huge pies were made with yeast dough and baked in out-door ovens of white limestone, some of which still stand. So great were the supplies of linen accumulated in large households that the women laundered but once a year, when they brought the soiled clothing down from an attic storeroom, scrubbed it with home-made soft soap by the creek, and spread it on grassy banks to dry.

Some of the old festivals are still celebrated. Maypoles are conspicuous in front of Belgian homes on May Day, and the famous harvest feast of Kirmess still occupies three days of each week for six consecutive weeks, with games, fairs, dancing in national costume, and many private celebrations. Choral groups, too, stroll about during feast days, and at other times sing before shrines.

At 32.5 m. is TORNADO PARK, a rough clearing where tiny pines and popple shrubs are springing up in tall grass. Two brick pillars each bear a bronze plaque inscribed with the story of the disaster commemorated by the park. In 1871 a series of forest fires, the worst conflagrations in Wisconsin's history, swept seven counties in this region (see Tour 2). When the fire was at its height a tornado arose over the blazing forests, sucked up flames, and became a whirlwind of fire. Sixty-one of Williamsonville's 77 inhabitants had taken refuge in an open field; the tornado swept across and left 61 charred corpses.

State 57 angles away from the Green Bay shore toward central Sturgeon Bay, and the escarpment slope is now imperceptible.

At 36 m. is the junction with State 42 (see Tour 1C).

The first of the Door County CHERRY ORCHARDS appears at 40.4 m. From plantings set here in 1893, the northern end of the peninsula has become one of the most concentrated cherry-growing districts in America. Though in 1930 Wisconsin's 719,000 trees ranked sixth in the Nation, 606,000 of them were in this one rather small county, whose annual production ranges between 6,000 and 9,000 tons and in 1933 was valued roughly at $325,000 gross. During blossomtime 25,000 to 30,000 tourists a day drive through clouds of fragrant blossoms along the country roads north of Sturgeon Bay. In fall thousands more come to take advantage of the "pick-your-own" plan offered by most orchardists. This plan allows visitors to pick what cherries they want and pay on leaving. Some of the cherries are exported fresh, but most are canned or frozen.

At 42.1 m., within the subdivision of Sturgeon Bay known as Sawyer, is the junction with County C.

Left on County C (poorly marked), which winds along the south bank of the Sturgeon Bay harbor, where boats and barges anchor near the coal docks, and bridges and overheads span the narrow bay. The route passes an old Government-owned QUARRY, 0.7 m., and continues along the bay over flat, moss-patched limestone ledges into a forest of tall Norway pine. Here is the entrance to 1,046-acre POTAWATOMI STATE PARK, 2.4 m. (camping facilities; trails).

At 3.4 m. is a BEACON LIGHT, from which point the wooded north shore is visible across an expanse of bay lively with boats and buoys. Mossy limestone outcroppings rise in the shade of the woods (L) and shelter a large, well-equipped CAMPGROUND at 3.8 m. Here the road forks.

Right the road climbs steeply to the top of GOVERNMENT BLUFF, a limestone promontory topped with a 75-foot wooden stair-type TOWER which overlooks the entire isthmus. When the State established the park in 1928, the bluff was included as a gift from the Federal Government. At its foot is Sawyer's Harbor, encircled by a curving arm of dense cedar thicket and marshland. Across Sturgeon Bay is the clifflike face of the largest quarry operated by electricity in this part of the country, virtually a longitudinal cross section of the whole northern headland. Behind lies the city of Sturgeon Bay, half hidden among the trees and hills surrounding its harbor.

At 42.4 m. a bridge crosses Sturgeon Bay into the main part of the city of the same name.

STURGEON BAY, 42.6 *m.* (590 alt., 4,983 pop.), is at the head of a long narrow harbor extending almost 1,000 feet into the narrowest part of the peninsula. From earliest times travelers between the frontier settlement of Green Bay and the Lake Michigan ports portaged across the isthmus here, eliminating the 100-mile voyage around the tip of the peninsula. In 1878 a 6,600-foot canal was blasted through the limestone.

Father Jacques Marquette, who came in 1673, was the first white man to record stopping here. In 1680 four survivors of La Salle's first disastrous expedition, led by Henri de Tonty, came crawling on their hands and knees through a frozen Indian cornfield near the portage, clawing the snow away for stray kernels. La Salle had left Tonty in command of Fort Crèvecoeur near the headwaters of the Illinois, but the Indians at the fort mutinied, and the Frenchmen were forced to flee into the deep woods of Wisconsin. Weak and exhausted, they paddled out of Sturgeon Bay and up the shore 12 miles to Egg Harbor, where they squatted for five days in a November sleet storm, chewing their moccasins for food. When the storm died they struggled back to Sturgeon Bay where they had seen dry firewood, in order, according to Tonty, "that they might die warm." Here they were saved by Onanguisse, a mighty Potawatomi chief.

Almost two centuries later Crandall and Bradley's sawmill employed more than 50 men who lived here in the wilderness the year around, receiving their supplies from Green Bay by steamboat. In 1857 the freeze came early and the steamer *Ogontz,* bringing the last salt pork, tobacco, and whisky the men would be able to obtain until spring, was blocked from entering the bay by a four-mile sheet of ice. While the woodsmen watched in despair, the ship hovered briefly about the harbor, then disappeared northward. Later a messenger brought word that it had made its way into landlocked Egg Harbor, and the men organized their own rescue expedition. Unpaid by their employers, who said "chop or starve," within three weeks they had hewn a perilous path across the swamps and through the frozen forests. When it was finished all the inhabitants of both communities gathered at Levi Thorpe's big log house at Egg Harbor for a frontier celebration. A week later, when the Egg Harborites came down to Sturgeon Bay on Christmas Eve, the lumberjacks roasted a whole bear, smoked sturgeons, baked suet pie, danced until dawn, and then fell asleep drunk in the corners. This road, oldest in the region, is now part of State 42 (*see Tour 1B*). The relative speed with which it was built led to the cutting of another through the Belgian settlements down to Green Bay, and before spring sleigh bells jingled all up and down the southern half of the peninsula.

Today Sturgeon Bay derives its income from tourists, industries connected with the cherry orchards, quarrying, shipbuilding, and the handling of water freight. It is one of the few Wisconsin cities that have a municipal central heating plant; its electric plant also is municipally owned. On the outskirts of the city are a STATE FISH HATCHERY and a branch of the State University's AGRICULTURAL EXPERIMENT STATION. In one of the dry docks are old ships once famous on the Great Lakes—the *Lucia Simpson*, last of the tall-sailed lake schooners; the *Petoskey*, celebrated for its luck; the *City of Saugatuck;* the *City of Holland;* the *Swift;* the *Beaver;* and others once noted for their speed and palatial comfort.

For years the section lying south of the bay was an independent community named Sawyer, founded in 1874 as Bay View. Though Sawyer became the Fourth Ward of Sturgeon Bay, it retains its own waterworks, school system, and baseball team, and has an independent post office and postal name.

Section b.   STURGEON BAY to SISTER BAY; 30.5 m., State 57

North of STURGEON BAY, 0 *m.,* State 57 traverses a region filled with cherry orchards, which crosshatch the hillsides and line both sides of the road.

At 3.5 *m.* is the junction with State 42 (*see Tour 1B*). Northward the cherry orchards are less frequent, and the road runs through good open pasture land with here and there an apple or pear orchard. IN-STITUTE, 6.5 *m.* (16 pop.), named for a large Roman Catholic orphanage that once stood here, consists of little more than the SEVAS-TOPOL CONSOLIDATED SCHOOL, erected in the early 1920's to serve seven districts.

At 9.5 *m.* is the junction with a graveled road marked with a small weathered sign reading, "Cave Point."

Right on this town road through green flat farmland, squared off by fences of heaped white field stones. The road becomes more narrow and rutted; small cutover growth appears; and by 1.9 *m.* it traverses a waste of rotting stumps, bleached slashing, and half-burned swamps, which at 2.3 *m.* give way to wind-heaped sand dunes thinly patched with long grasses. At 3.1 *m.* the road enters a hardwood forest, in which a profusion of green undergrowth waves beneath tall trees, and trilliums, honeysuckles, and other wild flowers grow among the mosses. At 3.7 *m.* is a fork in the road.

Right here to a point within 100 yards of Lake Michigan, whose water is practically hidden by the forest and the half-dozen cottages and boathouses along the sandy shore. At about 0.8 *m.* the road is opposite the most attractive parts (R) of CAVE POINT (*park car in woods*). A short walk leads to the brink of 30- to 50-foot cliffs overlooking Lake Michigan. For a mile above and below this point waves have carved the cliffs into a variety of fantastic arches, ledges, and caves. Wildlife is abundant; tracks of mink, raccoon, and water-fowl appear on the sand, and not infrequently the animals themselves are seen in the woods or on the beach.

At the base, sometimes above and sometimes below the water, a flat, thin shelf of rock extends outward, in places almost 200 yards. This wafer-like ledge is pitted with holes, some worn completely through, so that the graveled bottom of the lake is revealed through the water below. These holes were bored by round stones caught in crannies and whirled about by inrushing waves like miniature grindstones. The beach is littered with rocks, bleached white and worn round as doorknobs from having been driven back and forth upon the shingle.

Some of the caves at the waterline appear to run far back under the cliff, and one is believed to extend under the peninsula to the Green Bay side, 10 miles away. Many years ago a lake steamer loaded with corn was wrecked and washed ashore here; corn was later found floating on Green Bay at a point roughly opposite.

On the main road beyond the fork is a large sign at 4.2 *m.* on the edge of a black spruce swamp indicating CLARK'S LAKE, 400 feet L. At 5.4 *m.* the hardwood forest gives way to a smaller stand of young birch and aspen, which in turn thins out as farms appear.

At 6.8 *m.* is the junction with State 57 (*see below*).

The rolling, pleasant farmland grows rougher as State 57 veers toward the shore of Lake Michigan. At 13.8 *m.* is the junction with a graveled road to Cave Point (*see above*).

JACKSONPORT, 14.4 *m.* (200 pop.), a fishing village, occupies the site of an Indian village and a once prosperous lake-port lumber town. Ships from all the Great Lakes touched here during the post-Civil War period, but the port's prosperity dwindled with the forests. Now the beach is lined with old gray pilings, docks and nets drying on reels, and children in makeshift bathing suits playing on the sand.

North of Jacksonport the highway runs along the lake shore, pro-tected from drifting sand in places by a low rock wall. Daisies, honey-suckles, cowslips, fringed gentians, and trilliums spangle the ditches, and rarer flowers are occasionally seen. Door County contains at least 35 varieties of orchid and 25 varieties of fern and is almost the only place in Wisconsin where the dwarf iris or the bird's-eye primrose is found. At 18.8 *m.* is KANGAROO LAKE (L), a winding sheet of water on whose shores are some of the oldest resorts in the county.

BAILEY'S HARBOR, 20.8 *m.* (375 pop.), strung out along a curving beach at the foot of a sharp descent, is the oldest village in Door County. Its harbor, perhaps the best on the eastern side of the peninsula, was discovered in 1848 and settled by fishermen in 1851. Under the name Gibraltar the village was the first seat of Door County (1851-57). A Coast Guard station is here, and the old LIGHTHOUSE, built about 1868, is still in service.

At 23.1 *m.* the highway, crossing once more to the Green Bay shore, traverses a long swamp. Dark, sharply-pointed spruce protrude from the light green cedar bush, and in the burnt-over places tottering dead trees litter a blueberry marsh. By 24.9 *m.* the interlaced cedars crowd close upon the road, which proceeds along a built-up right-of-way as through a deep green tunnel. Farther north cherry orchards and some dairy farms appear. At 30.1 *m.* State 57 begins to wind down a long wooded slope, and at 30.4 *m.* is the junction with State 42 (*see Tour 1B*).

The hillside village of SISTER BAY, 30.5 *m.* (238 pop.), lies in the shadow of the SISTER BLUFFS, 130 and 190 feet high. The SISTER ISLANDS offshore are a breeding ground for herring gulls and terns; birds banded here have been recaptured as far away as Panama and Martinique.

Tour 1A

Sister Bay—Ellison Bay—Gills Rock—Washington Island; 11.2 *m.*
State 42 and ferry.

Hard-surfaced roadbed on mainland; dirt roadbed on island.
Small-town and resort accommodations.

This section of State 42 follows the rugged Green Bay shore from Sister Bay to Gills Rock, a Scandinavian fishing village at the tip of the peninsula. The water is almost always in view as State 42 rises to the tops of the bluffs or skirts shallow bays. Washington Island is reached by ferry across treacherous Porte des Morts.

State 42 branches north from SISTER BAY, 0 *m.* (350 pop.), which is at the junction with State 57 (*see Tour 1*) and State 42 (*see Tour 1B*).

ELLISON BAY, 5.5 *m.*, at the foot of 190-foot ELLISON BLUFF, is a fishing village, sharing with Gills Rock a catch approximating $100,000 annually, the largest on the Wisconsin shore of Lake Michigan. In Ellison Bay the landscape architect, Jens Jensen, has his colony, "The Clearings," which accommodates 50 year-around students working and living co-operatively.

GILLS ROCK, 10.4 *m.*, is at the tip of the peninsula from which TABLE BLUFF, 170-foot DEATH'S DOOR BLUFF, and the U. S. BIRD PRESERVE FOR GULLS AND TERNS overlook Lake Michigan. In the 1830's there came to Gills Rock a man named Allen Bradley, who measured more than four feet around the chest, had hands as broad as shovels, wore moccasins because he could find no shoes to fit him, and performed feats commensurate with his dimensions. The settlers referred to him as "Old Bradley, the timber chap who lives like an Indian and can cut seven cords of body maple in a day." He could drag a heavy fishing boat up on the shore singlehanded, or lift huge rocks, timbers, and heavy barrels. A genial giant, he would let men cling to his long, luxuriant beard as he carried them about the room; once on a bet he thus carried a 250-pound man until the latter became weary and let go.

Gills Rock is a fishing village, the home of Scandinavians whose fathers and grandfathers have fished the lake for a living. Along the water front are small boats, nets drying on rocks, weathered sheds where fish are cleaned and nets strung. Every day men put out in their little boats to the gill and pound nets set some miles from shore, and bring home the catch for shipment or for sale to the tourists who come to the sheds to choose their whitefish, trout, or perch.

At 10 6 *m.* is the junction with a dirt road.

In the Cities and Towns

THE CAPITOL AT MADISON

A. M. Vinje

WISCONSIN GENERAL HOSPITAL

YERKES OBSERVATORY AT WILLIAMS BAY, LAKE GENEVA. HERE IS THE LARGEST REFRACTING TELESCOPE IN THE WORLD

PLAQUE, ENTRANCE TO THE
MAIN BUILDING, UNIVERSITY
OF WISCONSIN, MADISON

"WHATEVER MAY BE THE
LIMITATIONS WHICH TRAMMEL
INQUIRY ELSEWHERE WE BE
LIEVE THAT THE GREAT STATE
UNIVERSITY OF WISCONSIN
SHOULD EVER ENCOURAGE
THAT CONTINUAL AND FEAR
LESS SIFTING AND WINNOWING
BY WHICH ALONE THE TRUTH
CAN BE FOUND" (TAKEN FROM A
REPORT OF THE BOARD OF REGENTS
IN 1894)
MEMORIAL CLASS OF 1910

BASCOM HALL, UNIVERSITY OF WISCONSIN

WISCONSIN'S OLDEST COURTHOUSE (1859)
DODGEVILLE

THE VILLA LOUIS, PRAIRIE DU CHIEN, BUILT BY
HERCULES DOUSMAN IN 1843

CORNISH MINERS' HOMES, BUILT BETWEEN 1835
AND 1840, MINERAL POINT

THE WISCONSIN UNION THEATER, UNIVERSITY OF
WISCONSIN, MADISON

OFFICE BUILDING OF THE S. C. JOHNSON AND SON
COMPANY, RACINE, DESIGNED BY FRANK LLOYD
WRIGHT

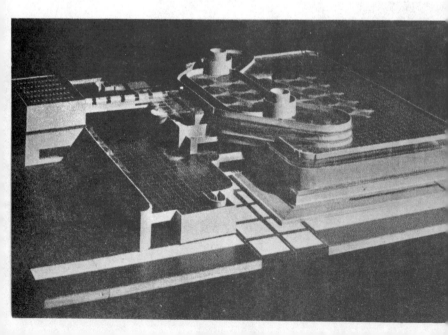

RACINE COUNTY COURTHOUSE

TALIESEN, THE HOME OF FRANK LLOYD WRIGHT, NEAR SPRING GREEN

PARKLAWN, FEDERAL HOUSING PROJECT AT MILWAUKEE

Right on this road to the junction with another road, 0.6 *m.*; R. here 1 *m.* to the junction with a third road; L. here 1.4 *m.* to EUROPE LAKE, once a bay in Lake Michigan. Waves and currents piled sand bars across its mouth, eventually converting it into a completely enclosed, forest-walled lake.

At 2.4 *m.* on the first road, at the very tip of the peninsula, is a pier used in rough weather by the Washington Island ferry.

The LANDING OF THE WASHINGTON ISLAND FERRY is at 10.7 *m.* on State 42. (*Ferry leaves for Washington Island at 10:30 a.m. and 5:30 p.m.; leaves island for Gills Rock at 9:15 a.m. and 4:30 p.m. Round trip fare for passengers, $1; for autos, $3 to $5.*)

The half-mile strait between Washington Island and the Door Peninsula has long been known as the PORTE DES MORTS (Death's Door). The treacherous undercurrents here rise so suddenly and rush so swiftly that they can undermine two feet of solid ice within 12 hours. On St. Patrick's Day, 1914, the mail was taken across the strait in the morning by motorboat, in the afternoon three horse-drawn vehicles crossed the ice, and at night an automobile was driven from island to mainland.

Indian canoeists dreaded this passage, and the French, who came after Nicolet's voyage in 1634 (*see Tour 1*), learned to share their fear. It is supposed that Robert La Salle's *Griffon,* first sailing vessel on the Great Lakes, was wrecked here in 1679, while carrying furs from Washington Island to a post just above Niagara Falls. Some sailors on the Great Lakes still insist that the vessel did not go down. The *Griffon* or its ghost, they say, has been seen scudding over the water in the teeth of a never-ending gale that blew up at Death's Door more than 250 years ago. In 1871 almost 100 vessels were officially reported shipwrecked here.

Not far from the mainland is PILOT ISLAND, little more than a rock in the heavy-pounding seas. The PILOT ISLAND LIGHTHOUSE has a 10-inch steam whistle that can pierce a fog for many miles. Though the light has probably witnessed as many shipwrecks as any on the Great Lakes, and its keepers have a long record of thrilling rescues, life on the rock used to be intolerably dreary. On the Fourth of July, 1874, the keeper entered in his log-book: "Independence Day came in fine after a heavy southeast gale. This island affords about as much independence and liberty as Libby Prison, with the difference in guards in favor of this place, and chance for outside communication in favor of the other."

A short distance beyond Pilot Island is PLUM ISLAND, so called because it is plumb in the center of Death's Door. Here nets dry on reels while fishermen clean and pack their fish in sheds near the ferry dock.

The ferry lands at DETROIT HARBOR on the southern side of WASHINGTON ISLAND. The sandy shore here slopes gently down to shallow water, but the northern and western shores have heavy, wood-capped cliffs. Washington Island, about 20 square miles in area, is a prolongation of the Niagara Cuesta that forms the Door Peninsula. Sites of Indian villages, mounds, cemeteries, and cornfields are numerous. Its first known inhabitants, the Potawatomi, moved temporarily to the mainland sometime before 1653, and for a time the island was deserted. Then in 1653 or 1654 the Ottawa and Petun Huron, fleeing the whole length of the Great Lakes from relentless Iroquois, stopped here for a year.

Sometime before 1656 the Potawatomi returned. In the winter of 1657 they were visited by two French traders, Pierre Esprit Radisson, and his brother-in-law, Médard Chouart, Sieur de Groseilliers. Years later, in the quiet of an English cottage, Radisson wrote in English a journal curiously entitled *The Auxoticiat Voyage into the Great and Filthy Lake of the Hurons, Upper Sea of the East, and Bay of the North*. (Nobody has discovered what he meant by *Auxoticiat*.) The manuscript was unknown until about 1880, when it was discovered among some papers in the Bodleian Library at Oxford. Written long after the voyage, its chronology is not clear, and its exact date cannot be ascertained. Of his visit to Washington Island Radisson wrote: "I can assure you I liked noe country as I have that wherein we wintered; for whatever a man could desire was to be had in great plenty; viz. staggs, fishes in abundance, and all sort of meat, corne enough."

In 1679 when Robert La Salle brought his ship *Griffon* into Detroit Harbor, he was met by Potawatomi under Chief Onanguisse, who sent runners through the Wisconsin forest. Tribesmen came by hundreds with canoe loads of furs. After that there is no notable mention of the island in history until about 1830, when fishermen established the first permanent settlements here. They were soon joined by Danish and Norwegian farmers and, in 1870, by the first colony of Icelanders to settle as a group in the United States. The descendants of the Icelanders now constitute a fifth of the island's population.

The difficulties experienced by most pioneers were augmented here by the isolation of the island. During the summer, mail and supplies were brought in weekly by fish buyers from Green Bay. In winter the islanders had to depend upon H. D. Miner, who would make the six-day trip across the blinding ice to Green Bay and back for $20 a trip.

Though the isolation has been broken, community ties on Washington Island are still unusually strong. Many of the enterprises, though not formally organized as co-operatives, are communally owned. The 25-year-old telephone system, connected with the mainland by cable, is run at cost with charges prorated among the customers. Strangers are charged 5¢ for each call. The operator knows the voice of everyone on the island, and when a stranger calls, she holds the wire until the toll has been paid to the owner of the telephone. The doctor is communally supported according to a plan that guarantees him $3,000 to $5,000 a year. Fire insurance and fire fighting are on a community basis. Each household is furnished with a fire extinguisher; alarms are broadcast by the telephone operator, who rings all homes at once with a special call; and all able-bodied men are compelled by ordinance to come forth with their extinguishers and help fight any blaze.

LITTLE LAKE, a commercial resort on Little Lake Rd., has a

small MUSEUM exhibiting specimens of rock, coral, and Indian relics. A short distance from the museum is a PREACHING CROSS, from which Jesuit missionaries preached to the Indians. Nearby (*inquire locally*) are evidences of ancient Indian habitation—cornfields, fireplaces, and sites of log longhouses.

At the end of the Potawatomi Trail on the island is BOWYER'S BLUFF, an imposing limestone ledge 200 feet above the water. Caves and fissures seam the cliff, and at places the erosion of water and wind have whittled grotesque formations in the rock. Topping the bluff is BOWYER'S BLUFF LIGHT TOWER.

JACKSON HARBOR, at the northeast corner of the island, is an important fishing village. All along the water front huge fishing nets are stretched to dry upon the rocks. Fishermen daily go out to their gill nets anchored 25 or 30 miles offshore. The nets are hauled by machinery into the boats, where the fish are cleaned and washed as innumerable gulls flutter about snapping up the entrails. Brought to the fish sheds at Jackson Harbor, the fish are packed for shipment.

Opposite Jackson Harbor is 1,000-acre ROCK ISLAND, which, like Washington Island, shows the contours of the Niagara escarpment. Trappers and fishermen settled Rock Island about 1835. Among the early comers was David Kennison, longest-lived member of the Boston Tea Party, who died in 1852 at the age of 116 and is buried in Lincoln Park, Chicago.

Since the Civil War, Rock Island has been virtually deserted and is now the estate of a Chicago manufacturer. At the head of its single harbor he has built a boathouse and great hall of cobblestones, roughly patterned after feudal Icelandic manors, with great beams bracing the pointed, unceilinged roof and an enormous fireplace at one end. The only other structure on Rock Island is the POTAWATOMIE LIGHTHOUSE, oldest in the State, erected in 1837 and rebuilt in 1858.

Tour 1B

Junction with State 57—Egg Harbor—Ephraim—Sister Bay; 28.1 *m.* State 42.

Asphalt roadbed.
Resort accommodations.

State 42 runs northeast along the Green Bay shore, sometimes on top of craggy coastal cliffs, sometimes dipping down abruptly to resort and fishing villages along the shore. When lumberjacks, cut off from winter supplies, first hacked out this route in 1857 (*see Tour 1*), the countryside was a succession of thickly wooded hills and dank swamps.

North of the junction with State 57, 0 *m*. (*see Tour 1*), State 42 traverses a smooth open countryside. Rows of trees in orchards form checks on the hillsides, elms and poplars plume the plain, and only an occasional woodlot intercepts the view.

CARLSVILLE, 5.7 *m.*, was founded as a stopping place for hungry teams and teamsters. North of the village the soil is light and sandy; many of the big barns have never been painted, and a few primitive log sheds are still in use. Ringing the plain—sometimes near, sometimes far, but always within sight—is a low green wall of ragged second-growth forest. At 12 *m*. State 42 suddenly dips down the escarpment face.

EGG HARBOR, 13.4 *m*. (200 pop.), the southernmost resort village along the Green Bay shore, lies below the wooded sides of overhanging bluffs. It was named for an incident on a boat trip made by some prominent Wisconsin citizens and their wives in 1825. Mrs. Elizabeth Fisher Baird, wife of Henry Baird, one of Green Bay's first lawyers, described it thus:

As we rowed away from the Red Banks on that most charming June morning, many were the amusements that followed each other. The boats would sometimes come near enough to allow an interchange of conversation, jest, and play. This began that morning, by the throwing of hard tack at each other. This, however, did not last long, the prospect of needing the biscuits, later, serving to save them. . . . Shortly after the war of the biscuits ceased, we began to see eggs flying in the air, and a very pretty sight they made too. . . . I crawled under the tarpaulin, where I was comparatively safe, although an occasional egg would strike me on the head.

The frolic continued after the party landed on the shore here that evening.

The next morning the field of battle presented a strange appearance, strewn as it was with egg shells, and many were the regrets expressed that the ammunition was exhausted. Before leaving the shore, speeches befitting the occasion were made by most of the gentlemen, and the place was formally christened "Egg Harbor."

State 42 emerges from the Egg Harbor basin and crosses a rough plateau. Throughout the rest of the route cherry orchards and cultivated fields alternate with woodland and cutover.

FISH CREEK, 19.5 *m*. (225 pop.) (*boats for trips to Chambers and Strawberry Islands for rent*), occupies another cleft in the escarpment. A group from St. Louis has developed a vacation suburb on a ledge of the towering west bluff. To the east SVEN'S BLUFF, a bold promontory of white limestone jutting out into the harbor, dominates the whole basin.

The first settler here was Increase Claflin, a rock-jawed, fringe-whiskered New Yorker. Before coming to Fish Creek he had lived farther south at Little Sturgeon Bay, where he bred horses and traded with the Indians. His relations with the savages were excellent until his hired man, Robert Stevenson, married the eldest Miss Claflin and took over the trading; Stevenson plied the natives with liquor and cheated them unmercifully. Finally a group under Chief Silver Band leaped from ambush and overpowered Claflin, who suggested a conference over a keg of whisky. The Indians agreed that this would help negotiations considerably; but when Claflin rolled out his keg and ripped off its cover, the Indians saw that it was full of gunpowder. Standing with a foot on the keg and a lighted torch in his hand, Claflin threatened to blow up the parley if his peace proposals were rejected.

In 1844 Claflin moved here to Fish Creek and built a large two-story log house overlooking the harbor. Its foundations are visible in Peninsula State Park (see below). In 1853 Asa Thorp built a pier and brought in men to cut and cord wood for passing ships. Fish Creek became successively a fishing village, a farming town, and a resort center.

Between Fish Creek and Ephraim, State 42 crosses the base of a gigantic headland set aside as PENINSULA STATE PARK (camping, picnicking, hiking, golfing, and bathing facilities). The main entrance, 23.1 m., is at a golf course with a TOTEM POLE standing prominently in the middle of a fairway.

Through this 3,400-acre tract runs a network of roads and 15 miles of foot and bridle paths, which wind through a forest of pine, hemlock, balsam, and hardwoods, and around rocks and ledges covered with juniper or shrubbery yew. Pileated woodpeckers, rose-breasted grosbeaks, purple finches, scarlet tanagers, and indigo buntings flash through the green; the crested flycatcher carefully places a discarded snakeskin before his hollow tree to frighten marauders; a pair of bald eagles has for years nested in a pine tree on the summit of 180-foot EAGLE BLUFF.

This bluff and two others, SVEN'S BLUFF and NORWAY BLUFF, rise in precipitous cliffs above the water and are the principal landmarks. A 75-foot OBSERVATION TOWER on Eagle Bluff reveals the rocky lakeshore and precipitious headland, shows little Ephraim (see below) shining clean and white amid heavy foliage, and overlooks the water to the Strawberry Islands, and, far out on the horizon, to Chambers Island. On this bluff, 30 feet above the present water level, is a wave-worn cave formed by the rolling of Glacial Lake Algonquin, predecessor of Lake Michigan. Another observation tower on Sven's Bluff reveals the south side of the peninsula.

Near the totem pole, a slim wooden shaft with symbolic carvings of Indian clan relationships, a nine-ton boulder marks the GRAVE OF CHIEF SIMON ONANGUISSE KAHQUADOS (1851-1930), last hereditary chief of the Wisconsin Potawatomi and lineal descendant of Chief Onanguisse, who rescued Tonty's starving band in 1680 (see Tour 1). When the totem pole was dedicated in 1927, Chief Kahquados attended in full ceremonial dress and accepted it on behalf of all Wisconsin

Indians as a memorial to their culture. Four years later he was buried near its foot amid ceremonies even more impressive.

Brought up in the forest of northern Door County, Simon Kahquados was first a lumber scaler, then a self-educated surveyor, having learned to read and write by copying from his children's schoolbooks. He lived most of his adult life in a primitive plank shack far back in the popple thickets of Forest County. Though handicapped by poverty and lack of education, he studied the history and genealogy of his tribe, recording for the first time the meanings and derivations of many Indian names and phrases. Eager to better the conditions of his people, he journeyed many times to Washington to consult the Bureau of Indian Affairs, which gave him a number of medals but disregarded his proposals. Kahquados died November 27, 1930, shortly before his eightieth birthday, and was buried six months later on Memorial Day, 1931. Both Indians and whites did him honor at his elaborate funeral, on which was spent more money than Kahquados had enjoyed during his entire lifetime.

EPHRAIM (Heb., very fruitful), 24.7 m. (191 pop.), on Eagle Harbor near the base of Eagle Bluff, was founded in 1853 by a colony of Moravians. Its story is intimately bound up with that of Nils Otto Tank, wealthy Norwegian aristocrat, who in 1849 was persuaded by a young theological student, A. M. Iverson, to aid some Moravian emigrants in the pioneer settlement of Milwaukee. Tank arrived with $1,500,000 in gold, bought a stretch of fertile land at the head of Green Bay, and transplanted there the Milwaukee colony with its pastor, the Rev. Mr. Fett. This settlement, then named Ephraim, is now the Eighth Ward of the city of Green Bay, locally known as Tanktown (*see Green Bay*).

In accordance with Moravian doctrines, all land was held in common by the General Economy at Bethlehem, Pa., where the Moravians had founded a central American church in the first half of the eighteenth century. Tank laid out dwelling lots, with farms adjoining, and set aside grounds for parks, a church, schools, and a college. A deserted Indian mission was equipped for religious purposes. Tank himself taught history, languages, and science, while Iverson expounded the scriptures and religion.

For a year the colony prospered, and Tank's dreams of Christian Communism seemed close to fulfillment. The size, population, and prestige of his colony increased; in the settlement only one man was unhappy, Pastor Fett, who from the beginning had been skeptical of Tank's motives. Fett whispered his doubts to Iverson, questioning Tank's sincerity, pointing out his previous failures in missionary work. Why, he asked, should this wealthy aristocrat bury himself here in the wilderness?

Fett's suspicion spread. These people had fled from the semi-feudal tenant system of Norway and could be only too easily persuaded to fear the same system here. When Tank refused to give them title to the lots they occupied, arguing that it was contrary to the fundamental doctrines of their faith, the group fell apart, literally fled. Some pushed on into the western wilderness; others went to Sturgeon Bay. A larger group, led by Iverson, obtained a $500 grant from H. A. Schultz of the Bethlehem authority, bought land here at Eagle Harbor, and established the present village of Ephraim. Tank stayed behind in his cottage at Green Bay, living there until he died. Fifty years later Iverson confessed that his suspicions had been wholly ill-founded.

Here, at the second Ephraim, the Moravians under Iverson fought anew the pioneer battle against the wilderness, fishing through the ice in winter, from boats in summer, clearing tiny patches for farms, cutting trees and shipping cedar fence posts and telegraph poles to Chicago. IVERSON'S COTTAGE still stands, as does the first MORAVIAN CHURCH, built in 1857 and since remodeled. In the church are the massive paneled pulpit, tables, chairs, and lamps the first settlers used. The records and Iverson's journal, written in Norwegian, are still intact. Plans are being made to restore the old chapel and to refurnish it with the original hand-hewn pews. In modified form the Moravian faith continues to flourish among the descendants of the first Moravians.

Predominantly a resort village, probably the most noted along this coast, Ephraim has a superb harbor; an annual regatta has been held here for many years, and wealthy summer residents are planning the Ephraim Yacht Club, which will promote weekly sailboat races during the summer. The PENINSULA ART ASSOCIATION, headed by Dr. Frederick Stock, director of the Chicago Symphony Orchestra, has its headquarters in the village. The Association was organized to provide a place where "a limited number of sincere, qualified artists—painters, musicians, writers, architects, sculptors, dancers, hand craft workers, decorative designers—at a minimum cost may join together for inspiration, study, and creative accomplishment." Although plans and housing facilities are not yet complete, in the summer of 1938 the Association gave 12 public entertainments, including lectures, an art show, a hobby show, and a concert; free handicraft classes for children and botany classes for adults were also held.

State 42 winds uphill out of the village. The view south from the hilltop, looking far across little Ephraim and its rippling bay to the high wall of Eagle Bluff, is one of the finest in the State. On the desolate plateau to the north the highway passes a few farms, a few stumpy pastures, an occasional young and struggling orchard, all encircled by the brush of the cutover.

SISTER BAY, 28.1 *m.* (238 pop.), is at the junction with State 57 (*see Tour 1*), and State 42 (*see Tour 1A*).

Tour 1C

Junction with State 57—Kewaunee—Two Rivers—Manitowoc; 56.7 *m.* State 42.

Hard-surfaced roadbed.
Adequate accommodations.

This route links Door Peninsula, with its rocky fields, wild brush, and old villages, to the eastern lakeshore with its broad, rich farms and crowded industrial cities.

South of the junction with State 57, 0 *m.* (*see Tour 1*), State 42 crosses a swamp overgrown with cedar and spruce. Six-foot ditches, like muddy canals, border the highway and drain both swamp and roadbed. For years construction engineers dumped tons of material into this swamp, but always the roadbed sank. Finally they dynamited the muck, allowed the highway to drop to the bottom of the bog, then graded it up to its present surface. The highway angles across broad farm land, and from a hilltop at 5.8 *m.* overlooks a wide plain and the white houses and black rooftops of FORESTVILLE, 6.7 *m.* (550 pop.), sleepy and sunny market center for the surrounding farm area. South of Forestville State 42 runs along the crest of a ridge overlooking lazily undulating countryside.

ALGOMA (Ind., sandy place), 12.8 *m.* (590 alt., 2,202 pop.), has an L-shaped business section. On top of the lakeshore bluff on the southern side of the city is a picnic and camping ground, and at its foot a public beach. Seen from this bluff, the fields and hills surrounding Algoma taper down to a wavering yellow line of sandy beach; the breakwaters form a pattern in white against the blue background of the lake; and a bright red lighthouse darts a sliver of vivid color into the windswept landscape.

Beyond the DOOR-KEWAUNEE COUNTY NORMAL SCHOOL, 13.1 *m.,* the highway traverses an open countryside with occasional farms and then sweeps into the marshy valley of the Kewaunee River at 23.8 *m.* Across the swamp (L) are the harbor and breakwater of Kewaunee's port; in the swamp rows of pilings show where railroad trestles once spanned the mile-wide flood plain.

KEWAUNEE (Ind., prairie hen), 24.7 *m.* (586 alt., 2,409 pop.), lies clustered around the harbor at the southern edge of the flood plain, sloping upward to the surrounding red clay banks. Though Jean Nicolet passed here in 1634, there was no settlement until 1795, when Jacques Vieau, agent for the North West Fur Company of Montreal, established a trading post here. Immigration was slow until 1836, when a rumored gold discovery brought a rush of land speculators and fortune hunters. The settlement became a potential rival of rapidly expanding Chicago. Land prices soared; lots in a swamp brought $1,000 apiece.

After the collapse of the boom, Kewaunee turned to lumbering. In 1842 appeared John Volk, a pious-looking gentleman in frock coat and tall silk hat, who purchased several mill sites and began large-scale cutting of Government timber. For 12 years he prospered, evading queries as to the exact limits of his holdings, and stripping thousands of acres. Confronted finally with accurate Government maps proving the land not his, he dropped his claims and sold his power sites, but by that time most of the timber was gone.

With a natural harbor navigable for 7 miles from its mouth, Kewaunee had hopes of becoming a large shipping center, but the hope was destroyed by the development of Chicago and the coming of overland communications by rail. Today its principal industry is the manufacture of school and office furniture, though the city is better known as the home of the Swoboda Church Furniture Company, which failed during the depression. This firm's artisans traveled throughout the country carving the interior woodwork and decorations of large churches. Some examples of their work are displayed in Kewaunee hotels and furniture stores.

The COAST GUARD STATION is one block east of the Kewaunee River bridge. Beside it is the terminus of the Pere Marquette freight ferries, whose busy docks are visible from the highway near the bridge.

TWO RIVERS, 49.3 m. (597 alt., 10,083 pop.), at the confluence of the Mishicot (Ind., great branch) and Neshoto Rivers, which unite here to flow into Lake Michigan through a single channel, was once the busiest port in the region, but lost its position in the 1870's to Manitowoc. Though commercial traffic is small, Two Rivers is still the home port of 11 powerful little fishing tugs.

Commercial fishing for whitefish began in 1836 with a 10-barrel catch. French Canadians soon came to fish in their flat-bottomed, two-masted mackinaw boats, and many of the city's present fishermen are their descendants. Brought in by chunky little motorboats, the city's 500,000-pound annual catch is shipped as far as Boston.

After the fishermen had founded the settlement, traders arrived; then a sawmill was built. The next settlers were New England lumberjacks and German immigrant farmers. As lumbering declined about 1860 these people found employment in woodworking industries. A chair factory, established in 1856, and a pail factory in 1857, merged as the Two Rivers Manufacturing Company. Shipbuilding also flourished between 1850 and 1875. In 1880 James E. Hamilton, a craftsman employed by this company, was asked by the local editor to cut some wooden type larger than that which he had in metal, and thus was founded the Hamilton Manufacturing Company, today one of four largest concerns in America making wooden type.

Largest industrial unit in Two Rivers is the $3,200,000 ALUMINUM

GOODS MANUFACTURING COMPANY PLANT, which covers five square blocks and employs 800 workers. In 1893, when aluminum was still a rather expensive curiosity, Joseph Koenig, a young German who had been in charge of the aluminum exhibit at the 1893 Columbian Exposition in Chicago, came here on a visit. Hamilton, interested in the product, leased Koenig space and power in his type factory. When Koenig took his first manufactured articles to Chicago in 1895, he received orders for more goods in two hours than he could manufacture in three months. Aided by the city, which provided $2,000 toward an aluminum novelties factory, Koenig attained such success that William and Henry Vits of Manitowoc converted their tannery into a competing plant. In 1909 these two factories were merged with the New Jersey Aluminum Company and incorporated as the Aluminum Goods Manufacturing Company, a Mellon-controlled concern.

MANITOWOC, 56.7 *m.* (595 alt., 22,963 pop.) (*see Tour 18*), is at the junction with US 141 (*see Tour 3*), US 151 (*see Tour 6*), and US 10 (*see Tour 18*).

Tour 2

(Menominee, Mich.)—Marinette—Green Bay—Oshkosh—Fond du Lac—Milwaukee—(Chicago, Ill.); US 41.
Michigan Line to Illinois Line, 225.5 *m.*

Chicago & North Western Ry. parallels route between Marinette and Fond du Lac; Soo Line between Fond du Lac and Richfield; Chicago, Milwaukee, St. Paul & Pacific R.R. between Milwaukee and Illinois Line.
Concrete roadbed.
Many camp sites and picnic grounds; good city accommodations.

Between Marinette and Oshkosh US 41 crosses territory known to three centuries of white men; it follows in part the Fox River-Lake Winnebago waterway, early route of French missionaries, explorers, traders, and soldiers. South of Fond du Lac the highway winds through the kettle moraine country and out into flat lakeshore farmlands settled in the 1830's by farmers from the East.

Section a. MARINETTE to GREEN BAY; 55.1 m., US 41

US 41 crosses the INTERSTATE BRIDGE spanning the Menominee River, the boundary between Wisconsin and Michigan, from Menominee, Michigan.

MARINETTE, 0 *m.* (600 alt., 13,734 pop.), on the Green Bay

shore at the mouth of the river, is an active city with a long and varied history, having passed through three distinct phases. From the spacious city square, through surrounding suburbs, streets lead eventually to the water front, dwindling into narrow, cobbled alleys. Here, among shacks and tiny bungalows, fishing nets dry in the sun, and children gather coal and wood from railroad tracks and lumberyards. Lake freighters load from docks and warehouses. Along the river, beyond high piles of peeled logs and the black waters of power dams, stand the mansions of those who profited in the days when Marinette was a fur-trading post and later a lumbering center.

In 1795 Stanislaus Chappu, agent for the American Fur Company, built a trading post on the river here. In 1822 his trading monopoly was challenged by William Farnsworth, an independent trader, who obtained the favor of the Indians, married the daughter of a Menominee chief, Marinette Chevalier (for whom the city is named), and finally gained the major portion of the Indian fur-trade. Around 1831 Farnsworth and his partner, Charles R. Brush, built the first wing dam and sawmill. Other mills and trading posts sprang up, and laborers settled in the region. But the panic of 1857 and the Civil War halted this development.

When lumbering operations moved north Marinette rallied, becoming for a while the center of the largest lumbering area in Wisconsin. Yankees, Southerners, Europeans crowded in to work at the lumberyards and mills. By 1900 lumber had created a city of 16,000 people, but when the timber vanished, only two of the 27 mills remained active, and Marinette was left destitute.

Again a new start was made, this time on a broader footing. A municipal bond issue built a city dock; Federal aid improved the harbor; new railroads were constructed. Marinette developed into a community of diversified industries. Among its present industrial establishments are paper mills, knitting mills, a chemical plant, a box factory that turns out both wood and paper boxes, granite works, a glove factory and a paper converting plant. A substantial dairy industry has been developed, and the city has four operating dairies and a condensery. In 1938 the Marinette fishing fleet numbered 50 vessels, and the fishing industry gave employment to approximately 300 workers.

Smelt fishing is the annual sport of Marinette citizens; each year when the smelts go up river to spawn, tourists and townspople turn out with dipnets or seines. The smelt run in greatest number at night, and from 9 p.m. until midnight all Marinette is festive. The Interstate Bridge is closed to traffic, every foot is crowded with poles, flashlights, machines for lifting the seines, and baskets full of shining fish. The riverbank is a blaze of light from bonfires; old automobile tires, thrown on the fires, send up heavy black clouds of smoke. Men, women, and children stand knee deep in the river, catching large numbers of fish in each drag of the seine. Barkers yell their wares, fireworks light the whole sky, and beer flows freely. The festival reaches a climax with the crowning of the Smelt Queen.

In a park running the length of Riverside Dr., R. from Interstate Bridge, is a MONUMENT TO ISAAC STEPHENSON (1829-1918), wealthy pioneer lumberman, who represented Wisconsin at Washington for many years, both in the House of Representatives and the Senate. Near by, a bronze tablet set in a red granite boulder marks the SITE OF WILLIAM FARNSWORTH'S FIRST DAM. The MERRYMAN MANSION, 2701 Riverside Ave., Victorian in style, was once the social center of local mill owners and railroad executives.

US 41 goes south from Marinette, past a free picnic ground (L), 3.8 m. Occasional tamarack swamps and pine forests break the monotony of flat land that ages ago was the bottom of a great body of water that has shrunk to the confines of Green Bay. Along the route are the homesteads of Polish, Irish, and Bohemian settlers who, when the Marinette sawmills closed, bought up land and began farming the cutover.

At 7.3 m., on the western outskirts of Peshtigo, is a MONUMENT TO THE GREAT FIRE OF 1871 (see Tour 1), a blaze that ravaged the northeast, killed 1,200 people, wiped out whole villages, and destroyed over $5,000,000 worth of property. During an unprecedented drought in the summer of 1871 many small fires burned sporadically in northeastern Wisconsin. Then on October 8, fanned by high winds, a tornado of fire broke out and swept up the shore, destroyed Peshtigo, and sped on toward Marinette. Between the cities the flame split; one part swirled out over the bay, the other, narrowly missing Marinette, consumed part of Menominee, Mich., and continued on up the peninsula, stripping the forest bare. Within four hours the fire swept a path 40 miles long and 10 miles wide along the western bay shore. Desolation was greatest here at Peshtigo where 600 persons were killed, hundreds horribly burned. Only two wooden structures survived the holocaust—a small shack and a crude cross in the cemetery.

PESHTIGO, 7.6 m. (609 alt., 1,579 pop.), has wide, planned streets and row after row of one-story bungalows, many dating from the rebuilding of the town after the fire. A PAPER MILL, employing approximately 500 workers, is the most important industrial unit in Peshtigo. An interesting by-product of lumbering is the manufacture of hand-made canoes, sailboats, and motor launches. Retail trade with farmers also helps support the city, although/ the land southward is alternately burned, eroded, and wooded. Much of the farm land is being reconditioned with lime or manure, which in spring lies in piles across the fields. Adjacent woodlots are crowded with brush or with jack pine and a fast-growing, sweet-smelling, soft popple, which lumberjacks called bumgillian, said to be a garbled form of Balm of Gilead.

OCONTO, 21.7 m. (590 alt., 5,030 pop.), spreading over a flat sand plain near the Oconto River, is one of the more prosperous cities in this northern section. Incorporated in 1869, the city has grown by fits and starts. Old wooden houses, modern brick hotels, Victorian dwellings, suburban bungalows, and story-and-a-half houses stand shoulder to shoulder, unaware of differences in age and style. All have a common ancestor—lumber. Oconto was almost as important a lumbering center as Marinette and had her share of German and Irish lumberjacks who stampeded the town after the spring drives and interrupted the quiet life of the French-Canadian residents. Today the boisterous lumberjack has been supplanted by the law-abiding mill worker. A sawmill here supports 30 per cent of the population.

Long before it became a lumbering camp, Oconto was the site of an Indian village and French mission. On Chicago St. ALLOUEZ CROSS (R), commemorates the founding of the first Jesuit mission in eastern Wisconsin, established in 1669 by Father Claude Allouez, who had come to the Green Bay region from his La Pointe mission (see Tour 14A). ·

The NICHOLAS PERROT MONUMENT, Main and Congress Sts., was erected in honor of Nicholas Perrot (1644-1718), one of the bravest and most astute fur traders and diplomats of the French regime. Appointed commandant of the Wisconsin territory in 1685, Perrot built fortified trading posts, opened up trade with the Sioux and other tribes, and discovered and worked lead mines in southwestern Wisconsin. He staged an elaborate pageant in 1689 and took possession of all the Upper Mississippi in the name of Louis XIV. Perrot succeeded in keeping friendly relations with the Indians and prospered until the King revoked all trading licenses in 1696. Then he retired. In 1698 he returned to Lower Canada where he spent the remainder of his life in poverty, acting occasionally as an interpreter and writing a long memoir of his life in the Northwest.

In a triangle at W. Main and Chicago Sts. stands a small wooden building, the FIRST CHURCH BUILT BY CHRISTIAN SCIENTISTS. A small congregation was organized here in 1886 by the Reverend Lanson P. Norcross, who conducted the first services in the new church in October of that year. Three years later he was called to Boston as pastor of the original Church of Christ, Scientist. A letter from Mrs. Mary Baker Eddy to "this little church that built the first temple for Christian Science worship" has been preserved.

At 35.1 m. is the junction with US 141 (see Tour 3); between this junction and Green Bay US 41 and US 141 are one route.

South of the junction the new concrete highway traverses what was once the bottom of the bay—flat wind-swept country cut by long sand ridges. Prosperous dairy farms alternate with stumpy fields on which appear dilapidated barns, tar-paper shacks, and weatherbeaten houses bearing signs, "This Place for Sale." Much of this submarginal land, reverting to the county because of tax delinquency, is being set aside for reforestation or recreational purposes.

SUAMICO, 45.4 m. (605 alt., 206 pop.), a recreational center scattered along the Suamico River, has a TOURIST CAMP (free), a general store that sells hunting and fishing equipment, and log tourist cabins. Southward US 41 traverses wild country, the home of deer, pheasant, and grouse, to DUCK CREEK, 51 m., which has a TRAILER CAMP (free) and a swimming pool.

GREEN BAY, 55.1 *m*. (590 alt., 37,415 pop.) (*see Green Bay*). Green Bay is at the junction with State 57 (*see Tour 1*), US 141 (*see Tour 3*), and State 29 (*see Tour 17*).

Section b.   GREEN BAY to FOND DU LAC; 70.9 m., US 41

South of GREEN BAY, 0 *m*., US 41 curves down the Fox River Valley, one of the richest historical regions in the State. In 1673 Father Jacques Marquette and Louis Joliet canoed up the Fox on the voyage that led to the first recorded discovery of the Upper Mississippi and the Fox-Wisconsin riverway, linking the Mississippi with the Great Lakes. For a century and a half thereafter this waterway was the axis about which the exploration and early development of Wisconsin turned. Green Bay, De Pere, Kaukauna, Little Chute, Neenah-Menasha, and Oshkosh, growing up at the six most advantageous points along the route, owed their development to the trade and resources along the waterway.

At 2.9 *m*., on a broad terrace overlooking the Fox River, a granite marker (R) indicates the SITE OF SHANTYTOWN. About 1818 Colonel Joseph Lee Smith, commanding officer at Fort Howard, Green Bay, became dissatisfied with the site and abandoned the fort, moving his troops here and constructing a stockade and barracks named Camp Smith. Merchants, saloonkeepers, and other camp followers built their stores between the stockades and the river; French-Canadian farmers, seeing a new market for their produce, squatted along the river on claims which, only a few rods wide, extended back from one to three miles into the wilderness. The soldiers, ridiculing the farmers, called their plowed tracts "all long and no wide."

Two years later, in 1820, this camp was abandoned, and the fort in Green Bay was again occupied; but Shantytown continued to grow. Before 1824 the first courthouse west of Lake Michigan was built here, and on June 20 of that year the first session convened. When no judge appeared, the court was adjourned until the next day. For nine days the court waited for a judge, and on the tenth adjourned *sine die*. Finally, late in October, James Duane Doty, a 23-year-old lawyer from New England, new to the Northwest, held the first regular session in the small courthouse, calling it "no better than a hovel." Shantytown was also the site of the first jail west of Lake Michigan; the town declined after Navarino and De Pere had been platted.

US 41 continues south through high farming country, as beautiful today as in 1854 when an early writer noted that the country between Green Bay and De Pere "has in some degree the appearance of an extended village . . . and on looking down the river, the expanded sheet of water, with its banks studded with white houses, green gardens, and yellow harvest fields, and bounded on the Northeast by the villages of Green Bay and Fort Howard, together with the masts of the Shipping and the tall iron chimneys of the steamboats overtopping the house roofs all combine in forming a most delightful summer picture."

DE PERE, 5 m. (595 alt., 5,521 pop.), approached through a wide street arched with heavy trees, is today a typical midwestern city, an agricultural and manufacturing center. Many well-to-do citizens working in Green Bay have built their homes here along one of the most beautiful sections of the river.

The handsome concrete and steel CLAUDE ALLOUEZ BRIDGE was erected in 1933 at a cost of $458,000. A bronze tablet attached to the railing on the eastern end indicates the SITE OF ST. FRANCIS XAVIER MISSION, the first permanent Jesuit mission on the Fox River, established by Father Claude Allouez in 1671. Allouez used this mission as headquarters for his work among the Wisconsin Indians. In 1676 he removed to Kaskaskia where he took charge of the Illinois mission of Father Marquette, who had died in 1675. In 1686 Father Nouvel was in charge of St. Francis Xavier when Perrot, military commandant of the Green Bay region (see above), presented a silver ostensorium to the mission. This ostensorium, earliest relic af the French regime in Wisconsin, is now in the Green Bay museum. In 1687 the mission house and its valuable store of peltry were burned by the Fox Indians, and the Jesuits retreated to Mackinac. The mission was reopened, however, and continued until the erection of Fort La Baye in 1717; in that year Father Chadron closed St. Francis Xavier and removed to Fort La Baye.

The DE PERE DAM, which furnishes power for mills and nearby villages, was erected in 1849 as part of a project to unite Lake Michigan and the Mississippi River by improving and connecting the Fox and Wisconsin Rivers (see Tour 21). Construction of the first Government dam and locks at the rapids here began in 1836, attracting many reckless speculators who bought all the adjacent land, sold it at fabulous prices, and circulated a quantity of worthless scrip that had been issued to finance the enterprise. The rapid expansion of De Pere was checked in 1847 when a storm swept the dam down the river. In 1849 the erection of a stronger dam was made possible by Federal land grants along the Fox River, and the city developed into a prosperous trading, shipping, and lumbering center.

Around the dam sprang up a gristmill, three sawmills, two lathing mills, three shingle-making machines, one planing machine, and two turning lathes. Docks and a three-story warehouse were built along the locks. Five million feet of lumber were cut yearly and marketed at Milwaukee, Chicago, and Buffalo. Fishing, too, was important. In one season 800 to 1,000 barrels of pike and pickerel were caught, salted, and sold at $5 to $8 a barrel. But the Fox-Wisconsin River development was never very practical; before the improvement was completed the northward expansion of the railroad had nullified its value, and the bright prospects of De Pere faded. Nevertheless, today De Pere has a diversified source of income, manufacturing glassine paper, butcher paper, boats, medicines and feeds. It has a steel works and a foundry and stoker plant. At the dam, the last on the Fox River, lake boats frequently transfer their cargoes to up-river barges.

In De Pere is St. Norbert College, a Catholic College which began in 1898 when the Praemonstratensian Fathers, recently arrived from Heeswijk, Holland, offered a few courses to local young men who aspired to priesthood. So successful was this educational venture, that six years later it was decided to enlarge the preparatory seminary into an American Catholic College. Today, St. Norbert College, still administered by its first President, the Right Reverend Abbott, Bernard H. Pennings, O. Praem., offers a collegiate course to Catholics and non-Catholics alike.

At 7 m. is the junction with a county road.

Left on this road to the Hickory Grove Sanatorium, 1.5 m. On the bluff (R), just south of the sanatorium is the Homestead of Eleazer Williams (1788-1858), an Episcopalian missionary of Indian descent who led a group of Oneida and Stockbridge Indians to Wisconsin in 1821 (see Tour 4). Promising to build schools and to make improvements, he persuaded the Menominee residing in the Green Bay region to sell some land; but disputes occurred, the Menominee became bitter, and eventually the New York Indians were forced to move again. In 1832, disgusted with Williams, they severed all connections with him, forbidding him to speak in their name or to mix in their affairs.

Suddenly in 1853 he publicly presented himself as Louis XVII, the "lost dauphin," whose disappearance during the French Revolution was of sufficient mystery to produce more than two dozen pretenders. Williams' assertions, based on a superficial coincidence of bodily markings and chronological events, created widespread attention, but the color and texture of his skin and the testimony of his Indian relatives betrayed him. Furthermore, there is no reason to doubt that Louis XVII died of neglect in his cell when he was ten years old (1795). Yet the legend of Wisconsin's "lost dauphin" still persists; in 1937 Metro-Goldwyn-Mayer dramatized it in a movie short entitled *A King Without a Crown*.

US 41 continues south among the small hills and ravines of the Fox River Valley. At first prized as agricultural land, the immediate vicinity of the riverbank has become highly industrialized; even in rural areas cheese factories, powerhouses, and other plants dot the smooth meadows and gentle valley slopes.

At 20 m. is the junction with State 55 (see Tour 4).

KAUKAUNA (Fr.-Ind., Grand Kakalin, long portage), 20 m. (709 alt., 6,581 pop.), grew around the portage used by early travelers in avoiding the long cascade in the Fox. In 1793, executing the oldest deed in the State, Dominique Ducharme purchased the site from Indians for two barrels of rum. Ducharme's brother Paul took over the trading business; purchasing supplies from shrewd Judge John Lawe of Green Bay, he soon fell so deeply into debt that the judge took over the property. In 1818 it was owned by Augustin Grignon, grandson of Charles de Langlade (see Tour 4). The Grignon family lived at the Grand Kakalin for years, controlled the local fur trade, built the first gristmill and sawmill in Wisconsin, and was prominent in the Fox River improvement speculation (see Tour 21). As water traffic increased, a dam was built here; paper mills were established to take advantage of the power. By 1875 farming had been successfully developed in the surrounding country, and Kaukauna began making dairy products, chief source of its income today.

Left from Tobanoir St. on the parkway parallel with the canal is the GRIGNON HOUSE (*fee 10¢*), built in 1838 of lumber shipped from Buffalo and occupied until 1933. Now in disrepair, the house has high, narrow windows and an ornamental balcony. The interior is notable for its fine wood trim and its black walnut stair rails with an elaborately hand-carved newel post. Four large fireplaces are still intact. Elms planted more than 100 years ago shade the overgrown grounds.

At 22.5 *m*. is the junction with County N.

Left on County N to LITTLE CHUTE, 0.8 *m*. (714 alt., 2,833 pop.), on the rapids in the Fox. The construction of a dam and lock led the city to hope for great size and prosperity, but it never succeeded in rivaling Kaukauna or Appleton. Today it is inhabited largely by workers in the large Kimberly Clark Paper Mill in Kimberly, across the river.

APPLETON, 29.2 *m*. (723 alt., 25,267 pop.) (*see Tour 18*), is at the junction with US 10 (*see Tour 18*). Between Appleton and a point at 30.7 *m*. US 41 and US 10 are one route.

At 36.4 *m*. is the junction with State 150.

Left on State 150 to the twin cities, NEENAH, 1.2 *m*. (747 alt., 9,151 pop.), and MENASHA, 2.4 *m*. (755 alt., 9,062 pop.), so closely united that Wisconsin people refer to them as one community, Neenah-Menasha. They lie on both sides of the two channels through which Lake Winnebago empties into the north-flowing Fox. Settled at approximately the same time and sharing the same development, they present a sharp contrast: Menasha is a city of small neat homes, populated by Scandinavian, Irish, and Polish factory workers; Neenah is a city of landowners, financiers, and industrialists who have built large palatial homes.

When French missionaries and traders first penetrated this section it was occupied by Menominee, Winnebago, and Fox. In 1766 Jonathan Carver stopped for several days at the island as the guest of Ho-po-ko-ekaw (Glory of the Morning), heroine of William Ellery Leonard's poetic drama, *Glory of the Morning* (*see Literature*). Her French husband, Sabrevoir de Carrie, was killed before Quebec; one of her sons, Chief Spoon Decorah, ruled the Winnebago of western Wisconsin.

In 1835-36 the U. S. Government built here for the Indians a sawmill, gristmill, wing dam, and dwellings. But the Indians tore up the wooden floors of their houses and built lodges inside the walls. Ceding the land to the Federal Government (1836), the Menominee moved away, and the site was deserted until 1843 when the War Department sold land, buildings, and water-power rights to Harrison Reed. To obtain capital, Reed took Harvey Jones of New York as his partner, and the community of Neenah was formed. However, after quarrels about their agreement had arisen, Jones ousted Reed from the venture. Reed, his brother Curtis Reed, and Charles Doty thereupon established Menasha. The Menasha group was awarded the charter to develop the water power; hence Menasha became the more industrialized city.

The completion of locks and dams attracted permanent settlers. The first sawmill and gristmill were built in Neenah in 1849, and the same year Elisha D. Smith established in Menasha a wooden-pail factory, still in operation, manufacturing woodenware of all kinds for an international market. Other industries followed and in 1857 Menasha was known as the best hardwood market in this section, while Neenah became a great flour-milling city. In

1870, when wheat production in Wisconsin dropped off, Neenah turned to the manufacture of paper, at first using wheat straw as raw material. Today Neenah has six paper mills, three machine shops, a knitting mill, and cellu-cotton factory; Menasha has seven paper mills, four machine shops, a pulley factory, a pump factory, a tannery, a wire mill, three paper-specialty factories, a boiler works, and two large printing houses.

DOTY ISLAND, in the center of the channels between the two cities, was a meeting place of Indians and explorers for many years. It is named for Judge James Duane Doty, speculator and Territorial Governor of Wisconsin, who acquired the island in the early 1830's. Nicolet Blvd. divides the island between Neenah and Menasha. DOTY PARK, on Neenah's half, preserves the GRAND LOGGERY (*open to public*), the log house in which Doty entertained prominent politicians, adventurers, and Indians. RIVERSIDE PARK, another of several in Neenah, is at the mouth of the Fox and contains the SITE OF THE GREAT COUNCIL TREE, scene of negotiations between Indians and whites.

In the Menasha half of Doty Island is CITY PARK, with three INDIAN EFFIGY MOUNDS and a marker at the SITE OF JEAN NICOLET'S LANDING in 1634. Menasha also has E. D. SMITH PARK (*tennis and bathing facilities*), with formal gardens and lagoons, and a memorial hall; GILBERT LAGOON, a landscaped bit of lakeshore; and the CITY BATHING BEACH.

At 40.5 *m.* is the junction with US 45 (*see Tour 5*); between this junction and a point at 48.2 *m.* US 45 and US 41 are one route (*see Tour 5*). At 48.2 *m.* US 41 turns L. on Murdock St. to Main; R. on Main to a second junction with US 45 (*see Tour 5*) at 51.8 *m.*

OSHKOSH, 51.8 m. (761 alt., 40,108 pop.) (*see Oshkosh*).

Between 51.8 *m.* and a point at 54.8 *m.* US 41 and US 45 (*see Tour 5*) are on one route. Fields are wide and pastures level as US 41 swings inland from LAKE WINNEBAGO (*see Tour 5*) through fields of corn, wheat, barley, and oats, green and golden in the sun. White-trimmed farmhouses and red barns appear on all sides, cows graze in timothy and clover stubble, pigs wallow in barnyard mud.

VAN DYNE, 60.2 *m.* (791 alt., 150 pop.), was named for an early Dutch settler during the 1860's. The village was hopefully founded to share the prosperity that the incoming railroad was to bring, but the trains between Oshkosh and Fond du Lac whizzed by without stopping. Many railroad men live in the village, however, and commute daily to their work in NORTH FOND DU LAC, 65.6 *m.* (749 alt., 2,244 pop.), which changed from a small farming community to a bustling railroad center when the Soo Line and Chicago & North Western Ry. transferred their shops here in the early 1900's.

FOND DU LAC, 70.9 m. (759 alt., 26,449 pop.) (*see Tour 5*), is at the junction with US 45 (*see Tour 5*), State 55 (*see Tour 4*), State 23 (*see Tour 5A*), and US 151 (*see Tour 6*).

Section c.　FOND DU LAC to ILLINOIS LINE; 99.5 m., US 41

South of FOND DU LAC, 0 *m.*, appears the Niagara escarpment, a long ridge patched with farms and woodlots; as the highway climbs a ridge spur, Hamilton stone shows close to the surface. Flaked off, the dull yellow rock is used as facing in modern houses.

BYRON, 8.2 m. (1,058 alt., 39 pop.), flanks the highway, a one-street village where fields creep up to back doors, where a single building combines post office, general store, and filling station, where every house has a weathered barn. The aviator S. J. Wittman, one of the outstanding speed pilots of the United States, winner of many races and trophies, lived here as a boy.

Southward is LOMIRA, 12.5 m. (1,019 alt., 603 pop.). The village, founded in 1849, was named Elmira for the young daughter of a pioneer, but its name got twisted with the years. The highway passes through the oldest section, for most of Lomira has moved eastward to follow a shift in railroad lines.

THERESA, 17.5 m. (940 alt., 427 pop.), lying on several knobby hills, was started by Solomon Juneau, one of the founders of Milwaukee, who named it for his daughter. The small brown frame JUNEAU HOUSE still tops the village's highest point (L). Most of Theresa's citizens are descendants of German immigrants. The village lies in the kettle moraine country, a land of rough hills, potholes, and gravelly soil difficult for farming. Eventually the State hopes to make an outdoor playground in this region, a narrow ribbon-like strip 85 miles long and two or three miles wide, that will extend from near Sheboygan through six counties and provide recreational facilities for the crowded lakeshore cities.

SLINGER, 33.7 m. (1,053 alt., 760 pop.), in a V-shaped groove of hills, was founded in the late 1840's by B. Schleisinger Weil, a German-Alsatian, who started a general store and named his settlement Schleisinger. The name was shortened to Slinger in 1921 at the request of the residents, most of whom are retired farmers and workers employed in the local brewery or engineering plant. Three miles northeast is BIG CEDAR LAKE, where vacationers throng to fish and swim.

RICHFIELD, 41.2 m. (968 alt., 214 pop.), was founded in 1842 by Philipp Laubenheimer, who proved an exception to the adage that lightning never strikes twice in the same place. Laubenheimer spent two weeks building a log house, only to learn that it was in the path of the Milwaukee-Fond du Lac road that Solomon Juneau was planning. So he built a tavern at what he considered a safe distance away, but inexorable road builders moved up and forced his second building off their right-of-way. Richfield is a village of small white frame houses, with old hitching posts, lawn swings, and pumps in their front yards; its few business places have false fronts and are backed by fields. Over 75 per cent of the population is of German descent.

At 41.5 m. is the junction with County P, a graveled road.

Right on County P along an attractive valley, then through swamps of tamarack and cedar, and up into the large rounded hills of the kettle moraine. At 5.1 m. HOLY HILL (1,361 alt.) (L), appears far above. At 7.8 m. the highway reaches the hill crest with its castle-like CHURCH and HOLY HILL MONASTERY of the Carmelite Fathers. Many tales center around this shrine, including one of the miraculous cure of François Soubris, a Quebec monk. Legend says that Soubris became paralyzed as he journeyed toward this consecrated spot. He climbed the slope on his hands and knees, and after spending the night in prayer recovered the use of his limbs.

In 1855 the Rev. Francis Paulhuber bought the land and later built a log chapel on the brow of the hill. Today his original building has been replaced by one of brick; a brick church also crowns the summit. Along the winding lane that leads to the crest are 14 Stations of the Cross, before which the devout kneel in prayer on their way to the shrine.

MENOMONEE FALLS, 48 m. (881 alt., 1,291 pop.), on the tumbling rapids of the Menominee River that flows through the center of town, was founded in 1843 by Frederic Nehs, who bought up 700 acres of land here, realizing the water-power possibilities of the site. German friends and immigrants followed him; population increased as a bottling plant, a flour mill, a sugar beet factory, and a ginseng plant were opened. These have long since closed their doors, and today the people of Menomonee Falls work principally in Milwaukee. A quarter-mile south three great LIME KILN RUINS stand near the river, pale yellow structures, lined with firebrick and yoked at the top by massive charred oak beams.

Southward, US 41 descends easily into the level lake region, a strip of rich black loam early farmed by land-hungry Germans who disembarked by the thousands every year at Sheboygan, Milwaukee, Racine, and other pioneer shore settlements.

At 52.5 m. is the junction with US 45 (see Tour 5), and at 56.5 m. is the junction with St. 190 (see Tour 21).

MILWAUKEE, 61.2 m. (592 alt., 578,249 pop.) (see Milwaukee).

Milwaukee is at the junction with US 41 (see Tour 3), State 42 (see Tour 3A), and US 18 (see Tour 23). Between this point and the Illinois Line, US 41 is divided into separate traffic lanes by a narrow parkway. The JACOB NUNNEMACHER HOMESTEAD DISTILLERY, 65.9 m., appears in the midst of a thick grove of evergreens. The cream brick house is now a tavern; in the grove is a tourist camp. Nunnemacher, an enterprising Swiss, gained a small fortune during the Civil War; he had stored up great quantities of liquor, and as the wartime Federal whisky tax did not have to be paid on these, he could undersell all competitors.

ST. JOHN'S LUTHERAN CHURCH AND CEMETERY are at 74.3 m. (L). In the grassy graveyard are stones dating from 1855, obsolete in design, some lettered "Vater" or "Mutter" in German script; others, toppled and weatherbeaten, are illegible. The sluggish Root River, 75.3 m., was named in 1698 by Father Jean François Buisson de St. Cosme, who found its channel tangled with roots. At 85.5 m. is the junction with State 11 (see Tour 24). The broad fields here are a continuation of the Illinois corn belt; straggling unkempt woodlots and fences darkened with weeds break a chain of shabby farmsteads, roadside markets, taverns, and filling stations. The twisting course of the Des Plaines River (R), 95.5 m., is marked by a feathery willow growth.

US 41 crosses the Illinois Line, 99.5 *m.,* 49.5 miles north of Chicago, Illinois.

Tour 3

(Iron Mountain, Mich.)—Green Bay—Manitowoc—Sheboygan—Milwaukee; US 141.
Michigan Line to Milwaukee, 219.9 *m.*

Chicago, Milwaukee, St. Paul & Pacific R.R. parallels route between Michigan Line and Green Bay; Chicago & North Western Ry. between Green Bay and Milwaukee.
Concrete roadbed.
Resorts and camp sites in north; city accommodations at Green Bay, Manitowoc, Sheboygan, Port Washington, and Milwaukee.

In the northern section US 141 cuts an almost straight path through a country of marshes and upland, desolate timber-stripped cutover, dark spruce forests, and swift rivers tumbling over granite thrusts. Little villages, once busy lumbering centers, now serve as trading posts for farmers living in crude cabins and tar-paper shacks. If this land is the farmers' despair, it is the vacationists' paradise with its wild natural beauty, camp sites and resorts, and deep streams stocked with fish.

Near Green Bay the terrain becomes less rough and the country less wild, as the highway enters a strip of rich arable land that continues to the end of the route. Communities established by hardworking and frugal Bohemians, Poles, Luxembourgers, Irish, Dutch, and Germans dot this green region. These people have been good to the land, and their bright red barns, clean creameries, busy factories, and trading centers testify that the land has been good to them.

Section a. MICHIGAN LINE *to* MANITOWOC; *133.1 m.,*
US 141

US 141 crosses the Interstate Bridge, 0 *m.,* 3 miles south of Iron Mountain, Michigan. The bridge spans the Menominee River, the boundary line between Michigan and Wisconsin. Although the river is not in sight, the highway parallels the Menominee's course as it cuts through the eastern end of the Northern Upland. Here is the only large area of exposed pre-Cambrian rock in the State; outcroppings of quartzite, granite, schist, and lava crowd an otherwise moderately flat landscape. Winding down a long steep granite ridge streaked with red veins of iron and pink veins of feldspar, US 141 reaches the banks of the Menominee at a point where its waters rush down the red rock in turbulent falls.

NIAGARA, 2 *m.* (2,033 pop.), named for these falls, lies along the river on small, ladder-like bluffs opposite the main ridge. The KIMBERLY-CLARK PAPER MILL PLANT, employing one-fourth of the population, cleaves to the top and side of the main ridge, a sprawling concrete structure hanging over the village like a medieval fortress. At night the village seems very small, very silent, and very dark under the lights of the mill, the incessant roar of the falls, and the long deep shadows from the high ridge.

A steel bridge over the falls connects the main factory building with the lumber yards, piled high with peeled balsam and spruce logs. The mill has operated since 1898, producing paper for several popular magazines. Up to 1907 pulpwood from forests upstream were floated down and caught above the falls by the peavies and pickaroons of sure-footed lumberjacks. Men who once handled the jams now sit around the stove in the lumberyard office, conferring by telephone about the arrival of carloads of pulpwood from Michigan, Minnesota, and northern Wisconsin.

South of Niagara US 141 follows the winding floodplain of the river through a rock ridge into hummocky, uneven and poorly drained land. Between Niagara and Green Bay there once stretched a magnificent spruce and pine forest, but within the short space of 30 years lumbering and settlement ripped the land of its natural growth, fires burned out the humus and left a coarse intractable clay. Where there has been any return of vegetation it is usually aspen and slim birch, though in areas where burning and cutting have been small, strips of vigorous spruce have sprung up, giving promise of future forests.

At 5 *m.* is the junction with US 8 (*see Tour 16*); between this junction and a point at 14.8 *m.* US 141 and US 8 are one route.

The highway crosses the North Branch of the Pem Bon Won River, 8.4 *m.,* one of a series of deep fast-running rivers with brush-lined banks and mossy rocks hiding rue anemone and trout lily. Integral parts of the plan to make this region a recreational area, these rivers are stocked every spring with game fish. Temporary and permanent covers, food patches, game refuges, and bird sanctuaries attract deer, grouse, pheasant, wood duck, teal, warblers, and scarlet tanagers. Trailing arbutus flourishes under the yearly layers of pine needles.

At 12.8 *m.* is the junction with a dirt road.

Left on the dirt road to the PEMBINE FIRE TOWER, 1.3 *m.* (R), set back from the road. At 1.8 *m.* near SMITH FALLS, along the Pem Bon Won River, there is a small settlement (*camping facilities*).

Between the North Branch of the Pem Bon Won River and the South Branch at 13.8 *m.,* US 141 traverses a forest-protection area—a first step in the solution of the immense problem created by the cutover. The fire lanes serrating the forest, the drainage ditches dug along the highway, the many seedlings planted, the strategically placed fire towers, the new campsites laid out, all are parts of a coordinated plan to save the remaining forest, provide a new supply of timber, and create recreational areas (*see Natural Setting*). At 14.2 *m*. is the junction with US 8 (*see Tour 16*).

PEMBINE (Ind., waterberries), 14.4 *m*. (971 alt., 254 pop.), 60 years ago a busy logging center, is now a railroad crossing with a general store, a post office, and a tavern. Pembine is typical of the lonely, one-street villages that happen along the roadside with no apparent relation to the natural sites. Here a great forest of red cedar and pine was exploited between 1860 and 1890. During that period a sawmill meant a town, a town meant false-front taverns to slake the prodigious thirsts of spendthrift lumberjacks. The railroad bought up great tracts of land, only to sell it later to peasant immigrants and naive city people; rival railroad companies laid down tracks now overgrown with bluegrass and ragweed. The timber disappeared, fires burned out the soil, lakes dried up. Then followed the arduous task of plowing a soil that could produce only the coarsest of feed crops, unrewarding labor that left the farmers embittered. Still living in crude log cabins and tarpaper shacks, these farmers are piecing out an existence in the backwoods. As they relinquish the struggle one by one and are removed elsewhere, the submarginal lands are put to use in accordance with a scientific conservation plan.

BEECHER LAKE, 18 *m*. (R), small but well stocked, surrounded by marsh and some upland country, is being developed as a hunting and fishing resort.

No part of this region is open for public sale; every square mile has been zoned; no new settlements may be developed; all land not now farmed has been designated as county or State forests. Crude and usually futile attempts are still being made to carry on agriculture. Here and there are the small barns, wooden silos, and the cheap farmhouses of those who cling to these submarginal lands, using stumpy wasteland for pasture, glacial boulders and logs for fences, scrub-oak patches for woodlots, and dry uplands for feed crops.

US 141 crosses the Pike River, 22.9 *m.,* another clear-flowing stream, which here roars over a granite outcropping in a five-foot falls (R). The highway now begins a long ascent to the crest of a hill overlooking a forest of aspen and birch, with some hardwoods and pine. Thin and of recent origin, it is typical of the forests that have grown up all over the north since county zoning ordinances were put into effect (*see Agriculture*). Reforestation is still in an experimental state, for scientists are not yet certain what more useful varieties of trees will thrive in these aspen-growing regions. In the fall this rolling valley is a mass of brilliant color with scarlet maples, yellow popple, and wine-red oak.

WAUSAUKEE (Ind., far away land), 31.7 *m*. (745 alt., 663 pop.), built on a good natural site at the end of the Wausaukee River Valley, lies at the northern tip of the dairy belt. Like Wausau (*see*

Tour 7), with which it shares its Indian name, the village passed through the usual pioneer phases of lumbering and railroad land speculation.

The FRONTIER HOUSE (L), constructed in 1884, still rests on the layers of peeled logs that served as its original foundation. The two log wings were built first; later the two-story center, built of slack wood, was wedged between the wings. Originally a private dwelling, the house became a stagecoach tavern and inn, and is now a summer residence.

On the bank of the river stand two buildings representative of the new era that has come to Wausaukee: the district FOREST RANGER HEADQUARTERS (R), an attractive building in landscaped grounds; and the RECREATION BUILDING (L), a gayly colored round structure, with free tourist camp, swimming pool, and picnic tables.

The young forests south of Wausaukee are transected by many creeks and small rivers. Off the highway are numerous resorts, tourist cabins, settlements around well-stocked lakes, and public and private camps, which are rapidly taking the place of the unproductive dairy and cattle farms that formerly occupied the entire region.

MIDDLE INLET, 38 *m.* (711 alt., 41 pop.), has a GRANGER MEETING HALL, built in the 1870's, shortly after the organization of the National Grange of the Patrons of Husbandry in 1867. After the panic of 1873 the Grange movement grew rapidly, entered politics, and by educational and agitational means directed the attention of the country to the farmers' serious problems. The hall still serves a wide community as a center for agricultural improvement programs and for political and social activities.

CRIVITZ, 42.4 *m.* (680 alt., 450 pop.), "gateway to the lakes and streams of the Thunder Mountain region," stretches out along the level flood plain of the Peshtigo River. A flat-roofed frame village, its streets wide and without plan, Crivitz played its part in the changing history of the river from fur-trading and lumbering days to the present time, when it has become the center of a recreational area. Back from the highway the country is beautiful, the streams are fresh and full of game fish. The grim business of making a living from fluctuating tourist trade has stripped the village of everything but restaurants, gas stations, garages, and stores displaying fishing tackle, guns, and tents.

At 44 *m.* US 141 crosses the Peshtigo River, a black and swirling stream known for its fishing and hunting, the chief tourist attraction of the region. Southward the highway enters a more extensively cultivated area. Hard-working Polish and Czech peasants settled here during the 1900's and have been able to wrest a scant living from the soil. Three or four cows, 40 acres of sandy soil fenced with stumps, crude plows, and a few tired sway-back horses constitute their stock in trade. Schoolhouses in this forest-protection area have no trees around them; high sand dunes shift across the windswept land; flooded creeks rush down eroded gullies. Whatever land is not now tenanted is being left to mature back to its natural vegetation.

POUND, 52.4 *m.* (723 alt., 246 pop.), and COLEMAN, 55.2 *m.* (715 alt., 407 pop.), are trading centers for the Polish and Bohemian farmers. At Pound is a POLISH BAPTIST CHURCH erected in 1908, a red brick Gothic structure with stained-glass windows and arched doors. The village also has a large ITALIAN CHEESE FACTORY.

LENA, 63 *m.* (714 alt., 413 pop.), with its flour mill, cooperative cheese factory and creamery, several farm equipment stores, and a large district school, indicates that farming is better here than in the regions farther north. Its several cooperatives are helping to lay the base for a modern economy.

At 73.8 *m.* is the junction with US 41 (*see Tour 2*); between this junction and Green Bay US 141 and US 41 are one route (*see Tour 2*).

GREEN BAY, 93.8 *m.* (590 alt., 37,415 pop.) (*see Green Bay*).

Green Bay is at the junction with State 57 (*see Tour 1*), US 41 (*see Tour 2*), and State 29 (*see Tour 17*). US 141 continues east on Main St. through a district of small residences and out into the open country. Far right is the great limestone outline of the Niagara escarpment (*see Natural Setting*).

In the late 1830's this section of US 141 was part of the Green Bay-Chicago mail route, a narrow Indian trail that was the main line of communication between the Lake Michigan settlements. Menaced by Indians and often suffering from cold and hunger, mail carriers were paid only $60 for the month-long round trip. Along the broad concrete highway that today sweeps past woodlots, truck gardens, fields, and wide pastures, the modern traveler can complete the same trip in five hours.

The solid farmhouses along the road were built by early settlers, who quarried great masses of limestone bedrock and fashioned them into foundation blocks to support the thick yellow brick walls of steep-roofed houses. An earlier type is represented by the abandoned house and barn, 98.8 *m.*, built of rough-hewn logs dovetailed at the corners and chinked with plaster rubble.

Farmers of the district haul their milk to the condensery depots on the outskirts of BELLEVUE, 100.7 *m.*, and PINE GROVE, 103.5 *m.*, the neat little trading centers for neighboring farms. At 103.8 *m.* is the small pine clump that gave Pine Grove its name. The houses of LANGE'S CORNERS, 106.3 *m.*, cluster about a small well-kept cheese factory, a familiar sight at crossroads in the dairy region.

The village of DENMARK, 109.5 *m.* (874 alt., 779 pop.), in the township of New Denmark, was settled in 1848 by Danes, who named the capital of their new "kingdom" Copenhagen, and spoke of the leading family, Niels Hans Gotfredsen and his wife, as "the king and queen of Denmark." East of the highway live the village's Danish descendants; newer communities of Irish, German, and Polish stock have settled west of it.

The suddenly rougher country southeast of Denmark marks the beginning of an interlobar moraine that becomes more pronounced in the kettle moraine country farther south (*see Natural Setting*). "Erratics," boulders brought from a distance and dropped by the glacier, are used as barn and house foundations. There are few smooth fields in this region of rocks.

In the years when the stagecoach rumbled through COOPERS-TOWN, 113.5 m., the HALFWAY HOUSE (L) was a lively hostelry for travelers. A village store and tavern now occupy its brick and frame structure. Beyond Cooperstown the road sweeps down to ROCK FALLS GROVE, 114.1 m., in a heavily wooded valley. Rock Falls Creek (R) breaks into little rapids as it plunges down the small gorges cut in the ancient bedrock, part of the Niagara Cuesta. Formations unusual for a glaciated area are the low limestone caves in this vicinity; one has been transformed into the MARIBEL CAVES INN, 115.6 m., a bizarre castle-like structure built by a priest. Sturdy log houses and barns, still in use though built by pioneers, appear frequently as the road leaves the interlobate region for the calmer land along Lake Michigan.

At 127.8 m. is the junction with US 10 (see Tour 18); between this junction and a point at 133.1 m. US 141 and US 10 are one route, three lanes wide.

MANITOWOC, 133.1 m. (595 alt., 22,963 pop.) (see Tour 18), is at the junction with US 10 (see Tour 18), State 42 (see Tour 1C), and US 151 (see Tour 6).

Section b. *MANITOWOC to MILWAUKEE; 87 m., US 141*

The route, leading south from MANITOWOC, 0 m., roughly parallels the Lake Michigan shore. At 2.9 m. is the junction with US 151 (see Tour 6). As the highway zigzags into open countryside, flat farmlands roll away from the road, revealing farmhouses white and sprawling, or gray and gaunt. The road passes through several villages consisting of little but a name, a church, a filling station, a few squarish houses, and occasionally a long gray creamery. The region is less interesting for its scenery than for its people—Germans, Belgians, Hollanders and Luxembourgers—who farm and fish along this shore which their immigrant fathers settled. Fishing is as important as dairying here, and "Fish" is advertised more frequently than "Chicken, Southern Fried" in the villages, whose restaurants and taverns offer lake trout, whitefish, pike, and perch, as well as black caviar, the roe of Lake Michigan whitefish. The lakeshore of these villages is spotted with fishing tugs, piers, and coal docks, and reel nets set out to dry.

US 141 slips through the village of NEWTON, 10.4 m. (660 alt., 102 pop.), dips suddenly into a wooded ravine, and at 18 m. passes ST. WENDEL, scarcely more than a name and a tall-spired brick church. Beyond HAVEN, 22.8 m., the road sweeps over a low hill that affords a view of Sheboygan, whose smokestacks and gleaming water tanks thrust jaggedly against the sky. The Pigeon River, crossed at 27.5 m., was named for the wild pigeons that once flocked so thickly in the upper

river valley that this region was known simply as "The Pigeon."
Along the riverbank at 27.6 *m.* stretches a shady little park laid out by
the Wisconsin Highway Commission. Roadside factories and dingy
houses line the highway as it enters Sheboygan.

SHEBOYGAN, 29.5 *m.* (589 alt., 39,251 pop.) (*see Sheboygan*).

South of Sheboygan US 141 travels over the brick streets of an old
residential section, past (R) the delicate antenna tower of Station
WHBL, 31.8 *m.*, a streamlined structure of cream brick.

At 36.5 *m.* is the junction with County KK.

Left on County KK to TERRY ANDRAE STATE PARK, 2 *m.* (*drinking
water, sanitary facilities, custodian and police protection, and campsites*).
This park, given to the State in 1928 by Mrs. F. Terry Andrae of Milwaukee
as a memorial to her husband, consists of 112 acres of sand dunes, groves of
white pine, and beach. Here is abundant plant and bird life; in the southern
end of the park is a bird sanctuary designed particularly for the protection of
wild waterfowl. Paths and roads wind through the grounds, under heavy
foliage, and along the sand dunes.

OOSTBURG, 39.2 *m.* (L) (701 alt., 671 pop.), of the township
of Holland, was settled in the late 1840's by Hollanders who left the
Netherlands because of State interference with their religious practices.
Led by the Reverend Peter Zonne, the Hollanders bought Government
land along Lake Michigan, a fertile section divided today into prosperous
farms of 40 to 80 acres. Fishing, a local milk condensery, and canning
factories supplement the village's farmer trade.

Life at Oostburg still centers in religion, and services in its four
churches are conducted in Dutch as well as English. There are no
dance halls or moving pictures, and only two taverns operate in the
village. Everything closes on Sundays, even the filling stations. Sunday
dinners are prepared on Saturday by Dutch housewives who still cook
the good things their mothers made—*khuete,* a vegetable and pork
roast stew; *oliebollen,* fried dumplings; *vetbollen,* coffee cake dough
sugared and raisined and fried in deep fat; and *babalaars,* a taffy-like
candy.

A tragedy that struck one of the early Dutch migrations is described
briefly on a roadside sign (R), 41.9 *m.*, outside a cemetery where many
of the first Dutch settlers are buried. The sign reads: "Holland
Settlement—Settlers came to this vicinity in 1846 under the leadership
of G. H. Te Kolste. Just north of here in 1847 the steamboat 'Phoenix'
with many new recruits to this colony was burned. 127 Hollanders
were lost in this disaster." Local people still speak of the ominously
named *Phoenix,* on which 209 immigrants had safely crossed the stormy
Great Lakes only to have the ship burst into flames on the last leg of
the journey between Manitowoc and Sheboygan. Tormented by the
sight of the near-by Wisconsin shore, the passengers were at the mercy
of the flames for two hours. A rescue ship that finally arrived found
that all but 46 had been drowned or burned to death.

At 41.9 *m.* is the junction with a side road.

Left on this road to the LAKE MICHIGAN SHORE, 1 *m.*, a sandy beach that sweeps in a curve for many miles. Here descendants of Dutch settlers, still wearing shoes with wooden soles and leather tops, fish for pike, pickerel, and bass to supply the hungry markets of Sheboygan, Port Washington, and Milwaukee. Fishing boats roll near their great nets planted like hedges in the lake, creak against the piers, or rest in cradles on the shore. There are few lake views lovelier than this one, where sand, boats and broad blue waters give the illusion of a long seacoast.

A marker, 44 *m.,* commemorates the fact that Louis Joliet and Jacques Marquette coasted this shore northward in 1673 on their return from the discovery of the Mississippi, and that La Salle and his party passed south in 1679, a century and a half before Hollanders first fished and farmed along the shore. Today the route followed by these intrepid explorers in their frail canoes is roughly paralleled by US 141's three lanes of concrete one mile inland.

At 46.9 *m.* are the RUINS OF TWO STONE HOUSES (L), massive structures pierced by a few small windows, typical of the gloomy homes built by the Flemish people who settled this region. Along the road are smaller fortress-like houses, still used as poultry sheds, cellars, workshops, storerooms, and mill houses by descendants of the builders. Left appears LAKE CHURCH, named for the church whose white bell tower and green spire emerge from the foliage that screens the hillside village. Lake Michigan swells into view at 54.6 *m.,* and for thirty miles US 141 runs intermittently along the lakeshore.

PORT WASHINGTON, 58 *m.* (671 alt., 3,693 pop.), an L-shaped city lying in a lake coast basin, overflows into the seven hills that ring the outskirts. In the artificial harbor lies a welter of boats, along its southern bank fishing shacks and nets; the black smoke of a modern power plant blends with that of coal tugs in the harbor. Two great bluffs overshadow the city, the north one the site of a tall church, the south one the historic site of a bitter fight waged by Ozaukee County farmers against being drafted during the Civil War.

Groups of Yankee, Irish, Luxembourger, and German settlers, who had filled the county, favored the Democratic Party and were opposed to taking up the quarrel between the North and the South. To the Luxembourgers especially the Civil War seemed a nightmare, for many had migrated from Europe so that their sons might escape military service; now they were being asked to fight for a country to which they owed no hereditary allegiance. Every man taken away from the grim business of clearing the wooded farms meant a family left in hardship on half-cleared, only half-productive land. In 1862, therefore, when Governor Edward Salomon (1862-64) ordered all able-bodied citizens to enroll, a mob gathered on the streets of Port Washington. On the morning of November 10 a thousand people surged through the city to the courthouse, destroyed the rolls, and threw Draft Commissioner Pors down the steps. Then the mob ransacked the Pors house, damaged the chimney, windows and doors. Later the rioting men seized a small cannon, used ordinarily for Fourth of July celebrations, and loaded it with the single cannonball in Port Washington. When Government troops sailed into the harbor that night to round up the rebels, they found them defiantly gathered on South Bluff, armed with pitchforks, clubs, and their little cannon. The ship captain slipped a detachment of men around to the back of the bluff and captured 80 men, which broke all further resistance. The rambling old PORS HOUSE, 405 Wisconsin St., scene of the draft attack, stands on a hilltop just a little distance from the highway.

Men settled Port Washington in the hope that it would become a strategic shipping point, but the city's artificial harbor was so poor that it never became more than a refueling stop for Great Lakes steamers. The Federal Government has spent more than $5,000,000 for improvements, but whenever storms threaten, fishermen and shippers still rush their boats out into the lake to keep them from being dashed to pieces inside the concrete breakwaters.

Port Washington is intensely industrial for its size, manufacturing clothing, chairs, office equipment, bent woodwork, rubber goods, and machinery. Another important industry is commercial fishing, which yields great catches of whitefish, trout, chubs, herring, perch, carp, suckers, and burbots. At dawn, warmly dressed and prepared for hard work, long hours, and rough weather, the fishermen set out in steel tugs and power launches. The tugs head toward the gill nets floating in the deep water off the Sheboygan reefs. Each boat is equipped with power machinery to haul up the nets so that fishermen can take off the fish caught by their gills in the fine mesh. The launches chug along shore a few miles to the pound box nets staked to the bottom of the lake. Fish enter these traps through a small opening, toward which they are steered by a long leader net extending hundreds of feet from shore. Eight hundred pounds of fish is a fair catch for five such traps.

At the entrance to the power plant is the OLD PEBBLE HOUSE, built in 1848 by Edward Dodge and his wife with pebbles picked up along the lakeshore. Two other landmarks are the century-old BLAKE HOUSE, 511 Grand Ave., which has been in the continuous possession of the Blake family since it was built, and the BLONG HOUSE, 317 Pier St., built in 1835 by the city's founder, General Worcester Harrison. It was at the Blong House that Abraham Lincoln stayed for a short time after the death of Ann Rutledge. In 1850 Leland Stanford, founder of the Stanford University, lived for a short time at Port Washington where he attempted to establish a law practice.

The highway crosses Sauk Creek, 58 *m.,* whose waters roughly divide the business and residential sections of the city, and continues south into rich open country skirted by distant stretches of woods. The red OCTAGONAL BARN (R), 68 *m.,* is representative of an architectural style favored in this region, and for several miles such many-sided barns, topped with shuttered cupolas, rise frequently from the fields.

THIENSVILLE, 71.6 *m.* (666 alt., 500 pop.), little more than a store-tavern-filling-station interruption in the rural scene, was for many years the post office address of Victor L. Berger (1860-1929), Milwaukee Socialist, editor, and Congressman.

In 1901 Berger, a mild-mannered, genial Austrian, became editor of the weekly *Social Democratic Herald,* which had been brought to Milwaukee from Chicago. In 1911, after the Socialists had captured control of the city government, he helped to found and edit the Milwaukee *Leader,* which eventually absorbed the *Herald* and became the outstanding Socialist daily newspaper in the United States (*see Newspapers and Radio*). Berger became the first Socialist member of Congress when elected to the House of Representatives in 1910. During the World War Berger was tried before Judge Kenesaw Mountain Landis in Chicago on a charge of having violated the espionage act with his anti-war publications and was sentenced to 20 years imprisonment. Freed on bail while his case was being appealed, Berger was again elected to Congress by his loyal Wisconsin constituents, but the House of Representatives repeatedly refused to seat "this convict." Completely exonerated in 1921 when the Supreme Court reversed Judge Landis' decision, Berger was returned to Congress in 1922, and served two more terms. He was chairman of the national executive committee of the Socialist Party from 1927 until his death in 1929.

At 73.6 *m.* US 141 swings left toward the lake and follows the crest of its wooded bluffs into Milwaukee. The countryside changes suddenly from farmlands dotted with houses and fat barns to a suburban district of lake-view mansions, built by well-to-do Milwaukeeans. A realtor's dream, this attractive suburb gives no hint of the industrial city beyond.

FOX POINT, 76.2 *m.* (689 alt., 474 pop.), is a long, wooded village set among gardens and trees along the lake; many a "Private Road" sign lists in gilt letters the names of those who live behind the fences and hedges that shield their houses from the road.

WHITEFISH BAY, 82 *m.* (656 alt., 5,362 pop.) (*see Milwaukee*), is an even more exclusive suburb.

SHOREWOOD, 82.8 *m.* (592 alt., 13,479 pop.) (*see Milwaukee*), is at the junction with St. 190 (*see Tour 21*). Left is SHOREWOOD PARK, green spaces looking north across the wide lake, blue to a far fringe of land; below is a public beach and stone piers. US 141 turns right on State St. away from the lake; at State and Milwaukee Sts. is the junction with St. 32 (*see Tour 3A*).

MILWAUKEE, 87 *m.* (592 alt., 578,249 pop.) (*see Milwaukee*).

Milwaukee is at the junction with US 41 (*see Tour 2*) and US 18 (*see Tour 23*).

Tour 3A

Milwaukee—Racine—Kenosha—Illinois Line; 43.9 *m.* State 32.

Chicago & North Western Ry., Chicago & North Shore Line, and Milwaukee
Electric Ry. and Transit Co. parallel route.
Cement-paved roadbed.
City accommodations.

Following the Green Bay-Chicago military road of the 1830's,
State 42, a continuation of the lakeshore route of US 141, directly
connects the chief industrial section of Wisconsin with Chicago, Illinois.

MILWAUKEE, 0 *m.* (592 alt., 578,249 pop.) (*see Milwaukee*).

Milwaukee is at the junction with US 41 (*see Tour 2*), US 141
(*see Tour 3*), and US 18 (*see Tour 23*).

From the junction with US 141 at E. State and Milwaukee Sts.,
State 32 runs south on Milwaukee Ave., following a twisting course
through an older factory and warehouse district. At 4.6 *m.* is (L) the
SOUTH SHORE PARK with its bathing beach. ST. MARY'S ACADEMY
(R), 5.5 *m.*, was founded in 1904 by The Sisters of St. Francis of
Assisi. The present buildings, which include the original structure,
with a new wing added in 1921, and a large building erected in 1930,
stand on a site overlooking Lake Michigan. St. Mary's is both a day
and boarding school; the high school enrollment is about 500, the grade
department 60. Immediately adjoining is ST. FRANCIS SEMINARY, built
in 1856 on a wooded, 100-acre tract overlooking Lake Michigan. This
seminary serves as a training school for priests; its former rector, the
Rev. Francis J. Haas, has gained national recognition as a mediator in
recent labor disputes. Next to the seminary are the ruins of the ST.
AEMILIANUS ORPHAN ASYLUM, destroyed by fire in 1930. St. Peter's
Church, the first Roman Catholic Church in Milwaukee (1839), has
recently been removed to the seminary grounds.

The Township of Lake, 5.6 *m.*, one of the richest in the United
States, contains the gigantic LAKESIDE POWER PLANT. According to
law, a certain proportion of the State taxes paid by this utility are
returned to the town, which since 1930 has paid all the State and county
taxes of its 9,000 inhabitants out of surplus funds, the only charges upon
the latter being taxes levied by school districts and assessments made by
the city of Milwaukee for sewage disposal.

State 32 winds southward a few rods from the lakeshore. From the
water level, the land rises in two broad terraces, marking the shore
line of former Glacial Lake Chicago, which once covered all of this
flat country (*see Natural Setting*).

CUDAHY, 7.4 *m.* (714 alt., 10,631 pop.), was founded by Patrick

Cudahy, who in 1893 moved his meat-packing plant from Milwaukee to a 700-acre tract that he had purchased here along the Lake Michigan shore. Cudahy became the promoter as well as the founder of the present city, and he named the first streets and avenues for prominent packers of the Middle West—Swift, Armour, Plankinton, and Layton. The city was incorporated in 1907 when it had a population of 2,700. Today (1940), besides the Cudahy plant, it has a dozen diversified industries, including a tannery, drop-forge plant, box factory, vinegar distillery, shoe factory, and the world's largest manufactory of machinery for washing, pasteurizing, and filling bottles. At least two persons of national fame have come from here. John Cudahy, a son of Patrick, was vice president of the packing plant in 1919; later he served as ambassador to Poland, minister to Eire, and minister to Belgium. And it was here in Pulaski Hall that Mary Michalski perfected the "shimmy" that in the early 1920's swept her to international stage and screen fame as Gilda Gray.

SHERIDAN PARK, 7.8 m. (L), dedicated in 1931, occupies one of the highest points on the western shore of Lake Michigan. GRANT PARK, 9.7 m. (*bathing and picnicking facilities; golf course, tourist camp*), consists of 360 acres on the bluffs overlooking Lake Michigan. In the north end of the park is a game refuge; within the park is a 40-acre county nursery that raises plants, trees, shrubs, and wild flowers for use in Milwaukee County parks and parkways.

SOUTH MILWAUKEE, 10.2 m. (674 alt., 10,706 pop.), once known as Oak Creek for the stream which here flows into Lake Michigan, is one of Milwaukee's largest industrial suburbs. The first permanent white settler here was Elihu Higgins, who came in 1835 and built a dam and sawmill on the river. He was followed later in the same year by John Fowle, who built a gristmill and a second sawmill. Rising waters washed out the dam in 1852, and the mills were abandoned.

Poor transportation facilities and the depression of 1837 retarded the city's growth, but in 1840 there were enough settlers here to organize the town of Oak Creek. Not until 1891, however, did industrial plants enter the city. Economically a part of Milwaukee, South Milwaukee has 17 industrial plants manufacturing steam shovels and dredges, malleable castings, shoes, phenol, gelatine, road tars, roofing and waterproofing pitches, creosotes, outdoor electrical equipment, glue, tile, and wood products.

CARROLLVILLE, 14.3 m., with a population of less than 600, employs more than 1,000 persons in its glue and chemical factories. The village, founded in 1899 by the United States Glue Company, is the only company town in Milwaukee County.

State 32 traverses the flat farmland of Racine County, tracing the route of an old Indian trail that became a military road. A century ago post riders and stagecoaches linked the lake settlements with Chicago. The Wisconsin Society of Chicago has erected markers along the route which serves as the sole memorials of the past.

RACINE, 26.1 *m.* (629 alt., 67,542 pop.) (*see Racine*).
Racine is at the junction with State 11 (*see Tour 24*).

Southward State 32 runs close to the Lake Michigan shore; here again the terracing caused by the receding waters of the ancient glacial lake appear (R) on the higher ground several miles distant. The Pike River, cutting through the soft soil at 34.6 *m.,* has formed a small ravine, the site of the ghost village of Pike River, settled in 1835. The village passed out of existence when its few settlers packed their belongings and moved to the larger lakeshore communities in 1842.

South of Pike River, State 32 continues down the valley between small bluffs and passes (R) a GROVE (*picnic tables and fireplaces*), 35.4 *m.* At 36.4 *m.* the highway, now a city street in Kenosha, is called Sheridan Road, a name it bears between this point and Chicago.

KENOSHA, 37.4 *m.* (612 alt., 50,262 pop.) (*see Kenosha*).

State 32 crosses the Illinois Line, 43.9 *m.,* 49 miles north of Chicago, Illinois.

Tour 4

Crandon—Shawano—Kaukauna—Fond du Lac; 159.1 *m.* State 55.

Dustless and concrete roadbed.
Adequate accommodations.

State 55 twists southward through an almost unpeopled country, the cutover wasteland of northern Wisconsin and the heavy forest of the Menominee Indian Reservation. Farther south there is a slow transition; gradually the wilderness recedes and farms and pastures appear. In its southern section State 55 traverses a rich land devoted to farming and grazing.

Section a. CRANDON to SHAWANO; 70.4 m., State 55

CRANDON, 0 *m.* (1,635 alt., 1,679 pop.) (*see Tour 16*), is at the junction with US 8 (*see Tour 16*). State 55 skirts the northern end of LAKE METONCA, then swings southward at 0.8 *m.* into a rough and stony country where high boulder-strewn uplands sink suddenly to swamps and ponds. In the low forest of popple, birch, and balsam along the roadside, wild animals occasionally are seen: a deer or rabbit moving swiftly through the brush, porcupines dozing in the forks of higher trees, more rarely a black bear nosing clumsily through the cutover. Farming on this land is spare and unproductive. In some fields stones are as thick as a crop of potatoes newly dug; the farm-steads themselves are low log huts with sloping lean-tos where pigs, chickens, and perhaps a cow are sheltered during the bitter winter.

State 55 crosses Swamp Creek and passes RICE LAKE (R), 7.7 *m.,* half hidden by the wild rice growing in still, shallow coves. Once the Menominee Indians came here regularly to harvest the grain. Seated in canoes, they pulled in the top of the stalks, beat the kernels loose with staves, then carried the grain ashore and winnowed it. For centuries wild rice was the principal food of the Menominee, whose tribal name means the people of the beneficent seed. Chippewa Indians living on MOLE LAKE, 8.3 *m.,* still come to Rice Lake to harvest in the same primitive way; but instead of using the rice themselves they sell it to dealers.

The irregular swamp and hill country continues as State 55 passes a cluster of lakes—ROLLING STONE LAKE (L), 10.8 *m.;* DEAD-MAN LAKE (L), 15.5 *m.;* and BIG TWIN and LITTLE TWIN LAKES (R) and (L), 19.2 *m.*. At 20.7 *m.* is a camp site (*free*) on the Wolf River, which the highway follows for 50 miles through the Menominee Indian Reservation (*see below*). For 60 years the Wolf River carried logs southward to Lake Winnebago and the sawmill towns of Oshkosh, Fond du Lac, and Neenah-Menasha. Along its lower reaches, where the stream ran deep and strong, logging was easy, inexpensive. But falls, rapids, and boulders upstream jammed the drives, sometimes stranding a winter's cut of logs far from the mills, until lumbermen formed improvement companies and built dams that stored enough water to float the logs over the rough spots.

LILY, 24.6 *m.,* only a few houses and a brick schoolhouse, lies near the Lily River, which once carried logs to the local sawmills. State 55 continues south through rough unproductive land to NINE MILE CREEK, 30.5 *m.,* and NINE MILE HILL (R), 32.4 *m.,* with a ladder-type fire tower surmounting it. A wire fence encloses a DEER PARK (*private*), 34 *m.,* in which deer live unmolested by hunters and predatory animals. Under such conditions deer breed fast, and every year scores are slaughtered and sold to provide a costly delicacy for restaurants.

LANGLADE, 36.2 *m.,* was named for Charles Michel de Langlade (1729-1800), fur trader, son of Augustin de Langlade, soldier and trader on the Great Lakes. As his mother was an Ottawa Indian, Charles de Langlade had great influence among the tribes of the North-west and used it to organize and lead them against the British during the French and Indian War. He helped to defeat Braddock in 1755, forced back Rogers' Rangers at Lake Champlain in 1757, and fought in the Quebec campaign of 1759. After the war he became a British subject and lived in patriarchal style at Green Bay, where he maintained a trading post. During the Revolutionary War, Langlade once more led Indian forces, but this time for the British and against the Colonies.

Southeast of Langlade, State 55 threads its way among jagged rocks and thick boulders, running close to the banks of the Wolf as it crosses a corner of the NICOLET NATIONAL FOREST, 40.4 *m.*

At 40.9 *m.* is the junction with County M.

Right on County M to the observation tower, cottages, and camp buildings of the GARDNER DAM CAMP, 0.7 *m.*, maintained by the Boy Scouts' Valley Council. An old and decrepit suspension bridge swings over the dam built years ago by lumbermen who released its waters every spring to float their logs down the Wolf River.

At 43.8 *m.* is the 231,000-acre MENOMINEE INDIAN RESERVATION (*picnic grounds; no overnight accommodations; taking of plants, picking of flowers, and fishing prohibited*). Here is a wild heavy forest. White pine, maple, birch, oak, and hemlock trees block out the sun; branches and dead leaves lie rotting in the gloom of the forest floor. Flowers rare to Wisconsin grow in the dampness: Indian pipe, false beech drops, delicate touch-me-nots, trillium, and trailing arbutus, first flower of spring. Through the reservation flows the Wolf River, now turbulent and rushing, now gliding smoothly beneath the shade of century-old trees.

In 1634 Jean Nicolet found the Menominee living on Green Bay at the mouth of the Menominee River. They had moved their settlements south and inland by 1836, in which year they ceded 4,000,000 acres along the Wolf River to the whites. In 1848 they relinquished all their territory north and west of the Fox and Wisconsin Rivers; but four years later, when a Government-supervised migration to new lands began, the tribe asked that a small portion of their former domain be returned. In 1854, with the aid of Father Florimond T. Bonduel, the Menominee obtained the land of their present reservation here in Shawano and Oconto Counties.

All land and timber in the reservation are owned in common by the tribe, which numbers 2,300 and is the wealthiest in Wisconsin. Lumbering is the main source of income, and the trees are carefully harvested on a sustained-yield basis. Profits from the sawmills are paid into a common fund held in the United States Treasury and used to pay school, hospital, and administrative expenses, old age pensions, workmen's compensation insurance, and small yearly allowances to tribal members. Most of the Indians work in the sawmill, and some 200 families cultivate subsistence farms ranging from 4 to 60 acres. Their dwellings are small one- or two-room huts, poorly painted, often squalid and unsanitary. Though most of the Indians have adopted the white man's clothes, cars, and religion, deep in the forest live some 100 pagans —solitary, shy, and a bit unfriendly. They are the older people who still follow the ways of their ancestors, hunting, fishing, and making maple sugar. Few work in mills.

Every spring the pagans hold their own ancient and secret Mitawin ceremony. At dusk on a prearranged evening the men come quietly through the forest to their private lodge, a framework of rough willow branches covered with skins and blankets. Each carries a medicine bag stuffed with "good medicine" charms—bird skins, bits of fur, animal teeth.   Inside the lodge burns a small ceremonial fire, and around it stand intent men beating the water drums that have been handed down in the tribe for generations.   In the semidarkness the medicine man intones the ceremonial chant telling the story of creation.   After the admission of new members, one for each who has died during the year, the tribal dance begins, with moccasined feet shuffling to the slow monotonous drum beats.   Through the cool spring night the ceremony continues; at dawn the Indians strip the lodge of its blankets and skins and silently leave.

Entering the reservation, State 55 winds southward through the thick forest.   In many stretches the only evidence of man's existence is the pale line of the highway, which here follows the route of the old military road that ran from Fort Howard, at Green Bay, to Fort Wilkins, at the tip of the Keweenaw peninsula.

At 44.2 *m.* (R) a sign marks the Scene of a Stagecoach Hold-up in 1894 by the notorious Raymond Holzse.   Holzse, the Dick Turpin of Wisconsin, used to practice marksmanship by riding at full speed around a tree, firing at a small target.   His career ended when he was sentenced to life imprisonment for emptying two guns into the passengers of a stagecoach he had halted.

The Shotgun Eddy of the Wolf River is visible at 45.5 *m.* The Gauthier Place, 46.4 m. (R), built about 1871, is one of several old taverns in this vicinity dating back to pioneer days.

At 51.5 *m.* is the junction with a forest road.

Right on this road to the junction with another forest road, 0.5 *m.;* L. here to BIG SMOKY FALLS (*adm. 10¢; approach to falls must be made on foot*). Here the Wolf River plunges over a three-foot ledge and down a narrow granite chute, generating the mist for which the falls are named.   According to Indian legend, a spirit dwells in a cave behind the falls, and it is the smoke from his pipe that mortals see.

At 2.2 *m.* on the forest road to the DALLES OF THE WOLF RIVER (*adm. 10¢; picnic tables*).   An eight-minute walk over bare granite with intricate and varicolored seams leads to the top of a cliff, from which the Wolf River is visible for miles as it pours through a deep gorge to spread out lazily on the flat plain below.

The Democratic Platform, 52.5 *m.,* is a broad flat slab of granite bearing a sign reading: "On this rock the early tote teamsters pledged anew their faith and drank to the success of their party."   The highway passes another old tavern, the Beaupre Place, 54.5 *m.*

At 54.8 *m.* is the junction with a narrow forest footpath (*parking for car, 15¢*).

The pathway leads through thick pines to the banks of the Wolf River. Here in a quiet spot, densely forested to the water's edge, is sparkling WHITE RAPIDS FALLS.

At 56.3 *m.* is the junction with a forest road.

Right on this road to BIG EDDY FALLS, 2 *m.* (*adm. 25¢ per car*).   Here the Wolf River glides over a red granite bed between walls of heavy pine.

A Menominee legend declares that spirit·children play on the forest greens near the falls and that by listening very closely one may hear their laughter on moonlit nights.

The highway has been widened at 59.9 *m.* to include historic SPIRIT ROCK, a crumbling granite boulder within an enclosure of white posts. "To this rock the Menominee Tribe brought their gifts to the Great Spirit," reads the marker. "It was then believed that the crumbling of the rock foretold the passing of the race and that upon its complete disintegration the race would be extinct." According to legend, the rock is the body of an Indian whose meritorious deeds attracted the attention of the Manitou. When the god told him he could have anything he wanted, the Indian asked for everlasting life. The Manitou, angry that a mortal should ask so great a boon, seized him by the shoulders, thrust him into the ground, and saying, "You shall have your wish!" turned him to stone.

In an INDIAN ROUNDHOUSE (R), 61.8 *m.,* a structure of poles and bark, Christian Indians hold commercialized ceremonial festivities for tourists (*fee varies*). About Labor Day every year an all-Indian cast presents *Otcikona,* an Indian play based on the Menominee story of the North Star Woman. The play graphically pictures the mode of living, dress, occupation, and customs of the Indian, and presents authentic ceremonials. (*Small fee for programs explaining the play and ceremonials; free parking.*) Most of the Menominee are Roman Catholic, and every year hundreds of visitors come to the reservation to participate in or watch the Indian observance of Corpus Christi, on the first Thursday after Trinity Sunday.

At 62.2 m. is the junction with State 47 (*see Tour 4A*). KESHENA (Ind., flying swiftly), 62.8 *m.,* is one of two villages on the reservation. Here are the Indian agency buildings, a tribe-owned school and hospital, and a Roman Catholic mission and girls' school.

At 63 *m.* is the junction with a dirt road.

Right on this road to the junction with a dirt road, 0.1 *m.;* R. here to a fork in the road, 0.5 *m.;* R. here across the Wolf River. The road, little more than two grass-grown ruts, leads upward to a ridge. At 0.7 *m.* (R) an immense white pine stands on the brink of the hill a few feet from the road (*park car here*). Ahead, perhaps 50 yards distant, is the OSHKOSH CLAN BURIAL PLOT, a 60-foot square tract enclosed by a barbed wire fence.

Most of the graves are covered with the customary Indian gravehouses. Members of the Oshkosh Clan who resisted conversion to Christianity are buried here, among them Wau-pau-o-ma-tam-oe, wife of Neopit Oshkosh. Above the inscription on her gravestone is an engraved representation of a tepee village with a woman grinding corn in front of a fire, over which hangs a kettle. On top of the stone has been carved a mythical animal with the head of an otter, the body of a rabbit, the legs of a dog or wolf, and the tail of a fox. Another stone marks the grave of Kin-eah-kiew We-so (Ind., daughter of a chief). The We-so stone has a deer carved on it. Three other graves are marked by smaller, simpler stones, one of which bears the inscription "Neopit Oshkosh."

At 69.6 *m.* is the junction with County H.

Left on County H to oak-shaded SHAWANO COUNTY PARK, 5.7 *m.* (*overnight camping charge*), near SHAWANO LAKE (*bathing beach; amusement equipment for children; camping and picnicking facilities*). On the grounds is a small zoo of animals native to Wisconsin.

SHAWANO, 70.4 *m.* (824 alt., 4,188 pop.) (*see Tour 17*), is at the junction with State 29 (*see Tour 17*).

Section b. SHAWANO to FOND DU LAC; 88.7 m., State 55

Between SHAWANO, 0 *m.,* and BONDUEL, 9 *m.* (884 alt., 534 pop.) (*see Tour 17*), State 55 and State 29 (*see Tour 17*) are one route (*see Tour 17*).

South of Bonduel, State 55 passes WHITE LAKE, 13.5 *m.,* set in a hollow stumpy pasture land. Gradually the northern cutover disappears as the highway approaches the Fox River Valley through land which, though long settled, has not yet been completely subjugated. The fields are choked with old pine stumps, burned, blasted, and splintered; gray rail fences surround pastures in which a few cattle graze; abandoned tar-paper shacks sag in clearings half obliterated by encroaching overgrowth. Tumbled hills cut the land as State 55 swings westward toward the lowlands of eastern Outagamie County. The twisted landscape levels out; although chiefly devoted to dairying and feed crops, the plain is brightened by a few small apple orchards.

SEYMOUR, 30.8 *m.* (791 alt., 1,201 pop.), a city sprawling over the flat countryside, has a cheesebox factory, two flour mills, and a canning factory. In the northern part of town are the fairgrounds of the Seymour Fair and Driving Park Association, incorporated to advance county agriculture and stock breeding.

South of Seymour fields are better cultivated. In uncleared areas a few dark pines and spruce rise above slender birch and popple; sumac and berry bushes cling to roadside ditches. Gradually the stones, stumps, spruce swamps, and the rank ragged vegetation of the transitional area disappear.

At 48.7 *m.* is the junction with US 41 (*see Tour 2*), on the outskirts of KAUKAUNA (709 alt., 6,581 pop.) (*see Tour 2*). State 55 crosses a long bridge, 49.4 *m.,* that spans a canal with its gaping locks (R) and the Fox River. Upstream is a high concrete dam; below and left the river trickles thinly over the graveled river bed. Under the south end of the bridge is the concrete-walled flow that carries the water away from the giant turbines of a paper plant.

At 54.4 *m.* is the junction with US 10 (*see Tour 18*). No sign of the cutover remains here. Fields of wheat, hay, and barley blend with the clean brightness of pasture land; scattered clumps of trees darken fence lines, grow thick along lowland creeks, cap the low distant hills that ring the plain. Ahead, a bulky ridge walls the horizon, at first a wavering blue line that grows slowly more distinct—the escarpment of the great Niagara Cuesta, a ridge of tilted limestone.

At SHERWOOD, 57.7 *m.* (834 alt., 375 pop.), the cuesta emerges from the plain and sweeps upward in a long slope, stretching southward for 75 miles to the tumbled kettle moraines below Fond du Lac. State 55 ascends to the escarpment's crest, then curves southward along the back slope, with the view (L) across lovely fields and meadows to farmsteads far below.

At 60 *m.* a gaudy sign marks the junction with a side road.

Right on this road to HIGHCLIFF PARK, 1.3 *m.* (*privately owned; adm. free except on special occasions; picnic and sanitary facilities, refreshment stands; amusement devices and playground; no bathing*). At 1.4 *m.* the road ends on the brink of the escarpment. Here the limestone cliffs have a straight 50-foot drop, below which a steep heavily-wooded talus slope descends for another 75 feet. During the past 55 years portions of the cliff have split off from the main escarpment and now stand as flat-topped battlements connected with the "mainland" by little bridges. At the foot of the cliff, between the split-off sections and the main rock, are densely shaded footpaths.

Almost all of LAKE WINNEBAGO is visible, lying blue and ruffled in its shallow basin. Almost directly opposite, a projecting point of land hides the twin cities of Neenah-Menasha; near the center of the western shore, plumes of smoke mark Oshkosh, and 25 miles away at the southern lake tip, Fond du Lac.

A path leads along the crest of the cliff. At one place a wooden Indian looks out over the scene, shading his eyes with one hand. Though a sign at his feet reads "Don't Harm the Chief. He Was a Good Indian," his left arm is missing. Back from the cliff is the shady park, with playground and an old merry-go-round, powered by a battered steam engine. On Sundays, when dance music plays and the merry-go-round goes round, hundreds come here to dance and relax.

State 55 continues south along the back slope of the cuesta through long stretches of thick woods and underbrush. Here and there the underlying limestone appears in small winding terraces, split and seamed so regularly that the work might have been done by stone masons. Veering to the crest of the escarpment, the highway then descends its western side.

STOCKBRIDGE, 65.3 *m.* (828 alt., 377 pop.), trim farmers' village, was once the home of the Stockbridge Indians, who, with the Brothertown tribe, had moved from New England to New York during and after the Revolutionary War. Between 1822 and 1833 these Indians and those of the Oneida and Munsee tribes, aided by land speculators and missionaries, migrated from New York to this section of Wisconsin (*see Indians*). The Oneida, under the leadership of Eleazer Williams (*see Tour 2*), settled near Green Bay, the Brothertown (*see Tour 6*) in the region east of Lake Winnebago.

The Stockbridge, peaceful and well educated, cultivated small farms. Bishop Jackson Kemper visited them in 1838 and wrote of one family in whose home he spent the night: "The young woman of the house is modest, intelligent and talks well. She has books, ink, a workstand &c. We had good beds and a good supper which closed with a fine slice of pompcin pie."

In 1843 the Stockbridge sold half of their land here to the Federal

Government and agreed to move to a new reservation across the Mississippi. On the unsold half the village of Stockbridge was platted, and here the Government unsuccessfully attempted to settle those Indians who desired to become United States citizens. When dissension arose, the tribe was reunited and tribal government restored. In 1856 the Stockbridge, after negotiating a final treaty with the Federal Government, relinquished all rights to their land here in return for a cash settlement and a new reservation adjoining the Menominee Indian Reservation (*see above*), where their descendants still live (*see Tour 17*).

South of Stockbridge, State 55 runs along the escarpment face. Below, the broad countryside is squared into fields, dotted with big barns and houses, intersected by thin files of trees. From the higher points almost all of Lake Winnebago is visible on clear days.

At 70.4 *m.* is the junction with US 151 (*see Tour 6*); between this junction and Fond du Lac State 55 and US 151 are one route (*see Tour 6*).

FOND DU LAC, 88.7 *m.* (759 alt., 26,449 pop.) (*see Tour 5*), is at the junction with US 41 (*see Tour 2*), US 45 (*see Tour 5*), State 23 (*see Tour 5A*), and US 151 (*see Tour 6*).

Tour 4A

Keshena—Neopit—Junction with US 45; 30.3 *m.* State 47.

Hard-surfaced roadbed.

State 47 travels a narrow path westward through the wooded wilderness of the Menominee Indian Reservation. More than 2,300 Indians live and work in the forest but are seen only occasionally following trails among the trees or driving truckloads of logs to their sawmill at Neopit.

KESHENA (Ind., swift-flying), 0 *m.* (*see Tour 4*), is at the junction with State 55 (*see Tour 4*). State 47 crosses the Wolf River, 0.3 *m.*, just below Keshena Falls, where Chief Reginald Oshkosh operated a trading post for both Indians and whites. At 1.7 *m.* is the frame of a ceremonial lodge, which is covered with skins and blankets when used for traditional Menominee dances.

At 8.4 *m.* is the junction with a dirt road (*impassable for cars when wet*).

Right on this rough and tortuous road to PEAVEY FALLS (*adm. 25¢ per car*), 0.6 *m.*, on the West Branch of the Wolf River, which spills over a red granite ledge and roars downstream through a narrow chute of solid rock. Churned to a creamy foam in their fall, the waters resume their coffee-brown color in a swirling pool below. At the head of the falls an improvised footbridge crosses the river to trails through the forest.

State 47 continues through the dense forest to the PECORE TRADING POST (*picnic tables, tennis courts, cabins*), 9.5 *m.,* where moccasins, blankets, beadwork, and souvenirs are sold by the Indian manager.

Right from the Pecore Trading Post on a forest trail along the west branch of the Wolf River to RAINBOW FALLS (*adm. 25¢ per car*), 0.7 *m.,* a series of falls that drop into a granite-walled gorge.

The forest thins out as the highway enters NEOPIT, 11.4 *m.* (1,077 alt., 300 pop.), a village of one- and two-room houses, their sagging porches unscreened, their unpainted siding curled and split. Here live the Menominee with their many children and dogs. The Indians have forsaken their traditional dress for overalls, gaudy shirts, and caps; their children play with toys of the white man's invention. A giant tepee serves as a tourist refreshment stand.

On the Wolf River, dammed within the village limits, slender booms confine thousands of logs destined to feed the SAWMILL on the riverbank (R). The first sawmill on the reservation was built in 1909, a year after its authorization by Congress. At first the trees were cut under the "designating" system devised and supervised by the Forest Service of the Department of Agriculture; since 1926, however, selective cutting has been practiced exclusively by the Indian Service here. Thus the Menominee are assured of a constant supply of timber for lumbering. In 1924 the old mill burned and was replaced by this modern sawmill, one of the best equipped in Wisconsin. Since 1936 the annual payroll has averaged about $400,000, 60 per cent of which goes to Indian workers in the mill and forest. Lumbering profits and stumpage payments are credited to the tribal account at Washington (*see Tour 4*).

Brought in on trucks, logs are kept in the booms until dragged into the "hot pond," water warmed by exhaust steam from the mill's engines. Here they are steered with pike poles to a conveyor which carries them to the second floor of the mill. A cradle-shaped "winch" releases the logs one at a time; two spiked arms called the "nigger" hoist them upon the carriage and roll them into the grip of the sharp-toothed, rachet-operated iron jaws known as "dogs." Controlled by a sawyer in an enclosed booth, the carriage is driven against the ribbon-like band saw. Two men ride the carriage, one to shift the log on the "dogs," the other to adjust the width of the cut. Sawyer and riders communicate by signs, for the loudest shouts are inaudible above the screech of the band saw. The carriage moves inexorably forward toward the blade and springs swiftly back; cut sections tumble down a ramp while sawdust streams from the blade.

Beyond the band saw, planks are given a preliminary sorting as they run over a roller conveyor. Slabs and bark edgings are taken off, some to be used as fuel, others to be made into lath, box lumber, or other byproducts. The larger pieces, roughly cut from the log, are resawed by circular ripsaws or another band saw. Then the boards go sidewise down a ramp under a set of crosscut saws controlled by another sawyer, one of the most highly skilled men in the mill, who sits in a booth above and scans each board. With a set of levers he brings his whirling saws down on the planks and cuts out knots, rotten spots, and other defective sections.

The planks are then run through a planing mill and given a smooth surface, after which they emerge from the mill on a long roofed platform. Here a grader marks each plank with a heavy pencil according to kind of wood, length, dimension, quality, and use. Other men with heavy gloves and leather aprons take the boards of each type as they arrive and load them into wagons or small cars for stacking and seasoning in the yards. The mill uses all waste, even burning sawdust by mixing it with coal.

At the PUBLIC SCHOOL (L) standard State courses are taught through the tenth grade. A recent Federal census shows that illiteracy is low among the Menominee; all but six of 548 children attend school. Beyond the school are several long decks of logs held as a reserve for emergencies.

State 47 continues westward through the half gloom of the forest. Off from the main road in this district live the pagan (non-Christianized) Indians. Standing by the houses are wigwams, used in all but the cold winter months. These full-blooded Menominee speak little or no English; the women like bright colors and spend much of their time weaving and doing beadwork. Some of the younger men work in mills, but the older pagans live by hunting, fishing, and gathering wild ferns to sell to florists.

Wild game supplies a large part of the Menominee diet, for the Indians are allowed at all seasons to hunt and fish on the reservation, but are forbidden to sell game or fish to tourists. Trials for all minor offenses are held before two Indian judges appointed by the superintendent for their fairness and ability; criminal cases are handled by the U. S. District Attorney.

Virgin hardwood trees flank the highway to the western boundary of the reservation, 21.6 m., beyond which State 47 passes the well-kept farmsteads and neat fields of white farmers.

At 30.3 m. is the junction with US 45 (see Tour 5).

Tour 5

(Watersmeet, Mich.)—Antigo—Wittenberg—Oshkosh—Fond du Lac
—(Chicago, Ill.) ; US 45.

Michigan Line to Illinois Line, 312.7 *m.*

Chicago & North Western Ry. parallels route between Michigan Line and
Milwaukee.
Oiled-graveled and hard-surfaced roadbed.
Resort accommodations north of Antigo; village and city accommodations be-
tween Antigo and Illinois Line.

US 45 plunges southward for some 80 miles through the concentrated lakes area of northern Wisconsin. Slashed cutover, old lumber
towns, worthless farming land, and thriving resorts reflect the historical
development of this region—from the short-lived prosperity of lumbering through poverty to the present day when the region is reviving as
a recreational area. South of Antigo the highway passes through a
transitional area of none-too-prosperous farms into the richer fields of
the Fox River Valley and Lake Michigan farmland.

Section a. MICHIGAN LINE to WITTENBERG; 106.6 m.,
US 45

As it crosses the Michigan Line, 0 *m.,* 9 miles south of Watersmeet,
Michigan, US 45 is on the "top o' the world," the local name for two
divides 1,700 feet above sea level. Here water is shed in three directions: southwest to the Mississippi, eastward to Lake Michigan, and
northward to Lake Superior.
At 0.1 *m.* is the junction with County B.

Right on County B to LAND O' LAKES, 0.5 *m.* (1,708 alt., 275 pop.), a
center of tourist traffic bound for the interconnected Cisco Lakes that loop
in a 140-mile chain along the State Line. Old portage paths used by Indians,
traders, and explorers were made public thoroughfares by the Northwest
Ordinance of 1787.

Southward in the cutover US 45 crosses a tiny forest stream, 1.4 *m.,*
the headwater of the Wisconsin River that flows almost the entire
length of the State in its gradually widening course to the Mississippi.
At 2.4 *m.* is the junction with County E.

Left on County E to LAC VIEUX DESERT, 3 *m.,* source of the Wisconsin
River. Though the literal translation of its name is "old deserted lake," Captain T. J. Cram, surveyor of the Wisconsin-Michigan boundary, said: "On

South Island there is an old [Indian] potato-planting ground; hence the appellation of 'Vieux Desert,' which, in mongrel French, means 'old planting-ground.' "   In early days scouts and trappers ascended the Ontonagon River from Lake Superior, portaged to this lake, then followed the Wisconsin to the Mississippi.   Ten square miles in extent, Lac Vieux Desert lies in an almost undisturbed forest, visited chiefly by fishermen, for it offers some of the State's best fishing for muskellunge, largest and most ferocious of fresh-water fishes.

To catch a muskie requires heavy tackle—a 5-foot, 9-ounce rod, a 20-pound test line, wire leaders, and large, sound plugs; more than one muskie has straightened the hooks of a four-inch plug with the violence of his plunges. Though muskellunge habitually feed at night, they may be angered into striking in daytime, launching an attack from any angle with a smashing impact that strains a fisherman's wrists, and continuing to fight with a strength and cunning unmatched in Wisconsin waters.   The battle may last an hour or more.   Running up to 50 or more pounds in weight, muskie is most easily distinguished from large northern pike by the scaling of its gill covers.   By present (1940) legal standards, no fish of less than 30-inch length may be caught.

County E continues through a dense stand of large birch to PHELPS, 8.7 m. (1,681 alt., 510 pop.) (see Tour 15), at the junction with State 70 (see Tour 15).

Rising and falling through ragged cutover and across low-lying marshes, US 45 passes small LAKE PLEASANT, 4.4 m. (private; fishing prohibited), to CONOVER, 8.3 m. (1,685 alt., 139 pop.), tourist trade center founded as a lumber camp in the late 1870's by Seth Conover.   Sometimes old logging roads, hardpacked by the hoofs of oxen, twist back into the tangled brush; occasionally deer stand motionless, in summer watching passing cars, in winter watching men with rifles creep toward them.

At 15 m. is the junction with State 17 (see Tour 15); between this junction and EAGLE RIVER, 19 m. (1,636 alt., 1,389 pop.), US 45 and State 17 are one route.   Surrounding and southward is a water-strewn wilderness: CATFISH LAKE, 21.5 m., is one of the Eagle Lakes chain; THREE LAKES, 29.3 m. (1,658 alt., 590 pop.), was named by disgruntled surveyors who started off in three different directions one day and each time found their survey blocked by a lake. Though a summer pleasure land for vacationists, this is a grudging land for farmers who must toil long months with double-bitted ax, grub hoe, and dynamite to win a few submarginal acres.   Often the only evidence of such labor is an abandoned shack with sashless windows gaping at the young trees creeping back to reclaim the clearings.

MONICO, 48.3 m. (1,597 alt., 180 pop.), a cluster of white frame houses about a red water tank, was founded on lumber and is still partly supported by a small portable sawmill cutting logs trucked in by farmers or brought in by the railroad.   The village is at the junction with US 8 (see Tour 16).

PELICAN LAKE, 53.7 m. (1,605 alt., 210 pop.), was built on the shore of the lake of the same name in 1882 when the Milwaukee Lakeshore & Western R. R. came through.   Lumberjacks who settled this region were of so many nationalities that their descendants call themselves the "League of Nations."   The most recent settlers are scattered groups of Kentuckians, who came about 1900 and made Crandon their headquarters (*see Tour 16*).

ELCHO, 59.3 *m*. (1,635 alt., 450 pop.), owes much of its present appearance to Charles W. Fish, former sailor, gold prospector, and structural iron worker, who came here in 1903 as a $35-a-month mill hand. Having saved $50, he bought near-by timberland, resold it to his employer for $3,300, and bought a share in the latter's mill. Left penniless when it burned, Fish worked for a year and a half in Michigan, returned to Elcho and built his own mill. By 1922 he had large plants at Birnamwood, Crandon, and Antigo as well. Once again fire destroyed the local mill and the business section. Fish then built the formal, Tudor-style building that extends the length of one block and houses the general store, bank, barbershop, and physicians' offices. When lumbering declined Fish retired. In 1935 fire destroyed Elcho's only other industrial plant; today, with one-sixth of its population on relief, the village is attempting to attract vacation trade.

The village of SUMMIT LAKE, 63.5 *m*. (1,723 alt., 64 pop.), straggles down a hillside from the shore of a lake of the same name, the highest in Wisconsin. Southward the soil gradually improves as US 45 enters the northern dairy belt, a strip of good farming country between the central sand plains and the northern cutover. Cattle graze in stumpy pastures; forest growth thins out into chunky woodlots; in some places drainage is so poor that standing water keeps farmers out of the fields in spring.

ANTIGO (Ind., the balsam evergreen river), 81.8 *m*. (1,496 alt., 8,610 pop.), was founded after the Civil War by Francis Augustine Deleglise, a Swiss. The city's early sawmills have been replaced by woodworking plants that make heel planks, shoe lasts, and plugs to fill spike holes in railroad ties. The Kraft-Phoenix processed-cheese factory here is one of the largest of its kind. A cooperative creamery founded in 1930 has 900 members and has a capacity to handle 200,000 pounds of milk daily; there is also a cooperative grocery that did a $177,000 business in 1937, as well as a cooperative hatchery, a 20-year-old cooperative feed warehouse, and a State-supervised cooperative maple syrup evaporating plant. The city is also a center for potato growers, who ship some 2,500 carloads annually.

The city's oldest building is the DELEGLISE HOUSE, built in 1877; it stands on the lawn of the ANTIGO PUBLIC LIBRARY. The library houses an HISTORICAL MUSEUM (*open to public; 1 p.m. to 5:30 p.m. daily except Sun.*), sponsored by the Langlade County Historical Society. Here are displayed pioneer documents, Indian relics, weapons, old lumbering tools, and a clock built in 1772 in Holland.

The highway skirts the Antigo Flats, a small sandy plain that produces more potatoes than any equal area in the State.

At 87.5 *m*. is the junction with State 47 (*see Tour 4A*).

At 91 *m*. is the junction with State 52.

Right on State 52 to the DELLS OF THE EAU CLAIRE RIVER, 4.7 *m*., a county park (*camping and picnicking facilities; shelter house*). Upstream the river flows smoothly over granite boulders, then suddenly, shortly beyond the bridge, it runs riot over fingerlike masses of igneous rock worn smooth as weathered wood and tumbles down a rocky gorge in a dozen cascades. Trails overlook the rapids and lead to the water's edge.

South of BIRNAMWOOD, 97.6 *m.* (1,286 alt., 557 pop.), US 45 is well within the northern dairy belt in which cement silos and freshly painted barns indicate the relative newness of the farms. The red brick HOMME ORPHAN HOME, 105.6 *m.,* established 50 years ago by the Reverend E. J. Homme, is now conducted by the Lutheran Church of Wittenberg.

WITTENBERG, 106.6 *m.* (1,168 alt., 863 pop.), named for the German university town where Martin Luther began the Reformation, was founded during the religious revival of the late nineteenth century by Norwegian Lutherans under the Reverend E. J. Homme. Homme first built the orphanage north of the village, then a high school subsequently destroyed by fire, finally a new and larger orphanage with a supporting farm. Spurred to emulation, German Lutherans in the village founded another orphanage, now used as the NORWEGIAN HOME FOR THE AGED. The BETHANY INDIAN MISSION BOARDING SCHOOL here closed its doors in 1933 when funds ran low, and the Indian children now attend public school. A few Indians, chiefly Winnebago, live in shacks near the town, making a meager living by weaving baskets or doing odd jobs in the forest.

Wittenberg is at the junction with State 29 (*see Tour 17*).

Section b. WITTENBERG to FOND DU LAC; 102.5 m., US 45

Between WITTENBERG, 0 *m.,* and a point at 2.2 *m.,* US 45 and State 29 (*see Tour 17*) are one route. TIGERTON, 9.6 *m.* (1,024 alt., 831 pop.), at the confluence of Tiger Creek and the Embarrass River, is a company-owned town. East and west stand the houses of Oneida Indians who work in the smokestacked mill, one of the few large sawmills still operating in Wisconsin. About it are yards piled high with rough-sawed lumber. Maplewood from this region is prized for furniture making, and some 5,000,000 board feet are trucked to Chicago and Milwaukee annually. The village has a cooperative creamery, for most of the German and Scandinavian farmers in this vicinity "live on their milk checks."

At 14 *m.* is the junction with County M.

Left on County M to TIGERTON MUNICIPAL PARK, 0.6 *m.* (*picnic and camping facilities*), on the DELLS OF THE EMBARRASS RIVER, a charming stretch of water flanked by red granite walls.

MARION, 21.2 *m.* (857 alt., 992 pop.), founded in 1856 on the Pigeon River and named for the first child born here, is one of the early northern lumber villages. In the 1920's its last sawmill closed; today Marion has eight cheese factories, as well as plants producing maple syrup, excelsior, and cheeseboxes.

Right on County F from Marion to the GRAVE OF SAM WAUPACA, 2.4 *m.*, Potawatomi chief, who dropped dead near present Waupaca while mounting his pony after a long speech to persuade his braves not to massacre white settlers. Buried on the spot, his body was later removed here. Both Waupaca County and the city of Waupaca (*see Tour 18*) were named for the chief.

Farms improve, stretching back from the road for many miles, as US 45 reaches CLINTONVILLE, 29.5 m. (824 alt., 3,572 pop.), at the junction of Bear Creek and the Embarrass River. The city was founded in 1855 by Norman Clinton when his ox became sick, halting his journey to the north woods. In 1857 a sawmill was built and the settlement was named Pigeon, for wild pigeons are said to have been so abundant that they could be knocked down in flight with a long pole. When Clinton was made postmaster the following year, the registrar, having forgotten the name "Pigeon," mailed the commission simply to "Clinton of Clintonville," and the name was retained.

This city was the home of Chet Bennett, famous woodsman who explored and named many northern lakes. When surveyors came to stake the railroad route in 1878, they scorned his guidance because he dressed so shabbily. Only after months of fruitless work among the swamps and hills did they turn to him. "Just fold up your instruments and put your stakes in my footsteps," said Bennett, and today the railroad goes north along the route Chet Bennett paced.

Although its sawmills ceased operations long ago, Clintonville is the most highly industrialized city in this agricultural region. In 1900 William Besserdich extracted his one-cylinder Reo automobile from the mud by turning the front wheels by hand while the motor drove the rear wheels. He returned home to his small machine shop, which he owned with Otto Zachow, convinced of the desirability of a four-wheel drive automobile. Together they founded the FOUR WHEEL DRIVE COMPANY PLANT (*open by permission*), foot of E. 12th St., which manufactures FWD trucks, employing more than 1,200 men at peak production. It is the principal industrial support of the city.

In the flat dairy land south of Clintonville stands a TYPICAL CHEESE FACTORY, 35 m., one of 2,500 such factories in Wisconsin— long and low, with white-painted siding, gable roof, and large smoke-stack. Most State cheese factories are more or less alike, built accord-ing to standardized plans supplied by the University of Wisconsin Agricultural College. Milk, delivered in the morning by farmers, is spilled into a copper vat heated from below. Rennet, made from the inner membrane of a calf's stomach, is added to coagulate the milk. As the curds form, the cheesemaker tests the progress of the process by plunging his bare arms into the vat and feeling the curds with his fingers. Then with a curd breaker, sometimes called a "Swiss Harp" because of its closely spaced wires, the whole mass is scooped up on a tray. After the whey has been pressed out on a wooden table, the curd is placed in containers for curing. As temperature must be kept uniform and the cheese treated at all hours of the day, the cheesemaker usually lives in the factory.

NEW LONDON, 49.4 *m.* (767 alt., 4,661 pop.), straddling the Wolf River near its junction with the Embarrass, was settled by a half-breed trader named Johnson who in 1853 sold out his claims to Lucius Taft and Ira Millerd, the real founders of the city. Named for his home in Connecticut by Reeder Smith, builder of the plank road between Appleton and Stevens Point, New London became a lumber center and the terminus of steamboats plying the Wolf River from Oshkosh. Though logging drives on the Wolf ceased about 1900 and those on the Embarrass about 1910, a large mill still operates full time on logs shipped in from northern Wisconsin and Michigan, producing 15,000,000 feet of lumber a year.

The CARR MUSEUM (*open Wed. to Fri. 2 p.m. to 5:30 p.m.*), erected in 1934, was founded by Charles Carr, a local newspaperman and naturalist. In its natural history exhibit are some 10,000 specimens; it also contains thousands of historical documents, letters and clippings concerning New London and its environment, a department of archeology, and a library specializing in works on ornithology. Among other relics are an Indian dugout canoe and a sturgeon-hook. Once the Wolf teemed with sturgeon, which were taken by the thousands with three-pronged spears as they lay half-submerged in the gravel of the bottom, only to be stacked like cordwood on the riverbank. On the outskirts of the city is an OCTAGON HOUSE, built 60 years ago, one of the few remaining in the State.

The countryside grows steadily richer around HORTONVILLE, 56.7 *m.* (805 alt., 906 pop.), whose post office occupies a former lumberjack barracks. Farms are larger and better developed, with small apple orchards and double silos. In season, vegetables and fruits from neighboring fields are sold at roadside stands.

At 64.6 *m.* is the junction with US 10 (*see Tour 18*). At 76 *m.* is the junction with US 41 (*see Tour 2*). From this point US 45 and US 41 are one route into the city of Oshkosh, located at the point where upper Fox River flows into Lake Winnebago.

OSHKOSH, 82.8 *m.* (762 alt., 40,108 pop.) (*see Oshkosh*).

Between 82.8 *m.* and a point at 85.8 *m.* US 45 and US 41 (*see Tour 2*) are one route. The highway skirts LAKE WINNEBAGO along a strip of willow swamp lined with cottages, boathouses, and the shacks of "pot hunters," who live by doing a little fishing and a few odd jobs. The first white man known to have visited this vicinity was Father Claude Allouez, who read a mass for the Indians near the site of Oshkosh in 1670. Farmers coming down the Fox River Valley from Green Bay settled this region in the 1830's; for a time there was much water commerce between towns along its shore, carried on at first with Durham boats, vessels 50 feet long but drawing less than two feet of water, propelled like punts with poles. Then came steamers, the first of which was probably the *Manchester* (1848). Throughout this period the lake was so crowded with enormous lumber rafts that it once took the *Manchester* 11 days to make a 20-mile trip.

FOND DU LAC (Fr., end of the lake), 102.5 *m.* (759 alt., 26,449 pop.), became a French trading post when Laurent Ducharme arrived in 1785. In 1835 Judge James Duane Doty organized a company and bought land in the vicinity, for a time even considering this site for the State capital. The first permanent white settlers, Colwert and Edward Pier, came in 1836. A sawmill and gristmill were built in the 1840's, and population slowly increased until it reached 400 in 1847.

Yet young Fond du Lac was poverty-stricken. When the sheriff bought a pair of handcuffs in 1845, townspeople called a mass meeting to protest the extravagance; a young lawyer, too proud to acknowledge his poverty by wearing worn shoes, appeared in court barefoot. By the 1850's, however, logs began coming down the Wolf to Lake Winnebago, and within a few years the town had two sawmills, a lath mill, and two sash and door factories. In 1869, eleven sawmills in Fond du Lac cut 61,500,000 feet of lumber. Ten years later this production had dropped by half as the timber line receded and sawmills moved nearer the source of supply.

Fond du Lac retained its importance as a concentration point for all forms of traffic. In the early 1850's one of the earliest and most successful plank roads was built between Fond du Lac and Sheboygan; at the same time John B. Macy (*see below*) organized what is now the Chicago and North Western Ry. The first 20 miles of track were laid between Fond du Lac and East Waupun in 1853, but as there were no rail connections to any point, it was impossible to get a locomotive or cars to the line. The owners of the plank road, insisting that their charter obligated them to pass only "horse-drawn passenger vehicles," refused to permit the ponderous engine to be hauled over their roadbed. The railroad officials thereupon hitched 20 teams of horses and oxen to the locomotive, loaded a few "passengers" into the cab, and successfully demanded passage. In 1859 the railroad was completed to Chicago; but the celebration train, loaded with notables and careening along at 10 miles per hour, was wrecked when an ox got stuck between the ties on a trestle and derailed the train.

Other railroad lines and highways converging at the lake tip helped Fond du Lac survive the transition from lumbering days to modern industrialism. In 1936 over 60 industrial plants produced $20,000,000 worth of products; among the larger plants are a precision tool foundry and factories manufacturing leather, burial caskets, and refrigerators.

ST. PAUL'S CATHEDRAL and GRAFTON HALL, formerly a girls' school, just off Main St. on W. Division and N. Sophia Sts., are institutions of the Episcopal Church. The interior of the limestone cathedral is American Gothic, richly studded with wood-carvings from Oberammergau, stained glass windows from various European and American studios, and many memorial gifts. It contains the effigy-tomb of Bishop Charles Chapman Grafton (1830-1912), for 23 years Bishop at Fond du Lac, and the death masks of Bishops Jackson Kemper (1789-1870) (*see Tour 23A*), John Henry Hobart Brown (1831-88), who delivered the 50th anniversary sermon at Christ's Church in Green Bay, and Reginald Heber Weller (1857-1935), Bishop coadjutor at Fond du Lac and author of the Hale Memorial Service of 1909. LAKE-SIDE PARK, foot of N. Main St. on the shore of Lake Winnebago, has a small zoo, beach, and boat docks.

In Fond du Lac is the junction with US 41 (*see Tour 2*), State 55 (*see Tour 4*), State 23 (*see Tour 5A*), and US 151 (*see Tour 6*).

Section c.   FOND DU LAC to ILLINOIS LINE; 103.6 m., US 45

South of Western and Main Sts. in FOND DU LAC, 0 *m.*, US 45 passes through a section of weathered frame houses. The JOHN B. MACY HOUSE (*private*), 3.6 *m.*, stands square and cream-colored in a plot of weeds, a century-old building with a two-story hexagonal Tower joined to it by an enclosed passageway leading from the master's bedroom upstairs. Macy, promoter of the Chicago & North Western Ry., had the tower built as a library and refuge, and often sought quiet there. He died in 1856 when the steamer *Niagara* burned within sight of Port Washington. Wearing a money belt filled with gold, Macy jumped from the blazing deck to a crowded lifeboat, capsized it, and drowned himself and all its occupants.

EDEN, 8.1 *m.* (1,015 alt., 223 pop.), was settled by Britishers around 1845 and so named when the townsmen decided that it was only proper that one of their members, Adam Holiday, should live in Eden. When the first settlers came here, all of the land stretching southward along Lake Michigan belonged to the Potawatomi tribe, which ceded its holdings to the whites and moved peaceably westward.

KEWASKUM (Ind., his tracks are homeward), 24.8 *m.* (951 alt., 799 pop.), on the banks of the Milwaukee, has mansions ornate with the columns, dormers, and scrollwork of the 1880's. An aluminum company and a malting plant each employ about 75 men.

US 45 threads its way southward through the kettle moraine country. Clusters of birch screen paintless gray farm buildings; grapevines ramble along roadside fences. Erosion has become so serious in this shallow-soiled land that the State has tentatively planned to make a recreation forest of its mounded hills and deep pot holes (*see Tour 2*).

BARTON, 30.9 *m.* (905 alt., 811 pop.), virtually a suburb of West Bend, is inhabited almost entirely by people of German stock, most of whom are employed by the Barton Washing Machine Co., the Sand Brick Co., and the Northern Sand and Gravel Co., or in West Bend industries.

WEST BEND, 32.5 *m.* (896 alt., 4,760 pop.), largest city between Fond du Lac and Milwaukee, was founded in 1845, when Dr. E. B. Wolcott of Milwaukee, on a surveying trip, decided that the bend here in the Milwaukee River would make an excellent halfway stop between Fond du Lac and his home city. When the first farmers, from Ohio and New York, began to migrate farther west, Germans came to the city in such large numbers that today 90 per cent of the population consists of their descendants. At the corner of Beech and Main Sts. is a massive STONE BREWERY, one of the first buildings erected by these settlers. A busy industrial center, West Bend manufactures aluminum goods, evaporated milk, auto parts, farm machinery, stokers, canned goods, pocketbooks and other leather products.

South of West Bend and the kettle moraine area, US 45 winds deviously through rock-strewn pastures. Churches appear frequently on the hilly horizon; in DHEINSBURG, 38.5 m., a village of six houses, is one of the largest, the 75-year-old Evangelical CHRISTUS KIRCHE.

Signs in German script guide the traveler into GERMANTOWN, 48 m. (858 alt., 255 pop.), settled about 1850 by Germans from Milwaukee. German is still spoken in the village, and German foods are offered in its few restaurants: *Springerle, Dampfnudel, Marzipan, Senfgurken,* and *Lebkuchen.* Germantown has only two streets with names, Main and Grand; the latter is known locally as John's, because so many men answering to that name live on it.

At 55.7 m. is the junction with US 41 (*see Tour 2*); at 59.1 m. is the junction with St. 190 (*see Tour 21*). Left is the 165-acre JAMES CURRIE PARK (*golf course, skating, swimming*). At 62.6 m. is the junction with US 18 (*see Tour 23A*).

US 45 skirts Milwaukee, passing through LINCOLN MANOR, 64.2 m., a residential suburb built in a medley of styles, with bright tile roofs of red, blue, and green. HALES CORNERS, 67.6 m. (357 pop.), is widely known for the fairs held here the first Monday of each month, when this otherwise quiet village is suddenly transformed. Almost a century old, the monthly fairs began in the days when the plank road between Janesville and Milwaukee passed through the village and Hales Corners was a center for horse traders. Bands of gypsies brought in their ponies, farmers traveled many miles to trade, card sharks and gamblers operated freely. As the scope of the fair widened, farmers brought in pigs, cattle, and sheep; the fair became a monthly stock market.

Today almost everything is sold here. Early in the morning, the first Monday in the month, horse-drawn wagons crawl along the highway beside rumbling trucks and speeding cars on their way to the market. Soon the village is jammed with people, animals, and produce. A truckload of seed corn stands wedged between a roadster filled with dried tobacco leaves and a sedan laden with cabbages. A woman arrives in a small cart freighted with boxes of tender tomato plants. Old acquaintances exchange greetings loudly, shouting above bleating lambs, squealing hogs, and barking dogs.

At 67.6 m. is the junction with an improved dirt road.

Left on this road to GREENDALE, 3.3 m., one of three such communities built by the Resettlement Administration as an experiment in city planning and low-rental housing. Greendale offers the advantages of urban residence to low-income families with members employed in Milwaukee. The community is laid out in the form of a crescent, with single-family houses arranged around a nucleus of small stores, offices, a theater, playgrounds, and other public facilities. The houses, built of colored concrete, are equipped with electric stoves and refrigerators, hot-air coal furnaces, and modern plumbing.

Surrounding this 240-acre area is a girdle of open land that has been purchased by the Resettlement Administration to protect the community from the encroachment of undesirable industrial establishments and to prevent overcrowded housing. Part of this "green-belt" has been reserved for future building; some of it is used for recreational purposes, and other sections are leased to farmers who sell fresh foods to the Greendale grocers.

Rents go to the non-profit town corporation, which uses the money for State and county taxes, street and home maintenance, and the support of the police and fire departments, the public school, the waterworks, and the sewage system.

Left at 68 *m.* is 613-acre WHITNALL PARK, with rustic bridges, foot trails, and a spring-fed creek. The National Park Service has built an artificial lake and a large amphitheater here.

Proceeding through lowland country, ideal for truck farming, US 45 passes DURHAM, 76 *m.,* a tiny crossroads settlement named for the Durham cattle brought from England by the first farmers, and NORTH CAPE, 82.1 *m.,* named for the town in Norway from which its founders came. The latter is a market center for oats, barley, milk, and cabbages, and has a tile plant burning 250,000 feet of tile a year in two mound-shaped kilns. Used principally for draining marshlands, the tiles are molded by machinery, then air cured, and finally fired in kilns, the temperatures of which ultimately reach a maximum of 1,800 degrees.

UNION GROVE, 89.9 *m.* (780 alt., 755 pop.), has one of the largest tile factories in Wisconsin, a large sauerkraut factory, and, a short distance northeast, the huge POOLE DIXON DUCK FARM, where 55,000 White Pekin ducks are hatched yearly in a great battery of incubators, fed for 10 weeks in eight brooder houses, then killed for market. In the CONGREGATIONAL CHURCH, built in 1851 and rebuilt in 1878, is the AMMON P. ADAMS PLAQUE, honoring one of the first physicians of southeastern Wisconsin. It reads: In loving memory of Ammon P. Adams, M. D. 1795-1869 "Who Went About Doing Good."

Union Grove is at the junction with State 11 (*see Tour 24*).

BRISTOL, 98.8 *m.* (772 alt., 500 pop.), first established 3 miles east of its present site in 1838 by settlers from Vermont and Connecticut, was removed here in the 1850's when the railroad came through. The first Barnum circus to appear in Wisconsin played in Bristol before the Civil War. P. T. Barnum often came to visit a sister who lived near by, and as he was clean shaven in a day of beards and usually wore a stovepipe hat, he presented a striking figure on the village streets.

US 45 crosses the Illinois Line at 103.6 *m.,* 18 miles north of Libertyville, Illinois.

Tour 5A

Fond du Lac—Ripon—Junction with US 51; 56.8 *m*. State 23.

Chicago and North Western Ry. parallels route between Fond du Lac and Princeton.
Asphalt and concrete roadbed.
Village and resort accommodations.

State 23 crosses the sandy region west of Lake Winnebago, linking Fond du Lac and US 51, Wisconsin's main north-south highway.

FOND DU LAC, 0 *m*. (759 alt., 26,449 pop.) (*see Tour 5*), is at the junction with US 41 (*see Tour 2*), State 55 (*see Tour 4*), US 45 (*see Tour 5*), and US 151 (*see Tour 6*).

Passing through a factory district of Fond du Lac, State 23 emerges on a swelling plain where lines of trees appear to march and countermarch across the horizon. Behind Lake Winnebago is the Niagara escarpment; as the highway goes westward, the fields and buildings on the escarpment lose their clarity, fading slowly into the blue haze.

ROSENDALE, 11.9 *m*. (889 alt., 305 pop.), shady and pleasant, is known for the SISSON PEONY FARM, visited by thousands who come each year to admire the flowers.

RIPON, 19.4 *m*. (914 alt., 3,984 pop.), is called "the city of the twin spires," from the spires of the Grace Lutheran and Congregational churches that stand high on College Hill. The neat landscape contrasts sharply with the drab time-worn buildings that line the main street.

Ripon has had a lively and interesting history as a socialistic community, a stronghold of abolitionism, and the birthplace of a major political party. Its first settlers were followers of François Charles Marie Fourier, socialist of the early nineteenth century. Fourier's ideas were accepted by Horace Greeley, whose editorials in the New York *Tribune* reverberated across the country to Southport, now Kenosha. Here Warren Chase took up the cause and organized a stock company called the Wisconsin Phalanx, which in 1844 purchased 600 acres of land in the present township of Ripon. The Fourierites named their settlement Ceresco, for Ceres, Roman goddess of agriculture. For a time they prospered; then quarrels broke out among the members, and between Ceresco and a settlement that recent newcomers had founded on a hill nearby. Finally, in 1850, the Phalanx disbanded by mutual consent, and Ceresco was absorbed by the rapidly growing settlement, Ripon.

On the western outskirts of the city is the large LONG HOUSE (*private*) in which the Fourierites lived; adjacent is CERESCO PARK (*picnic facilities*). What was once Ceresco is now the working-class district of the city, inhabited largely by laborers and factory workers of German stock.

Ripon, during the 1850's, reflected the North's growing resentment against slavery; in 1860 it was the scene of an antislavery demonstration during "Booth's War" (1854-61). Sherman M. Booth of Milwaukee, ardent abolitionist, after aiding in the escape of the famous fugitive slave, Joshua Glover, was first arrested in Milwaukee in 1854. Booth was dismissed by Wisconsin courts but was fined and imprisoned by United States courts. During imprisonment in Milwaukee, Booth was delivered from jail; he escaped to Ripon where many of his friends assembled to protect him. Here and in near-by villages he made abolitionist speeches while sympathizers prevented the authorities from taking him. Then throughout the month of August 1860 he and his friends played a lively game of hare and hounds with the pursuing Federal agents. Ultimately Booth was seized again, but in 1861 his fine was remitted by order of President ·James Buchanan, and charges against him were dropped.

A block from main street are the vine-covered buildings of RIPON COLLEGE, a privately controlled college affiliated with the Congregational Church, with an enrollment of approximately 400. On the campus is a small frame building that disputes with a number of places the distinction of being the BIRTHPLACE OF THE REPUBLICAN PARTY. On March 20, 1854, a group of Whigs, Anti-Nebraska Democrats, and Free Soilers held here one of the earliest meetings for the discussion of those ideas that carried the Republican Party to power under Lincoln.

West of Ripon a chain of bluffs, not always visible from the curving highway, runs the entire distance to GREEN LAKE, 28.3 *m.* (805 alt., 569 pop.), on the east shore of a lake of the same name, a great irregular oval of dark green water. Winnebago Indians, who lived here, knew the lake as Day-Cho-Lah (Green Waters), translated later by the French as Lac du Verde. Widely known as a playground for well-to-do Chicago people, Green Lake has many lavish summer homes, with social life centered about the Lawsonia Country Club (*swimming, boating*). On the south shore are the cottages of less well-to-do people who, wearing straw hats and overalls, work in their gardens and clean fish in the sun.

PRINCETON, 37.8 *m.* (776 alt., 1,183 pop.), a quiet old city, was settled by Royal C. Treat, who staked out a claim here on July 2, 1848. Indians ripped the boards off his shanty, raided his flour and pork barrels, and carried off his blankets and kitchen utensils. Treat was not discouraged; in 1849 he and his brother journeyed to the land office at Green Bay and bought 132 acres of land here, which they laid out as the village of Princeton. Through the city flows the crooked Fox River, its banks crowded with buildings and houses. Near by is the straight water line of the MECAN-PRINCETON CANAL between the Mecan and Fox Rivers, authorized by the legislature in

1852. In 1861 it was widened from 10 to 40 feet in order to develop water power at the Princeton end; the several deepenings since 1900 have turned the natural flow down the canal and allowed the Mecan channel to become choked with willows, logs, and debris, rendering the control dam at the Mecan end useless. On the outskirts of Princeton a mossy little dam, shaded by trees, forms a miniature waterfall.

State 23 passes a grove of colorful mountain ash, 38.7 *m.*, which in early summer bear large white flowers that stand on the tips of branches like candles. By late summer these flowers have become clusters of bright orange berries, peeping out from glossy, dark green leaves. Along here the highway overlooks long miles of low marsh or valley pasture land; wild roses ramble in sunny ditches, and little streams wind through pastures and oak woods. Everywhere in this greenness gleams tawny yellow sand that is too infertile to nourish crops, too light and shifting to afford them proper foothold.

MONTELLO, 49.2 *m.* (772 alt., 1,245 pop.), is distinctive for the bold bluff of red granite that stands conspicuously in the center of its business section, only a short distance from the courthouse of Marquette County. Granite from the MONTELLO GRANITE QUARRY, on an elevation in the northern section of town, was used for the tomb of Ulysses S. Grant and for a variety of monumental and building purposes. Although hand tools have been replaced by a huge saw that cuts 12 linear feet of granite every eight hours, many of the workmen who began quarrying here years ago are still employed. On the western outskirts of town is LAKE MONTELLO (*bathing beach*).

West of Montello, the farmland, poor as it is, shows to advantage in midsummer when crops of winter rye are nearing harvest. Pink phlox and blue flags grow along the fences, and redwing blackbirds dart among the grasses. This whole area is rough, however, its pastures ragged, its marshes shaggy with broadleaved bushes and oak trees.

At 56.8 *m.* is the junction with US 51 (*see Tour 7*).

Tour 6

Manitowoc—Fond du Lac—Beaver Dam—Columbus—Madison; 128.2 *m.* US 151.

Chicago, Milwaukee, St. Paul & Pacific R.R. parallels route between Sun Prairie and Madison.
Cement-paved roadbed.
Adequate accommodations throughout.

US 151 goes southwestward across the State through a bright low country of sweeping fields and pasture land, of neat villages and small clean cities serving the farmers' commercial and industrial needs. Only the smokestacks, foundries, and general business clutter of Manitowoc and Fond du Lac break the rather pleasant monotony of the route, along which the main activities of both city and country are dependent upon the soil.

Section a.   *MANITOWOC to FOND DU LAC; 55.2 m., US 151*

MANITOWOC, 0 *m.* (595 alt., 22,963 pop.) (*see Tour 18*), is at the junction with US 10 (*see Tour 18*), US 141 (*see Tour 3*), and State 42 (*see Tour 1C*).

US 141-151 branches southwest from Manitowoc. At 2.9 *m.* US 141 (*see Tour 3*) turns L.; US 151 continues R. (straight ahead). A backward glance here reveals an irregular sky line of massed houses, smokestacks, oil tanks, and church spires of the receding city. Far out is the vanishing blue of Lake Michigan. The large and formal buildings of the HOLY FAMILY CONVENT (L), 4.6 *m.,* stand in a charmingly informal setting of green woods, knolls, and ravines. At 9 *m.* the route enters a region of round knolls, marshy basins, and abrupt little valleys at the northern tip of the kettle moraine country (*see Natural Setting*).

VALDERS, 12.7 *m.* (812 alt., 504 pop.), save for the steeple of its white hillside church and its one tall smokestack, lies half hidden in a hollow. The village was settled by Norwegians from the remote valley of Valders, attracted to the New World by J. R. Reiersen's *Pathfinder for Norwegian Emigrants to the North American States and Texas,* published at Christiania, Norway, in 1844. Among the settlers came the parents of Thorstein Veblen (1857-1929), economist of international reputation. Veblen was born and lived here until his family moved to Minnesota, when he was eight.

At 15.3 *m.* is the junction with County A.

Left on County A to ST. NAZIANZ, 2.5 *m.,* a small village on the slopes of a hill, developed from an experiment in Christian communism. Even today St. Nazianz is different from the ordinary Wisconsin village. Houses sprawl up hill slopes towards church buildings on the summits; the streets are narrow and old-worldish; something of monastic isolation still seems to hang over the village; and the strong German accent and idiom of its people take it as much out of the contemporary American world as do the habits of the male and female branches of the religious community here. At 2.7 *m.* (R), crowning a round summit, are two early structures of this erstwhile Utopia, now occupied by the Salvatorian Sisters of the Society of the Divine Savior. One of the buildings is worn with age; torn yellow plaster reveals patches of faded brick, which give the walls a pinkish hue. At 3.2 *m.* (L) appear the grounds of the SALVATORIAN SEMINARY and the CHURCH; west is the CEMETERY of the Society of the Divine Savior.

In 1854 Father Ambrose Oschwald, saintly idealist who hoped to free his co-religionists from governmental interference and to build a society patterned after the communistic life of the early Christians, led 113 people, members of his parish and others, from Baden, Germany, and purchased 3,840 acres of land in the forests here. On August 27 the company raised a tall wooden cross on the hillside; by New Year's the settlement had a church, four log houses, a large shed, blacksmith shop, smokehouse, barn and 20 head of cattle.

From the first life was organized on a communal basis. All worked, ate, and prayed together; money and land were jointly owned. Religion, the motive for the colony's founding, so governed life that in 1857, influenced by Father Oschwald, the unmarried Brothers and Sisters formally organized under the Third Order of St. Francis. A convent and the Loretto House were erected, and by 1866 there were 80 members of the male branch and 150 members of the female branch at St. Nazianz.

The Christian community prospered until the death of Father Oschwald in 1873 destroyed the bond that held the group together. The property of the community had been held in Father Oschwald's name, but on his death a joint stock company was created under the name of the Roman Catholic Religious Society of St. Nazianz. Immediately dissension arose; many members sued the Society for their original investment and some demanded back wages for labor. Policies were changed. No married people were admitted after 1874, no new members after 1896. Eventually a part of the property was taken over by the Salvatorian Fathers, who still possess it.

Community life has not greatly changed, however. Although the Utopian hope for Christian communism is gone, St. Nazianz is still dominated by its church, seminary, and convents. On special feast days solemn processions of the devout wind their way through the village, college grounds and fields to the Shrine of Our Lady of Loretto; the mellow tones of church bells still regulate the simple and active life of the inhabitants.

The ascent of the backslope of the Niagara cuesta, a pre-glacial limestone ridge (*see Natural Setting*), begins at 17.7 *m*. At 20.7 *m*. is the western junction with State 32.

Left on State 32 to KIEL, 8.8 *m*. (918 alt., 1,803 pop.), where wooden shoes were formerly manufactured. In 1844 an old Belgian trapper living in the woods near by began to carve wooden shoes for the German and Belgian farmers of Manitowoc County. Later, to satisfy the demand for the product, a small factory was built.

Typically Belgian in style, the shoes were made from basswood logs, some 15 inches in diameter, which were stripped while still green and cut into blocks. These blocks were put on lathes, the shoes were shaped, the inside hollowed out. Finishing touches were added by hand; then the shoes were put in huge kilns to be dried and shrunk. The factory, now closed, sold almost its entire production outside Wisconsin, half to mail order houses, some for use in the rice and cane fields of Louisiana, and the remainder to theatrical outfitting companies.

CHILTON, 28.6 *m*. (856 alt., 1,945 pop.), a white man's city now, was founded by a Negro, Moses Stanton, and his Indian wife. Elder Stanton, as he was called, was both preacher and doctor to his neighbors for miles around. His wife, a descendant of King Philip, warlike son of Massasoit, who befriended the Pilgrims at Plymouth, was a woman of courage and spirit. During the election contest with Stockbridge over the county seat in 1856, she saddled her husband's best horse, saying to him and the townspeople, "See that all our friends in this part of the country are awakened to the importance of voting, and I will capture enough of the western enemy to save the day. Elder, have a fresh horse for me at Stockbridge at noon tomorrow. Goodbye." For three days and two nights she rode through the wilderness from one isolated cabin to another.

The CALUMET COUNTY COURTHOUSE stands in a landscaped square, a memorial to the success of Mrs. Stanton's campaign. The first church built in Chilton, now the TRINITY PRESBYTERIAN, likewise attests the spirit of pioneer women. In 1877 the women raised funds and built a village church to be used by all faiths. From its pulpit spoke many itinerant ministers—Methodists, Baptists, Episcopalians, Congregationalists, Presbyterians. In 1883 the men offered to cover the white pine siding of the church with brick veneer if the women would agree to hold no temperance meetings and lectures in it. The women held bazaars, raised money in other ways, and veneered the church themselves.

Chilton today is a quiet little city. It has an aluminum factory, two flour mills, several grain elevators, a canning factory, a large malt house, and a brewery. Surrounding dairy farmers bring their milk produce to the Chilton cheese factory and dairy or the condensery. Calumet County has a very high concentration of milk production; in 1930 it produced 59,019 gallons per square mile.

West of Chilton, US 151 continues to ascend the escarpment to its crest at 36.4 m., where it overlooks the green fields that drop away rapidly to the narrow strip of farmland along the shore of Lake Winnebago. On clear days the far shore can be seen, along which appear the distant smokestacks, water tanks, piers, and blockish buildings of Fond du Lac to the south and Oshkosh directly opposite. Cottages line the lakeshore, and in summer the scene is peaceful, pleasant. Fishermen slouch over their lines; swimming rafts and pleasure boats drift at moorings inshore; the slanting sails of many boats move across the water.

Autumn brings a change; the fields lie bare, the vacationists leave. By mid-December the lake is a blinding ice plain, swept by winds swirling loose snow into stinging clouds or piling it high in drifts along the shore. Iceboats replace the sailboats; sail skaters, the swimmers. About mid-January other sportsmen come, the sturgeon fishermen, who drive their cars from three to six miles over the frozen lake, cut a hole in the ice, and erect their frail, three-sided shanties. Shapeless in their heavy woolens, so muffled in scarves that only their wind-reddened eyes and noses show, they begin their tedious watch, waiting hour after hour, long spears in hand, for the black shadow that indicates an approaching sturgeon.

The spears consist of barbed iron heads fitted to long shafts. Attached to lines made fast on the ice, the iron head comes free when a strike is made. The harpoons are held constantly in the water ready for use, and in the hands of skillful fishermen need only to be aimed and thrust downward for a catch. Sturgeons are large, ranging from 20 to 150 pounds. State conservation laws limit each fisherman to not more than five a season.

At 36.9 *m.* is the junction with State 55 (*see Tour 4*). Between this junction and 55.2 *m.* US 151 and State 55 are one route.

The highway runs along the narrow fertile plain between Lake Winnebago (R) and the bluffs of the escarpment (L). Indians once had villages all along the plain, pitching their wigwams at the ridge base, building their mounds on top.

BROTHERTOWN, 39 *m.* (175 pop.), was settled in 1832 by the Brothertown Indians, who had previously lived with the Stockbridge in New England and New York (*see Tour 4*). Here they built substantial log huts and cultivated small farms. In 1838 Bishop Jackson Kemper wrote of them and their settlement, "We now entered a thickly wooded country through which there is a military road [now US 151] that is truly bad. This country belongs to the Brothertown Indians, who have lost the Indian language. They are fragments of 7 nations who once occupied the New England States. There is no pure Indian blood among them—and they cannot trace their descent."

A mixture of Indian, white, and Negro blood, the Brothertown included many types. In their village could be seen the tall athletic Narragansett; the sturdy and powerful Montauk; the alert Mohican; and many halfbreeds, some with the curly black hair and broad features of the Negro, others with the fairer hair and skin of the white. All spoke English. Several were skilled in trades, and helped to build the first steamboat on Lake Winnebago.

Successful for a time, the Indians could not withstand the direct competition of the more aggressive white settlers who soon flooded the region. Gradually they lost more and more of their lands; their forests went through pioneer sawmills to become the barns and houses of white farmers. In 1930 there were 128 Indians in Calumet County, most of them descendants of the original Brothertown band. In the village that bears their name, consisting today of a few scattered houses and a little white church with bright blue windows, there is nothing to suggest that the Brothertown once hoped to establish a permanent home here.

CALUMETVILLE, 41.5 *m.* (125 pop.), is named for the stone pipe in which Indians once smoked a mixture of Hudson Bay plug tobacco, sumac leaves, and aromatic red osier bark (kinnikinnick). In 1831 Chief Little Wave had his Menominee village here; German immigrants began settling the region 15 years later. One of them wrote home enthusiastically describing this fertile land. Printed in the *Barmer Zeitung* in 1846, his letter brought more of his countrymen— among others, Dr. Carl de Haas, who built a house here in 1847 and sat down to write two volumes on the Calumet area, *Nordamerika, Wisconsin, Calumet. Winke für Auswanderer*. This work, more than any other, made Wisconsin known throughout Germany and started the German immigration that continued for 40 years.

At PIPE, 43.1 *m.,* is a junction with a dirt road.

Right on this road to COLUMBIA COUNTY PARK, 0.8 *m.,* on the former site of Calumet Harbor (*tourist accommodations, playground and boating equipment*).

TAYCHEEDAH (Ind., camp by a lake), 47 *m.* (751 alt., 112 pop.), was founded in 1839 by Francis D. McCarty, who hoped to build a great industrial and commercial city here. All signs then justified his hopes. The early travel routes, including the Military Road between Green Bay and Prairie du Chien, converged here. By 1840, when Fond du Lac consisted of a few huts huddled on a swamp at the lake tip, Taycheedah was a favorite stopping-off place for traders, soldiers, and settlers. Decline began shortly before the Civil War when many of its important families moved to Fond du Lac, attracted by the superior natural advantages. Today Taycheedah overlooks the lake, its harbor undeveloped, its hopes for metropolitanism shattered by the growth of Fond du Lac. Only an old TRADING POST AND DANCE HALL remains as evidence of the lively days when long wagon trains rolled in to stop overnight.

At Taycheedah is the junction with County K.

Left on County K are the WISCONSIN PRISON FOR WOMEN and the WISCONSIN INDUSTRIAL HOME FOR WOMEN (*visiting hous 9 to 11 a.m. and 2 to 4 p.m. on weekdays*), 1 *m.* Set in a 244-acre farm on the Niagara ridge, the attractive buildings are distinctly non-institutional in appearance, both inside and out. Girls and women in the prison are employed on the farm, in the bakery and laundry, or at other work; girls in the industrial school are taught some useful vocation.

South of Taycheedah cottages crowd the wooded bank as US 151 skirts the lakeshore.

FOND DU LAC, 55.2 *m.* (759 alt., 26,449 pop.) (*see Tour 5*), is at the junction with US 41 (*see Tour 2*), State 55 (*see Tour 4*), US 45 (*see Tour 5*), and State 23 (*see Tour 5A*).

Section b.   FOND DU LAC to MADISON; 73 m., US 151

Southwest of FOND DU LAC, 0 *m.,* US 151 follows the route of the old Green Bay-Prairie du Chien Military Road, passing the COUNTY ASYLUM, 1.9 *m.,* a building of bright red brick with sloping gray roofs. As the road proceeds southwesterly the Niagara escarpment recedes from view; the land on both sides is an open sweep of fields dotted with box-type windmills, warped barns, and weathered houses.

WAUPUN (Ind., early light of day), 19.2 *m.* (888 alt., 5,768 pop.), on the Rock River, was founded in 1838 by Seymour Wilcox. Other settlers soon followed him, pioneers from Ohio and Pennsylvania—Dutch, Irish, English, Scottish, and German. A haven for retired farmers, Waupun is slow, quiet, almost oppressively "pleasant," with shady streets, well-kept lawns, and Victorian buildings. At the

dam on the river is a REPLICA OF THE END OF THE TRAIL MONU-
MENT, executed for the Panama-Pacific Exposition (1915) by James
Earle Frazer. In the cemetery stands Lorado Taft's ANGEL OF PEACE
MONUMENT.

For two blocks along a shady residential street extend the battle-
mented walls and barred arches of the WISCONSIN STATE PRISON
(*visiting hours: daily except Sat. afternoons, Sun. and holidays; guide
every hour*). An overcrowded institution, it has 960 cells for men,
as well as workshops, kitchens, a bakery, and other buildings on its
23-acre grounds. In March 1938 there were 1,635 prisoners here.

In 1855, four years after the prison had been built, the legislature
authorized the contracting of convict labor to private employers, who
thereafter carried on their business largely at State expense, paying the
prison from 45 cents to 65 cents a day for each worker. Mounting
opposition brought this practice to an end in 1928. The prison today
employs some of the men in the making of shoes, clothing, paint, binder
twine, furniture, mattresses, automobile license plates, highway signs
and traffic markers, tin cans, metal furniture, and miscellaneous machine
and foundry products used mainly in maintenance work in this and
other State institutions. Twine is the only product sold on the open
market; all other products are used by the prison or sold to tax-
supported institutions in the State.

Prisoners are encouraged to take correspondence courses and vocational training; in 1937 approximately 250 men attended school all day
long. The men write, edit, and publish *The Candle,* a monthly magazine of stories, articles, and jokes. After the prisoners have read the
magazine, they send the used copies out to friends and relatives.

At 20 *m.* a turn in the road reveals a red-brick, white-trimmed milk
condensery (L) and a large pea cannery (R), both suggestive of the
main enterprises of the farmers in this region. At intervals along this
section of the route appear creameries, cheese factories, pea canneries,
and vinery sheds, with their huge odorous piles of pea vines.

US 151 enters BEAVER DAM, 34.9 *m.* (867 alt., 9,867 pop.),
along a well-shaded street lined with typical, small-town American
houses—spare frame structures, two-story for the most part, each with
wide windows, a pointed roof, and a pillared front porch. Here and
there bristles a house of brick; everywhere there is a generosity of lawn.
In the business section the almost uniform brick buildings are almost
uniformly two stories high.

Just how people make a living in Beaver Dam, a typical small
American city, has been revealed by the Bureau of Home Economics
of the Department of Agriculture in a study made of 19 small cities,
140 villages, and 66 farm counties throughout the country. The purpose of the survey was "to provide adequate and comprehensive data
on the way in which American families earn and spend their incomes."

Figures for Beaver Dam were based on information supplied by
453 white families which represented a typical cross-section of the city.
The average income of this group for 1935-36 was $1,309. The aver-

age for business and professional families was $1,952, while that of wage earning families, comprising almost 60 per cent of the total, was far lower at $1,219. Nine of every 10 families were supported by the earnings of only one person.

Approximately 11 per cent of all families received relief at some time during the year 1935-36, having an average income of $462 from all sources: 4 per cent more had incomes of less than $500; 21 per cent received from $500 to $1,000; 37 per cent, from $1,000 to $1,500; 15 per cent, from $1,500 to $2,000; 8 per cent, from $2,000 to $3,000; and 4 per cent, $3,000 or more.

The average size of families was 3.6 persons. The smallest families were in the middle income groups. Families receiving more than $3,000 averaged 4 persons; those on relief, 4.9 persons. Half of the families studied owned their own homes. Those who rented paid an average of $20 a month, the highest for any city studied in which average income was less than $1,500. No family paid less than $5 or more than $45 a month. Average rent increased progressively with income, ranging from $17 for those receiving less than $1,000 to $30 for those with incomes of $3,000 or more.

A typical small industrial city with 15 factories, which employ 1,800 workers, Beaver Dam produces shoes, soap, stoves, barn equipment, cheeseboxes, refrigerators, water heaters, beverages, confections, canned goods, and cream cheese. The mammoth plant where Monarch stoves and ranges are manufactured extends for almost a mile along the highway.

At times Beaver Dam has shown itself a conservative community in a generally liberal State. When a strike broke out in the Bear Brand Hosiery Plant in 1934, the company closed its local factory permanently and withdrew from the city, which suffered a pay roll loss of almost $500,000 a year. Most of the workers left for other cities; those that remained were thrown on relief.

When a strike threatened in a local foundry in September 1935, the businessmen of Beaver Dam organized a Law and Order League to keep out outside agitators and lawbreakers, whether they be "a walking delegate, traffic violator, a politician with a Republican, Democrat or Socialist label." One midnight almost six months later, with more than 100 members of the Law and Order League demonstrating in the street, city officials ordered two labor organizers to leave the city under police escort. Later that day the union signed an agreement with the foundry to accept a 5 to 15 per cent cut in hourly wage rates. The signing of this contract prevented action by State or Federal authorities. After an investigation, Henry Ohl, Jr., president of the State Federation of Labor, asked the State government to protect labor organizations in Beaver Dam and advised the union to carry out its agreement. Eventually the animosity between business and labor died down, and the Law and Order League disbanded. Today labor in Beaver Dam is 90 per cent organized and in a far stronger position than in 1936.

In the city is VITA SPRING PARK, laid out around Vita Spring, which was regarded as a holy place by the Winnebago and Potawatomi, who attributed healing properties to its waters. They cast into it human and animal bones, arrows, and other treasures as offerings to the spirit living there. When the white men came, they cleaned the spring and built a park about it. A dam across the Beaver Dam River nearby forms a long millpond, known locally for its bullhead fishing.

Southwest of Beaver Dam, US 151 enters rolling country; here and there red barns stand like bright signal towers on the hill crests.

COLUMBUS, 46.6 *m.* (842 alt., 2,514 pop.) (*see Tour 22*), is at the junction with US 16 (*see Tour 21*) and State 60 (*see Tour 22*).

On the high flat prairie land southwest of Columbus are broad acres of wheat, corn, barley, and peas; farmhouses are scattered and poorly kept. Drab and unpainted, they are insulated from biting prairie winds in winter by leaves or straw piled against their foundations; oaks or evergreens in the yard protect them against the hot sun of summer.

SUN PRAIRIE, 61.7 *m.* (936 alt., 1,337 pop.), a village with a small business section of two-story brick buildings and a widely-spaced residential district, lies sprawled over a slope facing the open prairie. The village was named in 1837 by a party passing this way from Milwaukee to erect the State capitol at Madison. Charles H. Bird, who became the first settler, was a member of the party, which after nine weary days of rain was "thrilled with sunshine upon this prairie and carved 'Sun Prairie' on a burr oak tree one mile and a half east of this village, June 9, 1837." Today the massive SACRED HEART CHURCH and CONVENT on top of the hill dominates the village. Georgia O'Keeffe, distinguished American painter, was born in Sun Prairie in 1887 (*see Painting and Sculpture*).

In the countryside between Sun Prairie and Madison signs of glaciation multiply in the form of huge boulder trains, oval drumlins, glacial drift filling natural valleys, terminal and recessional moraines. The unstratified and conglomerate character of the rock can be clearly seen as the highway skirts the edge of glacial dump heaps or cuts directly through glacial mounds.

In the 1870's many wealthy men bought great tracts in this section and set themselves up as "gentlemen farmers." Their farms today suggest prosperity more by their size than by their condition; the huge old barns are gloomy, badly drained, and poorly ventilated; the houses are oversized and drafty. But situated as they are on low hills far back from the road, surrounded by evergreens and lilac bushes, and overgrown with honeysuckle, the old farmhouses are still attractive.

This section of US 151 was originally an Indian trail from Koshkonong to Fort Winnebago, at Portage. When American soldiers blazed a road from Green Bay to Prairie du Chien between 1835-38, the trail became a part of the route. Later it became a stagecoach road dotted with two-story sandstone taverns, which served as combination hostelry-saloon-bordello-courthouse-social centers. The taverns vanished with the "horse and buggy" age, and today travel is swift along this old road, now a broad concrete highway.

At 67.9 *m.* is the junction with US 51 (*see Tour 7*); between this junction and 69.6 *m.* US. 151 and US 51 are one route. US 151 enters Madison by way of E. Washington Ave.

MADISON, 73 *m.* (859 alt., 57,899 pop.) (*see Madison*).

Madison is at the junction with US 12 (*see Tour 19*), State 113 (*see Tour 19B*), US 14 (*see Tour 20*), US 18 (*see Tour 23*), and State 30 (*see Tour 23A*).

Tour 7

(Ironwood, Mich.) — Hurley — Wausau — Madison — Beloit — Rockford, Ill.); US 51.
Michigan Line to Illinois Line, 341.2 *m.*

Chicago & North Western Ry. parallels route between Hurley and Woodruff, and between Madison and Beloit; Chicago, Milwaukee, St. Paul & Pacific R.R. between Woodruff and Stevens Point, and between Madison and Beloit; Soo Line between Stevens Point and Madison.
Hard-surfaced and oiled-gravel roadbed.
Good hotels and restaurants provide adequate facilities throughout entire route; many camps, resorts, lodges, and cabins in northern lakes region.

From the mine-scarred cutover of the far north US 51 winds southward the length of Wisconsin, revealing along its route the aspects of a State so diverse that wolves are still hunted in one section while tractors and X-ray tubes are manufactured in another. Much of the north is a cutover wilderness in which people depend upon seasonal tourist trade for income; the timber is gone, farming has failed. To the south the scene gradually changes; rich, intensively cultivated fields succeed the unproductive cutover; tidy farmsteads, the log huts; and highly industrialized cities, the lean farm villages, as the highway approaches the Illinois Line.

Section a. MICHIGAN LINE to WAUSAU; 130.1 m., US 51

South of the junction with US 2 (*see Tour 14*), 0 *m.*, US 51 follows the Montreal River, the boundary between Michigan and Wisconsin, toward Hurley which sprawls on the hillside (R).

HURLEY, 1.5 *m.* (1,493 alt., 3,264 pop.), only a few thin blocks along the riverbank, fans out and up the valley, a scattering of white cottages and bungalows, yellow brick buildings, and gaunt frame houses joined by a bridge with Ironwood, Michigan, her much larger sister city across the river. Siamese twins, Hurley and Ironwood were born in 1884 and grew rapidly into lusty infants on a diet of lumber and iron ore. By 1886 thousands of men were on the Gogebic Range, cutting timber, and digging ore from small open pits. Hurley soon sheltered 7,000 residents and hundreds of transient lumberjacks and miners. "The four toughest places in the world are Cumberland, Hayward, Hurley and Hell," it was said at the time, and Hurley was toughest of all. Lumberjacks and miners crowded its slab saloons; when dead drunk, they were methodically "rolled" and thrown into the streets. Near by were the stockades, shacks surrounded by high board fences, where prostitutes were housed.

As low-grade Wisconsin ore was forced from the market and Wisconsin forests were exhausted, Ironwood forged slowly ahead, becoming the business and commercial center of the twin cities. Hurley's population fell as Ironwood's rose. By 1910 little remained of its proud boom days except a reputation for bawdiness and crime, which led Edna Ferber (see Literature) to choose it as the setting of her novel Come and Get It. The name of the principal character, Barney Glasgow, is fictitious, but old-timers assert that they knew the original. Lotta Morgan, his dance-hall sweetheart, lived and worked under that name at the old Central Gardens, a tavern now known as MICKEY'S PLACE. Both in real life and in Miss Ferber's book, Lotta was found one morning in the alley behind the Dew Drop Inn, now TROLLA'S MEAT MARKET, her touseled head split with an ax.

Through it transitional years Hurley was a rendezvous for booze runners, gunmen, and criminals. In 1924, during prohibition days, there were 51 "soft drink" parlors; in 1938, 80 of its 115 business establishments were taverns, which so solidly lined six blocks of Silver St. that it was difficult to buy a meal. In gambling dens, where silver dollars serve as chips, suave operators often sit behind 30 or 40 stacks of "cartwheels" piled a foot high. Local bosses run the city but their names are seldom mentioned, for it is safer not to talk or snoop in Hurley. Late one night during prohibition days, three men encountered another with a suitcase and asked what he had in it. The man replied by drawing his revolver and shooting his questioner dead. At the preliminary hearing it was ruled that he had shot in self-defense.

Although some logging still continues, Hurley subsists largely as a shipping center for ore from both the Michigan and Wisconsin mines, which employ most of its working population. In recent years the city has publicized itself as a recreation center, hoping to attract some of the vacationers who crowd north every summer.

Right from Hurley on State 77 along the Penokee Iron Range, past the dumps and buildings of the CAREY MINE, 2 m. MONTREAL, 3.2 m. (1,819 pop.), is a one-industry community, engaged in the mining of iron ore. Of the 400 houses in the city about 125 are owned by the Montreal Mining Company, which supplies small trees and shrubs from its nursery to householders who wish to landscape their lots.

South of the residential section, largely screened by a maple forest, is Montreal's industrial area. Here is a power house where immense rotary converters transform alternating current to direct current. Here also are huge hoists, each with two one-and-a-half inch steel cables. These cables, 4,000 feet long, are wound on drums 10 feet in diameter.

They run to the top of a 165-foot tower, called a headframe, which rises directly above the mine shaft. Skips carrying ore from 3,000 feet below the ground are hoisted at the rate of 1,800 feet a minute. A cage handling men and materials runs swiftly up and down the shaft. As many as 40 men at a time can be lowered or hoisted in this cage.

The iron ore lies more than half a mile below the ground in irregular, roughly triangular, trough-shaped bodies. Some 600 men, a majority from Montreal, work in two shifts, drilling and blasting the ore, digging it out, hauling it to the shafts, loading the skips, hoisting the ore to the surface, crushing it, stocking it in large piles during winter, and loading it onto railroad cars in summer. The ore is stocked from steel trestles, 40 feet high. Sixteen-ton electrically-operated cars carry the ore from the headframe to the proper pile.

During the shipping season large steam shovels scoop up the ore and load it in railroad cars which are usually routed to Ashland for shipment on Great Lakes steamers to eastern steel plants. The Montreal Mine has a capacity of approximately 1,000,000 tons a year. In 1937, 1,174,096 tons were shipped.

State 77 goes westward through a half-deserted, desolate land, a wilderness crossed by fire lanes. Farmsteads huddle in the brush; rock clogs the rust-stained soil. Overhead eagles soar, usually in pairs, wheeling tirelessly in great circles. Sighting prey, they glide down in ever narrowing circles, poising in mid-air 50 or 60 feet above the ground. Then suddenly, wings folded to their bodies, they plummet down, striking their victim with outspread claws.

Most of the small mining towns along the route are impoverished. PENCE, 5.3 m. (1,623 alt.), is built close to sidings where cars loaded with reddish lumps of iron ore stand ready to be hooked on west-bound locomotives. IRON BELT, 8.3 m. (1,548 alt., 860 pop.), has small shabby homes, for the mines here produce low grade ore that is mined only when prices are high. State 77 crosses the coffee-colored Potato River, 12.8 m., passes the single deserted shack of MOORE, 18 m., and the empty depot of TYLER'S FORK, 19.4 m. MELLEN, 26.2 m. (1,242 alt., 1,629 pop.) (see Tour 8), is at the junction with State 13 (see Tour 8).

Screened by miles of ragged trees and brush, US 51 runs southward through a barren, rocky land. From a hilltop, 6.5 m., a backward glance reveals Hurley, Ironwood, the Penokee Iron Range, and in the far distance the great dumps and mine housings of the CAREY and the MONTREAL IRON MINES (see above). Farms here are few and little cultivated; buildings are small, cheaply built, and often in disrepair. In compliance with county rural zoning ordinances (see Agriculture), much of the land is now abandoned to quack grass and rough undergrowth, spotted with patches of blueberry swamp. In late summer overalled children and women can be seen along the highway, waist deep in the brush, gleaning what they can from the devastation man and fires have made.

Forest fires have gutted much of this region, and the State's growing concern about the problem of conservation is manifest in the MERCOMA COUNTY FOREST, 14.6 m., and the NORTHERN STATE FOREST, 26.7 m. The latter contains lakes, streams, and free campsites. Although the trees are mainly scrub they give promise of future beauty and utility, provided the present conservation program is maintained. Forest rangers and fire wardens willingly explain their solitary work, warn against carelessness with campfires and cigarettes, give directions and advice.

MERCER, 24.1 *m.* (1,598 alt., 200 pop.), at the northern entrance to Wisconsin's famed Northern Lakes Region, still retains a relic of logging days, a GO-DEVIL. These go-devils consisted of two huge, 10-foot wheels on a great axle, drawn by oxen or horses. Heavy logs were chained under the axle and "snaked" out of the woods to be "decked" by the roadside. Now the logs are "snaked" out by a tractor or a gasoline-motor winch.

South of Mercer US 51 enters the Northern Lakes Region, which in ratio of water to land surface is paralleled only by two other places: one includes part of Minnesota and the Province of Ontario, northwest of Lake Superior; the other includes part of southern Finland, east of the Gulf of Bothnia. In Iron, Vilas, and Oneida Counties alone, lakes comprise 15 per cent of the total area, swamps an additional 21 per cent. Shaped as irregularly as ink blots, the lakes range in size from a few acres to several square miles. On the shores of some are sophisticated summer resorts; elaborate dance halls, taverns, and luxurious private homes set in the heavy forest strike a strangely discordant note. Almost all the lakes contain game fish native to Wisconsin— walleyed and northern pike, muskellunge, black and rock bass, perch, and sunfish.

MANITOWISH, 27.6 *m.* (1,591 alt., 75 pop.), lies in the center of the Manitowish Waters, which merge and branch in a patternless tangle of wooded waterways, providing some of the State's best "muskie" fishing. In a day a motorboat can travel for miles through this chain with only one or two windlass hoists. Near the village the Manitowish River flows through flat marshland covered with dogwood, or "kinnikinnick," as it was known to the Indians, who mixed it with Hudson Bay plug tobacco. Kinnikinnick gives tobacco a pungent aromatic quality, and even today is used in small quantities by many manufacturers.

At 34.2 *m.* a bridge carries US 51 over the outlet of REST LAKE (L); directly below is the MANITOWISH WATERS FISH HATCHERY (R), the only locally maintained hatchery in Wisconsin. Owned and operated by the town of Spider Lake, it supplies the Manitowish Waters with approximately 25,000,000 pike, muskellunge, and bass each year, helping to keep the lakes and streams well stocked. Tourist trade is the life and hope of this district. Flamboyant signs cluster at every crossroad, announcing that this region "offers you everything for a perfect vacation." This is the modern north, far removed from the older one whose life revolved about such logging camps as that at 34.3 *m.* —its buildings now abandoned, the dinner bell, rusted and silent, still on its pole above the sagging roofs and rotting logs of mess hall and bunkhouses.

LITTLE BOHEMIA, 36.5 *m.*, reached through scattered pines, is the resort where John Dillinger and his gang hid in 1934 and from which all but their "molls" escaped after a desperate gun fight with

G-men, one of whom was killed. Right, near the lodge, is a small green CABIN (*adm. 25¢*), occupied and cared for by John Dillinger, Sr. Here are displayed personal belongings of such gangsters as Dillinger, Tommy Carroll, Homer Van Meter, John Hamilton, and Baby Face Nelson. A gigantic red sign by the roadside announces that 51,687 visitors stopped here in 1937.

A small bridge spans the junction of MANITOWISH LAKE (R) and SPIDER LAKE (L), 37.8 *m.* US 51 cuts across the northeastern corner of the LAC DU FLAMBEAU INDIAN RESERVATION (*see Tour 15*), 43.3 *m.,* past the TROUT LAKE GAME REFUGE, 44.8 *m.,* half-hidden TROUT LAKE (R), 45.2 *m.,* and DIAMOND LAKE, 45.7 *m.* Southward, popple grows thickly, and State forest roads fight their way deep into the lake-strewn wilderness beyond. Although resorts and lodges are still numerous, a few farms begin to appear along the road-side.

At 54.6 *m.* is the junction with State 70 (*see Tour 15*); between this junction and a point at 57.2 *m.,* US 51 and State 70 are one route (*see Tour 15*).

MINOCQUA, 58.4 *m.* (1,600 alt., 475 pop.), on a bulb-shaped isthmus protruding into LAKE KEWAGUESAGA, is the center of the Northern Lakes Region. Its white cottages and freshly painted hotels fit naturally into the half-wild setting of lakes and timberland. When the first railroad reached here in 1887, opening southern markets for lumber, Minocqua became a natural logging center. River hogs and sawyers walked its streets and peopled its sawdust-floored saloons; but as the forests gave out, the timber cutters and their masters left; warehouses, homes, and stores were boarded up, deserted.

Tourist trade brought a revival; saloons became elaborate dance halls and speakeasies, crowded with vacationists. By 1931, within a 40-mile radius, there were 3,000 summer homes, 218 resorts, and 32 boys' and girls' camps. Every summer brings not only tourists but sharpers, "operators," and confidence men. By the Fourth of July the village is booming, its streets filled with cars from many parts of the country. In winter Minocqua hibernates in the northern snows. The spring brings more than a house cleaning. Supplies are stocked; "Tourist Rooms" signs are hung out; plans are laid to snare the gay birds whose migration north in summer provides the money that keeps Minocqua's winters warm.

HAZELHURST, 63.8 *m.* (1,592 alt., 302 pop.), once a company-owned lumber town that had more than 1,000 people, is today only a tiny retail center for near-by cottagers. On the wooded shore of LAKE KATHERINE (L) is a rambling, barracks-like hotel, formerly a boarding house for mill hands. In the undulating country to the south, spotted with blueberry swamps and patches of scrawny popple and jack pine, farms are few and poor. Hay, potatoes, and some livestock are raised, but the growing season is too short for most crops. So, like the townspeople, the farmers of the region wait for the seasonal vacation trade, sell the tourists poultry, dairy produce, and wild berries, rent them boats and cabins, and act as guides.

At 75.9 *m.* is the junction with US 8 (*see Tour 16*). Between this junction and a point at 80.9 *m.* US 51 and US 8 are one route (*see Tour 16*).

TOMAHAWK, 88 *m.* (1,449 alt., 2,919 pop.), built on a half-dozen lakelike sloughs formed by power and mill dams on the Wisconsin River, is a city of farmers and mill hands. Paper and pulp, furs and farming keep the city alive through the winter; in summer it earns what it can from selling fishing tackle and bait, groceries, gasoline, and bathing suits to the gay tourists hurrying northward.

Up to 1886 there was only a lonely tavern here, kept by Germain Bouchard. Fur traders and Indians stopped overnight at this outpost, which was called Tomahawk because one of the near-by lakes vaguely resembled an ax blade. Then in 1886 the Tomahawk Land and Boom Co. chose this site for a sawmill, the railroad came through, and the settlement grew with startling speed. By 1890 the population was 1,816; four sawmills were hard at work, cutting 75,000,000 feet of lumber and 25,000,000 shingles annually; mill hands, tradespeople, industrialists, and the railroad were all making money. But the boom collapsed as suddenly as it began. With the timber exhausted, the sawmills closed, then the paper and pulp mills; only one continues to operate, working sporadically. The city's population has increased little more than 500 in the last 30 years.

Lying at the gateway to the north woods, Tomahawk is State headquarters for forest-fire protection. During the months of extreme hazard all rangers and supervisors report here by telephone. With 120 watch towers placed throughout the north, each commanding a radius of about 10 miles, all of the forest-protection area is within range of some observer (*see Natural Setting*).

South of Tomahawk farms increase in number, size, and value stretching across the rough and sharply rolling land, which marks the boundary of the terminal moraine formed by the Chippewa lobe of the Wisconsin glacier. Between here and Wausau the highway continues through the main northern dairy region. Gross farm income here in Lincoln County averaged $917 in 1931, far above the $525 average for Iron County in the extreme north.

MERRILL, 110.9 *m.* (1,257 alt., 8,458 pop.), angularly sprawled along the confluence of the Prairie and Wisconsin Rivers, was originally called Jenny Bull Falls, then Jenny, and finally Merrill. As early as 1847 Andrew Warren, Jr., the first permanent settler, built a sawmill here. Jenny's growth was slow until 1874 when the Wisconsin Valley R. R. arrived. Enjoying new prosperity, in 1881 the city was renamed Merrill for S. S. Merrill, general manager of the railroad. Mills sprang up on every slough and backwater on the Wisconsin River, and the city grew around them, following the twists and bends of the stream. Lumber mill hands in rival east and west sections fought along the banks of the Prairie River; log drives on both streams reached enormous proportions; in 1892 the annual cut reached 150,000,000 feet of lumber and 86,000,000 shingles.

The biggest log jam in Wisconsin history occurred at GRAND-FATHER FALLS on the Wisconsin River a few miles above Merrill. Here 80,000,000 feet of timber piled up in a great mass, damming the river for miles; heavy logs were stacked like jackstraws to heights of 20 feet of more. Searching for the single key log, lumberjacks and river hogs dragged out sticks until a cave was formed in the head of the jam. Each log was removed at great peril, for with the removal of the unidentifiable key log the whole mass would come crashing downstream, crushing anyone caught within the cave. Blasting finally broke the jam without loss of life.

With the decline of lumbering after 1895, Merrill turned to other fields and today produces paper and pulp, sashes and doors, knitted woolen goods, shoes, and iron parts. A large condensery uses the milk produced by the surrounding dairy farmers. Part of the fortunes made in early days by local lumber kings has been devoted to making Merrill a city of parks. RIVERSIDE PARK and STANGE PARK are pleasant in their conventional way. COUNCIL GROUNDS STATE FOREST, a 277-acre tract of timber in almost its virgin state, was formerly a city park.

Between Merrill and Wausau the highway climbs up and over a series of long steep hills. Along this route in the late 1870's mail was brought daily from Wausau by Etta Space, intrepid 18-year-old girl who rode horseback through rainstorms and blizzards along roads that were often all but impassable. Miss Space later became first lady of Arizona as the wife of a lumberman of this region, Myron H. McCord, who was appointed Governor of Arizona Territory (1897-99). US 51 crosses the Wisconsin River on HIGH BRIDGE, 129.9 m.

WAUSAU (Ind., *wassa,* far away place), 130.1 m. (1,191 alt., 23,758 pop.), a hurrying commercial and industrial city scattered along a rapids in the Wisconsin River, has clean, well-paved streets, green, clipped lawns, well-kept houses, and a number of factories manufacturing paper and wood products. About 1836 Robert Wakely ventured up the Wisconsin River as far as the rapids here, then known from the descriptions of other explorers as Gros Taureau (Fr., big bull). In his own words, when Wakely first encountered the vast pine forests he "became enamoured with it"; later in St. Louis he told George Stevens fabulous stories of the wealth to be gleaned in the north. Stevens investigated the region, and then in 1839 bought machinery and built several sawmills. He also established a supply depot at Stevens Point (*see Tour 18*).

Big Bull expanded rapidly. Walter McIndoe, the Plumer brothers, and Alexander Stewart erected sawmills; Charley Single built the Forest House, the first hotel. A sled road was constructed in 1846, a plank road to the county line was built, and in 1850 the settlement was renamed Wausau. In 1864 August Kickbusch was village president, and the town was almost a city; but Kickbusch, a civic-minded Prussian, was not satisfied. Three years later he went to Germany, there chartered a ship, and returned with 702 immigrants to settle the Wisconsin River Valley. The first railroad, the Wisconsin Valley, came in 1874 and stimulated the logging industry.

By 1906 the timber was gone, but Wausau had grown wealthy. Rich lumbermen, who had built their mansions here, were unwilling to leave them and opened other channels of interest and profit. As sawmills farther north still required machinery, a factory was established to provide it; paper mills sprang up in Rothschild and Brokaw, near-by towns. Woodworking and veneer plants, two shoe factories, an abrasive factory, a cheese plant, an electric motor works, feed and flour mills were built and grew slowly. A mutual insurance company established home offices here and expanded to other cities. Wausau also prospered as the wholesale and retail trade center of an extensive agricultural region.

MARATHON PARK (*picnic and tourist facilities*), an 80-acre tract of white pine, lies on the west side of the city; STEWART PARK, corner of Grey Place and Scott Sts., is a natural amphitheater; RIVERSIDE PARK has a 50-yard municipal swimming pool, recently constructed.

Wausau is at the junction with State 29 (*see Tour 17*).

Left from Wausau on graveled County N (11th Ave.) to a fork in the road, 2.6 *m.* The R. fork leads to the entrance of the WINTER SPORTS AREA, 1.1 *m.*, at Rib Mountain. In 1938 this area included an open slope, 2,500 feet long and 300 feet wide, six ski trails of varied terrene and length, a ski tow 3,000 feet long, a snow shoe trail, and a temporary shelter building. The slalom, downhill, and combined ski champion meet, the first of its kind in the central United States, was held here in March 1938, in conjunction with Wausau's annual Winter Frolic, and was attended by 3,000 people. The ski tow takes skiers to the top of the slope in seven minutes (*service $1 per day, 50¢ per half day during week; $1.50 and 75¢ on Sat., Sun., and holidays; skiing free*). Plans have been made to build toboggan slides and a large new shelter.

Continue on County N to the junction with a graveled road marked by a large sign, 4.4 *m.;* R. here. The road rises along the mountain side, edged by trees that cut off the view, until it reaches the mountain top and RIB MOUNTAIN STATE PARK (*parking space; camping and picnicking facilities*), 7 *m.* (1,940 alt.). Here trails lead to spots of particular interest, such as the QUEEN'S CHAIR, SLIDING ROCK, SUNSET POINT, which are marked with the geological story of the mountain. An enormous granite hogsback, 3 miles long and a mile wide, Rib Mountain is one of the few remnants of a mountain range that in the far distant past occupied the whole of Wisconsin. From various vantage points a wide expanse of land can be seen far below and northeast the city of Wausau glistening on the green plain along the Wisconsin River, a streak of silver in the sun.

Section b. WAUSAU to MADISON; 153.6 m., US 51

Between WAUSAU, 0 *m.,* and Schofield, US 51 and State 29 (*see Tour 17*) are one route. SCHOFIELD, 3.9 *m.* (1,206 alt., 1,287 pop.), and ROTHSCHILD, 5.9 *m.* (499 pop.), Wausau suburbs, depend for their livelihood on the great Marathon Paper Mills that sprawl along the Wisconsin River at 5.6 *m.* Back from the highway stretch enormous piles of pulpwood; behind them is the river. The mills have added two subsidiary factories in Wausau recently and have experimented with new methods of paper making and new uses of by-products. Chemists have discovered that liquids distilled by the sulphite cooking process are not worthless, as formerly supposed, but contain substances of commercial value. By-products of the process include tanning material, thermosetting resins, vanillin, and parafilm, the last used in food-packing, tree surgery, and as a moisture-proof lamination agent.

At 13.8 *m.* is the junction with State 153.

Right on State 153 across the Wisconsin River to MOSINEE (Ind., *mosinig,* moose), 0.3 *m.* (1,154 alt., 1,229 pop.), another village almost completely dependent upon the paper-making industry. Right of the bridge is the power dam and below it the rapids of Little Bull Falls; L. are the mills. Almost all the inhabitants here work in the mills, breathing throughout their lives the heavy, dank smell of the sulphite paper-making process.

After pursuing an almost straight course across the level drainage basin of the Wisconsin River, US 51 enters the central sandy plain. Farms appear poor here, and the ragged, jack-pine forest closes in upon the highway once more. Roughly following the course of the river, US 51 swings through KNOWLTON, 21.5 *m.* (1,121 alt., 225 pop.), former stopping place for loggers and rafters, today shrunk to a gas station, a handful of stores, a sandwich stand. Many fences along the road here are built of logs that are being seasoned before taken to the "square" in STEVENS POINT, 33.8 *m.* (1,085 alt., 13,623 pop.) (*see Tour 18*), at the junction with US 10 (*see Tour 18*).

PLOVER, 40.1 *m.* (1,076 alt., 326 pop.), is the ghost of a hustling lumber camp that, like so many of its rivals, once dreamed of becoming a great metropolis. Because John Batten's tavern was here, Plover was chosen in 1844 as the seat of Portage County; in 1849 a courthouse was built. Not until 1867 was the seat moved to Stevens Point.

Between Plover and Plainfield, US 51 runs between two very different types of country. East is the terminal moraine; west, the unglaciated driftless area; this middle land between is nondescript country, now rocky, now flat, typical of neither section.

South of PLAINFIELD, 60.3 m. (1,108 alt., 537 pop.), the highway swings into a flat sandy land, the State's chief rye-growing district; during 1929-33 Waushara, Marquette, and Adams Counties produced more than 900,000 bushels of rye. Farmers plant the rye in fall; before the first frost it generally grows from 2 to 4 inches high. After lying buried all winter under the snow, the grain comes up in early spring and matures by midsummer.

The University of Wisconsin maintains one of its seven experimental farms near HANCOCK, 67.5 *m.* (1,088 alt., 420 pop.), where it studies crop growth and fertilization methods for this sandy loam soil. The Conservation Commission is also concerned with soil erosion here, for the wind has free sweep over the flat sand plain. Recently strips of pines have been planted, and by 1941 it is expected that these windbreaks will be large enough to "nail down" the soil. Farmers must cooperate with the commission, which provides nursery trees free for the planting (*see Natural Setting*).

At 73.2 *m.* ROCHE A CRIS MOUND appears faintly (R), and on the clearest days FRIENDSHIP MOUND can be seen, both rising like ships of stone far across the plain.

WESTFIELD, 85.5 *m.* (856 alt., 769 pop.), a pleasant and shady village, is a "going-through place" for vacationists. Men and women in shorts and gay bandanas hurry through in summer; in winter come muffled hunters with their shaggy dogs bound for the deer country. North of the railroad is a STATE FISH HATCHERY; at the filling station on the bend of the road is a pool of trout and giant goldfish.

At 92.5 *m.* is the junction with State 23 (*see Tour 5A*).

ENDEAVOR, 101.2 *m.* (781 alt., 405 pop.), in the heart of the sand country, was fathered by the Reverend R. L. Cheney, who established a revival camp here in the 1890's. Later he decided that his tent camp offered an ideal site for a Christian Endeavor academy. On a hill overlooking the roadway he built Cheney Hall, which in its 23 years of existence sent out 94 graduates, "missionaries, pastors, teachers, businessmen, a noble body, positively contributing to the bettering of the world after the program of Christ." Among students there was to be no "use of intoxicating liquors, profane or low language, tobacco or cigarettes, attendance upon a public dance and gambling of any sort," and the Sabbath was to be observed strictly by quiet and devotion to prayer. Cheney Hall still stands though the academy was removed in 1913; Endeavor remains a small farm town that started in the days when the village and the academy grew as one.

PORTAGE, 113.2 *m.* (785 alt., 6,308 pop.) (*see Tour 21*) is at the junction with US 16 (*see Tour 21*). Between Portage and a point at 116.3 *m.* US 51 and US 16 are one route.

A blue sign, 124.1 *m.,* indicates that US 51 here follows the route of the old MILITARY ROAD (*see Tour 23*), built in 1835 between Fort Howard, at Green Bay, and Fort Crawford, at Prairie du Chien. Southward the landscape changes: the long flat stretch of a sand plain is succeeded by rolling hills and valleys planted to grain and corn. Farmhouses are set deep in shade between hill crests splashed with tawny sunlight.

POYNETTE, 125.1 *m.* (845 alt., 672 pop.), once a fur-trading post, is now a "Saturday town," to which farmers come weekly to sell their produce and buy sufficient "store goods" for another seven days.

Left from Poynette on a dirt road to the STATE EXPERIMENTAL GAME AND FUR FARM (*visitors welcome, guides*), 1.8 *m.,* maintained by the Wisconsin Conservation Commission for the propagation of birds, game, and fur-bearing animals. Deer, fox, raccoon, otter, mink, karakul sheep, pheasants and other birds are bred and raised under close observation to determine what conditions are best suited to their needs. For the study and control of contagious disease, autopsies are performed on dead birds and animals; sick animals are segregated in a quarantine section. Experiments have been made in mating pure-bred karakul rams with grade ewes for the production of Persian lamb fur, with a view to the possibility of raising such sheep in the brushy cutover.

Black raccoons are raised and released in the woods to mate with the native Wisconsin gray raccoon; from the hybrid offspring has come a pelt of greater value than that of either parent. Other game animals and birds are raised for liberation throughout hunting areas. Over 1,000 black raccoons were released during the 1937 season, while more than 175,000 pheasants were produced on the farm.

The Experimental Game and Fur Farm, as established in 1934, consisted of 150 acres; in 1937, 133 acres were added. One of the largest and best equipped institutions of its kind, it has a lecture room, feed farm, feed and equipment building, refrigeration plant and storage warehouse, slaughter house, bunk-house, carpenter shop, machine shed, and a chemical and pathological laboratory. A zoo is planned so that visitors may see the animals and birds without disturbing those in the breeding sections.

At 126 *m.* a small sign (R) marks the JOHN MUIR VIEW, a prospect that the renowned naturalist enjoyed as a boy.

US 51 reaches the crest of the Upper Magnesian Cuesta, 128.3 *m.*, and begins to descend the gradual backslope, whose rich black loam indicates limestone parent rock. Here is one of the rich agricultural belts in Wisconsin; farms are large and prosperous, well-developed and systematically cropped to produce tobacco, peas, corn, and small grain.

At 130.6 *m.* is the junction with State 60 (*see Tour 22*); between this junction and a point at 132.7 *m.* US 51 and State 60 are one route.

At 141.9 *m.* LAKE MENDOTA (R) sparkles in the distance, with the white capitol dome gleaming above the trees blanketing Madison.

At 148.2 *m.* is the junction with US 151 (*see Tour 6*); between this point and a many-cornered street intersection, 149.9 *m.*, US 51 and US 151 are one route. Here US 51 turns L. and skirts Madison.

Right from the many-cornered intersection on US 151 (E. Washington Ave.) to the center of MADISON, 3.7 *m.* (859 alt., 57,899 pop.) (*see Madison*).

Madison is at the junction with US 12 (*see Tour 19*), US 14 (*see Tour 20*), US 18 (*see Tour 23*), and US 151 (*see Tour 6*).

Section c. MADISON to ILLINOIS LINE; 57.5 m., US 51

US 51 turns L. from the many-cornered intersection, 0 *m.*, on Winnebago St., which it follows to the junction with Atwood Ave.; R. on Atwood Ave. At 3 *m.* the highway follows the shore of Lake Monona through a pleasant shady stretch of fields and meadows, past the MISSION OF NORBERTINE FATHERS (R), 3.1 *m.*, the MONONA FARM (L), maintained by the Quaker Oats Company as a demonstration project, and the MONONA GOLF COURSE (L), 3.6 *m.*

At 5.1 *m.* is the junction with US 12 (*see Tour 19*) and US 18 (*see Tour 23*). Between this junction and a point at 6.1 *m.* US 51, US 12, and US 18 are one route.

At 5.6 *m.* US 51 cuts through the end of a slight ridge; all around the land is low and marshy, as unproductive now as when Black Hawk and his hungry Sauk passed through here in 1832 after flight along the Indian trail from Beloit. For years all of the southern tribes used this trail; as late as 1850 they passed through every spring and fall, headed for their hunting and fishing grounds.

Through trees and summer cottages at 7.6 *m.* appears LAKE WAUBESA, one of the Four Lakes. Old settlers called them by number: Kegonsa, First; Waubesa, Second; Monona, Third; and Mendota, Fourth. All are connected by the little Yahara River, 8.9 *m.,* whose north bank is crowded with cottages, fishing gear, flat-bottomed boats, and drying carp nets. At 11.8 *m.* is LAKE KEGONSA, tree-fringed and wide.

STOUGHTON, 17.8 *m.* (859 alt., 4,497 pop.), sloping down to the Yahara, has pleasant streets lined with drooping shade trees. In 1838 Daniel Webster bought a section of land here; in 1847 this same land was acquired by Luke Stoughton, for whom the city is named. Soon pioneers, attracted by water power and transportation possibilities, filtered in from New England. Though the railroad arrived in 1853, Stoughton's growth was slow.

Then in 1865 a local farm youth, 19-year-old T. G. Mandt, invested the whole of his $100 savings to found the first of the industrial enterprises to bear his name, the T. G. Mandt Wagon Company. Stoughton became known as the "Wagon City." This plant survived several fires and panics and three reorganizations before it finally went into receivership in 1936 under the name of the New Stoughton Company. At the sale held in connection with the receivership, the city made a futile bid of $25,000 to keep alive its oldest enterprise.

Mandt had lost control of his first factory in 1889. In 1896 he started another, the T. G. Mandt Vehicle Company, which was purchased by the Moline Plow Company in 1902. In the early twenties, when the Moline Plow Company closed its branch plant here and threatened to raze the property, Stoughton purchased the plant and machinery for $100,000. In 1926 the city leased most of this property to the Highway Trailer Company, which employs about 200 men at the peak of production. The Stoughton Cab and Body Company and the Stoughton Manufacturing Company are also housed in the former Mandt buildings.

Three of every four citizens of Stoughton are of Norwegian stock, and many residents still speak the mother tongue. The main Norwegian immigration to this locality occurred about 1870; for several years bewildered newcomers descended almost daily from the train and trudged through dusty streets to the homes of fellow countrymen.

Annual *lutefisk* suppers are held in the Norwegian churches, and people come from miles around to eat the flaky fish. The meal usually begins with *fruktsuppe,* a soup made of raisins, prunes, grapes, and dried apples, thickened with sago and flavored with cinnamon. For those who do not like *lutefisk,* there are *fiskeboller* (fish balls) and *kaöppboller* (meat balls). New boiled potatoes fill huge bowls on the heavily laden tables. *Lefse, knakkebröd* and *flatbröd* are the breads;

lyngon berries are the relish. For desert there is usually *flötegröt* (a cream pudding), *risentrö gröt* (a rice pudding), or *kräm* (fruit custard), with *kringla* (coffee cake), and several varieties of cookies such as *pepperkakar*. Plump and beaming matrons insist that guests ever devour more, apologizing the while for a scarcity of food on groaning tables.

ALBION, 28.3 *m.* (200 pop.), a somnolent and tidy village, was settled in 1841 by English and Norwegian families. In 1853 Seventh Day Baptists from New York and Vermont arrived and almost immediately founded ALBION ACADEMY AND NORMAL INSTITUTE (R), 28.4 *m.* On the old campus, now a city park, two of the original buildings still stand, three-story brick structures with the stern and uncompromising lines associated with early American pedagogy. Coeducational, Albion Academy strictly forbade smoking, indulgence in liquor, games of chance and profane language. It opened and closed intermittently until 1901 when the Norwegian district synod acquired it and made it a Lutheran school. · In 1914 the academy closed its doors permanently.

Opposite the Academy is the SEVENTH DAY BAPTIST CHURCH, white, simple in design, with great high windows and doors. During the Civil War an excavation under the church was the meeting place of the local Union League, organized to ferret out and punish Confederate sympathizers. It also served, according to local tradition, as a station of the Underground Railroad.

EDGERTON, 32.7 *m.* (822 alt., 2,906 pop.), has, like Stoughton, passed the flush of youth and seems well content to settle down peacefully in gardened homes built simply for comfort. Although eastern speculators made a few land entries here in 1836, most of the land was owned by the Government as late as 1845. In 1854 a celebrating throng watched the first railroad locomotive chug up the tracks to Edgerton; later in the year the engine stalled in a snowbank and was ignominiously dragged out by four yoke of oxen.

Tobacco was first grown in this district in 1854, and the new crop proved so profitable that 500 cases were shipped east for sale in 1860. Tobacco companies sent buyers to the fields, production began seriously, and warehouses were erected. Today the tremendous importance of tobacco to Edgerton is reflected on the main street, lined for several blocks with tobacco warehouses, immense yellow-brick structures. In the surrounding area are small tobacco fields of bushy, broad-leafed plants. To divert the strength of the plant to the leaves, the pale bell-shaped blossoms are removed before the seeds are formed; young shoots that will not develop fully are clipped in an operation known as "suckering." At harvest time the stalks are cut near the ground, laid out to wilt, then strung on laths for curing in TOBACCO SHEDS, such as those at 33 *m..* Scattered through the district, these buildings are rarely painted, alternate gray strips of siding are hinged to permit controlled ventilation for curing. In December the tobacco is baled, sold to buyers, and stored in Edgerton warehouses.

INDIAN FORD, 35.5 *m.,* a handful of shacks and houses, crouches at either end of a bridge spanning the Rock River. Below the bridge the river pours in a white froth over a low dam. For centuries wild animals came to ford the river at the shallow flats here; the Indians followed their path, and later the white men. In 1837 William Foster started a ferry, and the settlement, first known as Foster's Ferry, was successively called Morse's Landing, Fulton Center, and Indian Ford. In 1860 Foster constructed an 85-foot steamboat, *Star of the West.* Soon he quarreled with the Milwaukee and Mississippi R. R. when he demanded that it build a drawbridge over the Rock River in order that his boat might pass. In the midst of the wrangle *Star of the West* mysteriously disappeared; years later its hulk was found at the bottom of the river, laden with stones.

US 51 climbs out of the river valley and continues southward to JANESVILLE, 46 *m.* (801 alt., 21,628 pop.), industrial city on the Rock River. In the eastern part of town, about the courthouse, old mansions reflect the wealth of their owners. Still farther east toward the city limits are numerous small houses, modern as today's newspaper, equipped with air-conditioning and labor-saving devices. West of the river are the workers' houses. Flanking all the streets are the gracious shade trees that early brought Janesville the name of the "Bower City."

Janesville indirectly owes its founding to the Black Hawk War, for the praise of soldiers returning home advertised its fertile valley. Hearing of the new country, Henry F. Janes, pioneer and visionary, reached the Rock River in 1836 and carved his initials on a tree at the junction of present Main and Milwaukee Sts. In 1837 he started a ferry and built a tavern on the east bank. When a petition was made for a post office, the new settlement was named for Janes, who became the first postmaster. In 1839, however, feeling uncomfortably crowded in the growing settlement, Janes moved his family westward, giving his name to Janesville, Iowa, and Janesville, Minn. By 1849 he had reached the west coast and written to the Janesville *Gazette:* ". . . I have been constantly working westward till the nasty Pacific has made a stop to farther progress in that direction. . . . and yet the sun sets west of me, and my wife positively refuses to go to the Sandwich Islands."

Janesville grew rapidly. Stagecoach lines were routed through the village; flat-bottomed boats propelled by horses on treadmills plied the shallow Rock River; three steamboats came up from the Mississippi to dock at the Janesville landing. The tavern became an institution, posting such regulations as:

> Four pence a night for a bed,
> Six pence with supper,
> No more than five to sleep in one bed,
> Organ grinders to sleep in Wash House,
> No dogs allowed upstairs,
> No beer allowed in the kitchen,
> No Razor Grinders or Tinkers taken in.

By 1845 there were 817 persons in Janesville, and the saws in Charles Stephens' year-old mill bit hungrily into logs floated down the river to serve the building boom. The village had a single drug store which offered such remedies as "Fresh Soda Crackers for Invalids" and a "Small Supply of the Finest Swedish Leeches for Bleeding."

Depending on its fertile hinterland to buy its products and provide the necessary labor for its small industries, Janesville grew steadily until in 1920 it had a population of 13,000. Meantime, in 1919, the General Motors Corporation had come here, bought the old Janesville Machine Company, and begun the manufacture of tractors. The character of the city began to change, slowly at first, then more rapidly as it lost its homogeneity and compactness. Transient factory workers converged upon the city from all parts of the country. With housing facilities inadequate, a building boom developed and real estate prices rose sharply.

General Motors discontinued the manufacture of tractors in the early 1920's, but established a Fisher Body and a Chevrolet plant here in 1922. By 1925 half of Janesville's industrial workers were employed by General Motors; the prosperity of the city had become inextricably involved with the fortunes of the corporation. After the depression struck in 1929, relief costs mounted steadily for two years; in September 1932 came the blow the city had most feared: General Motors closed its two Janesville plants. By 1933 three of every four workers in the larger local factories had lost their jobs. As more and more came on the relief rolls, county relief expenditures jumped to $628,000, an 11-fold advance in two years. After a 15-month lay-off, General Motors resumed operations here and gradually expanded, and from 1935 to late 1937 an all-time peak was reached in the number of men employed. In late 1937 and 1938, another business recession occurred. During this period, however, employment did not drop as low as previously but work hours per man were considerably reduced.

Next largest employer in Janesville is the Parker Pen Company, incorporated in 1892 by George Parker, employing 800 men in 1937. The city also manufactures punch presses, cotton batting, cotton goods, woolen goods, shades and awnings.

Through the center of the city tumbles the shallow Rock River, held in its bed by riprapped walls of stone. At Monterey Ford, a pioneer crossing now spanned by the bridge over which US 51 crosses, business buildings have been erected on piers over the water. One block south at Court and Main Sts. is COURTHOUSE PARK, on a steep hillside. Here a mob gathered in 1855 to lynch David F. Maberry for the robbery and murder of a lumberjack who had given him a ride. By the following morning the tree on which he was hanged had been hacked to pieces by souvenir hunters; part of the cell occupied by Maberry is in the MUSEUM (*open to public upon request*), on the second floor of the PUBLIC LIBRARY, Main St. and St. Lawrence Ave. Here, too, are Indian relics, old books from New England, and a "draft wheel," used for drawing names during the Civil War.

In and about Janesville are reminders of three women. At Johnstown Center, 7 miles east on County A, Ella Wheeler Wilcox (1850-1919), who wrote *Poems of Passion,* lived in childhood. One mile west of US 51 on Milwaukee St. is the home of Carrie Jacobs Bond, composer of "A Perfect Day," and 3 miles south is the former home of Frances E. Willard (1839-98), ardent feminist and founder and leader of the W. C. T. U.

Janesville is at the junction with US 14 (*see Tour 20*) and State 11 (*see Tour 24*).

South of the city the land is flat, rich, and well cultivated, with thin lines of windbreak checkering the plain to the far horizon. US 51 veers R. along the Rock River, deceivingly well behaved in summer but a terror in late winter and early spring when it goes on its annual rampage, flooding the flats on both sides, heaping up cakes of ice almost to the road. US 51 follows its winding course into Beloit.

At 55.4 *m.* (L) is the largest of Beloit's many industrial units, the FAIRBANKS-MORSE COMPANY PLANT, a great sprawling factory manufacturing Diesel engines and the Fairbanks-Morse scales. Here on a spot marked by an inscribed boulder Abraham Lincoln, then captain of militia, camped during the Black Hawk War in 1832. Across the river is BIG HILL, today a city park, where Black Hawk's scouts kept watch. On an electioneering tour in 1859 Lincoln retraveled the old war trail and located landmarks along the way; at Beloit he spoke in HANCHETT'S HALL (*marked*), Broad and State Sts., where he declared "the fundamental principle of the Republican Party is the hatred of the institution of slavery."

BELOIT, 55.5 *m.* (743 alt., 23,611 pop.), is at the confluence of Turtle Creek and the Rock River. As early as 1824 Joseph Thibault, a French Canadian, traded with the Winnebago here. When the Indians were removed westward after the Black Hawk War, Thibault sold to Caleb Blodgett of Vermont as much of his claim as could be encompassed by "three looks," a standard Indian unit of measurement. In 1837 Dr. Horace White, agent of the New England Emigrating Company, bought one third of Blodgett's tract; in the same year a large part of Colebrook, New Hampshire, moved here bag and baggage.

Known successively as Turtle, Blodgett's Settlement, and New Albany, the village was given the name of Beloit in 1857. In 1886 when times were hard and "Beloit was whistling to keep its courage up," local businessmen formed an association to publicize the city through a folder, intimating that Beloit was not only beautiful, but also willing to make concessions to new businesses. In 1887 the association brought to the city the Berlin Machine Works, now the Yates-American Machine Company, which in 1937 employed 500 workers in the manufacture of 200 different types of woodworking machines. The Williams Engine Works, with Charles Hosmer Morse its sales manager, came to the city in 1889 when citizens raised $10,000 to encourage development and donated 10 acres of land. Later this concern combined with the Eclipse Wind Engine Company to become the Fairbanks, Morse Company (*see above*).

In 1935 some 60 industrial plants in Beloit paid $7,350,000 in wages to 6,100 workers and produced wares valued at more than $29,000,000. These products included pumps, stokers, home water plants, light plants, automobile radiators, shoes, refrigerating units, X-ray tubes, powdered milk, farm engines, electric brakes, fireworks and hosiery. The Beloit Iron Works has built more than 600 paper-making machines since 1858; each of these machines is almost 400 feet long and so large that a train of 65 cars is required to ship it.

Beloit early gained the reputation of being "refined, cultured, and elegant," for members of the New England Emigrating Company had resolved "to unite in sustaining institutions of science and religion and all the adjuncts that contribute to happiness, thrift and the elevation of society." Soon after their arrival they built a church and chartered Beloit Seminary, a coeducational school. In 1847 the Congregational Church founded BELOIT COLLEGE, Bushnell and College Sts., on the east riverbank. Two professors were hired at a salary of $600 a year, but their contract contained the proviso "if we can raise it." The early buildings gave no architectural unity to the campus, for each was in a different style. Later buildings are Georgian Colonial, with slight adaptations. The college has approximately 400 students and an exchange professorship with Harvard. One of its strongest departments is that of anthropology and archeology; an alumnus, Roy Chapman Andrews, writer and explorer for the American Museum of Natural History, has become famous in these fields.

On the campus is the LOGAN MUSEUM (*free; open during school year from 8:30 a.m. to 12 m. and 1:30 p.m. to 5 p.m. Mon. through Fri.; 8:30 a.m. to 12 m. Sat.; 2 p.m. to 4:30 p.m. Sun.*), originally planned to depict the culture of the American Indian but later expanded to present a record of prehistoric man. More than 1,000,000 aboriginal artifacts are displayed here, centered about the extensive Rust collection, donated by the founder of the museum, the late Dr. Frank G. Logan, famous art collector, trustee, benefactor, and honorary president of the Art Institute of Chicago, and founder of the chair of anthropology and evolution at Beloit College. The most interesting object in the collection is the Aurignacian necklace fashioned by a Cro-Magnon craftsman 35,000 years ago. Twelve murals by John W. Norton (1876-1934) illustrate man's development from earliest times; in 1935 Dr. Logan presented other murals of American Indians by Elmer C. Winterberg. The many Indian mounds in the vicinity (22 on the campus alone) have stimulated local interest and the study of anthropology and ethnology.

At 57.5 *m.* is the Illinois Line, where Beloit, Wis., merges imperceptibly into South Beloit, Illinois.

Tour 8

Ashland — Park Falls — Marshfield — Wisconsin Rapids — Wisconsin Dells; 286 *m.* State 13.

Soo Line parallels route between Ashland and Wisconsin Rapids.
Asphalt and concrete roadbed.
Accommodations throughout; complete recreational facilities at Wisconsin Dells.

State 13 drops southward from Lake Superior through north-central Wisconsin, paralleling the tracks of one of the first northern railroads. The route traverses a great expanse of cutover forest, still raw with the wounds of timber saws and forest fires, where settlers have tried again and again to smooth the rough stony soil into fields, to build homes for themselves. Many have grown discouraged and abandoned the land, leaving their empty shacks to gape at the passing traveler.

Most of the cities and villages along the way grew up about sawmills or railroad stations. The age and character of each depend upon when the railroads first came and upon what resources remained after the loggers had gone. Some have turned to quarrying and shipping, others to dairy industries and recreation, others to small-scale wood industries. Few signs remain to indicate their original roles.

Section a. ASHLAND to ABBOTSFORD; 149.2 m., State 13

ASHLAND, 0 *m.* (666 alt., 10,622 pop.), lies on a sunken plain, with streets sweeping in a long semicircle around the southern shore of Chequamegon Bay. From December until April the windows of Front Street glitter with cold reflections from the frozen harbor. When the ice breaks and snow trickles off the docks, ships appear on the Lake Superior horizon to the north, bringing heavy cargoes of coal and raw materials for the factories of the Middle West, carrying away great blocks of gabbro (black granite) or iron for the steel mills of America. Clouds of smoke from steamer funnels drift in the sky above the brownish waters of the bay, and the city hears battered old smacks creaking at the docks. Four railroads, one from Duluth and three from Chicago, have terminals here with facilities for dumping directly from flatcars to ship decks. When the harbor is open, all is rumble and big business along the water front. Back in the depths of the city, however, life is more quiet, fanned by pleasant lake breezes.

In the seventeenth century a sand spit stretched across the mouth of Chequamegon Bay. On their second voyage into the western country in 1659, Pierre Esprit Radisson and Médard Chouart, Sieur de Groseilliers, first white men to penetrate beyond the Great Lakes, had to be portaged across the spit by Indians. Paddling down the bay, the Frenchmen landed on the western shore, somewhere between Ashland and Washburn. Here they built a rude fort of stakes and boughs, presumably near the mouth of Whittlesey Creek.

In 1665, four years after Ménard, the first missionary to Wisconsin, had visited Chequamegon Bay, Father Claude Allouez erected a chapel of bark, probably not far from the site of the fort. He labored fruitlessly among the Indian bands that had come here to escape the fury of the Iroquois until 1669 when he relinquished the mission to Father Marquette and set out for the Green Bay region to establish St. Francis Xavier (*see Tour 2*). After two years of zealous but unsuccessful work here, Marquette closed the mission and journeyed to the Straits of Mackinac, where he founded the mission of St. Ignace. In 1673 he and Joliet set out from St. Ignace to explore the Mississippi River (*see Tour 19*).

Almost 200 years later, in 1854, Asaph Whittlesey rounded the bay in a rowboat, landed, and built a cabin on what is now the corner of 18th Avenue and Front Street. As the first tree he felled was a great ash, he wrote to Washington to gain approval of the name Ashland. Isolated in a pine wilderness, the little settlement opened negotiations in Chicago for a railroad to provide an outlet for immense resources of timber and brownstone. Rumors that railroad surveys were under way brought an influx of settlers in 1871 and 1872; 200 buildings were hastily built; some 1,300 men, working on the Wisconsin Central R. R., made Ashland their headquarters.

One morning in December 1872 the foreman in charge of construction near-by received orders "to shut down all work on the line, pay off and discharge all the men, and transport them and all others who desired to leave, out of the country." With more than a thousand people directly dependent on railroad work, Ashland immediately became tense. Besides, no boats could enter the frozen bay, and there were few wagons and no railroads. A journey on foot to Superior, 80 miles away, seemed to offer the only escape from starvation.

Plans were made for a mass removal. When delay developed at the paymaster's office, some of the workers tried to storm the place and seize their money. Leveled revolvers held them off while the paymaster and his force fled in a wagon. Later the checks were peacefully distributed and the scare proved unfounded. The company had merely been debating whether or not to finish the expensive construction of 60 bridges in the final 30-mile stretch of roadbed. On June 2, 1877, Chequamegon Bay and the harbors on Lake Michigan were finally bound together by bands of steel, and regular train service began on the Wisconsin Central R. R.

The city of Ashland boomed. Brownstone quarrying started on a big scale, and sawmills were busier than they have been at any time since. Geologic surveys in 1849 had revealed deposits of iron ore in the high Penokee-Gogebic Range that crosses Wisconsin into the Upper Peninsula of Michigan. "Clean hematic ore" was sighted under the roots of a fallen tree, and prospectors began combing the wilderness for similar deposits. By 1886 the whole north country was seized with mining fever, and fabulous amounts were paid for a few acres of unproved ground. Exchanges were set up at Milwaukee, Hurley, and Ashland to buy and sell mining stock. Every acre of land within a mile of the iron range was pitted and gashed with holes, ore was hauled overland to the bay for shipment, and the road between Ashland and Ironwood, Michigan, became one of the most heavily traveled in Wisconsin. People of Ashland set up small uncomfortable cots in their homes to take care of the overflow from hotels and charged hotel prices. First settlers sold their properties to outsiders breathless to pay whatever was asked, sight unseen.

The crash came late in 1887; stock prices and real estate values were reduced to reasonable levels. The sawmills, strung along the bay front from Brettings to Fish Creek, continued operations until the forests gave out about 1900. Brownstone quarrying has also decreased. During the first half of the 1890's a half dozen quarries were busy providing reddish blocks for the building of offices and houses throughout the Middle West; now only a few pits are sporadically active.

As lumbermen and mill hands moved farther west, leaving their log carriers to rot at the wharves, Ashland began to establish industries not dependent upon exhaustible natural resources. Today it has a large paper mill, manufacturing toilet tissue and napkins, a large black-gabbro polishing plant, shipping products as far east as New York and as far west as the Rocky Mountains. Most important, however, is its natural harbor. Millions of tons of iron ore from the Gogebic Range are shipped annually to the lower lakes. Through the three large coal docks move hundreds of tons of Ohio and Pennsylvania coal, bound for northern Wisconsin, Minnesota, and Michigan, for North and South Dakota and Montana. And in the harbor lie huge rafts of pulpwood, towed across from Canada for transhipment to the paper mills of Central Wisconsin.

Ashland has a reputation among Wisconsin municipalities for its many musical groups, among them a Boy's Band of 268 pieces, a 50-piece symphony orchestra, an American Legion Fife and Drum Corps, a community choral club of 100 voices, and a local North Woods Band, which appears in checkered flannel shirts and corduroy trousers as it parades playing the old songs beloved by lumbermen and railroad men. The favorites include "Casey Jones," "How Dry I Am," "I Been Working on the Railroad," "My Name Is Yon Yonson (I Come From Wisconsin)." Music has a prominent place in the curriculum of NORTHLAND COLLEGE, Ellis Ave. and 14th St.

In Ashland is the junction with US 63 (see Tour 9), US 2 (see Tour 14), and upper State 13 (see Tour 14A).

As State 13 leaves the thinning suburbs of Ashland, the blue and irregular summit of the Gogebic Range looms to the south beyond the greener, more level crest of the Keweenawan Range. The Keweenawan contains layer upon layer of ancient crystallized rock, heaving out of the flat upland in a long slope, which the highway ascends. Close by the road among the little sheltering knobs and higher hills are scraggy farm huts, some with no curtains in their windows, others with balls of rags stuffed into broken panes, all with sagging fences and yards cluttered with rusty and broken machinery. Like all submarginal farms of upper Wisconsin, they show plainly the signs of struggle.

State 13 curves down into the broad interval between the Keweenawan and Gogebic Ranges, cuts through small popple shooting up silver and green from low undergrowth, and enters MELLEN, 35.4 m. (1,242 alt., 1,629 pop.), at the base of the Gogebic Range. Northland forests crowd up close to its tilted streets; not far off among the trees are foaming streams filled with trout and other game fishes. During the winter Mellen is heaped with bulky snowdrifts that now and again shut out the farmer trade for days at a time. Lying as it does on the flat below Penokee Gap, the town receives the full force of every storm on the upland; giant snow plows battle with the drifts 24 hours a day, guided at night by powerful headlights shining through veils of flying snow. Paul Bunyan's "big snows" are a fact here.

The promise of minerals and the coming of the Wisconsin Central in 1886 brought the first settlers to Mellen, who named it Iron City even before they built their houses. Ten years later a fur tannery and several sawmills were constructed here. Today Mellen ships much iron ore, and has a gabbro quarry, a creamery, and veneer, boxwood, and lumber mills.

Left from Mellen on County K to the AMERICAN BLACK GRANITE COMPANY QUARRIES, 1.7 m., from which 2,000 to 2,500 tons of crushed black gabbro are shipped each month. Drilling is done with a compressed-air jack hammer and is the most grueling and highly paid work in the quarry. The stone masses, 8 to 10 feet square and from 4 to 6 feet thick, are split to any size required. A big crane in the center of the quarry lifts 100-ton blocks on railroad cars. There is no waste, for all gabbro fragments are crushed and used for terrazzo flooring. Monument stone is shipped to Ashland to be dressed and polished in the factory there.

Rounding a bend, County K passes through the cutover and brush of the MELLEN PUBLIC SCHOOL FOREST, 1.9 m., 80 acres of second-growth timber. This is one of Wisconsin's 151 school forests, ranging in size from 40 to 320 acres, used by school children as conservation laboratories.

The road dips sharply to enter COPPER FALLS STATE PARK, 3.5 m., where foot trails lead through a dense tangle of hemlock and hardwoods to the Bad River, which here plunges over the Keweenawan Trap Ledge in a tumult of copper, yellow, and white foam. In winter the far-flung spray coats the surrounding trees with such a thick layer of yellowed ice that they bend with the weight. The foot trail crosses a bridge over a 150-foot gorge and branches right to BROWNSTONE FALLS, where Tyler's Fork joins the Bad River in a 75-foot leap.

Mellen is at the junction with State 77 (see Tour 7). State 13 swings westward with the railroad and passes through Penokee Gap in the Gogebic Range, here narrow, high, and choked with brush, as it is throughout most of its 80-mile length. Back from the road the hills are scarred with grass-covered heaps of rock and dirt shoveled out years ago by prospectors sounding the range for iron and copper. Decaying cabins, big and little, stand beside yawning holes and rotting scaffoldings; scattered in the surrounding brush are the battered buckets and hand winches once used for hoisting the dirt above the surface.

During the past 50 years millions of tons of iron ore have been taken from the long elliptical hills of the Gogebic Range. The western-most end, known as the Penokee, was named by surveyor Charles Whittlesey, who was sent by the Government in 1849 to examine the belt of iron-bearing slates in this region. He called it Pewabic (Ind., iron), but the compositor misread the name and set it in type as Penokie. It has also been suggested that Penokee is merely a corruption of *opinikan* (Ind., wild potato ground).

From the summit of the range the view to the south reveals a vast and monotonous expanse of level treetops, broken here and there by small lakes glittering in pine swamps, or by great charred patches filled with blackened tamarack and hemlock. The few farmers who have broken the stony brown soil raise some grain; corn seldom attains more than a stunted 3- or 4-foot growth. The highway, walled in by tangled cutover, passes through small settlements, such as CAYUGA (Ind., the place where locusts are taken out), 45.1 *m.* (1,457 alt., 100 pop.), and GLIDDEN, 52.7 *m.* (1,521 alt., 610 pop.). Now and then, as in the village of BUTTERNUT, 65.4 *m.* (1,504 alt., 604 pop.), a lone fire tower appears like a giant box kite in the sky, guarding miles of second-growth cedar and hemlock, stump prairies, and bare wastes of fire-stricken timber. Along the road great piles of stones collected with the aid of a stone boat, a wooden sled with heavy runners, have been heaped up in the fields or about the foot of telephone poles, partly for support, partly for protection against the many little fires that run stealthily through the slashed underbrush.

PARK FALLS, 72.3 *m.* (1,494 alt., 3,036 pop.), at the intersection of the Flambeau River and the Soo Line Railroad, is an old lumbering city which has survived the exhaustion of the great pine forests. "A child of the railroad and the lumbering industry," it grew out of a lumber camp and sawmill settlement which sprang up here in the early 1870's. With the decline of lumbering, about 1900, Park Falls, unlike its neighbors, developed a flourishing pulp and paper industry, which has given it a slow but constant growth. Today it is still a practically "one-industry" town, with a large paper manufacturing company, a tie mill, and two sawmills. In recent years Park Falls has also become increasingly conscious of its possibilities as the center of a recreation area.

FIFIELD, 76.8 *m.* (1,464 alt., 310 pop.) (*see Tour 15*), is at the junction with State 70 (*see Tour 15*). Left here lies the CHEQUA-MEGON NATIONAL FOREST, out of which come many Christmas trees. Every tree taken from a national forest is tied with a red tag bearing the inscription: "This tree brings a Christmas message from the great outdoors. Its cutting was not destructive but gave needed room for neighboring trees to grow faster and better. It was cut under the supervision of the United States forest service from a crowded stand on the .... national forest."

Tall fire towers rise above the forest, and along the road are other evidences of the watchful care now given the cutover lands. Government crews are clearing out the old stumps and fallen trees that choke growth; at regular intervals appear signs reading, "Prevent Forest Fires"; furrows are ploughed through the forest to form firebreaks. The cutover serves the Federal and State Governments as a great laboratory to study the problems of the timberland.

When the railroad first hewed its way through this region towards Ashland, it needed cheap labor for the task; logging companies at the same time were seeking buyers for stripped timberlands. Both railroad and lumber companies sought workers and settlers on the docks of New York and among the peasants of Europe; they sent out agents and thousands of pamphlets urging poor people to come to Wisconsin. They advertised that "the country along the Wisconsin Central railroad possesses all the advantages necessary to make it easy for immigrants, even those without means"; that crops could be obtained by merely harrowing; that by seasonal work in northern lumber camps the new settler could earn enough money to buy a farm.

The railroad company provided houses in which 75 to 100 persons were accommodated free of charge for two weeks. The settlers attracted were largely Bavarians and Bohemians. Mail boxes along the highway bear such names as Kolnick, Valiga, Yborsky, indicating the Bohemian ancestry of those who live in the small houses back among the trees.

PHILLIPS, 91 m. (1,456 alt., 1,901 pop.), was founded in 1874 and named for a president of the Wisconsin Central R. R. White pine grew tall near Phillips then; but in 1894 a great fire ravaged the district and left only 13 buildings standing in the settlement. Rebuilt to its former size within a year, Phillips held a great celebration, which was so successful that for several years the city's rebirth was commemorated annually on July 27.

The Bohemian strain in the town's population is revealed on store fronts, in membership lists of lodges, churches, and schools. The LIBRARY has books written in Czech; certain restaurants offer *kolaces,* sauerkraut, dumplings, and other Bohemian foods. Except during national festivals, the Bohemians speak English and dress like other citizens, having set aside their bright clothes for more conventional garb. Many are employed in the local flooring and fiber mill and the wood-products mill, which turns out a popple fiber that looks much like shredded wheat and is used for paper boxes, corrugated papers, and incubators.

Between Phillips and Prentice, State 13 clears a swath through jumbled miles of cutover, in which wagon and foot trails begin nowhere and end nowhere, cutting across the road at right angles and disappearing in green and black mazes of trees. Some are as old as the first white settlements back in the brush, so well worn by pioneer horses, wagons, and boots that nothing has grown on them since. Many houses appear germ-ridden and badly insulated; some lack floors and beds. What little income the farmers here earn comes from primitive roadside stands, small milk checks, or scraggly potato crops.

At intervals back in the woods stand the empty ramshackle sheds of ginseng growers, who but a few years ago were carefully watching the plant through its long cycle from seed to maturity. China bought Wisconsin ginseng in large quantities up to the invasion of Manchuria in 1931 by the Japanese, who have forced the Chinese to buy Manchurian ginseng exclusively. Now the crop, whose culture had spread all over Wisconsin from its native habitat in the Driftless Area has no market whatever.

PRENTICE, 114.8 m. (1,542 alt., 437 pop.), where the old north-south and the new east-west lines of the Soo intersect, is a single long main street. Its population has dwindled since the day its two tanneries burned down soon after they were built. The Prentice Cooperative Creamery on the banks of the Jump River indicates that State 13 is entering the northern dairy belt.

Prentice is at the junction with US 8 (*see Tour 16*). Between Prentice and Westboro the highway overlooks a wavering green monotony of forest, broken only by little wild morainic hills. Old black tree trunks standing high above the popple indicate where fires crossed 20 to 25 years ago.

WESTBORO, 119.5 m. (1,504 alt.), headquarters for fishermen in the nearby lakes and streams and hunters in the Chequamegon National Forest, has a small veneer factory producing berry boxes and crates from maple and birch. Fishing is particularly good in JAMES LAKE, E. of the village.

MEDFORD, 135.6 m. (1,410 alt., 1,918 pop.), built in terraces on a hill facing open green pasture country, has a large creamery, a box factory, a sash and door factory, a pea cannery, and claims the largest LITTLE PIG MARKET in the world. Squirming and squealing, pink and almost hairless, little pigs only a few weeks old are brought from the farms to be sold in the market and shipped in all directions.

The Wisconsin Central R. R. determined the site of the local court-house. An election was held in 1875 to choose between two offered sites. That offered by the railroad was overwhelmingly rejected. Work on the new courthouse had already begun when an injunction was suddenly issued forbidding further construction. "For some reason" that Medford could never quite understand, the courthouse was finally built where the Wisconsin Central wanted it.

Mennonites from a colony a short distance west of the town appear at times on Medford's streets—bearded men in wide-brimmed hats and homemade, ankle-length coats; women in voluminous dark dresses, the severity of their costumes brightened only by little white caps. The Mennonite colony covers about 36 square miles. Only necessary work is done on Sundays when German services, accompanied by hymn singing and Bible study, are held in private homes. The preacher is selected by lot, and any adult man is eligible. The Mennonite faith appears to stress simplicity, hard work, and a deep-seated pacifism. Ernest L. Meyer, Wisconsin writer (*see Literature*), has described the intensity of their pacifism during the World War in his book, *Hey Yellowbacks!*

Between Medford and Marshfield, the land becomes increasingly richer, although there are still wide stretches of cutover. Settled by pioneer loggers as early as 1840, Marathon County is a transitional area between the northern cutover and the central sandy plain.

STETSONVILLE, 139.2 m. (1,447 alt., 625 pop.), a prairie town, named for the pioneer who built the first sawmill on a pond here, still has a sawmill in operation, a tie mill, and a cheese factory that utilizes 10,000 pounds of milk daily. The village is populated largely by retired dairy farmers, many of them German Catholics and Lutherans.

ABBOTSFORD, 149.2 m. (1,422 alt., 781 pop.), still has many German families, descendants of the early loggers. One day of each month the entire village turns out to a free auction at which anything and everything, from vegetables to furniture, are sold by an auctioneer hired by Abbotsford storekeepers. Foot races and other contests help attract trade. In the village are a cooperative factory, making Colby and American cheeses, and a large milk condensery.

Abbotsford is at the junction with State 29 (*see Tour 17*).

Section b. *ABBOTSFORD to WISCONSIN DELLS; 136.8 m., State 13*

South of ABBOTSFORD, 0 m., State 13 is deep in the northern dairy belt, a pleasant open land whose economic life revolves around the squat cheese factories in cities and villages.

COLBY, 2.7 m. (1,355 alt., 849 pop.), once two settlements named Colby and Hull, was incorporated as a single community in 1891. Settlers occupied the region before the Civil War, during which twelve families hid in the heavy woods near by to escape being drafted and were discovered only when crews began construction of the road to Wausau. This district has given its name to Colby cheese, which is known throughout the United States, although its market centers in the Northwest.

A few small wooden houses scattered up and over a slope, and one restaurant fashioned from a cast-off railroad coach mark UNITY, 6.8 m. (1,333 alt., 319 pop.); while SPENCER, 13.6 m. (1,308 alt., 456 pop.), has only one large modern building, the red and white Trinity Lutheran Church. Its feed stores, farmers co-ops, theater, and lumber sheds are worn with use and age. Here the two main northern lines of the Soo divide, one branching toward Ashland, the other running in a long straight line toward Superior.

MARSHFIELD, 23.9 m. (1,271 alt., 8,778 pop.), sprinkled out on a flat green prairie, is a busy center of the northern dairy belt. The city is patterned as rigidly as a chessboard, and industries are as diverse as pawns, knights, bishops, queens, and kings. Many of its establishments handle milk and milk products, including casein and ice cream. Its factories manufacture veneer, steel and sheet-metal products, shoes, beekeepers' supplies, farm equipment, gloves, beer, butter tubs, and bedding for farmer markets over a wide radius. Smaller business houses line both sides of Central Avenue, Marshfield's broad and brilliantly lighted "White Way."

The present city is the second of two Marshfields. The first settlers, Louis Rivers and his brother Frank, came in 1868 and built a tavern to serve railroad construction gangs. By 1872 swaths had been cut through the forest, and the Wisconsin Central tracks passed directly in front of the Rivers' tavern door. Six years later a depot—an empty boxcar—stood shakily in the midst of a litter of stumps and felled trees. Marshfield had no main street as yet, not even a road; only a few trails wound their way among enormous pines, around boulders, through swamps, and over hills.

Gashed out of the forest near the center of the State, the settlement soon had other railroads—the Omaha, the Princeton, and branch lines. Little complicated engines bumped and fiercely chugged their way up grades and rattled around curves banked the wrong way at 30 and 40 miles an hour. Tall pine stumps, too tough to grub and too strongly rooted to be pulled with oxen or horses, were left to rot around the settlement; standing timber was burned carelessly. By 1887 Marshfield had a monster sawmill, a furniture factory, stave and hub factories, boiler works, harness shops, nine hotels, 19 saloons, and two newspapers—one in English, the other in German.

That year a great fire, caused by sparks from a locomotive, broke out in the lumber piles in the center of the city. Mill whistles screeched as a strong wind fanned the flames. Horse-drawn brass-cylindered engines galloped towards Marshfield from Stevens Point, Spencer, and other settlements; but hoses were burned off at hydrants, and wooden ladders quickly caught fire. By nightfall the greater part of Marshfield was smouldering in ashes, having burned steadily since noon.

"Thieves and thugs rushed into the city on all trains and the home gang was out in full force," wrote the local *Times* in a graphic account of the catastrophe. "During the raging of the fire there was no expressed grief—not a tear stained eye to be seen—everybody was intent on saving what little they could from the wreck, but when telegrams of condolence and offers of assistance began to come in, many a stout heart failed and tears fell from many an eye. No city on earth suffering such a dire calamity ever received such expressions of sympathy." . . . "Phoenix like we have come out of the ashes, with a full stock of Dry Goods, Groceries, Boots and Shoes, Yankee Notions &c. . . .—Adv."

Within a few years a second city had been built; wooden frame gave way to solid brick; cheese making and dairying replaced lumbering. Today per capita sales in Marshfield are larger than in any other city in the State with the exception of Madison. Wood industries are still represented by a factory in which Wisconsin birch, basswood, and maple are cut, boiled, barked, sawed, dried, and sanded into golden veneer panels. When working at capacity, the factory consumes 65,000 feet of logs a day. The casein warehouse represents a more quiet and typical Marshfield industry. Into this small plant, smelling constantly of cheese curds, come quantities of coagulated skim milk to be dried in narrow 40-foot tunnels and shipped to larger factories.

At 26.8 *m.* is the junction with US 10 (*see Tour 18*); between this junction and a point at 28.6 *m.,* State 13 and US 10 are one route.

The countryside sinks suddenly from pleasant dairy farms and fields to soggy marshland. Tamaracks form a jagged landscape, shot through with white vertical poles of rotted birch. Stretches of marsh hay border fields torn up by dynamite, left with rain-filled tadpole ponds and reddish-yellow heaps of earth.

PITTSVILLE, 57.6 *m.* (1,030 alt., 508 pop.), the exact geographical center of Wisconsin, is a small, dust-blown community that has dwindled considerably since its first years as a sawmill town. Here in late summer are held the council and festivities of a band of Winnebago, who dance in war paint and buckskins under a wigwam made of tree branches. Just a step from Pittsville's side streets is the quiet Yellow River.

Between Pittsville and Wisconsin Rapids the highway proceeds east and then south across swampy farmlands and patches of second-growth poplar and tall ragged pines. Greenish-blue fertilizer stands in piles just inside farmers' fences. Little shacks give way gradually to bigger ones, and then to frame houses, brick residences, stores, and factories as State 13 enters Wisconsin Rapids.

WISCONSIN RAPIDS, 74.7 *m.* (1,005 alt., 8,726 pop.), seat of Wood County, through which the Wisconsin River tumbles headlong, is noisy with the brawling of water and the booming of paper mills and factories. Pulpwood logs lie jammed in a runway above the dam, over which water spills to the rocks below. The banks upstream are crowded with smoky houses and factories, but downstream they are free, with wooded parks, a public swimming pool, and streets arched over by elms. North of the bridge is the LEFEBVRE HOUSE, First Ave. N., an old white frame building with simple New England lines. Now a studio, it was formerly a saloon from whose willow-lined terrace people used to watch the ferry chugging across the river.

Wisconsin Rapids was once two settlements, Centralia on the west river-bank, Grand Rapids on the east. One midnight in June 1880, after the villagers had gone to bed exhausted from fighting a fire the previous night, the river began to rise rapidly and soon a flood was raging through the swamp, taking out a hundred feet of railroad bed, two bridges, embankments, barns, outhouses. Whole stores floated away on the torrent, with chicken coops, board walks, and desperately swimming livestock. Grand Rapids and Centralia rebuilt their houses and industries and turned from lumbering to woodworking, hardware, and pulp factories. In 1900 the two towns were consolidated under the name of Grand Rapids: because of confusion with Grand Rapids, Michigan, the city was renamed Wisconsin Rapids in 1920.

The CONSOLIDATED WATER POWER AND PAPER COMPANY PLANT, First Ave. N. and Jackson Sts. (*conducted tours on weekdays: 10:30 a.m. and 3:30 p.m.*), has the largest of its four plants on the western side of the river. Tours of the plant begin at the mill office entrance. Visitors are taken first to the wood room where hemlock, spruce, and poplar logs are cut to two-foot lengths and conveyed to barking drums. Blocks are reduced to chips which are cooked in sulphite digesters, while some of the wood is conveyed in two-foot lengths to grinders. The pulp in a thin milky form is first pumped through paper machines which remove the water by drainage through a screen or "wire," then sent to the presses. After passing over dryers and through calenders, the pulp is ready for super-calendering. From here it is shipped in the form of rolls or taken to the sheet department and cut into specified sizes. At the end of the trip visitors are presented with souvenir tablets containing paper made in the plant.

Advertised as the "Heart of Wisconsin," Wisconsin Rapids has four railroads connecting it with Chicago, Milwaukee, Green Bay and St. Paul, hauling paper and pulp, camp equipment, dairy products, refrigeration equipment, fiber, cranberries, and boxes and cartons. Cranberries are brought in from swamps and marshes formed by old beaver dams. In the city is the WISCONSIN CRANBERRY SALES COMPANY CENTRAL OFFICE, 171 2nd St., representing 90 per cent of the State's growers. At yearly cranberry festivals raking contests similar to corn-husking contests in other regions are held in the marshes.

South of Wisconsin Rapids, State 13 levels out over uninteresting country, with small dairy-farm clearings in the cutover. Rutted trails lead through tangles of low pine out of sight, heading toward cranberry marshes, off-road farms, and villages. Streams here trickle slowly through plantations and pine barrens, flowing over the sand bed of ancient glacial Lake Wisconsin (*see Natural Setting*). Great rocks that have resisted erosion by water and wind stand isolated on the flat prairie, turreted and towered like castles, their crevices choked with ragged pines. ROCHE A CRIS MOUND (R), 103.8 *m.*, rises 300 feet above the surrounding green plain.

FRIENDSHIP, 107.6 *m.* (956 alt., 438 pop.), seat of Adams County, and ADAMS, 108.5 *m.* (956 alt., 1,231 pop.), are one town except in name; both are railroad settlements. Friendship was founded first, in 1856, and through it the Wisconsin Central planned to chart its route; but when two men bought up ground on the planned right-of-way and asked $75 an acre for land not worth $5 or $6, the rails were laid where Adams now stands, and a new settlement was formed, calling itself Lower Friendship.

For a time the two villages were friendly; then a bitter conflict occurred over the selection of a school site. An election was held in Upper Friendship to which Lower Friendship citizens came in force. "But by some accident," say the old settlers, "the kerosene lights went out and couldn't be fixed," so the Lower Friendship people went home, only to learn the next morning that a vote had been taken in their absence and that Upper Friendship had won the school. Angered, Lower Friendship took steps immediately to build a high school of its own; a second district was organized and Adams was incorporated.

The rivalry has been largely forgotten, preserved only on names on schools and buildings. Although Friendship is primarily a farmer's trading center, both villages have a common interest in the railroad. The Adams public library and American Legion Post are housed in old parlor coaches contributed by the railroad; there are several lodges of the railroad brotherhoods. A high school, built in 1929 and supported jointly by both towns, is located halfway between the two business sections.

Farmers about Friendship and Adams do much of their trading by barter, exchanging wood and potatoes (one farmer even traded his canary) for canned goods and other necessities. "It would be good farm country," they say, "if we could have two rains a week all year round."

WISCONSIN DELLS, 136.8 *m.* (893 alt., 1,489 pop.), began in the late 1850's when the Chicago, Milwaukee, St. Paul & Pacific R. R. ran its tracks across the Wisconsin River here. There had previously been a few settlers, but the center of settlement and river traffic was Newport, now a ghost town, some 5 miles south on the west bank. There rivermen reassembled their cribs after running them through the crashing dells, smoky little steamboats unloaded their cargoes, and main overland routes converged. When the railroad was routed north to Wisconsin Dells, Newport died overnight. It was "not long before there was a procession of buildings moving like prehistoric monsters across the landscape to Kilbourn [Wisconsin Dells] and elsewhere."

A citizen of Wisconsin Dells, Lieutenant Colonel Joseph Bailey, of the Fourth Wisconsin, used his lumberjack knowledge of river drives through such spots as the dells to save the Louisiana Red River campaign from disaster during the Civil War. Bailey was with the Union fleet when low water stranded it above the rapids at Alexandria, Louisiana, leaving it exposed to Confederate attacks from shore. As chief engineer, he suggested the construction of a large dam to store up enough water to wash the fleet over the rapids. In lumbering country this trick was called a "lift," used to float stranded log fleets. Although his idea was laughed at, Bailey was given 3,000 men and told to go ahead with his nonsense; he immediately requisitioned the lumberjack boys of the 23rd and 29th Wisconsin, who worked without rest for eight days completing the dam. Early on the morning of May 12, 1864, the heavy gunboats weighed anchor and crashed through, with a great roar of plunging water and flying splinters from the wooden dam. The Navy Department commended Bailey for saving the fleet, and naval officers gave him a sword and silver bowl, which are now in the State Historical Museum at Madison. He was brevetted a brigadier-general soon after the Red River expedition.

Wisconsin Dells, once called Kilbourn, changed its name in 1931 in the hope that the more descriptive title would attract tourists, for the city is a starting point for water trips up and down the Wisconsin River, here walled with carved and freakish rock. The Dells, according to Winnebago legend, were formed when a giant serpent moved southward, battering its way through great masses of rocks, leaving the land rent and broken. Today excursion boats (*fee $2, boats leave at frequent intervals*) follow the serpent's path in exploration of three scenic landings in Upper Dells and the beautiful Rock Islands in the Lower Dells, passing DEVIL'S ELBOW, FAT MAN'S MISERY, NARROWS, NAVY YARDS, CAVE OF THE DARK WATERS, SUGAR BOWL, GIANT ARROW HEAD, GRAND PIANO, HAWK'S BILLS, and others. Near the Dells are seven miles of sandstone rock, some of which can be seen from the bridge that divides Upper Dells from the Lower. At this point high ledges of old Potsdam sandstone are crowned with foliage; ferns, vines and flowers hang from the crevices in the rock walls. Now wide and now narrow, the river has carved a deep channel in solid sandstone, creating many unusual forms. As a geologist wrote in 1847, "Architraves, sculptured cornices, moulded capitals, scrolls, and fluted columns are seen on every hand; presenting, altogether, a mixture of the grand, the beautiful and the fantastic."

Wisconsin Dells is at the junction with US 16 (*see Tour 21*).

Tour 9

Ashland—Spooner—Hager City—(Red Wing, Minn.); US 63.
Ashland to Minnesota Line, 201 *m.*

Chicago, St. Paul, Minneapolis & Omaha R.R. parallels route between Ashland and Turtle Lake.
Asphalt and oiled-gravel roadbed.
Accommodations scant except in resort area.

US 63 slants southwest from Lake Superior through a country of sand and jack pine, a region of lakes, streams, and low young forests to which hundreds of sportsmen come each year to hunt and fish. This district offers simple rugged backwoods entertainment; it has not yet acquired the superficial sophistication, the glittering dance halls and bars of older resort regions. Something of lumbering days still lingers in the villages and cities whose older residents remember a time when the caulks of logging boots were as important a part of a man's everyday armament as his fists or his teeth. Farther south US 63 traverses a long stretch of farmland within 30 miles of the Twin Cities market.

Section a. ASHLAND *to* SPOONER; *90.1 m., US 63*

ASHLAND, 0 *m.* (666 alt., 10,622 pop.) (*see Tour 8*), is at the junction with US 2 (*see Tour 14*) and State 13 (*see Tour 8*). US 63 turns R. along 6th St. at Vaugh Ave. At 1.4 *m.* is the junction with US 2 (*see Tour 14*).

US 63 climbs gently up from the bayshore plain. The soil here is heavy clay, tinctured with red. Indians once used it for making pottery, shaping it by hand into large round-bottomed pots which they lined with green leaves and dried over slow fires. Sometimes they added glue made from the vertebrae of sturgeons, from deer horns, or even from shell shards. At 14 *m.* the highway runs through a forest of young birch and popple, which is visible for miles ahead as the land rises in a series of long grades. Gradually the red soil disappears until at GRAND VIEW, 26.8 *m.* (1,021 alt., 412 pop.), US 63 is on the edge of the Northern Highland ·(*see Natural Setting*).

DRUMMOND, 34.9 *m.* (1,299 alt., 300 pop.), in the CHEQUA-MEGON NATIONAL FOREST, is a decayed lumber mill town that rests its hopes for the future on the nearby Drummond Forest Community. Faded paint peels from the sides of small houses huddled among outcroppings of dark crystalline rock. The mill that supported the community for more than 40 years has been abandoned and torn down, and on its site by the mill pond a public park and playground have been built. A FOREST RANGER HEADQUARTERS, on the northern outskirts of town, houses the offices, equipment, and personnel that supervises this section of the Chequamegon Forest and its Drummond Forest Community.

At 37 *m.* is the junction with a town road, locally known as Birchwood Rd.

Right on this road to the northernmost and largest of the farm groups of the DRUMMOND FOREST COMMUNITY, 4 *m.* Here farm owners and tenants from the nearby jack-pine barrens have been relocated by the Forest Service upon better land within the national forest; their former farms have been purchased for reforestation. Thirty-two farm homes have been built and equipped here, and in May 1938, 25 were occupied by farmers with their families. Each man is offered six months' work in the forest annually, for which he is paid about $400 in cash a year. The rest of the time he can devote to the partly improved 20-acre tract surrounding his modern dwelling.

Each of these units cost the Government an average of $6,500, of which $2,750 went to build the four-room houses and $950 the barn. The Government plans to retain ownership of these farmsteads and rent them on long-term leases. Monthly rents range from $14.50 to $15.50. The buildings are well built and insulated; barns and outbuildings were constructed from specifications provided by the University of Wisconsin. Running water, heating, sewage disposal, schools, and roads are all provided. The dwellings are wired for electricity.

Each of the 25 farmers has been selected on his record. All had maintained their sub-marginal farms neatly, had worked hard and remained out of debt, had demonstrated industry, intelligence, and a desire to maintain a high standard of living.

Recreation

ON LAKE MENDOTA

ON LAKE MENDOTA

GERMAN BROWN TROUT

WAITING FOR THE WHITE BASS RUN, OSHKOSH

THE BEACH NEAR THE YACHT CLUB, MILWAUKEE

DEVIL'S LAKE STATE PARK

LOOKOUT AT RIB MOUNTAIN (1940 ALT.),
HIGHEST ELEVATION IN WISCONSIN

A SKIING LESSON

WINTER SPORTS IN THE CHEQUAMAGON
NATIONAL FOREST

TOBOGGAN SLIDE,
PERKINSTOWN WINTER SPORTS AREA

Courtesy of the Wisconsin Conservation Commission

SKI MEET, MOUNT VALHALLA

DOG SLEDDING

Courtesy of the Wisconsin Conservation Commission

AFTER THE HUNT

CABLE, 45 *m.* (1,372 alt., 240 pop.), is a community of neat and well-kept homes, supported partly by a sawmill, partly by tourist trade. In 1880 the Omaha R. R., then building toward the timberland of the lakes region, stopped its construction at this point for two years, and settlement began. Cable became the jumping-off place and trading center for the wild northland beyond, and during those two years few settlements equaled it for turbulence and vice. After the Omaha resumed construction, the village was soon almost deserted; forest fires swept over it and obliterated the boom-camp saloons, the boarded-up stores and shanties. Rebuilt on a more modest scale, Cable had become by 1907 a center for fishermen seeking trout in near-by Namekagon River. Now there are about 45 resorts and many private cabins and cottages on the lakes near the village.

LEONARD'S SPUR, 48.2 *m.,* is a small neat village whose inhabitants work in the local planing mill and two sawmills. These mills buy logs from settlers, and during the 1936-1937 season cut more than 4,000,000 feet of lumber.

At 52.3 *m.* are the few buildings of SEELEY (1,274 alt., 50 pop.), whose people in 1937 were employed at a portable sawmill. Such mills seldom remain on a site for more than a year or two. An old threshing machine, a tractor, or any other available engine supplies their power; saws and carriages, housed in temporary board shelters, are easily demounted. Often mere collections of spare parts picked up by the operator and somehow made to run, such improvised mills can cut 8,000 to 10,000 feet of lumber a day.

HAYWARD, 62.5 *m.* (1,196 alt., 1,207 pop.), is one of those elastic northern Wisconsin communities that can expand to five or six times its normal size during the summer without discomfort either to residents or visitors. From the middle of May to Labor Day, Hayward is transformed; the whole town thrills to the joy of apartment dwellers expanding into the "Great Outdoors." Storerooms and cellars disgorge elaborate displays of souvenirs, camping equipment, bathing suits, mosquito dope, fishing tackle, pennants, and picture post cards; the supplies of clothing and groceries increase, as do prices; stores are gaily lighted from front to back; lemonade and hot-dog stands appear along the sidewalks. Girls in shorts, sun-blacked youths in slacks, women in khaki shirts, and pink-faced men mopping their bald heads, jostle on the streets; occasionally a couple of lanky backwoodsmen slink diffidently along the edge of the sidewalks, thinking perhaps of the days when only Hell, Hurley, and Cumberland could match Hayward for hard-fisted bravado.

About 50 resorts and innumerable private cottages scattered throughout the surrounding woods and lakes have Hayward as their mailing address and obtain all their supplies here. Hunters know this region as probably the best deer country in Wisconsin, and during open season hundreds of cars pass through the city with dead bucks strapped across their fenders. Skiing and skating meets are now held here (*see*

Recreation). An airport provides a landing field for weekend visitors from Chicago and St. Lous.

Near by are two STATE FISH HATCHERIES; one hatches about 150,-000,000 pike fry each year; the other raises trout and muskellunge. A 140-acre GOVERNMENT NURSERY, of which 80 acres are now under cultivation, is completely equipped with an overhead watering system. Some 26,000,000 trees are raised by successive transplantings from seeds to saplings; thus nursed, more than 85 per cent survive when finally put out in the forests.

In the city is CAMP HAYWARD, the only transient camp remaining in the State. Here drifters temporarily or permanently laid up from the road are permitted to stay as long as they abide by camp rules. It would be hard to recruit a logging gang, a harvest crew, or a section gang without such men; but when they grow old or can find no work they are glad to find some shelter like this. The number of men at Camp Hayward varies with the season from about 225 to 530. Most of them are migratory workers. . Though some are rather young, the average age is 63 years, and 80 per cent have some physical infirmity.

Camp Hayward was founded in 1934, when the State Public Welfare Department, aided by the Wisconsin Emergency Relief Administration, took over the buildings of an abandoned Indian school and began the acquisition of its present 240-acre farm. All improvements have been made by the men themselves; the camp is almost self-sufficient and often has surplus products for sale. The men are paid from 50¢ to $4.50 a week, depending upon their skills; with leave from the director, they may go on short furloughs.

As one is an experienced butcher, the camp director can buy meat on the hoof and utilize the whole carcass. Another, who once owned his own bakery, has trained an assistant, and together they make bread, pies, cakes, and pastries. The camp kitchen is in charge of two ex-cooks who prepare big, family-style meals at a cost of from 25¢ to 28¢ each. Washing for the entire camp is done in a repaired steam laundry.

A logging-camp blacksmith once appeared here. Dissatisfied with farm work, he asked for a forge and was given one. Immediately he set to work, endangering his health by 18-hour vigils over his glowing irons as he wrought ornamental ironwork. He had learned his trade in Europe and remembered it through all the years he spent repairing chains and forging hooks in the lumber camps. Soon he took other transient blacksmiths as his apprentices and trained them in his craft. Although he is now dead, Camp Hayward's reputation for its wrought ironwork is still maintained; in 1937 it sold $5,000 worth of lamps, brackets, candelabra, and similar articles handmade by its expert smiths.

South of Hayward, US 63 crosses a well-farmed district, then dives into the jack-pine forest again. STINNET, 68.5 *m.* (1,149 alt., 50 pop.), is a railroad siding where truckloads of pulpwood are loaded for shipment to paper mills. Farmers in the vicinity cut pulpwood bolts and pile them at the edges of clearings or in littered farmyards. Portable sawmills occasionally come through and set up by the roadside to handle the sawlogs found among the smaller pulpwood growth.

SPRING BROOK, 75.8 *m.* (1,090 alt., 51 pop.), consists of two-score buildings and a loading platform at the railroad tracks. US 63 crosses the Namekagon River, 81 *m.,* celebrated for its trout fishing and for a popular and exciting 50-mile canoe trip between Hayward and the St. Croix.

At 82.6 *m.* is the junction with US 53 (*see Tour 10*); between this junction and Spooner, US 63 and US 53 are one route. The highway crosses the Namekagon River into TREGO, 83 *m.* (1,090 alt., 110 pop.).

SPOONER, 90.1 *m.* (1,095 alt., 2,426 pop.), a railroad junction, is the trading and shipping center for a large but poor and thinly settled area. The McKenzie Lake Region, clustered within a 10-mile radius of Big McKenzie Lake, 12 miles northwest of the city, attracts many tourists. On the outskirts of Spooner are a STATE FISH HATCH-ERY and a branch of the University of Wisconsin's AGRICULTURAL EXPERIMENT STATION, which is working on the problems of the sandy jack-pine country; as early as 1895 its experiments laid the foundation for the present use of windbreak growths and shelterbelts to check wind erosion and hold light soils.

Spooner was named for John Coit Spooner (1843-1919), one of the railroad and lumber kings who dominated the State in the late nineteenth century. Soon after he had been admitted to the bar in 1867, the Omaha R. R. hired Spooner to lead its battle against revocation of land grants in territory where it had accepted land but had made no gesture toward building a line; the railroad won its case. As protégé of Philetus Sawyer (*see Tour 15*), Spooner became a U. S. Senator in 1885 and again fought against restoring to the public domain land grants made to the Omaha system.

Retired temporarily to private life in 1890, when the Democrats captured the State, Spooner was appointed counsel to Henry C. Payne, one of three receivers appointed to take over the affairs of the Northern Pacific R. R. after its financial collapse in 1893. The receivers immediately ordered a 15 to 30 per cent wage cut on the railroad, thus precipitating the great railway strike of that year. The railroad broke the strike by obtaining an injunction forbidding the workers to "conspire" or under any circumstances to leave work, and a supplementary injunction prohibiting anyone from talking to others about quitting work. The House Judiciary Committee at Washington denounced these injunctions as a clear violation of the Constitution and an abuse of judicial power with no authority in law.

Spooner rode back to the U. S. Senate on the anti-Bryan flood in 1897, but the storm clouds soon began to gather about him. Young Robert M. La Follette, the avowed enemy of Spooner and the interests he spoke for, was chosen to lead the State's delegation to the Republican National Convention in 1904. The crisis came later in the year when *McClure's Magazine* published Lincoln Steffens' article on the means by which Spooner had been elevated to power, offering Isaac Stephenson's confession that he and Philetus Sawyer had between them contributed $50,000 to the fund that had secured Spooner his seat. Although La Follette carried the State, the legislature again returned Spooner to the Senate.

But in the middle of his term, with all Wisconsin roaring at the scandals of the Sawyer-Spooner machine (*see Political History*), Spooner suddenly resigned and retired to New York to become one of the prominent corporation lawyers of his time, rarely returning to Wisconsin.

At Spooner is the junction with State 70 (*see Tour 15*).

Section b. SPOONER to HAGER CITY; 110.9 m., US 63

Between SPOONER, 0 *m.*, and a point at 2.1 *m.* US 63 and US 53 (*see Tour 10*) are one route. The land along the highway is cleared and farmed, but the farther slopes are covered with oak and softwoods. At 5.2 *m.* is a view of the wide bottoms and distant hills enclosing Shell Lake, and the village of SHELL LAKE, 6.4 *m.* (1,242 alt., 826 pop.), which has two factories building rowboats, skiffs, and motorboats for use on northern Wisconsin lakes. On the shore of Shell Lake is a TOURIST PARK with a dance pavilion and public bathhouses along the sandy beach.

US 63 continues south through ragged popple and birch. The sandy loam becomes more fertile and agriculture more profitable as the highway approaches Barron County, which, within range of the markets of Minneapolis and St. Paul, is one of the leading counties in production of butter, potatoes, and general farm produce. Crossing a series of hills, US 63 passes GRANITE LAKE (L), 20.4 *m.*, with a PUBLIC CAMP on its shores, and BEAVER DAM LAKE (R), 22.7 *m.*, with a TOURIST PARK.

CUMBERLAND, 23.4 *m.* (1,242 alt., 1,532 pop.), lies on what was formerly an island in Beaver Dam Lake; filled ground now connects it with the mainland. In 1874, hearing that a railroad was to cross the island, O. A. Ritan and Gunder O. Dahlby staked homesteads on it. After a number of delays the railroad finally came through in 1878, and the cheers of a score or more settlers drowned out the whistle of the locomotive as the first train steamed across the island. Within a year some 300 colonists arrived; a number of Italians, brought in from St. Paul to break a strike on the railroad, settled near by, the nucleus of the present colony of some 150 Italian families.

During the next two decades the town was one of the toughest lumber camps in Wisconsin, a member of the notorious quartette, "Cumberland, Hurley, Hayward, and Hell." The first three, it was said, were tougher than the fourth. In 1884 Cumberland had 24 saloons to serve a few hundred inhabitants; in 1886 the number of saloon licenses was restricted to five at any one time; in 1896 the townspeople voted against the licensing of saloons.

In the 1870's and 1880's the more sober elements of Cumberland engaged Pat Varley, an outsider, as town marshal at the then munificent salary of $100 a month. Varley made a formal call on every saloon in town, introduced himself as the new marshal, and warned the boys to behave. At dusk that evening, as he was passing a lumberyard, a dozen men led by Nels Paulson, a saloonkeeper, leaped upon him and dragged him among the stacks. All peeled off their coats and began rolling up their sleeves.

"Nels," said Varley, "you look like a real man to me. You shouldn't be party to a raw deal like this." Paulson grimly continued his preparations. "You'd better kill me then, Paulson, because I'm not the kind of man you can drive out of town; and every one of you is going to have to settle with me afterward." Paulson did not seem averse to killing. "Paulson, I'll bargain with you," Varley said. "We'll settle it in a fair fight. If you lick me I'll get out of town; if I lick you, I stay on as marshal." Paulson accepted the challenge. Stripped to the waist, the men fought 45 minutes without rules until Pat Varley won. For years thereafter the marshal of Cumberland maintained some semblance of order among his unruly flock.

Cumberland has twice become excited at the rumors of oil that have swept Wisconsin since 1860. In 1925 a certain Colonel Noble, agent for several oil companies, happened up into the Turtle Lake country (*see below*), decided that Barron County looked very much like Oklahoma, and wrote glowingly of the virgin oil territory he had discovered. The only evidence for the Colonel's claims was a mysterious instrument, invented by himself, which he declared to be an infallible oil detector. Without waiting for authorization of his employers, Noble hastened to Madison to obtain permission to drill. The State Geologist, positive that there was no oil in the region but averse to hurting the Colonel's feelings, granted him permission, provided his companies sold no stock in the venture. Nothing more was done.

About the same time Cumberland again became excited when W. J. Gavin started acquiring leases and options in the region. Gavin had found a "geologist" who told him that prospects of finding oil were very good. There was a new and better rumor every hour; the billboards and vacant stores of Cumberland flaunted great signs announcing the coming boom. Nevertheless, Cumberland still gets its oil and gasoline from tank cars.

The city prides itself on its rutabagas, which have an unusually fine and delicate flavor. Every September there is a weekend celebration in honor of the rutabaga, with bands, speakers, entertainers, and parades of gayly-decorated floats. At the close of the festival local gourmands compete in eating mashed 'bagies for a prize of $10 and the honor of being crowned Rutabaga King. The 1937 unofficial champion of the world was Ed Mizer, who got down eight pints of rutabagas with every appearance of pleasure.

South of Cumberland, US 63 crosses a region of swampland, scrub growth, and rough hills, with occasional fertile spots as at COM-

STOCK, 29.1 *m.* (1,282 alt., 100 pop.), which has a cooperative creamery and a cooperative store affiliated with the large cooperatives of Superior (*see Cooperative Movement*).

At 35.6 *m.* is the junction with US 8 (*see Tour 16*); between this junction and a point at 37.2 *m.*, US 63 and US 8 are one route (*see Tour 16*).

In CLAYTON, 41.8 *m.* (1,201 alt., 341 pop.), on the shores of Lake Camelia, is the STELLA CHEESE COMPANY PLANT, owned by Count Giulio Bolognesi, maker of Italian cheeses. The company maintains another plant at Campbellsport to make types that can be produced only farther south. The plant here employs a relatively large number of skilled workmen, most of them Italians. Using imported rennet and processes quite different from those traditional in Wisconsin, this plant, taking in more than 40,000 pounds of milk a day, produces such table cheeses as provolone, salama, scarmoze, encanestrato, and ricotta, and such special cheeses as parmesan, romano, modean, and asiago.

South of CLEAR LAKE, 49.4 *m.* (1,199 alt., 733 pop.), a neat village with a seasonally busy canning factory, the highway traverses high rolling prairie, wooded only in the draws. Farmed for more than 75 years, this was one of the State's great wheat-growing areas for half a century. With the decline of wheat growing (*see Agriculture*), it has turned successfully to dairy farming, specializing in butter production.

At 74 *m.* is the junction with US 12 (*see Tour 19*). Here US 63 is well within the Twin Cities trade area, which has stimulated agriculture in this region.

At 83.5 *m.* is the junction with State 29 (*see Tour 17*); between this junction and a point at 85.8 *m.* US 63 and State 29 are one route.

MARTELL, 84.9 *m.* (125 pop.), a small village among dense groves of second-growth pine, grew up around the sawmill now in ruins on the bank of the Rush River. Martell was named for one of the four French Canadians who settled here in 1847: Joseph Martell, Lewis Lepeau, John Doe, and Xerxes Jock.

Xerxes Jock was a famous hunter. Short, thick, and exceedingly strong, he knew woodcraft as well as any Indian. According to stories of old settlers, Jock went out after dinner one winter day in 1857 and shot five elk. On another occasion in 1858 he killed a mother bear and three cubs, captured a fourth cub alive, and brought in all five at once to his cabin some four miles away. He had much less trouble dragging in the dead four than in protecting himself against the live cub tucked inside his jacket. This feat was nothing compared with Jock's most famous exploit. Setting forth with his long rifle to get a celebrated bear in the vicinity, Jock missed with his first shot. Before he could reload, the bear charged. Jock drew his knife, but it was knocked from his hand; rushing in barehanded, he held the beast back by the throat until he could recover his knife and stab it through the heart. Badly injured in this fight, Jock lay between life and death for several weeks; on his first day out of bed he went bear hunting.

On the sandy soil south of Martell some turkeys are raised; near holiday time flocks of as many as 1,500 birds troop in the fields along the roadside. Maple syrup and sugar provide supplementary income. Each spring, when the snow begins to melt in the open places, farmers bore small holes about two inches deep in rock or black maples, drive notched metal spouts into them, and hang up 12-quart pails equipped with lids to keep out twigs and dirt. Daily the whole family makes the rounds, towing a big barrel or can on a stoneboat from tree to tree and emptying the pails. The sap flows fastest at times of alternate thawing and freezing, and under unusually favorable conditions several trips a day are necessary; there is a record of one tree that yielded 50 gallons of sap in a single day. When the time for refining arrives, people gather to boil the sap in large shallow pans over open fires and make a festival of the occasion. While the pans bubble, they sing, play games, and eat. It requires 30 to 40 gallons of sap to produce one gallon of standard syrup weighing 11 pounds.

At 94.6 m. is the junction with US 10 (see Tour 18); between this junction and a point at 97.9 m. US 63 and US 10 are one route (see Tour 18).

US 63 traverses an old and well-developed farming region. From the Civil War to the turn of the century it was renowned for its wheat (see Agriculture). At the once dreaded Hager Hill, 106.6 m., the highway drops sharply from the ramparts of the river bluffs to waterside terraces leveled by the Mississippi. Halfway down, the Mississippi Valley bursts into view. Across a gray-green mat of brush and trees a massive sweep of bare rock glows in a shadowed valley in the Minnesota bluffs three miles away.

HAGER CITY, 107.8 m. (719 alt., 104 pop.), has a few buildings crowded under the bluff which here rises in two terraces, each about 40 feet high. At 108.3 m. is an emergency landing field for the Twin Cities-Chicago airmail route. US 63 descends into the Mississippi bottoms, crossing a slough to an island largely occupied by rivermen and fishermen. The fish here tend to seek the quiet waters of the inshore sloughs, and, when the water level sinks, are often trapped in shallow pools on the flats. Formerly they were allowed to die as the pools dried up, but the State now gathers them up and transfers them to inland lakes and streams.

At 110.9 m. US 63 crosses the bridge at the Minnesota Line.

Tour 10

(Duluth, Minn.)—Superior—Spooner—Eau Claire—La Crosse—(La Crescent, Minn.); US 53.
Minnesota Line to Minnesota Line, 249.3 *m.*

Chicago, St. Paul, Minneapolis & Omaha R.R. parallels route between Superior and Eau Claire.
Oiled-gravel, asphalt, and concrete roadbed.
Accommodations average; resorts and cottages in north during summer.

South of the Lake Superior basin, US 53 climbs over the rough ridges of the northern highland, splits a waste of cutover land, skirts the western lakes districts, and descends into the Chippewa Valley, oldest of the State's lumber and flour-mill regions. In its southern section US 53 enters the unglaciated Driftless Area (*see Natural Setting*), winding through oddly eroded coulees, finally descending the Mississippi bluffs to La Crosse crowded on the river terrace.

Section a.   *MINNESOTA LINE to SPOONER; 73.6 m., US 53*

US 53 crosses the MINNESOTA LINE, 0 *m.,* from Duluth, Minnesota, on the ARROWHEAD TOLL BRIDGE (*10¢ auto and driver, 5¢ each additional passenger; trucks 25¢ to 35¢*).
SUPERIOR, 2.1 *m.* (629 alt., 36,113 pop.) (*see Superior*).
Superior is at the junction with State 35.(*see Tour 13*), US 2 (*see Tour 14*), and State 13 (*see Tour 14A*).
Southeast of Superior US 53 parallels the lakeshore and crosses the Nemadji River, 7 *m.* Here the NORTHERN PACIFIC ORE DOCKS and the GREAT NORTHERN ORE DOCKS (*see Superior*) extend far out into the bay. Ascending the gentle sides of the bowl-shaped Superior basin, so sheltered by the highlands to the south that it forms a separate climatic region, the route traverses a plateau through ragged cutover scarred with fire. In 1936 almost half of Douglas County was burned over.
At 8.2 *m.* is the junction with State 13 (*see Tour 14A*); at 16 *m.* is the junction with US 2 (*see Tour 14*).
SOLON SPRINGS, 34.7 *m.* (1,138 alt., 282 pop.), with its little church topping a hill (R) and its taverns set back under pines and white birch, is situated in a fine stand of tall timber. Here a marker indicates the route of the BOIS-BRULE-ST. CROIX PORTAGE, by which priests, soldiers, and traders for almost two centuries traveled from Lake Superior to the Mississippi. Somewhere on this mile-and-a-half

trail Daniel Greysolon Duluth probably built a supply post in 1683, one of the earliest forts in interior Wisconsin. The village is supported largely by the trade of tourists who are attracted here by crescent-shaped LAKE ST. CROIX, glimpsed at 36.3 *m.*

In the 20,000-acre DOUGLAS COUNTY BIRD SANCTUARY, 38.7 *m.,* hoppers of food are provided for game and songbirds during the winter, but it is expected that with the growth of natural cover and the sowing of patches of grain the necessity of hopper feeding will soon end. In May and September local organizations of sportsmen sponsor field trials for bird dogs here. In the sanctuary are riding and hiking trails; a clubhouse (*open on arrangement with Superior Chamber of Commerce*); an animal cemetery, where pets may be buried free; and a Memorial Cemetery for field-trial dogs, many of which have been honored with marble markers inscribed with their names, their pedigrees, and the names of their owners.

GORDON, 42.3 *m.* (1,038 alt., 305 pop.), a small village at the northernmost tip of the western lakes region, has a STATE NURSERY, the smallest of three maintained by the State for purposes of reforestation. WASCOTT, 47.2 *m.,* and MINONG, 52.3 *m.* (1,069 alt., 292 pop.), live largely on trade with summer tourists, drawn in increasing numbers every year to the relatively wild and unspoiled lake region of northwestern Wisconsin. US 53 runs through a ragged land, skirting SILVER LAKE, 58.9 *m.,* and WHALEN LAKE, 63.9 *m.* What farming occurs in this sandy region is largely a subsistence type of dairying, poultry raising, and potato growing. Many families live back in the cutover in huts of logs, planks, or lath and tar paper. Often in winter they become snowbound and must be rescued by dog teams; generally when spring thaw begins, the back roads become morasses even less passable than the snow drifts.

At 66.1 *m.* is the junction with US 63 (*see Tour 9*); between this junction and SPOONER, 73.6 *m.* (1,095 alt., 2,426 pop.) (*see Tour 9*), US 53 and US 63 are one route (*see Tour 9*).

At Spooner is the junction with State 70 (*see Tour 15*).

Section b. SPOONER to EAU CLAIRE; 83.6 m., US 53

Between SPOONER, 0 *m.* (*see Tour 9*), and a point at 2.1 *m.* US 53 and US 63 (*see Tour 9*) are one route.

East of the highway lie LONG, BASS, RED CEDAR, RICE, PRAIRIE, and the two CHETEK LAKES, with their smaller outlying waters, all beautifully wooded. At 11.2 *m.* a black fire scar almost five miles wide reveals the terrible devastation wrought by the great blazes that have swept through the forests in recent drought years.

A big forest fire quickly and completely alters life in an entire county. Every able-bodied man is subject to draft by the fire wardens. The sky is a mass of smoke by day, an inferno of red clouds by night.

Every stump smoulders; little flames crackle along the branches or race up the trunks of trees still standing; a tree crashes in a shower of sparks.

Men on the fire line labor 20 hours a day, cutting lanes through the trees, plowing up fresh earth, throwing dirt on little outrunning blazes. Heat and smoke sting the lungs and eyes of smoke-begrimed fire fighters who protect themselves as well as they can by tying handkerchiefs across the lower parts of their faces.

When the wind is high the fire races through the treetops so furiously that it can leap a 150-foot river. Again, it creeps along the ground, spreading through the underbrush or burrowing into the peat of bogs, where it may smoulder submerged until long after snowfall, revealed only by thin wisps of smoke. The year following a fire the charred ground is covered with tall, flame-colored fireweed, succeeded in time by a green fuzz of berrybushes, brush, and poplar saplings. Not for a generation does the wood grow large enough to be used even for ties, posts, or pulpwood; not for two generations does it reach mature saw-log size.

RICE LAKE, 24.4 m. (1,112 alt., 5,177 pop.), largest city in Barron County, stretches along the shores of RICE LAKE and the Red Cedar River. Both city and lake are named for the wild rice that once grew in the stagnant marshes offshore and was harvested annually by roving bands of Indians. In the 1850's Chief Na-nong-ga-bee of the Chippewa had an encampment here; he and his eldest son were killed by Sioux in 1854 while returning from La Pointe, where they had signed a treaty ceding the last of their lands in Wisconsin to the U. S. Government (see Tour 14A).

Along the lakeshore, amid stacks and piles of bolts and short sections of logs, sprawl the wood factories, reminders of early lumbering days when hundreds of millions of board feet were cut here. Today the city is the busy and prosperous trading center for the surrounding dairy farmers and the hundreds of vacationists who come annually to the near-by lakes.

Left from Rice Lake on County N to the junction with a town road, 8.5 m.; R. on this second road to the Anderson Farm, 9 m., whose owners can give directions to the PIPESTONE QUARRY. Pipestone is fine in .texture, dull red in color. Though soft enough to be cut with a knife, it hardens quickly when exposed to air.

According to Indian accounts, this quarry once supplied pipestone to all the tribes in the Great Lakes region, being prized above the more plentiful but plainer stone of western Minnesota. For several generations prior to 1850 the Chippewa used it as one of their principal items of barter.

As the pipes served ceremonial and religious purposes, the Chippewa kept the location of this deposit a secret from all but a half-dozen braves, who quarried and carved here. In one battle with the Sioux all the braves who knew the secret of the quarry's location were killed. For many years the Chippewa vainly searched the western slopes of the Barron Hills to rediscover it. Later the tract was included in holdings of Ezra Cornell (1807-1874), co-founder of Cornell University. Given to the university as part of its endowment, the land was subsequently sold to loggers.

The workings are now badly caved in; some stone has been taken out for ornamental building purposes; pieces of vessels or pipes are still found in the vicinity. In the Milwaukee Public Museum is an environmental miniature group of Indians at work in this quarry.

CAMERON, 30.9 m. (1,099 alt., 760 pop.), a quiet little Scandinavian farm town, gained considerable renown from the exploits of John Dietz, "Defender of Cameron Dam." In 1904 Dietz moved to a 160-acre tract on the Thornapple River, but just as his first crop was showing green above the ground, the Chippewa Log and Boom Company opened its dam and flooded the farm with water and a winter's accumulation of logs. After vain appeals to the company for redress, Dietz, armed with a rifle, mounted guard on the dam, vowing to hold it until he was recompensed, driving off deputies who sought to serve an injunction and routing a posse of 20 men. Dietz not only barricaded his house but built a small stone fort at the dam.

After much preliminary skirmishing the first "Battle of Cameron Dam" occurred on July 25, 1906, when six Milwaukeeans under Sheriff Gylland crept up to the edge of the Dietz clearing. Mrs. Dietz spied them, and they were driven off after one man on each side had been wounded. Although forced to be vigilant, Dietz moved about freely until October 1, 1910, when three members of his family ran into an ambush and were wounded. A small army of 60 men then besieged the Dietz cabin and on the seventh day surprised Leslie Dietz, a son, alone in a clearing. Escaping to the cabin through a hail of bullets, he and his father stood off the besiegers for three hours. Mrs. Dietz and a small daughter were in the cabin, and, to save them, old John finally sent out his daughter with a white flag.

Father and son were brought into town and charged with the murder of Oscar Harp, a deputy. At his trial Dietz refused to be represented by a lawyer and was given a life sentence that was later commuted to 20 years. In 1921 Dietz was pardoned by Governor John Blaine. He died three years later, broken in spirit.

Cameron is at the junction with US 8 (*see Tour 16*).

Long and narrow PRAIRIE LAKE, 37.5 m., has six or seven floating islands consisting of detached bits of tamarack swampland held together by interlaced tree roots. The floating islands are anchored to keep them from drifting with crushing force against piers and boats. On Cranberry Island, several acres in extent, a cottage owner has cut a hole through his back lawn so that he can let a line down and fish for the bass and pike that hide among the roots on the under side.

CHETEK, 39.1 m. (1,048 alt., 1,076 pop.), once a stopover on an important Indian trail, was the temporary home for some Mormons, fleeing from the Nauvoo persecution in the late 1840's. Here on LAKE CHETEK young Presbyterians of northern Wisconsin hold a yearly encampment.

BLOOMER, 56.6 m. (1,006 alt., 1,865 pop.), was named for Jacob Bloomer, wealthy merchant from Galena, Illinois, who built the first dam and mill here in 1818. Farmers in the vicinity first raised wheat, and flour milling became Bloomer's main industry. Later a large potato-growing center, Bloomer now depends increasingly on dairying; potato warehouses have been supplanted by a creamery-condensery receiving 500,000 pounds of milk daily. Bloomer also has a pea cannery, a brewery, and a large retail co-operative, with branches in near-by communities.

CHIPPEWA FALLS, 72.4 *m.* (859 alt., 9,539 pop.) (*see Tour 17*), is at the junction with State 29 (*see Tour 17*). The highway crosses the Chippewa River, 72.8 *m.,* and heads south on a wide embankment with long sweeping curves.

EAU CLAIRE (Fr., clear water), 83.6 *m.* (880 alt., 26,287 pop.), a compact and busy industrial city at the confluence of the Eau Claire and Chippewa Rivers, has a narrow crooked main street bright with plate glass by day, glaring with neon lights at night; its many factories lie back along the tracks that parallel the cramped and curving rivers.

In 1784 a trapper and trader named Le Duc was living here among the Sioux. Logging near the banks of the Chippewa began about 1822, and two decades later Jeremiah Thomas and Stephen S. McCann, first permanent white settlers, staked claims and built shanties here. In 1856, when word came that a railroad was to pass through, Eau Claire County was organized and settlers began coming in large numbers.

From the beginning the white pine of the Chippewa Valley became the foundation of prosperity in Eau Claire as well as in Chippewa Falls on the river above, and for years lumbering interests and rivalries determined the life in both cities. Soon after settlement an intricate series of conflicts arose over control of the many-branched Chippewa, main outlet for northwestern Wisconsin's wealth of timber. Dams and booms built at any one place on the river impeded the drive of logs to other communities downstream; quarrels based on this economic fact soon grew into feuds. When Eau Claire men proposed to build a dam in 1860, Chippewa Falls interests fought the project in the legislature and courts for more than 15 years, only to lose eventually; and when Eau Claire sought incorporation as a city, Chippewa Falls again opposed strenuously but vainly.

Such civic rivalries were complicated by the conflicts of individual lumbermen, who formed and reformed alliances and stratagems without particular regard to community loyalties. These business conflicts centered chiefly around projects to develop Beef Slough, the great log harbor at the mouth of the Chippewa. The Beef Slough men wished to use the Chippewa only as a driving stream and to have all sawing done on the Mississippi. The dams, mills, and booms at Chippewa Falls and Eau Claire were a hindrance both to the business unity of the project and to its log drives, and the rivalry between loggers sometimes flared into open battle. In the spring of 1867 the firm of Bacon and Davis hired a hard-fisted crew of rivermen who smashed a whole winter's cut through the booms at the falls, sweeping all logs with their own toward the Mississippi. The great mass of timber, extending from shore to shore, swept toward the Eau Claire mills, but before it arrived the sheriff and a posse of armed Eau Claire riverhogs stopped the Bacon and Davis crew. Eventually the Mississippi rivermen, partly by battle and partly by compromise, attracted most of their rivals into the Beef Slough Improvement Company and settled the logging disputes.

The railroad was completed in 1870. Eau Claire County had shrewdly inserted "may" instead of "shall" into its promise to float a $60,000 bond issue to subsidize construction, and, consequently, was one of a very few Wisconsin counties that escaped paying heavily for rail service. At this time 22 sawmills operated in Eau Claire. Then, as logging declined along the Chippewa, paper and pulp mills began to replace the sawmills, and the flow of timber over the dam fell to almost nothing. In place of heavy saw-logs came pulpwood for paper and pulp plants; much of the water of the rivers was diverted to drive hydroelectric turbines. Factories making furniture, sashes and doors, and other wood products sprang up. Today Eau Claire also produces kitchen utensils, farm machinery, books and stationery, mill tools, mechanics' supplies, sewer pipe, refrigerators, automobile tires and accessories. The Gillette Rubber Company Plant, the largest in the city, covers three city blocks and employs 2,500 men at peak production.

The Northwest Wisconsin golf, tennis, softball, and district basketball tournaments, and skiing and boxing meets are held here annually. There is a STATE FISH HATCHERY on Putnam Drive, which runs in a two-mile curve along the base of the southern bluffs. CARSON PARK (*boating and bathing facilities; picnic grounds; tennis courts, baseball and football fields*), occupies a peninsula extending out into HALF MOON LAKE, a narrow, spring-fed body of water in the western part of the city. In the park is a PAUL BUNYAN CAMP (*free; open daily*), consisting of a cook shack, bunkhouse, stable, and black-smith shop equipped as they were in the old lumber camps. The city also has a STATE TEACHERS COLLEGE. MOUNT TOM, a pyramidal rock rising abruptly from the plain in the northern section of the city, has been made into a municipal park.

Eau Claire is at the junction with US 12 (*see Tour 19*).

Section c. *EAU CLAIRE to MINNESOTA LINE; 92.1 m., US 53*

South of Eau Claire, 0 *m.,* US 53 ascends the face of the bluffs encircling Putnam Park. At 2.8 *m.* is the junction with US 12 (*see Tour 19*). From the bluffs, 4.4 *m.,* is a view of the city far below. The highway turns southeast out of the Eau Claire Valley, and at 11 *m.* rides a ridge of the Western Upland.

FOSTER, 15.9 *m.,* a cluster of houses at a railroad crossing, was named for a wealthy eccentric who built and managed a railroad between this village and small Fairchild, 15 miles to the east. He called his line the Fairchild & North Eastern, but people generally referred to the F & NE as the "Foster and Nobody Else's." According to local tradition, Foster once told the president of the New York Central: "My line may not be as long as some, but it's just as wide as any."

At 18.4 *m.* is the junction with US 10 (*see Tour 18*) ; between this junction and Osseo US 53 and US 10 are one route. Cutting through more rugged country, with farm buildings tucked away comfortably against the sheltering slopes of rounded hills, the highway sweeps down across the valley of the Buffalo River, 18.9 *m.*, to an OLD BUCKWHEAT MILL, which has been grinding grain for the neighborhood since the 1850's.

OSSEO, 21.3 *m.* (955 alt., 933 pop.), was settled in 1857 by Richland County farmers who had heard that a railroad was to pass here. Though the railroad never arrived, Osseo has become the trading center for the Norwegians who settled the surrounding coulees. The village is supported by milling, cheese making, a creamery, a pickle station, and a condensery.

At Osseo is the junction with US 10 (*see Tour 18*).

US 53 swings southward across the highlands to the brink of the escarpment at a point called BUENA VISTA (*lookout and parking space*), 26.2 *m.* The NICHOLAS BOURLIER MONUMENT here commemorates the hermit who found this his favorite view.

WHITEHALL, 42.2 *m.* (821 alt., 915 pop.), is a shady village with one block of false-front business buildings. The first settlers arrived in this township in 1855, but the scarcity of wood and hay in the region discouraged growth until 1873, when the arrival of the railroad made it a local trading and shipping center. Now it has three grain elevators, a tobacco warehouse, and a creamery. Across from the courthouse is the HOUSE OF MEMORIES, a small museum containing World War souvenirs, Sioux and Blackfoot Indian relics, pioneer household utensils, old weapons, a number of portraits of politicians, and a copy of the first issue of the first county newspaper.

BLAIR, 51.9 *m.* (849 alt., 702 pop.), founded in 1873 when the railroad arrived, has changed from a gristmill settlement to a small stock-shipping center. Here in 1889 occurred one of the State's few lynchings, that of Hans Jacob Olson, a man known for his great strength and for his surliness when in his cups. When he returned from serving a five-year term for arson, his wife had him put under peace bond. A mob of 40 or 50 men, including Olson's own son, gathered to run him out of the country. Led by Charles Johnson, self-appointed guardian of the law, who had brought two ropes with him, the group seized and bound Olson while he slept, and ordered him to leave at once on penalty of death. Olson refused to leave the house he had built. Twice the lynchers strung him up, strangled him into unconsciousness, and revived him. Still Olson refused to depart. Finally he was left dangling from the limb of a tree in the yard.

Next day a coroner's jury, with Charles Johnson as foreman, found that Olson had come to his death at the hands of persons unknown, but a young district attorney issued warrants for the arrest of 30 of the mob. Johnson, Olson's wife and son, and another lyncher were convicted of murder, sentenced to life imprisonment, and pardoned five years later. More than 50 others, convicted on a charge of riot, were fined.

South of Blair the soil changes to heavy yellow clay, sticky in wet weather, hard and crumbling after drought. ETTRICK, 58.8 *m.* (772 alt., 310 pop.), a one-street village with a creamery and flour and woolen mills, was founded in the 1870's when Norwegian farmers penetrated the hills and began to till the valleys and creek banks.

At 64.7 *m.* is the junction with County T.

Right on County T to the GRAVE OF PRINCESS MARINUKA, 1.1 *m.*, with a tepee built of concrete beside it. Marinuka was the daughter of Chief Winneshiek (*see Tour 13*) and the granddaughter of the famous Winnebago Chief Decorah (*see below*). When she died in 1884 at the age of 82, the last of a celebrated family, she was buried with pagan rites at midnight, her head pointing to the north.

GALESVILLE, 67 *m.* (712 alt., 1,069 pop.), on a hilltop overlooking LAKE MARINUKA, is built around a shady village square. Gale College, now a Lutheran junior college offering two years of post-high-school work, was founded here in 1854.

In Galesville is the junction with State 35 (*see Tour 13*); between this junction and La Crosse, State 35 and US 53 are one route.

South of Galesville DECORAH'S PEAK (L) juts out of the rough landscape, a wooded cone rising steeply to a pinnacle of bare rock. Here Chief Decorah, descendant of Queen Glory of the Morning and Sabrevoir de Carrie (*see Tour 2*), sat one day and watched his Winnebago braves battle with the Chippewa on the plain below. When the Winnebago were defeated, Decorah hid in a cave near by until nightfall, then crept to his white friends at La Crosse. Although undistinguished for valor, he was a shrewd diplomat and a persistent suitor for the friendship of the whites, ceding much Indian land to the Federal Government, surrendering Black Hawk to the military authorities after the Battle of the Bad Axe. Decorah died in 1864.

At 75.7 *m.* is the junction with State 93 (*see Tour 13*).

After passing through the Mississippi bluffs, which rise from 300 to 400 feet above the river, US 53 runs along the broad river terrace to ONALASKA, 84.8 *m.* (679 alt., 1,408 pop.), a suburb of La Crosse.

LA CROSSE, 91.2 m. (649 alt., 39,614 pop.) (*see La Crosse*).

La Crosse is at the junction with State 35 (*see Tour 13*), US 14 (*see Tour 20*), and US 16 (*see Tour 21*). US 53 zigzags along brick-paved streets past smoke-grimed warehouses to the river front, crosses a bridge (*free*) to PETTIBONE ISLAND, and at 92.1 *m.* crosses another bridge (*free*) to the Minnesota Line, 2 miles east of La Crescent, Minnesota.

Tour 11

Readstown—Boscobel—Fennimore—Lancaster—(Dubuque, Iowa);
US 61.
Readstown to Iowa Line, 76.7 *m.*

Hard-surfaced and oiled-gravel roadbed.
Accommodations in small cities.

US 61 traverses the coulee country immortalized in American literature by Hamlin Garland; the Wisconsin River, part of the most famous
waterway in the State; and the southwestern lead mining district—all
rich in history and legends of river days and frontier mining life.
Although in the seventeenth century Marquette and Joliet canoed
along the Wisconsin River, it was not until the 1820's that the discovery of lead in the region 25 miles south brought permanent settlers
to southwestern Wisconsin and made the river an important water
route for lead and farm-produce shipments.

On the southern outskirts of READSTOWN, 0 *m.* (754 alt., 544
pop.), is the junction with US 14 (*see Tour 20*).

The coulee country extends along the Mississippi River one-third
of the State's length. Here valleys, narrow and secluded, branch out
like tributary streams from a river system, all eventually coming to
an abrupt blind end. Their steeper sides for the most part lie unplowed;
occasionally white birches range the upper ridges; here and there gray
limestone outcroppings bulge from the green of sod and foliage.

SOLDIERS GROVE, 3.9 *m.* (726 alt., 710 pop.), near the
entrance of a deep coulee, lies scattered about a church and a general
store. Originally known as Pine Grove, its name was changed during
the Civil War when soldiers camped nearby.

At 8.1 *m.* is the junction with State 171.

Right on State 171 to GAYS MILLS, 5 *m.* (703 alt., 579 pop.), named for
John Gay who settled here in 1848. Here is the center of the Kickapoo apple
region, a district to which thousands of visitors come every spring or fall to
see the blossoming or the harvest.

Right from Gays Mills on State 131 to the junction with a dirt road, 5.4 *m.;*
R. here to the 800-acre KICKAPOO ORCHARDS, 7.4 *m.*, in the Kickapoo (Ind.,
kiwiganawa; he stands about) Valley, named for an Algonquian tribe. In
1908, when the Wisconsin Horticultural Society was searching for good spots
to plant trial apple orchards, J. H. Hayes offered his land here. So successful
was the experiment that apples are now grown in abundance. In the fall
people from surrounding farms and villages come to pick the crop which, in
normal years, is 350,000 bushels. A near by OBSERVATION TOWER affords a
sweeping view of orchards that spread down the valley.

Continuing through rugged wooded country, the highway dips in and out of steep-sided coulees, often no wider than an ordinary field. At 23.4 *m.* is the junction with State 60 (*see Tour 22*); between this junction and a point at 24.6 *m.* US 61 and State 60 are one route following the banks of the Wisconsin River. Then US 61 swings left across the river over a new steel and concrete bridge, 24.6 *m.*, which replaced one of the last covered bridges in Wisconsin. The original span, built in 1874, had sides almost completely enclosed by boards and a roof, shingled and painted red. On Armistice Day, 1937, the new bridge was dedicated to John J. Blaine, a leader of Wisconsin Progressivism (*see below*).

The Wisconsin River was once an important waterway. The Indians named its lower reaches the "Stream of a Thousand Isles"; and in his journal Marquette speaks of its many "vine-clad islets." It was these very islands and the shifting channels about them that later prevented the use of large steamboats on the lower Wisconsin and limited river traffic to rafts, barges, and flatboats.

In 1843 the steamer *Rock River,* owned by Haraszthy and Bryant of Sauk City (*see Tour 19*), provided the first regular freight and passenger service on the stream, penetrating as far east on the Wisconsin as Portage. For a time the lead mines farther south helped to increase river traffic. Although the first lead was shipped overland to Galena and down the Mississippi, the route was too long and slow. Early miners conceived the plan of shipping up the Wisconsin, across the portage to the Fox, down that river, and thence to New York by way of the Great Lakes. This route proved little better. Lead shipment on the Wisconsin was never large, although it was continued until land routes diverted the greater share of the ore traffic to Milwaukee.

Yet even before ore shipments on the Wisconsin ceased, lumber rafts made of the great pines in the north were sweeping downstream every year with the spring tides. Soon there arose a class of rivermen experienced in running the falls and rapids of the upper Wisconsin and in weaving through the islands and channels of the lower Wisconsin. In their stories they created a mythical riverman, great as Paul Bunyan in proportions and prowess, Whiskey Jack, who, with his rowdy crew, roamed up and down the river, performing amazing feats of strength and endurance. Then lumbering in turn died down; today river travel in other than small boats is impossible, for the channels are clogged with the mud washed in from tilled fields.

BOSCOBEL (Fr.-Ind., beautiful woods), 26.1 *m.* (673 alt., 1,762 pop.), clustered at the end of a high fill across the river swamp, though now a farm trade center, was formerly an important shipping point and stopping place for river traffic. Here the few steamboats that plied the Wisconsin discharged provisions as they went upstream; on the return trip they stopped to pick up freight and farm produce. Stagecoaches brought travelers from the interior to the river port; ox teams plodded over rutted roads with wagonloads of wheat or other produce;

rowdy raftsmen bound for Mississippi ports stopped off for food, drink, and frolic.

The Christian Commercial Travelers Association of America, more commonly known as the Gideons, whose Bibles are found in hotel rooms throughout the country, was founded in Boscobel in 1899. One night in that year two traveling salesmen were forced to share a common room. Before retiring, one drew forth a Bible, asked to be pardoned for the delay in turning out the light, and prepared to read to himself. The other recognized the book and said, "I am a Christian also. Let us have our devotions together."

Later the two men discussed the dismal evenings of Christian traveling men, who in the search for innocent entertainment often fished out old newspapers from the bottoms of bureau drawers or read telephone books from cover to cover. Suddenly they conceived the plan of the Gideons Society for Christian traveling men. The new organization was interdenominational; its members wore buttons as means of recognition; by 1907 the membership had reached 23,000. The society undertook to place a Bible in every hotel room in the United States and in every stateroom on vessels plying inland waters or engaging in coastwise trade. Most hotel keepers were willing to cooperate, and by 1914, 237,846 Bibles had been placed in 3,500 hotels. Pasted on the inside cover of each volume were such useful suggestions as these: "If trade is poor, read Psalm 37; John 15"; "If discouraged or in trouble, read Psalm 126; John 14"; "If you are out of sorts, read Hebrews 12."

Across a small bridge and opposite a little hospital in the center of town is the RESIDENCE OF JOHN J. BLAINE (1875-1934), Governor of Wisconsin (1921-27), United States Senator (1927-33), for a generation one of the outstanding liberal leaders in Wisconsin politics (*see Government*).

Crossing the floorlike, sandy flood plain of the Wisconsin, where great river bluffs range skyward on either side, US 61 once more enters coulee country, ascending imperceptibly the 10-mile escarpment of the Galena-Black River cuesta. In the folds and clefts of the hillsides lie half-hidden farms. Some of the farmsteads are old rectangular pioneer structures with high roofs and thick walls built of sandstone blocks; others are small frame houses; a few are crude log cabins set back against slopes amid sprawling outbuildings.

FENNIMORE, 37.6 m. (1,196 alt., 1,341 pop.) (*see Tour 23*), is at the junction with US 18 (*see Tour 23*).

LANCASTER, 49.2 m. (1,086 alt., 2,432 pop.), since 1837 the seat of Grant County, is old, shady, placid. Its business buildings straggle around the courthouse square, its residences spread irregularly beyond.

In the center of the GEORGE W. RYLAND PARK is the PUBLIC LIBRARY, an old white building with the flat siding and ornate roof popular in the 1880's. In shady Courthouse Square is the red brick COURTHOUSE with a gleaming dome of copper and green glass. Within the building a sealed box bears the inscription, "Accursed be he who peneth me ere a hundred years are gone." The box was sealed in 1876 during the country's celebration of the 100th anniversary of American Independence and contains issues of the county newspapers, agricultural products raised at that time, and the like. A CIVIL WAR MONUMENT, one of the first erected in the United States, and a STATUE OF NELSON DEWEY, the State's first Governor (1848-1852), stand in the square. Dewey (*see below*) is buried in the local Episcopalian cemetery.

The GRANT COUNTY ASYLUM (L), 51.6 *m.*, consists of a group of big brick buildings set on level wooded grounds. The soil here is rich and black; farm buildings are large and well painted, all but concealed behind cool screens of shade trees. Across an undulating plain is (R) the blue wall of the Iowa bluffs that line the Mississippi.

BRITISH HOLLOW, 60.1 *m.*, with its tumble-down buildings and stone ruins set against a steep low ridge, is old and shabby with the years. Tiny arched bridges of weathered stone span creeks into farmyards; cultivated fields are pocked with the sod-covered test holes sunk by early lead miners; occasionally a square outline of mossy yellow stone, the foundation of some pioneer's house, lies half buried in the pasture sod.

Right on State 129 to POTOSI, 1 *m.* (786 alt., 447 pop.), and tiny POTOSI STATION, 2.5 *m.*, the former a famous mining town, the latter a river port that rivaled Galena, Ill. From Potosi Station lead was shipped out on river barges, and supplies were brought in for distribution through the backwoods. One of the great lead strikes of the region occurred in 1829 when prospectors from Dubuque and Galena uncovered a rich vein in this hollow. Immediately miners rushed in with pick and shovel, ripped the ore from the ground, and shipped it down the Mississippi in grimy barges. Pocked with the scars of old pits, Potosi winds along the narrow valley floor, a drowsy and well-worn village. The brewery, its oldest part built solidly of stone about 1852, still operates. During prohibition it manufactured a cereal beverage. Frame or stone houses are often niched into the hillside; vaultlike root cellars penetrate the coulee walls behind them.

At 3.3 *m.* is the junction with County O; R. on County O along the Mississippi bluffs to CASSVILLE, 10.1 *m.* (620 alt., 575 pop.), a thriving village connected with the Iowa shore by a paddle-wheeled ferry. In 1831 Glendower Price settled here and opened a general store. Five years later Garrett V. Denniston and Lucius Lyon, land speculators from the East, came and platted the village, reserving a place for the future State capitol. When the seat of government was established elsewhere, the village first became a lead- and wheat-shipping port, finally a farmers' trade center.

At 10.9 *m.* is the junction with State 133; straight ahead on State 133 to NELSON DEWEY FARMSTEAD STATE PARK, 11.9 *m.*, former estate of Nelson Dewey, first Governor of Wisconsin (1848-1852). Dewey settled in Cassville in 1836, and he died here in 1889 after a long life of political service. The estate, which has been restored, includes the red brick mansion house, rebuilt after fire destroyed it in 1873; a two-story stone building with dormer windows, used as storehouse and servants' living quarters; an old smokehouse; a stone milk house with floor sunk two feet below the ground; a poultry house; and a barn with huge loft, iron-barred stalls for horses, tack room, and granary. Stone for all these buildings except the mansion house was hauled by ox teams from a quarry near Rock Flat, seven miles away. A circus at present leases the barn from the State. In the park are picnic tables and outdoor fireplaces.

The highway crosses Platte River, 65.5 *m.,* at a point where a ferry once operated. Even after the first bridge had been built the ferry continued its work, for every heavy backwater would tear the flimsy structure loose and carry it downstream or lodge it in the trees along the banks. From the crest of a ridge appear (R) the jagged blue outline of the Iowa bluffs and (L) the Platte Mounds, 10 to 15 miles distant (*see Tour 12*).

DICKEYVILLE, 68.7 *m.* (955 alt., 85 pop.) (*see Tour 12*), is at the junction with US 151 (*see Tour 12*). Between Dickeyville and the Iowa Line, 76.7 *m.,* US 61 and US 151 are one route (*see Tour 12*).

Tour 12

Dodgeville — Mineral Point — Platteville — Dickeyville — (Dubuque, Iowa); US 151.
Dodgeville to Iowa Line, 51.2 *m.*

Oiled-gravel and concrete roadbed.
Village and city accommodations; few resorts and campsites.

US 151 traverses the oldest settled region in Wisconsin, the unglaciated mining country. Here in the southwest is the only area in the State that was not covered by the great glacier (*see Natural Setting*), and here, too, is the only region where the invading seas of preglacial eras deposited rich veins of lead and zinc. Thousands of years later it was lead that attracted the first large group of permanent white settlers to Wisconsin and made mining the first stable industry in the State.

How early the Indians mined the lead is not known, but toward the end of the eighteenth century the more enterprising among them owned small diggings and were smelting the metal over open fires. By 1824, in spite of the hostility of the Winnebagoes, the earliest Badger mining settlements were founded at Hardscrabble, now Hazel Green (*see Tour 24*), and New Diggings. Three years later hundreds of lead miners came, the "Suckers" and "Badgers" from Missouri, Kentucky, Tennessee, and southern Illinois. The former came north in early spring and retreated south in fall; the latter dug homes in the hillsides and stayed the year around. Wisconsin's nickname, the "Badger State," comes from them.

These miners settled wherever lead was found. By 1828 the three focal cities of Dodgeville, Mineral Point, and Platteville were founded, and a mining boom swept the region. Between 1832-5 the Cornish came—thrifty, industrious, resourceful men of the same type as Simon Carfax in *Lorna Doone*. They lived in solid little houses built of native limestone, and worked in the diggings, buying up their own land when the mineral-bearing region was thrown open to sale by the Federal Government in 1846.

Meantime, the Military Road between Green Bay and Prairie du Chien, now US 18 (*see Tour 23*), was being built, and in 1835 the portion between Lake Winnebago and Prairie du Chien was opened to traffic. Two years later a spur branching off from it at Dodgeville was constructed through Mineral Point to the river port of Galena, Illinois. During mining days this highway, now US 151, became as busy and colorful a thoroughfare as ever existed in Wisconsin. People swarmed westward in a steady stream, churned the road into knee-deep mud in spring, then ground it into deep ruts and pulverized it to dust in summer. Traffic was confused and noisy; oxen, cattle, horses, and mules; traveling coaches, light carriages, covered wagons, and prairie schooners; jobless men seeking opportunity, adventurers seeking excitement, gamblers seeking prey, criminals fleeing from the law, and professional men and artisans searching for new communities. They crossed the streams on ferries where such were provided; otherwise they forded.

Men became rich overnight; promotion schemes thrived; land purchased as non-mineral bearing at the Government price of $1.25 an acre sold for $10,000 to $30,000 when rich ore deposits were discovered on it. Diggings and burrows became mushroom towns, frequented by miners, Indian fighters, Government officials, prospectors, swindlers, professional gamblers, and hangers-on. In 1828, when Milwaukee was only a trading post and Racine still a sand bar, the lead-mining district reported a population of 10,000.

Lead production reached its peak between 1845 and 1847 with an annual average output of 18,000 tons; but within five years a 50-per cent decline occurred, caused by the scarcity of easily accessible ores, the decreased price of lead, and the exodus of miners to the California gold fields. Hope that this region would become the focal center of the State faded as population declined and enterprising Easterners settled along the Lake Michigan shore. The miners turned to farming, and today US 151 crosses one of the State's richest dairy and corn-hog districts, where mining is now largely a matter of legend. Here the pastures are still pocked with sod-covered pits, remnants of the test holes and one-man mines sunk a hundred years ago; in the villages stand century-old houses, many of them occupied by descendants of the "Badgers" who built them so laboriously by hand.

US 151 branches south from US 18 (*see Tour 23*), 0 *m.*, on the northern outskirts of Dodgeville.

DODGEVILLE, 1.6 *m.* (1,253 alt., 1,937 pop.), named for Governor Henry Dodge (*see below*), was the metropolis of the lead region between 1827 and 1829; one of the earliest lead furnaces was built here. Then lead prices slumped, miners left, and before Dodgeville

regained prosperity in the 1850's it had lost primacy to Mineral Point
In 1859, after boundary changes had made Dodgeville more centrall
situated in Iowa County, the county seat was established here. Th
election was hotly contested, and Mineral Pointers delayed the officia
transfer by litigation. Feeling ran so high that after one temporar
victory the Pointers sent to Warren, Illinois, for a cannon, a 12-pounde
the only thing in the region loud enough to express their jubilatior
All day long they derisively bombarded Dodgeville with noise. How
ever, in 1860 the courts decided in favor of Dodgeville.

Today the city is a retail and shipping center for one of the bes
dairy and corn-hog districts in the State and a fine pea-growing regior
The COURTHOUSE, erected in 1859 in anticipation of the court decisior
is the oldest in Wisconsin. A building of buff native limestone, wit
a wooden cupola like those on New England churches and a facade c
fluted white pillars in the style of the South, it is a curious minglin
of local materials and imported tastes. CENTENNIAL PARK on th
southern outskirts, L. at 2.1 m:,. is a community picnic area and play
ground.

South of Dodgeville US 151 crosses a rich and varied farm regior
The land sweeps downward (L) as far as Blue Mounds, 15 mile
east, whose tilled flanks are clearly visible rising from the plain. Th
two Platte Mounds loom (R) in silhouette on the horizon 25 mile
southwest.

At 5.2 m. is the junction (L) with a graveled road.

Left on this road to the SITE OF GOVERNOR DODGE'S HOMESTEAD (L), 1.1 n
The site is marked by an unobtrusive granite stone almost hidden by wil
shrubbery at the bottom of a ravine.

Henry Dodge (1782-1867) swaggered through early Wisconsin history or
of the most brilliant and colorful characters the State has known. A ig
handed but forthright man, he carried a bowie knife and horrified sedate Eas
erners with his language. Before coming here he had been implicated in th
Aaron Burr conspiracy and indicted for treason by a grand jury. Outrage
by the charge, Dodge thrashed nine of the jurors, and the indictment w
dropped. In 1827 he came to Wisconsin and illegally settled on Indian lan
here. The Indians protested and the Indian agent threatened military actio
but Dodge blandly continued mining until the Indians gave up their title to th
land; then he bought more than 1,000 acres.

At the outbreak of the Black Hawk War, Dodge scoured the settlement
built forts, and gathered his famous mobile rangers. Black Hawk later d
clared that except for "Hairy Face" and his band of miners, his party woul
have escaped massacre. Thus becoming prominent, Dodge was appointe
first Territorial Governor in 1836. In 1841 he was displaced by his Whi
opponent and life-long rival, the wily speculator, Judge James Duane Dot
Reappointed Governor by President Polk in 1845, Dodge held office until th
State of Wisconsin was created in 1848, then served as United States Senat
until he retired in 1857. Though a former slaveholder, Dodge voted again
the Kansas-Nebraska bill and the extension of slavery.

The LEVI STERLING HOUSE (R), 7.2 m., is a rambling old re
brick structure. Sterling came here from Kentucky in 1828, was mar
times sheriff of Iowa County, and served in the Territorial legislatu
in 1838.

MINERAL POINT, 10.1 *m*. (944 alt., 2,274 pop.), is rich in relics of a vigorous past. Its streets are crooked, narrow, and steeply sloping; many of its buildings are a century old, covered with grime that has been accumulating since the earliest lead furnaces belched forth smoke over the valley.

Nat Morris, a roving prospector, discovered the great deposits in Mineral Point Hill in 1828. The community grew swiftly, settled first by Southern prospectors, then by Cornishmen after 1832. The city became locally known as Shake Rag because of its principal street, Shake Rag under the Hill, where Cornish miners built small houses of solid limestone blocks. At dinnertime dishcloths were waved to summon the men home from their mines on the opposite hillside; hence the name.

In 1836, when the Territorial government was organized, Henry Dodge was inaugurated first Governor here amid the acclamations of the town's 2,000 inhabitants, for Belmont, then temporary capital, was too small for a suitable celebration of the occasion. At that time Mineral Point was entering a period of growth that survived the depression of 1837, the disturbances of the California gold rush period, and a serious cholera epidemic. Noted leaders came here; William Hamilton, son of Alexander Hamilton; Charles Dunn, first Chief Justice during Territorial days; Moses M. Strong, early politician; and others.

From lead mining Mineral Point turned to zinc, and then, as mining declined, successfully effected a transition to retailing, shipping, and small dairy manufactures.

A small stone LODGE dedicated to Governor Dodge stands in a park at the intersection of Ridge St. (US 151) and High St. At 109 Ridge St., across the road, is the HENRY PLOWMAN HOUSE, where Dodge lived in a rented room. A long, shuttered limestone structure set at a slight angle to the street, the house was erected by one of the founders of the *Miner's Free Press,* the city's second newspaper (1838).

At the corner of High, Iowa, and Doty Sts., are the TRINITY CHURCH, the PARISH HOUSE (L), and the METHODIST CHURCH (R). The Trinity congregation was founded in 1836 by Episcopalians. The cornerstone of the plain red-brick building was laid in 1839, but because the trustee of the building fund "appropriated it to other and baser uses," the building itself was not erected until 1845. The Methodist congregation, said to be the first in Wisconsin, built a log building in 1834, replaced it with a small stone church in 1838, and erected the present large buttressed structure in 1867-71. The parish house, a barnlike structure of yellow vertical siding, stands on the site of the once famous Bank of Mineral Point, one of the first banks in the State.

Chartered in 1836 with a capital of $200,000, this bank, after a financial struggle involving Judge Doty, came under the management of S. B. Knapp and Porter Brace. Most of its business was in bills of exchange to and from Eastern cities, and the bank began issuing to its creditors "red dogs" (90-day bills endorsed in red ink) and "blue bellies" (6-month paper endorsed in blue ink). This practice infuriated the townspeople; an investigation was started and Knapp fled. When captured at Rockford, Illinois, he had nothing with him but several books, which he gave to the editor of the local paper. Suspicious, his captors scrutinized these books and found over $50,000 in notes and bills pasted in the fly-leaves. The creditors of the defunct bank then sent W. H. Banks east to collect on their bills of exchange. But Banks never returned.

The MINERAL POINT BANK was housed in a small red-brick building that stands at 324 High St. Its two founders, Cadwallader C. Washburn and Cyrus Woodman, had been law partners. After the partnership dissolved in 1855 Woodman retired. Washburn served as Congressman in 1855-61 and 1867-71, rose to the rank of major general during the Civil War, was Governor in 1872-4, and helped found the Washburn-Crosby flour mills in Minneapolis. The building has since been occupied by shops.

A row of CORNISH MINERS' HOUSES, with walls one foot thick, still stands on Shake Rag St., which runs parallel to a slow-flowing creek in the cleft of the valley. One of the most noted is the PENDARVIS HOUSE, built in the early 1830's, now a restaurant (*reservations must be made in advance*) and antique shop. Here are served pasties, clotted cream, saffron cakes, and other Cornish dishes. On the steep hillside across the river is SOLDIERS MEMORIAL PARK, containing a fine modern swimming pool built into the slope.

GUNDRY HOUSE, corner of Pine and Davis Sts., is a large stone mansion on a hilltop overlooking most of the city. Though built by a Cornishman, Joseph Gundry, the cupola on top, the great colonnaded porch, the stepping block at the driveway the cupolated outbuildings and pavilions scattered about the estate, all are reminiscent of the original Southern influence that still tinges local culture. Since 1940 the building has housed the MINERAL POINT HISTORICAL SOCIETY MUSEUM (*adm. to grounds and museum 25¢; open 1-5 daily from May 1 to Nov. 1*), where articles of historical interest, including old costumes, furniture, china and glassware, Indian relics, and minerals, are displayed. The mineral collection is one of the finest in the Middle West.

Partly built in 1836, the WALKER HOTEL, Commerce St. at the depot, is a long, balconied, three-story stone building, the oldest remaining hotel in the city. Almost directly opposite it occurred one of Wisconsin's few legal hangings. The victim was William Caffee, who was tried and condemned in 1842 for shooting Samuel Southwick.

The FIRST ODD FELLOWS' HALL, corner of Front and S. Vine Sts., has been converted into an Odd Fellow's museum (*open daily; free*). The building, of yellow-painted matched planks with green shutters and white trimming, was erected in 1838. The wrought-iron insignia with the words "Iowa No. 1" remain in the iron railing of the porch. Iowa No. 1 was founded in 1835 and was the first lodge of the Odd Fellows organized in the Northwest.

COTHREN HOUSE, one block east of Front St. in the 400 block on the easternmost edge of the city, is the still-inhabited ruin of a lordly mansion. The heavy limestone walls, necessitating window frames two feet thick, were once embellished with wrought-iron balconies; only a few damp mossy planks remain and some of the ironwork has collapsed. The shutters dangle in pieces, vines climb to the roof, banks of lilac trees grow wild at the side, and, in the rear, a crevice of rotting stone splits the building from top to bottom.

Southwest of Mineral Point US 151 rides a ridge overlooking small beautiful valleys on either side. The countryside in broken by steep, low ridges and hills, among which are cornfields enormous for Wisconsin. The Platte Mounds (R) become clearer and appear lower as they are approached.

BELMONT, 23.2 m. (1,010 alt., 452 pop.), is a small farm village. At the northern edge of the town is the junction with a clay-gravel road.

Right (straight ahead) on this road up the flanks of the smaller PLATTE MOUND, 2.8 m. Here the mound appears hardly more than a knoll. The land falls away imperceptibly to great distances, for it is a gradual swell rather than loftiness that enables this hill and its twin to dominate the skyline throughout most of southwestern Wisconsin. These mounds are 1,420 and 1,380 feet above sea level. In 1827 Major John H. Rountree and a friend, exploring in the region, climbed one of them to view the surrounding country and carved their names in rocks where Indian signal fires once burned. Rountree later became owner of one of the most profitable mines in the Platteville district.

At 3.2 m. is the FIRST CAPITOL BUILDING set in a small lawn now preserved as a State historical park. When the Territory of Wisconsin was created by Congress in 1836, the government seat was temporarily established at Old Belmont, a village that stood upon this site. The first legislature rented the frame building for its capitol and met there for 46 days. Lumber for this structure, like that for other plank or frame buildings in the Territory at that time, was bought in Pittsburgh and shipped here via the Ohio and Mississippi Rivers.

In 1836, after a long struggle, the legislature was influenced by James Duane Doty (see Madison) to locate the permanent capitol at the then unoccupied site of Madison. Old Belmont vanished; the first capitol building was abandoned to menial uses and at one time became the wing of a barn. It was restored to its original place and appearance in 1924.

PLATTEVILLE, 31.5 m. (918 alt., 4,047 pop.), a city of hilly streets, old false-front buildings, and irregular layout, is the present metropolis of the mining country. Around it are many marginal mines. The WISCONSIN INSTITUTE OF TECHNOLOGY, 20 N. Elm St., established in 1907, provides three- and four-year training courses for practical mining engineers and foremen, and, in late years, for highway construction engineers. The PLATTEVILLE STATE TEACHERS COLLEGE, 722 W. Pine St., is the State's first normal school. The HOUSE OF MAJOR JOHN H. ROUNTREE (not open), one block south on 3rd St. from its intersection with Pine St., is a red-brick, two-story Georgian building of L-shaped design. Interesting features are the Greek pediment, the gingerbread type of decoration in the cornices, a two-story, wooden porch, and long windows which reach almost to the floor. A bronze tablet states that this was the home of Rountree, one of the founders of Platteville in 1827. The building is now an apartment house.

Platteville is at the junction with State 81.

Right on State 81 to the ROUNTREE HOUSE (*not open*), 0.3 *m.* (R), on the outskirts of the city. A small cottage with low roof and dormer windows, half-concealed amid shady grounds on a small knoll, it was built about 1837 by the Reverend Samuel Mitchell. Later it was purchased and inhabited for many years by Major Rountree (*see above*) and is still owned by descendants of his family. Regarded as a charming example of early pioneer architecture, it contains some valuable old furniture.

Southwest of Platteville US 151 passes a small abandoned lead mine (R), 33.4 *m.,* and traverses more rugged country broken by deep twisting valleys. The road descends from its ridge and winds through the valley of the Little Platte River.

DICKEYVILLE, 43.2 *m.* (955 alt., 85 pop.), is the site of Father Wernerus' "sermons in stone," which were visited by more than 40,000 people in 1937. The GROTTO OF CHRIST THE KING AND MARY HIS MOTHER and its surrounding edifices were built between 1920 and 1930 as an act of devotion by the Reverend Father Mathias Wernerus and his cousin and housekeeper, Miss Mary Wernerus. The grotto contains a figure of the Virgin Mary holding the Infant Jesus, carved from a single slab of marble at Carrara, Italy, by a friend of Father Wernerus. Surrounding the grotto is a wall in which are set the statues of the Apostles and St. Paul and St. Joseph. Behind it is an elaborate exedra called PATRIOTISM IN STONE, in which a statue of Columbus is flanked by smaller statues of Lincoln and Washington. Another canopy shelters the figure of Jesus Christ.

These structures are composed of thousands of bits of broken glass and china, colored pebbles, turned rock balls, petrified wood, shells, and other bright objects, all set into a base of cement. The stones were imported from all parts of the world, and some of the old pieces of china and glassware are very valuable. The grotto is lined with unpolished Arizona onyx, the ceiling hung with crystals and snow-white stalactites. The surrounding garden contains sculptured animals and strange plants, all made of the same bristling mosaic that encrusts the posts and chains of the low fencing. An elaborate gateway to the cemetery in the rear of the grounds is of the same type.

At Dickeyville is the junction with US 61 (*see Tour 11*); between this junction and the Iowa line US 151 and US 61 are one route.

US 151 continues along the ridge top, overlooking many miles of bare rounded hills. Here erosion has laid waste frequent acres of farmland; though corn is grown on some of the hilltops, most of the land along the roadside is given over to pasturage. Suddenly the highway comes to the edge of the bluffs that look across the Mississippi River flood plain to Dubuque, Iowa, along the opposite shore; then, through a gap in the hills, the road winds downward to the floor of the flood plain near EAGLE POINT (R). Farther upstream appears a line of the precipitous bluffs that wall the river as far as the Twin Cities. US 61 runs alongside a reservoir dike, designed to hold the backwater of the great dam directly ahead.

At 51.2 *m.* is EAGLE POINT BRIDGE (*35¢ for car and driver, 5¢ each additional passenger*) which crosses the Mississippi to Dubuque.

Tour 13

Superior—Hudson—La Crosse—Prairie du Chien; 348.2 *m.* State 35 and State 27.

Soo Line parallels route between Superior and Osceola: Chicago, St. Paul, Minneapolis and Omaha R.R. between Hudson and Ellsworth; Chicago, Burlington and Quincy R.R. between Maiden Rock and Prairie du Chien.
Hard-surfaced or graveled roadbed.
Excellent facilities in cities; resort accommodations in summer.

Beginning at Lake Superior, State 35 crosses a waste of sand and cutover forest, whose monotony is broken by the great falls and pine-banked gorge of the Black River at Pattison State Park. The variety and beauty of lower sections of the route, which for long stretches skirt the palisaded banks of the Mississippi River, have been suggested by William Cullen Bryant, who, writing of a representative region, said, "This place ought to be visited by every poet and every painter in America. . . . It is a grief that Americans should wander off to the Rhine and the Danube, when in the Mississippi they have countless Rhines and Danubes. . . . Is Drachenfels one whit more castellated than any of the nameless bluffs about and around Trempealeau? All that is beautiful in lake-scenery, in lower mountain-scenery and river-scenery is garnered here." But Bryant apologized for the absence of "the dismantled walls of . . . robber barons' dens," unaware that the French occupation and the frontier life of steamboat days were to contribute romantic interest to many a faded river village along this highway.

Section a.   SUPERIOR to HUDSON; 145.1 m., State 35

SUPERIOR, 0 *m.* (629 alt., 36,113 pop.) (*see Superior*).
At Tower Ave. and Belknap St. is the junction with US 53 (*see Tour 10*), US 2 (*see Tour 14*), and State 13 (*see Tour 14A*). South of this junction State 35 ascends the slowly rising plain of the Superior Basin.

At 3.8 *m.* is the junction with State 105.

Right on State 105 to the only FREE BRIDGE, 4.5 *m.*, over the St. Louis River between Superior and Duluth, Minn.

State 35 ascends an irregular slope to the plateau along the route of the old Hudson Bay-La Pointe trail, a frontier forest route. This northern rim of the plateau is known as the Douglas Copper Range, for traces of the metal have been found here since the days when the Indians picked up occasional bits of almost pure copper. Attempts to develop the deposits have been unsuccessful, however, for the copper occurs in small and scattered pockets.

PATTISON STATE PARK, 13 *m.* (*camping, boating and bathing; no overnight accommodations*), is a 1,140-acre tract high above the Superior basin, named for its donor, Martin Pattison. Here the Black River rushes over a ledge to form the highest waterfall in Wisconsin, BIG MANITOU FALLS (Ind., *Gitchee Monido,* Falls of the Great Spirit), which plunges down 165 feet through a narrow notch of sandstone. Footpaths lead along the cliffs on both sides of the gorge; at the far end of the gorge the Mesaba Range appears beyond a vast wooded basin.

At 14.1 *m.* is the junction with a dirt park road.

Left on this road to 30-foot LITTLE MANITOU FALLS, 0.3 *m.* Although this drop is small in comparison with Gitchee Monido, the falls are broad, rocky, and hemmed in by timber.

For 100 miles State 35 runs through a wilderness of saplings and brush that blanket stumps left by the loggers. In summer the whang of portable sawmills rings through the woods; here and there freshly cut planks are stacked along the roadside. The only buildings are a few gray shacks and stores, covered with dented tin signs. At night the feeblest yellow light from the windows of a store-tavern seems warm and companionable.

DAIRYLAND, 35.3 *m.*, a small village of tarpaper shacks in the midst of charred stumps, was the scene of an experiment that attracted considerable attention in the early 1930's. When millions of workers were idle, editors, industrialists, and certain officials advocated a back-to-the-land movement as a partial solution of unemployment. With thousands of acres on its hands as a result of tax delinquencies, Douglas County devised its own homestead plan, offering land at $2 an acre cash, $3 on time. Throughout the country it advertised its cheap land, and between 1930 and 1932 allocated 103 sales, totaling 7,031 acres. But most families to whom land was assigned did little more than bargain; fewer than half moved on their land. Moreover, the plan attracted not a single one of the urban unemployed for whom it was primarily designed.

State 35 crosses the ST. CROIX RIVER, 47.9 *m.*, five miles above the point where it becomes the boundary between Wisconsin and Minnesota. The St. Croix was an important artery of travel and commerce both for the French and the early lumbermen, who every spring floated their logs down its rapids to sawmills at Hudson, Lakeland, and Stillwater. The highway twists among rough hills, past a number of small lakes, to the Yellow River, 55.8 *m.,* near which stand a few scattered Indian huts, covered with tarpaper or painted bright blue.

At 56.5 *m.* is the junction with State 152.

Right on State 152 to DANBURY, 0.3 *m.* (932 alt., 315 pop.), main trading center for the Indians living in the nearby woods. The Indians are usually seen slouching along the highway or working in their gardens, dressed in the ordinary garb of backwoods Wisconsin except for a feather or a touch of bright color.

State 35 crosses an open, partly tilled plateau past LONG LAKE, 58.1 *m.,* and YELLOW LAKE (R), 63.1 *m.* Over the brush (R) rises the wavering line of the Minnesota Hills.

At 69.9 *m.* is the junction with State 70 (*see Tour 15*) ; between this junction and SIREN, 72.2 *m.* (24 pop.), State 35 and State 70 are one route. The highway passes through a number of small villages, among them MILLTOWN, 92.9 *m.* (1,239 alt., 450 pop.), home of the farmer-politician, George Nelson (1873-   ), a former Progressive Republican who joined the Socialist Party during the depression and became its candidate for Vice President of the United States in 1936. Nelson provided leadership when his Scandinavian farmer supporters needed it most, helping them to organize and direct their strength in a fight against farm foreclosure sales. The Federal Land Bank, holder of many mortgages, and large financial trust houses were persuaded by angry crowds of Polk County men and women to postpone sales, reduce rates of interest and even the principal itself. Under the slogan, "heads together and our heels out, boys," the farmers succeeded in saving their homes.

At 103.9 *m.* is the junction with US 8 (*see Tour 16*) ; between this junction and a point at 108 *m.,* State 35 and US 8 are one route.

OSCEOLA, 115.2 *m.* (809 alt., 607 pop.), platted in 1855, served for several years as the Polk County seat. Though Osceola is the name of a famous Florida Seminole chief, the name of the village is probably a corruption of *"asi-yahole"* (black drink halloer), a phrase the Indians used when drinking in turn from a river.

A pea viner is on the outskirts of FARMINGTON, 120 *m.* Beyond SOMERSET, 129.6 *m.* (922 alt., 480 pop.), which occupies a flat on the southwestern bank of the Apple River, State 35 descends rapidly through irregular country to the bank of the St. Croix.

HUDSON, 145.1 *m.* (700 alt., 2,725 pop.), the largest city on State 35 between Superior and La Crosse, is an old community built upon land which slopes gently down to the St. Croix between the mouth of the Willow River and two great bluffs half a mile to the south. In 1838 Louis Massey, French-Canadian trapper, built a dugout here and married an Indian squaw. After quarreling with her for 25 years, Massey built a separate dugout for his mate, and for the remaining 15 years of their lives they lived in close separation.

In 1840, when the boundaries of St. Croix County extended far beyond their present limits, its seat was established at Brown's Warehouse (now Hastings, Minnesota). In 1846, when this settlement became part of Minnesota, the county seat was shifted to Stillwater; then in 1848 Stillwater also was given to Minnesota. The discouraged settlers on the Wisconsin side of the river established no other county government until 1853 when present St. Croix County was laid out, with Hudson as the seat.

After a period of boom the city declined during the 1870's when near-by Minneapolis and St. Paul began to flourish as wheat-milling centers, dominating the trade of the entire region. As the nearest Wisconsin gateway to the Twin Cities, Hudson still attracts considerable trade and traffic both by rail and highway.

A small landscaped MUNICIPAL PARK AND BATHING BEACH lies at the entrance of a TOLL BRIDGE (*15¢ for car and driver; 5¢ for each passenger; trucks and trailers 25¢ to $1*), which crosses the St. Croix River into Minnesota, 15 miles east of St. Paul. Below the bridge the river widens and stretches away between high wood-grown walls, losing itself around a curve of hazy hills far downstream. PROSPECT PARK (*free; kitchen and public dining room*), overlooks Hudson and the upper river.

Hudson is at the junction with US 12 (*see Tour 19*).

Section b.   HUDSON to LA CROSSE; 135.2 m., State 35

State 35 climbs out of HUDSON, 0 *m.*; at 0.6 *m.* two markers indicate the entrance (R) to BIRKMOSE PARK, overlooking the lower river and Lake St. Croix. Among the trees on the crest are several Indian mounds. The highway follows a low ridge, curving southward and eastward by turns to the valley of the Kinnikinnic River, where it winds among mesa-like hills covered with trees.

RIVER FALLS, 12.1 *m.* (887 alt., 2,363 pop.), straddling the Pierce-St. Croix County line, is strung loosely along the Kinnikinnic River. In 1849 Joel Foster of Connecticut stopped in a Stillwater saloon and heard a drunk say: ". . . if I had a section or two in the Kinnikinnick Valley I would not ask General Jackson to be my aunt." Foster explored the valley, considered it promising, and founded a settlement here, naming it Greenwood. Within two years it had two sawmills, a planing mill, and a large flour mill. Greenwood was soon rechristened Kinnikinnick, a name it bore when Bill Nye (*see Literature*) came here from Maine in 1852.

In Civil War times River Falls had a teacher-training academy called the Seminary. This was replaced in 1870 by Hinckley's Military Academy, a coeducational boarding school, founded by a former cadet at West Point. In 1872 a State Normal School was established here. The city, in those days, had eight handsome bridges spanning its streams, mill races, and waterfalls. According to a local history published in 1900, young ladies would frequent the Glen, a well-bred place "tremu-

Lumbering ; Conservation

REFORESTATION, CHEQUAMAGON
NATIONAL FOREST

WHITE PINE STAND

LOGGING CAMP, MENOMINEE INDIAN
RESERVATION

STUBBLE OF A FOREST CROP

CATERPILLAR TRACTOR HAULING LOGS

Above Left

UNITED STATES FOREST PRODUCTS LABORATORY, MADISON. HERE THROUGH EXTENSIVE RESEARCH THE GOVERNMENT SEEKS TO IMPROVE AND DEVELOP METHODS OF USING WOOD, AS SHOWN IN THESE PHOTOGRAPHS

Below Left

PREFABRICATED PLY-WOOD HOUSE, BUILT AT THE FOREST PRODUCTS LABORATORY

Above Right

TESTING FENCE POSTS

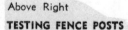

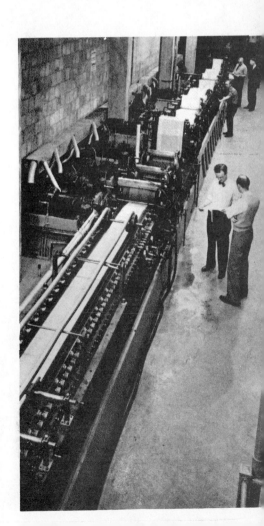

Below Right

TESTING PAPER IN PRECISION MACHINE

LAKE IN KELLOGG BIRD SANCTUARY

CENSUS TAKERS BRANDING A SNOWSHOE HARE

FEED HOPPER AND LEAN-TO SHELTER FOR PHEASANTS

WHITE-TAILED DEER IN WINTER YARDS

OLD LUMBER CAMP

PULPWOOD FOR PAPER, WISCONSIN RAPIDS

lous with the finer activities of the forest," and there, "like celestial companies of modern Dianas, console themselves for the lack of social briskness." In 1876 a fire consumed most of the business section, and in 1894 "the Kinnikinnick went on a startling frolic, in the course of which it broke down the mill dam, tied two of the iron bridges into bow knots and after undermining the stone arch, carried two of the wooden structures, in company with a saw mill and starch factory, over the falls and down the gorges toward the St. Croix."

GLEN PARK (*tourist camp, picnic lodge, swimming pool*), near the western end of Cascade Ave., is a wooded tract on the high bank above the junction of the South Fork and Kinnikinnic Rivers. A 100-foot suspension bridge for pedestrians, over the deep glen of the South Fork, connects the park with the city. On the southeastern outskirts of the city is River Falls STATE TEACHERS COLLEGE.

River Falls is at the junction with State 29 (*see Tour 17*); for 1.4 miles from this junction, State 35 and State 29 are one route.

The road follows along valleys into BELDENVILLE, 21.6 *m.*, where soft limestone is quarried, then crushed and used for fertilizer, and continues through hills capped with white stone outcroppings to ELLSWORTH, 26.5 *m.* (1,069 alt., 1,124 pop.) (*see Tour 18*), at the junction with US 10 (*see Tour 18*) and US 63 (*see Tour 9*). Between Ellsworth and a point at 28.2 *m.* US 10, US 63, and State 35 are one route; between Ellsworth and a point at 31.3 *m.* US 10 and State 35 are one route.

Turning south toward the Mississippi, State 35 traverses a hilly region to the river bluffs. The fields and pastures bordering the road are plumed with elms and dotted with bright farm buildings. In the middle distance the gentler slopes are patterned and many-tinted; thin lines of windbreak wander over the hillsides and up the gullies toward the heavy woodlots on the heights.

LAKE PEPIN, 40.3 *m.*, lies between 700-foot bluffs, extending far south through wooded palisades, a frozen sheet of white in winter, in summer a shimmering blue. The lake, an enlargment of the Mississippi, is formed by the sand bars heaped up by the swift Chippewa River where it enters the sluggish Mississippi. Of the two bluffs that shut off the view to the south, MAIDEN ROCK, on the Wisconsin side, is the loftier, rising sheer above the lake. The village of MAIDEN ROCK, 44 *m.* (692 alt., 311 pop.), is at the junction with County S.

Left on County S to the MAIDEN ROCK SILICA SAND COMPANY MINE, 0.3 *m.* (*visiting by permission of the owner, M. J. Gore*). Large shafts tunnel into the bluff, intersected at 100-foot intervals by cross shafts. Used for sandblasting, the silicate rock is blasted loose and hauled by truck to the refining plant, where it is dried, sifted, and sorted into various grades.

The highway winds along the narrow terrace between the river and the bluffs; in places the wooded slopes slant down almost to the water. The angular bluffs cast cubistic shadows in changing patterns of gray and blue. On these heights and in the ravines below the Sioux and the Chippewa waged war as late as 1851.

STOCKHOLM, 50.7 m. (688 alt., 205 pop.), has several carp ponds that supply live fish to kosher markets in large cities. Though clams are dredged for their shells, which are sold to button factories, clam fishing in the Mississippi is restricted by the Government, which is trying to preserve the mussels from extinction. A flour mill at Stockholm dates from the time when Wisconsin was a great wheat State and grain traffic supported many river barges.

PEPIN, 57.1 m. (683 alt., 603 pop.), first settled in 1846, has quiet streets, sloping lazily toward the river. Along the water front are sleepy hotels where fishermen gather about the stove and spend the long winter hours swapping yarns. Their speech draws many images from the great river. Seeing a drunken man staggering up the street in early spring, an idler remarks, "He's sure goin' up the river," and his crony replies, "Yep, he's gonna burn all the ice out of Lake Pepin."

Much in Pepin is reminiscent of the time when the river brought a steady flow of commerce and strangers; many of the people here remember the life Mark Twain wrote about, when boats shallow enough to "flat on a heavy dew" moved slowly among the bars and bottoms of the river. The Fuller brothers, celebrated steamboat engineers of the upper Mississippi, lived in Pepin; it is said that they were among the Mississippi steamboat men who helped to popularize the word "stateroom" as applied to ship cabins. The rooms were named for States, so that a passenger might, for instance, have a choice of residing temporarily in "Alabama" or "Texas."

State 35 crosses the CHIPPEWA RIVER, 59.7 m., which, draining the entire northwest portion of the State, was an important early highway for loggers and settlers. Millions of logs came crashing down from the Northwest every spring to be caught here at Beef Slough, the name given a great net of stagnant waterways along the Mississippi and Chippewa channels, once one of the biggest log harbors in the State. The logs were drawn into the bayous and sorted; each log bore the stamp of its owner punched into an end with a mall-driven die. Rafters then took the logs into the sheltered coves, and built them into rafts, which were floated down the river to St. Louis. These great brownish platforms, which sometimes covered the width of the Mississippi, were steered by a pilot and crew who lived in shanties built on them and labored with sweep oars to guide them down the channel.

The Chippewa was also an important navigable waterway for Eau Claire, Chippewa Falls, and other communities (see Tour 10). A bitter fight arose when the Beef Slough Improvement Company, organized by lumbermen along the Chippewa, proposed to close the mouth of the river with booms; the company's charter, finally granted in 1867, stated specifically that the river had to be kept open for navigation. The loggers thereupon devised swinging booms to allow boats to pass. Mills and yards were built back in the sloughs off the steamboat route.

NELSON, 64.9 *m.* (680 alt., 232 pop.), built on the edges of a maze of valleys and coulees and overshadowed by RATTLESNAKE BLUFF (R), was founded in 1844 by James Nelson, an Englishman. For a time it was a popular stopping place for lumberjacks en route to the Chippewa Valley camps.

Right from Nelson on the county road to a TOLL BRIDGE (*50¢ for passanger cars; trucks 75 to $1*), *4 m.*, into Wabasha, Minn.

ALMA, 73.3 *m.* (674 alt., 1,009 pop.), like other river towns, clings to the lower slopes of the bluffs. It is shady and old, with buildings of aged brick or weathered wood. Rising sharply out of its back yards is TWELVE MILE BLUFF, so called by rivermen because it was 12 miles from the mouth of the Chippewa. At one time a huge rock hung on the point of this bluff, a landmark for river travelers by day and night. It stood directly over the lower part of the village, where it caused considerable fear. When it finally fell in 1891, plowing great holes in the talus slope, only a fragment reached the road.

South of Alma State 35 is in the unglaciated country (*see Natural Setting*). In the flats along the Mississippi wood cutters occasionally work, chopping out railroad ties and other rough wood products. Overhead the crags rise like medieval battlements, with bastions, balconies, and gargoyles of wind-eroded rock.

COCHRANE, 81.7 *m.* (683 alt., 418 pop.), is L. below the highway.

MERRICK STATE PARK, 88.1 *m.* (*picnicking, camping, swimming, fishing, golf, sanitary facilities; no overnight accommodations*), a 291-acre tract facing on Fountain City Bay, has one of the best bathing beaches on the Upper Mississippi. The park was acquired by gift and named in honor of George Byron Merrick, Mississippi pilot, who became a historian of the upper river.

FOUNTAIN CITY, 90.5 *m.* (662 alt., 880 pop.), spills down EAGLE BLUFF and INDIAN HEAD ROCK. Stone walls hold terraced gardens on the steep cliffs; houses seem to hang precariously on the hills. Lots along the main street, which begins and ends near old breweries, were once sold at high prices by two brothers named Pierce, who had acquired title to the section of land designated as the Trempealeau County seat. Later they discovered that Section 1-19N-12W, set aside as the county seat plat, was not at Fountain City at all, but some distance upstream. They rushed up the river, seized a stray lumber raft, clapped together a shack, and called it a courthouse, notifying Fountain City officials that the county offices must be moved to the new site. Lawyers supported their claim, the offices were moved, and a new settlement arose, called Upper Fountain City. Old Fountain City built a stately courthouse and offered it dirt cheap to the county, which accepted it. But the following year, 1860, the settlement of Alma built still another courthouse, and the seat was finally moved there.

South of Fountain City the highway cuts into the yellow sandstone of the bluff. Birches climb the talus to bare limestone crags; down in the river white channel markers give warnings of submerged sand bars.

At 96.5 *m.* is the junction with State 54.

Right on State 54 to a FREE BRIDGE, 2 *m.*, leading into Winona, Minnesota.

State 35 turns east into the rough back country, where frequent coulees break the even ranks of the hills. Fields and pastures cover the ridge tops and level floor of the valleys, where numerous creameries stand at crossroads.

At CENTERVILLE, 105.8 *m.* (738 alt., 100 pop.), is the junction with State 93.

Right on State 93 through a coulee to TREMPEALEAU, 5 *m.* (712 alt., 541 pop.), founded by James Allen Reed, a Kentuckian who had served as scout for the garrisons at Prairie du Chien, and his son-in-law, James Douville. William Cullen Bryant was lyrical in describing Trempealeau and its environs, and the Reverend David Van Slyke, a local Methodist minister, attempted to prove that this was the site of the Garden of Eden.

The Reverend Van Slyke combined farming with preaching, but found time to publish a pamphlet entitled *The Garden of Eden* in 1886, in which he pointed out that according to Biblical description "the Garden" consisted of a valley with four rivers, one of them being the Euphrates, the Greek name for *the great river*. Trempealeau had the Mississippi, certainly a great river, the Beaver, the Trempealeau, and the Black. Finally, concluded the author, the two promontories framing the valley were the exact counterpart of the gates to Eden.

In Trempealeau is the junction with County K.

Right on this road, which descends to the water front and turns R. to 1,050-acre PERROT STATE PARK (*camping, picnicking, hiking, drinking water and sanitary facilities*), presented to the State in 1918 by John A. Latsch, of Winona, Minnesota.

A park road runs northeast near the Mississippi, past a number of log cabins and old stone houses clinging to the slopes of forested bluffs. Creeping around EAGLE BLUFF, southern extremity of the curving TREMPEALEAU BLUFFS, the road runs under THUNDER MOUNTAIN, BALD KNOB, BUNNIBLE BLUFF, REED'S PEAK, and PERROT RIDGE. The road continues along the edge of a meadow, with TREMPEALEAU BLUFFS forming the skyline (R), to a group of INDIAN MOUNDS and the SITE OF A FRENCH FORT, 1.9 *m.*, occupying a broad point on the shore of a slough (L). A marker explains that the site was identified about 1885, 200 years after Perrot (*see TOUR 2*) had built his trading post stockade here. In 1731 Linctot, a French officer, built a fort on the site and maintained it for five years. Rounding Brady's Bluff, the road comes to one of the mouths of the Trempealeau River, 2.7 *m.* where the water trickles among sloughs.

Across the river, but still within the park, is TREMPEALEAU MOUN-TAIN, a Mississippi landmark for 250 years. Called Hay-nee-ah-chah (Soaking Mountain) by the Winnebago and Minnechonkaha (Bluff in the Water) by the Chippewa, because from a distance it appears to rise directly out of the water, the mountain was known by the French equivalent, *"la montagne qui trempe a l'eau,"* as early as 1731. From this designation Trempealeau River, County, and village derive their present name.

The road turns R. along the east banks of the river, whose backwater forms OLD LAKE, 3.4 *m.*, passing a cluster of PICTURED ROCKS, another group of INDIAN MOUNDS, and a grove of butternut trees. Except for this grove, almost the entire drive is heavily shaded by oak and birch. The road loops east and south behind the isolated Trempealeau Bluffs and returns to the village, 7.8 *m.* North from Trempealeau on State 93 to Galesville, 15.8 *m.*

At GALESVILLE, 111 *m.* (712 alt., 1,069 pop.) (*see Tour 10*), is the junction with US 53 (*see Tour 10*); between this junction and La Crosse, State 35 and US 53 are one route (*see Tour 10*). At 119.7 *m.* is the junction with State 93 (*see above*).

LA CROSSE, 135.2 *m.* (649 alt., 39,614 pop.) (*see La Crosse*).

La Crosse is at the junction with US 53 (*see Tour 10*), US 16 (*see Tour 21*), and US 14 (*see Tour 20*).

Section c.   LA CROSSE to PRAIRIE DU CHIEN; 67.9 m.,
State 35 and State 27

Between LA CROSSE, 0 *m.,* and a point at 5 *m.* State 35 and US 14 (*see Tour 20*) are one route.

State 35 proceeds south past interconnected Bluff Slough, Wigwam Slough, Running Slough, and others to CHIPMUNK COULEE, which opens (L) opposite a dirt road leading to GOOSE ISLAND. Here begin the upper reaches of an artificial lake formed by the navigation dam at Genoa, 12 miles downstream. Southward similar lakes make the highway an almost continuous lakeshore drive. This stretch, part of a 284-mile strip of bottoms between Wabasha, Minn., and Rock Island, Ill., is a small section of the UPPER MISSISSIPPI RIVER WILD LIFE AND FISH REFUGE.

STODDARD, 12 *m.* (643 alt., 316 pop.), lies partly on the low-land, partly on the face of a gently sloping bluff. Like many river villages it grew up around the rough-and-tumble shanties of fishermen and woodcutters and now sustains itself by retail trading and fishing. Work of the Coon Creek Soil Conservation District (*see Tour 20*) is evident at 13 *m.*

GENOA, 19.2 *m.* (639 alt., 300 pop.), is peopled by Italian fisher-men and farmers whose ancestors came up the river in 1848 from lead mines at Galena, Illinois. In Genoa they began work as fishermen; a few English, New England and German families moved in later, but the community remained distinctively Italian. In early days tremendous flocks of wild pigeons flew close to the cliffs behind the village, and men standing on the bluffs knocked them down with long willow branches. One year, when nesting pigeons covered the islands for 7 miles up and downstream, people went out with nets and brought back as many as two barrels of pigeons each.

After passing a dam that forms the artificial lake, 19.6 *m.,* State 35 reaches the Bad Axe River, 23.4 *m.* The county was originally named for this stream, but believing that "Bad Axe" frightened away prospective settlers, in 1862 the inhabitants changed the name to Vernon County.

A marker, 23.6 *m.,* indicates the SITE OF THE RED BIRD RAID OF 1827, sometimes referred to as the "Red Bird War." Chief Red Bird and his Winnebagoes had been friendly with the whites until they heard rumors that two of their tribe, arrested for murder, had been clubbed to death. In retaliation Red Bird and three warriors made a swift raid and killed Register Gagnier, a farmer near Prairie du Chien, and his hired man. Then they proceeded north to a Winnebago encampment here at the mouth of the Bad Axe River, where they held a drunken celebration of the raid. A few days later two keelboats approached along the Mississippi and the drunken Indians attacked them; although the boats escaped, several of the crew were killed. American troops came in pursuit, and Red Bird and several of his tribesmen surrendered to prevent open warfare and the destruction of the Winnebago. Red Bird died in prison a few months later; in time the others were pardoned. William Ellery Leonard (*see Literature*) has based a play, *Red Bird,* on this incident.

A second marker points out the probable SITE OF THE BATTLE OF THE BAD AXE, which ended the Black Hawk War (*see Indians*) and led indirectly to the settlement of Wisconsin. The battle that took place here on August 1-2, 1832, was Black Hawk's last stand. With an exhausted and famished band that had fled the width of Wisconsin, Black Hawk reached the river bottoms here within sight of the Minnesota shore. Hemmed in on Wisconsin land by soldiers and frontiersmen, the Indians attempted to protect the women and children by sending them downstream in boats or on rafts. But the steamer *Warrior,* in the middle of the river, discharged its cannister on truce parties, warriors, women, and children alike. Caught between cross fire the Indians were all but wiped out. Those who reached the Minnesota shore were betrayed by the Sioux; though Black Hawk escaped eastward, he was later captured by the Winnebago and surrendered to the Indian agent at Prairie du Chien.

VICTORY, 26.1 *m.,* is named in memory of the Bad Axe battle. At one time the region surrounding the village suffered from raft pirates and horse thieves who then infested the upper river. They raided lumber rafts, boats, and farms in Wisconsin, selling their loot to Minnesota farmers.

DE SOTO, 30.8 *m.* (636 alt., 322 pop.), founded by New Englanders, lies on the Crawford County line near the head of a man-made lake formed by the Lynxville dam. WINNESHIEK BLUFF nearby was named for a Winnebago chief (*see Tour 10*).

At 31.7 *m.* is the junction with a dirt road.

Right on this road to the BLACK HAWK TOLL BRIDGE (*car and driver, 50¢; extra passengers, 10¢; trucks, 50¢-$1.50; pedestrians 10¢*) leading into Lansing, Iowa.

FERRYVILLE, 38.9 *m.* (635 alt., 266 pop.), was named in anticipation of ferry service between this point and Lansing during Civil War years. Local tradition says that an ordinance passed at the time of incorporation stipulated that the village should cover more than a mile before liquor could be sold; for this reason Ferryville is exceptionally long.

LYNXVILLE, 47.4 *m.* (635 alt., 230 pop.), is another faded village on a river bluff. The Federal dam here, completed in 1938, cost

$3,000,000 and created a 25-mile backwater. Southward State 35 winds inland, climbing through wooded ravines and over broad shoulders of tilled land. Trees thread the intervening valleys, and cattle graze on rounded pastures.

At Linxville take road left to junction with State 27, then turn right on State 27.

EASTMAN, 55 m. (1,224 alt., 271 pop.), essentially a farm town, has a neat double row of taverns and stores facing the highway, with their back yards dropping sharply downward into ravines. South of the village the fields are fairly level, but as the highway edges toward the Mississippi again, the terrain becomes rougher. After descending through a narrow wooded gulch, State 35 emerges upon a flood-plain and runs straight west across an oval prairie. South is the great bulk of SENTINEL RIDGE, part of Wyalusing State Park (see Tour 23).

PRAIRIE DU CHIEN, 67.9 m. (643 alt., 3,943 pop.), the second oldest settlement in the State, lies on a broad terrace overlooking the Mississippi, three miles north of the confluence of the Mississippi and the Wisconsin Rivers. Since 1880 its importance as a trade and transportation point has gradually diminished; today the city is a sleepy and spacious settlement looking to recent improvements on the Mississippi for new energy and new purpose.

The Mississippi flows sluggishly here, its course diverted by innumerable islands; the oldest section of the city is built on one of these islands, ST. FRIOL, connected by bridges with the city's other sections, which stretch back from the river towards the bluffs. Soon after the journey of Joliet and Marquette down the Wisconsin to the Mississippi in June, 1673, the site of Prairie du Chien became an important gathering place for Indians and fur traders, and a stopping place for adventurers. It is believed that Nicholas Perrot (see Tour 2) erected Fort St. Nicholas at or very near the site of Prairie du Chien in 1685. Jonathan Carver, who stopped here in 1766, found a village of several hundred Indian families. Although a land claim made in 1781 by three French Canadians sets that year as the date of the first permanent white settlement, it is believed that French stragglers had settled here before 1761 and had named the place for a Fox chief whom they called *Le Chien* (Fr., the dog).

Each spring and through the summer until late fall, flatboats laden with trinkets, food, and "firewater" arrived at the village; Indian tribes from the remotest sections of the Mississippi and the Wisconsin came with great packs of furs. A market was set up on St. Friol Island and the settlement was alive with tremendous activity. Prosperous traders, boisterous *coureurs de bois* and voyageurs swaggered about in buckskins, bright caps and scarves, with ornaments dangling from their ears and bracelets on their arms. Habitants, those white farmers, boatmen, and mechanics who lived at the village, gathered at the market place to buy calico shirts, scarves, caps, and deerskin *culottes* from the traders. Resident traders and military officers appeared in silk and velvet costumes or in uniform. Mingling with these frontiersmen were half-naked Indians, their bodies painted, their long hair bedecked with feathers. As winter approached, the traders went back to Mackinac or New Orleans, the Indians returned to their villages, and Prairie du Chien became once more a lonely frontier outpost.

The AMERICAN FUR COMPANY POST (*private*), Bolvin and First Sts., is a two-and-one-half-story stone structure built in 1835 by Joseph Rolette. In 1842 Rolette rented this building to the American Fur Company, which had been organized by John Jacob Astor in 1808. Astor's company first started operations in Prairie du Chien in 1817. This building, now a private residence and store, served mostly as a storage place for furs.

Joseph Rolette, the first agent of the American Fur Company at this post, is buried in the OLD FRENCH CEMETERY, north of the city on County F. The BRISBOIS HOUSE (*private*), 324 N. First St., was built in 1815 by Michel Brisbois, who came to Prairie du Chien in 1781 and became a trader for the American Fur Company. The house, one of the oldest stone buildings in Wisconsin, has a five-bay front, a small pedimented portico supported on corner posts, and a lean-to clapboard wing.

Hercules L. Dousman, the most influential of Astor's agents here, amassed a fortune from his fur-trading activities. The DOUSMAN HOTEL (*private*), Fisher and First Sts., is a large stone building, built in 1863 by the railroad to assure accommodations for its patrons. Deserted for years, it has recently been repaired and is now used as a meat packing plant. VILLA LOUIS (*open from May 1 to Nov. 1, daily 9 a.m. to 5 p.m.; hourly trips with guide: adults 25¢, children 10¢*), is in DOUSMAN PARK (*swimming pool and golf course*), end of Third St. Villa Louis is the mansion built by Dousman in 1843 and remodeled by his son in 1872. Although the present structure has been altered and is now a long rectangular building with twin end chimneys and a glass-enclosed veranda, it has been refurnished with the dishes, ornaments, paintings, and furniture brought here by Dousman and his wife, and with carpets and wallpaper in the style of the original. Villa Louis and the 80-acre park were presented to the city in 1935 by the Dousman heirs.

Villa Louis is on the site of Fort Shelby and the first Fort Crawford. Fort Shelby was built by the Americans in 1814 to insure possession of Prairie du Chien. The same year a British force seized the fort, repaired it, and named it McKay in honor of the British commanding officer. At the end of the War of 1812 the British were ordered to evacuate Fort McKay; they did so, but burned the stockade to the ground when they departed.

In 1816 Brevet Brigadier General Thomas A. Smith and several companies of the United States Army erected Fort Crawford here. The American officers who commanded the fort during the first years treated the British sympathizers severely; they accused Brisbois of treason, sent him to St. Louis, and banished Rolette. The Indians were troublesome and restless until the treaty of 1825, when they met in council with the white men and pledged themselves to remain peaceful, to respect the government of the United States, and to form certain boundaries for themselves.

In 1829, because of unsanitary conditions caused by high water, the first Fort Crawford was abandoned and a second was built a mile southeast on the riverbank; its site is now occupied by ST. MARY'S COLLEGE, Beaumont Rd. and Dunn St., a Roman Catholic boarding school for girls. The same year Colonel Zachary Taylor took over the command of the garrison, with dashing Lieutenant Jefferson Davis as one of his assistants. It was while he was stationed here that Davis fell in love with Sarah Knox Taylor, whom he married in 1835 in spite of the colonel's opposition. After his marriage Davis retired from the army and took his bride to his Mississippi plantation, where she died of fever a few months later.

In 1856 the United States abandoned Fort Crawford. Though it was used temporarily during the Civil War, military occupation ended in 1865; the buildings were either moved away or torn down. Today all that remains on the site is the FORT CRAWFORD MILITARY HOSPITAL, end of S. Beaumont Rd., which has been restored as a historical museum (*free*). In front of the hospital is the BEAUMONT MARKER, erected in memory of Dr. William Beaumont (1785-1853), post surgeon at Fort Crawford. In 1822 Dr. Beaumont, as surgeon at a Mackinac fort, cared for a young half-breed, Alexis St. Martin, who had been seriously shot through the stomach. After a long illness St. Martin recovered, but the wound only partially healed, leaving a permanent opening into the stomach. In 1825 Beaumont, employing his unusual patient as a subject, began experiments on the processes of digestion. This work was soon interrupted by the sudden disappearance of St. Martin. In 1829, however, after his transfer to Fort Crawford, Beaumont recovered his subject, and the experiments were continued intermittently until November, 1833. That year the doctor published his results in a book called *Experiments and Observations on the Gastric Juice and the Physiology of Digestion,* which to this day remains one of the chief source works for the study of gastric digestion.

Other points of interest in Prairie du Chien are the FORT CRAWFORD MILITARY CEMETERY, near the intersection of S. Beaumont Rd. and Webster St., one of the smallest in the United States maintained at Federal expense; the DIAMOND JO STEAMSHIP LINE WAREHOUSE on the riverbank, a long, one-story, stone building, erected in 1863 and used for loading and unloading railroad and river freight; the NORTH WEST FUR COMPANY BUILDING, N. Beaumont Rd., now used as a taxi office and barber shop; and the LEAGUE OF WOMEN VOTERS' BUILDING, Blackhawk Ave., a one-and-one-half-story stone house built in 1842. Captain Wiram Knowlton, commander of a volunteer company, had his office here after the regular fort troops had been withdrawn in 1846 to serve in the Mexican War.

Prairie du Chien is at the junction with US 18 (*see Tour 23*) and State 60 (*see Tour 22*).

Tour 14

(Ironwood, Mich.)—Ashland—Superior—(Duluth, Minn.); US 2. Michigan Line to Minnesota Line, 106.3 *m.*

Chicago and North Western Ry. parallels route between Hurley and Ashland; Northern Pacific Ry. between Ashland and Superior.
Concrete and oiled-gravel roadbed.
Accommodations good in Hurley, Ashland, and Superior; tourist camps and cabins scattered along the route.

US 2, shortest highway between the Michigan and Minnesota boundaries, cuts across the top of Wisconsin through cutover and swamps, a region of red clay and ferrous soil. It joins Ashland and Superior, shipping and factory cities, and links the small farm villages scattered through the cutover.

US 2 crosses the MICHIGAN LINE, 0 *m.*, from Ironwood, Michigan. At 0.1 *m.* is the junction with US 51 (*see Tour 7*), 1.5 miles north of HURLEY (1,497 alt., 3,264 pop.) (*see Tour 7*).

West of the junction US 2 passes through a gap in the Penokee-Gogebic Iron Range, enters a dense forest of second-growth popple and birch, with occasional farms in the clearings, then crosses the Montreal River, 4.4 *m.* Somewhere in this wooded region, according to Indian legend, there was a mysterious lodestone so highly magnetized that it drew to itself all metal objects. A malignant spirit fallen from the sky or cast down by the Thunderbirds was believed to inhabit the stone. It was said that once a Dakota war party armed with metal weapons passed by and all but one man disappeared. Lumber cruisers used to complain that their compasses would not work in this region; lumberjacks occasionally claimed that axes, saws, and peavies mysteriously disappeared from the woods.

SAXON, 11.2 *m.* (1,117 alt., 300 pop.), is a former lumber town trying to subsist on trade with farmers who themselves are living at virtually a subsistence level. In 1936 the average gross income per farm in Iron County was $547, the second lowest in Wisconsin. A few cattle graze in unfenced fields; farm buildings are rude, constructed of logs, planks, or tar paper.

From LAKE VIEW CEMETERY (R), 11.6 *m.*, is a view of shallow Oconto Bay to the north, and, far out on Lake Superior, the Apostle Islands (*see Tour 14A*). To the south the saw-tooth peaks of the Penokee Range rim the Lake Superior basin eastward to the Porcupine Mountains in Michigan, a blue haze in the distance. At the stair-type BIRCH HILL FIRE TOWER, 18.1 *m.*, is the unmarked boundary of the BAD RIVER RESERVATION (La Pointe Indian Reservation), established in 1854. It occupies most of the northern part of Ashland County, providing a home for 1,191 (1937) Chippewa, of whom less than one-fifth are full-blooded Indians. The highway crosses the Bad River into ODANAH (Ind., town or village), 27.7 m. (613 alt., 600 pop.), a drab and dilapidated Indian village which, near the confluence of the White and Bad Rivers, is often inundated during spring floods. In the western outskirts are ST. MARY'S CHURCH, a yellow frame structure, and the two rambling buildings comprising ST. MARY'S SCHOOL.

Most of the Bad River Reservation, once heavily wooded, is now a wasteland. At one time a lumber mill owned by whites ran day and night at Odanah, cutting timber by arrangement with the Government. When the forest was exhausted, this barren tract was left to the Indians. The land is so poor and so poorly farmed that 18.4 per cent of Ashland County's relief costs in 1937 were expended on this tribe.

At the northern edge of the village, fanning out toward Lake Superior, are the Kakagan Sloughs (Ind., home of the wall-eyed pike), 12 square miles of wild rice fields cut by a series of tortuous and narrow channels. Also called Nin-duh-tah-so-win (Ind., my storehouse), it provides the Chippewa with wild rice for food and for sale. In the fall the Indians force their canoes into the liquid mud lining the channels, bend the heavily laden stalks over the gunwales of the canoe, and beat the kernels loose with sticks. Wild ducks nest and fatten here in one of the largest natural game preserves in Wisconsin; blue herons occasionally flap across the horizon; the channels are alive with trout, pike, pickerel, and bullheads.

Broad tilled farmlands appear as US 2 nears Ashland. The MARATHON PAPER MILLS (*guides provided*), 35.4 m., employ huge 100-foot machines in making paper from prepared pulp; among other specialties, they produce 8,000,000 paper napkins daily. In a cove beyond the mills thousands of logs, confined by a boom, carpet acre after acre of water, rising and falling gently with the lake swell. Pungent odors of pine fill the air; in rough weather the crunching of the logs is audible far inshore. Powerful tugs tow immense rafts of logs from Port Arthur to be stored here until they are shipped to the company's mills at Rothschild (*see Tour 7*) to be converted into sulphite.

ASHLAND, 37.2 m. (666 alt., 10,622 pop.) (*see Tour 8*), is at the junction with State 13 (*see Tour 8*) and US 63 (*see Tour 9*).

As US 2 emerges into the open countryside the cities of Barksdale and Washburn appear (R) on the rocky hills across Chequamegon Bay (*see Tour 14A*). Ten miles north is Long Island, a natural breakwater protecting the bay and making it one of the best harbors on the Great Lakes. According to Indian legend Nanabozho, Ojibway god, while trying to capture the Great Beaver in Lake Superior, built a dam from the south lakeshore, forming Long Island. Occasionally he threw a fistful of dirt far out into the lake, and each fistful as it fell formed one of the Apostle Islands. Thus the bay received the name Shaugawaumikong (Ind., place of the soft beaver dam), which the French corrupted into Chequamegon.

As US 2 enters the cutover, farms become more infrequent, their pastures more ragged, buildings poorer, and fences more straggling. From the top of a long rise, *50.5 m.*, is the last backward glimpse of Ashland, curving along the bayshore. Much of the cutover here has been settled by Slovaks, the first of whom took over the wild cutover land in 1909, centering their settlement around Moquah (Ind., bear) several miles north. These land-hungry immigrants were attracted by advertisements published in papers printed in their national language. They have retained much of the culture of their native land; colorful Slovak costumes are still worn at weddings and christenings.

At *55.2 m.* is the eastern boundary of the CHEQUAMEGON NATIONAL FOREST, an unbroken sheet of trees stretching across a great basin to distant hills. Soon red clay gives way to the yellow sand of THE BARRENS. Blueberries grow thickly here, ripening in mid-July; then begins a migration of berry pickers—transients, Indians, and neighboring farmers. Whole families come, setting up rude shelters and tents in little colonies, picking both to use and sell. Ten to 12 quarts of berries, an average daily pick, bring about $1.

At *61.9 m.* is the junction with a side road.

1. Right on this road to LONG LAKE, 1 *m.,* one of the few woodland recreational developments along US 2 (*campground and cottages; boating, fishing, and swimming*).

2. Left on this road to LAKE MILLICENT, 2 *m.,* one of the westernmost lakes of the Pike Lake Chain. Only seven lakes are actually stream-linked, but there are more than 50 in the straggling chain that runs roughly southeast for 15 miles. The road winds past and between many of them, and connects with a maze of town and private roads.

IRON RIVER, 64.9 *m.* (1,114 alt., 475 pop.), occupies a site once known to the Indians as Medicine Springs because of the mineral waters that gush here. The first white settler was John Pettingill, who established a trading post in 1887 in anticipation of the arrival of lumberjacks and settlers. A sawmill was soon built on the banks of the Iron River, and Pettingill erected a hotel, which, in 1892, when people came to settle on the townsite, once accommodated 156 people overnight. Several times during the next generation the village was virtually destroyed by fire.

As the lumber industry gradually declined, many lumberjacks settled down to become farmers. Some time later the Scandinavians, who now outnumber other nationalities in Iron River and the surrounding region, drifted in from the Michigan iron country and began farming. They sell their produce to a canning factory and a cooperative creamery in the village and truck in loads of pulpwood to be shipped by rail to paper mill towns. Summer trade with vacationists on the nearby lakes constitutes an increasing source of income.

West of Iron River US 2 traverses an area of swamps and wooded marshes to BRULE, 73.1 *m.* (994 alt., 151 pop.), the center of the region in which President Calvin Coolidge vacationed in 1928. Consisting of only a few tourist cabins, filling stations, and taverns, Brule gained fame overnight when Coolidge said, "The fishing around here, I can testify, is very excellent"; he added, "The climate is wonderful." The President stayed 88 days in his summer White House at the Pierce estate on the Bois Brule River.

It was this country along the shores of Lake Superior (shining Big-Sea-Water) that Henry Wadsworth Longfellow used in part as a setting for the poem *Hiawatha*. But Hiawatha, it appears, never saw this region, for he was a legendary hero of the Iroquois, bitterest enemy of the Ojibway, who inhabited this country. The error occurred when Schoolcraft in his *Algic Researches,* a record of the Ojibway legends, incorporated tales told of Hiawatha and identified him with Nana-bozho, an Ojibway deity. Longfellow went to Schoolcraft as the source of his material.

1. Left from Brule on County H to the D. A. R. FOREST, 0.3 *m.*, a section of the Brule River State Forest. At 2.9 *m.* is the junction with a dirt road.

Right on this dirt road to HOODOO LAKE, 0.9 *m.*, small and dark in its setting of gloomy spruce. At 1.1 *m.* is the junction with a car trail; L. here, winding uphill through Norway pine to the 99-foot stair-type STONY HILL FIRE TOWER, 1.4 *m.* Far below is the Bois Brule River, wriggling like a silver snake.

At 3.1 *m.* on County H is the junction with County B which the route now follows. Nearby is an old railroad station named WINNEBOUJOU for a deity of the Chippewa Indians, a roving god who guarded the Chippewa from enemies and occasionally administered a rough and impulsive justice. The forge of this gigantic blacksmith was supposed to be in the Smoky Mountains, some 20 miles to the south, where he fashioned native copper into weapons. Much of his forging was done by moonlight, and the ringing blows of his hammer were heard by Indians along the entire shore of Lake Superior. On cold moonlight nights, when the ice of the lake cracks with great booming explosions and the northern lights hang in flickering curtains across the sky, the blows of old Winneboujou can still be heard as the glow of his forge lights the horizon. When an Indian heard this sound, he was supposed to be endowed with greater strength and industry; it was consequently welcome to the Chippewa and dreaded by their hereditary enemies, the Siouan Dakota. Amik, the grandmother of Winneboujou, was a disobedient old goddess who rebelled against his authority and was transformed into a beaver. Her descendants are still busy building dams on the twisting Bois Brule River.

Between Winneboujou and Poplar, County B is known as the COOLIDGE MEMORIAL HIGHWAY. For several miles it cuts through spruce and cedar where occasional Norway pine, 70 feet or more high, lift above the lower growth. At 5.1 *m.* and again at 6.3 *m.* are well-kept dairy barns, set up by an Italian count, Giulio Bolognesi, who started a factory for making Italian cheeses at Lake Nebagamon. Finding the country not suitable for dairying, he later moved to Clayton (*see Tour 9*) and Campbellsport. County B continues west past the shore of LAKE NEBAGAMON (Ind., watching for game at night in a boat) to the village of LAKE NEBAGAMON, 8.1 *m.* (1,153 alt., 367 pop.), consisting of two blocks of stores and taverns. Within the village is CAMP NEBAGAMON, a camp for Jewish boys, occupying 60 acres on the former Weyerhaeuser estate (*see Tour 16*). Near the lakeshore stood the old mill, parent institution of the far-flung Weyerhaeuser enterprises.

At 9.1 *m.* is the junction with County P; R. on County P is POPLAR, 15 *m.* (984 alt., 449 pop.), at the junction with US 2.

2. Right from Brule on County H to the small white PRESBYTERIAN CHURCH, 0.2 *m.*, which President Coolidge attended although many of the larger churches in Superior had more elaborate arrangements to receive him. The fields

along the highway are thick with charred pine stumps, some 40 and 50 years old, still rooted in the earth like broken teeth in a jawbone. To remove them farmers drill holes in the snags, pour in kerosene until it permeates the wood, then set them afire. Days later the farmers dynamite the remaining portions and grub out any of the tenacious roots that remain.

At 4.2 *m.* is the junction with a side road; L. on this road to the NORTHERN WISCONSIN CO-OPERATIVE PARK, 4.6 *m.* Finnish people coming here from their original settlements along Lake Superior brought the cooperative movement into this region. In 1930 an association, with a present membership of 450 individuals and 25 organizations, was formed to buy and equip this tract at a cost of $10,000. Pleasantly wooded, its 80 acres are transected by the Bois Brule River and contain housing quarters for 75 people, a community building with store, kitchen, dining room, and recreation room. The park is in almost constant use. Children's camps operate at capacity throughout the summer, and on Saturday nights large crowds throng to dances in the community hall. Sunday is reserved for group picnics. In the late summer the Harvest Festival is held.

The best farmers and housewives are honored, and all compete in games both American and Finnish. In addition to baseball diamonds, a swimming pool, and horseshoe courts, there is a Finnish steam bath. Within it hardy Finns sprinkle water on heated rocks to produce the clouds of steam in which they take their sweat baths.

West of Brule US 2 rises and dips with the sharply rolling ground. From the higher hills the glinting blue waters of Lake Superior are visible (R); the hulking iron range of Minnesota looms vaguely on the skyline ahead.

POPLAR, 84.7 *m.* (984 alt., 449 pop.), is a village with 12 square miles of cutover and farmland within the generous limits provided for its future growth. Poplar's wide cement-paved main street is only two blocks long. The villagers, chiefly of Swedish and Norwegian stock, are seasonally employed in the local pea cannery, which is also equipped to freeze fresh peas.

Poplar is at the junction with County P (*see above*).

WENTWORTH, 86.3 *m.,* consists of a depot, church, and two stores, huddled near the West Branch of the Middle River, a noisy stream racing through a deep narrow gorge of granite.

At 89.3 *m.* is the junction with a town road.

Right on this road to JAMES BARDON PARK 0.3 *m.* (*road near river difficult or dangerous in wet weather*). Situated on the banks of the Amnicon River (Ind., spawning ground), the park is near a series of waterfalls. Adjacent to a parking space for cars, the swift waters of the river break over two cascades, then glide down a granite bed through a grove of white and Norway pine. A footpath follows the river approximately 0.3 miles downstream to a fork where the left branch breaks over a series of shelves in a long cascade and is lost from sight in the dense wood growth which clothes its narrow banks.

The trail follows the right branch of the Amnicon, which plunges over a low precipice, then races 100 yards farther downstream and drops over a 20-foot fall into a sandstone gorge. Between the falls and the rapids, a bridge spans the Amnicon to the rocky pine-covered island dividing the two branches of the river. The path follows the right branch of the river to the lower edge of the island and returns on the left side to a second waterfall, the larger of the two. This 35-foot fall is difficult to see, for the crumbling rock about the gorge offers no safe approach.

Farms become more numerous west of the Amnicon River, many of them with berry patches near the highway. Strawberries grow here in mats of interlaced vines; their white, yellow-centered blossoms star the fields briefly in spring; red berries peep from under the green leaves in late summer. The raspberries cultivated here have much the tang of the wild varieties that grow in the surrounding cutover. Some farmers receive a gross income of $300 to $400 an acre from their berry patches. Numerous apple orchards appear at the roadside, for here is one of the principal apple-growing districts of the State.

At 90.3 *m.* is the junction with US 53 (*see Tour 10*); between this junction and the Minnesota Line, US 2 and US 53 are one route (*see Tour 10*). At 96 *m.* is the junction with State 13 (*see Tour 14A*).

SUPERIOR, 104.2 *m.* (629 alt., 36,113 pop.) (*see Superior*).

Superior is at the junction with US 53 (*see Tour 10*), State 35 (*see Tour 13*), and State 13 (*see Tour 14A*). US 2 reaches the ARROWHEAD BRIDGE (*toll: 5¢ each passenger; 10¢ for auto; 25¢ team and wagon or small truck; 35¢ large truck*) at the Minnesota Line, 106.3 *m.*

Tour 14 A

Ashland—Bayfield—Superior, 107.9 *m.;* State 13.

Oiled-gravel or asphalt roadbed.
Accommodations adequate. Good hotel and restaurant facilities at Bayfield and Washburn.

State 13, alternate route between Ashland and Superior, is almost 40 miles longer than US 2. Curving along the rocky shores of Lake Superior, it passes storm-beaten fishing villages, touches the Red Cliff Indian Reservation, and provides access to the Apostle Islands with their wave-carved cliffs and arches.

ASHLAND, 0 *m.* (666 alt., 10,622 pop.) (*see Tour 8*), is at the junction with US 2 (*see Tour 14*), US 63 (*see Tour 9*), and lower State 13 (*see Tour 8*). Passing grimy coal docks and the steam plant of the Lake Superior District Power Company, the highway rounds the head of Chequamegon Bay and ascends the steep ridge along its western shore.

WASHBURN, 11 *m.* (656 alt., 2,238 pop.), seat of Bayfield County, rises in tiers on the slope of a bluff. Many of its buildings, notably the courthouse, are constructed of reddish-brown stone quarried on Basswood Island (*see below*). Until 1883 not a tree had been cut in this district. In that year the Chicago, St. Paul, Minnesota & Omaha R. R. purchased this site and in 1884 founded a village named for Cadwallader C. Washburn, State Governor (1872-74). Within five years coal docks lined the bayshore, and a freight warehouse, an elevator, and three lumber mills were operating. In Washburn the MOQUAH RANGER STATION (*open to visitors*) guards the cutover.

North of Washburn are faded farmsteads. State 13 descends to the shore of Chequamegon Bay, 14.3 *m.*, and sweeps in a wide curve to densely timbered VAN TASSELL'S POINT, a great hogsback thrusting lakeward. A fire lane cuts straight from the water's edge over the ridge top; quartzite and sandstone shoulder up between the trees. The STATE FISH HATCHERY, 19.9 *m.*, breeds a strain of pure white trout from one- to three-year-old albinos.

BAYFIELD, 22.9 *m.* (617 alt., 1,195 pop.), at the foot of a steep hill, was named for Admiral Henry Bayfield of the British Navy, surveyor of the Great Lakes, who arrived here about 1823. Later, in 1857, nine men under Henry M. Rice of St. Paul arrived and started a village. For a long time Bayfield's only connection with the outside world was by lake and forest trails. Indians, bringing the mail from Superior on foot, required five days for the 85-mile journey; fare for the jolting wagon trip to St. Paul by logging road was $20. About 1880 the railroad came, and the lumbermen took over the region.

On the western outskirts of the city is the BAYFIELD FIRE TOWER, from which the Porcupine Mountains of Michigan, about 30 miles east, appear dimly on the horizon. Scattered in the middle distance are the Apostle Islands (*see below*), a maze of red cliffs, tawny beaches, and channels of cerulean blue, where wisps of smoke drift from the hidden huts of island fisherfolk.

Although trout trolling in Lake Superior has only recently become popular, some 5,000 fishermen now come here annually. (*Boats: $15 to $30 a day including pilot; most boats provide fishing equipment free.*) Fishing is best in the channels between Brownstone (or North Twin) Island, Devils Island, and Bear Island. To catch Lake Superior trout gear equivalent to the strongest muskellunge tackle is required. Heavy silk casting lines will do, though some fishermen insist upon copper or steel lines; large spoon hooks or ordinary casting plugs are adequate as bait. Most fishing is done from cabin cruisers in water 20 to 150 feet deep. Catches range from 5 to 40 pounds. A 35-pound trout, approximately 4 feet long, 10 to 12 inches wide, and 4 to 6 inches thick through the back, will fight desperately until brought to gaff.

The APOSTLE ISLANDS can be visited from Bayfield by an excursion boat (*daily except Sat. bet. July 1 and Sept. 1; leave Bayfield at 10:30 a.m., return at 3:15 p.m.; $1 each person; open for charter*). Fishing boats also take passengers (*$1 each*), and there is a ferry to Madeline Island (*see below*).

Gulls follow the ferry, swoop over the fishing boats, and hover above the cleaning shanties on the islands, which early Frenchmen referred to as the "Twelve Apostles," although there are more than 20 in the group. Most of them rise 20 to 150 feet from the water, and all are being modified by water action.

On Madeline, Michigan, Outer, Devils, Sand, and Raspberry Islands, and at Red Cliff Point on the mainland, are Government lighthouses. Oak, Manitou, Bear, South Twin, and North Twin Islands are inhabited during the summer; Madeline, Stockton, and Sand islands the year round. Wild game is plentiful—deer, mink, muskrat, beaver, otter, wolves, and an occasional bear; thousands of ducks and other migratory waterfowl nest here; and loons, herons, and owls are numerous.

The intricate and grotesque carving of the 10- to 60-foot cliffs have given the Apostle Islands wide fame. On STOCKTON ISLAND are several noteworthy formations: the SPHINX, LONE ROCK, and natural GROTTOS. On the northern point of OAK ISLAND (480 feet alt.) is THE HOLE IN THE WALL, where waves have undermined the entire point and created a natural bridge.

Perhaps the most striking examples of wave erosion are found on DEVILS ISLAND, where in a space of 200 yards there are more than 50 arches, some circular, others Gothic, resting on symmetrical pillars 6 to 12 feet in diameter. The arches overhang SEA CAVES, a few large enough to permit the passage of cabin cruisers. In the subdued light of these subterranean lakes the water is a pale translucent green, lapping gently against the overarching red rocks. There are two well-known formations on this island—TROUT CAVE and DEVILS PIANO.

On SAND ISLAND are the formations of TEMPLE GATE and the THREE-LEGGED STOOL.

HERMIT (Wilson) ISLAND is known for its legendary buried treasure. In the early 1860's a scholarly recluse named Wilson lived here. Because he spent money liberally, it was whispered that he possessed a treasure. After he had been found dead in his cabin, men rushed to the island with shovels and picks, tore up the ground about the cabin, but discovered only a few coins.

Largest and richest in historic associations is MADELINE ISLAND, the only one with roads, villages, and farms. (*Ferry fees: 15¢ one way; 25¢ round trip; car including passengers, $2; leaves Bayfield at 8, 10, and 11 a.m. and 2, 4:30, and 5:30 p.m.; leaves La Pointe at 7 and 9 a.m. and 1, 3, 5, and 7 p.m. Trip takes 20 minutes. Ferry docks at City Dock and Mission Inn Docks on Madeline Island.*)

At the southwestern tip of the island is the settlement of LA POINTE, a name first given to the Jesuit mission established on the mainland by Allouez in 1665. Several years later the name came to signify the entire Chequamegon Bay region; not until 1718, when Fort La Pointe was built here by St. Pierre and Linctot, did the name become closely associated with Madeline Island.

Fort La Pointe was the second French fort on the island; the first, erected by Le Sueur in 1693 and abandoned in 1698, held open the route from Lake Superior to the Mississippi for French trade. Fort La Pointe was established to maintain peace among the Indian tribes in this region. In 1727 Louis Denis, Sieur de la Ronde, was given command of the fort. While La Ronde was in charge, the fort was garrisoned; a dock and probably a mill were built; some agriculture was carried on.

The Indians at La Pointe told the French of an island of copper guarded by spirits; La Ronde, when he heard of the mineral, requested permission from the French Government to combine his duties at the fort with mining. He was not given permission to operate the mines until 1733, and in 1740 his mining activities were halted by an outbreak between the Sioux and the Chippewa. Nonetheless, La Ronde is known as the first practical miner on Lake Superior, and the man who opened this region for settlement by white men.

La Ronde was succeeded by his eldest son, Philippe. In 1749 Joseph Marin was given charge of the fort, which by this time was a subsidiary of a Mississippi river post and had lost much of its importance. In 1759, during the French and Indian War, the French commandant and the garrison were withdrawn.

Alexander Henry, English fur trader, revived trading activtiy here in 1765. Michel Cadotte built a post near the site of Fort La Pointe about 1800 and strengthened his influence as a trader with the Indians by marrying the daughter of the local Chippewa chief. First an agent of the North West Fur Company and later of Astor's American Fur Company, Cadotte was joined in 1818 by two Warren brothers, who married his half-breed daughters and remained as agents until La Pointe lost its commercial significance.

A PROTESTANT MISSION, built in 1832 near the western end of the island, is still used. Carefully restored, its inner walls are lined with birchbark, cut and fitted as accurately as wallpaper. In 1832 the American Fur Company moved its post to this part of the island. It was here, on the council grounds adjoining the warehouse, that the Chippewa signed the treaty of 1854 that established reservations for each of their separate bands.

RED CLIFF, 25 *m.*, lying in a glade between upland and bay, consists of scattered Indian huts, most of them unpainted. Indian children play and swarthy men loiter in bedraggled yards. The whites refer to these Indians as "shiftless bow-and-arrows," but their poverty and shiftlessness is largely owing to the infertility of their land and the allotment of individual holdings (*see Tour 15*). The INDIAN CATHOLIC CHURCH, 25.9 *m.*, is the cultural center of the community.

The RED CLIFF INDIAN RESERVATION encircles the rounded tip of the Bayfield Peninsula. Here live the descendants of a group of La Pointe Chippewa Indians (*see Tour 14*), who, given 14,142 acres of land by the treaty of 1854, settled here under the leadership of Chief Buffalo. Only 3,856 acres in the reservation remain in the hands of individual Indians, most of whom have sold their allotments. The Federal Government has purchased 930 acres to add to the reservation. Only a few rough country roads lead into the reservation from State 13. Lake fishing, the support of many coast settlements, is not open to these Indians because of the large amounts of capital required (*see below*). Most of the Indians on the barren reservation live on Government pensions and county relief.

In the reservation, near the mouth of the Sand River, is a DEER YARD, where hundreds of deer winter in the depths of a black spruce swamp. The whole yard reeks with their musky odor. Through the long winter the deer nibble the needles, bark, and twigs of spruce and swamp alder; but toward spring they become weak from hunger, hardly able to fend off the wolves, and fall easy victims to pneumonia. The State Conservation Department hauls hay into the yard, but even so the deer suffer greatly during a hard winter.

State 13 swings west through a gap in the hills and crosses the end of the peninsula. A few shabby farms dot the countryside. Here and there along the roadside is a portable sawmill, cutting boards from larger logs, sawing smaller ones into posts, ties, pulpwood, and cordwood. Cordwood, the principal fuel for both cooking and heating, sells at $1.50 to $2.50 a cord.

At 41 *m.* State 13 runs along the shore of Squaw Bay.

Northeast of this point (*accessible only by boat for rent at Holton Farm*) are some RED CLIFF CAVES, 3 *m.*, and rock formations almost as odd as those of the Apostle Islands. Several of the sea caves are large enough to admit a boat, many of them higher than those on Devils Island. At one point is a great cleft in the rock which goes back into the bluff some 300 feet; its walls rise in an overhanging arch 70 or 80 feet high. The water when quiet is crystal clear, and deep within it fish can be seen swimming in and out of the cove. Ferns and moss grow over the rocks, and mountain ash clings to the sides of the cliffs, its vermilion berries vivid against the green growth and the reddish brown of the stone. Owls nest in pockets of the rock, only their yellow eyes visible; a cautious climber can approach within a few feet of them. Woodchucks, gophers, and chipmunks scurry along the ledges; occasionally a deer appears on the brink of the cliffs.

EAGLE ISLAND, just opposite, was so named because eagles have nested there for years.

CORNUCOPIA, 44.4 *m.*, on Siskowitt Bay at the mouth of the Siskowitt River, is a fishing town. Stiff gray fishing nets hang drying on big reels; weathered shacks crowd to the shore line with its old docks; thousands of gulls flash white against the sky, wheeling and dipping in search of food.

In 1938, 18 fishing boats, from 26-foot cabin cruisers to 60-foot tugs, all equipped with gasoline engines, operated from this base. They range as far as Isle Royale for trout, whitefish, and longjaw, bringing in daily catches of from 300 to 1,000 pounds. The fishermen receive 10¢ to 14¢ pound. When the herring run, a lift of 3 or 4 tons a day is common; a load of 10 tons is not unknown. As herring bring from $30 to $40 a ton, fishermen receive large gross incomes during the season. The investment required for boats, nets, and equipment is high, ranging from $2,500 to $10,000 for each outfit; for 6 months the lake, choked with ice, is unnavigable; and during the remaining 6 months fishing is periodically restricted by conservation laws.

Left from Cornucopia on County C to the FALLS OF THE SISKOWITT RIVER, 0.8 *m.* Here a bridge crosses the river, a little cascade runs (R), and the falls proper are hidden in a dense tangle of underbrush between two high bluffs a short distance downstream. The falls consist of a series of 15 rocky shelves down which the water breaks.

State 13 traverses a swampy region drained by the West Siskowitt River and Bark Creek, 48.9 *m.*, a small trickle down a wide flood plain originally cut by a mighty post-glacial river.

HERBSTER, 52.8 *m.*, is at the junction with a town road.

Right on this town road along the shore of the lake to the tip of BARK POINT, 5 *m.* The road, lashed periodically by waves and spray, is often littered with driftwood. A few cottages and taverns line the bleak roadside. Right is a high bluff that gradually slopes down to Bark Point; beyond it is the entrance to Bark Point Bay and (L) the vast expanse of Lake Superior.

PORT WING, 60.1 *m.* (250 pop.), is a declining little fishing village. Like Herbster and other lakeshore villages, Port Wing is a trade center for neighboring farmers, most of them of Finnish stock and still addicted to their traditional steam baths. Many farms in this region have square, air-tight, log bathhouses; occasionally a group of families erects a large bathhouse in common. Once or twice a week, summer and winter, entire families, scantily clad and carrying pails of water, troop out to the bathhouses. Benches and bunks line the walls of the bathhouses from floor to ceiling; water is poured on stones heated in a fireplace or open stove; soon the room is clouded with steam; stretched out on the benches, the bathers "cook" in the vapor.

The Finnish immigration into the Lake Superior region began about 1864 and increased greatly in 1878 and 1899. The Finns first settled as miners in the copper country of Michigan, near Hancock, then drifted slowly down to the Ironwood and Hurley region. In the early 1880's they began filtering into northern Wisconsin. Some found employment in the iron mines; others, like those at Port Wing, began to take up farms all along the route from Michigan to Minnesota. By 1900 they were permanently settled, forming the cooperatives for which they are famous (*see Cooperative Movement*).

West of Port Wing, State 13 crosses an area little changed since the first settlers arrived here in the 1850's. Crossing Iron River, 67.5 *m.*, the highway continues through other deep, narrow, wooded valleys that reveal glimpses of winding, spruce-dark lowland, crosses streams tinted red by the iron-bearing soil, passes shiny milk cans on crude platforms at the roadside, and traverses occasional strips of farm-land. Beyond the Bois-Brule River, 77.4 *m.*, which flows between wooded and almost perpendicular banks, the trees gradually thin out. Silos and wire fences are common now, farms are better kept. Big shedlike pea vineries stand at crossroads, each backed by a stack of stripped vines. At 95.2 *m.* is a large WINDMILL made of white cement, built in 1885 by Nicholas Davidson, one of the earliest of the Finnish settlers. Until 1918 flour and grist were ground here between stones that Davidson had cut by hand.

At 95.3 *m.* is the junction with County V.

Left on County V to JAMES BARDON PARK, 5 *m.* (*see Tour 14*).

At 99.7 *m.* is the junction with US 2 (*see Tour 14*) and US 53 (*see Tour 10*); between this junction and Superior, State 13, US 53, and US 2 are one route (*see Tour 10*).

SUPERIOR, 107.9 *m.* (629 alt., 36,113 pop.) (*see Superior*).

Superior is at the junction with US 53 (*see Tour 10*), State 35 (*see Tour 13*), and US 2 (*see Tour 14*).

Tour 15

Michigan Line—Eagle River—Fifield—Spooner—Minnesota Line;
State 17 and State 70.
Michigan Line to Minnesota Line, 227.7 *m.*

Chicago, St. Paul, Minneapolis & Omaha R. R. parallels route between Draper
and Couderay.
Hard-surfaced and oiled-gravel roadbed.
Year-around accommodations in small villages; resorts, cabins, campgrounds,
and tourist homes in summer.

East-west highways, St. 17 and St. 70 reveal more of northern Wisconsin perhaps than any other single route. For miles it travels through virtually uninhabited cutover; agriculture and industry are often rudimentary. · Only two communities on the route have populations larger than 1,000, and in the 154 miles between them there is not an incorporated village. Both of the main northern lake regions—one on the stony highlands of the northern peneplain, the other on the sandy highlands of the Western Upland—are traversed, although the lakes are glimpsed only occasionally from the highway.

Section a. MICHIGAN LINE to FIFIELD; 93.5 m.,
State 17 and State 70

South of the MICHIGAN LINE, 0 *m.*, State 17 touches the wooded shore of SMOKY LAKE (R). The highway is here in the NICOLET NATIONAL FOREST where farms are set amid dense stands of hemlock, spruce, and hardwood. Created in 1936, the forest contains 985,400 acres within its boundaries. Stones are everywhere: they stand in ragged piles in pastures, dot plowed fields, are built into fences. In these grim surroundings frugal hard-working Finns have made neat and pleasant farms. Spruce-bordered LONG LAKE is at 3 *m.*

At 8.3 *m.* is the junction with a town road.

Right on this road to the stair-type MILITARY HILL FIRE TOWER, 0.4 *m.*, whose platform, rising above the summit of the hill, reveals a panorama of wild cutover land extending into Michigan and embracing Big Twin Lake.

PHELPS, 9 *m.* (1,681 alt., 510 pop.), was founded in 1900 when wealthy lumbermen chose its site for a sawmill, ran in a 10-mile railroad from Conover, and set up the Hackley-Phelps-Bonnell Company's plant. The present village is owned, for the most part, by the C. M. Christiansen Company. The only independent enterprise in Phelps is the Northwood Chemical Company, established in 1937 after the Christiansen Company had abandoned the chemical field. Soon after it had opened, one of the first manifestations of a labor movement in the north woods occurred here when a strike was called by the Timber Workers Union.

In Phelps is the junction with County E.

Right on County E to LAC VIEUX DESERT (*see Tour 5*), 5.6 *m.*, and the junction with US 45 (*see Tour 5*), 8.7 *m.*

State 17 skirts the southern shore of BIG TWIN LAKE, 10.7 *m.*, and passes out of the Nicolet National Forest. At 21.7 *m.* is the junction with US 45 (*see Tour 5*); between this junction and Eagle River US 45 and State 17 are one route.

EAGLE RIVER, 25.7 *m.* (1,638 alt., 1,386 pop.), center of a recreation area, like the near-by river and lake is named for the bald eagles that once lived in the surrounding woods. Fifty years ago it was a lumber camp. Although the arrival of the railroad in 1883 assured a certain stability, the village's present prosperity came with modern highways and motorcars. Eagle River was one of the first Wisconsin towns to develop winter sport facilities. In addition to a 35-foot ski jump, a 90-foot steel double toboggan slide, and a 50-foot "ash can alley" slide, it has a large municipal fieldhouse in which its professional hockey team plays teams from Minnesota and Michigan.

The town owns a GOLF COURSE (*fee: $1 for half day; $1.50 for full day*), a floodlighted beach at SILVER LAKE (*showers and lockers*), and a LANDING FIELD for those who week end by plane. There is only one small factory in the town; all the utilities are municipally owned.

Eagle River owes its attraction to the EAGLE WATERS, a chain of 27 lakes clustered irregularly along the river, the habitat of almost every variety of native Wisconsin fish. Some lakes have lavish resorts; others lie in the unbroken forests, frequented largely by wild animals.

Vilas County, of which Eagle River is the seat, was named for William Freeman Vilas (1840-1908), who early won fame as an orator, became professor of law at the University of Wisconsin at 28, revisor of statutes at 35, and a regent of the university at 41. He amassed a fortune through operations in northern timberland holdings. Rising to national prominence, Vilas became permanent chairman of the Democratic National Convention in 1884, State legislator in 1885, Postmaster General (1885-88), Secretary of the Interior (1888-89), and U. S. Senator (1891-97). While he was Secretary of the Interior, there was a Federal investigation of his Wisconsin timberland activities, but no report was made.

Vilas' will provided that upon the death of his daughter his entire fortune should be held in trust for the University of Wisconsin, except for certain permissible deductions from the income, until it amounted to $30,000,000. Then it was to be used to create professorships, to found fellowships and scholarships (one-fifth of which were to go to

Negroes), and to build a Greek theater, with reading and assembly rooms.

Eagle River is at the junction with State 70. Take latter right.

West of Eagle River, State 70 skirts WATERSMEET LAKE (R), then crosses the Wisconsin River, 29.7 m. The NORTHERN STATE FOREST, 33.2 m., contains 133,482 of the 170,190 acres of forest land owned by the State. Along the roadside appear (R) McDON-ALD LAKE, 34.9 m., and LITTLE ST. GERMAINE LAKE, 39 m., the first of some 500 lakes said to be within 20 miles of the highway between this point and the Lac du Flambeau Reservation. Passing small LAKE CONTENT and BIG ST. GERMAINE LAKE, State 70 loops over steep brush-clad hills to LITTLE ARBOR VITAE LAKE (L) and BIG ARBOR VITAE LAKE (R), on the shores of which lie the scattered houses of ARBOR VITAE, 48.7 m. (1,627 alt., 800 pop.), founded in 1893 by the John D. Ross Lumber Company and given the Latin name for cedar.

At 50.8 m. is the junction with US 51 (*see Tour 7*); between this junction and a point at 53.4 m. State 70 and US 51 are one route.

WOODRUFF, 52.5 m. (1,609 alt., 250 pop.), though small today, was once a lively settlement consisting largely of saloons and other pleasure resorts catering to lumberjacks in from the woods for a spree. Beyond LAKE MINOCQUA (L), the highway crosses a narrow ring of cleared farmland, where farmers advertise their skills as bricklayers, masons, carpenters, or guides on roadside signs. Through pine forests and spruce swamps the highway winds to the shores of LAKE SISSHEBOGEMA, 59.7 m., SUNDAY LAKE, 60.1 m., and PIKE LAKE, 61.2 m.

HASKELL LAKE, 64.9 m., is at the junction with County D, which leads back into the Lac du Flambeau Indian Reservation.

Right on County D to LONG LAKE (L) and CRAWLING STONE LAKE (R), 2.6 m., named for a series of stones extending into the lake, which legend says were dropped as stepping stones by an Indian fleeing from a bear. At 3.6 m. is MUD LAKE, and at 3.9 m. is the LAC DU FLAMBEAU (Fr., lake of the torch), so named for the torches of tightly rolled birchbark that the Indians used while traveling, hunting, or fishing by night.

On the lakeshore is the village of LAC DU FLAMBEAU, 3.9 m., where some 700 Indians live in poverty. Houses are small log or frame structures, some covered with tar paper, some gray and weather-beaten, a few painted in gaudy colors—red, green, blue, and yellow. About 4 p.m. on weekdays trucks discharge workers from the near-by CCC camp, the school bus full of swarthy children draws up, and the women, choosing this hour deliberately, come down to shop and visit; the otherwise dull village is then briefly active.

In a report published in 1934 the Land Planning Committee of the National Resources Board discusses this reservation as an outstanding example of mismanagement of Indian affairs. Under the General Allotment Act of 1887, repealed in 1934, land was given to individual Indians rather than to tribes or families. For 25 years the reservation was held in trust by the Government, which permitted outsiders to log off the timber, thus depriving the Indian owners of the only valuable property they had. By 1914 lumbering had ceased, and the Indians were left unemployed on denuded land. Eventually each Indian received a small tract, virtually worthless for farming, not large enough to be used for grazing or forestry. When he died it was divided among his heirs. This division has continued until today; in one instance more than 39 Indians own equities in one allotment of 80 acres. The use of land by its owners is thus rendered virtually impossible. If fortunate, they can sell it and spend the proceeds; or they can lease it and live idly on the small income.

After it had been turned over to its owners, the supposedly worthless Lac du Flambeau Reservation was found to contain some potentially valuable property. Some of the lakes within its 70,000 acres are among the most beautiful in the north, and palatial summer homes have been built on their shores. Under the conditions of the allotment act the valuable frontages did not long remain in Indian possession. Studies made by the National Resources Board show that about 32 per cent of the 70,000 acres in the reservation are swamplands claimed by the State. Of the remaining 48,000 acres, more than 30 per cent has been alienated by white purchase and about 27 per cent is tied up in the estates of deceased allottees. The land left in Indian ownership, largely swampland and cutover, is so broken and scattered that it is virtually impossible to block out tracts for effective use. Thus deprived of even the discarded submarginal land originally given them, many Indians are living almost at starvation level. Their only income is derived from selling trinkets, berries, or wild rice, or acting as guides or servants to occasional tourists.

At 4.3 m. is the junction with an oiled road. Left on this road past the village ball park, LONG LAKE (L), and LAKE POKEGAMMA (R) to the PRESBYTERIAN CHURCH (L) and ST. ANTHONY'S ROMAN CATHOLIC CHURCH (R), 4.6 m.; nearby is a large DAY SCHOOL, a few of whose graduates attend the high schools for Indians at Flandreau, South Dakota, or at Lawrence, Kansas.

Beyond the LAC DU FLAMBEAU FISH HATCHERY (R), 5.2 m., the road curves around the shore of the Lac du Flambeau to the reservation's CIVILIAN CONSERVATION CORPS CAMP, 5.8 m. The $30 a month wage paid at the camp has been the principal source of income to the people since the middle 1930's. Put to work at enterprises they understand, Indians have demonstrated remarkable ability to accomplish cooperative undertakings.

In a thick stand of pine near the CCC camp is the junction with a dirt road. Left on this road to the OLD INDIAN VILLAGE, 7.5 m., where about 150 pagan Indians try to live as their forefathers did. Though each family has a dilapidated shack for winter shelter, they live most of the year in low, dome-shaped wigwams made of wide strips of birchbark stretched over bent pole frames. In front of the wigwams are poles, often pine trees stripped of their branches, to which are hung bits of cloth, tin, or wooden flags, or perhaps a red sweater. Some of the flags bear crudely painted pictographs, for these shafts are a modification of the totem poles of ancient Indian ritual and custom. The MEDICINE LODGE (R), 7.6 m., is a low structure about three times as long as its width, covered with canvas, skins, and roofing. Here the semiannual medicine dances are held, for these Indians still seek happiness for the dead or cures for disease by ancient ceremonies. At 7.8 m. is a windowless, slab-sided octagonal DANCE HALL (ceremonies not open to visitors) with a conical roof, whose earthen floor has been packed hard by the trampling of many feet in tribal dances.

The road crosses the Bear River, 7.9 m., passes a few scattered Indian homes, and rounds the south shore of Lac du Flambeau through dense woods. At 11.3 m. is the rejunction with County D; right on County D to State 70, 13.8 m.

State 70 cuts across the northern part of the immense, multi-lobed CHEQUAMEGON NATIONAL FOREST, 68.8 m., which, created in 1936, contains 1,031,022 acres of sparsely settled land. Wildlife is abundant here; sometimes in sunny fire scars and slashings black bears waddle through solid miles of wild raspberry bushes, stopping occasionally to seize a bush between their paws and stuff leaves, thorns, berries, and all into their mouths. Westward an expanse of burnt-over land lines both sides of the road. The highway passes 100-foot FIFIELD FIRE TOWER, 88.6 *m.*, and follows the bank of the south fork of the Flambeau River into Fifield.

FIFIELD, 93.5 *m.* (1,454 alt., 310 pop.), named for Sam S. Fifield, Lieutenant Governor of Wisconsin (1882-87), was once the main lumbering town in this region. When Price County was organized, Fifield was certain it would become the county seat. Balloting was held at Phillips (*see Tour 8*). The story is told that, since many of the lumberjacks could not read or write, a Fifield printer gave them printed slips bearing the town's name to drop in the ballot boxes. A Phillips printer, observing this, asked the lumberjacks, "Why are you voting for Phillips? I thought you were for Fifield." "We are," they said. "Don't these tickets say Fifield?" "Naw—somebody's slipping one over on you. Here—I'll print you some slips for Fifield." He printed a number of cards reading "Phillips," and the lumberjacks dropped them in the ballot box; thus Phillips became the county seat.

Fifield is at the junction with State 13 (*see Tour 8*).

Section b. FIFIELD to MINNESOTA LINE; 134.2 m., State 70

West of FIFIELD, 0 *m.*, the roadside is a patchwork of small pastures, rocky fields, woods, and tamarack swamps. At the PIXLEY POWER DAM, 4.6 *m.*, State 70 reaches the Flambeau River, which appears intermittently for the next 15 miles. A moss-covered log bridge, 9.5 *m.*, and rotting decks of logs, 10.5 *m.*, recall the days when loggers conducted great spring drives down the Flambeau.

At 14.2 *m.* State 70 enters Sawyer County, named for Philetus Sawyer (1816-1900), one of the great lumber kings of Wisconsin. Born in Whiting, Vermont, Sawyer left home at 17 to work in a lumber mill; when the mill experienced financial difficulties, Sawyer leased it and resold at a profit. In 1847 he came to Fond du Lac County, Wisconsin, farmed, took over a failing mill at Algoma, and became a prosperous small businessman. Aware that the U. S. Government would sometime open northern timberlands for sale, he spent two years tramping the woods to find out where the finest timber stood. Then he bought the choicest tracts at Government auctions, and made $3,000,000 within two years by reselling them. Through speculations in Wolf River timberlands, he later doubled this capital.

Meantime, Sawyer's genius for reorganizing distressed companies led him to take over two small western Wisconsin railroads and affiliate them with the Omaha line, which then was fighting the Chicago, Milwaukee & St. Paul R. R. for land, timber, and rights-of-way. Obtaining control of the State government was part of the conflict. In 1881 Sawyer and the Omaha won the legislature, which elected Sawyer to the U. S. Senate, where he was later joined by his able protégé, John C. Spooner (*see Tour 9*). At the close of his life Sawyer became the central figure in a scandal. After losing the election of 1893, he was compelled to pay the surety bonds of Republican State treasurers who had failed to account for interest paid on deposits of public funds. Extricating himself from this difficulty, he undertook activities that brought a flat charge of bribery against him by young Robert M. La Follette, who rose to political power partly by exposing Sawyer's boss rule.

State 70 passes a few small farms scratched into the edge of a badly burned area and enters OXBO, 15.9 m., little more than a post office, named for the nearby oxbow bend on the Flambeau. Oxbo has a small Zoo containing bears, deer, wolves, foxes, raccoons, porcupines, and other wild animals found in the surrounding woods.

In the environs of WINTER, 35.3 m. (1,360 alt., 275 pop.), a village small and neat, the roadside is piled with decks of logs from small cuttings in the surrounding wilderness. Jim-poles hang like gallows over the railroad tracks, waiting to hoist the logs to the stake-sided flatcars on which they are transported to sawmills. South and east, in the Brunet, Thornapple, and Flambeau Valleys, game is as abundant as anywhere in Wisconsin. On nearby lakes and the sprawling Chippewa flowage are many resorts.

The seclusion of this region attracted Joe Saltis, noted Chicago gangster of the prohibition era, who came here every summer to relax. During one summer, while Saltis was entertaining local officials and newspapermen at Winter and making no secret of his identity, Chicago and Illinois authorities, spurred on by newspaper campaigns, were searching the country for him. The residents of Winter were amused each morning to read on the front page of a Chicago newspaper that "Joe Saltis has now been missing for .... days." Saltis remained undisturbed until, posting a circle of armed guards through the woods, he began fly fishing for trout within the prohibited 500 feet below a dam. A group of volunteer deputies led by a game warden flitted unseen past the city-wise guards and captured the whole gang. While the metropolitan journals announced the 90th day of fruitless search, Saltis was brought before a local magistrate, assessed the maximum fine, and released.

The OJIBWA STATE ROADSIDE PARK (camping and picnic facilities), 39.4 m., one of three small tracts maintained by the State, is a grove of young hardwood and spruce fronting the Chippewa River. OJIBWA, 40.8 m., built by a land-selling agency, is conspicuous in this half-deserted region for its neatly painted homes and regularly platted lots. Logs, ox yokes, old river boats, and other relics of logging days are displayed in a fenced enclosure at the roadside.

RADISSON, 46 m., was named for the French explorer Pierre Esprit Radisson (see Tour 1A). State 70 follows the Couderay River, which flows swiftly through a region of charred stubs, rotting slashings, granite outcropping, and boulders, to COUDERAY, 51.3 m. (1,260 alt., 171 pop.). Here is a small sawmill, which operates intermittently.

The LAC COURT OREILLES INDIAN RESERVATION, 55 m., is adjacent to the lake of the same name. During his second western voyage (1658-60), Radisson named this lake Ottawa for the Indians dwelling on its shores. When Radisson arrived the Ottawa were suffering from a famine, and shortly after his departure they moved into northern Minnesota. The Sioux subsequently settled here, but about 1740 they were driven out by the Chippewa, whose descendants now occupy this reservation.

An agent of the North West Fur Company, named Corbin, traded here from 1800 to 1852. In 1808 the Chippewa, hearing of the Tecumseh rebellion, burned his warehouse; Corbin hid in the woods during the excitement and then returned to continue trading for almost a half century.

The Federal Government allotted this region to the Chippewa in 1854, but in 1860 the lands were withdrawn by the General Land Office. In 1873 the Government reallotted 69,136 acres of this land to the Chippewa. The Indians have sold parts of the reservation, and now it consists of only 41,161 acres. In 1929 a Senate Subcommittee on Indian Affairs found tuberculosis, trachoma, and venereal disease widespread here, medical facilities inadequate, sanitation poor, illegitimacy common.

The land in the reservation is poor, barren, and rocky; yet the Lac Court Oreilles Indians have led the State in organizing Natagamie, or garden clubs, as a partial solution of their problems. Vegetables from these small plots, usually less than an acre, are sold to summer tourists or stored in root cellars.

State 70 crosses the Couderay River, 59.1 m. Just upstream is BILLY BOY DAM, named for an Indian, William Billy Boy, who lived until 1920 in a cabin above it. Here are exhibited what is said to be the first plow used in Sawyer County and a rusted slab of iron, known as Paul Bunyan's razor blade.

WHITEFISH LAKE (R), 62.3 m., with diving tower, docks, and cottages, is connected to Grindstone, Couderay, and Sand Lakes. For 50 miles State 70 now crosses the western area of sand-country lakes. West of the village of STONE LAKE, 67.4 m., State 70 passes a few of the tar-paper farmhouses and shacks that in this country so often serve as homes. Although the average farm income of Washburn County is relatively high among the counties along this route, even here about a third of the area is tax delinquent and much of it has been withdrawn from agriculture under the forest crop law.

Beyond ladder-type POTATO LAKE FIRE TOWER is POTATO LAKE, 75.5 m., where marl, a calcium carbonate clay used as fertilizer, is scooped from the lake bottom with a windlass. Crossing the Yellow River, 85.5 m., State 70 passes the branch station of the University of Wisconsin's Agricultural Experiment Station (see Tour 9).

SPOONER, 86.7 m. (1,095 alt., 2,426 pop.) (see Tour 9), is at the junction with US 63 (see Tour 9) and US 53 (see Tour 10).

The highway passes a number of lakes sparkling in the dark green of the lowland spruce and pine: CYCLONE LAKE, LONG LAKE, BIG SAND LAKE, VIOLA LAKE, and CLAM LAKE.

At 111.6 m. is the junction with State 35 (see Tour 13); between this junction and a point at 113.9 *m.* State 70 and State 35 are one route.

FALUN, 122.6 *m.* (956 alt., 175 pop.), lies on low land; late each summer farmers come here to harvest and stack wild hay. Above the swamps occasionally rise higher, gentler sweeps of meadow, dotted with clumps of osier and tamarack. ALPHA, 124.4 *m.,* is a small creamery settlement. Westward, State 70 crosses the long-settled butter-producing strip that runs along the State's western boundary. A two-mile-wide belt of cleared farmland borders the road; here are fences, silos, and other evidences of prosperous farming.

GRANTSBURG, 129.4 *m.* (905 alt., 777 pop.), seat of Burnett County, was founded in 1855 by Canute Anderson. The first white man here was John Drake, a trader, who was killed in 1847 by Indians. The village is the county metropolis, with modern school buildings, a hospital, and a golf course. On its outskirts are a stair-type FIRE TOWER and a FOREST RANGER STATION.

The TOURIST CAMP, 131.4 *m.,* is filled in summer with trailers, some jacked up on blocks and enlarged with board or canvas lean-tos, occupied by semitransients, who come here to cut pulpwood bolts. They fell trees not less than four inches in diameter, lop off the branches with axes, saw them into sections precisely eight feet four inches long, set them on sawhorses, and peel off the bark with drawshaves. A practised workman can turn out from 40 to 140 sticks and earn from $3 to $5 a day. From midspring to early fall the roadsides are lined with rows of bolts laid side by side, ready to be picked up by truck. The work stops with the first freeze, for frost makes the bark stick tightly to the wood and hinders peeling.

State 70 begins a sinuous descent into the St. Croix River Valley at 133.8 *m.* At 134.2 *m.* is the TOLL BRIDGE (*toll, 50¢ per car*) at the Minnesota Line.

Tour 16

(Norway,. Mich.)—Crandon—Rhinelander—Prentice—Ladysmith—St Croix Falls—(Taylors Falls, Minn.) ; US 8.
Michigan Line to Minnesota Line, 273 *m.*

Minneapolis, St. Paul & Sault Ste Marie R. R. parallels route throughout. Hard-surfaced and oiled-gravel roadbed.
Lodges and resorts in recreation areas. In central part of State, accommodations limited to larger villages.

US 8, trans-State highway between Michigan and Minnesota, tells the story of northern Wisconsin—of lumbermen and ragged cutover, of forest fires and useless soil, of impoverished farmers and abandoned land, and finally of recreation, on which the north depends increasingly for its livelihood.

Section a. MICHIGAN LINE to PRENTICE; 148.7 m., US 8

The MENOMINEE RIVER, 0 m., boundary between Wisconsin and Michigan, was once the logging highway of the northeast, each year carrying millions of feet of jostling pine logs down to sawmill towns. For years lumbering determined the economic life of this region; it brought in the railroad and lumberjacks, and, indirectly, the settlers who hoped to change the cutover into fertile and prosperous farms. But agriculture failed here, and lumbering is almost gone.

Along the eastern section of US 8 lie the farms, tar-paper shacks or log huts, set in clearings edged around by the encroaching brush. Forest stands are second-growth and straggling; stumps and great snags fill the cutover, which in summer is green with tangled brush and young saplings, in winter bleak with snow marked only by the tracks of animals or occasional trappers and loggers.

At 2.4 m. is the junction with US 141 (see Tour 3): between this junction and 12.2 m. US 8 and US 141 are one route (see Tour 3). This part of Marinette County is a peneplain, a worn-down mountain range, where the soil is thin, studded with rocks, and infertile; much of the land is abandoned or tax delinquent. Yet it is only recently that the north gave up its dream of farming this land and passed zoning ordinances (see Agriculture), recognizing that the land's value now lies in its timber possibilities. In keeping with this new emphasis, forest protection in Wisconsin is well organized (see Natural Setting); the north is divided into 10 districts, each with scattered ranger offices and fire towers.

DUNBAR, 23.2 m. (150 pop.), one of the ghost towns spaced at intervals throughout the north, is little more than an opening in the low forest of evergreen, popple, and hardwood.

GOODMAN, 33.2 m., in contrast with Dunbar, is still a lumbering village. Owned by the Goodman Lumber Company, it is neat and progressive in appearance, with tidy one- and two-story houses, a complete department store, a garage, a well-constructed community hall, and attractive school buildings. Here is one of Wisconsin's few sawmills maintained on a sustained-yield basis. Logs from Marinette, Forest and Florence Counties are brought to the village and manufactured into veneer, standard dimension stock and lumber, according to the kind and quality of the logs. A wood chemical plant turns the surplus wood and small logs into charcoal, wood alcohol, and acetate of lime.

Through its acceptance of the new forestry plan of sustained-yield logging, the Goodman Lumber Company has assured its mills an annual timber yield sufficient to maintain continuous operation, providing permanent part time work for its employees, some of whom own small farms nearby. The sawmill has operated continuously for 30 years, except for shutdowns during repair periods. The lumber camps are now located in Florence County and furnish seasonal employment for many farmers in that vicinity.

LAONA, 55.7 m. (1,533 alt., 350 pop.), a small village named for the daughter of a local businessman, stands on the eastern limits of the Wisconsin Lakes district. It is both a lumbering and recreation center. Railroad cars loaded with logs, huge yards piled high with lumber, and a gray and weathered sawmill, stand side by side with taverns, bright stores, and a modern hotel. The village is especially busy in summer when vacationists stop for supplies, guides, and fishing tips from the old-timers.

Laona is largely owned by the Connor Lumber & Land Company. Lumbering interests helped to build the school, the city hall, the library, and the only hospital in Forest County, all fine brick buildings; workers rent their houses for from $4 to $16 a month. The Connor Company plant consists of a three-band sawmill, a planing mill, flooring and lawn furniture factories, and modern drying kilns equipped to dry green lumber after it is sawed. The mill regularly employs 375 workers at wages ranging from 40 to 97 cents an hour; 250 are employed in the company's logging camps.

Near Laona and Crandon (*see below*) is the Forest County Potawatomi Indian Community, 13,640 acres of land purchased for the Potawatomi tribe by the Federal Government in 1937 but not yet set aside as a reservation. The first white men found this once powerful tribe all along the Lake Michigan shore. In 1833 when the Potawatomi ceded their lands and agreed to remove to a reservation on the Missouri River in Iowa Territory, about 400 remained in Wisconsin. Their descendants live in tar-paper shacks, one-room huts with sagging frames and dirt floors. A few have small gardens, usually untended, for the Indians prefer to spend the summer picking the wild berries that grow so abundantly in the cutover. In season they make maple sugar and syrup, hunt, trap, fish, and find occasional employment as lumberjacks or guides.

In the village of Blackwell nearby lived Simon Kahquados, last hereditary chief of the tribe, who is buried in Peninsula State Park (*see Tour 1B*).

The country between Laona and Crandon is wild, in some spots beautiful. After passing SILVER LAKE (L), 57.9 m., US 8 crosses the Rat River and comes to broad LAKE WABIKON (L), 61.7 m., with low evergreens hugging its shores and hardwoods covering the surrounding hillsides. Lake Wabikon is filled with a peculiar loose muck, fluid enough to swim through, which extends to within 2 or 3 feet of the surface. At spots where springs bubble up, rifts have formed, and these narrow channels, some 30 feet deep and perhaps 200 yards long, provide excellent trolling for great northern pike.

Wabikon is connected by a small stream with RILEY LAKE, hidden behind a wall of trees on the opposite shore.

US 8 climbs westward over several steep hills to a high crest, 63.3 *m.,* which offers a view of the country for miles around, including 1,951-foot SUGAR BUSH HILL (L), the highest measured elevation in Wisconsin. LAKE LUCERNE, 65.1 *m.,* long, narrow, and studded with islands, winds between two high hills covered with cedar and spruce. Numerous points jut out into the water; along its shores or halfway up the hillside cottages crouch half hidden in the forest. Cold, clear, and spring-fed, Lake Lucerne offers good fishing for bass, pike, and pan fish.

CRANDON, 69.2 *m.* (1,635 alt., 1,679 pop.), named for F. P. Crandon, railroad official, is built around and between four lakes: METONCA, which forms dead-end streets at its southern limits; SURPRISE LAKE, tiny and circular, a block from the courthouse; CLEAR LAKE, with old rotting booms; and PESHTIGO, stumpy and marshy "Mud Lake." Though periodic fires between 1920 and 1924 wiped out most of Crandon's lumberyards and woodworking industries, the city now has two lumberyards, a boat and special furniture factory, a sawmill, an excelsior mill, a creamery, and the only legal distillery in operation in Wisconsin.

Crandon is at the junction with State 55 (*see Tour 4*).

Westward the highway again enters the ragged cutover, where twisted stumps show above the weeds and scrawny brush. The first Wisconsin farmers named for the Government's Matanuska Valley Colony at Palmer, Alaska, were chosen from this region in 1935. One man, speaking of his land in Forest County, said: "Aw hell, there's nothing here. I've been in the army, and I've been to the west coast, and I've been to hell-and-gone in Canada, and I've never seen a spot where a man has less of a chance to make a go of farming. Yeh, there's a little hunting here, then what?"

MONICO, 82 *m.* (1,597 alt., 180 pop.) (*see Tour 5*), is at the junction with US 45 (*see Tour 5*). As US 8 continues westward, LAKE VENUS (R), 82.5 *m.,* and LAKE GEORGE (R), 91.2 *m.,* are bright spots in the cutover.

RHINELANDER, 97.1 *m.* (1,543 alt., 8,019 pop.), is the self-named "Capital of the Heart O' the Lakes" and the trading center for the surrounding resort area. Each spring, in anticipation of the tourist season, it brightens with activity; signs advertising "Rooms for Tourists" are hung out; stores, taverns and gambling houses prepare to receive the visitors who crowd the region from June through August. Although in summer primarily a resort trade center, Rhinelander is also an industrial city, founded on pine lumbering. The first logging was done here in the winter of 1857-8; by 1916 most of the timber in Oneida County was gone. Gradually Rhinelander turned from lumbering to wood products and paper manufacture. Today it claims one of the country's largest plants manufacturing glassine and wax paper.

A LOGGING MUSEUM (*open daily, 9 a.m. to 5 p.m.*), 924 Davenport St., on the Wisconsin River bank, exhibits relics of the city's early history. This long low museum building is a reproduction of an old-time logging camp. It consists of two rooms, one the bunkhouse and the other the kitchen, with a covered space between, such as was used in the old days for hanging venison and storing wood. Lumbering tools are displayed within, and on the grounds are gigantic log wheelers, a crude snow plow, a steam hauler, a sleigh water tank used to make ice roads, a narrow-gauge logging engine, and a batteau taken from the Rib River where the last known log drive was made.

Among other relics is a pair of shoes so huge that they could have been worn by no one but Paul Bunyan, hero of the north woods. The story goes that Paul once caught a baby muskellunge, carried it home, and put it in a rain barrel outside his cabin. Every day he took the little fish out of the barrel and placed it on the ground; in time the muskie learned to walk and, before many months, to abhor water. One day when Paul was walking along the Rib River, the fish followed him and tried to cross the fast stream on a fallen log. Halfway across, it lost its balance and fell in. Although Paul quickly pulled off his shoes and plunged into the river, his pet had drowned by the time he reached it. Overcome with grief, Paul returned to camp, forgetting his shoes, the pair now displayed in the museum.

Rhinelander's nickname, "the Hodag City," also comes down from the days of Paul Bunyan when a fabulous beast called the hodag roamed the forests. Although it was supposedly extinct, one man in Rhinelander, Eugene S. (Gene) Shepard, stubbornly maintained that some hodags still lived in the remoter swamps. Everybody scoffed at him until the day a strange carcass was found in the wild swampland and brought to the city. Shepard confidently identified it as a hodag, and it became a seven-day wonder. From all over the north visitors came to marvel at this weird beast with bulging eyes, huge horns, great hooked claws, and huge gaping mouth filled with dagger-like teeth. Its hide was tough and brown, and a row of pointed spikes ran down the ridge of its leathery back to the end of its tail. By the time Shepard confessed that he had made the hodag himself, Rhinelander had received its nickname. Today the hodag has become a symbol of the north's old traditions, and Rhinelander high school athletes wear a hodag emblem on their jerseys.

Beyond ONEIDA LAKE (L), 109.4 *m.,* hardwoods predominate in the forests. Because it was easier to cut and more marketable, the first lumbermen cut only pine, leaving the hardwoods. In this region sand drifts like fine snow around the roots of the jackpine, chokes the ditches at the roadside, and in places covers the oiled surface of the highway. Although farms are few among the wooded hills, some fine dairy cattle graze in stumpy roadside pastures as US 8 enters the northern dairy belt.

At 113.5 *m.* is the junction with US 51 (*see Tour 7*); between this junction and a point at 118.5 *m.* US 8 and US 51 are one route.

TRIPOLI, 133.7 *m.* (50 pop.), a one-street village, has been dwindling away since the closing of its lumber mills. When the depression became especially severe here, about 1931, one third of its small frame houses were sold to farmers and carted away on trucks. In the center of Tripoli is the CONGREGATIONAL CHURCH (L), a small log building, and on its western outskirts is the Tri-County State high school, maintained jointly by Lincoln, Oneida, and Price Counties, and a graded school maintained by Lincoln and Oneida Counties.

BRANTWOOD (R), 139.5 *m.* (pop. 150), looks as if some giant hand had carelessly tossed its buildings far and wide. A large general store is on the highway; scattered houses straggle up the side road (R); out of sight is the town hall and cheese factory. As Finns settled this district, such family names as Pajala, Kerttula, and Salonen are common, and many Finnish homes still have their squat log bathhouses for the Saturday night *sauna* or steam bath (*see Tour 14A*).

Both Finns and Bohemians, frugal patient folk, farm the near-by cutover. Occasionally rutted trails intersect the highway, and along these grassy tracks are deserted farms, each telling a story of defeat. Usually the settler came in early summer, built a crude house, and made a small clearing. During the winter he cut trees, sawed them into fuel lengths, and peddled them in the village from his home-made bobsled. Sometimes he received $2.50 a cord, usually $1.50, and often there was no market at all.

In spring, with snow still crusting the ground, the settler, his wife, and children chopped brush, dug up roots, burned refuse. In summer they blasted the stumps, cleared out stones, and laboriously built a fence of rocks and gnarled stumps. That same summer the new farmer planted a small patch of potatoes, gathered enough wild hay to feed a horse and a cow. After a year, perhaps two or three acres had been cleared, a small potato crop harvested; but by that time the settler's capital was gone, and he had no reserve to carry him through the pinched years and to build a self-sustaining homestead.

PRENTICE, 148.7 *m.* (1,542 alt., 437 pop.) (*see Tour 8*), is at the junction with State 13 (*see Tour 8*).

Section b. PRENTICE to MINNESOTA LINE; 124.3 m. US 8

PRENTICE, 0 *m.,* lies between two different sections of the north: the highly publicized recreational area to the east, and the dairy belt to the west. Both have a common past in large-scale lumbering, and both, with the exhaustion of the forests, have turned to new enterprise. Although the transition between the two areas is not abrupt, west of CATAWBA, 12.8 *m.* (1,493 alt., 282 pop.), farms increase in number and quality. After entering Rusk County, US 8 is bordered by pasture land, fields of peas, and the supporting feed crops of dairying, which provides the principal cash income for the farmers here.

The highway crosses the Flambeau River, 43.3 *m.* Old Abe, the

Wisconsin war eagle, was captured on the northern wilds of this river in the spring of 1861. As mascot of the Eagle Regiment or the Eighth Wisconsin Infantry, Old Abe, perched on a standard made for him, was carried on parades, marches, and into 39 battles and skirmishes during the Civil War. "During a battle, his appearance was perfectly magnificent. . . . At the sound of the regimental bugle, which he had learned to recognize, he would start suddenly, dart up his head, and then bend it gracefully, anticipating the coming shock. When the battle commenced, he would spring up and spread his wings, uttering his startling scream, heard, and felt, and gloried in by all the soldiers. The fiercer and louder the storm, the fiercer, louder, and wilder were his screams." After the war Old Abe lived in a large room fitted for him in the basement of the Wisconsin State Capitol, and there he died on March 26, 1881.

LADYSMITH, 43.7 m. (1,142 alt., 3,493 pop.), radiating outward from the falls of the Flambeau River, was a rendezvous in early days for voyageurs, trappers, and traders who came to rest at Bruno Vinette's hotel at the foot of the falls before continuing their journey upstream. Successively called Flambeau Falls, Warner, and Corbett, Ladysmith was given its present name in 1900 to honor the wife of E. D. Smith, who had selected the village as the site of a branch factory of the Menasha Wooden Ware Company. In early days a pulp mill, a paper mill, a sulphate mill, a sawmill, and several small factories attracted settlers; today, although the log drives are over, Ladysmith's activities still center around lumber and wood processing. A large cooperative creamery and a canning plant for peas and beans are important sources of income for villagers and surrounding farmers.

Draining 10,000 square miles of land, the Chippewa River, 51.8 m., with its six tributaries—the Flambeau, Yellow, Big Jump, Eau Claire, Red Cedar, and Thornapple—spreads out over northwest Wisconsin like an enormous, seven-fingered hand. Long after the south and east had been settled by permanent farmers, this region was known only to the Indians and lumbermen who traveled its streams. Though logging began in the 1820's along the lower Chippewa, not until the 1860's did it move up the main stream and each tributary into the far north. In 1860 the Chippewa carried 60,000,000 feet of lumber down to the Mississippi; 11 years later, 436,000,000. By 1870 thousands of loggers thronged the forests, and the golden age of lumbering had begun. For 30 years the north resounded with the noise of axes biting deep into century-old trees, the rasping drag of crosscut saws, the lusty shout of "T--im--ber." Then suddenly the forests were gone and the lumber barons moved on, leaving a waste behind them.

WEYERHAUSER, 59.9 m. (1,200 alt., 321 pop.), is named for Frederick Weyerhaeuser (1834-1914), an enterprising German immigrant who rose from a sawmill worker to become one of the greatest of the lumber kings. Weyerhaeuser began logging operations in the Chippewa region in 1864. Unlike his contemporaries, Sawyer (*see*

Tour 15), Spooner (*see Tour 9*), and Vilas (see *Tour 15*), Weyerhaeuser was interested only in Wisconsin's timber resources, not in its government, its people, or its future. Working alone or with partners, he quietly began acquiring land and timber rights, buying from inexperienced Indians, working hand in hand with land-hungry railroad companies. As early as 1870 he organized the Mississippi River Logging Company (*see Tour 10*), the greatest lumber syndicate of its time.

As his business grew, Weyerhaeuser formed new partnerships until eventually he controlled the largest lumbering interests within the State. His camps employed hundreds of men; his timber holdings were enormous; his economic power was far-flung and autocratic. When he built his first logging railroad through this region in 1885, Chippewa Falls, the nearest rail center, was 40 miles away. Regardless of distance and cost, Weyerhaeuser had all materials—rails, ties, flatcars, and locomotives—hauled laboriously from Chippewa Falls during the winter when snow allowed the use of great sleds, each drawn by many yokes of oxen. Ten miles long, the line was one of the first in this region.

Weyerhaeuser's mills sawed their way swiftly through the white pine timber of Wisconsin, then of Minnesota. Although rich in lands on the Pacific coast, which were a subsidy from the Government, in 1900 the Northern Pacific Ry. found itself short of ready cash. So Weyerhaeuser organized another timber company and for $6 an acre bought the enormous Northern Pacific land holdings in Washington and Oregon—some 1,000,000 acres of the richest timberland in the world. There his heirs continue operations.

When Weyerhaeuser transferred his lumbering activities westward, life in the north slowed down, the village of Weyerhaeuser became almost deserted. Though thousands of acres lay raw and jagged with tree stumps, the land was partially cleared for incoming settlers. The lumberjacks disappeared, either following the pineries west or staking out farms on the cutover. They left behind them, however, the legends of Paul Bunyan and Babe, the Blue Ox, who measured "seven axe handles between the eyes." Out of their Viking lore, the Scandinavian lumberjacks in Wisconsin had multiplied the legends that followed the westward march of the lumbermen from the northeastern Atlantic coast. They gave Paul a logging crew of mighty Norsemen—Big Ole, Chris Crosshaul, Axel Axelson, Happy Olson, Hels Helsen, and Shot Gunderson. Big Ole, the blacksmith, forged Babe's shoes, which were so enormous that each set exhausted an iron mine and so heavy that when Ole lifted them he sank knee-deep in solid rock. Shot Gunderson was equally powerful and adept. Shot used to roll a 75-foot log right out of its bark, then walk nonchalantly ashore on the bubbles.

The deep purple range of the BARRON HILLS (R), 66.5 *m.,* rises 300 to 600 feet above the plain. The highway is now in the richest and best developed agricultural district along its route. Low roadside creameries squat on hillsides, for both Barron and Polk Counties to the west are important butter-producing areas in the northern dairy belt. Proximity to the Twin Cities market has helped develop this region.

WILD RICE CREEK, 74.8 *m.*, is named for the wild grain that grows in its shallow sluggish water. Requiring neither sowing nor cultivation, wild rice was long an important Indian food, so important, in fact, that many a warrior died in the constant warfare the Sioux and Chippewa waged for possession of the larger fields in this region. Although the wars have ended now, swarthy Indians still gather the grain in the simple and laborious way of their ancestors (*see Tour 4*).

CAMERON, 76.6 *m.* (1,099 alt., 760 pop.) (*see Tour 10*), is at the junction with US 53 (*see Tour 10*).

Two logging tributaries of the Chippewa River, the Red Cedar and the Yellow, are crossed at 78.3 *m.* and 81.3 *m.* The land is more thickly settled, with Scandinavians predominating in population. The early Scandinavian immigrants settled in southeastern Wisconsin; finding the best land taken, later arrivals pushed far north to the wilderness of the upper Mississippi Valley. · Here they worked as railroad laborers or as lumberjacks; many settled on the land, farming in summer, working as loggers in winter. By 1880 Scandinavians predominated in the pineries.

BARRON, 82.1 *m.* (1,120 alt., 1,863 pop.), seat of Barron County, became an actual community in 1878 when a sawmill was built on the Yellow River here. The arrival of the Minneapolis, St. Paul & Sault Ste Marie R. R. in 1884 led to the erection of another sawmill and a flour mill, which helped support the community after the pine forest was gone. As the lumberjacks turned to farming they were forced to remove the hitherto undesirable hardwood. A stave mill and woodenware factory arose in Barron, and on winter days bobsleds lined up, a hundred in a row, to unload hardwood logs. Several small brickyards were founded in clay deposits nearby, and in 1901 the city acquired water power sites and built an electric light plant. In 1902 the Barron Co-operative Creamery Company was organized, and for years it ranked as one of the largest cooperative creameries in the world. Development of transportation facilities in the region has enlarged the city's trade area, and it is now one of the more important trade centers in the county.

US 8 passes pastures, pea fields, and woodlots, crosses the small Vermillion River, 85.9 *m.*, and skirts Turtle Lake (R), 94.8 *m.*

At 98 *m.* is the junction with US 63 (*see Tour 9*); between this junction and a point at 99.6 *m.*, US 8 and US 63 are one route.

TURTLE LAKE, 98.3 *m.* (1,267 alt., 598 pop.), began in 1879 when Stephen F. Richardson built a sawmill here. In 1877 the Omaha R. R. reached the village, and the Soo Line came through in 1884. The station was rebuilt after a Soo train had run into an Omaha train here in 1901, injuring several people and hurling cars into the station, which burned to the ground. A feed mill operates here, but the village depends largely for its livelihood upon a cooperative creamery and a pea cannery. Agricultural development in this region has reached its maximum.

Much of the land has been zoned for recreational and forest development (*see Agriculture*), and both private and public land is under the State's forest crop law (*see Natural Setting*). The region is turning to recreation in the hope of attracting visitors from the Twin Cities to its lakes and streams. At 109.7 *m.* is (L) a CAMPING GROUND, and at 117.8 *m.*, DEER LAKE, a large body of water looping through the woods.

At 119.4 *m.* is the junction with State 35 (*see Tour 13*); between this junction and a point at 123.5 *m.*, US 8 and State 35 are one route.

ST. CROIX FALLS, 124 *m.* (922 alt., 952 pop.), on the St. Croix River, is the largest village in Polk County. Its early history is the county's history, for here in 1837 the first permanent white settlers staked out claims and built their cabins. Soon lumber mills and trading posts sprang up. Lumbering was the important activity of the village, and farming was so neglected that when supplies were cut off in the winter of 1844, a two-month famine occurred.

Ray Stannard Baker (1870-   ), magazine feature writer, biographer, and essayist, spent his early life at St. Croix Falls. Under the pen name of David Grayson he wrote sketches of rural life.

At 124.2 *m.* is (L) INTERSTATE PARK (*camping, picnicking, and bathing accommodations; complete sanitary facilities*). The oldest of Wisconsin's State parks, created cooperatively with Minnesota in 1900, contains 730 acres, 580 of which are in Wisconsin. Here the river pours through a canyon cut from traprock of the Keweenawan period, remnant of an ancient lava flow. Red cliffs and pine-grown terraces hang above the seething stream; trails pass from shadowed gloom to sunswept patches of bare rock on the castellated bluffs that wall the St. Croix River for miles.

There are several remarkable geological formations in the park. The OLD MAN OF THE DALLES (*see below*), a grim rock profile, tops the Wisconsin bank where the river turns southwest. Farther downstream a slender red shaft, the DEVIL'S CHAIR, spires high above the Minnesota side. On both banks, far above the present water level, are pot holes or kettles, ground by spherical boulders that were swirled about in rock crevices by prehistoric rapids. These holes, in many of which the boulders are visible, vary in diameter from one to 12 feet and sometimes reach a depth of 141 feet.

Almost the entire park is covered with a network of roads and hiking trails that lead through the forest into deep rifts in the rocky floor or high among the crags that rise 200 feet above the riverbanks.

1. Right on the park road, past camping grounds near the riverbank, to the STATE FISH HATCHERY and its trout ponds at the north end of the park.

2. Left on the park road through heavily shaded PICNIC GROUNDS and along a wall of rocky cliffs to the OLD MAN OF THE DALLES. The Chippewa regarded this remarkable head as that of Winneboujou, mythical giant-hero of their nation, who performed great exploits for his people throughout northwestern Wisconsin. Watching ceaselessly from on high, he more than once caused the river here to destroy canoe fleets of the warring Sioux, the Chippewa's inveterate enemies. HORIZON ROCK shows (L) just as the road reaches the

bathing beach of tiny LAKE O' THE DALLES, and the rocky slopes continue past SOUTH PEAK to the end of the park.

At 124.3 *m.* is the INTERSTATE BRIDGE (*free*) into Taylors Falls, Minnesota.

Tour 17

Green Bay—Wausau—Chippewa Falls—Prescott—(St. Paul, Minn.); State· 29.
Green Bay to Minnesota Line,˙ 266.2 *m.*

Chicago and North Western Ry. parallels route between Green Bay and Wausau; the Soo Line between Abbotsford and Chippewa Falls.
Cement-paved and oiled-gravel roadbed.
Accommodations adequate in larger cities; poor in villages.

State 29 traverses the State from Green Bay in the east to Prescott in the west, both renowned in the past, one as a fur-trading capital, the other as a lumbering center. Today the fur-bearing animals and tall forests are gone; along much of its route State 29 crosses dreary cutover, which only here and there has been converted into farms.

Section a.   GREEN BAY to WAUSAU; 94.2 m. State 29

GREEN BAY, 0 *m.* (590 alt., 37,415 pop.) (*see Green Bay*).
Green Bay is at the junction with State 57 (*see Tour 1*), US 41 (*see Tour 2*), and US 141 (*see Tour 3*).
In 1745 French fur traders, in quest of mink, beaver, muskrat, marten, and fisher, built a trading post on the site of Green Bay. About a century later Americans and immigrants from Europe began clearing the land around Green Bay, raising wheat and shipping it east or down to Wisconsin's lakeshore cities. As the once fertile soil became impoverished, the farmers of this region turned to dairying.
Villages in the moderately rich dairy country west of Green Bay are small, some of them mere crossroad settlements: MILL CENTER, 9.7 *m.;* PITTSFIELD, 14.1 *m.;* and ANGELICA, 20.3 *m.,* are in the heart of a district settled in the 1880's by freedom-loving Polish immigrants. These religious, hard-working people have many tiny farming centers within a radius of 20 miles—Pulaski, Zachow, Krakow, Kunesh, and Sobieski.
Beyond Angelica State 29 enters the rugged, twisted moraine coun-

try. On both sides of the highway stretch fields of half-cleared farmland and miles of sparse second growth.

BONDUEL, 28.4 *m.* (884 alt., 534 pop.), though named for Father Florimond T. Bonduel, a French missionary, is now, paradoxically, a village of preponderantly German stock.

Bonduel is at the junction with State 55 (*see Tour 4*); between Bonduel and Shawano State 55 and State 29 are one route.

Twisting up and down over moraines covered with young growth, the highway ascends LIME KILN HILL, 32.2 *m.,* and passes a ruined stone kiln, 32.4 *m.* Other kilns are scattered in the woods farther along the slope. The use of lime began in Wisconsin in the days when transportation was so difficult and hazardous that building materials could not be shipped in. When pioneers wanted new homes for their families, several of them united to build a lime kiln. After producing enough lime for the purpose, and perhaps for the local sale of a few tons, the 40-foot stone and firebrick shafts would be abandoned until needed again. When transportation improved, the kilns were left to crumble and fall. Those that remain here are allowed to stand only because farmers have found no other use for the limestone hill.

SHAWANO (Ind., south), 37.4 *m.* (824 alt., 4,188 pop.), approached through acres of timberland and small farms, is a quiet city, a retail center for farmers, through-vacationists, and the Indians on the nearby Menominee Reservation (*see Tour 4*).

Like many other Wisconsin cities, Shawano was the site of an Indian village before the coming of the white men. In the nineteenth century a band of Menominee moved westward from Green Bay in search of a lake wherein game and fish abounded. They found SHAWANO LAKE, settled near by, and began to fish for sturgeon. When the white men came, however, it was not the fish but the timber that attracted them. The Wolf River promised water power for mills and a convenient waterway for floating logs. Lumbering started with Samuel Farnsworth's mill in 1843. Shawano flourished for a time and then declined; after the big timber had been depleted, Shawano turned to paper making, woodworking, and the sale of Indian pottery, baskets, and other souvenirs.

After crossing the Wolf in the outskirts of the city, State 29 passes through a sandy and desolate lowland, dotted with rank, thick spruce swamps. North of here is the SITE OF THE STOCKBRIDGE INDIAN RESERVATION, given to the Stockbridge by the Federal Government in 1856 in exchange for their lands on the eastern shores of Lake Winnebago (*see Tour 4*).

"In the early 1870's," according to Dr. Joseph Schafer, superintendent of the State Historical Society, "these pine lands were sold, under an act of congress passed without notice to the tribe, as they claimed, to a corporation of which a prominent Wisconsin politician was a leading member, thus reducing the Stockbridge reserve to the dimensions of half a township. . . ." When the timber had been exhausted, the lumbermen moved on, leaving the Stockbridge with no land and no means of subsistence except the sale of produce from their meager gardens and odd jobs at near-by villages and farms. Recently the Bureau of Indian Affairs has acquired 14,423 acres of the original Stockbridge Reservation. It plans to reforest the land and allot it to the Indians under trust patent.

The highway enters Forest Protection District No. 4 on the banks of the Embarass (Fr., obstruction) River, so named by French *voyageurs,* who, canoeing down the stream, frequently found their passage blocked by fallen logs.

At 63.8 *m.* is the junction with US 45 (*see Tour 5*); between this junction and WITTENBERG, 66 *m.* (1,168 alt., 863 pop.) (*see Tour 5*), State 29 and US 45 are one route (*see Tour 5*).

West of Wittenberg the northern dairy belt begins to improve. Although spruce and cedar swamps are still numerous, field crops appear along the roadside; pastures are fresh and green in summer.

At 82 *m.* RIB MOUNTAIN (*see Tour 7*) appears as a lofty shadow on the horizon straight ahead; soon LITTLE RIB HILL becomes visible, nestled like a calf against the flank of the mountain. Left, MOSINEE HILL dominates the sky line. The farms improve in size, number, and development. A large Fox Ranch is (R) at 89.8 *m.*

SCHOFIELD, 90.3 *m.* (1,206 alt., 1,287 pop.) (*see Tour 7*), is at the junction with US 51 (*see Tour 7*). State 29 and US 51 are one route between Schofield and WAUSAU, 94.2 *m.* (1,191 alt., 23,758 pop.) (*see Tour 7*).

Section b. WAUSAU to MINNESOTA LINE; 172 m. State 29

West of Scott and Third Sts., 0 *m.,* State 29 continues along Scott St. to the High Bridge spanning the Wisconsin River. At 0.6 *m.* is the junction with US 51 (*see Tour 7*).

Passing Marathon Park, 1.1 *m.,* State 29 emerges into open farmlands, some of the best in the northern dairy belt. The long flank of Rib Mountain, undulating beneath a cover of hardwoods and conifers, looms up (L) parallel to the highway. Here in Marathon County, largest in Wisconsin, farmers depend largely on dairying, but many horses graze in roadside pastures, for this is one of the State's main horse-breeding sections.

During the depression many Wisconsin farmers reverted to the use of draft horses in place of tractors, which were more expensive to maintain. Every year during the last decade 20,000 shaggy and half-wild horses from the western plains have been shipped into the State. Horse-breeding farms have been established to supply the demand for good stock, and the Wisconsin Horse Breeders' Association, the College of Agriculture of the University of Wisconsin, and the State Department of Agriculture and Markets have cooperated with them to improve the breed of Wisconsin draft horses. In 1920 almost 30 per cent of the State's licensed stallions were of mixed breed; in 1937 only about 2 per cent were of inferior stock.

ABBOTSFORD, 34.6 *m.* (1,422 alt., 781 pop.) (*see Tour 8*), is at the junction with State 13 (*see Tour 8*).

The highway crosses the Black River, 50.4 *m.,* at one time an important lumbering stream (*see Tour 19*). Here, as elsewhere in Marathon County, American cheese is the main agricultural product. Supplementary income is derived from condensed milk, butter, potatoes, peas, poultry and eggs, honey, maple sugar, and canned vegetables.

THORP, 58.5 *m.,* (1,129 alt., 892 pop.), has a small PARK (L) containing a tiny pond, a bit of lawn, a decorative miniature windmill, and a few flowering shrubs.

STANLEY, 65.3 *m.* (1,079 alt., 1,988 pop.), a farm trading center, has one of the largest apiaries in Wisconsin, 800 colonies of bees, owned by Charles Giauque. Small apiaries are scattered over Wisconsin; here in the dairy region they produce clover honey. The broad view of the wooded countryside, from a hill, 76.1 *m.,* is bordered by the distant escarpment of the upper Magnesian cuesta (*see Natural Setting*).

CADOTT, 77.6 *m.* (979 alt., 631 pop.), has a curious conglomeration of racial strains. It was perhaps named for the father of Michel Cadotte (*see Tour 14A*), Jean Baptiste Cadotte, a French-Indian trapper who settled here on the Yellow River in 1838. Later other Frenchmen came from Canada; Germans, Irish, English, and Norwegians arrived after the passage of the Homestead Law of 1862; and many Czechs and a few Slovaks came about 1900. This mixture of nationalities created a problem in the churches. In the local Roman Catholic church a single service was conducted in French, English, and German, and later even in Czech, so that on Sundays the devout spent four hours in kneeling, standing, and sitting until the polyglot devotions were ended.

West of Cadott the highway runs through a region of sandy soil and marshland and then along the shore of LAKE WISSOTA, 84.1 *m.,* backwater from the power dam at Chippewa Falls.

CHIPPEWA FALLS, 89.8 *m.* (859 alt., 9,539 pop.), is an industrial community. Probably the first white man to visit the Indian village on this site was Jonathan Carver, English explorer, on his expedition of 1766. He described it in bitter terms: ". . . the inhabitants, in general, seemed to be the nastiest people I have ever been among. I observed that the women and children indulged themselves in a custom . . . that of searching each other's head, and eating the prey caught therein." Nevertheless, apparently he thought well enough of the Chippewa Valley to contemplate asking the King to sanction a grant of land that the Indians had given him here. Whether or not the King granted his plea is a matter of conjecture, but for many years thereafter his heirs periodically asserted title to an enormous tract of valley land. Even when the present city was founded, numerous Carvers still claimed the valley.

Whether or not their title was valid, the Chippewa Valley was then considered public property, since the Indians had ceded their right to it in 1837. In 1836 Jean Brunet had established the first sawmill here and built a dam on the Chippewa River. Other settlers built mills, and soon Chippewa Falls became a bustling lumber town, filled with French-Canadian and Indian lumberjacks. The village was important, too, as a trading post and retail center. The Government established a blacksmith shop here, and while Wisconsin remained one of the Nation's leading wheat-producing States, numerous gristmills lined the riverbank.

The flour mills were the first to vanish. When lumber in turn declined, the city turned to hydroelectric power, generated at the falls. Today the NORTHERN STATES POWER COMPANY HYDRO PLANT dominates the city, the reflection of its lights visible for many miles at night. This plant has an installed capacity of 30,000 horsepower, and is one of three in Chippewa County on the Chippewa River; it supplies electrical energy to a transmission line system in western Wisconsin, which in turn is interconnected with hydroelectric plants on the Wisconsin River, steam and hydro plants in eastern Wisconsin, and steam plants in Minnesota.

Chippewa Falls has three large shoe factories, a woolen mill, and two small meat packing and food processing plants. The city is also the headquarters of the State branch of the Farmers Union, one of the largest and most powerful of farmer organizations.

Chippewa Falls is at the junction with US 53 (see Tour 10). State 29 plunges downhill out of residential Chippewa Falls and follows the green gorge of the Chippewa River (L). Leaving the river, the highway runs through land so level that it presents no water erosion problem. But the wind that sweeps across the broad flats carries away tons of soil every year.

At 108.1 m. is the junction with US 12 (see Tour 19); between this junction and Menomonie, State 29 and US 12 are one route. The red brick DUNN COUNTY ASYLUM (R), 115.8 m. is backed by the white barns of its modern dairy. The highway skirts a bluff 60 feet above RED CEDAR LAKE, broad and still, its distant opposite shores dark with small pines.

MENOMONIE, 118.2 m. (803 alt., 5,595 pop.), on the banks of the swift Red Cedar River, began when lumbermen saw that the Red Cedar was a natural highway for logs and Menomonie a logical sawmill site. Platted in 1859, Menomonie, by the 1870's, was headquarters of one of the largest lumber corporations in Wisconsin, which owned 115,-000 acres of timberland and employed from 1,200 to 1,500 men. The situation confronting the county's first resident preacher, Joshua Pittman, who arrived here in 1854, indicates the energy of this early frontier settlement. Although Pittman came to preach, he found his duties more complex, for he was expected to "preach Sundays, teach school week-days, and pack shingles nights."

After the supply of timber had been exhausted, Menomonie declined rapidly. With its sawmills silent, slowly rotting away in piles of pungent sawdust, the fading city was saved by new enterprises, notably a power plant on the Red Cedar River, and STOUT INSTITUTE, Main and 2nd Sts., the only college in the country devoted wholly to training teachers in industrial and household arts. In 1889 James H. Stout, a pioneer lumberman, incorporated courses in vocational training into the Menomonie public school system. In 1903 he founded Stout Institute (then Stout Training School) as a private, coeducational training college. Taken over by the State in 1911, the institute was given the privilege of granting degrees in 1917; in 1935 graduate work for the Master of Science degree was begun. Training courses are divided into two groups—industrial arts and household arts.

Although largely a college town, Menomonie is frequented by farmers of the vicinity, who come to sell their milk to the condensery and trade at the local stores.

Menomonie is at the junction with US 12 (*see Tour 19*).

West of Menomonie State 29 curves down a wooded hill, crosses the Red Cedar River, 118.6 *m.*, then plunges into open rolling farm land dotted with rugged hills. In spite of their ruggedness, Pierce and St. Croix Counties contain a large portion of fertile land. Dairying is important here, and farm land not planted in crops is used to pasture sheep, cattle, and horses.

On the banks of the Eau Galle River, 136.1 *m.*, squats (R) a tiny, make-shift sawmill powered by a threshing machine engine. In the days when timber was to be had for the taking, many such primitive sawmills worked the Wisconsin woods.

SPRING VALLEY, 137 *m.* (941 alt., 896 pop.), seems a half-forgotten village, as drowsy as the region about it. Spring Valley was an ordinary logging camp about 1890, when a prospector from the West discovered iron deposits near by. A furnace was erected; railway tracks were extended to the town; large mills were built to cut staves, spokes, and heading. In the summer of 1892 a typical mining boom began, and Spring Valley grew rapidly. The panic of 1893 closed the furnace; when it reopened, iron was being produced more cheaply elsewhere; in 1908 the furnace ceased operations. Lack of timber soon caused the woodworking plants to move away, although two small sawmills operate part-time.

West of this point State 29 climbs by fits and starts, following a tortuous course through the western section of the hills country.

At 144.3 *m.* is the junction with US 63 (*see Tour 9*); between this junction and a point at 146.6 *m.* State 29 and US 63 are one route (*see Tour 9*).

RIVER FALLS, 159.1 *m.* (887 alt., 2,363 pop.) (*see Tour 13*), on the Kinnikinnic River, is at the junction with State 35 (*see Tour 13*). Between this point and 160.5 *m.* State 29 and State 35 are one route.

West of River Falls the rolling hills and valleys are well cultivated, although occasionally a great barren monadnock rises out of the fields and pastures: farms are large, farmsteads widely separated.

At 170.7 *m.* is the junction with US 10 (*see Tour 18*); between this junction and the Minnesota Line, State 29 and US 10 are one route.

PRESCOTT, 171.6 *m.* (702 alt., 755 pop.) (*see Tour 18*), borders the Mississippi. US 10 and State 29 cross the Minnesota Line, 172 *m.*, by a BRIDGE (*toll: 15¢ for driver and car; 5¢ for each additional passenger; children under 12 free*), 16 miles southeast of St. Paul, Minnesota.

Tour 18

Manitowoc—Appleton—Stevens Point—Prescott—(St. Paul, Minn.); US 10.
Manitowoc to Minnesota Line, 290.4 *m.*

Chicago & North Western Ry. parallels route between Manitowoc and Appleton; Soo Line between Appleton and Auburndale; the Chicago, St. Paul, Minneapolis & Omaha R. R. between Neillsville and Mondovi.
Cement-paved, oiled-gravel, or low-type bituminous roadbed.
Good accommodations at Manitowoc, Appleton, Waupaca, and Stevens Point; otherwise village hotels and restaurants.

US 10 cuts across the fertile eastern Wisconsin grain belt along Lake Michigan, then the glaciated sandy soils of middle Wisconsin, and finally the high slopes of the Western Uplands. Transportation and water power first brought settlers to Manitowoc, Appleton, and Stevens Point, and later gave industry a chance to grow there. For the most part, however, the highway passes only tiny soot-free villages, their size and activity determined by agriculture alone.

Section a. MANITOWOC to STEVENS POINT; 115 m., US 10

MANITOWOC, 0 *m.* (595 alt., 22,963 pop.), sprawls around the harbor where the Manitowoc River enters Lake Michigan, a city in which maritime sights and sounds mingle with those of industrial activity. The lake and river were dotted with Indian fishermen when Colonel A. Edwards passed in a canoe in 1818, en route to Chicago from Green Bay; for years after his passage the harbor was a stopover station on the month-long journey between the cities. As Wisconsin grew and new paths were cut through the wilderness, Manitowoc became in turn a lumber camp, a fishing town, a shipbuilding center, and finally the commercial and industrial capital of Manitowoc County. Though ships and shipping are not so important as they once were, Manitowoc still takes color from the blue-capped sailors who walk its streets. Evenings, when workers in other towns are at home, fishermen trudge its dark streets near the waterfront, coming home to a late dinner, or pause in lakeside taverns to drink beer and whisky with officers, tugmasters, and others who sail the Great Lakes.

Manitowoc rose with the land boom of 1835, then floundered in the subsequent depression of 1837. With recovery a few eastern and English farmers came in, followed almost immediately by Germans, Norwegians, and Irish. Bohemians arrived in 1854-56, Poles in the late 1860's. Among the German immigrants was Carl von Brause who, though a baron from the Palatinate, was a freethinker and revolutionary. He and his delicate wife came to Manitowoc in 1848, where they tried to scratch a living from Wisconsin soil. Pioneering proved too rigorous for the gentle baroness, and her death provided Manitowoc with one of its most persistent legends. In Phantom Hollow, where they built their New World home, her spirit can be seen on cold nights by anyone who will brave the dark and the chill.

In 1850 business was brisk, fisheries were hauling 175-barrel catches of whitefish in the lake and river. A cholera epidemic struck in the summer of 1850 and again in 1854. All but a few diehards deserted the settlement, and it was several years before Manitowoc recovered. By 1860 the city was growing up again with a new industry—shipbuilding. As commerce on the Great Lakes expanded, Manitowoc built ships in ever increasing numbers until, in the late 1880's, shipping and shipbuilding began to lose importance. When iron vessels began to replace the old wooden ones, about 1890, Manitowoc could not keep pace with larger manufacturing centers. Not until the World War did the shipyards operate again at full capacity, manufacturing ships and iron parts; at the peak of production one of the largest plants employed 2,500 men. Since then shipbuilding has continued at a leisurely pace.

Post-war prosperity was as rosy here as anywhere; in 1929 industrial plants manufactured tinsel ornaments for Christmas trees, aluminum goods, cement, tires, condensed milk, malt, beer, coaster wagons, machinery, knit goods, metal furniture, flour, and pleasure yachts. Though the depression meant retrenchment for many companies and bankruptcy for a few, some of the larger held their ground, even prospered. The ALUMINUM GOODS MANUFACTURING COMPANY (*see Tour 1*), 16th and Washington Sts., was one of the latter.

The RAHR MALTING COMPANY PLANT, 6th and Washington Sts., founded in 1847, is another survivor of the industrial slump. Within its great storage elevators and workhouses here and at Minneapolis and Shakopee, Minnesota, 6,500,000 bushels of grain and malt can be stored at a time, and in the three cities its present production capacity is 11,000,000 bushels of malt a year. The company manufactures malt from barley, wheat, and rye for breweries, distilleries, and the food products industries.

From SCHUETTE'S PARK, Huron and 11th Sts., on a high bluff

overlooking the river, is a fine view of the city lying like a half-moon on the blue harbor.

The PERE MARQUETTE AUTO FERRY (*passengers, $3 each; cars, $5 each*), which provides transportation between Manitowoc and Ludington, Mich., docks at the mouth of the Manitowoc River.

Manitowoc is at the junction with State 42 (*see Tour 1C*), US 141 (*see Tour 3*), and US 151 (*see Tour 6*). Between Manitowoc and a point at 5.3 *m*. US 10 and US 141 are one route.

US 10 turns R. on 8th St. and at 0.5 *m*. crosses the dirt-brown Manitowoc River, whose waters empty into the harbor a few hundred yards downstream. As the route passes through residential Manitowoc, the scene shifts from city to prosperous countryside. Farms, barns, and silos are large. The pattern varies little—pasture, hayfield, cornfield, barleyfield, and oatfield. Only the small cherry and plum orchards in every farmyard briefly break the green monotony when they blossom for a fortnight each spring.

At 5.3 *m*. is the junction with US 141 (*see Tour 3*).

Villages in this region are small. Most of them were settled by Germans between 1857 and 1865, when Pomeranians, West Prussians, and North Germans poured in during the great Teutonic influx that populated so much of Wisconsin.

BRILLION, 23.9 *m*. (825 alt., 1,167 pop.), is a trading center for neighboring farmers who come to buy and sell, to visit with friends, to talk crops in the taverns, spicing the familiar terms of farming with a scientific phrase or two culled from recent university bulletins. Although most of the population of Brillion is of German stock, there are a few descendants here of the Italians who performed much of the heavy labor when railroads first cut through the Wisconsin wilderness.

West of Brillion, US 10 traverses the northern section of the great malt barley area of eastern Wisconsin. With the repeal of the prohibition amendment the value of barley soared and farmers began planting more and more of it; even by 1934 barley occupied 8.4 per cent of Wisconsin's farm acreage. The landscape becomes more rolling and more heavily wooded as the highway enters Calumet County. Just beyond FOREST JUNCTION, 28.9 *m*. (250 pop.), US 10 reaches the crest of the Niagara cuesta.

At 35.8 *m*. is the junction with State 55 (*see Tour 4*). Soon an occasional break in the trees reveals LAKE WINNEBAGO (*see Tour 5*). Between this point and Appleton the land is flat and fertile, almost wholly under cultivation. In the distance appear the industrial sky lines of Appleton (R) and Neenah-Menasha (L) (*see Tour 2*). US 10 crosses the Fox River at 42.2 *m*.

APPLETON, 48.7 *m*. (723 alt., 25,267 pop.), both a college and an industrial city, lies on the rapids of the Fox River. Although Lawrence College came first, industrial Appleton followed soon after. In 1848, a year after Amos A. Lawrence had donated $10,000 for the establishment of a Methodist college at the Grand Chute, the first sawmill was built here. Grand Chute was renamed Appleton for Lawrence's Bostonian father-in-law.

Although the Rock River Conference of the Methodist Episcopal Church chose this site for a college solely because of its beauty, incoming industrialists saw other advantages. The Fox, which has a fall of 38 feet within the present city limits, promised ample water power for industrial plants. By 1854 a paper mill, a cabinet factory, and several flour mills were operating here, each drawing its power from the swift stream. During the Civil War other wood products factories and a woolen mill sprang up; flour milling became a $1,000,000 industry, and not until the 1890's, when wheat production declined, did the paper and pulp industry replace it.

Appleton had one of the first streetcar lines in the United States. When Charles J. Van Depoele was demonstrating his electric streetcar in Chicago in 1883, Judge J. E. Harriman of Appleton made a special trip to see the wonder work and returned full of plans and enthusiasm. He organized a corporation, obtained a franchise, and in 1886 set five streetcars going on the muddy streets. Within 10 years the company was bankrupt, but a year later the reorganized corporation built interurban lines to Kaukauna and Neenah (*see Tour 2*). This time the project was successful, and it was not until 1928 that the rails were torn up and buses substituted for cars.

Paper is Appleton's most important product today; the city is largely supported by six large paper manufacturing plants. Other enterprises contribute to the city's prosperity. In 1930 a total of 60 industrial plants had an annual pay roll of $4,500,000. The student body and faculty of Lawrence College had spending power of $1,200,000.

Meanwhile, Lawrence had become a thriving denominational college. In the beginning grave penalties were provided for smoking, drinking, or failing to observe the Sabbath. The school was coeducational, and an early regulation provided: "If any male student have a relative in the female department whom he wishes to see, he will be permitted to go to the steward's room, request her to be sent for and there converse with her. Brothers can also walk out with their sisters by permission from someone of the faculty, but with no others."

Lawrence has come a long way from the stringent regulations and restricted curriculum of its youth. During the past 20 years the program at Lawrence College has undergone major changes. An art rental service and sophomore tutorials have been instituted at Lawrence. In addition, the college program includes all the recognized advances of recent years, including comprehensive examinations, inter-departmental majors, and other procedures designed to make the curriculum flexible and adapted to individual student needs. The college also includes a well recognized conservatory of music offering professional work leading to the degree of bachelor of music.

In 1929 Lawrence College began a unique experiment in adult education. The Institute of Paper Chemistry, a post-graduate institution, was organized to train college and university graduates for scientific work in a relatively unexplored field. In addition to its educational activities, it is engaged in research for the pulp and paper industry and for other industries having problems of a related nature. Originally the institution was sponsored by a group of Wisconsin paper mill companies, but the group now includes companies from all important paper-making States of the Union. The first institution of its kind in the United States, it offers a four year course leading to the degree of doctor of philosophy. A master of science degree is awarded at the end of the second year. Courses are offered in the fields of organic, analytical, and physical chemistry; physics; wood technology; and pulp and paper chemistry and technology.

Harry Houdini (1874-1926), whose real name was Ehrich Weiss, was born in Appleton, the fifth child of a Jewish rabbi. His parents, both from cultured families, had fled to America from Budapest after a duel in which Dr. Weiss was reported to have killed a gentile. Ehrich first manifested the skill that later made him famous as a magician by picking the locks his mother kept on her pastry cupboard. Pies and cookies frequently disappeared, but Mrs. Weiss could not see that the lock had been touched, and it was only through circumstantial evidence that she was able to prove Ehrich was the thief. Whenever a circus came to Appleton, Ehrich immediately visited the side show where the magician performed, and, after the show had moved on, spent many hours practicing the feats he had observed. At the age of nine, the boy got a job as a performer in a circus, but his parents would not let him leave Appleton with the show. A few weeks after his twelfth birthday, however, Ehrich ran away from home, and shortly thereafter the Weiss family removed to New York.

At 52.1 m. is junction with US 45 (*Tour 5*) and US 41 (*Tour 2*).

West of Appleton US 10 enters the sandy plain of middle Wisconsin, whose chief products are potatoes and cattle.

FREMONT, 68.1 m. (778 alt., 387 pop.), on the Wolf River, was a thriving lumber camp in the 1890's. But the last log drive came down the swift Wolf in 1911, and it has been even longer since the last pine was cut near Fremont. Only the river is unchanged—clear and deep, teeming with fish. In April, when the pike come down after spawning in the swamps upstream, the bridge is lined with fishermen, and the river is filled with boats, each with from one to three anglers. For several Sundays during the great pike run thousands come from Wisconsin and Illinois to drop their baited hooks into the water here. And from May to October fishermen come to Fremont for pickerel, white bass, black bass, and other varieties of pan fish. All summer, men in hip boots, using long rakes called "crow's feet," take clams from the Wolf and its tributaries, selling their shells to the WOLF RIVER PEARL BUTTON WORKS, which manufactures them into button blanks and ships them to finishing plants.

Northwest of Fremont, US 10 winds for 70 miles through the typical sandy drift of Wisconsin's leading potato area. This is part of the principal area of commercial production, which centers in Waupaca, Portage, and Waushara Counties. Among potato-growing States, Wisconsin ranked sixth in 1930 and second in 1934; the farm value of the crop varies with the year from $14,000,000 to $40,000,000.

WEYAUWEGA (Ind., he embodies it), 75.2 m. (778 alt., 1,067 pop.), named for an Indian chief, was settled in 1852 by Yankees and Germans. Lumbering and flour milling kept it alive until the turn of the century when both these industries began to pass from the Wisconsin scene. Then, as agriculture in the north expanded, Weyauwega became a farmers' trading center.

WAUPACA (Ind., white sand bottom), 83.1 m. (868 alt., 3,131 pop.), early became the center of Wisconsin potato production, when other northern towns were occupied with lumbering. Although farmers still market their potato crops here, Waupaca is important also as a recreation center. The 23 lakes in the chain southwest of Waupaca and the well-stocked trout streams draw sportsmen from many States to fish the clear water for pickerel, bass, small pan fish, and trout. Occasionally a 10- or 12-pound German brown is caught in a lake, a rare phenomenon, for German browns seldom inhabit any but running water. The entire chain, spring-fed, cold, and clear, set in deep hollows between low rounded hills, offers long leisurely canoe trips or more speedy ones in power launches.

Northwest of Waupaca, the highway enters the terminal moraine country, formed by the last great ice sheet which blanketed Wisconsin hundreds of thousands of years ago (*see Natural Setting*). The land becomes rougher; mounds and hills rise on every side; many of the valleys are swamps filled with lush vegetation.

STEVENS POINT, 115 m. (1,085 alt., 13,623 pop.), lying in a natural basin formed by the Wisconsin River (W) and the Plover River (E), was founded in 1839 when, with timber cutting starting along the Wisconsin River, George Stevens chose this spot, "the Point," as the most convenient stopping place on the long pull upriver from Wisconsin Rapids to Mosinee. Tradesmen and pioneers followed, hewed logs for their houses, began work on a dam. But Stevens Point never became an important lumber city; the forests near by were too sparse for large-scale logging operations. Although it boasted half a dozen sawmills during the timber rush, the Point did not approach its present size until the timber line had receded north and Portage County had turned to paper making and agriculture. Today paper plants line the riverbanks in the heart of the city.

The Hardware Mutual Casualty Company, organized here in 1914, is one of the outstanding companies of its kind in the United States, writing much automobile insurance.

In Stevens Point are the WEBER LIFELIKE FLY COMPANY PLANT, 133 Ellis St. and G. W. FROST & SONS PLANT, 322-324 Strongs Ave., manufacturers of flies and tackles for all fresh-water game fish. Using feathers, hair, silk thread, and other materials, these companies produce flies and lures in hundreds of patterns. G. W. Frost & Sons manufacture such favorites as the *Royal Coachman, Yellow May, Parmachenee Belle, Jenny Lind, Bannock Chief, and Durham Ranger.*

At the west end of Main St. is the PUBLIC SQUARE, once known as "the Potato Capital of Wisconsin." Consisting of two blocks of brick-paved open market, donated in 1847 by Mathias ("Big Mitch") Mitchell, it has been a market since the Civil War. Store and office space on the four sides of the rectangle has been allotted to 11 taverns, two Polska Apteks (Polish druggists), two harness shops, and a medley of hardware, grocery, shoe, and clothing stores. In the windowed rooms above the stores are some half-a-dozen law offices. Here in the square, summer and winter, especially on Thursdays and Saturdays, farmers come to hawk their wares and talk crops, farm prices, and politics in the taverns about the market. They crowd their trucks, trailers, or wagons in the center of the square, where they pile high their fruit, vegetables, wood, meat, and potatoes. The language they speak among themselves is often Polish, for Stevens Point is the Warsaw of the many Polish communities in Portage County.

The first Poles migrated to Portage County in 1857, an overflow from the landless peasant class in the Old Country. The first stragglers were assimilated, but when the emigration reached full tide whole communities simply transplanted themselves from one world to another and settled down to live their old lives more prosperously in a new land. At first many worked in the mills and lumber camps; later they bought land and commenced the grueling task of farming the scrubby, unfertile sand. Gradually they improved the hard land, planted more crops, earned a little more each year. From 1870 to 1895 the number of Polish immigrants diminished; after 1921, when the immigration quota laws were passed, few came. Even today in Portage County some of the older people can speak only their native tongue fluently and read no newspapers but those printed in Polish.

Some of the Poles have also retained the complex ritual of their wedding festival. Beginning in early morning, the festivities continue all day and end near dawn when the bride, the groom, and the guests have tired of celebrating. After the church ceremony the guests return to the bride's home to eat boiled chicken, roast pork, vegetables, cookies, pies, cakes, biscuits, and, most indispensable of all, czarina, or blood soup. All through the afternoon and evening the bar is open; "wiskey" (any alcoholic beverage) is served to all comers. At nightfall comes the long awaited bridal dance. *"Jecz cha nacha!"* shouts the bride's father (Polish, Yes, sir, she is still ours!). *"Jecz cha nacha"* echo the musicians, the guests, and all who have come to watch the festival. The music begins, the men form a circle, in the center of which the bride begins her exhausting dance. Her father stands with her—collecting the money the guests throw on a plate in exchange for a whirl around the floor with his daughter. The dance ends when gifts cease or the bride is too tired to continue. Polish grandmothers then take off her veil and toss a pin or a bit of lace to the throng. Finally the bride's mother dances with her, kisses her, and gives her to her husband; the celebration continues until the last of the guests have gone.

Stevens Point is at the junction with US 51 (*see Tour 7*).

Section b. STEVENS POINT to MINNESOTA LINE; 175.4 m., US 10

West of STEVENS POINT, 0 *m.,* US 10 follows the Wisconsin River for several miles, winding through its sparsely populated river valley. Most of the land here is idle, covered with small maple, birch, and oak. The few scattered farms grow potatoes or corn and are fenced with glacial stones or gnarled stumps piled in rows. After crossing the terminal moraine, the highway passes into the more fertile lowlands of the west, where farms are more numerous and more prosperous.

MILLADORE, 16 *m.* (1,194 alt., 222 pop.), is a railroad junction and warehouse village fringing the highway. A short distance away (*inquire locally for directions*), in a small clearing in the midst of the cutover, is the FIRST SOAPSTONE MINE (*closed*) in Wisconsin and one of the few in the Middle West. Operated between 1926 and 1931 by the American Talc Company, it produced a carload of soapstone a day. Soapstone is used in the manufacture of tubs and sinks for chemical laboratories because it is acid-resisting, and of furnace blocks because it can withstand great heat.

In the green hills to the west herds of cattle graze; there is scarcely a village without its cheese factory. At 31.2 *m.,* across stubby fields and swampy wood growth, appear (R) the church spires and smoke-stacks of MARSHFIELD (*see Tour 8*).

At 33.3 *m.* is the junction with State 13 (*see Tour 8*); between this junction and a point at 35.1 *m.* US 10 and State 13 are one route.

The highway dips into the valley that cradles LYNN, 47 *m.* (50 pop.), then rises again. Westward the land continues to roll more and more sharply until, at 50.2 *m.,* US 10 climbs a hill to reveal for the first time the jagged blue line of the distant Western Upland, with a peak or two where rock has been exposed. An early geologist wrote of this region: "The whole combination suggests the idea, not of an aboriginal wilderness, inhabited by savage tribes, but of a country lately under a high state of cultivation and suddenly deserted by its inhabitants; their dwellings indeed gone, but the castle-homes of their chieftains only partially destroyed, and showing, in ruins, on the rocky summits around."

NEILLSVILLE, 58.3 *m.* (997 alt., 2,118 pop.), seat of Clark County, lies scattered over several hills and valleys. On the highest hill stands a white sandstone water tower. Neat and quiet, Neillsville is supported chiefly by surrounding dairy farmers who sell their produce to the cooperative creamery, the milk condensery, the dairy, and pea cannery.

On the banks of the Black River is the WINNEBAGO INDIAN

MISSION SCHOOL, 59.5 *m*. In 1878 the Reverend Jacob Hauser opened an Indian mission school 7 miles northeast of Black River Falls. It grew rapidly, and in 1921 was replaced by the larger building here. For nine months of the year it provides a home and school for 115 Winnebago children, who are taught carpentry, cement work, simple house building, domestic science, infant hygiene, fence construction, and the Bible, in addition to the more usual subjects. Those who show talent in drawing, painting, and modeling are given special instruction. The Winnebago have no reservation in Wisconsin, but about 1,500 of them are scattered throughout the west-central counties. Having been moved about by the Government from Iowa to Minnesota, then to South Dakota, and finally to Nebraska, many returned to Wisconsin, their ancestral home.

For several miles west of Neillsville there are no farms—only brush, a few high-topped pines, and low swampy woodlands. The region is wild enough for deer to roam freely, and they may be glimpsed occasionally, moving through the forest by day or, with their great luminous eyes, watching the lights of automobiles at night.

At 75.9 *m*. is the junction with US 12 (*see Tour 19*); between this junction and FAIRCHILD, 78.6 *m*. (1,066 alt., 634 pop.), US 10 and US 12 are one route.

West of this junction the road ascends and descends steep hills on whose sides twisted pines thrust up through rocky soil. Ahead the horizon is banked by the towering bluffs that roll and tumble in the distance.

OSSEO, 91.1 *m*. (955 alt., 933 pop.) (*see Tour 10*), is at the junction with US 53 (*see Tour 10*); between Osseo and a point at 94 *m*. US 10 and US 53 are one route.

Besides cattle, occasional flocks of sheep graze in the pasture lands to the west, for US 10 is here in the State's main sheep-breeding district. The green troughs between the rolling hills clearly reveal the drainage pattern of the region, and the sheep and the cattle follow these depressions as they graze. At 124.1 *m*. the highway is in the jagged uplands, where hills are badly eroded, some of them almost bare rock.

DURAND, 129.6 *m*. (728 alt., 1,590 pop.), on the banks of the Chippewa River, was laid out by Myles Durand Prindle in 1856 and in 1861 became the seat of Pepin County. First built in a valley to the north, it abandoned its old site after having been flooded twice by high spring waters.

Notorious in Durand's early history were the Maxwell brothers, known as Ed and Lon Williams, outlaws and horse thieves. In 1881 they killed the deputy sheriff of Pepin County in a gun fight and during the remainder of that year turned up occasionally in Wisconsin and neighboring States, always as principal actors in dramas of gunplay and robbery. Ed was finally caught in Nebraska and returned to Durand to stand trial; but vigilantes took him from the custody of the law and hanged him from an oak on the courthouse lawn. The tree still stands, a reminder of one of Wisconsin's few lynchings.

Durand was a busy and exciting river port in lumbering days, when great log rafts were made up in neighboring sloughs, and steamers from the Mississippi brought with them all the gayety and license of the rivermen. When the rafts ceased to go downstream and the steamers stopped coming up, Durand declined. Every year more stores along its once lively main street were boarded up and abandoned, and a few more families left the town. Today Durand is supported by its farm trade.

West of Durand, US 10 crosses the swift Chippewa River, then winds through green hilly country where the valleys are short and narrow. From a bluff, 137.9 *m.*, the road overlooks the prosperous farms that lie on the intensively cultivated valley floor.

At 153.4 *m.* is the junction with State 35 (*see Tour 13*); between this junction and a point at 158.2 *m.* US 10 and State 35 are one route. At 156.5 *m.* is the junction with US 63 (*see Tour 9*); between this junction and a point at 159.8 *m.* US 10 and US 63 are one route.

ELLSWORTH, 158.1 *m.* (1,069. alt., 1,124 pop.), is a village of two distinct parts, one built in a valley, the other on a hill. In 1890 business was brisk here, and the ambitious inhabitants of what is now West Ellsworth eagerly awaited a railroad connection with outside markets. When railroad officials finally agreed to build their line through Ellsworth, the people were wildly enthusiastic. "Where do you want the station?" the executives asked them. "Oh, anywhere within a mile of the courthouse," they answered hurriedly. So the company built the station exactly 5,276 feet from the courthouse, thus saving many dollars in trackage. A settlement quickly sprang up near the station, and Ellsworth, in spite of its small size, divided into two parts. US 10 passes through East Ellsworth and into the countryside before entering West Ellsworth.

Westward the land is well settled. The bluffs are barren and sere, but the soil eroded from them has gone to enrich the farms in the valleys below. Each successive rise in the road reveals long stretches of gently dipping and rolling farmland. As the road descends from the upland into the wide valley at the confluence of the St. Croix and Mississippi Rivers the two streams are visible, the broad Mississippi dotted with islands and sand bars.

At 174.1 *m.* is the junction with State 29 (*see Tour 17*); between this junction and a point at 175.4 *m.* US 10 and State 29 are one route.

PRESCOTT, 175 *m.* (702 alt., 755 pop.), at the mouth of the St. Croix, was the first settlement in Pierce County. In 1827 a government interpreter, Philander Prescott, agent for army officers stationed at Fort Snelling, staked claims and built a claim cabin where the village now stands. Not until 1851, when these holdings were sold, did a community spring up.

From the beginning Prescott was a river town, carried along with the tide of river navigation and northern lumbering. Prescott has never quite forgotten some of the riotous pay nights of her golden era. Old-timers still tell stories of the terror that struck the hearts of peace-loving men when the rafters came to town for sprees, which often ended in free fights between rival crews. Sometimes a hundred men would fight in the muddy streets while the city marshal, revolver in hand, sat "watching the affair with the enlightened eye of an expert and the enjoyment of a connoisseur."

In 1853, when Pierce County was formed, Prescott became the county seat. Then in 1861, by popular vote, Ellsworth became the legal seat of government, and a long battle between the two places began. For eight years Prescott forces defeated all appropriations to erect county buildings; records were kept almost anywhere, sometimes in attics, sometimes in wagons. It was only after a long struggle that Ellsworth undisputedly won the county seat.

At 175.4 m. US 10 crosses the Minnesota Line by a BRIDGE (*toll: 15¢ for driver and car; 5¢ for each additional passenger; children under 12 free*), 16 miles southeast of St. Paul, Minnesota.

Tour 19

(Chicago, Ill.)—Lake Geneva—Madison—Wisconsin Dells—Tomah —Eau Claire—Hudson—(St. Paul, Minn.); US 12.
Illinois Line to Minnesota Line, 341.6 m.

Chicago, Milwaukee, St. Paul & Pacific R. R. parallels route between Wisconsin Dells and Tomah; the Chicago, St. Paul, Minneapolis & Omaha between Camp Douglas and Hudson.
Cement-paved roadbed.
Accommodations excellent in cities and in and around the Lake Geneva and Wisconsin Dells resort region. Resort rates higher during summer.

In a long arc between the Illinois Line and the Mississippi River, US 12 runs successively across southern farmland, central wastes of marsh and sand, and the hilly Chippewa Valley. In its central section much of the route is monotonous; here are long miles of sheer sand, broken occasionally by small cities and villages, lonely bluffs, buttes and crags, and narrow unmarked side roads. The highway links two of Wisconsin's oldest resort regions—Lake Geneva and the Wisconsin Dells.

Section a. ILLINOIS LINE to MADISON; 82.2 m., US 12

US 12 crosses the ILLINOIS LINE, 0 m., about a mile north of Solon Mills, Illinois. Cultivated for more than a hundred years, this farmland is still rich, its pastures kept fresh by underground water, numerous duck ponds, and lakes. Recreation is important here in southern Walworth County, and intersecting State and county roads lead to tourist cabins, live-bait markets, golf courses, hotels, and resorts.

At 1.4 *m.* is the junction with County B.

Right 4.1 *m.* on County B to POWERS LAKE (L). At 5.6 *m.* a branch road leads directly to the edge of LAKE MARIE, the lower of the twin lakes (R); LAKE ELIZABETH, the upper, first glimpsed at 5.8 *m.*, is considerably longer than Lake Marie, with cottages and summer homes crowding its shores. At the east end of the lake is the straggling resort village of TWIN LAKES. The COMMODORE BARRY CLUB, 7.1 *m.*, is at the junction with County D.

Left on County D across a farm region of choppy hills. At 11.8 *m.* the Lower Fox River appears (L), its channel lost in a maze of oak clumps and bayous. A COUNTY PARK has been built at this excellent fishing spot; along the bayou are parking grounds (L). Across the lowlands SILVER LAKE and the vacation settlement on its shores are visible at 12.5 *m.* County D passes through the small business section of Silver Lake Village at 12.9 *m.* At 14.5 *m.* is the junction with State 50; L. on State 50 to Lake Geneva, 22.5 *m.* (*see below*).

LAKE GENEVA, 10.3 *m.* (892 alt., 3,073 pop.), is a summer city frequented by well-to-do people, many of whom live on enormous estates hidden from the city by long lake bluffs. More casual visitors stop at the hotel designed by Frank Lloyd Wright, or live in small cottages at near-by Fontana or Williams Bay.

Lake Geneva began to grow after 1840 when a stage route was established between Kenosha (then Southport) and Beloit. In 1844 the settlement was incorporated as a village, and for the next three decades it owed its existence to the power generated by the White River, the lake's only outlet. In 1870 the population was still small, but within the next 10 years wealthy people began coming in large numbers, settling the pleasant lakeshore. During the Chicago fire of 1871 many rich Chicagoans, including the mayor, rushed their families to Lake Geneva. "The Newport of Chicago society," Lake Geneva is known in Wisconsin for the wealth of its summer residents.

LAKE GENEVA, on which the city lies, is a body of clear water, hemmed in by hills thickly wooded with oak, maple, and elm. It has a maximum depth of 140 feet, is partly spring fed, and contains such game fishes as large-mouthed and small-mouthed bass, northern pike, and the celebrated cisco.

ELKHORN, 20.7 *m.* (996 alt., 2,340 pop.) (*see Tour 24*), is at the junction with State 11 (*see Tour 24*). The highway continues north through flat corn land and fields of feed grains. County roads form a network of trails to numerous small lakes. US 12 skirts the shores of LAUDERDALE LAKE and GREEN LAKE (*camp grounds and an 18-hole golf course*), 26.7 *m.*

WHITEWATER, 39.2 *m.* (822 alt., 3,465 pop.), is a city of wide streets and deep green lawns shaded by immense trees. On Whitewater Creek stands an OLD MILL (R), built in 1839. A store and tavern soon sprang up near the mill. Every morning, so local history has it, the surveyor hired to lay out the streets would start from the tavern, survey for a time, return for a drink, and then survey some more. Thus the streets were platted in their curiously irregulal pattern.

In 1852 the Milwaukee and Mississippi R. R. came through, and in 1857 George Esterly moved his reaper plant north from La Grange to Whitewater. Lacking a direct rail connection with Chicago, the reaper plant, which had employed about 500 men and occupied 12 spacious buildings, was moved to Minneapolis in 1893. Today the city has a brewery, a condensery, and several small plants producing canned goods, clothing, pumps, and electric wire fences.

The STATE TEACHERS COLLEGE, for the construction of which Whitewater donated $25,000, has an enrollment of 800. The MORRIS PRATT INSTITUTE, founded in 1902 by Morris Pratt, is a duly organized and endowed school, designed to prepare its students for the Spiritualist ministry. In 1883 Pratt, a Spiritualist, consulted a Madison medium and was advised through her "control" to purchase land near Ironwood. Following this advice, Pratt invested $4,000 in land rich in iron ore, selling it later for $125,000, a part of which he used to erect the institute. Students, ranging in age from 15 to 60 years, are admitted without an educational examination. In the psychic room seances are held regularly every Thursday evening for the students or faculty members who desire to develop their psychic powers.

Busy FORT ATKINSON, 50 m. (794 alt., 5,793 pop.), contrasts sharply with quiet, almost rural Whitewater. Blocky factories stand on the banks of the Rock River near the heart of the city.

In 1832 General Henry Atkinson, pursuing Black Hawk, stopped to set up a stockade with two blockhouses at the confluence of the Rock and Bark Rivers. In 1836 the first permanent settler, Dwight Foster, built a house near the half demolished fort. Later, in 1844, a Mississippi steamboat, coming up the Rock River with a load of pleasure-seeking passengers from Janesville, found its way blocked by a low bridge. An early chronicler writes: ". . . since the passengers outnumbered the entire population, they took out a bent, allowing the boat to pass."

In 1873 William Dempster Hoard, later Governor of Wisconsin (1889-91), who was responsible more than any other man for Wisconsin's development as a dairying State, began to publish the *Jefferson County Union* here. The year before Hoard, realizing that the continued planting of soil-depleting grains was destroying land fertility, had organized the Wisconsin State Dairyman's Association with the aid of six other men. Elected secretary, he toured the State, preaching the virtues of the cow, "the foster mother of the human race." His success was phenomenal. When Babcock discovered a method of testing butterfat in 1890, Hoard agreed with the creamery owner who declared that "this will make the farmers more honest than the Ten Commandments ever did." In 1885, still campaigning, he expanded the dairying column of the *Jefferson County Union* into the *Hoard's*

Dairyman, which today is read by farmers throughout the country. As Governor, Hoard sponsored anti-oleomargarine legislation.

Besides being an important shipping and trading point for the regional dairy farmers, Fort Atkinson also has a cannery and plants that manufacture barn equipment and poultry supplies, "little pig" sausages, dairy equipment, hose, and saws, both ordinary and musical. The musical saws ground here are subjected to more rigid specifications than carpentry saws. Manufactured as alto, tenor, baritone, and bass blades, they are made straight-backed to permit a consecutive scale, and of smooth, homogeneous steel so that notes may run all through. For purity and clarity of tone they are the same thickness from tooth-edge to back, not tapered for clearance as are utility saws. Most ornate of the company's musical saws is a gold-plated model, its mahogany handles studded thickly with jewels. The local company not only offers a correspondence course in saw playing, but also publishes an annual called *Sawing News of the World.*

In the basement of the PUBLIC LIBRARY, one block right on Milwaukee Ave., is the FORT ATKINSON HISTORICAL SOCIETY MUSEUM (*open Sat., 10-12 a.m. and 2-5 p.m.*). Here is Governor Hoard's cradle; a knitting machine invented by Thomas Crane; the editorial desk of an ardent temperance newspaper; Fort Atkinson's first "post office," a desk with a drawer in which the mail was stored; ox yokes; early china; arrowheads; flintlock muskets; spinning wheels; carders; and several early books, including *Asserting the Rights of Great Britain against the Claims of America,* printed in 1776.

US 12 swings northwest out of the city into rolling dairy country where Holsteins stand white and black against green pastures.

At 60.8 *m.* is the junction with a town road.

Right on this road which curves along LAKE RIPLEY. At 2.6 *m.* is the junction with County A; L. on County A to the CAMBRIDGE COMMUNITY PARK (*adm. free: playgrounds, baseball and kittenball grounds, tennis courts*), 3.1 *m.,* a 17-acre tract of land. The sand beach is lined with diving stands built according to Olympic standards.

At 3.3 *m.* is the junction with US 12, 0.5 miles southwest of Cambridge (*see below*).

CAMBRIDGE, 62.7 *m.* (500 pop.), was settled by Joseph Keyes in 1847. Near the river is the stone SCANDINAVIAN METHODIST CHURCH, said to be "the oldest Methodist Episcopal Church ever built by Norwegians, Danes or Swedes in this or any other country." In 1850 the Reverend C. P. Agrelius was sent to Cambridge to sow the seeds of Methodism. In 1851 a second preacher, Christian B. Willerup, a Dane, planned a $4,000 stone church. The first drive netted $400 and the determined minister laid a cornerstone and went to New York to solicit funds from the Methodist Board of Missions. Jenny Lind, the famous Swedish singer, then touring the country, sent him a check for $200. That fall Willerup mortgaged his horse and buggy, and many farmers their farms, to finish the building. Knute Nelson (1843-

1923), U. S. Senator from Minnesota, was once a Sunday school teacher here.

At 63.3 *m.* is the junction with US 18 (*see Tour 23*); between this junction and Madison, US 12 and US 18 are one route (*see Tour 23*).

MADISON, 82.2 *m.* (859 alt., 57,899 pop.) (*see Madison*).

Madison is at the junction with US 151 (*see Tour 6*), US 51 (*see Tour 7*), State 113 (*see Tour 19B*), US 14 (*see Tour 20*), US 18 (*see Tour 23*), and State 30 (*see Tour 23A*).

Section b. *MADISON to TOMAH; 101.1 m., US 12*

Between Madison and Middleton, 6.4 *m.* (931 alt., 983 pop.) (*see Tour 20*), US 12 and US 14 are one route (*see Tour 20*).

Northwest of Middleton the highway narrows from four lanes to two and rises slowly among patternless hills. On the valley floors are fertile farmlands developed by farmers quick to realize their adaptability to dairying purposes. These farmers built L-shaped, two-story sandstone houses which still stand, and planted pines in rows on both sides of the slab walks leading to their doorways. This modesty of color is broken by bright orange-painted plows in the fields, by brilliant paint on the old carriage barns where polished black carriages were kept. Among the crevices in the stones grow violets; wild flowers border the walks.

US 12 crosses the bridge, 24.5 *m.,* spanning the WISCONSIN RIVER (*see Tour 22*).

SAUK CITY, 24.7 *m.* (757 alt., 1,137 pop.), and PRAIRIE DU SAC, 26.1 *m.* (758 alt., 949 pop.), are twin cities strung along the high west bank of the river. Each is named for the Sauk tribe whose villages once stood here on the prairie. The main streets of both, 30 feet above the river bottoms, are separated only by a town line; a long-standing rivalry began nearly a century ago when Sauk City was known as Lower Sauk and Prairie du Sac as Upper Sauk.

Sauk City's advantage was the business daring and acumen of its founder, "Count" Agoston Haraszthy, an Hungarian nobleman who settled here with his family in the summer of 1841. Stories abound in the countryside concerning Haraszthy's personality, his bearded hooked-nosed face, his bright sashes and shirts, his manners, and his prowess as a hunter. More than any other of the European refugees who fled here, he helped Sauk City to keep in touch with world events, bringing in "at one time and another noted personages and public speakers, not usual in such out-of-the-way places." In 1842 he founded the Humanist Society, which on October 24, 1852, several years after he had left Sauk City for the West, was incorporated as the *Freie Gemeinde,* the Free Congregation of Sauk City. The first hall was built about 1853 on land deeded by Haraszthy; in 1884 it was replaced by the large gray FREIE GEMEINDE HALL, two blocks west of US 12 in the northern part of town. Sauk City became known all over Europe as the "Freethinkers Heaven," and such nationally known speakers as Carl Schurz, Franz Siegel, Karl Heinzen, and Robert Ingersoll spoke here. Between 1854 and 1888 Eduard Schroeter was the speaker of the congregation.

Today the Sauk City hall is the only one in the United States used exclusively by the Freethinkers Society; here meetings are held monthly, occasional lectures and dances are given, and a Freethinker library, one of the most complete in the country, is kept. Members of the Congregation are buried in the Freethinker Cemetery, which is in the Town of Honey Creek.

Before his disillusionment and eventual migration to California in 1849, Haraszthy had built a store; when the time came for the two villages to bid for the Sauk county seat, the store was offered by Lower Sauk as a prospective courthouse. Upper Sauk, however, volunteered several vacant lots and was temporarily selected for the county center. Haraszthy countered by campaigning for the Baraboo Valley, where the one small village of Baraboo Rapids was located. His efforts, together with a last-minute disclosure of a trick proviso in the Upper Sauk deed of gift, influenced the voters who made Baraboo Rapids, now Baraboo, the permanent county seat.

During the early years taverns and businesses sprang up in both villages. In Sauk City private enterprise constructed the ASTOR HOUSE, now a brick tavern, and the CURTIS HOTEL, now the town hall and public library. There, too, trade flourished in Haraszthy's hopyard, the first in the State. Sauk City academy taught French, fencing, and music. The two villages had sawmills, lumberyards, a cannery, a brickyard, and a brewery, many of which operated only until about 1880 when business declined and the citizens turned to farming and occasional river trade. Today the rivalry continues most keenly in the schools and churches. Sauk City is predominantly German Catholic, while Prairie du Sac is preponderantly Protestant.

Sauk City's two novelists, August Derleth and Mark Schorer (see Literature), treat of the town's history. Derleth has begun his Sac Prairie Saga, picturing the town and environs as they were a hundred years ago; Schorer has written of Haraszthy in A House Too Old.

Sauk City and Prairie du Sac are at the junction with State 60 (see Tour 22).

North of the twin cities US 12 continues on the long pancake surface of SAUK PRAIRIE. The third London edition of Jonathan Carver's Travels in Wisconsin (see Literature) describes the prairie in the eighteenth century: "On the 8th of October we got our canoes into the Ouisconsin River, which at this place is more than a hundred yards wide; and the next day arrived at the Great Town of the Saukies. This is the largest and best built Indian town I ever saw. It contains about ninety houses, each large enough for several families. These are built of hewn plank neatly jointed, and covered with bark so compactly as to keep out the most penetrating rains. Before the doors are placed comfortable sheds, in which the inhabitants sit, when the weather will permit and smoak their pipes. The streets are regular and spacious;

so that it appears more like a civilized town than the abode of savages. The land near the town is very good. In their plantations, which lie adjacent to their houses, and which are neatly laid out, they raise great quantities of Indian corn, beans, melons, etc., so that this place is esteemed the best market for traders to furnish themselves with provisions, of any within eight hundred miles of it."

Today on Sauk Prairie the homes of the Indians have been replaced by the solid farmsteads of German-American farmers. The land is extensively farmed; in summer corn grows tall and green in roadside fields; in late fall hogs root in the dry stubble left by the harvesters. This land was once the river bed, which in thousands of years has shifted from the foot of one bluff line to the other. US 12 crosses the prairie and commences to climb the Baraboo Range, 34.5 m. Both road banks were blasted from red purplish rock, back of which are the steeply wooded walls of the range; from higher points the highway overlooks a wilderness of timbered country that slopes down toward the tableland.

At 38.2 m. is the junction with State 159.

Right on State 159, one of the shortest highways in the State system, to the junction with State 123, 1.3 m.; R. on State 123 to the entrance to the 1,440-acre DEVIL'S LAKE STATE PARK, 1.7 m. (*cottages, campsites, and supplies. Camping free first two weeks; thereafter 50¢ a week or $10 a season. Police protection. Golf and bathing facilities. CCC guides conduct hiking tours, leaving at 9 a.m. for east bluff and 2 p.m. for west bluff*).

The campground tapers off to the shore of clear, oval-shaped DEVILS LAKE, hemmed in by a towering horseshoe of cliffs rising from 400 to 500 feet above water level in tumbled piles of rocks, purple under a wild covering of green pines. Seven hundred million years ago the Baraboo Range was a series of high quartzite peaks, which have been eroded down to their present height by wind, rain, and the waves of pre-glacial seas. When the great glacier moved down over Wisconsin, the Baraboo Range slowed its progress, and lobes of ice shunted off north and south. Then, before the ice could cover the area, its forward movement ceased and its borders began to retreat. Devils Lake was formed when debris, deposited by the glacier at both ends of a valley, choked off the course of a stream then running through it. Because of its geological oddities Devil's Lake is a sort of geologist's sample box. Students from universities in the Middle West camp here annually on field trips, scrambling over the cliffs to observe glacier scratches on the rock, the pot holes, and the petrified sand waves of the ancient sea. There are also a number of Indian mounds and unusual rock formations. No public road goes around the lake, but hiking trails make most spots accessible.

At 39.5 m. US 12 divides: one highway is marked in yellow, the other in white.

Right on the yellow-marked US 12 to BARABOO, 1.7 m. (864 alt., 5,545 pop.), Sauk County seat, which radiates crookedly up and over small hills. It has the narrow, tree-filled streets of an old city; almost all its business houses are centered on the square. Named for a French trader, Jean Baribault, who is said to have built a post at the confluence of the Wisconsin-Baraboo rivers, this land was once owned by the Winnebago, who ceded it to the United States in 1837. During early years the Baraboo bluffs proved such a formidable obstacle that the stage line coming up from Prairie du Sac did not establish regular service until 1855. Even then passengers had to walk up the steep slope of the range.

In the center of Baraboo are the old brick and stone buildings that once served as the RINGLING BROTHERS CIRCUS WINTER QUARTERS. The Ringlings, who were sons of a German harnessmaker, chose their career early, inspired by a circus boat which they had seen during their boyhood days in McGregor, Iowa. Sometime after coming to Baraboo five of the seven brothers—Charles, Otto, Albert, John, and Alfred (Henry and August never took a very active part in the circus enterprise)—organized the Ringling Brothers' Classic and Comic Concert Company, which they advertised as "Moral, Elevating, Instructive and Fascinating." After their opening performance at Mazomanie before an audience of 59 persons in November, 1882, the brothers toured Wisconsin, Iowa, Dakota Territory, and Minnesota. The next year, renamed the Ringling Brothers' Grand Carnival of Fun, they again covered practically the same circuit; by 1884 they had earned more than $800. With this money they bought equipment for a one-ring tent show, which by 1888 had grown to a railroad show with 30 cars of menagerie and circus props. As this in turn grew, Ringling Brothers' signed an agreement with Barnum and Bailey whereby the Ringlings toured the Middle West and Barnum and Bailey the East. In 1907 Bailey's widow sold the Barnum and Bailey show for $410,000 to the Ringlings, thus making their combined circus "the Greatest Show on Earth."

Baraboo is at the junction with State 113 (*see Tour 19B*). Yellow-marked US 12 proceeds through Baraboo to the junction with white-marked US 12 (*see below*).

From the junction of yellow-marked US 12 (*see above*) and white-marked US 12, 40.6 *m.,* the highway climbs steadily out of the Baraboo Valley, then descends the north foothills into flat scrawny country of poor farms and woodlots of scrub oak on the fringe of the Wisconsin Dells recreation area. At 48.6 *m.,* LAKE DELTON AIRPORT and the LAKE DELTON GOLF COURSE lie near LAKE DELTON, 48.8 *m.,* which reaches far back into a rough gorge.

At 49.2 *m.* is the junction with State 23.

Left on State 23 to the junction with a dirt road, 0.5 *m.;* L. on a bridge over the gorge. Below is the dam that forms MIRROR LAKE (R), which, like Lake Delton, is a widening of Dell Creek. Near the north end of the bridge a little road turns (L) and winds downhill to a pancake flour mill. A footbridge here hangs over the river just above the dam, and nearby, on both sides of the gorge, are docks and landings, where boats can be hired. A board walk suspended from the sides of the rock leads a half mile downstream. Both Lake Delton and Mirror Lake offer good fishing for bass, perch, and great northern pike.

At 51.8 *m.* is the junction with State 13 (*see Tour 8*) and US 16 (*see Tour 21*); between this junction and a point at 99.3 *m.* on the southern outskirts of Tomah, US 12 and US 16 are one route.

ROCKY ARBOR ROADSIDE PARK (*camping facilities*), 53.2 *m.,* is deeply shaded by hardwoods and mixed growth. Masses of mossy rock protrude from the hillside, weathered into queer shapes half hidden by foliage. The surrounding country is a sandy plain, which shimmers with heat waves in summer. On both sides of the road are patches of scrub oak and spindly birch varied occasionally by small baked fields cultivated by Chippewa Indians living in the vicinity. The Indians here set up birch pole shelters to display baskets, moccasins, beads, and Indian dolls offered for sale.

The highway presently enters a region of bluffs, buttes, and crags, outliers of the Magnesian cuesta. Some are hills that rise abruptly from the sandy plain, covered with wild wood growth; others are strange bare monuments of tan sandstone, untouched by glaciation and carved fantastically by wind and water. At 66.4 *m.* is SHEEP PASTURE BLUFF (R*'*), on which is SWISTALL MOUND. MILE BLUFF (L), an arm of the escarpment, prolongs its line to form an immense wall across the landscape.

MAUSTON, 72 *m.* (880 alt., 2,107 pop.), borders the stagnant marshy backwater of the Lemonweir River, a bog encrusted with cattails and lily pads. In 1840 the poor timber blanketing this region was cut, and a settlement called Maughston grew up around General M. M. Maughs' sawmill. A marker at the roadside here indicates the old INDIAN BOUNDARY LINE drawn in 1825 by U. S. Commissioners Lewis Cass and William Clark, to define the lands of the Chippewa and the Menominee tribes.

Northwest of Mauston US 12 continues along the flat plain to NEW LISBON (892 alt., 1,076 pop.), a railroad junction village, and on through sandy country spotted with willow swamps. Attempts to drain these swamps have ended in failure; their dark muck is too acid for cultivation; drainage ruins cranberry growing in the marshes.

At 85.5 *m.* is the junction with a side road.

Right on this road to an auto parking space, 0.3 *m.*, at the foot of CASTLE ROCK. A long ladder has been placed on the west side for climbing; otherwise the sides are difficult to scale. About 200 yards distant on foot across the plain is the base of LONG BLUFF, whose rocky sides are steep and bristling with trees. The ledges, however, are worn enough for easy climbing. On top of the bluff is a high stair-type fire tower. Long Bluff, rising about 350 feet above the plain, offers a view for 20 miles in every direction. Both Long Bluff and Castle Rock are on the grounds of the Camp Williams Military Reservation.

At 85.9 *m.* is the military village of CAMP DOUGLAS, with high rocky TARGET BLUFF rising directly from the roadside (L). On annual Governor's Day, Camp Douglas is overrun with visitors, veterans, tourists, and children, who come to witness demonstrations by the soldiers of the local camp.

At Target Bluff is the junction with a side road.

Right on this road to the entrance of CAMP WILLIAMS MILITARY RESERVATION, 0.3 *m.;* R. here toward Long Bluff, which rises only a few hundred yards to the east. The road passes barracks, mess halls, and other camp buildings.' At 0.6 *m.* it runs along the rifle range, then rises steeply up a spur of the bluff, which affords a view of the camp, and is a vantage point from which to watch target practice.

US 12 veers northwest past CHINAMAN'S BLUFF (R), DELLS NEEDLE (L), and RAGGED ROCK. The Magnesian escarpment (L) shoulders the sky in an unbroken line.

TOMAH, 101.1 *m.* (958 alt., 3,354 pop.), was named for Tomau, a Menominee chief during the British regime. The city lies on a rise in the far-reaching plain, and over its wide brick and cobbled streets rattle army and Indian wagons from near-by military stations and farms. On pay day the city is virtually under martial law, or rather is martially unlawful, for soldiers skylark in the tavern and on the streets most of the night.

Until 1934 Tomah had one of the State's several boarding schools for Indian children whose parents were unable to care for them adequately. Today needy children are put in foster homes or in the Sparta School for dependent children (*see Tour 21*). The Federal Government still maintains a fully equipped INDIAN HOSPITAL, with itinerant clinics in the Indian population centers in this region. At the northern outskirts of Tomah are the large buildings of the old INDIAN SCHOOL (R), built of brick and fronted with pale yellow barns and a high black water tower.

At the southern edge of Tomah is the junction with US 16 (*see Tour 21*).

Section c.   *TOMAH to MINNESOTA LINE; 158.3 m.*

North of TOMAH, 0 *m.*, the sandy soil continues, lying level between lines of hills. Gradually the countryside roughens until the highway winds among jumbled hills, emerging again on a barren lowland. Indian families squat in bark shelters and tents at the side of the road, offering handmade baskets and leather or bead souvenirs for sale, thus adding to the small income they receive from the soil and from their Government allowances. CASTLE MOUND PARK (L), 27.9 *m.* (*drinking water, camping and sanitary facilities, trails*), is a county-owned tract surrounding a great rock with queer toothlike battlements.

BLACK RIVER FALLS, 29.4 *m.* (805 alt., 1,950 pop.), lies on the western bank of the BLACK RIVER at a spot where logs once tumbled over a high falls. The business section of the city occupies a plateau above the river; the high school, courthouse, churches, and houses are scattered up the hillside. In 1819, when the Black River countryside was a wilderness of pine, one of the first sawmills in Wisconsin was built here. In spite of unfriendly Indians, who probably burned the mill, the settlement established itself and continued logging all through the nineteenth century.

Among the early settlers came a group of Mormons from Nauvoo, Illinois. Once encamped here, the Mormon elder told his flock that the wilderness belonged to the Lord, and that the Saints should not respect any Gentile boundaries. Accordingly, they started to log off the claim of Jacob Spaulding, one of the influential settlers. Hearing of the Mormons' activities, Spaulding immediately gathered 20 men and led them to his property. There they halted, and Spaulding went alone to the Mormon camp, where he found that some 300 trees had already been felled. Having gone indignantly to the elder, who refused him satisfaction, Spaulding summoned his followers and drove the Mormons off. When the elder left, he complained that his tormenters were "worse than the Missourians."

Back at the main camp the Mormons determined to go to war with the Gentiles and sent to Nauvoo for armed men. Spaulding countered by threatening to get military aid from Prairie du Chien. His strategy and warning were successful, and when armed men came by boat from Nauvoo they were transformed into peaceful loggers. Shortly afterward Joseph Smith, the Mormon leader, was murdered, and the group returned to Nauvoo.

One wild night Black River Falls was awakened by 40 brawlers who, out on a spree, had found a breaking-plow and were busy plowing up two blocks of the main street. They smashed into a feed store and took several sacks of oats, scattering them over the furrowed streets, roaring that they were sowing their wild oats. They finally exhausted themselves after emptying sacks of flour on one another. That was in the days when a Neillsville lawyer advertised in the local *Banner:*

N. M. CLAPP
Eternally at Law
Solicitor at the Bar, Register of Deeds, makes
out conveyances and raises h——l generally.

Today Black River Falls is quiet, with a large Indian population. The flow of water over the falls has been diminished by a large power dam; the surrounding forests have been leveled. Below the bridge crossing the 350-foot wide defile of the river, the channel is heaped with slabs and blocks of quartzite. In the spring, when the snow melts, the power plant opens the floodgates of the dam, and the water is allowed to roar downstream as it once did.

In MERRILLAN, 41.4 *m.* (938 alt., 554 pop.), is the junction with State 95.

Right on State 95 to the junction with a dirt road, 0.8 *m.;* straight ahead on the dirt road to a fork, 2 *m.;* R. to BRUCE MOUND, 2.6 *m.* A footpath, following an opening in the woods cut for the telephone line, leads to a 70-foot, ladder-type fire tower. From this tower Bruce Mound appears to be an S-shaped ridge coiling around two glens. Highest crags stand out 350 feet above the plain. In places the crumbling rock juts out bare and yellow on the lower slopes, weathered fantastically. Surrounding mounds and ridges stand out in bold relief against the horizon; marshes fill the low places; scrub oak, pine and popple blanket thousands of acres of country.

At 52.4 *m.* is the junction with US 10 (*see Tour 18*); between this junction and FAIRCHILD, 55.1 *m.* (1,066 alt., 634 pop.), US 12 and US 10 are one route.

AUGUSTA, 67.4 *m.* (968 alt., 1,359 pop.), reflects the increased fertility of the land as the highway approaches the Chippewa River system. FALL CREEK, 75.4 *m.* (937 alt., 528 pop.), is a busy little village on a creek of the same name. An old MILL DAM (R), 75.7 *m.*, forms a shady pool of brown water.

US 12 runs through a cleft locally known as the Gap, 77 *m.*, between high and abrupt hills, and crosses a region of small rough hills. Forest growth clusters on their summits and spills smoothly down their sides.

At 85.1 *m.* is the junction with US 53 (*see Tour 10*); between this junction and EAU CLAIRE, 87.9 *m.* (791 alt., 26,287 pop.) (*see Tour 10*), US 12 and US 53 are one route.

Westward, US 12 heads towards the Mississippi River through sandy plain. The highway runs close to the foot of shaggy ELK MOUND, 98.7 *m.*, with its name spelled in white stones on a grassy slope. At the village of ELK MOUND, 98.9 *m.* (929 alt., 376 pop.), is the junction with a graveled road.

Right on this road to a small county PARK (*picnic tables*) on ELK MOUND, 1 *m.* The highest point overlooks the Western Upland plateau ringed by hills, some buttes identifiable 20 to 30 miles distant.

At 101 *m.* is the junction with State 29 (*see Tour 17*); between this junction and MENOMONIE, 111.1 *m.* (803 alt., 5,595 pop.) (*see Tour 17*), US 12 and State 29 are one route (*see Tour 17*).

Northwestward the land becomes suddenly hilly, and the road winds between steep rounded slopes—some topped with woods, others thinly sprinkled with trees and pastures, still others bald and exposed to erosion. US 12 climbs a hillside filled with lime pits, the site of much activity until cement began to replace slaked lime. The shaft of the old kiln is near the base of the hill, 125.8 *m.* US 12 now enters a flat open plain, its surface varied only slightly by low earth swells. Much of the ground is bare, a natural prairie that never bore forest cover. Farmers here grew wheat long after it had ceased to be a major State crop (*see Agriculture*), and the villages of HERSEY, 128.5 *m.* (1,204 alt., 296 pop.), WOODVILLE, 132.2 *m.* (1,171 alt., 403 pop.), and BALDWIN, 136.6 *m.* (1,136 alt., 808 pop.), all had flour mills, branches of the great mills of Minneapolis and St. Paul. Today these villages are trade centers for farmers who after 1900 turned from wheat raising to dairying. West of HAMMOND, 140.1 *m.* (1,103 alt., 395 pop.), the land surface becomes rougher, the marshes disappear, and the soil is a heavier loam. Alfalfa, spring wheat, and various feed grains wave in the fields by the roadside.

HUDSON, 157.4 *m.* (700 alt., 2,725 pop.) (*see Tour 13*), is at the junction with State 35 (*see Tour 13*).

US 12 crosses the Minnesota Line, 158.3 *m.*, on a toll bridge (*15¢ for auto and driver; 5¢ for additional passengers*) over the St. Croix River, 16.9 miles east of St. Paul, Minnesota.

Tour 19 A

Lake Geneva—Williams Bay—Fontana—Lake Geneva; State 36, town roads, County BB, State 120.
Lake Geneva to Lake Geneva, 19.7 *m.*

Hard-surfaced roadbed.
Resort and hotel accommodations at villages.

This route circles Lake Geneva, closely following its shore, skirting comfortable estates and summer homes. Crowding the shore from one end to the other, the houses are often completely hidden by foliage, walls, or hills. As in Williams Bay and Fontana, the estates are headquarters for lake sports, both summer and winter.

LAKE GENEVA, 0 *m.* (892 alt., 3,073 pop.) (*see Tour 19*), is at the junction with US 12 (*see Tour 19*). State 36 goes L. one block to the lake front and turns R., first following the beach, then running inland away from the lake. On the slopes are country gentlemen's estates; some are farmed; others have well-pruned orchards; still others are rambling groves of woods. Beyond, shut off from view by trees and hills and wrought-iron fences interlaced with vines, wealthy Chicagoans have summer mansions, which bear such names as Flowerside Farms, Bonnie Brae, Alta Vista, Wychwood, and Jersey Hurst. At 1.3 *m.* is the entrance to GREEN GABLES, formerly the summer home of William Wrigley, Jr. (1861-1932). Here the heirs of the chewing-gum manufacturer maintain a large stock farm, with poultry, cattle, and high-bred riding horses.

In the winter, on the ice near the Wrigley estate, fishermen set up a "fourth ward" of the city of Lake Geneva, a colony of tarpaper, piano-box, and galvanized-iron shacks. These shacks are arranged in rude streets presided over by a mock mayor and a mock council. When the men are fishing, all light is shut out from the shelters so that the green glow of the depths below the ice is visible. One or two men occupy each building, using kerosene stoves for heat, angling through chopped holes in the ice. Ciscos, which are fished for chiefly, require a number 8 hook baited with a brightly colored bead. The fish sights such a bait 75 feet away and fights savagely when hooked.

State 36 climbs a ridge, and at 4 *m.* appears (R) COMO LAKE, with CISCO BEACH (L). Como Lake ends in a straggling swampland at 4.6 *m.* as the highway swings L. towards the shore of Williams Bay, 5.4 *m.* (*swimming, boating, refreshments, bait, licensed fishing guides; all round lake trip $1; speedboat trip 25¢*). In summer sails gleam and motorboats fly in a cloud of spray across the water. Ahead on the wooded slope across the Bay, the dome of Yerkes Observatory (*see below*) rises above the cottages, docks, and pavilions that fringe the shore. A Potawatomi Indian village once stood here at the water's edge. State 36 runs along the sandy bayshore, then goes uphill to the village of WILLIAMS BAY, 5.7 *m.* (630 pop.). Here, as elsewhere in the Lake Geneva region, attempts are being made to inaugurate large-scale winter sports carnivals with tobogganing, skiing, skating, and ice-boating; during the cold winter months a regatta of graceful boats skims over the ice. The Bay shore extends outward in two arms; on the western one are CONFERENCE POINT CAMP, and ELEANOR CAMP, the first for boys, the second for girls.

At 6.6 *m.* is the entrance to the world-renowned YERKES OBSERVA-TORY (*open on Sat. only; 1:30 p.m. to 4:30 p.m. from June through Sept.; 10 a.m. to 12 a.m. other seasons*). Operated by the University of Chicago, the brick and terra-cotta observatory houses the world's largest refracting telescope, set within a mammoth dome. The telescope and observatory, which were the gift of Charles T. Yerkes (1837-1905), was completed in 1897. The 40-inch refractor is 62 feet in focal length and weighs over 20 tons. It is used principally for visual work and photographs of celestial bodies, which are later studied and closely measured. Trained on the heavens every clear hour of the night and during a large part of the day, the refractor has made important con-tributions to the study of the stars and of the sun. Important work has been done in photographing the Milky Way, in measuring the distances of the stars, the size of double stars, and the spectra of the stars. Besides the giant telescope there are a 12-inch equatorial refractor, and a 24-inch reflector in the smaller twin domes of the observatory.

At 6.8 *m.* is the junction with a blacktop road; L. on this road, the route continues past the entrance of COLLEGE CAMP, 7.2 *m.,* summer home of the YMCA College of Chicago, where hundreds of young people stay during summer preparing for YMCA careers. Halfway down the hill the road turns sharply to OLIVET INSTITUTE CAMP (L). Beyond, the road passes through thick woods, through which the lake is intermittently visible below (L); side roads branch off to hidden estates.

FONTANA, 9.1 *m.* (385 pop.), was named for its many springs (*swimming, boating; suits for rent 25¢; private bathhouses 15¢*). When the first white men came through this region in 1832, they went to visit Big Foot, one of the leading chiefs of the Wisconsin Potawatomi, whose wigwam was pitched on the present village site. Here in the fall of 1836 the Van Slykes built a cabin near the Indian encampment, and soon won the respect of the tribe. The following year Mrs. Van Slyke amputated the frozen toes of a man, performing the operation with an ordinary pair of scissors and sewing up the wound with common needle and thread. Fontana was incorporated in 1924, rather late for a Wis-consin village; its homes are new and modern, half hidden by trees and foliage.

Eastward the route follows the old Chicago-Lake Geneva trail, marked on both sides by several Potawatomi campsites. Summer homes nestle among heavy woods of white and red oak and maple; flowers and ferns spill out on the roadside. Some of the larger estates (L) are shut in by walls and fences extending a quarter of a mile; between the estates, smaller summer homes cluster in little communities. The road runs up and downhill, cutting across the gullies that lead to the lake.

The LAKE GENEVA YACHT CLUB has its headquarters (L), 11.5 m. From the docks here start most of the sailboat races, among them the Sheridan Cup Race, held on the last Saturday in August, at the close of the boating season. The NORTHWESTERN NAVAL AND MILITARY ACADEMY, 12 m., has large and gracious stone dormitories set far back on spreading grounds. On the academy grounds are some Indian burial mounds, several large springs, a paddock, and a toboggan slide. At 12.7 m. is (L) a GOLF COURSE. Here the road slants away from the lakeshore, passing through wooded hills and steep farmland.

At 15.1 m. is the junction with County BB; L. on County BB to the junction with State 120, 16.8 m.; L. on State 120 along the water's edge, where hills enclose the lake narrowly on both sides. Near the road is (R) a bass rearing pond, and beyond it at 17.6 m., a private shooting ground (R), licensed by the State Conservation Commission.

The ESTATE OF SIDNEY SMITH (1877-1935), the cartoonist, is at 18.8 m.; shields on the gateposts bear the initials S. S.; at the end of the long lawn nearest the highway is a plaster STATUE OF ANDY GUMP.

At 19.4 m. is the junction with US 12; at 19.7 m. the route reaches the center of Lake Geneva.

Tour 19 B

Madison to Baraboo; 43 m. State 113.

Chicago and North Western Ry. parallels route.
Blacktop roadbed.
Poor accommodations at villages; resorts at Merrimac and Baraboo; camping grounds.

State 113, an alternate route to US 12 (*see Tour 19*) between Madison and Baraboo, mounts through a fertile farm and dairy region into the rocks and high hills of the Baraboo Range.

MADISON, 0 m. (859 alt., 57,899 pop.) (*see Madison*).

At Madison is the junction with US 151 (*see Tour 6*), US 12 (*see Tour 19*), US 14 (*see Tour 20*), US 18 (*see Tour 23*), and State 30 (*see Tour 23A*). From Park St. State 113 follows University Ave. to Bassett St., L. on W. Washington Ave. to Capitol Square, around the square to Hamilton St., R. on Hamilton St. to E. Johnson

St., then R. on E. Johnson to TENNEY PARK. After winding through the park on Thornton Ave., State 113 leaves Madison on Sherman Ave., curving near LAKE MENDOTA (L) for some distance.

The LAKEVIEW SANATORIUM is (R) at 6.3 m., and the STATE HOSPITAL FOR THE INSANE is visible (L) at 7.3 m. Northward are rolling fertile fields, planted with tobacco or waving grain. This land was broken to the plow about 1845 by Irish and German farmers who settled here in northern Dane County. When the price of wheat soared during the Crimean War in 1855, many of these settlers migrated to the better grain land, the previously neglected prairies of southern Wisconsin.

WAUNAKEE, 13.2 m. (926 alt., 640 pop.), is a trading and canning center. Except in summer, when the pea and corn crops make canneries hum, the village is a quiet gathering place for farmers.

Northward corn, grain, and hay cover the dark brown earth, and the highway climbs gradually in long swells to sunny DANE, 19.5 m. (1,062 alt., 280 pop.), near the crest of the Magnesian cuesta. In the surrounding dairy farms great areas are used for pasturage.

North of Dane the road climbs to the crest of the cuesta (see Natural Setting), 22 m., then drops almost 300 feet into LODI, 25 m. (852 alt., 1,065 pop.) (see Tour 22), at the junction with State 60 (see Tour 22). State 113 follows Spring Creek Valley through rich fields under the shoulders of tall round hills and the high massive profile of Gibraltar Rock (L).

OKEE, 29.2 m., on Spring Creek, is at the junction with a dirt road.

1. Right on this road to PINE BLUFF, a peninsula that juts out into the waters of LAKE WISCONSIN. Prickly-pear cactus and bright orange bittersweet grow on the southern slope of the bluff; on the top and eastern side is SUMMERVILLE PARK (public picnic grounds).

2. Left from State 113 on the dirt road to a fork in the road, 0.5 m.; L. here to the entrance to RICHMOND MEMORIAL PARK, 1 m., donated by Albert and Ruth Richmond in memory of "James and Emma F. Richmond and other early pioneers," and dedicated in 1929. A footpath leads upward through heavy growth, a climb of half a mile, to the top of GIBRALTAR ROCK (1,240 alt.), highest straight cliff in Wisconsin. The forest land on the crest of the hill is unfenced and untended, littered with stones and boulders. The unrailed brink of the precipice is bare rock; tiny rock platforms overlook the sheer drop. Small cedars, tough and gnarled, cling to crevices below and split the rock with their roots; green forest sweeps up the talus slope; through the tops of the trees can be seen great mossy boulders that have fallen from the crags. Far out, beyond the slope, stretch farms and pasture land, seamed with brown roads and glistening rivers. Twenty-five miles away is the flat cone of Blue Mounds (see Tour 23), half seen, half imagined.

Northwest of Okee the highway follows the southern bank of artificial Lake Wisconsin, formed by the Prairie du Sac power dam. At 31.4 m. is a STATE-OPERATED FERRY across the Wisconsin River (free, 24 hr. service; open from April 15 to Nov. 20). On the north bank of the river is MERRIMAC (800 alt., 490 pop.); here is the junction with State 78.

Right on State 78 to the junction with a dirt road, 5.5 *m.;* L. on this road to DURWARD'S GLEN (*parking 10¢; closes at 8 p.m.*), 6.5 *m.* Just beyond the parking area here is an old frame STUDIO (L), and straight ahead is the ST. CAMILLUS NOVITIATE (*daily services open to public*), a small log chapel and living quarters for the father and brothers, built by the Camillian Fathers of Milwaukee in 1935.

A posted trail (R) leads to the old DURWARD HOME. Bernard Isaac Durward (*see Painting and Sculpture*) of Scotland, artist and poet, found this secluded place in 1861. He bought 40 acres and built a house, a studio, and a chapel of native stone. In the ROCK STUDIO, built in 1887, are paintings by Bernard and his son Charles, as well as some of the family possessions (*adm. 10¢; gallery open from middle of May to end of October*). A foot trail leads among pines to the glen (L) and up the side of a hill to the CHAPEL (*mass every Sunday during summer, only on special occasions otherwise; visitors welcome*).

At 31.6 *m.* in Merrimac is the junction with State 78.

Left on State 78 to the junction with a town road, 0.2 *m.;* R. here to the junction with another road, 2.6 *m.;* L. here to the junction with a farm road, 3.1 *m.,* where a sign announces Parfrey's Glen; R. on the farm road to a PARKING SPACE, 3.5 *m.* A footpath leads up a gentle, rock-strewn slope to PARFREY'S GLEN, 3.7 *m.* The trail follows the bank of a little creek that tumbles among the trees from a cleft in the hills. Great hemlocks, three centuries old, line the gorge, shutting out the direct rays of the sun. As the path ascends, the outcroppings become higher and higher, until the creek emerges between two sheer, 100-foot precipices of gray stone, so close together that they almost shut out the sky. The stream bed is blocked with great slabs that have split off from the cliffs, and the water runs around them in trickling rivulets.

State 113 swings away from Lake Wisconsin toward the Baraboo Range (R). The ascent of the range commences at 36.3 *m.,* at the bottom of a heavily forested gully. At 36.7 *m.* a side road turns left to the southern end of DEVILS LAKE (*see Tour 19*), and at 37.7 *m.* another leads to the northern end. State 113 continues climbing, until at 39.5 *m.* Baraboo comes into view, filling the western end of a broad shallow valley. The white cottages of its outskirts are scattered eastward, trailing off into farm land dotted with red barns, farmhouses, and shining windmills. The road slopes down the bluff to the valley floor, crosses the Baraboo River to BARABOO, 43 *m.* (864 alt., 5,545 pop.) (*see Tour 19*), at the junction with the yellow-marked alternate route of US 12 (*see Tour 19*).

Tour 20

(Chicago, Ill.)—Madison—Richland Center—La Crosse—(La Crescent, Minn.); US 14.
Illinois Line to Minnesota Line, 206.1 *m.*

Chicago, Milwaukee, St. Paul & Pacific R. R. parallels route between Illinois Line and Janesville and between Madison and Richland Center; Chicago & North Western Ry. between Janesville and Madison.
Hard-surfaced roadbed.
Accommodations limited in villages.

US 14, marking off a triangular corner of Wisconsin, crosses the fertile, long-cultivated lowlands of the south, the sandy corn lands of the Wisconsin River Valley, and the rough country of the rocky Western Upland to the Mississippi River terrace. Along the way are Madison, lake-surrounded, tree-framed capital of the State; Tower Hill State Park, rich in historical associations; Taliesin, home of Frank Lloyd Wright and his architects' fellowship; and, finally, the great hills and dark valleys of the half-wild coulee country.

Section a. *ILLINOIS LINE to MADISON; 68.8 m., US 14*

US 14 crosses the ILLINOIS LINE, 0 *m.,* 68 miles north of Chicago, into WALWORTH, 2 *m.* (1,004 alt., 920 pop.), built around a shady square with a green slatted bandstand. Streets lead past small residences into open fields. An aged frame hotel fronts the square; nailed to one of the veranda posts is a sign announcing "A lawyer will be here on Thursdays."

US 14 swings northwestward through a gently rolling country, which has long been farmed. Buildings all about are shabby and run-down, attesting years of depression. In the villages sale notices are common:

"Having sold our farm we will sell at Public Auction on the late P. D. Smith Farm located on the SW ¼ section of 25 township of Darien 2 miles E of the overhead bridge on highway 15 to E. of Little Stream where County Road turns North one quarter mile from the third sideroad.

There will be lunch served on the grounds.

20 Holsteins all young, and most of them are springing. A good dairy, all of them being home raised.

7 good horses.

Farm machinery.

Some antiques and other articles too numerous to mention."

DARIEN, 9.7 *m.* (946 alt., 1,220 pop.), grew up along an old Indian trail, later the pioneer military road between Chicago and Madison. A bronze-plaqued boulder in the DARIEN CITY PARK (R) marks the trail and commemorates John Bruce, first settler. Each year cavalry troops pass over this road between Ft. Sheridan in Illinois and Camp McCoy near Sparta.

At 14 *m.* is the junction with State 11 (*see Tour 24*); between this junction and Janesville US 14 and State 11 are one route.

West of this junction small knolls begin to break the smooth ground; the highway is now entering an outwash plain (*see Natural Setting*). Dairying and hog raising are important here; every farm has its corncrib, hogpen, big barn, and silo. Farther west the dark green of sugar beets shows in roadside fields.

One of the MACARTHUR PHEASANT FARMS, 22.5 *m.*, supplies eggs and carload lots of birds to shooting preserves throughout the United States and in foreign countries. The farm has a breeding stock of 2,000 ring-necked pheasants that lay 50,000 eggs a year; 10,000 birds are hatched annually; some of them are released in a 1,000-acre tract here to be shot at by hunters, largely from Chicago, who pay $3 for each bird bagged. The farm also produces 1,000 mallard ducks each season, all of which are turned out here for shooting. Hunters are provided with dogs, guides, and shelters. For years Wisconsin farmers protested that during the short open season pheasant hunters ignored property rights, killed livestock, and destroyed fences. In 1931 the State legislature, in an attempt to prevent quarrels between hunters and farmers, authorized the establishment of licensed pheasant preserves to assure hunters good pheasant shooting from October 1 to February 1. In 1935 there were about 75 such preserves, averaging 1,000 acres each; the number has since increased.

JANESVILLE, 29.3 *m.* (801 alt., 21,628 pop.) (*see Tour 7*), is at the junction with US 51 (*see Tour 7*) and State 11 (*see Tour 24*). US 14 crosses the Rock River, passing factories, dingy homes, and old mansions, speeding across flat fields toward small hills in the distance.

EVANSVILLE, 45.7 *m.* (897 alt., 2,269 pop.), has false-front, two-story shops along its main street, their ground floor used as stores, their upper floors as living quarters.

The first settlers staked a claim here beside a spring in 1839; more arrived the next year and built houses, sheds, and a schoolhouse of white oak. They named their community "The Grove" for the fine timber surrounding it, timber that disappeared as the land was broken to farms. In 1845 a chair factory was established, only to close shortly; a sawmill was built, and when the timber gave out a gristmill succeeded it.

In 1855 the Reverend Asa Wood, itinerant preacher, persuaded the Methodist Church to found Evansville Seminary, now WYLER SCHOOL at the end of W. Church St. A Yale graduate was engaged as teacher, and school opened in November. Charles R. Van Hise, President of the University of Wisconsin (1903-18), and Robert M. La Follette, Sr. attended this seminary.

When the railroad came in 1864 the business of the region turned to Evansville; the village grew and was incorporated in 1867. Later in the century "Colonel" George W. Hall, pioneer showman, established his home here. Hall had begun his circus career at the Boston Centennial, where he sold popcorn in so beguiling a fashion that Horace Greeley wrote of him in the New York *Tribune*. Having established his own circus, Hall made Evansville his headquarters for more than a half century. The city was also the home of Theodore Robinson (*see Painting and Sculpture*), who lived here as a child and youth, and of Clinch Calkins (*see Literature*), author of *Spy Overhead* and *Some Folks Won't Work*.

Contemporary Evansville, besides being a trading center, has an auto-trailer factory, tobacco warehouses and coal sheds, miscellaneous dairy and farm products industries, and a plant that manufactures windmills, farm machinery, and gasoline engines. LEONARD PARK lies on LAKE LEOTA, once a mill pond. In Evansville is the central office of the Wisconsin Raccoon and Fox Hunters Association, which, together with the Wisconsin Conservation Department, releases hundreds of bred female raccoons every year. In the fall, usually in October, as many as 5,000 spectators attend the Association's field trials for coon and fox hounds. Raccoons are dipped in water, led over a prescribed course, and then placed in a tree. Dogs are unleashed, eight at a time, and the first to scent the trail and the first to bark at the treed coon qualify for the final trials. First, second, and third prizes are awarded both for trailing and treeing.

A sign "Jesus Saves" announces the HALLELUJAH CAMP-GROUNDS (R), 57.4 *m.,* with its central building, tabernacle, refectory, small hotel and identical cottages bearing such names as Beulah, Ezekial, Mizpah, Rock of Ages, and Genesis. This interdenominational, evangelistic institution was founded in 1923 by a former Congregationalist minister, the Reverend C. H. Linn, its present director. During the three weeks' revival meetings in August, three services are held daily; the rest of the tourist season the cabins are rented.

OREGON, 58 *m.* (948 alt., 857 pop.), is built about a triangle walled by stubby brick and frame buildings. The first white settler in this region was Oliver Emil, a Frenchman, who later married a Winnebago squaw and migrated westward with the tribe. By 1842 permanent settlers had come; in 1856 they platted a village, which became an agricultural trading center. Subsequently, with the arrival of Norwegians, tobacco-growing brought new prosperity to village and country.

John Muir (*see Tour 7*) once taught in a near-by rural school. While teaching he found use for many of his ingenious, if fantastic, inventions. He had one clock that would tip him out of bed, and another that would start a fire in the school stove an hour before class time.

North of Oregon the soil is rich and black, and the ground swells in long low hills. LAKE WAUBESA (R), 62.1 *m.*, glints between the wooded clefts of higher and sharper hills. From a long smooth slope, 64.7 *m.*, appears the whitish dome of the State capitol. The highway passes the Burr Oaks Golf Course (L), 66.5 *m.*, and LAKE WINGRA (L), 66.8 *m.*

MADISON, 68.8 *m.* (859 alt., 57,899 pop.) (*see Madison*).

At Madison is the junction with US 151 (*see Tour 6*), US 51 (*see Tour 7*), US 12 (*see Tour 19*), State 113 (*see Tour 19B*), US 18 (*see Tour 23*), and State 30 (*see Tour 23A*).

Section b.   MADISON to RICHLAND CENTER; 64.2 m. US 14

Between MADISON, 0 *m.*, and Middleton (*see below*) US 14 and US 12 (*see Tour 19*) are one route. US 14 follows University Ave. westward from its junction with Park St., passing (R) the University Campus (*see Madison*), and skirting the edge of University Heights (L), the professorial residential district.

At 5.6 *m.* is the junction with a side road.

Right on this road to TRAILER TOWN, 0.3 *m.* (*50¢ a night, $3 a week, $10 a month per trailer*), in a tract of 48 acres in the woods overlooking Lake Mendota. (*Electric connections for trailers, modern comfort and bathing facilities, laundry equipment, gas station, store, and riding stable.*)

MIDDLETON, 6.4 *m.* (931 alt., 983 pop.), successively called Peatville, Mendota, Middleton Station, and Middleton, was settled by English and Germans. In the middle 1860's it was a milling and grain and stock shipping point; now it is a dairying center.

At Middleton is the junction with US 12 (*see Tour 19*).

Named for its situation at the intersection of two early military roads, CROSS PLAINS, 14.1 *m.* (861 alt., 302 pop.), is a mile-long street of frame, stucco, and limestone houses standing flush with the highway. Among the oldest buildings in the village are the white frame Christina House, now a residence, erected as a tavern during stage-coach days; the Post Office, built in 1860 as a general store; the two-story Roller Mill, constructed of native limestone.

Soldiers of the War of 1812, chiefly from South Carolina and Maryland, settled here between 1832 and 1850 on veteran grants; many left during the California gold rush of 1849. In 1852 a German baron, Peter L. Mohr, erected about 30 stone and frame buildings; in 1855 he recorded a plat of the village and named it Christina, for his wife. He called the streets "Gerda", "Jovina", "Celina", and "Eulalia" for his children, and resorted to history for a "Julius" and a "Caesar." The incorporated part of Cross Plains fuses a part of Christina with the whole of near-by Foxville. Retired farmers constitute the major part of the population.

BLACK EARTH, 19.5 *m.* (816 alt., 490 pop.), lies in the valley of a Wisconsin River tributary. When the English and Norwegians settled the surrounding hills in the early 1850's, their farms looked down upon a great marsh in the middle of a sandy plain, which was later drained to uncover miles of rich dark earth. Black Earth was platted in 1850, and soon afterwards one of the first gristmills to operate west of Madison was built here. It was constructed of native oak and equipped with a burr stone brought from France. First a grain shipping center, the village today subsists almost entirely on rural trade. The Patrons' Mercantile Company, one of the oldest farmer cooperative stores in Wisconsin (*see Cooperative Movement*), does a yearly business of $200,000.

Northwest of Black Earth US 14 enters the broad sandy floodplain of the Wisconsin River, part of the unglaciated Driftless Area (*see Natural Setting*).

MAZOMANIE (Ind., the iron that walks), 23.1 *m.* (780 alt., 747 pop.), is a half-mile stretch of·small houses and business buildings. Though the plain on which the village lies was early crossed by explorers, fur traders, and missionaries, there was no settlement in the vicinity until three members of the British Temperance Emigration Society arrived in 1843. They were followed the next years by other members of the society, inexperienced farmers from Yorkshire and Lancashire. German immigrants later settled here; their influence can be seen in such buildings as a house above the railroad tracks, built in the style of a Rhine castle with turrets, high gables, and elaborately carved borders. The SALEM KIRCHE is also distinctively foreign and old in its delicate lines and hand-wrought stone blocks.

In 1856 Haskell University was incorporated by a minister from New York. The school building was erected the following year, and two instructors came to teach Latin, French, mathematics, music, drawing, and "some of the common branches" to about 50 pupils. Within three years the university closed. The small building it occupied is now a store. Mazomanie remains a shipping point and trading center for the dairy farmers who live on the plain and uplands around the village.

` ARENA, 29.3 *m.* (738 alt., 273 pop.), is the successor of old Arena and Hayworth, villages that were boat stops 5 miles west on the Wisconsin River. Beef cattle were brought there "on the hoof"; long wagon trains hauled in wheat for shipment and returned home with supplies and lumber that had been rafted down the river. The extension of the railroad to the present site of Arena in 1855 caused the inhabitants of old Arena and Hayworth to remove here. Arena is linked to these "ghost towns" only by a house and a hotel, both still standing, which were hauled across the prairie by oxen.

For a time the prairie surrounding Arena became a corn land for feeding pigs. Early each winter the farmers pooled their drivers, teams, and feed corn, set out on long expeditions to herd the pigs, and "hogged" from 100 to 500 of the squealing animals down the crude roads to the Arena depot. Present Arena, centered about a one-block graveled street bordered with shops of wood and cement blocks, is now the trading center for the surrounding dairy farmers.

At 30.8 *m.* is the junction with County H.

Left on County H to COON BLUFF CAVE (*descent into cave difficult, though still passable*), 7 *m.*, one of the smaller of the caves scattered throughout the Driftless Area. Passages lead into the side of the bluff, then are blocked off abruptly. Old-timers say that gold and silver ingots and other loot of an early counterfeiting gang are hidden in the cave.

US 14 lifts off the plain, then sweeps down a hill to historic TOWER HILL STATE PARK, 36.5 *m.* (*camping and picnicking facilities; no overnight accommodations*). Here at the base of a perpendicular bluff is the SITE OF HELENA, a village platted in 1828. Three years later the construction of a shot tower on the hilltop above the park entrance was begun. Work was interrupted during the Black Hawk War (1832), the houses in Helena were torn down and their logs used for rafts to move soldiers across the river. After the war the shot tower was completed, and by 1835 Helena was again a thriving village, where lead from the mineral region to the south was made into shot and shipped down the river. Production was reduced by the panic of 1837, but speeded up again in 1839 when rising lead prices started a period of prosperity. After closing several times, the shot tower shut down permanently in 1861. Most of the miners enlisted in the Civil War, and the village of Helena disappeared.

TOWER HILL itself is a soaring peak overlooking the placid Wisconsin River as it flows through a sand-yellow valley. On the cliff above Mill Creek, a muddy slough, is the 120-foot SHOT TOWER SHAFT, a hole bored through sandstone, largely by hand, to a cave at the bottom of the cliff. The cave was filled with spring water, and melted lead, dropped down the shaft, came out below, cooled and hardened, in perfectly shaped balls. The several sizes were weighed, sacked, put into kegs, and loaded on steamboats tied up on Mill Creek. From 5,000 to 10,000 pounds of shot could be turned out in a day.

In 1889 this land was sold for $60 to the Reverend Jenkin Lloyd-Jones, former Chicago minister and uncle of Frank Lloyd Wright. The same year Lloyd-Jones organized the Tower Hill Pleasure Company as "a summer resort and resting place for ministers, teachers, and others who might enjoy . . . a simple, economical retirement from the city." A camping ground, lecture pavilion, public dining room, and cottages were provided, and a summer school was conducted on the grounds. The grounds were given to the State in 1922.

The road descends past the hillside CEMETERY (L), where a few of the old settlers of Helena are buried. Although the three-foot headstones are badly worn, it is possible to decipher inscriptions dating back to 1829.

At 37.3 *m.* is the junction with State 23.

Left (*straight ahead*) on State 23 to TALIESIN, 0.6 *m.* (*No meal, lodging, or picnicking facilities. Conducted tour of grounds $1 per person. Moving picture, Sun. 3 p.m., included in tour fee; otherwise 50¢ per person.*)

"About four miles from Spring Green, Wis.," said the magazine *Time* in its Jan. 17, 1938, issue, "the hills splay into two soft ranges to let a fast stream flow toward the Wisconsin River. Facing southwest over this valley a big, long house folds around the summit of one hill, its roof lines parallel to the line of ridges, its masonry the same red-yellow sandstone that crops out in ledges along the stream. Under the snow the house melts easily into the landscape. Its name is Taliesin, a Welsh word meaning 'shining brow.' Its history is one of tragic irony. Its character is one of extraordinary repose. It is the home of Frank Lloyd Wright." (*See Architecture.*)

In 1911 Mr. Wright took possession of this 200-acre tract, which had belonged to his grandfather, Richard Lloyd-Jones. Taliesin I rose on the hilltop, only to be damaged by fire in 1914. In 1915 the house was rebuilt, and there Mr. Wright lived until he set out for Japan, where the greatest engineering feat of his career awaited him, the construction of Tokyo's earthquake-proof Imperial Hotel. The hotel was finished in 1920. Mr. Wright returned to Taliesin, and in 1924 a second fire destroyed the house, together with many antique works of art collected in the Orient. It was then that Taliesin III, in Mr. Wright's characteristic later style, took its present place on the hill. Built of native materials, largely gathered from the immediate vicinity, the Taliesin group constitutes an example of what Mr. Wright has chosen to describe as a "Usonian" type of architecture—that is, a type belonging to the United States, indigenous to the locality, an American type free of stylistic preconceptions whether "modern" or historic. The group was planned with a free sense of space relations, its numerous units being designed to form an organic ensemble in harmony with the character and contours of the land. Bankruptcy eventually lost the estate to a bank, and it was returned to its builder only when friends and sympathetic clients incorporated Mr. Wright in 1929.

In 1933 the Taliesin Fellowship was established. Since then, an average of 25 to 30 young men and women have yearly paid a $1,100 tuition fee to serve as Mr. Wright's apprentices, studying architecture, interior decoration, landscaping, painting, sculpture, and music. This is not a school in the ordinary sense, since there are no curricula, textbooks, classes, or degrees. Each apprentice spends approximately four hours daily working for the Fellowship, in the fields, about the buildings, or in the kitchen. The rest of the time he is free to follow his talent independently. Visiting artists occasionally give lectures and advice.

In this way, Mr. Wright believes "all begin again (if they can begin at all) to think of building as an interpretation of life from the ground upward. . . . The inexperienced have been getting the feel of materials into their hands after working on designs to be executed in the nature of those materials . . . getting correlation of hand and brain . . . meanwhile developing mastery over self by way of hard work and clear thinking. . . . Not a style at Taliesin. But a variety of daily effort all in the nature of Style."

SPRING GREEN, 39.9 *m.* (728 alt., 779 pop.), lies comfortably in the dark shade of aged elms and maples. In the business section is the old TOWN HALL, used for the town clerk's and deputy sheriff's offices and as a fire house; upstairs is the movie hall, its stage curtain displaying the ads of businessmen of the last generation. Side by side stand the churches and parsonages of Roman Catholics, Methodists, and Congregationalists, built on land donated by A. C. Daley in the early days. From 1860-80 Spring Green was a shipping point for hogs, beef cattle, and wheat; it is now a busy dairy center, seat of the Farmers Dairy Board of Trade.

A portable sawmill in this village is operated by Miss Maurice Cavanaugh, "Lady Logger," who began her career in Minnesota in 1926 and has since acquired 11 sawmills in two States.

At 41.3 *m.* is the junction with State 60 (*see Tour 22*); between this junction and 52.3 *m.* US 14 and State 60 are one route (*see Tour 22*).

SEXTONVILLE, 57.2 *m.*, in the shadow of a pointed crag, was settled in 1851 by New Englanders, many of whom deserted the village when the railroad line was laid elsewhere. Sextonville had the first high school in Richland County; in the school yard is a large bell from the original building.

RICHLAND CENTER, 64.2 *m.* (736 alt., 3,632 pop.), focal point for the surrounding dairy industry has a milk condensery, two cheese warehouses, a co-operative creamery, a casein plant, and a cheese box factory; there are also a wholesale grocery and coffee-roasting company, a button company, a farmers' co-operative oil company, and the largest co-operative stock shipping organization in the State.

Richland Center dates from 1849 when it was settled by easterners who were followed by Norwegians, Irish, Scots and English. The city, together with Madison, was the cradle of woman's suffrage in Wisconsin. Contending that "it is a mistake to think that all life (for women) is in marriage," several Richland Center wives held suffrage meetings in 1882 under the guise of cultural gatherings. By 1884 they were active in the State and national suffrage movement and they made an unsuccessful attempt to have a woman suffrage clause written in the charter when Richland Center was incorporated as a city in 1887.

Frank Lloyd Wright, born here in 1869, designed the WAREHOUSE of Simon Brothers' wholesale grocery. Its high windowless walls of weather-darkened maroon brick are patterned with narrow perpendicular strips of glass which rise at wide intervals almost from the street to an ornate cement frieze, suggestive of Mayan designs, which outlines the flat roof. The building incorporates a cooling system; this was a novelty of engineering when it was installed in 1918.

Right from Richland Center on State 80 along the rich dark-soiled valley of the Pine River to the junction with County D at ROCKBRIDGE, 7.4 *m.* Left on County D to a gate (*park car here*), 7.5 *m.*, near the road. Follow the path that leads along the left bank of the river, which flows beneath a great overhanging rock (R) some 150 feet high. At about 0.3 *m.* a tributary of the Pine River has cut an arch, 12 by 20 feet, shaped like an inverted "Y" through the rock, forming the NATURAL ROCK BRIDGE (*accessible only on foot*).

Near the gate another path, precariously railed, leads across a rickety bridge and up the bare face of the rock to a level platform, about 20 feet square, at the top. From this point there is a view of the entire valley, with Rockbridge to the east across a swamp of cattails and other rushes, through which the tributary creek snakes its way toward the natural bridge below.

Section c. RICHLAND CENTER to MINNESOTA LINE;
73.1 m. US 14

West of RICHLAND CENTER, 0 *m.*, US 14 enters coulee country. Here valleys become narrow, often mere slits between the hills, often watered by rivulets that trickle near the road, allowing space only for a cramped dairy farm or small tobacco field here or there. Oddly shaped rocks, with a reddish tinge, appear on the hills, and wooded ridge lines frequently end in a snout of harsh outcroppings.

READSTOWN, 24.8 *m.* (754 alt., 544 pop.), lies in the Kickapoo Valley on a ledge safe from the floods of the Kickapoo River. The village, once mostly on the west side of the river where a few buildings still remain from 1848, gradually shifted to the other side when the railroad was laid on the east bank. A factory for cheese, butter, and casein employs some 80 men, while others work in the tobacco warehouse, which draws half its stock from Edgerton, half from Vernon County.

At 25.3 *m.* is the junction with US 61 (*see Tour 11*). Westward US 14 continues up grade through a close-walled coulee which winds between overlapping bluff ends to a rounded plateau where trees thin out for a view over miles of fertile flat lands and woods.

VIROQUA, 37.4 *m.* (1,274 alt., 2,792 pop.), seat of Vernon County, has a water tower that flaunts "Viroqua Welcomes You," some 110 feet from the ground. The city stretches along the western edge of a plateau. A long, tapering promontory curves out into the broad valley below; at the very tip is the LOVER'S LEAP, from which, it is said, Viroqua, an Indian maiden, threw herself when her father forbade her to wed a white hunter and trapper.

First settled by easterners, the region roundabout was later cultivated for tobacco by Norwegian immigrants. Among early settlers was Jeremiah McLain Rusk (1830-93), who in 1853 came here with his family in a covered wagon. After six years as Republican Congressman from the Sixth Wisconsin District, Rusk served as State Governor for three successive terms (1882-89). Soon after his first inauguration, he was called upon to cope with a delicate labor problem when the Chicago, Portage and Superior R. R. failed, leaving a crew of 1,700 men stranded without food or money in a section remote from a railway. Property owners, fearing violence and rioting, called for military protection; to their plea the Governor made reply. "These men need bread, not bayonets!" Furthermore, he refused to allow liquidation of the company's other debts until the men had been paid full wages.

Though Vernon County is known as a rough county, some 40 per cent of its land is tillable. Dairying and tobacco-raising are important enterprises in the county. With three sorting houses (one cooperative, two private), Viroqua is today the pivot of a great industry in choice binder tobacco, as well as the seat of one of the largest creameries and milk depots in the State, the Viroqua Cooperative Creamery, which in 1938 had 422 stockholders and over 700 patrons. In 1937 this

creamery manufactured 1,603,569 pounds of butter and handled 1,613,-
931 pounds of milk, from which it produced 377,500 pounds of dried
milk powder and a large quantity of skim milk. The city's prosperity is reflected in the increase of its population from 2,500 to 3,500
during the last five years.

US 14 winds downhill into open country where dark walls of evergreen grow at the roadside and in farmyards, and masses of rock
thrust up from the fields.

At 40.2 m. is a junction with a town road.

Left on this road to THREE CHIMNEYS, first seen at 0.8 m., in the middle of a
field (R). The name suggests their form: three shafts of stone rising precariously from a single base.

In Viroqua they say that anyone who lives in WESTBY, 44.6 m.
(1,309 alt., 1,366 pop.), can be recognized by a peculiar tang in his
speech. The city was named for Ole Westby, Norwegian pioneer; 95
per cent of its citizens have come from western Norway; shop doors
and windows carry the names Iverson, Unseth, Nestingen, Stevlingson,
Borgen, Flugstad, Brettingen, Storbakken, Thorson. Norwegian is
heard as often as English on the streets; the theater shows pictures
with Norwegian dialogue; and *lutefisk* dinners in autumn and Norwegian Independence Day celebrations in May are established institutions.

The Westby countryside is heavily planted with tobacco which is
brought to the Westby warehouse. Here 120 men are employed, sorting cigar-filler and cigar-binder leaves. Subsidiary enterprises are dairying and the raising of white leghorns, whose eggs are trucked to
wholesale houses in other cities. Westby has a cooperative creamery,
a cooperative feed store, a cooperative electric company serving the whole
of Vernon County, and a locally owned telephone company.

This village is situated in the COON CREEK SOIL CONSER-
VATION DISTRICT, which began operations in January, 1940, as a
successor to the Coon Valley Soil Conservation Demonstrational Project. The Project, the first of its kind in the Nation, was undertaken
in 1933 by the United States Department of Agriculture, with the
co-operation of the University of Wisconsin, to work out and demon-
strate methods by which erosion control in a hilly area could be adapted
to practical farm management. More than 400 farmers in the Coon
Creek watershed, receiving free technical assistance from the Soil Erosion Service (now the Soil Conservation Service) through five-year
co-operative agreements, made such valuable improvements to their
farms that when the agreements expired they took steps to set up the
present District. After the presentation of petitions and the approval
of a special referendum, the District was created as an independent
governmental unit with its own taxing powers, much like a drainage
district. Similar districts are being created in Grant and Trempealeau
Counties. These districts receive technical assistance from the federal
Department of Agriculture and are given aid by the Civilian Conserv..

tion Corps in reforestation, the erection of erosion-control dams, and similar work. Meanwhile, through tours of the area, farmers in other parts of the State have been able to study the effectiveness of forest growth, strip cropping, terracing, gully control, the rearrangement of fields, and the realignment of crops as erosion-control measures.

COON VALLEY, 54.4 m. (753 alt., 462 pop.), is scattered below the high bluffs surrounding the long, northward-reaching valley of the same name, whose numerous creeks and springs attracted the early settlers. Here tobacco-growing and dairying provide the chief source of income for the Norwegian and Bohemian population. The Coon Valley Cooperative Creamery ships butter to faraway parts of the country, and the Federal Soil Conservation Project, set up in 1933, with its headquarters in an abandoned garage, exhibits a map showing the extent of cooperation by farmers.

The hills around the village are the largest that have yet appeared on US 14. Coulees continue—longer, deeper, and more intricately interwoven. This is the kind of country in which Hamlin Garland (*see Literature*) grew up and which has supplied the setting for many of his books. At 61 *m.* the highway turns due west toward the wavering blue line of the range that walls the Mississippi terrace on its western side. Ahead lies the broad flat of MORMON COULEE, named for the colony of Mormons who lived here briefly in 1844 (*see La Crosse*).

At 66.2 *m.*, is the junction with County MM.

Left on County MM to OEHLER'S CAVE (*fee 25¢*), 0.5 *m.*, a great opening in the sheer rock of a towering pine-grown hill beside a bend of MORMON CREEK. Here are PICNIC GROUNDS (*10¢ per person*) and the remains of an aged STONE DAM and GRINDING MILL, built by the Oehler Brothers in 1854.

At 67.2 *m.* is the junction with State 35 (*see Tour 13*); between this junction and a point at 72.2 *m.* US 14 and State 35 are one route.

The highway is now on the Mississippi River plain; for mile upon mile, on both sides of the river, immense bluffs enclose the valley like the wings of an old-fashioned stage-setting. US 14 travels across the plain to La Crosse.

LA CROSSE, 72.2 *m.* (649 alt., 39,614 pop.) (*see La Crosse*).

La Crosse is at the junction with State 35 (*see Tour 13*), US 53 (*see Tour 10*) and US 16 (*see Tour 21*).

US 14 crosses a channel of the Mississippi to PETTIBONE ISLAND. Another bridge (*free*) is at the Minnesota Line, 73.1 *m.*, 1.9 miles east of La Crescent, Minnesota.

Tour 21

Shorewood—Columbus—Wisconsin Dells—La Crosse—(La Crescent, Minn.) ; State 190 and US 16.
Shorewood to Minnesota Line, 214.6 *m.*

Chicago, Milwaukee, St. Paul & Pacific R. R. parallels route between Shorewood and Tomah; Chicago and North Western Ry. between Sparta and La Crosse.
Hard-surfaced roadbed.
Good accommodations.

From Lake Michigan the highway crosses dairy country onto Wisconsin's Central Sandy Plain, touching historic Watertown and Portage and the summer resort regions of Oconomowoc and Wisconsin Dells. West of the Dells the route passes through a wasteland of pine-grown sands and stark buttes to fertile farmlands in the coulee country. Beyond the westernmost bluffs lies the Mississippi; here the highway ends, at La Crosse, before the great crags that frame the river terrace.

Section a. *SHOREWOOD to COLUMBUS; 71.7 m. US 16*

SHOREWOOD, 0 *m.* (13,479 pop.) (*see Milwaukee*), is at the junction with US 141 (*see Tour 3*). The road goes west on Capitol Drive, passing ESTABROOK PARK (R), 1.4 *m.*, a pleasant strip of greenery. At 6.9 *m.* is the junction with US 41 (*see Tour 2*); at 9.2 *m.* is the junction with US 45 (*see Tour 5*), and proceeds on State 190.

West of the city, hills and shallow valleys warp the broad stretches of field and pasture. A Shetland pony "ranch" lies on a slope (R) at 11.6 *m.,* and at 12.9 *m.* are the buildings of the LAMBRECHT-MILLER HATCHERY. From a distance the long white barns with their curved roofs suggest a fleet of boats drawn up on shore, with keels turned upward. Near by are nine chicken coops with three-story porches along the sides, laid out with the precision of a government housing project. Across the rich farmlands is a brief glimpse of LAKE PEWAUKEE.

PEWAUKEE (Ind., either *pewaunawkee,* a flinty place, or *nibiwaki,* swampy), 20.9 *m.* (852 alt., 1,067 pop.), is half farm trade center, half a vacation resort. Across from the low wooden shops of the main street is the lake front and beach. Sailboats skim the blue lake in summer; in winter ice boats and skaters mark the frozen surface.

At Pewaukee is junction with US 16. Take latter right.

On the shores of PINE LAKE (R), 27.6 *m.,* Swedish immigrants, the first in Wisconsin, founded a short-lived settlement, New Upsala, in 1841. On the opposite shore lived a colony of Norwegians. The two groups, together with some Danish settlers, built a church and affiliated themselves with the Episcopalians, but retained such of the old practices as did not conflict with their new doctrines.

OKAUCHEE (Ind., either *okatci,* something small, or *okidji,* pipestem), 31 *m.,* is a resort village (R) on LAKE OKAUCHEE (*boating and fishing facilities, dance halls, cottages*).

At 32.4 *m.* is the junction with County P.

Right on County P to MAPLETON, 5 *m.,* fountainhead of the International Catholic Dramatic Movement (*see The Theater*). The PARSONAGE, now a dormitory and print shop for plays and books about the theater and for the organization's magazine *Practical Stage Work,* and the PARISH HALL, which serves as a theater, have become school buildings where 10 carefully chosen young students are being taught to stage and act plays, both religious and secular, with the expectation that they will return to their homes and direct community theaters. The students in the training school in drama support a professionally trained group of actors in staging plays in cities and villages of Wisconsin and neighboring States.

OCONOMOWOC (Ind., gathering of waters), 34.2 *m.* (866 alt., 4,190 pop.), lying along and between FOWLER LAKE and LAKE LA BELLE (R), has long been a noted watering place. In the 1880's and 1890's wealthy families from St. Louis, New Orleans, and other Southern places came with coachmen and carriages to spend the summer at white-pillared DRAPER HALL, 219 N. Main St., or at the great estates on the lakeshore. With better communications Oconomowoc developed a flourishing weekend trade that eventually turned many of the estates into summer hotels and clusters of cottages. In addition to the summer sports, Oconomowoc provides skating, sleigh riding, iceboating, and horse racing on the ice. A yearly ice carnival with a number of championship events, including the North American (United States and Canada) skating meet and the Central States champion ski jumping contests, is held here. Contestants and audience turn "Cooney," as Oconomowoc is locally called, into a lively town. They play tag and football on the ice between visits to the taverns for warming up, dash about from buffet suppers to dancing parties in the hotel ballrooms, or jingle over the countryside in bobsleds, 20 or 30 people crowded together for warmth, wrapped in blankets and mattressed with straw and heated bricks. Fashionable hostelries reopen for a brief season of gay parties, balls, and miscellaneous revelry.

Although mainly a resort city, Oconomowoc has a brewery, a pea cannery, a bottling works, a milk plant, and a boat factory. The highway continues through Oconomowoc, past DEVIL'S HOLLOW (R), 37.1 *m.,* where skiers compete on the jump during the winter carnival. The Rock River is crossed at 38.8 *m.*

Upon Richards' Hill on the eastern outskirts of Watertown is (L) the four-story cream-colored brick OCTAGON HOUSE (*adm. 25¢ for adults, 15¢ children under 13; open 10 to 12 a.m., 2 to 5 p.m. daily from May 30 to Nov. 1*), 45.5 *m.,* built between 1849 and 1852 by

John Richards, early local lawyer. This is the building that inspired George Fred Keck, former Watertown architect, to design the ultra-modern glass and steel "House of Tomorrow" at Chicago's Century of Progress Exposition in 1933-34. A spiral stairway runs up through a square stair-well beneath a cupola. The 57 rooms, including halls and closets, surround the stair-well; on each floor there are four large square rooms between which are wedged four smaller triangular rooms, often subdivided. The house has a Dutch oven large enough to bake two dozen loaves of bread at once, and one of the first furnaces in the region—a huge mechanism built to burn 4-foot logs.

WATERTOWN, 47.7 m. (822 alt., 10,613 pop.), lies on the Rock River, which here falls 20 feet within two miles. It was water power possibilities that attracted the first New Englanders who came about 1836 and built a settlement, harnessing the river to the machinery of sawmills and factories making wagons, carriages, firkins, and barrels.

German immigration began in the 1840's and continued for several decades, changing the character of the young settlement. Among the newcomers were political refugees, many of them university students and professional men. Unsuccessful at farming, the latter turned to the trades, with results equally discouraging. They made shoes that could not be worn and cigars that could not be smoked. They tried a short-lived experiment with a brewery. Passing farmers often heard the pigs squealing riotously in an adjacent sty, and knew that another brew had been spoiled and spilled out on the ground. The brewery soon closed, and its chief asset, a 35-gallon basin, became a kettledrum in a Watertown orchestra. These political refugees were locally known as the "Latin Farmers," for when they congregated in the Buena Vista House, they often conversed in Latin.

Most famous of them was Carl Schurz (*see Literature*), political reformer, who had to flee Germany after the ill-fated revolution of 1848. Schurz (1829-1906) arrived in Watertown in 1855. Although most of the German immigrants were Democrats, Schurz could not tolerate slavery and entered local politics on the ticket of the newly formed Republican Party (*see Tour 5A*). He was often showered with rotten eggs as *"ein verdammter Republikaner,"* but his logic and fiery eloquence won a fair portion of German votes. In 1857 he ran for the lieutenant governorship of Wisconsin but was defeated. The next year he campaigned for Lincoln in the contest with Douglas, thus gaining national prominence. In 1861 Lincoln made him Minister to Spain, and his career in Wisconsin was closed.

Other notable Watertown inhabitants were Mrs. Schurz, a pupil of Frederick Froebel, who in 1856 established the first kindergarten in America, in a building still standing near Memorial Park on N. Second St.; and Ralph Blumenfeld, author of *R. D. B's Diary, 1887-1914,* who introduced American journalistic methods into England with great success and became editor of the London *Daily Express.* Blumenfeld was born in Watertown and lived here through his boyhood.

Easy communication with the outside world was established in 1850 when a plank road was completed; the TOLL HOUSE still stands on Main St. In the 1850's Leopold Kadisch transplanted here the institution of *Viehmarkt,* or cattle fair, held on the second Tuesday of each month. Although the Gypsies, horse traders, and other colorful figures at the early fairs have vanished, this "community day" survives in the monthly marketing of *Spanferkel,* little pigs. The market is enlivened now and then by a pitchman vending his "slum goods" or by an Indian medicine man expounding the merits of his cure-alls. Another transplantation is the "noodling", or force-feeding of geese for a period of a month before they are brought to market. Large quantities of cooked noodles made of wheat, corn, and barley are shoved down the birds' throats with a wooden pestle; the geese grow to uncommon size, and their livers become greatly enlarged. Watertown geese are raised chiefly for these livers which are made into *pâté de foie gras.* At one time 50,000 pounds of Watertown geese were shipped to New York markets in a single season.

Watertown today is chiefly an industrial city, producing cutlery, cash registers, locks, furnaces, shoes, automobile linings, table slides, and canned peas. The city is also the seat of two small colleges. NORTHWESTERN COLLEGE, established by the Wisconsin Synod of the Evangelical Lutheran Church, opened in 1865. Originally modeled after the German *Gymnasium,* it now offers primarily a classical course. THE SACRED HEART JUNIORATE trains Catholic boys who wish to become teachers in any field as members of the Congregation of Holy Cross.

Northwest of Watertown US 16 crosses the black soil of the lowland dairy country, past cheese factories and farms with fields of hay, oats, clover, corn, and peas. Willow woodlots, common in this vicinity were first planted about 1864 at the instigation of manufacturers of reed furniture. Their bushy foliage makes good windbreak, for the trees grow in marshy areas that would otherwise be wasteland.

COLUMBUS, 71.7 *m.* (842 alt., 2,514 pop.) (*see Tour 22*), is at the junction with US 151 (*see Tour 6*) and State 60 (*see Tour 22*).

Section b. COLUMBUS to TOMAH, 97.3 m. US 16

West of COLUMBUS, 0 *m.,* the countryside changes, becoming more sandy, yet the farms are still well-kept and productive.

RIO, 15 *m.* (928 alt., 641 pop.), was the scene of a disastrous railroad wreck in 1886, when a "Limited," traveling at the then tremendous speed of 40 or 45 miles per hour, ran through an open switch into a string of freight cars on a sidetrack.

> When crash, and wails of terror
>   Were sent through the morning air,
> Wails from the crushed and dying,
>   Caught in a cruel snare;

> There midst the burning timbers,
>   Were those whom none could save;
> Some with thin hands ceased praying,
>   Waiting the hissing wave;
> (from *The Rio Disaster,* by Katie Le Daune Howard).

Stoves and lamps overturned, and in a few minutes fire was leaping along the aisles; some 16 of the 25 passengers perished in the holocaust. The charred remains of most of the victims were buried in a single grave in the little Rio cemetery, where a small monument commemorates the tragedy.

Between Rio and Portage the country becomes progressively more irregular; green hills block the view; the valley floor is uneven. US 16 mounts to a crest, 22.7 *m.,* from which, over stretches of rough country, there is a glimpse of the hills that bank the Wisconsin River, miles ahead, and the smoke-blue profile of the Baraboo Range beyond.

At 26.2 *m.* is the junction with US 51 (*see Tour 7*); between this junction and Portage US 16 and US 51 are one route.

US 16 parallels the WISCONSIN RIVER LEVEE (L), 26.1 *m.,* built in 1903 to prevent the Wisconsin from flooding the Fox River Valley, as it had done five or six times, carrying homes down to the headwaters of the Fox and destroying wild hay crops. The PORTAGE CANAL, 29.2 *m.,* connects the Fox River with the Wisconsin, thus forming a continuous waterway between the Great Lakes and the Mississippi River. On June 14, 1673, the mile and a half of marshy meadow here was crossed by the first expedition known to have used the Fox-Wisconsin waterway, that of Pere Marquette and Louis Joliet, sent by the King of France. The portage played an important part in the French fur trade, British military occupation, and American settlement.

From 1792 until the early 1850's the chief means of transportation from one river to the other was the ox team, which hauled supplies and passengers over a plank road at the rate of 50¢ per hundred pounds. The agitation for a continuous, easily navigable waterway between Green Bay and the Mississippi began about 1829 under the leadership of Morgan L. Martin, a Green Bay lawyer. In 1834 the Legislative Council of Michigan Territory incorporated the Portage Canal Company for the purpose of cutting a waterway across the lowlands here. This project soon fell through, but in 1836 the Fox River Hydraulic Company, incorporated by the Wisconsin Territorial Council, began construction of a dam, locks, and canal at the De Pere rapids. No other action was taken until 1848, when the Wisconsin Legislature accepted a Congressional grant of lands along the Fox River and at the portage which were to be sold to finance further improvements. A State Board of Public Works was then created to supervise the project and work was started at the portage and the several rapids of the lower Fox River.

In 1851 the portage canal was nearly completed. By this time, however, the land sales had dropped off alarmingly and the board found itself practically without funds; meanwhile the public was clamoring for a speedy completion of the project. The legislature in desperation now turned over the work on the lower Fox, between Lake Winnebago and Green Bay, to Martin, agreeing to pay him in State scrip, though this was a violation of the terms of the Federal grant and of the State constitution. By the end of 1852 the State's debt, together with estimated cost of finishing the work, amounted to $502,573, while credit based on the scrip was rapidly shrinking. To avert the necessity of paying the debt through direct taxation, the legislature decided to turn the work over to a private organization. Thereupon Martin formed the Fox and Wisconsin Improvement Company, which assumed responsibility for the entire project and agreed to pay the State debt in return for the remaining grant lands and a 20-year lease on the waterway.

Almost at once the company began to lobby for an enlargement of the Federal grant, and eventually Congress passed two acts (August 8, 1854, and March 3, 1855) allowing a "reinterpretation" of its original terms which added 424,310 acres to the previous 260,250. The success of Martin and his associates was gradually arousing intense jealousy and suspicion. Well-founded rumors declared that the company had bribed congressmen and that it was intending to use part of the grant lands to pay for official favors. Consequently, in 1856 the Legislature felt obliged to make a public investigation. The only result of the investigation was that the company was required to redeem the State scrip, complete, enlarge, and improve the work within three years, and perfect the titles of settlers along the route, under the supervision of a board of trustees appointed by the governor.

Despite the immense gain in grant lands, the enterprise was soon in difficulties again, owing to the financial panic of 1857 and the company's inability to sell its stocks. In 1866 a group of New York State capitalists, who had gradually obtained a controlling interest in the organization, bought in all the remaining lands, franchises, and personal property and formed the Green Bay and Mississippi Canal Company. In a short time the improvements on the Fox River were completed. But now it was discovered that the Wisconsin River, assumed all along to require only minor improvements, was hopelessly unnavigable. In 1872 the Federal Government was induced to buy out the Canal Company for $145,000, exclusive of franchises and personal property, and improvements along the Wisconsin were undertaken on a grand scale. Unfortunately, the government engineers employed a device which had already proved its inadequacy, with the result that after several years the river was still unnavigable. Eventually Congress grew tired of making appropriations, and the work lapsed. The Federal Government still owns and maintains the Fox River improvements and the Portage Canal, though several of the franchises remain in the possession of the Green Bay and Mississippi Canal Company.

PORTAGE, 29.3 m. (785 alt., 6,038 pop.), more than 100 years old, was founded by early traders and adventurers who traveled the

Fox-Wisconsin waterway. In time furs, military supplies, wheat, lumber, and railroads brought the city a livelihood. Later Portage developed a large and steady farm trade and some local industry, having a hosiery plant, brewery, shoe factory, and granite works. Out of steady trade and industry has grown a pleasant midwestern city with comparatively equal distribution of wealth.

Situated on high ground overlooking the Fox River marsh and the islands and sloughs of the Wisconsin, Portage is a lovely city, particularly in summer when the leaves are out and the water is clear and blue. Many shade trees line the avenues, and waterfowl fly down the Wisconsin to the Mississippi. In this environment of economic security and social peace the authors (*see Literature*), Frederick Jackson Turner, Zona Gale, Majorie Latimer, and Elinor Green were born.

Miss Gale (1874-1938), drew upon local setting and her experience with Portage people for the materials of her novels, *Birth, Friendship Village,* and *Miss Lulu Bett*. The last named book, when dramatized, was winner of the Pulitzer Prize. Frederick Jackson Turner (1861-1932), son of Andrew Turner, early historian and politician of Portage, was born in the city. His later works on the American frontier were inspired by a first-hand intimacy with frontier life and culture as he experienced it at Portage. To some extent, the local scene is also reflected in the work of Miss Latimer and Miss Green. John Muir (1838-1914) came to the Portage country when he was a small boy, and it was the swamps, prairies, and forests here that awakened his love of nature.

Points of interest within Portage include the JOLIET-MARQUETTE MARKER, Wisconsin St. and Wauona Ave., commemorating the first voyage over the portage; the Pauquette Marker, Edgewater and Mac Sts., indicating the SITE OF THE FIRST FERRY across the Wisconsin. The CURLING RINK, Canal and Mac Sts., is one of the largest in the world. Although curling is an old Scotch game, the interstate and international matches held here are called bonspiels, apparently a combination of the German words *Bahn,* or path, and *Spiel,* or play. The game is a variation of bowling and is played on ice. A 40-pound oval granite stone, having a handle like a flatiron, is skidded down a cleared alley as the bowler's teammate helps to guide it by vigorously sweeping the ice a foot or so in front of the sliding stone. The object of the game is to skid the stone so that it stops in the smallest of several concentric circles at the end of the ice lane.

At the corner of Wisconsin and Cook Sts. is the junction with State 33.

Right on State 33 to the junction with a dirt road, 2.1 *m.;* L. on this road to the INDIAN AGENCY HOUSE (*fee 25¢*), 3.1 *m.,* on a slight rise of ground overlooking the eastern end of the canal. Built in 1832 by John Harris Kinzie, Portage Indian agent, and his wife, Juliette, it is one of the few remaining structures of its kind in Wisconsin. Mrs. Kinzie, in her book, *Wau-Bun,* a collection of reminiscences of her early life in the Northwest, tells of the many years when her home was the only social center for the West Point graduates stationed at Fort Winnebago. The house, restored and redecorated by the D. A. R., is a white frame building with green shutters, massive fireplaces, and an old-fashioned kitchen. It contains charming colonial furniture.

Across the canal, opposite the Agency House on a small piece of ground where three roads meet, is the SITE OF FORT WINNEBAGO, built in 1828 to protect white settlers in the region. Only the SURGEON'S QUARTERS, a rough log building, still stands. Red Bird, the Winnebago chief, surrendered here in 1827, a year before the fort was built. Lieutenant Jefferson Davis, later President of the Confederate States of America, was one of the first officers to be stationed here and was in direct command of the construction of the fort.

Portage is at the junction with US 51 (*see Tour 7*).

West of Portage is (R) SILVER LAKE (*lifeguards, public bathhouses*), 31 *m.* Rich soil, profitably farmed, borders the highway, which soon enters a stretch of relatively flat land. In the distance (R) the steep, foliated CALEDONIA HILLS rise on the skyline. US 16 swings alternately from marsh to upland in a landscape whose cover changes quickly from swamp weeds and tamarack to pasture grass and oaks. Numerous tourist cabins, cottages, and campgrounds hug the road as it approaches the dalles of the Wisconsin River.

WISCONSIN DELLS, 49 *m.* (893 alt., 1,489 pop.) (*see Tour 8*), is at the junction with State 13 (*see Tour 8*).

US 16 crosses the shallow gorge of the Wisconsin, 49.2 *m.* Below the bridge, a leash has been put upon the river current in the form of a power dam, which supplies 10,000 horsepower of electricity at maximum flow and 3,000 at low to several nearby cities.

At 49.8 *m.* is the junction with US 12 (*see Tour 19*). Between this junction and TOMAH, 97.3 *m.* (958 alt., 3,354 pop.) (*see Tour 19*), US 16 and US 12 are one route (*see Tour 19*).

Section c. *TOMAH to MINNESOTA LINE; 45.6 m. US 16*

West of TOMAH, 0 *m.*, US 16 climbs gradually westward through stretches of oak and pine, interrupted here and there by fairly affluent farms, with the usual white houses, red barns, and occasional battery chargers, which look like dwarf windmills. Alfalfa and grain grow in the valleys or up the milder slopes; cattle are pastured among the woodlots on round low hills. The sandy soil here overlies a substratum of yellow sandstone, apparent in the roadcuts. From the crotch of a great yellow gap, 6 *m.*, is a far-reaching view over the spikes of forest pines and the orange-stained buttes.

US 16 descends between rocky hills to a stream (R), 8.5 *m.*, the southern boundary of CENTRAL WISCONSIN FARMS, a U. S. Resettlement Administration Project. "On the theory that it is better to provide the worthy family with means of encouragement and guidance to help itself, than to perpetuate an unsatisfactory condition through administering direct aid for temporary subsistence," families from poor land are resettled in areas where they can hope to attain decent standards of living.

Seventy-two farms near Marshfield were bought by the Administration for the inhabitants of submarginal land in Jackson, Monroe, and Juneau Counties. In 1937 the Resettlement Administration was taken over by the Farm Security Administration, and it is not intended to expand the program further.

At 12.5 m. is the junction with State 168.

Right on State 168 to CAMP McCOY, 1.3 m., the 14,206-acre maneuvering ground of the 6th Corps Area of the U. S. Army. Here 7,000 regular soldiers and reserves come each year to participate in summer maneuvers. Infantry, cavalry, field artillery, anti-aircraft, engineering, quartermaster, and medical corps, almost every branch of the army service, are represented, as well as the State Militia artillery batteries, which come here for target practice. In the camp are 100 buildings recently constructed and 775 tent floors, of which 48 per cent are framed. There are modern light, water, and sewer systems and a sewage disposal plant.

Right of the highway is CAMP McCOY ROADSIDE PARK, 13 m. (*stone fireplaces, picnic tables, log shelter, water, and sanitary facilities*). West of the park, sand and scrub-growth border US 16 as it crosses a tree-matted floor between the pyramids and loaves of sheer rock partially blanketed with forest-cover.

SPARTA, 17 m. (789 alt., 4,949 pop.), lying on a narrow plain between bluffs, greets the traveler with a sign stating that the city has a free tourist camp, free factory sites, water 99 per cent pure, good railroad facilities, access to one Federal and two State highways, good schools, and a modern hospital. In the city is a theater whose architecture suggests the style of Frank Lloyd Wright.

About 1850, when a road between Prairie du Chien and Hudson met another between Portage and La Crosse here, settlement began. Frank Petit, first settler, gave away lots to anyone who would promise to build a house. By 1852 logging had begun on the La Crosse River; when Monroe County was created in 1854, Sparta, after a struggle, became the official county seat. In the 1850's several industries were established: gristmills, an ironworks, and factories for woolens, furniture and farm machinery. A paper mill was constructed, and a newspaper established. At this time Sparta was the scene of a memorable hoax. A man from La Crosse bought some near-by land in 1865. By night he planted several barrels of crude oil and attached pipes and valves; then one morning oil began to flow. The amazed inhabitants flocked to the spot, and the owner kindly permitted his friends to buy stock in his "Gem Petroleum Company." The barrels were cleverly hidden and performed so well that oil always flowed when prospective buyers were investigating. One day the well failed, and it was discovered that the gentleman from La Crosse had disappeared with $50,000.

But from this saddening experience came good fortune: a medicinal mineral spring flowing 100 gallons a minute was struck in one of the "wells". By the early 1870's Sparta had become a much-frequented health resort. "Over the natural beauties of the place the 'Pleasure Season' throws her spell of life and gayety," read an advertisement of the Turkish Bath Institute. "As evening approaches ladies and gentlemen throng the porticos of hotels, or are wheeling about town behind fast steeds, or are dreamily lounging about the shady retreats in the public parks. Others, with cup in hand, can be seen seated within the enclosure of the Fountain, sipping the health-invigorating water."

All kinds of baths were to be had: Turkish, Russian, sitz, plunge, and others. It was believed that the water, when taken internally, effectively treated anemia, bladder stones, dyspepsia, throat affections, consumption, female diseases, hemorrhagic diseases, constipation, diarrhea, and malaria. Then, within the decade, the vogue diminished, and Sparta's days as a spa ended.

Contemporary Sparta subsists on its trade from farmers and Camp McCoy. It is the seat of two dairy organizations, Guernsey and Holstein, a cooperative creamery, a farmers' shipping association, and a fruit growers association. Carloads of raspberries, blackberries, and strawberries, grown on members' farms and picked by youngsters of the city, are shipped out each summer. Stock associations exhibit prize beef and dairy cattle in the courthouse square early each fall, and in September the county fair is held on the city streets.

In Sparta is the STATE PUBLIC SCHOOL, established in 1885, which educates and cares for neglected or dependent children committed to it by the State's juvenile courts. Of the approximate 1,100 children under the school's care, about 700 are placed in homes throughout the State, some for adoption, others to earn wages or work their way through school, under the supervision of the institution. Those who remain here are grouped according to age and sex, and live in 14 cottages on the grounds. The institution has a nursery school for some 50 or 60 children between the ages of two and four and a complete course from kindergarten through the eighth grade. In addition to the usual school work there are classes in domestic science, manual training, music, arts and crafts, and physical training.

At 23.1 m. is the junction with County J.

Left on County J to the entrance of the SNOW AND ICE CAVE (adm. 25¢), 6.8 m., covered with a low tin structure. Stairs lead down through a shaft in the hillside to the cave, dug out of shale rock in 1935. The temperature descends with the steps, reaching the freezing point in a deep fissure 20 feet below. Here a cold breeze circulates through crevices where ice forms and snow clings to the rocks during the hottest weather. This cavern belongs to the Hylandale Academy, which uses it as a summer ice box.

Near the cave entrance a side road (L) descends a gulch to the wooden buildings of HYLANDALE ACADEMY, 6.9 m., strung along the opposite hillside and in the ravine. Hylandale is a Seventh Day Adventist School. There are about 60 students, boys and girls, who take the ordinary high school work in addition to manual training, music, and Bible study; there are also 10 elementary pupils. The students earn their entire keep, except for a monthly tuition of $12, by working 24 hours a week about the school or on the 347-acre farm up in the hills; many work through the summer to pay the tuition. The teachers receive little remuneration other than their maintenance. The school is practically self-supporting.

Hylandale is locally known for such regulations on student conduct as: "Girls are asked to refrain the use of rouge, lipstick and eye-brow pencil," "All dresses worn by girls must be modest as to length, neckline, etc.," "Shoes of the spindle-heel type are not approved," "The taking of pictures on the Sabbath is regarded as out of harmony with the true spirit of Sabbath keeping."

The highway proceeds westward through a stretch of flat prairie. Roadcuts show yellow sandstone, but the topsoil is black loam, so fertile that 75 years of cultivation have not appreciably depleted it.

US 16 turns south and continues on a broad rolling plain to NESHONOC, 31.4 m., a village settled by easterners and Norwegians in 1850. Eight years later a disagreement with the villagers over land prices caused the railroad to lay its tracks a mile to the south, where West Salem now stands. Neshonoc's population of 200 dwindled speedily as the inhabitants moved nearer the railroad.

WEST SALEM, 32.8 m. (749 alt., 1,011 pop.), founded by people from Neshonoc in 1858, soon attracted Norwegian and German immigrants. A farm trade center, it has co-operative creamery which has been in operation since 1891. For many years this creamery has had an average output of over 1,000,000 pounds of butter annually as well as several carloads of powdered buttermilk. A local pea cannery produces from 60,000 to 120,000 cases yearly.

The HAMLIN GARLAND HOUSE, where the author lived, and which he describes in *A Son of the Middle Border,* stands in West Salem. It is a two-story wooden structure, painted dark green and suggestive of a kite with its broad gabled wings and long tail of kitchen and sheds. Garland (*see Literature*) was born in 1860 on a farm in Green's Coulee, north of near-by Onalaska. When he was eight, his family moved west, and it was not until 1893 that the novelist returned to the coulee country, which he was to describe and celebrate. Garland settled in West Salem and remained here until 1915, when he moved east. The house was then rented, and it has recently been offered for sale. According to West Salemites who knew him, it was not merely the inconvenience for his work that caused Mr. Garland to leave, but a "liberal turn of mind," which prevented him from getting on well with the straight-laced Norwegian Lutherans of the village when he tried to take a hand in community affairs.

US 16 takes a crescent-like course southwest from West Salem. On the bank of the La Crosse River, 33.9 m., in a thick grove of elms and other hardwoods, is (L) a PUBLIC PARK (*picnic facilities*). The highway spans a hill, ascends through an enormous roadcut, then dips gradually onto the Mississippi plain. Farms are scant, although a few cornfields cover the easier slopes and coulee bottoms. Hereabout the work of highway improvement is noticeable in the sodding of road shoulders, the terracing of roadside slopes with pegs interwoven with a riprapping of brush for erosion-control, the planting of young growth native to the region, and a landscape cleared of debris.

At 40.2 m. is the junction with County O.

Left on County O to BARRE MILLS, 1.7 *m.*, a crossroads settlement. On the Gust Horman farm near by is SAMUEL'S CAVE, or Pictured Rock Cave, notable for its records of the prehistoric and historic Indians of this region. Excavations among the layers of sand and ashes on the floor indicate that there were four distinct periods of human occupation, at considerable intervals. The walls are covered with crude carvings of birds, animals, and human figures, believed by archeologists to have been made from 300 to 800 years ago. The cave, partially blocked by debris from a dry-run among the cliffs above its entrance, was discovered by Frank Samuels in 1878. What the ravages of weathering had spared, the vandalism of early visitors, who carved initials and other marks, further effaced before the cave could be adequately protected. Several of the petroglyphs, however, remain in good condition.

US 16 continues toward the spires and stacks of industrial La Crosse, swinging around the foot of MILLER BLUFF and crossing the flats diagonally in view of GRANDAD'S BLUFF (L).

LA CROSSE, 44.7 *m.* (649 alt., 39,614 pop.) (*see La Crosse*).

La Crosse is at the junction with US 53 (*see Tour 10*), State 35 (*see Tour 13*), and US 14 (*see Tour. 20*).

US 16 crosses bridges (*free*) over the Mississippi to PETTIBONE ISLAND and the Minnesota Line, 45.6 *m.*, 1.9 miles east of La Crescent, Minnesota.

Tour 22

Columbus—Sauk City—Gotham—Prairie du Chien; 125 *m.*, State 60.

Chicago, Milwaukee, St. Paul & Pacific R. R. parallels route between Spring Green and Prairie du Chien.
Hard-surfaced and oiled-gravel roadbed.
Accommodations adequate at Prairie du Sac, Sauk City, and Prairie du Chien.

State 60 proceeds from the windy, actively farmed ridgetops of Columbia County to the quiet and beautiful Wisconsin River Valley. While the cities and people on the upland are "making history," as one editor says, in the river valley they only remember it from the days when the waterway opened the West to the East and the South to the North, when it attracted European exiles because it was believed to resemble the Rhine, and when it bore raftsmen and lumber fleets on their way to St. Louis. Along the first part of the route the farms are expansive; along the second they cling to hillsides and occupy rare patches of fertile river bottoms.

COLUMBUS, 0 *m.* (842 alt., 2,514 pop.), is at the junction with US 16 (*see Tour 21*) and US 151 (*see Tour 6*). In 1838 Major Elbert Dickason returned from the Indian wars and stopped here to hunt and fish on the banks of the Crawfish River. In 1839 he returned with oxen, horses, and workmen to construct the first log house and sawmill.

Within the city limits are a pea cannery, a dry-milk-products factory, a brewery, an antiquated gristmill that was once Dickason's sawmill, and a hotel, built in the 1840's. Standing among the ordinary two-story frame and brick business buildings is the FARMERS' AND MERCHANTS' UNION BANK, one block west on James St. Designed in 1919 by Louis Sullivan, this massive brick building ranks among his most notable works. The treatment of the main facade consists of a single powerful arch enclosing the main entrance and show window beneath an intricately designed lintel. On the side elevation five arched windows, grouped in a series, are the only accent. The ornamentation, concentrated to emphasize the structure of the building, follows complex interlaced patterns derived in part from Gothic precedents. The exterior is enriched by a striking color scheme in greens, browns, and yellows, harmonizing the stained-glass windows, the brickwork, and the glazed terra cotta. Inside, a sense of height and mass is achieved by smooth, even-colored walls and ceiling, high dim windows, and balcony and recesses of dark mahogany.

West of Columbus State 60 begins a slow ascent of the Magnesian Cuesta's backslope; the route overlooks broad acres of corn, distant hills, numerous small creeks, and near-by glacial humps. Here is some of the most productive small grain, corn, and pea-growing land in Wisconsin; along much of the highway during season lie abundant spreading crops broken only by oak clusters, farm buildings, and an occasional PEA VINERY such as that at 6.3 m. (R), a small open shed built to shelter a pea shelling machine. During June and July hayracks loaded with pea vines jolt along the highway to the vineries. The vines are unloaded on a continuous belt and drawn into a rotating drum, in which they are tossed around by wooden baffle-plates until the pods are cracked and the peas roll out through holes in the drum. The stripped vines are lifted on another belt, carried out of the vinery, and stacked for use as silage.

Peas are a delicate crop that must be harvested while still immature. Throughout the ripening season men from the canning companies go from field to field to determine the proper harvesting time. A delay of as little as 8 or 10 hours in cutting may result in an inferior quality and a lower price. Each acre yields about 1,300 pounds of peas, which are purchased by the cannery for an average of approximately 2½¢ a pound.

NORTH LEEDS, 15.2 m. (35 pop.), is a small crossroads village near the summit of the cuesta.

At 15.4 m. is the junction with US 51 (see Tour 7); between this junction and 17.5 m., State 60 and US 51 are one route.

ARLINGTON, 17.6 m. (1,047 alt., 161 pop.), the highest point on the route, serves the German farmers of the surrounding country. During the pea canning season the ARLINGTON CANNERY (open from *about June 20 to July 10*) is a noisy, busy place as the work of weighing, washing, grading, blanching, sealing, cooking, and cooling the peas proceeds efficiently through a three- to five-week season. Speed is essential, for the sooner the peas are processed after being cut, the better is their flavor in the cans; the quality of peas diminishes if more than a few hours elapse between harvesting and sealing. Intricate machines and conveyor systems hustle the peas along their route; workers handle cans with dexterity and amazing speed. When the machine is running at full speed an average of over 100 cans a minute comes from each production line.

Most of the seasonal workers—housewives, college students, young men and women who can meet the minimum age requirements established by State law—are drawn from the near-by farms and villages; a few transient workers are also employed. Because of the shortness of the canning season and the brief duration of the peak of heavy canning when abnormally long hours are required, only one shift of men is employed; the women, however, work in two shifts. During the busiest period machines work long into the night, stopping only when there is a mechanical breakdown or when grades and sizes must be changed. The skilled mechanics, processors, and managers often work during the off season repairing and replacing machines, sorting and processing seeds, making future contracts, and managing the company's farms.

The Arlington Cannery pays considerably more than the low minimum wages provided by Wisconsin law. The State minimum hourly wage for workers under 17 and for inexperienced women—those who have not had one year of experience—is 16 cents. The minimum hourly wage for experienced women and minors in cities with a population of 5,000 or more is 22½ cents, in cities with less than 5,000 population 20 cents; not more than 25 per cent of the total number of women and minors employed in any one cannery can be classed as inexperienced women and minors under 17. Because of powerful opposition from farmers, the regulations governing the employment of women and children in other industries are relaxed in regard to employment in factories canning peas, beans, tomatoes, and a few other highly perishable products. Girls between 16 and 17 years of age can be employed up to 54 hours a week during emergencies or rush periods, boys of the same age to 64 hours a week, and women more than 17 to 60 hours a week, though no minor under 17 or woman can be used as an emergency worker for more than 8 days in a canning season.

State 60 leads west from Arlington through dark-soiled country. Summer sees the valley sides of this fertile land green with barley, wheat, corn, and peas, but winter sees them steeped in snowdrifts. During heavy rains in spring and summer water gushes down the slopes, creating springs, gullies, and creeks. Finding a ready supply of water, immigrant farmers, particularly Norwegians, built old-country homes on the ribs of the ridge; those who could afford to dig wells settled on the smoother uplands. At 22.8 *m.* State 60 begins a precarious descent through steep bluffs that are hideouts for wild birds; coveys of quail frequently whir up from the roadside.

LODI, 25.8 *m.* (852 alt., 1,065 pop.), is at the junction with State 113 (*see Tour 19B*). The business section is set in the valley pocket, while the rest of the village spreads helter-skelter over the surrounding heights. Immediately back of the business district flows swift, crooked Spring Creek; on its bank is the dam of a crumbling GRISTMILL. This shaky yellow mill, once run by water, now operates by electricity. The mill still bears its name in Norwegian script high above its entrance. The first settlers here, Norwegians, chose this site because of its many springs. Soon their village became the hog- and horse-trading center of the region; many carloads of draft horses are still shipped in from the Dakotas and Montana.

Lodi, largely populated by Norwegians and Germans, is free from debt; it owns its light and power plant. The fairly recent establishment of two factories, a chocolate-manufacturing company and a pea cannery, has brought in Czechs and Poles, immigrants of the 1910-20 decade.

West of Lodi cornfields stretch from the road bank down to the edge of a BOG (L), a long stretch of humps covered with marsh grass lying on the surface of acres of stagnant water. Children in Lodi will tell how, by jumping up and down on a single hummock, they can make the whole bog shake like a raft.

State 60 dips for some five miles in and out of the bluffs hemming the Wisconsin River Valley. At 32.5 *m.* the northern end of CRYSTAL LAKE is glimpsed in the flat valley ahead. At 32.9 *m.* is smaller FISH LAKE, where each year during the hottest summer months the Egyptian lotus bursts into flower. The highway climbs to a ridgetop, more than 200 feet above the Wisconsin River flood plain; ahead is a view of the wooded BARABOO RANGE (R), which hundreds of thousands of years ago slowed the progress of the continental ice sheet. State 60 sweeps downward from the ridge, curving around isolated monadnocks to the PRAIRIE DU SAC BRIDGE, a low steel structure spanning the Wisconsin River. Upstream and downstream, rising sheer from the east riverbank, are wedge-shaped bluffs, cut by gorges and covered with scrub pine and oak. These bluffs form the riverbank; they are stratified sand dunes from 125 to 150 feet high that cave away easily when the water swings close.

PRAIRIE DU SAC, 40.2 *m.* (758 alt., 949 pop.) (*see Tour 19*), and SAUK CITY, 41.6 *m.* (757 alt., 1,137 pop.) (*see Tour 19*), are at the junction with US 12 (*see Tour 19*).

West of Sauk City, State 60 runs along or near the WISCONSIN RIVER, mingling scenes of historical interest with long clear river views. Almost always within shouting distance of the main channel, the highway at first diverges from the stream, then gradually moves in closer. Below Sauk City the river is wide and rambling, often split double by tree-covered, oval islands. As it winds westward, slowly the far bluffs edge closer and closer together, compressing the valley into a narrow funnel as it approaches the Mississippi.

The Wisconsin River has had a dramatic history. As early as 1673 Marquette described this section of the river as ". . . very wide; it has a sandy bottom, which forms various shoals that render its navigation very difficult. It is full of islands covered with vines." In 1766 Jonathan Carver (*see Literature*), working as a map-maker for Rogers' expedition seeking a northwest passage to the Pacific, wrote: "The Ouisconsin, from the Carrying Place to the part where it falls into the Mississippi, flows with a smooth but strong current; the water of it is exceedingly clear, and through it you may perceive a fine and sandy bottom, tolerably free from rocks. In it are a few islands, the soil of which appeared to be good, though somewhat woody. The land near the river also seemed to be, in general, excellent; but that at a distance is very full of mountains, where it is said there are many lead mines."

Though once traveled by Indians; *coureurs de bois, voyageurs,* missionaries, early settlers, and raftsmen, the river today lies shallow and sand-barred, unnavigable except for small boats. State 60 heads across SAUK PRAIRIE, where Jonathan Carver found "the Great Town of the Saukies" in 1766 (*see Tour 19*). At 45.9 *m.* are the RUINS OF LODDE'S MILL (R), an old landmark overshadowed by a high, bare limestone cliff.

State 60 swings right at 47 *m.* into FAIR VALLEY, a rich, dark-soiled tributary of the main valley. This is a coulee—narrow and steep-walled, winding back into the hills and eventually reaching a blind end. The valley floor is rich with good earth washed or blown down from the hills.

Toward the west State 60 curves down into BADGER SLOUGH, 52.6 *m.,* a typical offshoot of the main channel formed during periods of high water. The stagnant bottoms shelter more frogs, mossback turtles, and snakes than the river itself. February and June floods, however, keep the waters fresh enough for good pickerel, strawberry bass, sunfish, and bullhead fishing.

In summer small boys, using grasshoppers or worms for bait, and bamboo poles or willow switches for rods, patiently fish the sloughs. Bullheads are the favorite catch. When this fish bites it pulls the cork deep under water. While other slough fish are scaled, the bullhead is usually skinned with a pair of pliers. As a more profitable pastime the boys catch and sell bullfrogs and turtles. The latter, generally bought locally for soup, bring from 25 to 50 cents apiece. The frogs are sometimes bought for shipment to hotel markets or to Florida swamps to aid in insect control. Nine fair-sized bullfrogs average a pound, worth from 20 to 90 cents.

At 55.1 *m.* Badger Slough widens and joins the river. The few farmers in the valley across which the river cuts raise watermelons and muskmelons, which they sell at roadside stalls throughout the season. This is rattlesnake country, rocky and dry. A few persons earn their living by catching the rattlers, which net a bounty of about 50 cents each. The best months are in July and August, when the snake is shedding its skin and is blind; armed with lassoes, bags, forked sticks, or guns, the hunters then seize whole nests at once. Usually they carry along tourniquets and serum as precautions against a poisonous bite.

The water tower, church steeples, and elm-lined streets of SPRING GREEN (*see Tour 20*) appear (L) in the center of the valley. A bluff face (R) is bare except for an even line of oaks upright on its rim, which resemble the feathered headdress of an Indian chief.

At 61.7 *m.* is the junction with US 14 (*see Tour 20*); between this junction and 72.7 *m.*, State 60 and US 14 are one route.

State 60 now leads through pine-dotted, sandy prairie. Prosperous farmers in tributary valleys raise corn, some of the State's best dairy cattle, and much of its prize-winning 4-H livestock.

At 72.7 *m.* is the junction with US 14 (*see Tour 20*).

GOTHAM, 73.2 *m.* (701 alt., 300 pop.), with its frame houses in disrepair, lies near the indistinguishable river bottom SITE OF RICHLAND CITY, a ghost village platted at the fork of the Pine and Wisconsin Rivers during the lumbering days of the 1860's and 1870's. Richland City grew rapidly because of the river traffic. Six years after its founding a Platteville newspaper wrote of it: "The town, already the most populous in the county, can boast of five or six good stores, a good steam sawmill, and thanks to the energy of Henry Powell, Esq., has one of the best steam flouring mills in the State of Wisconsin."

When the Prairie du Chien division of the Chicago, Milwaukee, St. Paul and Pacific R. R. was built, the tracks followed the boundaries of Iowa and Grant Counties on the southern riverbank, ignoring Richland County trading spots. The Wisconsin River changed its channel, and eventually what houses had not already been moved from the site of Richland City were washed away.

State 60 continues on a bluff slope along the Wisconsin. The wide river bed stretches between two high ridges that mark the level of the land before the river wore out its groove. The main channel, less than 30 feet wide, twists among densely wooded islands, a nesting ground for herons and kingfishers; here turtles and frogs sun themselves on rotten logs. In the limestone bluffs cavelike formations have been left by the erratic waters.

BOGUS BLUFF (R), 74.2 *m.*, is a jutting 200-foot formation hiding COUNTERFEITER'S CAVE. Prior to and during the Civil War period, the counterfeiting of bank notes was rampant throughout the Mississippi region, for in such places of transient trade, spurious bills could be passed without detection. Counterfeiter's Cave sheltered a successful gang for many years before it was closed by Federal operatives.

PORT ANDREWS, 89.3 *m.* (35 pop.), is an old-looking village built on the sides and bottoms of a gorge-cut slope that fronts the river. COUMBE ISLAND looms up frequently in the middle of the channel, connected with the bank by catfish set-lines. The catfish caught in the Wisconsin sometimes weigh as much as 70 pounds, and resemble half-grown pigs. They are a sort of overgrown bullhead and have the same sleek black and yellow skin and the same teardrop build, broad and round at the head and tapering to a narrow tail.

It is along here that the "river rats"—so named by the towns-people—live easy, squalid, half-nomadic lives. These people, many of whom are illiterate, fish the river for redhorse, pickerel, slapjack, bass, and catfish; they live in makeshift tin and frame huts in the river bottoms, or houseboats in which they travel up and down the river, tuning pianos, and peddling woven baskets, patent medicines, and inexpensive supplies. At 92.6 *m.* State 60 crosses Knapp's Creek; the river swings L. and disappears behind a wall of underbrush.

At 97.3 *m.* is the junction with US 61 (*see Tour 11*); between this junction and 98.5 *m.,* State 60 and US 61 are one route (*see Tour 11*).

WAUZEKA, 108.7 *m.* (644 alt., 519 pop.), is at the confluence of the Kickapoo and Wisconsin Rivers; many of the town's inhabitants are retired dairy farmers. Other villagers work on the Kickapoo or the Milwaukee Railroads, in the box factory, which turns out thin, round, wooden cheese boxes, or in the cheese factory and creamery. Wauzeka grew rapidly during lumbering years, enjoying railroad, high-way, and river trade. The Kickapoo River drains the apple-orchard country to the north. Farmers in this rambling valley raise chickens, tobacco, and corn. Their speech is a distinct drawling nasal not found elsewhere in Wisconsin.

West of Wauzeka the flood plain is broad and parklike, with the river's underbrush visible at the foot of the L. ridge. At 119.4 *m.* is the junction with US 18 (*see Tour 23*); between this junction and PRAIRIE DU CHIEN, 125 *m.* (643 alt., 3,943 pop.) (*see Tour 13*), State 60 and US 18 are one route (*see Tour 23*).

Tour 23

Milwaukee—Madison—Prairie du Chien—(Marquette, Iowa); US 18. Milwaukee to Iowa Line, 181.1 *m.*

Chicago & North Western Ry. parallels route between Milwaukee and Fenni-more.
Hard-surfaced and oiled-gravel roadbed.
Accommodations adequate.

Once an Indian trail between the Lake Michigan shore and the Mississippi River, US 18 now bears the heavy trucks, pleasure cars, and hitchhikers of modern America. It swings westward across the breadth of the State, linking industrial Milwaukee, Wisconsin's largest city; harried Madison, its political center; and drowsy Prairie du Chien, its second oldest settlement. Everywhere along the route the land is rich in crops and dairy herds; barns and silos rise against rounded hills; honeysuckle grows on low farm house porches.

Section a.   MILWAUKEE to MADISON; 82.4 m., US 18

MILWAUKEE, 0 *m.* (592 alt., 578,249 pop.) (*see Milwaukee*). Milwaukee is at the junction with US 41 (*see Tour 2*), US 141 (*see Tour 3*), and State 42 (*see Tour 3A*).

From the Chicago and North Western Ry. depot, foot of Juneau Park, US 18 follows Prospect Ave. to E. State St., crosses the Wisconsin Ave. viaduct, then turns west on the W. Blue Mound Rd. and proceeds through the outlying districts of Milwaukee and WAUWA-TOSA (652 alt., 21,194 pop.) (*see Milwaukee*). Beyond the green-lawned suburbs the highway enters a truck gardening area, with many signs advertising fresh eggs and spring chickens. At 8.5 *m.* is the junction with US 45 (*see Tour 5*).

At GOERKES CORNERS, 14.6 *m.,* is the junction with State 30 (*see Tour 23A*).

The prosperity of the countryside west of Goerkes Corners is evinced in new white barns, silvery windmills, numerous tractors ranging heavily over planted hillsides, sleek cows grazing in lush pastures. Here the highway is in the fluid milk region that embraces half of Waukesha and part of Milwaukee Counties; milk from this district is sent daily to the lakeshore industrial belt of Wisconsin and Illinois. The butter-yellow barns of Fox's GOLDEN GUERNSEY FARM (*open to visitors*), 17.5 *m.,* lie in long slabs on the hilltop, an example of shining efficiency and mass production in the dairy business. Set solidly in stone, the buildings are weatherproof and clean. Inside, washed cows in steel stanchions, workers in neat denim, bright churns and pasteurizing coils tell the story of a constant vigilance against milk-borne disease.

WAUKESHA (Ind., little Fox), 18.5 *m.* (821 alt., 17,176 pop.), seat of Waukesha County, is an industrial city set in the midst of green agricultural acres. Almost all traces of the Waukesha that once was the "Saratoga of the West" have long since been obliterated.

In 1833 the Potawatomi, who had a village here on the Little Fox River, ceded their land to the Federal Government. The following year Alonzo and Morris Cutler, searching for a water-power site and timber for a sawmill, came upon this fertile valley and remained here. Other settlers soon came to the tiny village which was named Prairie-ville. The first were hard-bitten easterners, who, for reasons largely economic, left their homes and came west. On their heels arrived English, Irish, Scottish, Welsh, and Germans, and still later, Danes, Norwegians, Swedes, and Poles. In the 1840's and 1850's the Germans came in such numbers that they still constitute the dominant national stock.

When the supply of timber had been exhausted, a large gristmill replaced the sawmill, and flour making became a major industry, encouraged by William August Barstow, later Governor of Wisconsin (1854-6). As early as 1842 the village was manufacturing plows and other machinery for the rapidly developing farm lands in southern Wisconsin. Three separate companies began to quarry the pure limestone that went into many buildings in Milwaukee. The rails of Wisconsin's first railroad were laid between Milwaukee and Waukesha in 1851.

CARROLL COLLEGE, East and College Aves., founded in 1841 as Prairieville Academy, was renamed in 1846. An act of the legislature in 1857 established the House of Refuge for juvenile delinquents of both sexes, now the STATE INDUSTRIAL SCHOOL FOR BOYS, College Ave. and State St.

Waukesha was an abolitionist center in pre-Civil War days. The *American Freeman* (1844-8) was printed here and spread Waukesha's aggressive anti-slavery sentiments. As early as 1842 Waukesha, called "that abolition hole," was an important station on the Underground Railroad. Escaped slaves were spirited from one house to another as indignant slave owners or their agents pursued their property. Waukesha farmers and tradesmen left their plows and counters and drove long days and nights with hidden, frightened human cargoes until they had reached the Canadian border. A tablet in CUTLER PARK, in the center of the city, honors Lyman Goodnow, who conducted to Canada the first slave to escape northward through Wisconsin.

In post-Civil War years the city returned to calmer ways; milling and quarrying gained steadily in importance. Two new foundries were begun. Carroll College, now under the control of the Presbyterian synod, dedicated itself to furthering classical education and Christian conduct among its student body.

In 1869 Colonel Richard Dunbar, a visiting New Yorker, drank from Waukesha's numerous small springs and soon announced that the waters had cured his incurable ills. Through Dunbar's ardent sponsorship Waukesha spring waters became one of the Nation's most publicized nostrums, and Waukesha was suddenly a fashionable watering place. From all over the country came hypochondriacs and the genuinely ill, men and women of fashion, quacks, confidence men, and promoters. Some bathed, some drank, some scooped up the profits.

By day the streets were bright with ostrich plumes, taffeta gowns, and gay parasols of promenading elegance. Men in checked suits and fancy vests lolled in taverns or swung their canes outside the barber shops. At night the brilliantly lighted hotels were the stage on which the actors danced and played. At one time there were 34 boarding houses and hotels here. Many of the hotels, stone or brick structures fashioned in the heavy amplitudes of the period, often housed hundreds of guests apiece. The FOUNTAIN SPRINGS HOUSE, 200 S. Grand Ave., is now the only reminder of that golden past. As unaccountably as it had begun, the health fad waned in the late nineties; the great hotels were razed or put to other uses. By 1934 two mud baths were the only survivors of the institutions along the once gay road to health.

In 1905 the METROPOLITAN CHURCH ASSOCIATION, 200 S. Grand Ave., members of which are called Holy Jumpers or Shakers, bought the old Fountain Spring House and established national headquarters in the empty halls. This sect was founded in the nineteenth century by a strange pair of self-sacrificing Chicago missionaries who poured much of their considerable fortunes into the cause. From the first the association devoted itself to spreading the Word of God in Christian and heathen lands, to establishing orphanages and domestic science schools, to caring for the needy. In time, as the organization grew, the annual camp meetings at Waukesha attracted great crowds from all over the State and Nation.

For a while after the health boom, all local enterprise languished. But water power and Waukesha's nearness to the lakeshore cities soon attracted industry. New factories replaced the faded resorts. At the present time brewing, quarrying, and the manufacture of gasoline motors, church furniture, metal castings, aluminum, steel sashes, air conditioning units, bottlewashing machinery, cement tiles, gelatine dessert, malted milk, and dairy products employ the major part of the city's working population. Bottled spring, mineral, and distilled waters are still listed among Waukesha's products—both as curative drinks and as sparkling waters to make Scotch and rye highballs.

At 26.7 m. is the junction with State 83.

Left on State 83 to WALES (L), 1.6 m. (1,002 alt., 132 pop.). When John Hughes, a Welsh settler, first saw the country about Waukesha, then Prairieville, he was homesick for Cambria. Government Hill reminded him slightly of Snowdon; there was Wales in the landscape. After he had written his friends about the hills and the valleys between, the Welsh came in scores, contributed their share to the building of villages like Prairieville, and founded several almost completely Welsh settlements within Waukesha County. Wales is as homogeneous as any of them; the townspeople, steeped in the ways of their fathers, are loyal to things Cambrian. Music, singing in particular, is relished by a Welshman as much as the eternal kaus (cheese) and tea on his table. Wales, true to ancient pattern, was early celebrating the great Eisteddfod festival of harvest and song. Local singers and poets were rewarded in the same elaborate ceremony that accompanied the homeland's annual recognition of its bards. Though the Eisteddfod celebration has been discontinued, for the last seven years the Welsh have revived Gymanfa Ganu (see Music), a custom of the British Welsh. And still loyal to their honored Saint 300 to 400 people gather annually to observe St. David's Day.

The STATE SANATORIUM (R) was opened in 1907 when the campaign against tuberculosis was beginning to demand the attention of public-minded citizens. There are facilities here for the treatment of 238 tubercular patients. Although both convalescent men and women may remain in the sanatorium for treatment, some of the men are sent to Tomahawk Lake Camp north of Rhinelander for physical hardening through work.

US 18 now passes through the last miles of kettle moraine country, and the bumpy landscape levels away into Jefferson and Dane Counties.

Many of the farms here dispose of their milk to near-by condenseries and cheese factories. The WISCONSIN MASONIC HOME (L), 32.5 *m.*, was built 20 years ago on the site of one of the popular resort hotels of the Waukesha spa period to care for aged Masons and the wives, widows, or mothers of Masons. GOLDEN LAKE, 36.2 *m.*, emerges from surrounding swampland, its shores heavily wooded, its waters clean and clear. The highway has now passed out of the fluid milk belt; as the soil becomes more sandy, it is used as pasture and for growing feed crops. Fat hogs sleep in the sun or rub their bristled backs against the fence posts.

JEFFERSON, 49.5 *m.* (792 alt., 2,639 pop.), at the junction of the Rock and Crawfish Rivers, has two or three modern factories; other buildings are well kept but worn, some being nearly a century old.

In 1836 several wandering easterners settled here for the winter. Others followed, lured by the free land in the Wisconsin Territory. The first settlers were succeeded by Germans, part of the great flood that poured into Wisconsin in the 1840's. The settlement grew slowly; slow growth, indeed, is a characteristic of Jefferson's early history. There were few booms, no fads which flourished and died overnight; in 1845 there were less than 80 inhabitants. In 1866 the Reverend B. F. Rogers founded the Jefferson Liberal Institute, a free-thought academy, but 13 years later economic difficulties became so acute that the school building had to be sold to the city to pay the mortgage.

Local stories say that Jefferson's only boom came when a pair of sly metropolitan land sharks appeared in the 1840's, with a story of a canal shortly to be built between Milwaukee and Jefferson. Those were the days when communication by water with the Great Lakes or the Mississippi River sent land prices sky-high in Wisconsin. Jeffersonians fought for the privilege of buying useless land. When a steamboat, purposely sent by fraudulent promoters to stimulate the boom, actually came up the Rock River from St. Louis, local augurs cast aside all caution and predicted a future of metropolitan proportions for the little city at the river junction. Then, before the townsmen knew what had happened, the promoters departed; nothing remained but tracts of swampland with weather-beaten markers reading "SOLD."

A chair factory was established in 1856, a woolen mill in 1866, and in 1868, a shoe factory. After a hundred years the city also has an upholstery factory, a wood products factory, a packing plant, two carding mills, a condensed milk plant, and a creamery.

West of Jefferson the creamery and condensery area continues into the Rock River dairy region. Valleys and low tree-covered hills, elongated glacial drumlins, are sown to pasture. At 56.5 *m.* a tobacco farm introduces a new area. In midsummer and later, pale flowers on spindly stalks reach above broad tobacco leaves in these fields. To prevent cross fertilization with other strains, flower heads are sometimes tightly hooded with paper bags, and whole acres of strange paper blossoms rattle in the wind (*see Tour 7*).

At 63.5 *m.* is the junction with US 12 (*see Tour 19*); between this junction and Madison US 18 and US 12 are one route.

At 65.7 *m.* (R) a farmer has built a barn sturdy and round as a silo. The rugged stone base is surmounted with a few feet of board, a disc-shaped roof, and a picturesque turret. The building is set deep in the ground like a solid fortress. Though advocated by F. H. King of the University of Wisconsin, inventor of the round silo, the round barn has never become popular in Wisconsin. The limitations of the circular construction make enlargement difficult; storage space is inadequate; and because the barn cannot be built against a slope, it loses the natural advantage of two entrances at different levels.

At 77 *m.* is the junction with US 51 (*see Tour 7*); between this junction and a point at 78 *m.* US 18 and US 51 are one route.

From a hilltop, 79.2 *m.,* is a view of Lake Monona, its far shore fringed with houses; behind rise the smokestacks, office buildings, and the capitol dome of Madison. At 80.6 *m.* is the junction with US 14 (*see Tour 20*). US 18 follows Olin Ave. in Madison to Park St., R. on Park St. to University Ave.

MADISON, 82.4 *m.* (859 alt., 57,899 pop.) (*see Madison*).

Madison is at the junction with US 151 (*see Tour 6*), US 12 (*see Tour 19*), State 113 (*see Tour 19B*), US 14 (*see Tour 20*), and State 30 (*see Tour 23A*).

Section b.   MADISON to IOWA LINE; 98.7 m., US 18

South on Park St. from its junction with University Ave., 0 *m.,* to Regent St.; R. on Regent St. to Monroe St., 0.7 *m.;* Monroe St. leads L. out of Madison.

Outside of the city US 18 runs across a region bearing many signs of glaciation—swamps, dumpy little hills, pebbles, and glacial boulders strung out in pastures From the dairy farms here milk is shipped in several directions—south into Green County, the Swiss cheese area; east into Madison for fluid consumption; and northeast into Dodge County to be made into brick cheese. The Dane County ASYLUM AND POOR FARM, 8.1 *m.,* was built in 1854.

VERONA, 9.3 *m.* (983 alt., 455 pop.) (*see Tour 23B*), is at the junction with State 69 (*see Tour 23B*).

US 18 crosses a broad marsh and mounts one of a series of far-flung hills, outlying ribs of the greater Military Ridge to the west. Hills billow away in every direction, in summer a patchwork of dark green oak clumps, lighter green willow groves, silver-green birches, and the yellow-green of grass and corn. On the more accessible slopes stand patches of shoulder-high hazelnut bushes, with horned, fuzzy leaves, and gnarled, beautifully grained roots that old settlers whittle and oil into napkin rings. In spring these fields will be plowed, the hillsides half dark with the fecund colors of upturned earth; in the autumn corn will be cut and dried in shocks along the slopes or in cribs in the valleys.

MT. HOREB, 19.9 *m.* (1,230 alt., 1,425 pop.), crookedly spread out on the ridge, is one of the largest farm villages through which US 18 passes on its way to the Mississippi. The Norwegian and Swiss origin of many of its founders is revealed in the name of the townspeople and the games they play. One game, played now for more than forty years by Mt. Horeb and Monroe farmers, is *Le Hornuss* (Swiss, Hornet), named for the whizzing sound made by a hard rubber disc which the players whack from one end to the other of a 300-yard field. A sort of long distance ping-pong, *Le Hornuss* is fought with willow sticks called "switches," with shieldlike weapons, called "shingles," and with the hornet itself. With the offense team shouting *"Weit dr ne?"* (Bernese, can you take it?), and the defenders roaring back *"Gat ume!"* (Bernese, just give it to us!), the game commences. The attacking team starts from one end of the field, their switches batting out three hornets in succession; the other team attempts to intercept the discs with shingles. When every man on the attacking team has had three chances to knock the hornet behind the enemy goal the other team takes the offensive. On crisp Sunday autumn afternoons the Hornet field is abuzz.

There is also some fox hunting in the Mt. Horeb district. Hunters and hounds are driven in cars into the grassy countryside, where bushbeaters rout the fox into the open. Barking dogs and yelling people pursue; but instead of sounding the traditional curved fox horn, the hunters blare their auto horns.

At 23.5 *m.* is the junction with a dirt road.

Right on this road, which plunges down through densely banked woods to an open space on the valley floor. In a still lower hollow and surrounded by a spindling white picket fence, is (L) LITTLE NORWAY or NISSEDAHLE (Nor., valley of the elves), 1 *m.* (adm.: *adults 55¢; children 30¢; large groups by appointment, 30¢ a person*). On the north slope of the hollow several little hewn-oak houses, with sod roofs, bright blue window casements, and massive barred doors, look like a child's candystick village. Rooms are furnished in the heavy, brilliant style of Scandinavia; box beds covered with bright hand-made spreads are built against the walls. Various wooden chests are on display: "Tinas," used as lunch baskets; sailor's chests, with a broader base than top; and wedding chests, with inwrought designs. There are hand-turned articles, ranging from iron hinges and silverware to "lovespoons," chained together and carved from a single stick of wood. A large collection of Norwegiana includes a Grieg manuscript and umbrella, two canes of Ole Bull, six Emil Björn water colors of frolicking elves, a complete cobbling set, a set of "apostle spoons," dating back to 1694 (said to be one of two such sets in the world), gold looped earrings of the founder's sailor grandfather, two drinking glasses made in the motherland in 1811, and other carvings, furniture, and household effects.

This collection was made when Little Norway was founded in 1926 by Isak Dahle, a Norse-American businessman of Chicago, who acquired 160 acres here and set a crew of Norwegian artisans and craftsmen to work making the land look as much as possible like the Valley of the Elves in Norway. The guide, who has shown Little Norway to more than 50,000 visitors during the last decade, is a Latvian called Stikky, a tall rugged man who autographs pictures of himself: "H. A. Stikhevitz—there is not much wits." "A European at large," as he calls himself, Stikky is the only occupant of the houses; though the treasures are locked away in bank vaults during the winter, he stays on with a cat for company, reading and writing.

Right at 24 *m.* to the junction with a town road, where there is a sign pointing to the Cave of the Mounds.

Right on this road to the junction with a graveled road, 0.1 *m.;* L. here and downhill to the CAVE OF THE MOUNDS (*adm.: adults, 44¢; children, 28¢; groups of 25 or more, 28¢ per person before noon and after 6 p.m. weekdays; conducted tours every 10 minutes between 7 a.m. and 10 p.m. daily*), 0.2 *m.,* on the valley floor. The Cave of the Mounds is an underground cavern, which was formed by the action of subterranean waters. It was discovered on August 4, 1939, when workers blasting stone in a quarry here exposed one side of the cave, which had no natural entrance. The cave was opened to the public on May 30, 1940. The explored section is approximately 1,000 feet long and varies in height from 15 to 30 feet. The principal formations are stalactites, stalagmites, and helictites. In one of the "rooms" cave onyx is found in large quantities, and there are several specimens of an extremely rare formation of crystallized white limestone with black stripings caused by deposits of oxide of manganese. Many of the odd rock formations are colored with lines of red, orange, yellow, and brown, due to the presence of oxides of iron. One of the caverns contains a well-preserved fossil of a cephalopod, the largest animal of the Ordovician period, a geologic era when the galena limestone of this region was deposited at the bottom of the Ordovician Sea.

BLUE MOUNDS, 24.8 *m.* (1,301 alt., 182 pop.), confined to little more than a city block, lies in the shadow of a great hill of the same name.

Right from Blue Mounds village on a graveled road to the crest of BLUE MOUND, 0.9 *m.,* a huge, tapering, 1,716-foot cone rising above the surrounding counties. In the privately owned PARK here (*adm.: 40¢ for car; $1 for bus*) are facilities for community gatherings, ball playing, fishing, picnicking, and fireplace marshmallow roasts. Timber is cleared for splendid long views. To the east, south, and west are far-reaching plains and ridges; to the north, the heavily wooded valley of the Wisconsin River, and, beyond, the dark bulk of the Baraboo Range. Indians once used this windy spot as a lookout and flint quarry; they believed that the blue haze, that clouds the mound when it is seen from below, was smoke from the pipe of their god, Wakanda, the earth maker.

US 18 begins to climb and dip over steadily higher ridges until it joins the MILITARY ROAD on Military Ridge, the trail built between 1835-8 along which American soldiers marched, rode their horses, and drew their clumsy wagons the width of the State from Green Bay to Prairie du Chien. From the prairielike top of the ridge, bristling with tall prize corn, the land slopes down in long alluvial stretches of fields and pastures. Where US 18 runs close to the escarpment face, the land (R) is pitched and irregular.

At 41.6 *m.,* on the ridge above DODGEVILLE (1,253 alt., 1,937 pop.) (*see Tour 12*), is the junction with US 151 (*see Tour 12*).

This southwest section of Wisconsin, once the lead and zinc mining country (*see Tour 12*), is now a rich agricultural region. The first farming here began in the 1830's when the early miners planted small vegetable gardens and a few acres of crops. Later many combined farming and mining, and eventually, when mineral production fell off, they entirely abandoned their shafts and became successful farmers.

MONTFORT, 56.5 *m.* (1,119 alt., 554 pop.), rambling down a deep hillside, has a mining-town history dating back to 1827, when a wandering ox driver stopped here for water on his way from Galena, Illinois. Finding both a spring and lumps of pure lead crystals, he remained. Soon he was joined by other miners. They built makeshift log huts near the spring, chopped the forest off the hillside, and "gophered" the surrounding slopes and pastures with the holes and pits still visible near the muddy stream. After the lead mines had been exhausted, Montford started afresh as a farming community, leaving the old pits as relics of its past.

The soil west of Montfort is a rich, loose type of wind-blown loess suitable for diversified farming. All along US 18 are evidences of the fight against soil erosion. Large gullies have been dammed with concrete and earth; smaller gullies and eroded spots have been planted to trees or allowed to grow back to thick native vegetation; some cultivated fields have been terraced and a new pattern of farming which grows crops in alternate strips is noticeable. In an attempt to increase wildlife, patches of evergreen have been planted, each with bird feeding stations.

The Military Ridge slopes off gently to the south for mile upon rolling mile, suddenly breaking on the north into billowing hills; cattle are brown and white specks on the green slopes. In places farms spread out over as many as 400 acres; straight-planted rows of corn form rippling green hallways; in the pastureland sleek cows of a Baumgarten, Ketterer, Gottweiler, Bach, or Ruddersdorf, eat their fill of succulent bluegrass.

FENNIMORE, 67.9 *m.* (1,196 alt., 1,341 pop.), ordinary in appearance but extraordinary for its humming farmer trade, lies on a point of the Military Ridge that drains four ways: to the Blue, the Green, the Platte, and the Grant Rivers.

Fennimore is the southwestern headquarters for a Soil Conservation Service of the U. S. Department of Agriculture, and nearly 100 farmers (1938) in the project northeast of Fennimore cooperate with the local staff. The problem of soil erosion became recognized here only after serious damage. As social and economic factors increased the pressure on farmers to produce more corn, hogs, and dairy products, each year they cut more timber for pasture, plowed more prairie land for fields, cultivating up and down slopes. At first erosion and soil removal were gradual; then as the topsoil became thinner erosion accelerated. Large gullies, formerly confined to land adjoining streams, developed in the uplands; small gullies appeared in good fields, and the topsoil plowed into them was promptly washed out by the next heavy rain. Even the wildlife balance was destroyed with the destruction of cover, nesting areas, and food supplies. Although the farmers who own land on the demonstration projects benefit by cooperation with the Service, the main objective is to show by example how erosion can be checked, how nature's balance can be restored and at the same time provide the products needed by society.

Fennimore's CREAMERY has expanded with the growing herds of Guernsey, Holstein, Brown Swiss, and Jersey cattle in this district. Wisconsin dairying first became stabilized about 1890, when a hand-operated cream separator and the Babcock butterfat tester were put on the market, enabling milk producers and buyers to pay farmers on the basis of the butterfat content of their milk (*see Agriculture*).

Fennimore is at the junction with State 61 (*see Tour 11*).

Beyond Fennimore the outlines of Military Ridge disappear in a tumble of rugged hills and valleys on the Wisconsin side of the Mississippi bluffs, a steeply pitched country, shady with tremendous knotty trees, lined with cow trails, cut through by rushing creeks. V's in the hills lead back into clefts choked with wood-growth, sumac clumps, wild strawberry patches, or bare-faced greenish limestone, thinly touched with moss.

At 86.3 *m.* is the junction with County P.

Left on County P to the junction with County X, 4.6 *m.;* R. on County X to the junction with County Z, 7.6 *m.;* R. on County Z to WYALUSING STATE PARK, 8.8 *m.* (*facilities for camping, picnicking, hiking; no bathing*). A sign at each intersection indicates the correct road.

Wyalusing Park, a tract of 1,671 acres, lies high in the hills above the Mississippi River, second largest of Wisconsin's State parks. Created in 1917, it was first named for Nelson Dewey, but in 1937, when the Nelson Dewey homestead was purchased and made into a park (*see Tour 11*), the name was changed to its present form. From the park is a view far out over the river, west to Iowa and north to Prairie du Chien on the level plain. Below in the valley the historic waters of the Wisconsin River enter the Mississippi. The bluffs contain caves, waterfalls, odd rock formations; they are covered with heavy growth, sheltering wild birds, wild flowers, and small native animals.

Marquette and Joliet, the first white men known to have traveled the upper Mississippi, paddled among the islands that clog the Wisconsin's channel here. The trade route they established between Green Bay and Prairie du Chien, the Fox-Wisconsin waterway, was for a century and a half the main artery of travel in the Northwest.

SENTINEL RIDGE, the park's crest, stands 1,108 feet above sea level, 530 feet above the Mississippi. POINT LOOKOUT and SIGNAL POINT on the ridge offer views of both rivers. On Signal Point is a group of Indian earthworks, including three bear effigy mounds. SAND CAVE, a shallow cavern, is hidden among hardwood trees some distance behind the baseball grounds; TREASURE CAVE is an aperture in the rocks on the trail below Point Lookout. Other interesting points are BIG AND LITTLE CANYONS, PICTURED ROCK, EAGLE EYE BLUFF, BLACK HAWK MONUMENT, GLENN GROTTO, SUNSHINE HILL, PINE TRAIL, and THE KNOB.

West of the junction with County P, US 18 swerves downward through hills that steadily grow steeper and stonier, dotted with crazily leaning hardwood trees, pitted with quarries. A few farms are perched precariously on the hillsides. After crossing the bottoms of the Wisconsin River flood plain, US 18 reaches the great concrete bridge that lifts in a long arc over the river.

BRIDGEPORT, 92.2 *m.,* once a cattle market, is now a straggling river village; it was nearly destroyed by fire late in 1936.

At 92.4 *m.* is the junction with State 60 (*see Tour 22*); between this junction and a point at **98** *m.* State 60 and US 18 are one route. West of the junction the highway swings diagonally across the fan-shaped prairie on which Prairie du Chien lies. Ahead is the level hazy line of the Mississippi bluffs, with steep, tree-covered Sentinel Ridge (L).

PRAIRIE DU CHIEN, **98** *m.* (643 alt., 3,943 pop.) (*see Tour 13*), is at the junction with State 35 (*see Tour 13*) and State 60 (*see Tour 22*). US 18 crosses the Iowa Line, 98.7 *m.,* on the INTERSTATE TOLL BRIDGE (*70¢ for car and driver one way, $1.15 round trip; 10¢ each way for each additional passenger*), one mile east of Marquette, Iowa.

Tour 23A

Junction with US 18 to Madison; 67.6 *m.,* State 30.

Oiled-gravel and low-type bituminous roadbed.
Small village accommodations.

State 30 connects Milwaukee and Madison, providing an alternate route to US 18 (*see Tour 23*). The distance of the two routes is almost equal, but State 30 is narrower, less traveled, and not so well surfaced. Because of light traffic, it has been chosen as a Youth Hostel route, and now, in addition to being a thoroughfare for milk trucks rolling up and down its low hills in early morning, State 30 is a line of "safeguarded adventure" for hikers, cyclists, and horseback riders. Their overnight destination may be any one of the pleasant farmhouses along the way.

Branching right from US 18 (*see Tour 23*) at GOERKES CORNERS, 0 *m.,* State 30 leaves the noisy traffic of outer Milwaukee and enters peaceful moraine country, where the land surface is humped strangely in mounds and ridges, or sunken in duck ponds and grassy craters. For all its roughness, it is intensively cultivated, largely by truck gardeners, who haul their fresh lettuce and other vegetables to Goerkes Corners and Milwaukee.

DELAFIELD, 10.9 *m.,* with its white frame and yellow brick buildings, lies in the shade of old trees; at times from surrounding swamps and lakes can be heard the cries of marsh birds. The HOMESTEAD HOTEL, a frame building painted white and brown, with old ornate woodwork, was for years a stopping place for coaches on the old Milwaukee-Madison stage route.

Right from Delafield on County C past the STATE FISH HATCHERY and the Cox Stables to the junction with a dirt road, 0.2 *m.;* L. here to the campus of ST. JOHN'S MILITARY ACADEMY, 0.4 *m.,* Episcopal seminary for boys (*dress parade at 4 p.m. spring Sundays*). The buildings of St. John's are of native gray limestone, slab stone, and colored boulders, set well apart on level graveled grounds. Dormitories have Gothic archways and narrow medieval windows overgrown with ivy. In the center of the grounds is a shady park, marked with class stones. Right of the park is a beacon-topped monument, which carries such slogans as: "Don't be a molly-coddle," "The game is not over until the whistle blows," "Carry on," and "Play the game."

At 0.7 *m.* is the junction with County B; L. on County B to the junction with a dirt road, 1.2 *m.;* R. on the dirt road to NASHOTAH HOUSE, 1.8 *m.,* oldest Episcopal seminary in the Middle West. Encouraged by Bishop Jackson Kemper, three young men came here from the East in 1841 to found a monastic Anglo-Catholic mission, to serve Indians and whites, and to train candidates for the priesthood. They purchased from the Government 464 acres of heavily timbered land on Upper Nashotah Lake and built the BLUE HOUSE, which still stands though it has been moved from its original site. Their mission was supported by student labor, contributions from missionary societies and friends, and, to some extent, by the produce from their farm. In 1850 the monastic idea was abandoned.

A tall preaching cross of rough granite marks the original SITE OF RED CHAPEL, built in 1842 and dedicated to St. Silvanus, patron saint of the wilderness. Today Red Chapel stands beside the faded Blue House. Inside is a bare whitewashed room, with a simple altar, crude altar cross, wooden candlesticks, and rough wooden benches. A Requiem Eucharist is held here annually on Commencement Day. Overlooking Nashotah Lake is a CEMETERY (L), called "The Westminster of the American Church" because of the many graves of church founders and benefactors. The GRAVE OF JAMES LLOYD BRECK, one of Nashotah Mission's founders, is designated by a monumental cross. Near by is the GRAVE OF BISHOP KEMPER (1789-1870), first missionary bishop of the Protestant Episcopal Church, who founded three colleges, established seven dioceses, opened numerous schools and academies, and planted the Episcopal Church in the Northwest.

At 11.4 *m.* is the junction with a graveled road.

Right on this road across the reedy Bark River to CUSHING MEMORIAL PARK (*parking area, picnic facilities, refreshment stand*), 0.2 *m.,* on the old Cushing homestead. This park, a green hillside sloping down to the marsh, was established in 1915 by the State and the Waukesha County Historical Society. Since that time hundreds of trees have been planted as memorials to Wisconsin Civil War soldiers. High on the slope is an imposing granite shaft, commemorating the three Cushing brothers, all of whom won distinction for bravery during the Civil War. William (1842-74), a naval commander, with 14 officers and men sank the Confederate ram, *Albemarle,* in 1864. Alonzo (1841-63), a lieutenant colonel, was killed at Gettysburg. Howard (1838-71), a lieutenant, served during the war and was killed in 1871 fighting Indians on the Southwest border.

State 30 follows the edge of the Bark River marsh into NEMAHBIN, 13.1 *m.,* a few old houses and buildings huddled between the UPPER AND LOWER NEMAHBIN LAKES. A rickety ROLLER MILL (R) still grinds flour and feed as it did nearly a century ago. Westward the land spreads out into a flat sweep of grass country, where occasional fences of thickly netted wire screen white flocks of chickens from the road. Far back on both sides of the highway are rambling country-gentlemen estates, owned by Milwaukee industrialists. At about 16.7 *m.* State 30 enters a stretch of irregular, pleasant countryside, one of the three most concentrated drumlin regions in the United States. Wire and stone fences run helter-skelter across the land. Yellow-brick farmhouses are half hidden by hawthorn trees, red maple, and walls of bridal wreath; lawns are carefully mowed and raked, hedges neatly clipped.

JOHNSON CREEK, 31.8 *m.* (805 alt., 457 pop.), has a singular cleanliness about its buildings and lawns. Though this bright small village ships dairy produce all over America, its commercial and industrial activities are unsuspected, for it is nearly as quiet on the surface as the countryside in which it lies.

The H. C. CHRISTIANS COMPANY PLANT, with its home office and plant at Johnson Creek and a branch office at Chicago, is one of the largest wholesalers of butter and eggs in the Middle West. Butter is contracted from more than 75 creameries. The company's combined shipments aggregate some 2,000 carloads of butter and 500 carloads of eggs a year, the equivalent of a train 20 miles long. Other concerns in Johnson Creek supply condensed milk in barrel lots for the bakery, confectionery, and ice cream trades. The villagers, like the farmers who trade here, are largely of German stock.

In AZTALAN MOUND PARK (L), 35.9 *m.,* are ruins of a prehistoric Indian village built by an unknown people. Judge Nathaniel F. Hyer, who surveyed the site in 1837, named it Aztalan because he believed that the cultural remains might be those of Mexican Aztecs. Earthworks are heaped up on both banks of the Crawfish River; on the west bank are the foundations of two stockades of earth, covered with clay and grass, which protected the native homes scattered within. In the southwest corner of the enclosure are the ruins of a terraced pyramidal mound; in the northwest corner is a smaller ceremonial mound. Large numbers of human bones which archeologists have taken from the refuse pits indicate that the Indians, or whoever they were, were cannibalistic. Other relics—pottery, bones, shells, stones, copper artifacts—found in the pits and burial mounds prove that the culture of these tribes was alien to Wisconsin (*see Indians*). The terraces and truncated pyramids, the plastered walls and pits, the shells from the Gulf Coast identify Aztalan definitely with the culture of the Middle and Lower Mississippi rather than with the Upper Mississippi and Woodland culture found in other parts of the State.

LAKE MILLS, 38.7 *m.* (860 alt., 2,007 pop.), on the irregular shore of ROCK LAKE, is a city of broad lawns and shade trees. In the center of the city is a PARK with many trees fronting the business section. Near by are a shoe factory and dehydrated milk plant and on the city's outskirts are a pea-canning factory and a dairy equipment factory.

The CREAMERY PACKAGE MANUFACTURING COMPANY PLANT (*visitors allowed*), E. Lake and Creamery Sts., produces dairy equipment such as butter churns, printers, milk pumps, milk pasteurizers, bottle washers, cheese vats, and presses. Departments include an iron foundry, tank shop, woodworking shop, and sheet metal shop where stainless steel is formed, welded and polished.

After curving around Rock Lake, State 30 abruptly runs into higher and more steeply pitched countryside. Long red tobacco sheds begin to appear high on the hills, and many farms have cloth-covered hot-houses. Then the highway slopes down again to marshland and peat flats.

At 62.4 m. is the junction with US 51 (see Tour 7); between this junction and a point at 63.3 m., State 30 and US 51 are one route.

State 30 continues into the city to the junction of Park St. and University Ave.

MADISON, 67.6 m. (859 alt., 57,899 pop.) (see Madison).

Madison is at the junction with US 151 (see Tour 6), US 12 (see Tour 19), State 113 (see Tour 19B), US 14 (see Tour 20), and US 18 (see Tour 23).

Tour 23B

Verona—New Glarus—Monroe—(Orangeville, Ill.); State 69.
Verona to Illinois Line, 43.3 m.

Hard-surfaced roadbed.
Accommodations limited except at Monroe.

State 69 leads southward through the pleasant hills and valleys of the Wisconsin Swiss settlements. For some distance the Little Sugar River parallels the highway, its tiny tributaries threading through hummocky pastures on which Holstein and Brown Swiss cattle graze against a background of model farmsteads.

In VERONA, 0 m. (983 alt., 455 pop.), are small stores and pleasant shaded houses; behind the main street buildings rises (R) the white frame Auditorium Hotel, the Saturday-night meeting place for townsmen and farmers. Verona is at the junction with US 18 (see Tour 23).

State 69 cuts through a low ridge of bright pink and yellow sandstone, 4.5 m., then circles among low hills and woodlots covered with brush to BELLEVILLE (Fr., beautiful city), 10.1 m. (864 alt., 564 pop.). The village, lying on the Sugar River in the center of an oval plain, was named by an early settler, John Frederick, for his old home in Canada.

At 13.4 m. the highway descends the side of a ravine dark with massive rocks and wild-growth tangles. At 17.7 m. is a TOURIST CAMPGROUND.

NEW GLARUS, 18.4 *m.* (860 alt., 1,010 pop.), lies on the banks of the Little Sugar River. Old World patterns persist in this Swiss-settled community and on surrounding farms. Heavy bells, cast in some mountainous canton of Switzerland, hang from the necks of New Glarus cattle and chime with the slow movement of the herds; speech in street or field is often in the Swiss idiom; and quartets and choruses, fortified with *Schnitzel* and *Zuri beter,* yodel like the best of Europe's Alpine mountaineers.

The history of New Glarus begins in the central Europe of 1844 when, because of a partial crop failure and the rigorous times, the government of the Swiss Canton, Glarus, appropriated $600 for organized emigration to North America. An emigration society was formed, and $2,000 more was raised by private subscription. Early in 1845 the society dispatched Judge Nicholas Duerst, 48 years old, and Fridolin Streiff, a 29-year-old blacksmith, to America to find and purchase land for a colony. Carrying money in trust for each of 106 subscribers to the project, they were instructed to choose a locality similar to Glarus in climate, soil, and general characteristics. Each subscriber was to have a tract of 20 acres with timber, pasture, and tillable land.

The two men arrived in New York in May 1845; the next two months they traveled across the mountains and through Illinois, Iowa, Missouri, and Wisconsin seeking the ideal spot. On June 27 they finally found this oval valley, like a great natural amphitheater, and in its center the knoll on which the church now stands. Duerst and Streiff purchased 1,200 acres of farmland and 80 acres of good timber in the valley.

Back in Glarus the departure of the two pioneers had aroused an enthusiasm for emigration that permeated the whole canton. Finally on April 16, 1845, 193 men, women, and children set sail across the Atlantic.

The crossing took 49 days. After landing at Baltimore the Swiss immigrants traveled by rail and canal boat to Pittsburgh, where they embarked on river steamers that carried them down the Ohio to the Mississippi, then up the Mississippi to St. Louis. Here, where they were to meet Streiff and Duerst, they found only a letter from a man named Blumer, of Allentown, saying that the pioneers were somewhere in Illinois in search of land. Unfamiliar with the language of the country, the colonists waited in the frontier metropolis for guides. Some of them became disheartened and returned to the home country, some left for private employment, others died; from 193 their number dwindled to 108.

Finally the group sent out two men to search for Duerst and Streiff. These couriers went by water and land routes through Illinois and Wisconsin until one day, coming to an opening in the timber, they discovered Duerst and Streiff working on a cabin. Duerst immediately set out for St. Louis to guide the colonists to their new home in Wisconsin. Meanwhile, the distracted band had moved up the Mississippi to Galena, capital of the lead region. Duerst, who might as well have gone down the Illinois River, fortunately chose instead to follow the Old Lead Trail to the Mississippi; he, too, arrived at Galena and there encountered his fellow countrymen.

Though the party managed to hire teams to carry the women and children and provisions, all but the smallest and weakest had to take turns at walking. On August 15, almost four months after they had set forth across the ocean, the weary Swiss arrived at the long-sought goal and found there a wilderness, with only the hills to remind them of their homeland.

At first the entire group lived in a single shelter that had been quickly erected in three days. The land was soon divided satisfactorily, and each man set out to clear his own tract. Their implements were of their own manufacture; the methods and markets of the country were entirely new to them. The first year they laboriously planted a small crop of potatoes, beans, vegetables, and a little corn; after 1850 they began to plant a little wheat, which they hauled overland by oxen to Milwaukee.

For 20 years the group lived in relative poverty, raising wheat as the principal crop. Though stock raisers by tradition, they kept only a few cattle, and it was their custom to make a Swiss hard cheese from the skimmed milk for their own needs. After the Civil War, when the price of wheat fell and the worn-out land no longer produced an adequate wheat yield, these farmers, forced by necessity, turned to dairying. It was then that the prosperity of the community began. They built larger barns and silos, bought more land, used fertilizers, and pioneered in advanced methods of livestock breeding. Swiss cheese found a market in the East, and Wisconsin dairy produce became recognized.

Upon the knoll, where the first log building of the Swiss Evangelical and Reformed Church was built, is now a new red-brick CHURCH with high Gothic windows. In the churchyard is the GRAVE OF NICHOLAS DUERST.

At the foot of the hill is a SWISS PIONEER MONUMENT; on the sides of the red-brown pedestal are inscribed the names of the first settlers. Surmounting the shaft is the granite figure of a Swiss pioneer, whose hand at hat brim shades eyes that search the southern hills.

On the second Sunday and Monday of each September the village celebrates Kilbi, a festival that originated centuries ago in old Glarus on the occasion of the dedication of the Reformed Church. As part of the celebration, the names of those confirmed in the church since 1860 are read to the congregation, and as each confirmation year is called those who entered the church in that year rise. Throughout Monday the celebration continues, with parades, folk games, dancing, and the eating of Swiss dishes.

An old-country industry is also continued here. Though a milk condensery is the largest plant in New Glarus, the most interesting is a lace factory at the southern edge of town. Here artisans draw designs for the lace, and other workers enlarge the patterns six times and follow it with their stitches.

South of New Glarus State 69 crosses a valley to the NEW GLARUS WOODS 20.1 *m.*, a 40-acre tract of oak forest set aside as a State roadside park (*camping and sanitary facilities; picnic tables, fireplaces, and good drinking water*). In the center of the park at 20.5 *m.* is the junction with County H; a monument here commemorates this road as the OLD LEAD TRAIL (*see Tour 12*), early route to the lead and zinc mines of southwestern Wisconsin. In 1832 General Henry Dodge and his rangers passed along this route in their pursuit of Black Hawk; 13 years later the first band of Swiss colonists followed the same path to their new home at New Glarus.

When the Swiss arrived at New Glarus the lead mines of Wisconsin were already flourishing. In the near-by woods are a few of the deep "badger holes," which the miners of that early period dug by hand; today most of the diggings are concealed by tall grasses or choked with leaves.

At 22.6 *m.* State 69 dips into MONTICELLO (827 alt., 644 pop.), then swings out again into a broader and more level country.

MONROE, 35.2 *m.* (1,045 alt., 5,015 pop.), is at the junction with State 11 (*see Tour 24*). At 35.3 *m.* State 69 divides, the main route, white-marked, traversing a substantial residential area, the yellow-marked alternate road leading (R) to the square. The GREEN COUNTY COURTHOUSE is in the center of the square; business places are ranged closely along its sides.

Known as "the Swiss cheese capital of the United States," Monroe is the trade and shipping center for a small area whose 300 factories produce more than half of all the Swiss and Limburger cheeses made in America. Great golden, pungent wheels of cheese are brought here from the numerous wayside factories in the region and stored in long warehouses beside the tracks to await shipment; factories within the city greatly increase the amount of produce, and many of the prosperous homes in Monroe have been built with profits from cheese.

This city of cheeses and of many Schweitzers was settled by Irish, Scots, Scandinavians, and New Englanders. Though Monroe became the seat of Green County in 1839, it grew slowly. With the coming of the Milwaukee and Mississippi R. R. in 1857, it began to grow more rapidly. Farmers and people from neighboring towns began to bring their produce in for shipment. Thus in the early 1870's New Glarus cheese makers brought their odorous loads to Monroe and dispatched them to a growing eastern market. School children held their noses as wagons of Limburger passed, and an ordinance was once proposed in the Monroe common council to ban the product from the streets.

Reports of the flourishing dairy product industry at New Glarus reached the European homeland, and numerous ambitious men from Canton Berne crossed the Atlantic for Wisconsin and set up their factories in the favorable Monroe area. By 1883 there were 75 factories in Green County alone, and almost all of the product from the south-western Wisconsin cheese area went to market by way of Monroe. Cheese became less offensive when money as well as odors from the new industry began to pour into the city.

In 1914 a Cheese Day was inaugurated with the enthusiastic support of the city. The seventh cheese festival, held in 1935, attracted 50,000 people to watch an elaborate parade climaxed by the crowning of a cheese queen and to feast on eight tons of Swiss and Limburger cheese. In the same year cheese was stoutly defended when Monroe's postmaster engaged in a sniffing duel with a postmaster in Iowa to determine whether or not the odor of Limburger in transit was a fragrance or a stench. Well publicized by the press of the Nation, the duel ended when a decision was reached which held that Limburger merely exercised its constitutional right to hold its own against all comers.

Saturday afternoons in Monroe find the townspeople evincing great interest in the display of new cheese-making implements in the windows of hardware stores, mingling with the cheese makers and their assistants, who often walk slowly on stiff and aching legs made rheumatic by the water and steam of the factories.

Organized gymnastic groups meet regularly in a $35,000 TURNER HALL, one block south of the square, which replaced the old hall destroyed by fire in 1936. Typical Swiss dances are held here on occasion, and yodeling societies frequently fill the hall with throaty performances.

The alternate and main route of State 69 rejoin at 35.6 *m.*

State 69 crosses the Illinois Line, 43.3 *m.*, 4 miles north of Orangeville, Ill.

Tour 24

Racine — Burlington — Janesville — Monroe — Illinois Line; 165 *m.*, State 11.

Chicago, Milwaukee, St. Paul & Pacific R. R. parallels route between Racine and Shullsburg.
Hard-surfaced and oiled-gravel roadbed.
Adequate accommodations at Racine, Janesville, Monroe, and the resort region near Elkhorn and Delavan.

State 11 links two early settled regions in Wisconsin—the metropolitan Lake Michigan area and the southwestern mining country. Separated by distance and dissimilar in ideals, the two were political and economic rivals during Territorial days. At first the older southwest with its rich lead deposits dominated industry, and Southern miners from Kentucky and Missouri held the reins of government. However, soon after Wisconsin became a State in 1848, eastern enterprise gained control, eastern transportation facilities and growing factories superseded the lead industry, and eastern politicians directed the government (*see Political History*).

The highway, roughly paralleling the Illinois border, 15 miles south, reveals tangible evidence of this change. In the east are the great factories of Racine, one of the leading industrial cities of the State; in the west are hundreds of mines and test holes, sometimes a century old and generally abandoned. In the eastern and central parts of the route are thriving cities, recreation, farm-trade, or industrial centers; in the west are small, placid villages where crooked streets, old buildings, and surrounding mines are now only surface relics of a dynamic past.

Section a. *RACINE to JANESVILLE; 68.9 m., State 11*

RACINE, 0 *m.* (629 alt., 67,542 pop.) (*see Racine*).

Between Sixth and Main Sts. at Monument Square, 0 *m.*, and 1.5 *m.*, State 11 and State 42 (*see Tour 3A*) are one route. At 1.5 *m.* State 11 turns R. on 16th St. and traverses first a district of factories and shops, then a bright, fairly new zone of small residences.

The highway is in the open countryside at 3.5 *m.*, a flat, low, and gently undulating land, most of it divided into truck farms that raise fresh produce for the lake-shore cities. These Lake Michigan counties, some of the first land in the State to be systematically farmed, have been under cultivation for a hundred years or more.

Eastern farmers settled in Racine County during the 1830's. By 1839, when the Government threw the land open for sale, many of the better tracts had been taken. At the land sales each settler would bid in his claim, and frontier ethics, enforced by vigilante bodies of settlers, ruled that no other try to take it from him. An anonymous account written in 1842 describes the excitement of a land sale: "The suburbs of the town present the scene of a military camp. The settlers have flocked from far and near. The hotels are thronged to overflowing. Barrooms, dining rooms, and wagons are metamorphosed into bedrooms. Dinners are eaten from a table or a stump, and thirst is quenched from a bar or a brook."

When the rush for new lands was at its height, many squatters systematically exploited newcomers interested in buying farms. The squatters staked out claims on the best land available, waited until prospective buyers came along, then sold the land to them. After the transaction the squatters would move farther west to repeat their performance.

The SUNNY REST SANATORIUM (L), at 4.7 *m.*, is a county institution for tubercular patients. The road passes now under a highline that runs southward from the great Lakeside Plant at Milwaukee and supplies electricity to all the cities along the lakeshore. The derrick-like towers stretch across the plain; another file of them (R), turning off at right angles, carries current from the main line into Racine.

STURTEVANT, 7.8 m. (725 alt., 746 pop.), is an important railroad shipping point for the truck farming region. Much of the kraut that is commonly associated with Wisconsin and its large German population is produced from the cabbage raised by surrounding farmers. For a long time the Germans made kraut only for home consumption, but gradually popular demand warranted commercial production. Government surveys proved that the low, flat land of Racine, Kenosha, and Milwaukee Counties was especially well suited to the culture of cabbage, and today this district leads the State in the quantity grown. In sauerkraut production Wisconsin ranks second to New York State, and it success in growing the vegetable is a result of work done by the College of Agriculture's Experimental Station in fighting cabbage disease. Today many of the disease-resisting varieties of cabbage are results of Wisconsin experimentation.

The cabbage is taken to a cannery, allowed to wilt from 24 to 47 hours, then shredded and taken to the tanks. Salt is added, and the leaves are allowed to ferment. After fermentation, which generally requires 10 days, the kraut is canned. During the World War, when feeling against Germany ran high, sauerkraut was called "liberty cabbage."

At 10.3 m. is the junction with US 41 (see Tour 2). West of this junction a gradual change in the type of farming is noticeable; dairy cattle and hogs appear in pastures and barnyards, and corn grows in the roadside fields. At 12.5 m., as State 11 enters the terminal moraine country, the land begins to roll more heavily and woodlots are more frequent.

UNION GROVE, 15.5 m. (780 alt., 755 pop.) (see Tour 5), is at the junction with US 45 (see Tour 5).

West of the village almost every farm has corncribs and pig pens, although there are also the big barns and silos typical of a dairy region. Most of the milk produced here is shipped to Milwaukee and Chicago for fluid consumption. A PHEASANT FARM (L), 19.3 m., has pens fronting rows of small huts. The stocking of pheasants in Wisconsin was begun in 1929. By the end of 1936 it was estimated that the birds within the State numbered 200,000, some reared on the State Game Farm, others on private refuges. At 25.4 m. State 11 passes BROWN'S LAKE (R) and NORTON'S LAKE (L).

BURLINGTON, 27.5 m. (786 alt., 4,114 pop.), was called Fox-ville until a group of New Englanders came in 1835 and named it for their home in Vermont. Here the water power generated by the White and Fox Rivers, which had originally influenced the selection of the village site, encouraged the establishment of industrial plants, first a sawmill and a gristmill, later lime kilns and woolen mills. Yet it was the farmers in the environs who determined the trend of Burlington's chief industries. When sheep were raised, woolen mills dominated the city's industrial life. After 1880, when dairy cattle supplanted the sheep, dairy products plants sprang up; today Burlington's four plants have a handling capacity of 300,000 pounds of milk daily.

In recent years the city has become known as the headquarters of the LIARS' CLUB (*information available at Racine Journal Times, Chestnut and Pine Sts.*). People from all over the United States and Canada send in contributions; in 1934 popular interest warranted the first annual national broadcast of prize-winning stories. The club hopes "to preserve a little bit of Americana which vanished with the old-time grocery store when our granddads used to gather and spin their wonderfully concocted yarns."

The 1934 medal was won by the story: "My grandfather had a clock that was so old that the shadow from the pendulum swinging back and forth had worn a hole in the back of it." The same year a Kansas contributor wrote of the two- or three-day windstorms in his State. According to the contributor so much soil is blown away that when these storms finally end, the farmers emerge from hiding, build roofs on their wells, and thereafter use them for silos.

West of Burlington State 11 follows the banks of the White River. At 29.4 *m.* is the junction with a dirt road.

Left on this road to a QUARRY of Niagara pink limestone which is made into benches, sundials, arches, and other ornamental garden pieces. The limestone is also used for building purposes.

A marker on the riverbank at this junction is on the SITE OF VOREE, where a colony of Strangite Mormons established the Garden of Peace in 1844. Their leader was James J. Strang (1813-56), a brilliant but erratic lawyer converted to Mormonism and baptized by Joseph Smith (1805-44) shortly before the latter was killed by an angry mob. Immediately after Smith's death, Strang journeyed to a conference of elders and announced that the Lord had appeared to him in a vision and had ordained him the new Prophet. Several hundred Mormons followed him to Voree; the rest, under the leadership of Brigham Young, excommunicated him as an imposter.

Religious dissension soon arose in the Garden of Peace. In 1845, to quiet his followers, Strang claimed to have had another vision; obeying its dictates, he unearthed some metallic tablets hidden in a near-by hill. No one could decipher the jumbled hieroglyphics. So Strang had still another timely vision, which translated the tablets and set them forth as the Mormon law. The discovery increased Strang's power tremendously, silenced the doubters, and gained many new converts for the Voree colony. Religious fervor ran high, and the official colony organ, the *Voree Herald,* issued thousands of pamphlets that thundered forth ominous prophecies against those who refused to recognize Strang as Prophet.

In spite of Strang's authority, the Garden of Peace was an economic failure. Most of the good land had already been claimed by others;

the richer Mormons refused to pay $50 for a small plot; and many members rebelled against the rigorous asceticism enforced by the Church.

Finally in 1849 the colony abandoned Voree for Beaver Island, Michigan. There Strang's rule was despotic—he regulated the legal machinery, forced his followers to pay a tithe, forbade the use of tea, tobacco, and liquor, and commanded the women to wear bloomers rather than long skirts. Announcing that he had been divinely instructed to advocate polygamy, Strang married four women and urged the other men to take several wives.

Gentile officials, who violently opposed the Mormon settlement, set a price on the king's head but were unable to capture him. Public opinion forced President Fillmore to have Strang arrested and charged with robbing the mails, counterfeiting, and trespassing on public lands. Strang was tried only for robbing the mails, and he argued his own case so cleverly that he was acquitted. His victory increased his power tremendously and was responsible for his election to the Michigan House of Representatives.

Resentment among the Mormons grew, and in 1856 two rebellious subjects, one of whom had been publicly whipped for defending his wife's refusal to wear bloomers, assassinated their king. Today the GRAVE OF STRANG is a neglected grass-grown mound in the Voree burial ground.

State 11 winds across a succession of ridges and valleys where each summit is higher and each valley shallower than its predecessor. At 33 *m.* the level of the upland plain, about 200 feet higher than the preceding lowland, is reached, and by 36 *m.* the land has flattened out into a rolling plain with only occasional irregularities.

ELKHORN, 42.3 *m.* (996 alt., 2,340 pop.), founded in 1837 in the center of Walworth County, is a city of trim homes fronting narrow streets. Early settlers gave it this name because an elk's horn was found here imbedded in a fallen tree. Lack of water power and main lines of communication slowed Elkhorn's early development, but in 1849 a plank road was built between Janesville and Racine and in 1856 a railroad came through.

The hymn "Sweet Bye and Bye" was composed here in 1868 by Joseph P. Webster (1819-75), local musician, and S. F. Bennett (1836-98), druggist. In his drugstore one evening Bennett wrote the words to the song, Webster filled in the melody on his violin, and 30 minutes later a drugstore quartet was gingerly feeling its way through the hymn as it is today. Later, when "Sweet Bye and Bye" became popular, adverse rumors as to the circumstances of its composition arose. In 1892, to discredit them, Bennett wrote in a letter: "The press has given and is giving so many versions of the story of the 'Sweet By and By' many of them erroneous, that I feel impelled to give its true history to the world. In some of the accounts mentioned currency is given to the shameful story that Mr. Webster was drunk when he wrote the music and one excerpt sent me from Massachusetts has it that we were both drunk. And here I put on record for this and future generations the solemn and earnest assertion that the charge of being drunk is a false and shameful slander upon the memory of the noble dead."

By the turn of the century Elkhorn was a city of prosperous and thrifty retired farmers. In 1918 the citizens persuaded the FRANK HOLTON MUSICAL INSTRUMENT CO. PLANT, N. Church St., to move here from Chicago. The city raised $40,000 and constructed a factory, which became the property of the company when $500,000 had been paid in wages. The manufacture of wind instruments began, and Elkhorn became music conscious. Children got instruments and spent long hours puffing laboriously, singly or in groups. The Elkhorn Cornet Band, the nucleus of which, organized long before, had played at Abraham Lincoln's funeral, was merged with the Holton Company Band. In 1924 the city erected a $5,000 BAND SHELL in the Courthouse Square. Weekly concerts (*8:00 p.m. Wed.*) became the social high light of the summer. "Quiet, Please" signs appeared in the square and the blaring "Officer of the Day" was superseded by the "Poet and Peasant" overture.

Elkhorn's population rose from 1,700 in 1917 to 2,300 in 1930, and new homes went up in a building boom. By 1921 the company had paid out $500,000 in wages; to demonstrate its worth to the city, in the late 1920's it paid its bimonthly pay roll in silver dollars. About 350 employees started the "cartwheels" rolling, and Elkhorn citizens, joining the fun, kept them in circulation for nearly a month. The city rode high with the company's success and slumped when the depression came in 1929. Today Elkhorn citizens, still music conscious, hope for renewed prosperity. Commonplace to them is the sight of a small boy astride a bicycle, wedged solidly in the serpentine coils of a Sousaphone, delivering papers as he pedals purposefully home from band practice.

Elkhorn is at the junction with US 12 (*see Tour 19*).

DELAVAN, 48.5 *m.* (938 alt., 3,301 pop.), is clean, shady, and spacious. In 1836 Henry and Samuel Phoenix settled here and named the town for E. C. Delavan (1793-1871), a noted temperance leader of New York. The Phoenix brothers originally planned a temperance colony. It was no fault of theirs that the plan miscarried, for all property deeds made out by them contained a clause forbidding the sale of intoxicants. Delavan's leading industrial plant is the BRADLEY KNITTING MILL, which manufactures bathing suits and knitted outerwear.

Back in the days when circuses grew and thrived on Wisconsin soil, Ed and Jerry Mabie of New York established their circus headquarters here. By 1850 most of the villagers were engaged, directly or indirectly, in the circus business. Some citizens were executives, performers, teamsters, or animal trainers; others built wagons, seats, and tents; the women fashioned costumes; and the farmers and stock raisers furnished supplies and horses.

Left from Delavan on State 50 to the junction with a side road, 1 *m.; R.* here 1.3 *m.* to the BORG FARM. This estate, owned and operated by George Borg, produces fluid milk for Chicago markets. There are three immense barns, each flanked by two silos the size of grain elevators, and two large red and white feeding sheds.

At 2.2 *m.* on State 50 is (R) the LAKE LAWN HOTEL. Surrounding it are gray frame cottages with tar-paper roofs, close together but neat and orderly.

At 2.8 *m.* State 50 winds along the eastern end of DELAVAN LAKE, where a natural dike of marshy land has cut off a strip of water about 20 yards from the main shore. At 3.4 *m.* the highway crosses the outlet of the lake, a semistagnant stream (L) that sprawls out into a pond with docks and cottages on its borders. The property around Delavan Lake is privately owned (*no public recreation spots*). As the highway turns away from the lake a number of small summer cottages line the roadside. Signs on some of them advertise a variety of goods and services for vacationists—laundry, Irish terriers, repair work and antiques.

WILLIAMS BAY, an arm of Lake Geneva, is glimpsed at 6.3 *m.* (R), and the dome of the YERKES OBSERVATORY (*see Tour 19A*) gleams through the foliage.

At 7.4 *m.* is a long, narrow vista of symmetrical COMO LAKE.

At 7.7 *m.* is the junction with State 36 (*see Tour 19A*).

The WISCONSIN SCHOOL FOR THE DEAF, 48.9 *m.* (R), is set in a shady lawn with an Indian totem pole facing the main driveway. It was founded by Ebenezer Chesebro, but in 1852 its supervision and upkeep were taken over by the State.

At 53.6 *m.* is the junction with US 14 (*see Tour 19*). Between this junction and Janesville, State 11 and US 14 are one route (*see Tour 19*).

JANESVILLE, 68.9 *m.* (801 alt., 21,628 pop.) (*see Tour 7*), is at the junction with US 14 (*see Tour 19*) and US 51 (*see Tour 7*).

Section b. JANESVILLE *to* ILLINOIS LINE; *96.1 m. State 11*

West of S. Main and E. Milwaukee Sts. in JANESVILLE, 0 *m.,* and a point at 0.7 *m:,* State 11 and US 14 (*see Tour 20*) are one route.

West of Janesville are moundlike, closely bunched hills; rib-like moraines (L) with their intervening valleys sweep gradually downward from the roadside to a distant blue ridge. There are a few small chicken farms and one goat dairy, 4.5 *m.,* but dairying and attendant feed crops predominate throughout this region. The highway passes through FOOTVILLE, 9.5 *m.* (819 alt., 358 pop.) and ORFORDVILLE, 14.9 *m.* (883 alt., 502 pop.), both quiet farm trade centers. Farm buildings grow gradually more weather-beaten and shabby, as State 11 enters the Sugar River flats, a small area of light, sandy soil made useless by wind erosion. The surrounding farm region is one of the richest in the State; it leads in the production of alfalfa, corn, and feeds and is one of the foremost butter-making and condensery areas.

BRODHEAD, 21.7 *m.* (790 alt., 1,533 pop.), is old and pleasant. Just south of the central square is a shady PUBLIC PARK with a Civil War monument, a fountain, and a bandstand. Brodhead is on the site of a Winnebago village, and there are many Indian mounds in and near it.

The Sugar River, a regionally important drainage outlet, is at 24.9 *m.* Both Indians and whites once collected sap from the hard maples lining the riverbanks; in 1843 some 200 Indians camped here and made maple syrup and sugar. Picnic tables are (R) in the pine grove (*open to public*), but the land, like the dance hall and amusement park beyond, is privately owned.

JUDA, 30 *m.* (812 alt., 300 pop.), small in size, lies in a broad valley. Westward, woodlots are conspicuously absent; hills are bare; fence posts and telephone poles stand in stark rows against the sky line. Agriculturally this region is rich; the principal activity is dairying, though the raising of horses, corn, and hogs is almost as important. Farmhouses are old but in good condition; many barns have the names of their owners printed across their gables.

MONROE, 37.2 *m.* (1,045 alt., 5,015 pop.) (*see Tour 23B*), is at the junction with State 69 (*see Tour 23B*).

West of the city the land becomes rougher, and a variety of transitional formations marks the beginning of the Driftless Area. At 44.7 *m.* is (R) a straight drop of 25 feet; at 45.7 *m.* a small hill rises abruptly from the flat plain, and farther west more of these rocky humps stick up out of the valley floor like band shells.

BROWNTOWN, 46.4 *m.* (789 alt., 291 pop.), clusters on a long ridge of sod-covered rock overhanging the Pecatonica River. This was formerly an Indian camping site, and today arrowheads are occasionally to be found after a heavy rain. The Pecatonica (L) is virtually on a level with the roadbed, and during spring floods it inundates the countryside and blocks the highways. Early settlers used the river as a waterway, but it was too shallow for any but the lighter boats.

GRATIOT, 60.9 *m.* (797 alt., 287 pop.), is approached from the east across a pleasant undulating land where farm buildings sprawl on sunny hillsides, shaggy with loose open brush and small trees. The village, on the eastern edge of the lead mining district, is named for Henry Gratiot, a Southern miner who came to Wisconsin in 1826.

SHULLSBURG, 72.1 *m.* (930 alt., 1,041 pop.), is spread loosely upon two hill crests (L). The main street is narrow, old, and twisting, with flanking buildings of brick or clapboards. Streets bear such names as Peace, Truth, Judgment, Cyclops, Church, May, Wisdom, Friendship, Happy, and Faith.

Shullsburg was named for Jesse Shull, an early fur trader, who settled a little west of the present city. When Lafayette County was formed in 1847, Shullsburg became the county seat, which it remained until the courthouse was moved to Avon. In 1826 Henry and John Gratiot of Missouri began mining in GRATIOT'S GROVE south of Shullsburg. Soon six furnaces were operating, manned by 60 Frenchmen and Indians. During the Black Hawk War, Fort Gratiot, a nonmilitary refuge, was established at the grove for the protection of surrounding settlers. An old-timer, speaking of these forts scattered throughout the lead district, remarked that it was questionable which was the worse—being exposed to the quarrels inside the crowded forts or to the Indians outside. Several family feuds, begun in these stockades, colored local life long after the Indians had been pushed across the Mississippi.

West of Shullsburg, State 11 is in the old lead-mining country (*see Tour 12*), and along the route are relics of this once important industry. The first of these is an abandoned mine with its huge pile of tailings (R), 72.7 *m.*; another, with its gaunt gray buildings, stands at 74.3 *m.* Soon one mine after another, of indeterminate age, appears in roadside fields; in places the pastures are marked with century-old prospecting craters which make the land look like a war-torn battlefield. The Fever River, 78.3 *m.*, flows through low bluffs as it winds past more mines.

BENTON, 81.1 *m.* (846 alt., 869 pop.), though now only a farm village, occupies an important place in southwest mining annals. Lead was discovered here in the 1820's, and within three years hundreds of Southern miners were in the district. They built the village, naming it for Thomas H. Benton, U. S. Senator from Missouri and preacher of America's "manifest destiny" in the West, and founded an academy. In 1827 a flour mill, the first in the region, was built.

Two landmarks in Benton are the stone WATER TOWER, with its surmounting modern galvanized tank, and the JOHN TEMPLE HOUSE, built in the 1820's by Dennis Murphy. Murphy also built the American House, an early hostelry that served travelers for years. Such taverns dotting pioneer Wisconsin did more than furnish food, drink, and shelter for wilderness travelers and grimy teamsters; they also served as social centers where settlers met for amusements, dances, lectures, town meetings, elections, and conventions. During the late 1840's and early 1850's, when the roads were black with mile-long caravans of lead and produce wagons, these taverns often stood every two miles along the busier routes.

The countryside west of Benton is pocked with dozens of old mine sites and test-holes. State 11 proceeds toward the high blue ridge of the Mississippi bluffs on the Iowa shore.

HAZEL GREEN, 86.5 *m.* (601 pop.), first called Hardscrabble, one of the earliest permanent miners' settlements in Wisconsin, was established when lead was discovered here in 1824. U. S. Grant, later to be President of the United States, who lived with his brother at Galena, Illinois, occasionally visited here while gathering information for his reports on the lead and zinc deposits of southwestern Wisconsin. The GRAVE OF JAMES GATES PERCIVAL (1795-1856), eccentric poet and geologist, is in the local cemetery.

When lead deposits here were exhausted and the miners turned to large-scale farming, wheat was their first crop. In the late 1850's the price and local yield of wheat fell at the same time that the value of corn, pork, and beef rose. So corn and clover replaced the wheat, and farmers started raising stock. Today this area is one of the most highly concentrated corn-hog districts in Wisconsin.

State 11 turns R. at Hazel Green and heads directly toward the 285-foot SINSINAWA MOUND (Ind., *jinawe,* home of the young eagle). At 90.7 *m.* is the junction with a graveled road.

Left on this side road to SAINT CLARA ACADEMY, 1.5 *m.,* which stands about three-fourths of the way up Sinsinawa Mound and overlooks a great expanse of rich valley land. The sloping grounds and wide campus are shaded by great trees, isolated from the noise of the world, and very quiet. Against the steep slope of the mound the four-story buildings loom high. The center section of gray stone was built by Father Mazzuchelli in 1845 and 1856; the higher red brick structures are more recent.

In 1844 Father Samuel Mazzuchelli (1806-64), Italian priest, missionary, educator, and architect, bought Sinsinawa Mound. In 1845 he built a church, which was intended to be the nucleus of a religious and educational center comprising a college for men, a Dominican missionary school, and a convent and school where Dominican Sisters could be trained to conduct elementary and higher schools for girls. By 1849 the plan had been realized and Father Mazzuchelli considered his work here completed. He deeded the mound and property to the Dominican Fathers of the Kentucky Province and turned his attention to the educational work of the sisterhood. In Benton he built Saint Clara, a convent and school, which in 1852 was incorporated as the Benton Female Academy.

In 1867 it was transferred from Benton to Sinsinawa. In 1902 a college for women under the name of Saint Clara College was opened; here it continued until 1922 when it was transferred to River Forest, Illinois, and renamed Rosary College. The academy is now a boarding academy for girls and the mother house and novitiate of the Sinsinawa Congregation of Dominican Sisters.

FAIRPLAY, 93.8 *m.* (863 alt.), consists of a few buildings scattered among the oaks on a hillside (R). West of the village State 11 winds through the rough country bordering the Mississippi River, where road cuts reveal that the underlying rock occasionally extends up to the very grass roots. The highway continues along oak-covered slopes, then ascends from the valley.

On the ridge crest at 95.3 *m.* is the junction with State 35.

Right on State 35 from which the river plain far below (L) is visible through gaps in the sharply rolling hills. At 2.1 *m.* is the junction with US 61 (*see Tour 11*). US 61 crosses the river into Dubuque, Iowa, over the EAGLE POINT TOLL BRIDGE (*car and driver 35¢; additional passengers, 5¢ each*).

From the crest of the river bluff the lower hills on the Iowa shore are visible across the floodplain. The rooftops of Dubuque glimmer occasionally (R) among the trees.

The Illinois Line is at 96.1 *m.* Two miles farther, in East Dubuque, Illinois, spanning the Mississippi into Dubuque, Iowa, is a toll bridge (*car and driver 25¢; additional passengers, 5¢ each*).

PART IV
Appendices

Chronology

FRENCH DOMINION

1634 Jean Nicolet, emissary of New France, lands on shores of Green Bay.

1654–56 Médard Chouart, Sieur de Groseilliers, fur trader, with companion of uncertain identity, winters among Potawatomi around Green Bay; following spring ascends Fox River; crosses Wisconsin River at Portage.

1656–57 Groseilliers, with his brother-in-law, Pierre Esprit Radisson, visits Green Bay; proceeds south—route uncertain.

1658–60 Same two explorers skirt south shore of Lake Superior; somewhere between Ashland and Washburn build rude waterside hut—probably first white habitation in Wisconsin. Visit Ottawa on Lac Court Oreilles; accompany Sioux to site of city of Superior and into eastern Minnesota. Returning, build post of Chequamegon Bay; return to Montreal.

1660–61 Father René Ménard follows Hurons into Wisconsin; winters at Keweenaw Bay; starts to visit Hurons of Chippewa and Black Rivers; lost in dense forest along tributary of Chippewa River; is never heard from again.

1665–67 Father Claude Jean Allouez, Jesuit missionary, reopens Huron mission on shore of Chequamegon Bay.

1668–70 Nicolas Perrot, fur trader, visits Winnebago, Potawatomi, Fox, Sauk, and Mascouten villages near Green Bay; gains Potawatomi trade for New France.

1669 Father Jacques Marquette relieves Father Allouez who goes to Green Bay.

1670 May 20. Father Allouez returns to Sault Ste Marie after visiting Fox village on Wolf River and Mascouten village on upper Fox (near present Berlin). In autumn, he and Father Claude Dablon begin three missions; St. François, for Menominee and Potawatomi; St. Marc for Fox; and St. Jacques for Mascouten.

1671 Simon François Daumont, Sieur de St. Lusson, at Sault Ste Marie, takes official possession of Northwest in name of French King.

1672 Fathers Allouez and André build St. François Xavier mission at De Pere, center of Jesuit missionary work.

1673 May, Louis Joliet and Father Jacques Marquette leave Mackinac; enter Green Bay and Fox River; reach Mascouten village on June 7; portage into Wisconsin River. June 17 they discover Mississippi River.

1673–78 Father Allouez, aided by Fathers André and Silvy, continues missionary work around Green Bay.

1675 May 19. Death of Father Marquette on eastern shore of Lake Michigan.

1678–80 Daniel Greysolon, Sieur du Luth (du Lhut), discovers Bois Brulé-St. Croix route to Mississippi. (Historians differ, some believing that he went by way of St. Louis River into the interior.)

1679 September. Robert Cavelier, Sieur de la Salle, arrives off Green Bay in "Griffon," first sailing vessel on Great Lakes. Explores west coast Lake Michigan.

1680 Father Louis Hennepin explores upper Mississippi.

1683 Du Luth defends De Pere mission against Iroquois. Punishes Indian murderers of French at Sault Ste Marie; makes Lake Superior safe for French traders.

1684 First French post at Green Bay built by La Durantaye.

1685 Perrot is appointed "Commandant of the West." Crosses Fox-Wisconsin route with 20 soldiers; winters on east bank of Mississippi above Trempealeau.

1686 Perrot establishes trading posts on Mississippi, among them Fort St. Nicolas, near Prairie du Chien and Fort St. Antoine on Lake Pepin. Presents silver ostensorium to De Pere mission—oldest relic of Wisconsin; still preserved at Green Bay.

1689 Perrot takes possession for French King of Fort St. Antoine and of St. Croix, St. Peter, and upper Mississippi valleys.

1690–92 Perrot discovers and starts operating lead mines in Iowa and Wisconsin region; adjusts peace among Sioux, Fox, and their allies.

1693 Indian war makes Fox-Wisconsin waterway unsafe. Pierre le Sueur is sent to command Chequamegon and keep open route from Lake Superior to Mississippi. Builds stockade village at La Pointe.

1696 Fur trade licenses revoked. Posts evacuated.

1698 October 4. Father Jean François Buisson de St. Cosme camps at Potawatomi village on supposed site of Sheboygan. Visits sites of Milwaukee and Racine.

1700 Le Sueur and 30 French miners ascend the Mississippi and build fort on Blue Earth River (Minnesota).

1701 Peace between Iroquois and northwestern Indians. Wisconsin Indians invited to Detroit by Cadillac.

1702 Juchereau de St. Denis pays Fox Indians 1,000 crowns to pass his fleet of trading canoes to Mississippi by Fox-Wisconsin route.

1710 Many Fox Indians move to Detroit.

1712–16 Hostile Fox Indians from Green Bay imperil trade routes between Great Lakes and Mississippi.

1716 Louis de la Porte, Sieur de Louvigny, leads 800 men into Little Lake Buttes des Morts region; peace is negotiated with Fox.

1717 Fort is built at Green Bay; Philippe d'Amours, Sieur de la Morandière, commander.

1718   Paul le Gardeur, Sieur de St. Pierre, founds Chequamegon post.

1721   Father Pierre François Xavier de Charlevoix, Jesuit historian, visits Wisconsin with Jacques Testard, Sieur de Montigny, who supersedes La Morandière as commandant at La Baye.

1724–26   Marchand de Lignery, commandant at Mackinac, and François d'Amariton, commandant at Green Bay, aided by Jesuit missionaries, attempt to make peace among warring tribes. In 1726, truce permits building of post among Sioux.

1727   Fort Beauharnois is established on west bank of Lake Pepin (near Frontenac, Minnesota), to separate Sioux from their Fox allies; René Boucher, Sieur de la Perrière, in command.

1728   August. Lignery, with expedition of French and Indians, advances up Fox River; destroys villages and crops of Fox. On return, destroys French fort at La Baye; warns Fort Beauharnois garrison; fort is evacuated, October 3; roving Mascouten and Kickapoo capture and retain garrison as hostages.

1729   French captives detach Mascouten and Kickapoo from Fox alliance; make peace between them and Illinois. Commandant at Chequamegon reports copper mines on Lake Superior.

1730   Pierre Paul Marin, commanding Menominee, aids Winnebago against Fox on Little Lake Butte des Morts. In eastern Illinois, French defeat Fox seeking asylum with Iroquois.

1731   Kiala, principal Fox chief, surrenders as hostage to Commandant at Green Bay.

1732   Fort La Baye at Green Bay is rebuilt on later site of Fort Howard, under command of Nicolas Antoine Coulon de Villiers. René Godefroy, Sieur de Linctot, rebuilds Lake Pepin post.

1733   Sauk and Fox amalgamate after severe battle at Sauk village near Green Bay; retreat to lead regions.

1737   St. Pierre abandons Lake Pepin fort.

1738   Louis Denis Sieur de la Ronde gets permit to work Lake Superior copper mines.

1739–43   Marin pacifies all Wisconsin Indians, thus ending Fox wars. Lead mining is begun in southwestern Wisconsin.

1750   Marin reestablishes post among the Sioux. He and his partner, Governor Marquis de la Jonquière, obtain from Wisconsin fur trade an annual net profit of 150,000 livres.

1752   Joseph Marin relieves his father at Sioux post.

1753   La Baye post is granted to François Rigaud, brother of Governor Vaudreuil. Marin and St. Pierre make peace between Sioux, Cree, and Chippewa.

1755   Charles de Langlade and Indians take part in Braddock's defeat.

1756   Joseph Marin abandons Sioux post.

1757   Hubert Couterot last French commandant at La Baye; Pierre Joseph Hertel, Sieur de Beaubassin, last at Chequamegon.

1759   Wisconsin Indians take part in siege of Fort William Henry on Lake George and in defense of Quebec.

1760 Louis Liénard de Beaujeau-Villemonde, last French commandant, evacuates Fort Mackinac; retires to Mississippi; takes with him La Baye garrison.

BRITISH DOMINION

Upon surrender of New France to Britain, September 8, 1760, Wisconsin becomes British territory governed from Mackinac and Quebec.

1761 October 12. Capt. Henry Balfour, British Infantry, arrives at Green Bay to assume command of abandoned French stockade renamed Fort Edward Augustus; leaves garrison under command of Ensign James Gorrell.

1762 Gorrell makes treaties with Menominee, Winnebago, Ottawa, Sauk, Fox, and Iowa; promotes treaty between Chippewa and Menominee.

1763 Wisconsin, with other parts of New France, formally ceded to Britain.

Gorrell makes treaty with Sioux.

Pontiac's conspiracy: Indians attack British posts on upper Great Lakes.

June 21. Gorrell abandons Green Bay post, which is never again garrisoned by British.

1764 Augustin de Langlade, wife, and son Charles, from Mackinac, settle at La Baye.

1765 Alexander Henry and Jean Baptiste Cadotte reopen trading post on Chequamegon Bay.

1766 Jonathan Carver, colonial officer in French and Indian War, visits Wisconsin; leaves valuable records descriptive of region.

1773-75 Peter Pond, Connecticut fur trader, visits Wisconsin; writes of inhabitants. Finds French ex-soldier, Pinnashon, at Fox-Wisconsin portage (now Portage) transporting boats and cargoes.

1774 By Quebec Act, Wisconsin becomes part of British Province of Quebec.

1776-78 Langlade leads Indians to Canada to defend Montreal and Quebec against Americans.

1778 George Rogers Clark allies Wisconsin Indians with Americans.

1780 British build small fort at Prairie du Chien; send thence expedition against St. Louis. Spanish attack: fort burned by Langlade.

1781 Traditional date of settlement of Prairie du Chien by Basil Girard, Augustin Ange, and Pierre Antaya—although French traders long had dwelt there.

1783 Treaty of Paris is concluded; British territory east of Mississippi is ceded to United States.

AMERICAN DOMINION

(Under British influence until 1815)

1784 Northwest and Mackinac Fur Companies organized.

1785 Julien Dubuque visits Prairie du Chien; explores lead mines.

1787 July. Congress passes ordinance for government of Northwest Territory including Wisconsin.

1788 Fox Indians in general council at Prairie du Chien, allow Dubuque to work lead mines.

1791 Jacques Porlier comes to Green Bay.

1792 John Johnston builds trading post on Chequamegon Bay.

1792–93 Charles Reaume winters on St. Croix River; Porlier on upper Mississippi.

1792 Laurent Barth builds cabin at Fox-Wisconsin portage; transports boats and cargoes.

1795 Pierre Grignon, Sr., son-in-law of Charles de Langlade, dies at Green Bay.

Jacques Vieau establishes posts at Kewaunee, Sheboygan, Manitowoc, and Milwaukee.

1796 British evacuate western posts. Mackinac occupied by American garrison.

1797 Incited by Spanish, Sauk and Fox pillage British traders at Prairie du Chien. Sioux-Chippewa war in northern Wisconsin.

1799 XY Company organized to compete with Northwest & Mackinac Companies.

John Lawe, clerk for Jacob Franks, reaches Green Bay.

1800 May 7. Congress creates Territory of Indiana with jurisdiction over vast Northwest Territory, including Wisconsin.

1801 Charles de Langlade dies at Green Bay.

1802 John Campbell, British trader, is appointed Indian agent at Prairie du Chien.

Governor Harrison of Indiana grants commissions as justices of peace to John Campbell and Robert Dickson of Prairie du Chien; organizes militia.

1803 Charles Reaume commissioned American magistrate for Green Bay; Henry Monroe Fisher for Prairie du Chien.

1804 At St. Louis, Governor Harrison makes treaty with Sauk and Fox, who relinquish title to their lands, including lead mines, in southern Wisconsin. Northwest and XY Companies amalgamated.

1805–06 Lt. Zebulon M. Pike sent from St. Louis to inform Indians and traders along upper Mississippi of Louisiana Purchase; spends several days at Prairie du Chien.

1806 Nicolas Boilvin is appointed assistant Indian agent for Sauk and Fox.

1809 February 3. Act of Congress creates Territory of Illinois whose bounds include Wisconsin.

1810 John Jacob Astor purchases Mackinac Company; organizes Southwest Fur Company.

1812–13 Robert Dickson leads Wisconsin Indians to aid of British in Ohio and Michigan.

1814 Fort Shelby, first United States post in Wisconsin, built at Prairie du Chien.

1814   July 17. Fort Shelby surrenders to British and Indian forces led by Major William McKay and Robert Dickson.

August 4. Wisconsin traders, Indians, and British defend Mackinac against United States attack.

1815   British abandon Fort McKay after Treaty of Ghent. U. S. jurisdiction resumed under Nicolas Boilvin, Indian agent and justice of the peace.

1816   Gen. Thomas A. Smith erects Fort Crawford at Prairie du Chien on site of Fort McKay, formerly Fort Shelby. Col. John Miller erects Fort Howard at Green Bay on site of former French and British posts.

Act of Congress restricts fur trading to U. S. citizens.

Astor's American Fur Company continues operating in Wisconsin.

Government fur trade factories established at Green Bay and Prairie du Chien.

First flour mill, horse power, is built at Fort Crawford and makes flour for soldiers.

1817   February, first school in Wisconsin is opened at Green Bay. First priest visits Prairie du Chien.

1818   School opened at Prairie du Chien by Willard Keyes.

Brown, Crawford, and Michillimackinac Counties organized; embrace whole of present Wisconsin, part of Minnesota, and upper Michigan peninsula.

Solomon Juneau arrives at Milwaukee.

December 3. Wisconsin region attached to Michigan Territory upon elevation of Illinois Territory to statehood.

1818–21   French inhabitants of Green Bay plan to remove to Red River; finally become American citizens.

1820–21   Land claims of French settlers at Prairie du Chien and Green Bay adjusted.

1821   First steamer to navigate Lake Michigan brings New York Indians to arrange transfer to Wisconsin.

Code of Michigan Territory made basis of law; no courts organized except those of justice of peace.

1822   Government fur trade factory system abolished.

New York Indians begin removal to Wisconsin.

Speculators and prospectors rush to southwestern Wisconsin following opening of lead mines at Galena, Illinois.

1823   May 12. First session of Crawford County Court held, Prairie du Chien.

October 17. First session of U. S. Circuit Court held, Prairie du Chien; James D. Doty, judge.

Steamboat, the *Virginia,* is first to ascend the upper Mississippi.

1824   July 12. First session of Brown County Court opens at Green Bay, Jacques Porlier, chief justice.

October 4. Judge Doty holds first U. S. Circuit Court, Green Bay.

1825   William Clark and Lewis Cass, Government commissioners, conclude treaty at Prairie du Chien with Indians of Illinois, Minnesota, and Wisconsin; establish boundaries and make peace among the tribes.

1826   Fort Crawford's garrison removed.

1827   Winnebago outbreak causes remanning of Fort Crawford.
        Winnebago mining lands ceded to U. S. as condition of pardon for leaders of insurrection.

1828   September. Fort Winnebago is begun at Portage.

1829–32 Col. Zachary Taylor rebuilds Fort Crawford on new site at Prairie du Chien.

1829   July. Chippewa, Ottawa, and Potawatomi at Green Bay cede their lands between Rock and Wisconsin Rivers.
        Thousands of miners settle in lead regions.

1831   Daniel Whitney's company begins erection of shot tower at Old Helena on Wisconsin River.

1832   Black Hawk War; Indians defeated. Cede lands east and south of Fox and Wisconsin Rivers.

1833   Chippewa, Ottawa, and Potawatomi cede lands south and west of Milwaukee River.
        December 11. Green Bay *Intelligencer,* first Wisconsin newspaper, established.

1834   Land offices opened at Mineral Point and Green Bay. First public land sale at Mineral Point.
        First public road laid out.
        Settlers begin to arrive at Milwaukee.

1835   June 17. First steamboat at Milwaukee.
        First bank at Astor, part of Green Bay.
        Influx of settlers in southern and eastern Wisconsin.

1836   April 20. Territory of Wisconsin organized by Act of Congress. Henry Dodge, first Governor; John S. Horner, secretary. George W. Jones, first delegate to Congress.
        July 4. Officers sworn in at Mineral Point.
        Supreme Court constituted: Charles Dunn, David Irvin, and William Frazer, justices.
        October 25. First Territorial assembly meets at Old Belmont (now Leslie).
        November 24. Madison is chosen as capital.
        Because of depression, the four banks in Territory fail.
        Milwaukee *Advertiser* begun; land office opened here, no sales until 1839.

1836   Menominee cede to United States about 4,000,000 acres in Michigan and Wisconsin.

1837   Winnebago chiefs sign treaty at Washington ceding their Wisconsin lands; agree to remove from Territory.
        Townsite of Madison surveyed and platted; first capitol begun.

1838   Congress appropriates land to endow University of Territory of Wisconsin.
        Eighty post offices and thirty-five mail routes established.

Second Territorial assembly meets at Madison; lack of accommodations forces it to adjourn.

Milwaukee and Rock River Canal Company chartered.

1839 Adjourned session of second Territorial assembly meets at Madison. First school taxes levied.

Wisconsin Marine & Fire Insurance Company (Mitchell's Bank) chartered.

1840 Population 30,945 (U. S. census).

1841 James Duane Doty appointed Governor (1841-44).

1843 A cooperative industrial community, chiefly English, under Thomas Hunt, settles at North Prairie, Waukesha County.

1844 Wisconsin Phalanx, Utopian socialist community, settled at Ceresco (now Ripon). Promoted by Warren Chase.

Nathaniel P. Talmadge appointed Governor (1844-45).

1845 Talmadge removed; Dodge reappointed (1845-48).

Swiss colony settles at New Glarus.

Mormon colony organized near Burlington, Racine County.

1846 State government voted. Congress passes enabling act.

October 15. First constitutional convention opens at Madison.

1847 First constitution rejected by popular vote.

November 21. Propeller *Phoenix* burned off Sheboygan; 148 persons lost, 127 of whom were immigrants from Holland.

December 15. Second constitutional convention opens at Madison.

Population 219,456 (Special census).

1848 March 13. Second State constitution adopted.

May 29. Wisconsin is admitted as a State.

First State officers: Nelson Dewey, Governor (1848-52); Henry Dodge and Isaac P. Walker, U. S. Senators; Mason C. Darling and William P. Lynde, U. S. Representatives; Andrew G. Miller, Judge, U. S. District Court.

June 5. First State legislature convened.

Free school system established.

Land grant for university made by Congress; university chartered.

Menominee, by treaty, cede to the United States their lands east of Wisconsin and north of Fox Rivers.

Large number of Germans settle at Milwaukee and in eastern counties.

1849 Construction of railroad from Milwaukee westward is begun.

State historical Society organized.

University of Wisconsin opened at Madison.

First telegram received in Milwaukee.

Cholera epidemic State-wide.

Gold rush to California.

1850 Population 305,391.

1851 First railroad train in State run from Milwaukee to Waukesha.

1852 Several railroad enterprises in southern Wisconsin.

Leonard J. Farwell, Governor (1852-54).

1853   July. Act abolishing capital punishment in Wisconsin passed.
Milwaukee and Mississippi Railroad completed to Madison.

1854   February 28. State Republican Party founded at Ripon (reorganized at Madison, July 13).
University of Wisconsin graduates first class.
State Historical Society reorganized; Lyman C. Draper, secretary.
Fugitive Slave Act declared void by Wisconsin Supreme Court.

1856   Reelection of Gov. William A. Barstow, Democrat, declared fraudulent. Coles Bashford, Republican, declared elected (1856-58).

1857   Milwaukee & Mississippi Railroad completed to Praire du Chien.
Legislature passes law against kidnapping to neutralize effect of Fugitive Slave Law.
Severe monetary panic.

1858   Excursion train celebrating opening of Chicago and Fond du Lac Railway (now C&NW) wrecked at Johnson's Creek. Fourteen killed. Legislative investigation exposes bribery of officials by railways and improper use of United States railway land grants.
Alexander W. Randall, Governor (1858-62).

1859   Byron Payne elected to State Supreme Court on anti-slavery platform.
September 30. Abraham Lincoln delivers address at State Fair, Milwaukee.

1860   September 9. Milwaukee excursion steamer, *Lady Elgin* sinks; 225 persons drowned.
State votes for Lincoln.
Grand League of Farm Mortgagors organized.
Population 775,881.

1861   April 15. Gov. Alexander W. Randall calls for volunteers in Civil War. Sixteen regiments mustered during year.
July 2. George C. Drake, Co. A 1st Inf., dies at Falling Waters, Virginia; first Wisconsin soldier killed in the war.

1862   April 19. Gov. Louis P. Harvey, on visit to Wisconsin soldiers wounded at Shiloh, drowned in Tennessee River. Edward Saloman becomes Governor (1862-64).
April. 700 captured Confederate soldiers received at Camp Randall, Madison.
Wisconsin sends about 15,000 volunteers into war service during year.

1863   September 17. War Democrats hold convention in Janesville; repudiate Ryan address of September 3, 1862, criticizing Federal administration.
Military hospitals opened in Milwaukee and Prairie du Chien through efforts of Mrs. Harvey.

1864   James T. Lewis inaugurated fourth war-time Governor (1864-66).
Feb. 23. Death of Fr. Mazzuchelli, missionary to Green Bay and southwestern Wisconsin since 1833; founder and builder of churches, schools, and other public buildings; chaplain of first Territorial legislature.

Chester Hazen establishes first Wisconsin cheese factory at Ladoga, Fond du Lac County.

1865　April 13. Wisconsin recruiting ceases. Wisconsin furnished 91,379 men to North during war; losses by death, 10,752.

1866　February. Reorganization of State university; creation of college of agriculture under the Morrill Grant.

James R. Doolittle, U. S. Senator, asked by legislature to resign because he supported President Johnson's reconstruction policy.

Lucius Fairchild, Governor (1866-72).

1867　Invention of practical typewriter by Christopher Latham Sholes, of Milwaukee.

1869　March 9. Fifteenth Amendment to United States Constitution is ratified by Wisconsin.

Legislature defeats bill to regulate railway rates.

1870　May 24. Death at Delafield of Bishop Jackson Kemper, missionary of the West, builder and founder of schools, churches, colleges, and convents.

Contest over railway legislation continues; cities, towns, and villages authorized to issue bonds in aid of new railways.

Population 1,054,670.

1871　October 8-10. Great fires in Door, Oconto, Shawano, Kewaunee, Brown, and Manitowoc Counties; 1,000 perish; 3,000 homeless.

1872　Wisconsin Dairymen's Association organized at Watertown.

C. C. Washburn, Governor (1872-74).

1873　Financial panic.

Democrats, on issue of railway legislation, elect State ticket for first time since Civil War.

Winnebago forcibly removed to Nebraska.

1874　Potter Law, limiting railroad rates, enacted; law upheld in State Supreme Court.

William R. Taylor, Governor (1874-76).

1875　Republicans opposing Potter Law and "Grangerism," elect State ticket.

Women made eligible to vote for school offices.

April 28. Oshkosh almost entirely destroyed by fire.

September 14. Death of Increase A. Lapham, famous scientist.

1876　Potter Law repealed.

Harrison Ludington, Governor (1876-78).

1877　John F. Appleby perfects twine binder on principle of "knotter" invented by him in 1858.

Enactment of State law enabling women to practice law in Wisconsin.

1878　William E. Smith, Governor (1878-82).

1880　John Stevens of Neenah patents his roller flour mill.

October 19. Death of Chief Justice Edward G. Ryan.

Population 1,315,497.

1881　September. First serious labor disturbance: Eau Claire sawmill operatives demand reduction of hours; National Guard called out.

1882   Constitution amended to provide for biennial legislative sessions.
Jeremiah M. Rusk, Governor (1882-89).

1883   Agricultural Experiment Station established at Madison.

1885   March 6. William F. Vilas appointed Postmaster General in Cabinet of President Cleveland.
High grade iron ore discovered on Gogebic Range.

1886   Agricultural Short Course opened at college of agriculture.
Milwaukee workmen strike for 8-hour day. National Guard called out; several strikers killed. Gov. Rusk "seen his duty and done it."

1887   June 27. Marshfield almost destroyed by fire; property loss between $2,000,000 and $3,000,000.

1888   January 16. William F. Vilas appointed U. S. Secretary of the Interior.

1889   Legislature passes "Bennett Law" making English compulsory in schools.
March 4. Gen. Jeremiah M. Rusk appointed first U. S. Secretary of Agriculture.
William D. Hoard, Governor (1889-91).
Strike of railway builders at West Superior.

1890   Democrats elect entire State ticket on Anti-Bennett law platform.
Bible reading in public schools declared unconstitutional by Wisconsin Supreme Court.
Dr. S. M. Babcock discovers method of determining butterfat content of milk.
University dairy school established.
Population 1,686,880.

1891   "Bennett Law" repealed.
Reapportioned congressional and legislative districts under 1890 census unsatisfactory to Republicans.
George W. Peck, Governor (1891-95).

1892   Special legislative session adopts new apportionment; not contested.
October. Third Ward Fire, Milwaukee, causes $5,000,000 damage; 6 lives lost.

1893   Medford virtually destroyed by fire.
November 21. Death of Gen. Jeremiah Rusk, three times Governor.
Panic causes failure of several Milwaukee banks.

1895   William H. Upham, Governor (1895-97).

1896   May 23. Death of Gen. Lucius Fairchild, three times Governor, Minister to Spain, National Commander of G. A. R.
Wisconsin Free Library Commission organized. Traveling library system initiated in Dunn County.
Immigration into northern Wisconsin substantial.

1897   Corrupt Practices Act, requiring statements of campaign expenses, passes legislature.
Edward Schofield, Governor (1897-1901).

1898   Wisconsin raises 5,496 men for Spanish-American War; equips 4 regiments of infantry and 1 battery.
Strike of woodworkers in Oshkosh; violence.

Forest fires in Barron and Polk Counties cause $500,000 loss.

1899   Third Regiment mustered out in January and Fourth Regiment in February at Anniston, Alabama.

Anti-Railway-Pass Law enacted; State tax commission created.

June 12.   Tornado destroys New Richmond; $1,000,000 loss.

1900   May 1-8.   Forest fires on Chequamegon Bay and Menominee River; more than $1,000,000 damage.

June 12.   Belle Boyd, famous woman spy during Civil War, dies at Kilbourn.

October 19.   New State Historical Library Building, Madison, dedicated.

Revival of lead and zinc mining in southern Wisconsin.

Population 2,069,042.   Gain of 22.6% in 10 years.

1901   January 7.   Robert M. La Follette, first native-born Governor, inaugurated; twice reelected (1901-06).

1903   Primary election law passes.   Ad valorem railroad tax, mortgage tax, and inheritance tax chief features of year's legislation.

1904   February 27.   Fire destroys south wing and much of interior of State Capitol.

June 5-9.   State university celebrates golden jubilee; Charles R. Van Hise inaugurated president, first alumnus to hold that office.

November 8.   Voters endorse primary election law.

1905   January 25.   Gov. Robert M. La Follette elected to U. S. Senate.

Civil Service for State employees adopted.

State board of forestry organized.

Railroad Regulation Law passed: Railroad commission established.

1906   Gov. Robert M. La Follette resigns to take seat in U. S. Senate. (Served as Senator until his death, June 18, 1925.)

James O. Davidson, Governor (1906-11).

1907   Construction of new State Capitol begun.

Public utilities put under Railroad Commission.

1908   Will of former Senator William F. Vilas creates trust fund from which $30,000,000 eventually will accrue to State university.

1909   Significant legislation: cities permitted to adopt commission form of government.

1910   U. S. Forest Products Laboratory established at university.

Milwaukee elects Socialist municipal ticket—first large city to be governed by that party.

February 17.   Eau Claire adopts commission form of government.

November 8.   Socialists carry Milwaukee County and elect Victor Berger first Socialist Congressman.

Population 2,333,860.

1911   Two new commissions—public affairs and industrial—created.

State laws passed regarding income tax, labor regulations, workmen's compensation, State life insurance, corrupt practices, teachers' pensions, control of water power, second choice primary, board of vocational education.

Francis E. McGovern, Governor (1911-15).

1913 Legislation: mothers' pensions; minimum wage law for women; workmen's compensation made compulsory; water power control; eugenic marriage law.

October 22. Death of Dr. Reuben Gold Thwaites, Superintendent of State Historical Society.

1914 Wisconsin Cheese Federation organized.

John Muir, writer and naturalist, dies.

1915 Consolidation of State departments.

Creation of conservation commission, State board of agriculture, and State department of engineering, State board of education.

Mothers' Pension Act made compulsory.

Emanuel L. Philipp, Governor (1915-21).

1916 Wisconsin National Guard sent to Mexican border.

1917-18 World War.

1917 Wisconsin National Guard mobilized; equipped by State at an expense of $780,000; three companies transferred to 42nd Division at Camp Mills; remaining troops sent to Camp MacArthur.

State organized for war-time activities through State and County Councils of Defense.

Law enacted providing State aid and hospital treatment for crippled and deformed children.

State Capitol completed at total cost of $7,258,763.

October 21. Accidental death of U. S. Senator Paul O. Husting.

1918 Wisconsin has approximately 120,000 men in military service; losses by death, approximately 4,000.

Civil Service preference to veterans passed by legislature.

November 19. Charles R. Van Hise, president of university, dies.

November 22. William D. Hoard, former Governor, dies.

1919 Divisions of rural planning, markets, and land settlement board made part of State board of agriculture.

1920 Population 2,632,067.

1921 John J. Blaine, Governor (1921-27).

Legislation: teachers' retirement fund law; inheritance tax rates increased; several dairy standards laws.

March 4. Death of Charles McCarthy, promoter of "Wisconsin Idea."

1922 Law requires publication of income tax returns.

1923 Farmers and laborers obtain representation on board of university regents.

Military training at University of Wisconsin made optional.

1924 Wisconsin State General Hospital opened.

Senator Robert M. La Follette, Wisconsin's first candidate for the Presidency, runs on Progressive platform; carries only Wisconsin.

1925 January 5. Wisconsin wins when United States Supreme Court upholds injunction against Chicago's lowering level of Lake Michigan.

Glenn Frank, editor of *Century Magazine,* elected president of State university.

June 18.   Senator Robert M. La Follette dies in Washington.
Legislature unanimously chooses him for remaining place allotted
Wisconsin in National Hall of Fame.
Robert M. La Follette, Jr., elected U. S. Senator.
Legislation: sale of oleomargarine prohibited; constitutional amend-
ment for recall of elective official; absentee voters law liberalized;
ratification of child labor amendment; new minimum wage law for
women; old age pension law optional with counties.

1926   U. S. Supreme Court upholds Wisconsin's Workmen's Compensation and insurance laws.

1927   February 8.   Wisconsin's Progressive Republican Congressmen refuse to enter Republican caucus at Washington.
October 19.   Congressman Victor L. Berger, Milwaukee, chosen
national chairman of Socialist Party.
Fred R. Zimmerman, Governor (1927-29).

1928   President Coolidge makes Cedar Island Lodge on Brule River his
summer White House.

1929   Prof. Harry Steenbock, University of Wisconsin, announces com-
mercialization of his vitamin D patent; profit to go to university.
August 7.   Victor L. Berger, Socialist, dies.
Walter J. Kohler, Governor (1929-31).

1930   Gov. Walter J. Kohler exonerated of charges of violating Corrupt
Practices Act in 1928 campaign.
Population 2,939,006.

1931   Dr. Stephen Moulton Babcock, famous scientist, dies.
Chris L. Christensen appointed dean of college of agriculture.
Legislation: Wisconsin first State to enact labor code to protect
labor's rights in disputes with employers; workmen's compensation
act made compulsory for employers of three or more persons; enactment of compulsory old-age pension law effective in 1933.
Philip F. La Follette, Governor (1931-33).

1931-32   November 24-February 4.   Special session of legislature; first
American unemployment compensation law enacted.
Emergency chain store tax law enacted.

1932   For first time in 42 years, member of La Follette family defeated
by popular vote—Gov. Philip La Follette losing primary election.
State goes Democratic nationally for first time since 1912 by largest
majority in its history.   Albert G. Schmedeman elected Governor
—first Democrat since 1895.   F. Ryan Duffy elected Senator.
Federal Government advances $3,000,000 for highway construction
jobs.
New U. S. Forest Products Laboratory, world's largest wood research laboratory, erected at Madison; cost $737,000.

1933   Three farm strikes led by Wisconsin Cooperative Milk Pool and
Farmers Holiday Association involve more than 17,000 farmers;
rioting, milk dumping, and pitched battles between farmers and
deputies.   Gen. Immell calls out National Guard.   One farmer
fatally shot.

1934 Tercentenary of French discovery of Wisconsin celebrated for eight weeks at Green Bay.

Public Service Commission authorizes municipal competition with privately owned utility, and denies private utility damages in addition to purchase price in case of municipal acquisition of local plant.

One hundred and twenty strikes—65 of major importance.

Strike at Kohler most serious; rioting, two men killed, 40 wounded.

One man killed during Milwaukee Electric Railway and Light Company strike.

Philip La Follette elected Governor; Robert M. La Follette, Jr., reelected U. S. Senator.

1935 University launches Science Inquiry—new step in scientific appraisal and education.

1936 March 2. Death of Rasmus B. Anderson, diplomat, scholar, "father of Norse literature in America."

Centennial of organization of Territory celebrated at Madison and other cities.

Franklin D. Roosevelt and Philip F. La Follette sweep Wisconsin by large majorities.

Wisconsin, with 2.37 per cent of Nation's population, pays over $51,000,000 internal revenue tax.

Bibliography

GENERAL INFORMATION

Wisconsin. *The Wisconsin Blue Book, 1937.* Madison, 1937. 689 p., ill. Compiled by the Wisconsin Legislative Reference Library. ~~Biennial.~~ First pub. 1853.

DESCRIPTION AND TRAVEL

Carver, Jonathan. *Travels through the Interior Parts of North America in the Years 1766, 1767, and 1768.* London, Printed for the Author, 1778. 543 p.

Clemens, Samuel Langhorne (Mark Twain). *Life on the Mississippi.* Boston, J. R. Osgood and Co., 1883 (and in numerous later editions). 624 p., ill.

Cole, Harry Ellsworth. *Stagecoach and Tavern Tales of the Old Northwest,* ed. by Louise Phelps Kellogg. Cleveland, The Arthur H. Clark Co., 1930. 376 p.

Featherstonhaugh, George William. *A Canoe Voyage up the Minnay Sotor.* London, R. Bentley, 1847. 2 v., ill.

Gale, Zona. "Wisconsin, a Voice from the Middle Border." (In Gruening, Ernest, ed. *These United States.* 1st series. New York, Boni & Liveright, 1923. p. 172-184.)

Holmes, Frederick Lionel. *Alluring Wisconsin.* Milwaukee, E. M. Hale & Co., 1937. 480 p., ill.

Kellogg, Louise Phelps, ed. *Early Narratives of the Northwest, 1634-1699.* New York, Scribner, 1917. 382 p.

Kemper, Jackson. "Journal of an Episcopalian Missionary's Tour to Green Bay, 1834." *Wisconsin Historical Collections,* 1898, v. 14:394-449.

Leonard, William Ellery. "Wisconsin." *Wisconsin Magazine of History,* 1923, v. 6:247-260.

Nute, Grace Lee. *The Voyageur.* New York and London, D. Appleton & Co., 1931. 288 p., ill.

Smith, Glanville. "On Goes Wisconsin." *National Geographic Magazine,* 1937, v. 72:1-46.

The Trail Blazer. Madison, The State Guide Pub. Co., 1934, 1935, 1936.

Thwaites, Reuben Gold. *Historic Waterways.* Chicago, A. C. McClurg, 1888. 298 p.

GEOGRAPHY, GEOLOGY AND TOPOGRAPHY

Alden, W. C. *Quaternary Geology of Southwestern Wisconsin.* Washington, D. C., Govt. Print. Off., 1918. 356 p. (United States Geological Survey.)

Bean, Ernest F. "Description of the Surface Features of Wisconsin." *Wisconsin Blue Book,* 1925, p. 15-38.

Chamberlin, Thomas Chrowder, and others. *Geology of Wisconsin.* Madison, 1877-83. 4 v. and atlas. (Wisconsin Geological and Natural History Survey.)

Dopp, Mary. "Geographical Influences on the Development of Wisconsin." American Geographical Society *Bulletin,* 1913, v. 45:401-412, 490-499, 585-609, 653-663, 736-749, 831-846, 902-920.

Featherstonhaugh, George William. *Report of a Geological Reconnaissance Made in 1835.* Washington, Gales & Seaton, 1836. 168 p.

Martin, Lawrence. *The Physical Geography of Wisconsin.* Madison, 1916. 549 p., ill. (Wisconsin Geological and Natural History Survey. Bulletin 36.)

Smith, Guy-Harold. "The Settlement and Distribution of the Population in Wisconsin." *Transactions* of the Wisconsin Academy of Sciences, Arts and Letters, 1929, v. 24:53-107.

Wisconsin Geological and Natural History Survey. *Bulletins, 1898-1930,* 1-77a. Madison, 1898-1930.

CLIMATE

Miller, Eric Rexford. "A Century of Temperatures in Wisconsin." *Transactions* of the Wisconsin Academy of Sciences, Arts and Letters, 1929, v. 23:165-77.

Schafer, Joseph. "Praying for Rain—Droughts in Wisconsin." *Wisconsin Magazine of History,* 1937, v. 20:337-353.

U. S. Department of Agriculture. Weather Bureau. *Climatic Summary of the United States.* Section 47: Northwestern Wisconsin; Section 48: Central Wisconsin; Section 49: Eastern Wisconsin. Includes data through 1930.

Whitson, A. R., and O. E. Baker. *Climate of Wisconsin and Its Relation to Agriculture.* Madison, 1928. 2d rev. ed. (University of Wisconsin Agricultural Experiment Station. Bulletin 223.)

LAND

University of Wisconsin. College of Agriculture. Extension Service. *Making the Best Use of Wisconsin Land through Zoning.* Madison, The University, 1934. 19 p. (Special circular.)

Wisconsin Executive Office. Committee on Land Use and Forestry. Report. *Forest Land Use in Wisconsin.* Madison, 1932. 156 p. Contains extensive bibliography on all phases of conservation.

Wisconsin State Planning Board. *Wisconsin Regional Plan Report. 1934.* Madison ,1934. 501 p. (Bulletin 2.)

————. Land Economic Inventory Division. *Bulletin 3.* Madison, 1936. 40 p. Land economic inventories for all counties are in the making and a number have already been published. Obtainable free on request.

WATER

Fenneman, N. M. *On the Lakes of Southeastern Wisconsin.* Madison, 1901. (Wisconsin Geological and Natural History Survey. Bulletin 8.)

Kanneberg, Adolph. "The Water Power Situation in Wisconsin." *Wisconsin Blue Book,* 1929, p. 75-96.

University of Wisconsin. *The University and Conservation of Wisconsin Waters.* Madison, 1936. (Science Inquiry Publication II.)

Weidman, Samuel, and A. R. Schultz. *The Underground and Surface Waters of Wisconsin.* Madison, 1915. (Wisconsin Geological and Natural History Survey. Bulletin 35.)

MINERAL

Bean, Ernest F., and W. O. Hotchkiss. *Mineral Lands of Part of Northern Wisconsin.* Madison, 1929. (Wisconsin Geological and Natural History Survey. Bulletin 46.)

Grant, Ulysses S. *Report on the Lead and Zinc Deposits of Wisconsin, with an Atlas of Detailed Maps.* Madison, 1906. (Wisconsin Geological and Natural History Survey. Bulletin 14.)

Steidtmann, Edward. *Limestones and Marls of Wisconsin.* With a chapter on the economic possibilities of manufacturing cement in Wisconsin, by W. O. Hotchkiss and E. F. Bean. Madison, 1924. (Wisconsin Geological and Natural History Survey. Bulletin 66.)

University of Wisconsin. *The University and Conservation of Wisconsin Minerals.* Madison, 1937. 23 p. (Science Inquiry Publication VI.)

TREES AND FLOWERS

Clohisy, Matt. *Wisconsin Trees.* Milwaukee, The Milwaukee *Journal,* 1927. 148 p. Prepared in cooperation with the Botanical Department of the Milwaukee Public Museum.

Fassett, Norman Carter. *Spring Flora of Wisconsin.* Madison, The Author, 1931. 174 p., ill.

Roth, Filibert. *On the Forestry Conditions of Northern Wisconsin.* Madison, 1898. (Wisconsin Geological and Natural History Survey. Bulletin 1.)

Wilson, F. G. *Forest Trees of Wisconsin; How to Know Them.* Madison, 1928. 64 p., ill.

Wisconsin Wild Flowers. Milwaukee, The Milwaukee *Journal,* 1920. 122 p. Prepared in cooperation with the Botanical Department of the Milwaukee Public Museum.

FISH

Wisconsin Conservation Commission. Current publications free on request. *Wisconsin Fish.* Milwaukee, The Milwaukee *Journal,* 1928. 68 p. Prepared in cooperation with the Milwaukee Public Museum.

BIRDS AND ANIMALS

Kumlien, L., and N. Hollister. *Birds of Wisconsin.* Milwaukee, 1903. 143 p. (Wisconsin Geological and Natural History Survey.)

Nehrling, Henry. *Our Native Birds of Song and Beauty.* Milwaukee, George Brumder, 1893. 2 v., ill.

University of Wisconsin. *The University and Conservation of Wildlife.* Madison, 1937. 39 p. (Science Inquiry Publication III.)

Van Vuren, F. S., and H. M. Mackin. *Wisconsin Birds.* Milwaukee, The Milwaukee *Journal,* 1927. 87 p., ill. Prepared in cooperation with the Milwaukee Public Museum.)

Wisconsin Conservation Department. State Game and Experimental Fur Farm. *Guidebook.* Madison, 1937. 55 p.

INDIANS AND ARCHEOLOGY

Black Hawk. *Life of Black Hawk; Ma-ka-tai-me-she-kia-kiak.* Iowa City, Iowa State Historical Society, 1932. 155 p. "Dictated by himself."

Blair, Emma Helen, ed. *The Indian Tribes of the Upper Mississippi Valley and the Region of the Great Lakes.* Cleveland, The Arthur H. Clark Co., 1911. 2 v.

Davidson, John N. *In Unnamed Wisconsin.* Milwaukee, S. Chapman, 1895. 307 p.

Fish, Carl Russell. "The Relation Between Archeology and History." *Proceedings* of the Wisconsin State Historical Society, 1911, p. 146-152.

Kirsch, Mary Moran. "The Indians of Wisconsin." *Wisconsin Blue Book,* 1931, pp. 91-112.

Lapham, Increase A. *The Antiquities of Wisconsin.* Washington, Govt. Print. Off., 1852. 92 p. 60 plates. (Smithsonian Institution Publications, no. 70.)

Radin, Paul. "The Winnebago Tribe." Washington, Govt. Print. Off., 1915-16. ill. (In U. S. Bureau of American Ethnology *37th Annual Report,* pp. 35-560.)

Skinner, Alanson. *Material Culture of the Menomini.* New York, Museum of the American Indian, Heye Foundation, 1921. 478 p., ill.

Smith, Huron Herbert. *Ethnobotany of the Menomini Indians.* Milwaukee, 1923. 173 p. (Bulletin of the Public Museum of the City of Milwaukee, v. 4, no. 1.)

The Wisconsin Archeologist. Milwaukee, The Wisconsin Archeological Society, 1901-1937. 37 v., ill.

U. S. Bureau of American Ethnology. "Indian Tribes of Wisconsin." Washington, Govt. Print. Off., 1907-10. Mimeographed. (Bulletin 30.) Excerpts from the *Handbook of American Indians North of Mexico.*

GENERAL HISTORY

Campbell, Henry Colin. *Wisconsin in Three Centuries, 1634-1905.* New York, The Century History Co., 1906. 4 v.

Kellogg, Louise Phelps. "The Story of Wisconsin, 1634-1848." *Wisconsin Magazine of History.* 1919-1920, v. 2-3.

Paxson, Frederic Logan. *When the West is Gone.* New York, Holt, 1930. 137 p. (Brown University. The Colver Lectures: 1929.)

Quaife, Milo Milton. *Wisconsin, Its History and Its People, 1634-1924.* Chicago, The S. J. Clarke Pub. Co., 1924. 4 v.

Smith, Alice E. "Wisconsin's Historical Manuscripts." *Wisconsin Blue Book,* 1933, pp. 1-7.

Thwaites, Reuben Gold. *The Story of Wisconsin.* Boston, Lothrop, 1890 (rev. ed. 1899). 389 p., ill.

Wisconsin Historical Collections. Madison, The Wisconsin State Historical Society, 1854-1931. 31 v.

Wisconsin Magazine of History. Madison, Wisconsin State Historical Society, 1917 to date.

Wisconsin State Historical Society. Proceedings. Madison, 1887-1937. 46 v.

EARLIEST HISTORY

Draper, Lyman C. "Early French Forts in Western Wisconsin." *Wisconsin Historical Collections,* 1895, v. 13:293-334.

"The Fur Trade in Wisconsin, 1815-1817." *Wisconsin Historical Collections,* 1910, v. 19:375-488. A series of documents.

Kellogg, Louise Phelps. *The British Regime in Wisconsin and the Northwest.* Madison, Wisconsin State Historical Society, 1935. 361 p. (Wisconsin Historical Series, v. II.)

——. *The French Regime in Wisconsin and the Northwest.* Madison, Wisconsin State Historical Society, 1925. 474 p. (Wisconsin Historical Series, v. I.)

Malhiot, François Victor. "A Wisconsin Fur-Trader's Journal, 1804-05." *Wisconsin Historical Collections,* 1910, v. 19:163-233.

Thwaites, Reuben Gold. *Father Marquette.* New York, Appleton, 1902. 244 p., ill.

EARLY SETTLEMENT AND LATER DEVELOPMENT

Anderson, Rasmus Björn. *Life Story of Rasmus B. Anderson.* Madison, The Author, 1915. 678 p., ill.

Bartlett, William W. *History, Tradition and Adventure in the Chippewa Valley.* Chippewa Falls, Wis., The Author, 1929. 244 p., ill.

Burnham, Guy M. *The Lake Superior Country in History and in Story.* Ashland, Wis., Ashland Daily Press, 1929. 453 p.

Butterfield, Consul W., ed. "History of Wisconsin." (In his *History of Dane County, Wisconsin,* Chicago, Western Historical Pub. Co., 1880, pp. 19-109.)
Also by Butterfield are a number of detailed histories of separate counties. The Western Historical Publishing Company, Chicago, is the publisher of similar standard histories covering almost all of the counties.

Edwards, Everett E., comp. *The Early Writings of Frederick Jackson Turner.* Madison, The University of Wisconsin Press, 1938. 316 p.

Fitzpatrick, Edward A. *Wisconsin.* New York, The Bruce Pub. Co., 1931. 429 p., ill. *History of Northern Wisconsin.* Chicago, Western Historical Pub. Co., 1881. 1218 p., ill.

Holand, Hjalmar Rued. *Old Peninsula Days; Tales and Sketches of the Door County Peninsula.* Ephraim, Wis., Pioneer Pub. Co., 1925. 244 p., ill.

Kinzie, Juliette Augusta (Magill). *Wau-bun, the "Early Day" in the Northwest.* New York, Derby & Jackson, 1856. 498 p.

Merk, Frederick. *Economic History of Wisconsin during the Civil War Decade.* Madison, Wisconsin State Historical Society, 1916. 414 p.

Merrick, George B. *Old Times on the Upper Mississippi.* Cleveland, The Arthur H. Clark Co., 1909. 323 p.

Muir, John. *The Story of My Boyhood and Youth.* Boston and New York, Houghton, Mifflin & Co., 1913. 293 p., ill.

Nelligan, John E. "The Life of a Lumberman." *Wisconsin Magazine of History,* 1929, v. 13:3-65; 131-185; 1930, v. 13:241-304.

Strong, Moses McCure. *History of the Territory of Wisconsin, from 1836 to 1848.* Madison, 1885. 637 p., ill. Pub. by authority of the State.

Titus, William A. *History of the Fox River Valley, Lake Winnebago and the Green Bay Region.* Chicago, 1930. 3 v.

Turner, Frederick Jackson. *The Frontier in American History.* New York, Holt, 1920. 375 p.

Turner, Jennie McMullin. *Wisconsin Pioneers.* Appleton, C. C. Nelson Pub. Co., 1929. 111 p., ill.

Wisconsin State Historical Society. *The Wisconsin Domesday Book.* General Studies. Madison, The Society, 1922-1937. (v. 1. *A History of Agriculture in Wisconsin,* by Joseph Schafer. 1922. v. 2. *Four Wisconsin Counties, Prairie and Forest,* by Joseph Schafer. 1927. v. 3. *The Wisconsin Lead Region,* by Joseph Schafer. 1932. v. 4. *The Winnebago-Horicon Basin, a Type Study in Western History,* by Joseph Schafer. 1937.)

GOVERNMENT AND POLITICAL HISTORY

Barton, Albert Olaus. *La Follette's Winning of Wisconsin (1894-1904).* Madison, 1922. 478 p., ill.

Berger, Victor L. *Voice and Pen of Victor L. Berger.* Milwaukee, The Milwaukee *Leader,* 1929. 753 p.

Berryman, John R. *History of the Bench and Bar of Wisconsin.* Chicago, H. C. Cooper, Jr. and Co. 1898. 2 v.

Haugen, Nils P. *Pioneer and Political Reminiscences.* Evansville, Wis., The Antes Press, 1930. 198 p.

Hoan, Daniel Webster. *City Government; the Record of the Milwaukee Experiment.* New York, Harcourt, Brace & Co., 1936, 365 p.

Howe, Frederic Clemson. *Wisconsin: an Experiment in Democracy.* New York, Scribner, 1912. 202 p.

La Follette, Robert M. *Autobiography.* Madison, Robert M. La Follette Co., 1913. 807 p., ill.

McCarthy, Charles. *The Wisconsin Idea.* New York, Macmillan, 1912. 323 p.

Schurz, Carl. *The Reminiscences of Carl Schurz.* New York, Macmillan, 1907-8. 3 v.

Shaw, J. F. "Study in Wisconsin Civics." *Wisconsin Blue Book,* 1929, pp. 113-120.

Steffens, Lincoln. "Wisconsin: A State Where the People Have Restored Representative Government—the Story of Governor La Follette." *McClure's Magazine,* v. 23:563-79. (Series: "Enemies of the Republic.")

Stephenson, Isaac. *Recollections of a Long Life. 1829-1915.* Chicago, The Author, 1915. 264 p.

Thomson, Alexander McDonald. *A Political History of Wisconsin.* Milwaukee, E. C. Williams Co., 1900. 452 p.

Winslow, John Bradley. *The Story of a Great Court.* Chicago, Flood, 1912. 421 p.

AGRICULTURE AND FARM LIFE

Hibbard, Benjamin Horace, and Asher Hobson. *Cooperation in Wisconsin.* Madison, 1917. 44 p. (University of Wisconsin. Agricultural Experiment Station. Bulletin 282.)

Kirkpatrick, E. L., and Agnes M. Boynton. *Wisconsin's Human and Physical Resources.* Madison, 1936. 173 p. (Resettlement Administration Region II, Research Section.)

Kirsch, William. "Cooperative Marketing in Wisconsin." *Wisconsin Blue Book,* 1931, pp. 31-47.

Thompson, John Giffin. *The Rise and Decline of the Wheat-growing Industry in Wisconsin.* Madison, 1909. (University of Wisconsin. Bulletin 292. Economics and Political Science Series v. 5:295-344.)

Wisconsin Department of Agriculture and Markets. *Wisconsin*. Madison, 1935. 36 p. (Bulletin 160.)
——. *Wisconsin*. Madison, 1937. 62 p. (Bulletin 180.)
——. Crop and Livestock Reporting Service. *Wisconsin Agriculture*. Madison, 1932. 148 p. (Bulletin 140.)
——. Crop and Livestock Reporting Service. *Wisconsin Agriculture*. Madison, 1934. 109 p. (Bulletin 150.)
——. Crop and Livestock Reporting Service. *Wisconsin Dairying*. Madison, 1931. 136 p. (Bulletin 120.)
——. Crop and Livestock Reporting Service. *Wisconsin Agriculture: Statistical Atlas,* 1926-1927. Madison, 1928. (Bulletin 90.)

INDUSTRY, COMMERCE AND TRANSPORTATION

Alexander, J. H. H. "A Short Industrial History of Wisconsin." *Wisconsin Blue Book,* 1929, pp. 31-49.
Commons, John R. *Economic Survey of Wisconsin*. Madison, University of Wisconsin, 1931-32. 2 v. Mimeographed.
Holmes, Frederick L. *Regulation of Railroads and Public Utilities in Wisconsin*. New York and London, D. Appleton & Co., 1915. 375 p.
Merrill, J. A. *Industrial Geography of Wisconsin*. Chicago, Laurel Book Co., 1911. 175 p.
Phelan, Raymond Vincent. *Financial History of Wisconsin*. Madison, 1908. 294 p. (University of Wisconsin. Economic and Political Science Series v. 2, no. 2.)
University of Wisconsin. *The University and Transportation*. Madison, 1937. 23 p. (Science Inquiry Publication V.)

LABOR

Schmidt, Gertrude. *History of Labor Legislation in Wisconsin*. Madison, University of Wisconsin, 1933. 415 p. Typewritten. (Thesis, Ph.D.)
Bulletins and other publications of the Wisconsin Industrial Commission and the Wisconsin Labor Board contain explanations of labor code, summaries of laws, interpretations of rulings of these commissions.

RACIAL ELEMENTS

Alphonsa, Sister Mary. *The Story of Father van den Broek*. Chicago, 1907. 94 p., ill. (Lakeside Series of English Readings.) Describes Dutch settlement in Wisconsin.
Christensen, T. P. "Danish Settlement in Wisconsin." *Wisconsin Magazine of History,* 1928, v. 12:19-40.
Copeland, Louis Albert. "The Cornish in Southwest Wisconsin." *Wisconsin Historical Collections,* 1898, v. 15:301-334.

Doubrava, Ferdinand F. "Experiences of a Bohemian Emigrant Family." *Wisconsin Magazine of History*, 1925, v. 13:393-406.

Hansen, M. V. "The Swedish Settlement at Pine Lake." *Wisconsin Magazine of History*, 1924, v. 8:38-54.

Hense-Jensen, Wilhelm. *Wisconsin's Deutsch-Amerikaner.* Milwaukee, Die Deutsche Gesellschaft, 1900-02. 2 v.

Holand, Hjalmar Rued. *Wisconsin's Belgian Community.* Sturgeon Bay, Wis., Door County Historical Society, 1933. 105 p., ill.

Lacher, J. Henry A. *The German Element in Wisconsin.* Milwaukee, Pub. by Muehlenberg Unit 36, Steuben Society of America, 1925. 60 p.

Levi, Kate Everest. "Geographical Origin of German Immigration to Wisconsin." *Wisconsin Historical Collections*, 1898, v. 14:341-393.

Luchsinger, John. "The Swiss Colony of New Glarus." *Wisconsin Historical Collections*, 1879, v. 8:411-439.

Qualey, Carlton. *Norwegian Settlement in the United States.* Northfield, Minn., Norwegian American Historical Association, 1938. 258 p.

Ragatz, Oswald. "Memoirs of a Sauk Swiss." *Wisconsin Magazine of History*, 1935, v. 19:182-227.

Schafer, Joseph. "The Yankee and the Teuton." *Wisconsin Magazine of History*, 1923, v. 7:3-19; 148-171.

Wisconsin Jewish Chronicle. *Jewish Community Blue Book of Milwaukee and Wisconsin.* Milwaukee, 1924-26. 2 v. and supplement.

Ylvisaker, Erling. *Eminent Pioneers.* Minneapolis, Augsburg Pub. Co., 1934. 162 p.

FOLKLORE

Brown, Charles E. *Wigwam Tales,* Madison, The Author, 1920. 28 p.

Burlin, Natalie (Curtis), ed. *The Indians' Book.* New York and London, Harper, 1907. 572 p., ill. See Chapter "Lake Indians, Winnebago," pp. 243-295.

Davis, Susan Burdick. *Wisconsin Lore for Boys and Girls.* Eau Claire, Wis., E. M. Hale & Co., 1931. 283 p., ill.

Judson, Katherine Berry, ed. *Myths and Legends of the Mississippi Valley and the Great Lakes.* Chicago, A. C. McClurg, 1914. 215 p.

Kearney, Luke Sylvester. *The Hodag, and Other Tales of the Logging Camps.* Wausau, Wis., The Author, 1928. 158 p.

McDonald, James J. "Paul Bunyan and the Blue Ox," *Wisconsin Blue Book,* 1931, pp. 113-127.

McKern, Will Carleton. "A Winnebago Myth." *Year Book,* Public Museum, Milwaukee, 1929, v. 9:215-230.

Red River Lumber Co. *The Marvelous Exploits of Paul Bunyan.* Minneapolis, 1922. 25 p., ill.

EDUCATION

Bradford, Mary Lemira (Davison). *Memoirs of Mary D. Bradford.* Evansville, Wis., 1932. 542 p. Reprinted from *Wisconsin Magazine of History.*

Commons, John Rogers. *Myself.* New York, Macmillan, 1934. 201 p.

Hambrecht, George P. "The Work of the State Board of Vocational Education." *Wisconsin Blue Book,* 1929, pp. 415-437.

Patzer, Conrad E. *Public Education in Wisconsin.* Madison, 1924. 511 p. Issued by John Callahan, State Superintendent.

Stearns, John William, ed. *The Columbian History of Education in Wisconsin.* Milwaukee, 1893. Pub. under authority and by direction of the State Committee on Educational Exhibit. 720 p.

Thwaites, Reuben Gold, ed. *The University of Wisconsin; Its History and Its Alumni.* Madison, J. N. Purcell, 1900. 889 p.

Wisconsin State Board of Vocational Education. City Vocational School Division. *Biennial Report. 1926-1928.* 2 parts. Part I. Wisconsin Part-time and Evening Schools for Juvenile and Adult Workers. Madison, 1929. 144 p. Part II. Description of City Vocational Schools in Wisconsin. Madison, 1930. 74 p.

RELIGION

Bennett, P. S. *History of Methodism in Wisconsin.* Cincinnati, Cranston & Stowe, 1890. 517 p.

Breck, Charles, comp. *The Life of the Reverend James Lloyd Breck, D.D.* New York, E. & J. B. Young, 1883. 557 p., ill.

The Catholic Hal. Milwaukee. *Commemorating 300 Years of Catholic History in Wisconsin.* Milwaukee, 1934. 98 p., ill.

Dexter, Frank N. *A Hundred Years of Congregational History in Wisconsin.* Fond du Lac, Wisconsin Congregational Conference, 1933. 310 p.

Fallows, Alice Katherine. *Everybody's Bishop, Being the Life and Times of the Right Reverend Samuel Fallows, D.D., by His Daughter.* New York, J. H. Sears & Co., 1927. 461 p., ill.

Fry, C. Luther. *The New and the Old Immigrant on the Land.* New York, George H. Doran Co., 1922. 119 p. (Committee on Social and Religious Surveys.)

Greene, Howard. *The Reverend Richard Fish Cadle.* Waukesha, Wis., Priv. print by Davis-Greene Corporation, 1936. 163 p., ill.

Heming, Harry Hooper. *The Catholic Church in Wisconsin.* Milwaukee, Catholic Historical Pub. Co., 1895-1898. 1181 p., ill.

Sauer, Philip von Rohr. "Heinrich von Rohr and the Lutheran Immigration to New York and Wisconsin." *Wisconsin Magazine of History,* 1935, v. 18:182-227.

Scanlan, Peter Lawrence. "Pioneer Priests at Prairie du Chien." *Wisconsin Magazine of History,* v. 13:97-106.

LITERATURE

Derleth, August William, and Raymond E. F. Larsson, ed. *Poetry out of Wisconsin.* New York, Harrison, 1937. 334 p.

Doudna, Edgar G. "Wisconsin Writers." *Wisconsin Blue Book,* 1927, pp. 71-80.

Ferber, Edna. *A Peculiar Treasure. The Autobiography of Edna Ferber.* New York, Doubleday, Doran & Co., 1938. 398 p., ill.

Hazeltine, Mary Emogene. *One Hundred Years of Wisconsin Authorship, 1836-1937.* Madison, Wisconsin Library Association, 1937. 149 leaves. Mimeographed.

Leonard, William Ellery. *The Locomotive-God.* New York, London, The Century Co., 1927. 434 p., ill.

Rounds, Charles Ralph. *Wisconsin Authors and Their Works.* Madison, Parker Educational Co., 1918. 400 p.

Titus, William A. *Wisconsin Writers, Sketches, and Studies.* Chicago, 1930. 433 p.

DRAMA

Dickinson, Thomas H., ed. *Wisconsin Plays.* New York, B. W. Huebsch, 1914. 187 p.

————. *Wisconsin Plays. Second Series.* New York, B. W. Huebsch, 1918. 217 p.

The Play-Book, a Magazine of the Drama. Madison, 1913-15 2 v. Published monthly by the Wisconsin Dramatic Society.

PAGEANTS

Children of Old Wisconsin. Madison, Bureau of Dramatic Activities, University Extension Division, 1935. 51 p. Bulletin of the University of Wisconsin.

Davis, Susan Burdick. *Our Wisconsin.* Milwaukee, E. M. Hale, 1934. 48 p., ill.

Kellogg, Louise Phelps. *Under Three Flags.* Green Bay, Wis., 1934. 20 p.

Rockwell, Ethel Theodora. *The Centennial Cavalcade of Wisconsin.* Madison, 1936. 68 p.

ART

Butts, Porter. *Art in Wisconsin.* Madison, Madison Art Association, 1936. 213 p., ill.

Partridge, Charlotte Russell. "Wisconsin in the Field of Art." *Wisconsin Blue Book,* 1929, pp. 103-110.

MUSIC

Barton, Albert Olaus. "Ole Bull and his Wisconsin Contacts." *Wisconsin Magazine of History,* 1924, v. 7:417-444.

Miller, Winifred V. "Wisconsin's Place in the Field of Music." *Wisconsin Blue Book,* 1929, pp. 97-102.

ARCHITECTURE

Wright, Frank Lloyd. *An Autobiography*. London, New York, etc., Longmans, Green & Co., 1932. 371 p., ill.

RADIO

Gapen, Kenneth M. *Agricultural Broadcasting by Educational Institutions*. Madison, 1931. (Thesis [M.A.], University of Wisconsin.)

McCarty, Harold. "WHA, Wisconsin's Radio Pioneer; 20 Years of Public Service Broadcasting." *Wisconsin Blue Book*, 1937, pp. 195-207.

NEWSPAPERS AND PRINTING

McMurtrie, Douglas Crawford. *Early Printing in Wisconsin*. Seattle, Wash., McCaffrey, 1931. 220 p., ill.

Union List of Newspapers. American Newspapers 1821-1936, A Union List of Files Available in the United States and Canada, edited by Winifred Gregory under the auspices of the Bibliographical Society of America. New York, The H. W. Wilson Co., 1937. 791 p.

Wisconsin Historical Society. *Annotated catalogue of newspaper files in the Library of the State Historical Society of Wisconsin*. 2d ed. Madison, The Society, 1911. 591 p.

SPORTS AND RECREATION

Albers, J. M. "A Recreational Plan for Wisconsin." *The Municipality*, 1938, pp. 121, 122, 130, 131. Pub. by the League of Wisconsin Municipalities.

Harrington, C. L. "Wisconsin Parks." *Wisconsin Blue Book*, 1923, pp. 53-63.

Wehrwein, George Simon, and Kenneth H. Parsons. *Recreation as a Land Use*. Madison, 1932. 32 p. (University of Wisconsin. Agricultural Experiment Station. Bulletin 422.)

Wisconsin. Conservation Department. Recreational Publicity Division. *55,000 Square Miles of Vacation Land, Wisconsin*. Madison, 1938. (Also other publications, free on request.)

Wisconsin. State Planning Board. *A Conservation and Recreation Plan for Southeastern Wisconsin*. Madison, 1936. 28 p. (Bulletin 3.)

CITIES AND POINTS OF INTEREST

Beloit Daily News. *The Book of Beloit*. Beloit, Wis., 1936. 312 p., ill.

Bruce, Wm. George. *A Short History of Milwaukee*. Milwaukee, Bruce Pub. Co., 1936. 249 p., ill.

Bryant, Benjamin F., ed. *Memoirs of La Crosse County.* Madison, 1907. 428 p.

Conard, Howard L., ed. *History of Milwaukee from Its First Settlement to the Year 1895.* Chicago and New York, Am. Biographical Pub. Co., 1896. 2 v., ill.

Evans, Constance M., and Ona B. Earll. *Prairie du Chien and the Winnishiek.* Prairie du Chien, Wis., 1928. 32 p., ill.

Green Bay Historical Bulletins. Green Bay, Wis., Brown County Historical Society, 1925 to date.

Gregory, John Goadby. *History of Milwaukee, Wisconsin.* Chicago, The S. J. Clarke Pub. Co., 1931. 4 v., ill.

Koss, Rudolf. *Milwaukee.* Milwaukee, Milwaukee *Herold,* 1871. 473 p.

La Crosse County Historical Sketches, ed. by A. H. Sanford. La Crosse, La Crosse County Historical Society, 1931-38. Series 1-4, ill.

Madison, Dane County and Surrounding Towns. Madison, William J. Park & Co., 1877. 664 p., ill.

Nolen, John. *Madison: a Model City.* Boston, 1911. 168 p., ill.

Scanlan, Peter Lawrence. *Prairie du Chien: French, British, American.* Menasha, Wis., Geo. Banta Pub. Co., 1937. 258 p., ill.

Stewart, Lillian Kimball. *A Pioneer of Old Superior.* Boston, Christopher Pub. House, 1930. 322 p.

Titus, William A. "Historic Spots in Wisconsin." *Wisconsin Magazine of History,* 1919-1929, v. 3-5, 7-12.

Young, Kimball, J. L. Gillin, and C. L. Dedrick. *The Madison Community.* Madison, 1934. 229 p. (University of Wisconsin Studies in Social Sciences and History, no. 21.)

Population Figures, 1940 Census

(Final population figures for all incorporated cities, towns, and villages)

CITIES OF 10,000 OR MORE:

Appleton	28,436
Ashland	11,101
Beaver Dam	10,356
Beloit	25,365
Chippewa Falls	10,368
Cudahy	10,561
Eau Claire	30,745
Fond du Lac	27,209
Green Bay	46,235
Janesville	22,992
Kenosha	48,765
La Crosse	42,707
Madison	67,447
Manitowoc	24,404
Marinette	14,183
Marshfield	10,359
Menasha	10,481
Milwaukee	587,472
Neenah	10,645
Oshkosh	39,089
Racine	67,195
Sheboygan	40,638
Shorewood	15,184
South Milwaukee	11,134
Stevens Point	15,777
Superior	35,136
Two Rivers	10,302
Watertown	11,301
Waukesha	19,242
Wausau	27,268
Wauwatosa	27,769
West Allis	36,364
Wisconsin Rapids	11,416

2,500 TO 10,000

Algoma	2,652
Antigo	9,495
Baraboo	6,415
Berlin	4,247
Black River Falls	2,539
Burlington	4,414
Clintonville	4,134
Columbus	2,760
Delavan	3,444
De Pere	6,373
Edgerton	3,266
Fort Atkinson	6,153
Greendale	2,527
Hartford	3,910
Hudson	2,987
Hurley	3,375
Jefferson	3,059
Kaukauna	7,382
Kewaunee	2,533
Kimberly	2,618
Ladysmith	3,671
Lake Geneva	3,238
Lancaster	2,963
Little Chute	3,360
Mauston	2,621
Mayville	2,754
Menomonie	6,582
Merrill	8,711
Monroe	6,182
Neillsville	2,562
New London	4,825
Oconomowoc	4,562
Oconto	5,362
Park Falls	3,252
Platteville	4,762
Plymouth	4,170
Portage	7,016
Port Washington	4,046
Prairie du Chien	4,622
Reedsburg	3,608
Rhinelander	8,501

Rice Lake	5,719
Richland Center	4,364
Ripon	4,566
River Falls	2,806
Shawano	5,565
Sheboygan Falls	3,395
Sparta	5,820
Spooner	2,639
Stoughton	4,743
Sturgeon Bay	5,439
Tomah	3,817
Tomahawk	3,365
Viroqua	3,549
Waupaca	3,458
Waupun	6,798
West Bend	5,452
West Milwaukee	5,010
Whitefish Bay	9,651
Whitewater	3,689

LESS THAN 2,500

Abbotsford	920
Ableman	395
Adams	1,310
Adell	313
Albany	741
Alma	1,139
Alma Center	431
Almond	449
Altoona	1,239
Amery	1,461
Amherst	611
Amherst Junction	197
Aniwa	283
Arcadia	1,830
Arena	278
Argyle	735
Athens	856
Auburndale	342
Augusta	1,519
Avoca	417
Bagley	293
Baldwin	918
Balsam Lake	452
Bangor	847
Barneveld	358
Barron	2,059
Barton	900

Bay City	299
Bayfield	1,212
Bear Creek	409
Belgium	356
Bell Center	264
Belleville	594
Belmont	476
Benton	835
Big Bend	298
Big Falls	187
Birchwood	531
Birnamwood	556
Biron	475
Black Creek	542
Black Earth	531
Blair	856
Blanchardville	662
Bloomer	2,204
Bloomington	677
Blue Mounds	196
Blue River	381
Boaz	230
Bonduel	661
Boscobel	2,008
Bowler	315
Boyceville	533
Boyd	618
Brandon	708
Brillion	1,200
Brodhead	1,750
Brokaw	477
Brooklyn	449
Browntown	271
Bruce	596
Buffalo	293
Butler	778
Butternut	669
Cable	314
Cadott	676
Cambria	688
Cambridge	577
Cameron	807
Campbellsport	1,094
Camp Douglas	445
Cascade	358
Casco	292
Cashton	706
Cassville	956

Catawba	290	East Troy	925
Cazenovia	370	Eden	223
Cecil	370	Edgar	694
Cedarburg	2,245	Eland	296
Cedar Grove	907	Elderon	249
Centuria	411	Eleva	406
Chaseburg	258	Elkhart Lake	571
Chenequa	288	Elkhorn	2,382
Chetek	1,227	Elk Mound	338
Chilton	2,203	Ellsworth	1,340
Clayton	367	Elmwood	828
Clear Lake	676	Elroy	1,850
Clinton	903	Embarrass	335
Clyman	230	Ephraim	254
Cobb	276	Evansville	2,321
Cochrane	458	Exeland	194
Colby	903	Fairchild	639
Coleman	562	Fairwater	293
Colfax	992	Fall Creek	572
Combined Locks	625	Fall River	425
Conrath	128	Fennimore	1,592
Coon Valley	469	Fenwood	156
Cornell	1,759	Ferryville	306
Cottage Grove	310	Fontana on Geneva Lake	461
Couderay	189	Footville	459
Crandon	2,000	Fountain City	985
Cross Plains	374	Fox Lake	1,016
Cuba City	1,259	Fox Point	1,180
Cumberland	1,539	Frederic	725
Curtiss	171	Fredonia	356
Dallas	436	Fremont	437
Dane	301	Friendship	453
Darlington	2,002	Galesville	1,147
Deerfield	611	Gays Mills	737
Deer Park	203	Genoa	339
De Forest	598	Genoa City	715
Denmark	864	Germantown	292
De Soto	400	Gillett	1,145
Dodgeville	2,269	Gilman	440
Dorchester	456	Glenbeulah	357
Dousman	272	Glen Flora	140
Downing	308	Glenwood	811
Doylestown	253	Grafton	1,150
Dresser Junction	294	Granton	300
Durand	1,858	Grantsburg	874
Eagle	391	Gratiot	297
Eagle River	1,491	Green Lake	661
Eastman	348	Greenwood	776

Neosho	255	Princeton	1,247
Neshkoro	301	Pulaski	979
New Auburn	398	Randolph	1,146
New Glarus	1,068	Random Lake	613
New Holstein	1,502	Readstown	584
New Lisbon	1,215	Red Granite	857
New Richmond	2,388	Reedsville	729
Niagara	2,266	Reeseville	407
North Fond du Lac	2,083	Rewey	267
North Freedom	547	Rib Lake	1,042
North Hudson	595	Ridgeland	242
North Prairie	375	Ridgeway	431
Norwalk	551	Rio	696
Oakfield	655	River Hills	541
Oconto Falls	1,888	Rochester	288
Ogdensburg	207	Rockdale	136
Oliver	201	Rockland	171
Omro	1,401	Rosendale	317
Onalaska	1,742	Rosholt	523
Ontario	533	Rothschild	812
Oostburg	742	St. Cloud	353
Oregon	1,005	St. Croix Falls	1,007
Orfordville	510	Sauk City	1,325
Osceola	642	Saukville	431
Osseo	1,105	Scandinavia	295
Owen	1,083	Schofield	1,536
Oxford	404	Seymour	1,365
Palmyra	711	Sharon	812
Pardeeville	1,001	Sheldon	199
Park Ridge	210	Shell Lake	872
Patch Grove	195	Shiocton	592
Pepin	754	Shorewood Hills	1,064
Peshtigo	1,947	Shullsburg	1,197
Pewaukee	1,352	Silver Lake	365
Phillips	1,915	Sister Bay	309
Pittsville	556	Slinger	775
Plain	405	Soldiers Grove	778
Plainfield	571	Solon Springs	392
Plum City	368	Somerset	476
Poplar	462	South Wayne	331
Port Edwards	1,192	Spencer	506
Potosi	506	Spring Green	868
Pound	310	Spring Valley	973
Poynette	870	Stanley	2,021
Prairie du Sac	1,001	Star Prairie	250
Prairie Farm	335	Steuben	321
Prentice	452	Stockbridge	386
Prescott	857	Stockholm	179

MAP OF
WISCONSIN
IN NINE SECTIONS

Index to State Map Sections

LEGEND

State Boundaries ▬ ▬ ▬ ▬
County Boundaries ▬▬▬ ▬ ▬
National Highways ▬▬[63]▬▬
State Highways ▬▬[70]▬▬
Indian Reservations ▬ ▬ ▬ ▬ ▬

National Forests
State Forests
State Parks ▒
Points of Interest ■
Mounds ▲

Cities and Towns

Capital ⊛   County Seats ◉

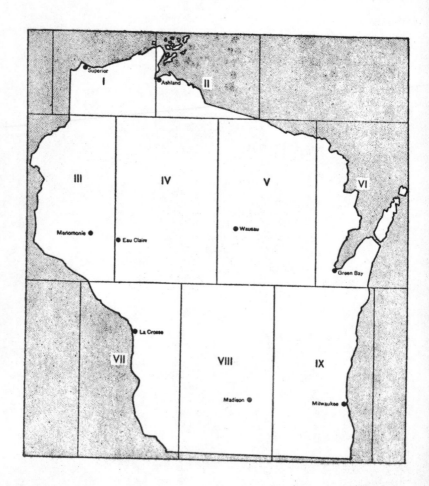

SECTION I

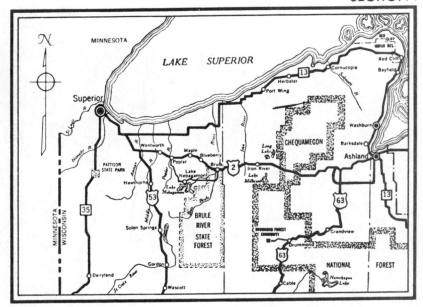

SECTION II

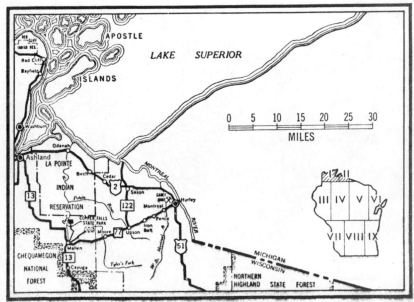

SECTION III

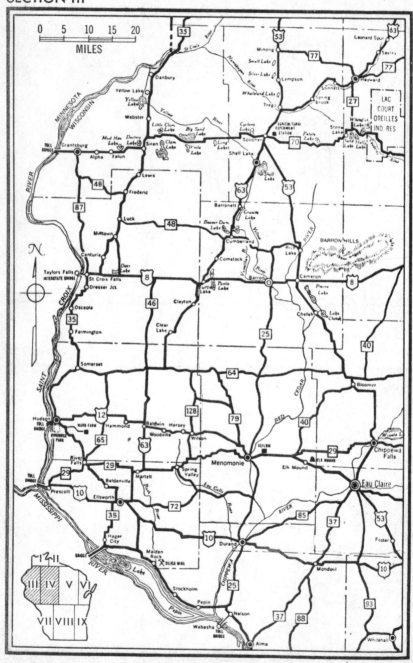

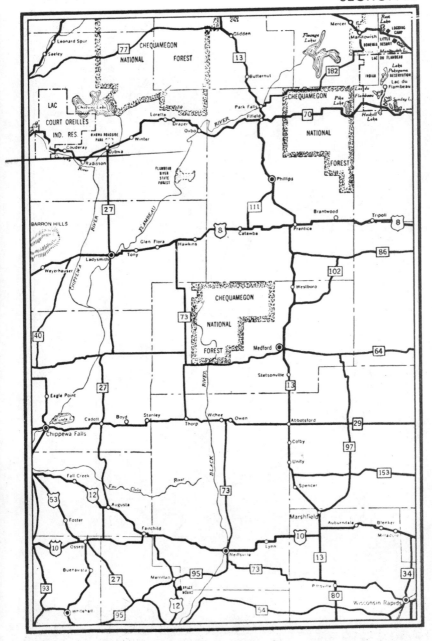

SECTION V

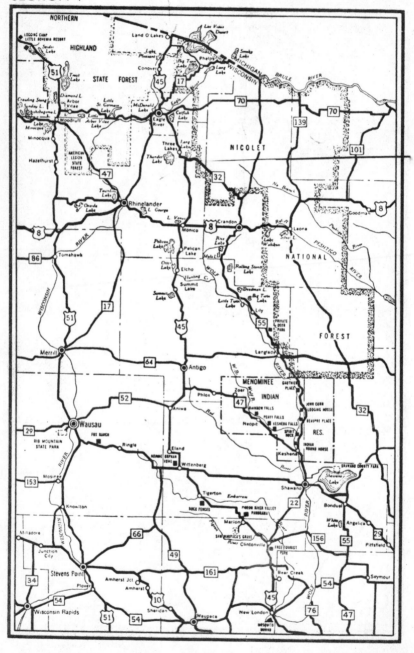

SECTION VII

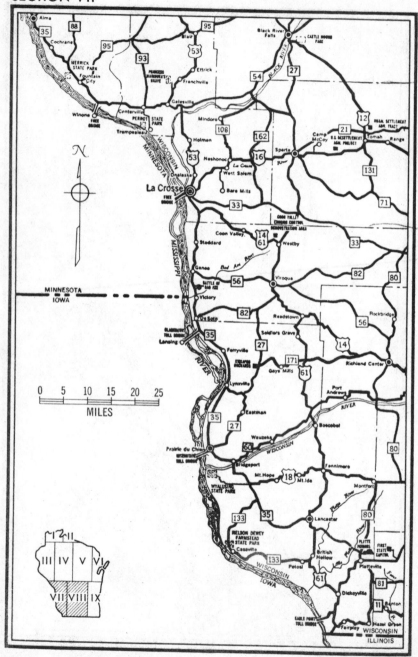

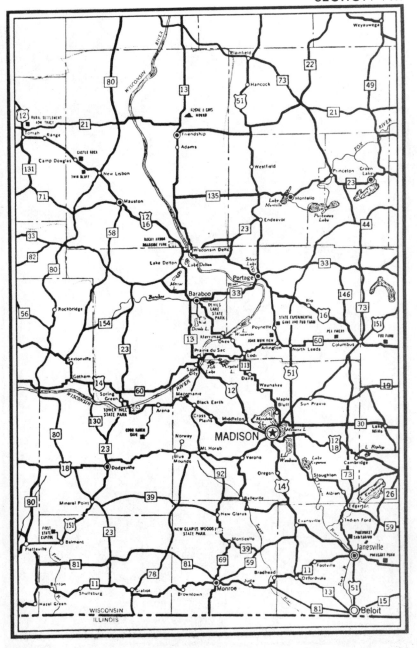

SECTION IX

Index